Natural and Prescribed Fire in Pacific Northwest Forests

Natural and Prescribed Fire in Pacific Northwest Forests

edited by

John D. Walstad
Steven R. Radosevich
David V. Sandberg

Oregon State University Press
Corvallis, Oregon

Cover photo courtesy of Joan Landsberg and the OSU Forestry Media Center.

The paper in this book meets the guidelines for permanence and durability of the Committee on Production Guidelines for Book Longevity of the Council on Library Resources and the minimum requirements of the American National Standard for Permanence of Paper for Printed Library Materials Z39.48-1984.

Library of Congress Cataloging-in-Publication Data
Natural and prescribed fire in Pacific Northwest forests / edited by John D. Walstad, Steven R. Radosevich, David V. Sandberg.
   p.   cm.
Includes bibliographical references.
ISBN 0-87071-359-0 (alk. paper).   ISBN 0-87071-086-9
1. Forest fires—Northwest, Pacific. 2. Prescribed burning—Northwest, Pacific.
3. Forest ecology—Northwest, Pacific. 4. Fire ecology—Northwest, Pacific. I.
Walstad, John D. (John Daniel), 1944-   . II. Radosevich, Steven R. III. Sandberg, David V., 1944-   .
SD421.32.N67N37   1990
634.9'618—dc20   89-36338
                                                                          CIP

Contributors

James K. Agee, College of Forest Resources, University of Washington, Seattle, Washington

Robert L. Beschta, College of Forestry, Oregon State University, Corvallis, Oregon

Jeffrey G. Borchers, College of Forestry, Oregon State University, Corvallis, Oregon

J. Douglas Brodie, College of Forestry, Oregon State University, Corvallis, Oregon

Robert G. Clark, USDI Bureau of Land Management, Washington, D.C.

David A. Cleaves, College of Forestry, Oregon State University, Corvallis, Oregon

James N. Craig, Pacific Northwest Region, USDA Forest Service, Portland, Oregon

Kermit Cromack, Jr., College of Forestry, Oregon State University, Corvallis, Oregon

David S. deCalesta, Northeastern Forest Experiment Station, USDA Forest Service, Warren, Pennsylvania

John E. Deeming, Professional Consultant, Bend, Oregon

Frank N. Dost, Department of Agricultural Chemistry, Oregon State University, Corvallis, Oregon

J. Boone Kauffman, Department of Rangeland Resources, Oregon State University, Corvallis, Oregon

Susan N. Little, Pacific Northwest Research Station, USDA Forest Service, Portland, Oregon

Robert E. Martin, Department of Forestry and Resource Management, University of California, Berkeley, California

Thomas E. McMahon, College of Forestry, Oregon State University, Corvallis, Oregon

David H. McNabb, College of Forestry, Oregon State University, Corvallis, Oregon

Richard E. Miller, Pacific Northwest Research Station, USDA Forest Service, Olympia, Washington

Russel G. Mitchell, Pacific Northwest Research Station, USDA Forest Service, Bend, Oregon

Logan A. Norris, College of Forestry, Oregon State University, Corvallis, Oregon

David A. Perry, College of Forestry, Oregon State University, Corvallis, Oregon

Steven R. Radosevich, College of Forestry, Oregon State University, Corvallis, Oregon

David V. Sandberg, Pacific Northwest Research Station, USDA Forest Service, Seattle, Washington

Kenneth W. Seidel, Pacific Northwest Research Station, USDA Forest Service, Bend, Oregon

Bo Shelby, College of Forestry, Oregon State University, Corvallis, Oregon

Robert W. Speaker, Department of Geography, Oregon State University, Corvallis, Oregon

Edward E. Starkey, USDI National Park Service and College of Forestry, Oregon State University, Corvallis, Oregon

Frederick J. Swanson, Pacific Northwest Research Station, USDA Forest Service, Corvallis, Oregon

Walter G. Thies, Pacific Northwest Research Station, USDA Forest Service, Corvallis, Oregon

John D. Walstad, College of Forestry, Oregon State University, Corvallis, Oregon

Acknowledgments

This text culminates three years of planning, synthesis, and review by the authors and editors involved in its production. The task would not have been accomplished, however, without the expert assistance of numerous individuals who provided key services along the way. Principal among them are Faye C. Dalton, Mary Beth Kemp, and Izella Stuivenga who furnished excellent secretarial support during preparation of the manuscript. Linda Haygarth provided the artistic talent for most of the graphs and charts included in this book. Joe Graff prepared the detailed index. Jo Alexander of OSU Press provided high quality editorial assistance during the production phase. Drs. Don Boelter, George Brown, and Steve Hobbs ensured financial support through the COPE (Coastal Oregon Productivity Enhancement) Program of Oregon State University and the Pacific Northwest Research Station of the USDA Forest Service with major funding from the USDI Bureau of Land Management. Finally, we are indebted to the following specialists who carefully reviewed relevant chapters and provided numerous suggestions to ensure the accuracy and completeness of the material presented:

Mr. Robert J. Anderson, Weyerhaeuser Company
Dr. Stephen F. Arno, USDA Forest Service
Mr. Gary W. Blanchard, Starker Forests, Inc.
Dr. George W. Brown, Oregon State University
Dr. James L. Clayton, USDA Forest Service
Dr. Patrick H. Cochran, USDA Forest Service
Mr. Stanley Coloff, USDI Bureau of Land Management
Mr. John Core, Oregon Department of Environmental Quality
Dr. Hannah J. Cortner, Professional Consultant
Dr. C. Theodore Dyrness, USDA Forest Service
Dr. David L. Eaton, University of Washington
Dr. Lee E. Eddleman, Oregon State University
Dr. Robert L. Edmonds, University of Washington
Mr. James Evans, USDA APHIS
Dr. Fred H. Everest, USDA Forest Service
Dr. George R. Fahnestock, University of Washington
Dr. Michael C. Feller, University of British Columbia
Dr. Roger D. Fight, USDA Forest Service
Mr. William C. Fischer, USDA Forest Service
Mr. Jeremy S. Fried, University of California
Mr. Robert D. Gale, USDA Forest Service
Mr. Armando Gonzalez-Caban, USDA Forest Service
Mr. Dennis V. Haddow, USDA Forest Service
Dr. James D. Hall, Oregon State University
Mr. Michael G. Harrington, USDA Forest Service

Dr. Alan E. Harvey, USDA Forest Service
Dr. J. David Helvey, USDA Forest Service
Ms. Charlotte J. Hopper, Professional Consultant
Dr. Walter E. Howard, University of California
Dr. Bruce M. Kilgore, USDI National Park Service
Dr. Jane Q. Koenig, University of Washington
Dr. William C. Krueger, Oregon State University
Mr. Theodore Lorensen, Oregon Department of Forestry
Dr. Douglas A. Maguire, University of Washington
Dr. Richard R. Mason, USDA Forest Service
Dr. William C. McComb, Oregon State University
Dr. Joseph E. Means, USDA Forest Service
Dr. Charles E. Meslow, Oregon State University
Mr. Robert E. Metzger, USDI Bureau of Land Management
Mr. James E. Miller, USDA Extension Service
Dr. Robert A. Monserud, USDA Forest Service
Dr. David D. Myrold, Oregon State University
Dr. Rodney A. Norum, USDI National Park Service
Dr. William W. Oliver, USDA Forest Service
Dr. Philip N. Omi, Colorado State University
Mr. Roger D. Ottmar, USDA Forest Service
Dr. David J. Parsons, USDI National Park Service
Mr. Howard Phronson, Washington State Department of Natural Resources
Mr. Richard N. Pierson, Weyerhaeuser Company

Dr. Raymond M. Rice, USDA Forest Service
Mr. Jerry Richeson, USDI Bureau of Land
 Management
Mr. Alvin Roberts, USDA Forest Service
Mr. Kenelm W. Russell, Washington State
 Department of Natural Resources
Mr. Charles Sartwell, Jr., USDA Forest Service
Mr. R. Gordon Schmidt, USDA Forest Service
Dr. James R. Sedell, USDA Forest Service
Mr. Robert M. Simmons, L.L.B., USDA Office of
 General Counsel
Mr. J.A. Kendall Snell, USDA Forest Service
Dr. Thomas A. Spies, USDA Forest Service
Dr. William I. Stein, USDA Forest Service
Dr. John D. Stuart, Humboldt State University
Dr. Jonathan Taylor, University of Wyoming
Dr. Thomas A. Terry, Weyerhaeuser Company
Dr. Byron R. Thomas, USDI Bureau of Land
 Management
Dr. Arthur R. Tiedemann, USDA Forest Service
Dr. Torolf R. Torgersen, USDA Forest Service
Dr. Michael R. Wagner, Northern Arizona University
Dr. Darold E. Ward, USDA Forest Service
Mr. Darrel Weaver, Washington State Department of
 Ecology
Mr. Boyd E. Wickman, USDA Forest Service
Mr. William Williams, Washington State Department
 of Natural Resources
Dr. Robert J. Zasoski, University of California

J.D.W.
S.R.R.
D.V.S.

Preface

"Our beautiful virgin forests of Douglas-fir followed fire. Since the advent of cutting and logging, burning has been found to be not always indispensable but often a useful tool in eliminating a fire hazard and preparing the site for a new stand. Foresters have learned under what conditions its use may be beneficial, and where its use may be harmful. It has also become evident that there is still much to learn about the biological and physical effects of burning in this forest type. Therefore, ecologists and foresters should hesitate a long while before they propose burning as a blanket rule, or before they try to eliminate burning as a prime factor in the ecology of the type. Instead, they should continue to use fire as a useful tool where its beneficial effects are known to outweigh any harmful effects of slash burning." (Isaac 1963, p. 16)

This advice, offered by Leo A. Isaac of the USDA Forest Service in 1963, is still applicable today. Indeed, the issues surrounding the control and use of fire in today's environment are even more complex and controversial than they were in Isaac's day. And identifying the situations and conditions under which fire is likely to be beneficial versus harmful is still very much a matter of judgment and experience.

But much has been learned since 1963. Enlightened management policies now allow natural fires to burn under certain specifications, thereby maintaining key ecological conditions. Slash burning is increasingly confined to areas where disposal of flammable logging residues is essential. Underburning is being perfected to maintain the vigor and fire resistance of overstory trees. Smoke management plans have been adopted to minimize impacts on air quality. Environmental assessments are routinely conducted to avoid adverse effects on soils, water, and wildlife. These and other developments over the past 25 years have greatly advanced the science and practice of using fire in the management of Pacific Northwest forests. This book compiles the knowledge and points the direction for additional work needed to further increase our understanding of fire and its appropriate level of application in forestry.

John D. Walstad
Steven R. Radosevich
David V. Sandberg

Isaac, L.A. 1963. Fire—A tool, not a blanket rule in Douglas-fir ecology. Tall Timbers Fire Ecol. Conf. Proc. 2:1-17.

Contents

I Overview and Introduction

1 Introduction to Natural and Prescribed Fire in Pacific Northwest Forests

John D. Walstad, Steven R. Radosevich, and David V. Sandberg

Introduction

Fire in the forest. The phrase evokes images of trees engulfed by roaring flames; of wildlife frantically searching for an escape route; of smoke and soot so dense it obscures the sun and chokes the air; of charred, blackened landscapes seemingly devoid of life. But not all forest fires lead to such destruction. Many of them are relatively benign, simply burning the undergrowth, a thin layer of duff, and woody debris. Whether benign or destructive, however, fire is a natural, recurring phenomenon in most forest ecosystems. Analyses of prehistoric conditions indicate that periodic fires have occurred for millenia in the Pacific Northwest (Chapter 3). Historical records for Oregon since settlement indicate major conflagrations have occurred every ten to twenty years somewhere in the state (Table 1-1). As modern day evidence, a series of dry lightning storms ignited major fires in eastern Oregon in 1986 and in southwest Oregon and northern California in 1987. And there were a number of devastating fires in Yellowstone National Park during the summer of 1988.

Fortunately, many plants and animals are adapted to the periodic disturbance created by fire. They have evolved a variety of mechanisms to recolonize areas after burning (Chapter 4). Thus, fire sets the stage for the natural cycle of forest renewal, the first step in secondary plant succession.

So the forests are going to burn, but the landscape will recover. Both are just a matter of time. With modern forest management, however, it is possible to reduce the level and extent of destruction. Wholesale devastation of timber and wildlife can be prevented. Damage to the forest floor and

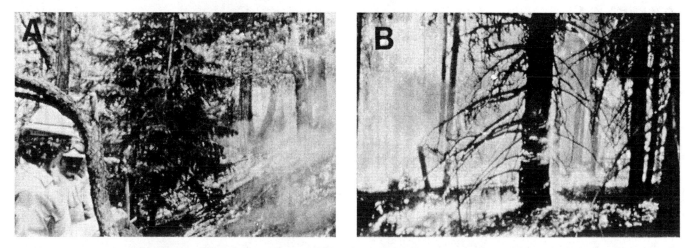

Figure 1-1 Prescribed fire (A) can be used to reduce fuel loads, thereby decreasing the likelihood of more severe stand-replacement fires (B). (Photos courtesy of J.B. Kauffman)

underlying soils can be minimized. Risks to human life and property can be avoided. And the time required to heal the landscape can be shortened considerably.

The key is management, which includes a variety of silvicultural techniques designed to mimic the beneficial effects of wildfire without incurring the disastrous consequences. Principal among them is *prescribed burning*, the controlled use of fire to achieve specific forest management objectives (Fig. 1-1). Such objectives include fire hazard reduction (through disposal of flammable fuels), control of competing vegetation, creation of seedbeds and planting spots, and overall improvement in the efficiency of silvicultural operations by removing impediments to reforestation and stand management (Chapter 6). Prescribed burning (including natural fires allowed to burn under carefully prescribed conditions) is also used to enhance range and wildlife conditions and to maintain ecological diversity and stability in natural areas (Chapters 3, 4, and 7).

Types & Methods of Prescribed Burning

Two major types of prescribed burning are done in forestry: *underburning* and *slash burning* (Chapters 5 and 6). Underburning, as its name implies, is burning beneath mature forest canopies. It is predominately practiced east of the Cascades and is done to interrupt "fuel ladders" extending into the canopy, to help perpetuate the pine type, and to improve habitat and forage conditions for wildlife and livestock.

Slash burning is a method of disposing of logging residues and other woody debris and vegetation that would otherwise impede reforestation and create a serious fire hazard (Chapter 8). Two methods are employed: *broadcast burning* and burning of piled or windrowed material, commonly referred to as *pile-and-burn*. Both methods are used throughout Oregon and Washington, but find their greatest application west of the Cascade Crest where fuel loads after harvesting tend to be large.

Key Questions

Thus, the multipurpose nature of prescribed fire makes it a convenient and cost-effective tool for preparing sites for reforestation, reducing the risk of subsequent wildfire, maintaining ecological diversity and stability, and enhancing animal habitat conditions. Nevertheless, the widespread use of prescribed fire has generated a plethora of complex questions and issues:

- Is fire truly unavoidable in Pacific Northwest forests?
- If so, how can we manage it to protect or create desired forest landscapes and resources?
- How do the frequency, intensity, and effects of natural wildfires compare to those for prescribed fires?
- In the process of using prescribed fire, how can we maintain the short- and long-term productivity of forest ecosystems?

Table 1-1. Summary of major historical forest fires in Oregon.

Year	Name and Location	Acreage
1848	Nestucca Fire near the north-central coast of Oregon between Tillamook and Lincoln City	295,000
1849	Siletz Fire between the Siuslaw and Siletz Rivers of the central coast of Oregon near Newport	800,000
1853	Yaquina Fire from Yaquina Bay near Newport to Corvallis	480,000
1865	Silverton Fire southeast of Salem near Silver Creek Falls State Park	990,000
1868	Coos Bay Fire on the south-central Oregon Coast	295,000
1902	Several, including the Columbia Fire near Mt. Hood	170,000+
1918	Several	Unspecified
1933	Tillamook Burn in northwestern Oregon near Hebo	240,000
1936	Bandon Fire in Coos and Curry counties on the southern Oregon coast	145,000
1939	2nd Tillamook Burn (Saddle Mountain Fire)	190,000
1945	3rd Tillamook Burn (Wilson River and Salmonberry Fires)	180,000
1951	Sardine Creek Fire in Linn and Marion counties	21,400
	4th Tillamook Burn (North Fork and Elkhorn Fires)	33,000
	Vincent Creek Fire in Lane County	30,000
1961	Cayuse Fire in Umatilla County	25,000+
	Ditch Creek Fire in Grant County	25,000+
1966	OxBow Burn in Lane County west of Eugene	43,000
1986	Eastern Oregon fires	85,000
1987	Southwest Oregon fires	200,000

- What are the costs, risks, benefits, and trade-offs associated with prescribed fire vis-a-vis other management alternatives?
- How can we avoid adverse side effects associated with prescribed fire such as site damage, escaped fire, smoke pollution, and aesthetic impacts?

These are only a few of the questions surrounding the topic of fire in forest resource management. Although this text cannot answer all the questions about fire, it does provide the basic information needed to approach the questions in an intelligent manner. Each chapter provides a synopsis of what is known about the topic it covers and notes those areas in which significant information is lacking. Chapter 2 presents a comprehensive summary of the entire book and includes important perspectives for forest resource managers, regulatory and legislative officials, and interested publics. The chapters have been prepared by qualified specialists and subjected to technical peer review to ensure accuracy. Collectively, they provide a comprehensive overview of the role, use, and impact of both natural and prescribed fire in Pacific Northwest forests. Techniques of fire prevention and fire suppression are not covered, however. These topics are adequately addressed in a variety of books and manuals.

Book Focus

The focus of this book is prescribed burning for silvicultural purposes. This is a major practice in Pacific Northwest forestry, and each year over 200,000 acres are burned in Oregon and Washington (Chapter 6). As mentioned earlier, prescribed burning (including carefully monitored natural fires allowed to burn) is also used for a variety of other purposes such as range enhancement, wildlife habitat improvement, and park maintenance, and these applications are discussed where they intersect with forestry (Chapter 7). Many of the principles and techniques mentioned are common to all uses of prescribed burning (Chapter 5).

Coverage is primarily restricted to Oregon and Washington. In many instances, however, the information can be extrapolated to adjacent states, provinces, and other regions with similar climate, topography, and timber types. Occasionally, some of the information presented is drawn from regions outside the Pacific Northwest because that was the best source.

We did not attempt to prepare an exhaustive literature review of each topic covered in the text. Such compilations already exist and are cited in our text where appropriate. Instead, our objective was to prepare an accurate, perceptive, and timely summary of the major features of fire and prescribed burning in forest settings. It is hoped that such a primer will be helpful to decision makers as they grapple with the issues surrounding the use and regulation of fire in Pacific Northwest forests.

2 An Overview and Synthesis of Knowledge Concerning Natural and Prescribed Fire in Pacific Northwest Forests

Logan A. Norris

Introduction

The purpose of this chapter is to provide an overview of the major elements of the book and to synthesize an integrated view of fire in natural resource management in the Pacific Northwest. The chapter is needed to accommodate those wishing an overview of the material in all of the chapters, and to bring together in summary form the essence of what is known, and the research which is needed to facilitate the best quality decisions about managing fire in the forests of the Pacific Northwest. For these purposes the chapter is divided into two parts: an overview of the key points from each chapter, and a synthesis which bridges and combines perspectives across chapters to present a more integrated view of fire and its impact and role in natural resource management.

Overview of Knowledge

The overview is divided into seven major sections, corresponding to the major sections in the body of the text. Each section covers material from two to four individual chapters.

Natural history and ecology

Fire in the forest evokes strong emotions because it is often associated with great destructive power. However, it is clear fire has long been a natural component of the forest and is in fact responsible for shaping many of the forests we enjoy today. The nature of many of our forests was largely determined by the frequency, intensity, and extent of the natural fire regimes associated with a particular area. These regimes reflect the moisture and temperature characteristic of these areas primarily during the period of low rainfall in the summer.

1987 was the most severe fire year in the last 50 years, and one of the two worst in the last 120 years, yet the acreage burned was only 30 percent of the average acreage historically burned by wildfire in Oregon. Modern fire suppression and fire management strategies have had a profound effect on natural fire frequency, intensity, and extent of occurrence, with significant implications for the species composition, vegetative density and forest structure of many current and future forests in the Pacific Northwest.

The characteristics of the mature forests we see today reflect the ecological adaptation of species both as individuals and as communities to the natural fire regime of a particular area. The adaptations which ensure species survival in one area may not be the same in another which has a different fire regime. Thus, if the fire regime changes significantly, it is likely the species composition and density will also change.

Examples include the increasing occurrence of shade-tolerant conifers in the ponderosa pine and mixed-conifer forests east of the Cascade crest where frequent but low-intensity fires were relatively common historically, but have been largely excluded for the last 80 years or so. On the west side, the infrequent (a return frequency of 250 to 500 years or more) but intense stand-replacement fires have been largely eliminated by 60- to 100-year rotations where harvesting in many instances is followed by prescribed fires, typically of much lower intensity and less extensive.

In the future it is unlikely humans will allow wildfire to occur as it did historically, regardless of the natural fire regime for the area. It may be possible in many instances for prescribed fire to be utilized in a positive manner to compensate in part for the effects of natural fire. The key to success in this is a thorough understanding of the response of all parts of the forest ecosystem to fire, and the influence of various fire management strategies on the forest.

Those policies and management programs which are in reasonable harmony with the ecological strategies of individual species and plant communities are most likely to result in forests with desirable composition and levels of productivity. The challenge for contemporary resource managers is to use fire (either natural or prescribed fire as long as they meet prescribed objectives) in a manner which is consistent with the ecological realities of the site.

Application of prescribed fire

Prescribed fire is one of the tools which can be used in meeting specified natural resource management objectives. However when fire is used, it is seldom the only tool used on a specific unit. Clear articulation of the management objectives for a unit, and an understanding of the effects of fire alone and in combination with other tools in meeting the objectives are essential to success.

The key to successful use of fire is the development of a prescription which includes elements which influence the behavior of the fire (fuels, weather, topography), the pattern of ignition, and the conditions of the vegetation and fauna on the site. Successful execution of the prescription requires good planning and the use of trained, experienced personnel. This involves a variety of activities prior to and during the burn, as well as mop-up. Postfire monitoring is essential to provide a basis for evaluating success and, when needed, for altering prescriptions for the future.

Prescribed fire can be used to accomplish many objectives, but the most common relate to improved reforestation and improved rangeland characteristics. Other natural resource values may be enhanced by prescribed fire, but these effects are usually secondary to attaining the primary objectives.

Reforestation can be accomplished either by artificial means such as planting seedlings (most common west of the Cascades) or by natural regeneration where seed from nearby desirable species produce seedlings on the area to be reforested. In either case some preparation of the site is usually advantageous and can often be accomplished by prescribed burning.

Prescribed burning favors natural conifer regeneration on many moist sites. It is also advantageous on dry sites but the intensity of burn is more critical because of the potential to lose more of the nutrient-rich forest floor. Prescribed burns resulting in about 40 percent of the area in exposed mineral soil, and the remainder with litter less than an inch deep, seem to be most favorable for natural regeneration in westside forests. Prescribed burning appears less favorable for natural regeneration at high elevations where true fir and mountain hemlock are common species. On the eastside, the situation is more variable because of the wider range of species, yet a high proportion of exposed mineral soil appears important in successful natural regeneration.

Extensive experience with prescribed burning in artificial regeneration has demonstrated its value, at least in the short term. Studies in the Coast Range show 28 percent greater survival, 36 percent greater height growth, and 68 percent greater diameter growth of planted seedlings in burned plots compared to unburned areas. Most of this benefit is attributed to reduced competition from shrubs.

The pattern of prescribed fire use in the Pacific Northwest has evolved in the last 50 years. Originally, prescribed fire was used almost exclusively for reduction of fire hazard by burning the large accumulations of logging slash associated with harvest of old-growth timber. With declining amounts of old growth being harvested, the increasing value and degree of utilization of logging residues and previously unimportant tree species, and the increasing recognition of the value of leaving woody debris on the site, the use of prescribed fire to dispose of hazardous slash accumulations is declining. Increasing in emphasis is the use of prescribed fire for site preparation prior to reforestation.

Prescribed fire in reforestation on all lands in the Pacific Northwest has declined slightly in the last ten years. In 1975 about 90,000 acres were burned. This level increased to more than 120,000 acres in 1980, but has declined to about 80,000 acres in

1987. The decline has been most pronounced on National Forests.

As in the forest, periodic wildfire (and in some areas the use of fire by Native Americans) historically was part of the ecology of rangelands (including forested rangelands), particularly those in the low-intensity fire regime areas of the intermountain west. These lands are important for forage for livestock and habitat for wildlife. The future structure of the vegetation communities on these lands will be influenced by current and future fire policy.

Prescribed burning on forested rangelands is used to:

• Improve forage and browse species for livestock and wildlife (a 2- to 3-fold increase in production in 5 years is common);

• Control the species composition of vegetation (such as reduction of the density of sagebrush species, although they may be replaced by other species such as rabbitbrush which are also not desirable);

• Maintain ecological diversity (by reducing the dominance of sagebrush species which in many instances form monocultures, excluding nearly all other species); and

• Reduce wildfire hazard (by reducing fuels around areas of heavy human activity and broad expanses of wildlands where natural fires are difficult and expensive to control).

A number of commonly held generalizations about burning on rangelands are not universally true. For example: "burning will double grazing capacity." While this is true in some instances, in others grazing capacity decreases due to reduced forage production and the increase in undesirable species.

Managing range and forest lands is complex and often involves tradeoffs among various resource values. Clearly established and articulated objectives for the management of these lands are essential in determining the tools and procedures to use.

Site-specific analysis and prescriptions are needed to optimize success both in reforestation and rangeland improvement. Prescribed burning can be a useful tool (sometimes the only practical tool) to ensure success, but a thorough knowledge of characteristics of the site and the ecology of the species is essential in developing prescribed burning prescriptions. Thoughtful analysis is needed to assure both short- and long-term management objectives are accomplished, and are within the limi-

tations imposed by site characteristics, species ecology, and regulatory framework.

Interactions between prescribed burning and forest protection

Forest resource values can be adversely affected by wildfire, insects, and disease, and young conifers can be damaged by animals. Because of the fire-adapted nature of natural forests, it is not surprising that these factors can be influenced by prescribed burning in managed forests.

The fuel load in Pacific Northwest forest and range ecosystems has increased significantly over the last century. This fuel load is composed of natural fuels, which are the normal accumulation of dead vegetation, and activity fuels such as logging slash. Over a century of wildfire control and fire prevention has prevented the consumption of the natural fuels which would normally occur in the frequent but low-intensity natural fire regime of the eastside. There has probably been little or no effect on fuel accumulation on the westside (with the exception of southwest Oregon) where the natural fire regime has a much longer return frequency. In addition, large quantities of activity fuels are produced in some areas (more than 25 million tons per year in western Oregon and Washington). Historically these have sometimes been responsible for increased extent of wildfires, some of which were of disastrous proportions.

Prescribed burning has been proposed as a solution to both of these problems, and has in fact been extensively used for hazard reduction in logging slash in western Oregon and Washington. The information needed to reduce fine and intermediate fuel classes is well developed, indicating burning prescriptions can be developed to accomplish hazard reduction with accuracy. However, less attention has been given to the cost effectiveness of this practice. In those situations where the cost of burning is low and wildfire risk and resource values are high, prescribed burning can be cost effective. However, in many situations it cannot be economically justified for wildfire protection alone. Escaped prescribed fires contribute significantly to the acreage of wildfire burns, accounting for nearly 30 percent of the burned forest acreage in western Oregon and Washington. There is a significant role for prescribed burning in reducing losses from wildfire, but highly site-specific analyses are required. General hazard reduction for most wildland situations is not economically viable. Combinations of site-specific hazard reduction, fuel breaks, and vegetation mosaics developed in landscape-level planning offer the optimum approach to protecting forest values from wildfire.

Damage by wildlife pests (such as bear, deer, porcupine, and pocket gophers) to conifer seedlings and saplings amounts to millions of dollars annually in the Pacific Northwest. Prescribed burning significantly alters wildlife habitat (at least in the short run) and may in some cases provide protection to seedlings. Specific studies of these effects are lacking, and impacts are inferred largely from experience and judgment.

Prescribed burning will cause a direct reduction in the numbers of many of the smaller pest animals living above ground, and increase the rate of predation on them because cover is reduced. In some instances reduced forage for small mammals may cause them to leave the area, but in other cases, if the preferred food source is gone and only tree seedlings are left, they will be consumed.

In general, prescribed burning can result in reduced damage to conifer seedlings by small mammals by direct reduction of the number of pests, and by alteration of habitat. Burning will have little effect on deer mice, but may provide 1 to 2 years of protection from shrews and chipmunks when direct seeding or natural regeneration are employed. Burning will have little or no effect on damage from large mammals, except as it is used with other techniques such as forage seeding, improved access for trapping (mountain beaver), and the installation of protective devices (such as tubing over seedlings). However, prescribed burning may also increase animal pest damage if preferred foods are removed by the fire and only the desired forest species are left. In this instance, other techniques of population control are necessary. The integration of prescribed burning with other silvicultural operations is most likely to ensure animal damage does not exceed acceptable levels.

Insects cause significant levels of damage in Pacific Northwest forests each year. In some years potential losses are very large, and major direct-control projects using chemical and biological insecticides are used. These programs are expensive, and in many instances controversial. Consequently there is substantial interest in minimizing the adverse effects of insects on forest values.

Wildfire control and, in some areas, selective harvesting of shade-intolerant species such as ponderosa pine, have resulted in substantial increases in the proportion of shade-tolerant true fir in stands. These species are a favored host for the Douglas-fir tussock moth and the western spruce budworm, both of which are serious pests when they periodically reach epidemic proportions. These pests (and a few others) are much more common and serious in western forests than they were 50 years ago. This problem is not restricted to eastside forests. It is also occurring at higher elevations in the Cascades where the shade-tolerant Pacific silver fir is replacing seral Douglas-fir in many areas. Pacific silver fir is susceptible to attack by the balsam wooly aphid, and these attacks are far more serious at the lower elevations into which this tree species is advancing. The effect of fire exclusion from these areas has been to increase the impact of the balsam wooly aphid over large areas of the Pacific Northwest. However, prescribed underburning may not be nearly as valuable a tool in this forest type as in the eastside forest types.

Prescribed burning is capable of altering species composition and stand density in these forests. Unfortunately, interactions between insect populations, stand composition, and the use of fire have not been critically evaluated, and it will be difficult to do so. Current concepts of these interactions are based on empirical evidence and plausible (but untested) inferences. While prescribed burning does present a few problems in these forests, the positive benefit from the standpoint of protection from insects is very high.

Tree diseases (such as root diseases, stem diseases, foliage diseases, and dwarf mistletoes) cause major loss of primarily timber values in the Pacific Northwest. The interaction between these types of disease and fire is poorly documented. Fire does not appear to have a significant direct effect on root diseases, but it can facilitate the progress of stem diseases. Foliage diseases can be directly controlled with fire, but are relatively unimportant in the region. Dwarf mistletoes are widespread and cause significant losses of timber value annually. Although undocumented, it is believed that the historic frequent but low-intensity fire regime of the Interior West may have reduced the incidence of dwarf mistletoe. With fire exclusion, the organism is not affected directly, and the stand is maintained in a susceptible seral stage for long periods. Prescribed burning could be an effective tool to control dwarf mistletoes, but information on the cost effectiveness of this practice is lacking.

The greatest research need involves the interaction between fire and root disease. Information from other regions can help forest managers and pathologists evaluate fire interactions with stem disease and dwarf mistletoes.

Effects of Fire on the Environment

Thus far the focus has been on the role of fire in the forest and its potential utility as a tool to accomplish specific management objectives. While we must be concerned with its efficacy, equally important in decisions regarding fire are its potential adverse impacts. These impacts involve the maintenance or sustainability of forest productivity with particular emphasis on the timber resource, and the effects on nontimber resources. An understanding of and appropriate balance among these competing interests and between efficacy and adverse impacts is needed in seeking rational decisions concerning the appropriate role and the techniques of use of fire in the forests of the Pacific Northwest.

Effects of fire on forest productivity

In this section productivity means primarily the sustainability of timber production; that is, the ability of the site to produce trees at a relatively constant level over many cycles of harvesting and regeneration. Assuming constancy in climate and a large number of other external factors, forest productivity is largely controlled by a number of soil physical and chemical properties (such as nutrient and organic matter levels, bulk density, and porosity) and biological properties (such as the species composition and abundance of a wide array of soil organisms).

Burning (both wildfire and prescribed fire) disrupts the cycling of nutrients in the forest because of effects on vegetation and through consumption of fuels which contain nutrients. In Pacific Northwest forests, nitrogen is most commonly the limiting nutrient resource, and it is also the one which is most likely affected by fire.

Substantial amounts of nitrogen can be lost through volatilization during burning. During burning, some nutrients are lost from the site by convection of ash in the smoke column, but these losses are believed relatively minor, and the elements are usually returned to the forest (at another site, but over time this probably balances out). Leaching and erosional losses may also occur, but relative to the magnitude of the nutrient capital on the site, these losses are quite small and of short duration since burned areas frequently revegetate quickly, and the plants absorb available nutrients from the soil solution.

The amount of nitrogen lost is usually proportional to the amount of fuel consumed by the fire. Estimates of loss range from 150 to more than 1,000 pounds per acre, with higher amounts associated with the loss of thick layers of forest floor in British Columbia forests. Mid-range values are from the Cascade Range where burning prescriptions included removal of coarse woody debris before burning to reduce fire intensity and burning when the forest floor was wet to minimize loss of the litter layer. Nitrogen losses from wildfire have seldom been reported, but estimates from the 1970 Entiat Fire in central Washington indicate a loss of about 800 lbs of nitrogen per acre.

Forest productivity is not always directly proportional to site nitrogen levels because on many sites much of the nitrogen capital is not readily available for uptake by plants. In western Oregon, less than 2 percent of the site nitrogen is available on many sites. Burning can decrease the total amount of nitrogen on the site but increase the amount of available nitrogen and, at least in the short run, increase the growth of the young forest. Burning is most likely to increase nitrogen availability in colder climates where decomposition of litter is slow. Sulfur and phosphorus are also subject to loss by volatilization; however, these elements appear less limiting than nitrogen, and attention to losses of nitrogen will minimize losses of sulfur and phosphorous. Uncertainty remains as to the long-term consequences of these changes.

Wildfires, at least those of significant intensity, probably result in greater nutrient loss than prescribed fires because of the severity of the burning conditions when these fires occur. The greater consumption of soil organic matter (and therefore nutrients) in severe wildfires distinguishes them from most prescribed fires. When evaluating the loss of nutrients associated with prescribed fire, it is important to remember that intense stand-replacement fires were historically part of the natural forest cycle, and the forests we see today are a reflection of them. Thus the long-term potential impacts of prescribed fire must be evaluated in context of their frequency and severity and in contrast to that associated with historic wildfire. Additionally, fire is not the only factor influencing nitrogen levels in the forest. Rotation length, the presence of nitrogen-fixing species, and the degree of utilization of the vegetation on the site at the time of harvest are also important.

Prescribed burning can be accomplished in such a way as to minimize the loss of nutrients. The most important criterion is to minimize the loss of the forest floor (litter) because it has the highest concentration of nitrogen of any dead fuel. This can be accomplished by burning when the forest floor moisture content is greater than 30 percent; hence the current increase in spring, winter, and early summer prescribed burning. Preburning removal of large woody debris will also reduce consumption of forest floor, but this practice may have other undesirable effects. Mass ignition techniques (those which initiate burning over a large portion of the unit in a very short period of time) are also helpful because they promote burning of fuels without a lot of advanced heating and drying associated with slow-moving flame fronts.

Soil organisms substantially influence forest productivity, in part because of their role in decomposition of organic matter and the cycling of nutrients, and in part because of the relationships they form with higher plants (such as mycorrhizae). In these complex interactions energy is transported from above to below ground. Here the energy is used by soil organisms to accomplish a large number of functions important in maintaining site productivity, such as nitrogen fixation and the solubilization of minerals. The organisms in turn, through their association with plant roots, can enhance nutrient and water uptake and protect the roots from pathogens. Soil organisms also influence some soil physical properties such as aggregation of soil particles.

Fire affects soil organisms, both directly as a function of fire intensity and indirectly through changes in the vegetation with which the soil organisms interact. Prescribed burning usually results in a short-term reduction in populations of soil organisms, but the effects are not predictable given current knowledge and the variations which

occur in fire intensity. On at least some sites, the formation of mycorrhizae is essential for survival and growth of seedlings. Current research suggests the speed and extent to which host species for mycorrhizal fungi reinvade burned areas is a key factor in assuring mycorrhizal fungi are on the site and available to promote the survival and growth of the seedlings. Prompt and effective reforestation is probably the best mechanism for this, but invasion of some native nonconiferous plants may also accomplish this purpose. Long periods of devegetation appear quite harmful in maintaining the integrity of the soil organism community, with serious consequences for eventual reforestation success.

Accelerated physical loss of soil (erosion) from the growing site is likely to result in loss of site productivity. Disturbance, including fire, usually accelerates erosion processes through its effect on vegetation and soil. Generally, as fire severity increases so does the loss of vegetation and forest floor. In addition, the hydraulic conductivity of the soil declines, which may inhibit infiltration of rain into the soil profile. The loss of soil as a result of prescribed burning is usually minor, except on the most erodible soils or during extreme precipitation events. Most soils of the Pacific Northwest have properties which are less conducive to this type of erosion than in some other areas of the West. In general, accelerated erosion from prescribed fire will have little effect on long-term productivity as long as the fire severity and frequency are not greater than is common for the natural fire regime. Those burning prescriptions which minimize loss of forest floor, minimize the loss of nutrients, and protect biota are also compatible with minimizing soil loss by erosion.

The most direct measure of the effects of burning on productivity for timber production would be through comparisons of timber growth on burned and unburned sites across the region, through several rotations of forest crops, with reasonable degree of uniformity of other cultural operations applied. Data such as this do not exist, even for one rotation.

The most comprehensive data set is for 44 burned and adjacent unburned plots in the Oregon and Washington Cascade Range. Measurements made 35 to 42 years after initial timber harvest and natural regeneration show no significant difference in average site quality between the burned and unburned sites, but the species mix was different, with more of the shade-tolerant species present on the unburned than the burned plots. However, there was substantial variation from location to location, emphasizing the wide array of factors which could influence these results, and the need for site-specific analysis and prescription of silvicultural treatments.

In western Oregon and Washington, positive prescribed burning effects in coast Douglas-fir are expected at most locations because of improved initial stocking and reduced cover of shrub species. However, where advanced regeneration is an important component of new stands, and where fire may stimulate germination of species such as ceanothus, growth is likely to be reduced. There is no direct evidence to indicate prescribed burning of slash reduces tree growth by affecting basic soil properties in the western Cascade Range. Analysis of projected stand growth using growth simulation models for those plots with more than 80 percent basal area in Douglas-fir show the current difference in volume between burned and unburned plots is significant, but will gradually disappear, being no more than 5 percent different at 100 years. Since the average tree diameter is the same on both plots at this point, it is the greater number of trees on the burned plots which account for the larger volume. These might be harvested in thinnings, thereby "capturing" the additional volume before it is lost through normal stand mortality.

The data are so limited for burning in eastside forests that meaningful conclusions are not possible. The limited studies which have been done show both negative and positive effects of burning on stand growth and yield.

Clearly there are few long-term data on stand-level responses to prescribed burning. While the theories are well developed, there has been little critical testing of their validity and interactions in the field. There is a significant need for the installation of these kinds of monitoring plots in connection with forestry operations. With the increased emphasis on performance monitoring and evaluation in public forestry agencies, and with the advent of computerized data management options, there now exists the technical ability to conduct such studies in a meaningful way.

Effects of prescribed fire on nontimber resources

Knowledge of the effects of prescribed fire on air quality and human health, on water quality and quantity, and on fish and wildlife is needed to help ensure technically sound decisions can be made concerning the use of prescribed fire in managed forests. Among these, the potential impacts of prescribed burning on air quality and on human health are the most vigorously debated and are the most likely to be the basis on which regulatory standards and strategies are established.

More than 200,000 acres of forest in Oregon and Washington are prescribed burned annually, emitting more than 110,000 tons of smoke (estimated 44 percent in Washington, 56 percent in Oregon). In Washington, 57 percent of the emissions are on the westside compared to 90 percent in Oregon. This burning is done within an increasingly stringent regulatory framework, guided primarily by the Clean Air Act of 1963, as amended. Prior to 1970, air quality considerations had little influence on prescribed burning strategies. Between 1970 and 1984, smoke management programs were effective in greatly reducing the intrusion of smoke into urban areas. In addition, through a combination of increased on-site utilization (resulting in less fuel) and improved burning techniques, particulate emissions per acre have been reduced about 30 percent. By using more summer burning, enhanced smoke dispersion has also been attained. Since 1984, the 1977 amendments to the Clean Air Act (which provided specific protection for visibility in National Parks and Wilderness) and a period of significant wildfire danger (when burning might otherwise have been done) have resulted in about a 33 percent reduction in total acreage burned.

The regulatory framework in the Pacific Northwest includes air quality management strategies which regulate:
* the amount, time, and location of emissions from burning;
* the use of specific emission standards to minimize the production of emissions; and
* risk management to minimize health risks for workers associated with burning.

These regulations will be increasingly stringent in the future. Air quality standards for particles which can be inhaled (those less than 10 micrometers in diameter) have been set, and new standards for fine particles (less than 2.5 micrometers in diameter) are expected in the near future. These two standards have important regulatory implications for prescribed burning because particles of these sizes are abundant in wood smoke. A case study in 1984 of visibility impairment in the Northwest indicated 44 percent was caused by slash burning. The situation is compounded significantly because residential wood combustion is also a significant source of these particles. When standards are exceeded, prescribed burning may be further restricted to ensure air quality standards are maintained, because it may be easier to control emissions from prescribed forest burning than by trying to control emissions from the countless number of home-heating devices.

Slash burning consumes on the average about 43 tons of fuel per acre in western Oregon and Washington (about 50 percent duff and fine litter and 25 percent each of pieces smaller than and greater than 3 inches in diameter). In eastside slash burning the fuel consumed is about 25 tons per acre. Burning to improve range and wildlife habitat on the eastside consumes about 5 tons of fuel per acre.

The chemistry of combustion has been well developed. Standards for the regulation of priority pollutants such as particulate matter, carbon monoxide, oxides of sulfur and nitrogen, lead, and ozone have been developed, and they guide regulatory strategies. Criteria remain to be developed for other classes of material such as polynuclear aromatic compounds, aldehydes, and a few other compounds which may have human health implications. The strategies for human health risk assessment are well established but are restricted in their utility because of the limited data on both exposure of humans and the toxicity characteristics of some of the products of combustion. However, even when maximizing assumptions are employed, it appears the health risk to humans from slash burning is no greater than living in a community where home heating is accomplished by wood, and is less than living in a home which is heated with wood combustion.

An excellent research base has been developed and is being improved to help managers conduct prescribed burns which minimize pollutant production. Mitigation strategies can influence the amount of air pollution caused by fires. These include specific measures which rely on:

- *avoidance*, in which burning is conducted under atmospheric conditions which avoid the incursion of smoke into sensitive areas;
- *dilution*, in which atmospheric conditions and dispersion in both time and space are used to assure the concentration of smoke will not exceed designated levels in sensitive locations; and
- *emission reduction*, in which scheduling and specific burning strategies are used to reduce the emissions per acre.

The smoke management programs in Washington and Oregon are unequaled in other states. They are quite advanced and have been largely successful in nearly eliminating smoke intrusions into designated sensitive areas. Both programs have been modified within the last 5 years to meet the criteria required by the the Clean Air Act. These smoke management programs relied largely on avoidance and dilution to accomplish their objectives in the 1970s, but more recently techniques for the reduction of emissions have assumed greater importance. Based on emission inventories conducted in western Oregon and Washington for 1984-85, particulate emissions declined about 29 percent since the baseline period of 1976-79. About half of this reduction is attributed to improved utilization of logging residues. As the proportion of harvesting in second-growth forests increases, emissions should continue to decline because there will be less unmerchantable material left after logging. Forest Service estimates indicate a further 37 percent reduction in emissions by 2000. If this is achieved, the total reductions in emissions since 1976-79 will be 55 percent. We don't know the degree to which these figures reflect trends on other land ownerships.

The effects of fire on water quality and quantity are also important considerations for the resource manager. The effects of fire on water quantity are relatively straightforward. If fire destroys the overstory vegetation, annual water yield will increase initially because of the reduced amount of water lost through transpiration from the canopy. Summer flows may be increased for a couple of years, but the total volume of increase is generally small. Initial increases of 20 inches in annual runoff were observed in the Coast Range and the westside of the Cascades, and 5 inches on the eastside. However, as revegetation occurs (as it usually does quite quickly) these increases will decrease and yields will return to predisturbance conditions (in 20 to 40 years). When prescribed fire is used in western Oregon and Washington, it is usually in areas where harvesting has been completed, and thus the overstory vegetation is already removed. In these conditions, burning will have little effect on water yield. We lack specific data for water yield as it is influenced by underburning on the eastside, but it is unlikely to have a very significant effect. There is no indication that the magnitude of peak flows (floods) are increased as a result of prescribed burning.

Burning which destroys the streamside vegetation that provides shade to the stream will cause an increase in water temperatures, particularly the high temperature extremes during the summer months. This is likely a factor along very small streams where buffer strips are not required, and may account for some increase in water temperature over that expected due to harvesting alone. This increase will be increasingly modified as revegetation along the stream course proceeds. In severely burned areas, this may take less than 10 years in the Coast Range to several decades in the high Cascades. The implications for aquatic habitat will depend on site-specific conditions.

Burning which consumes much of the forest floor material, particularly on steep slopes, can cause significant reductions in water quality, particularly due to surface erosion. Increased concentration and discharge of selected nutrients from watersheds may occur after prescribed burning, but these are typically confined to a short period of time after the burn. Little or no change is noted over a period of several years.

Generally speaking, relatively cool burns which leave most of the surface organic matter in place and relatively undisturbed produce insignificant effects on either water quality or quantity.

Fire can affect fish and other aquatic species in forest streams. Direct increases in stream temperature, increased sedimentation, and other effects have been observed, as have shifts in aquatic species composition and density. In some cases the effects were positive, with increased productivity of salmonids. Unfortunately, there is little research which has examined specifically the effects of fire and fire-induced changes in the local environment as distinct from logging, road building, and other management activities. It is difficult to partition effects among these activities.

Snags and dead and down woody material in the riparian zone are believed to be critical to the stability and the productivity of aquatic ecosystems. Strategies which protect the integrity of the riparian zone, especially its living vegetation and dead logs, minimize potential impacts of prescribed burning on aquatic species.

The effects of burning on intermittent and small headwater streams are poorly documented. These streams are commonly not buffered because they do not directly support fish. Yet they frequently account for 70 percent of the total stream miles in a forested area. The cumulative effects of fire on these small streams need to be evaluated with a basin-wide perspective.

Fire can impact wildlife directly, but mortality is insignificant both in terms of the numbers of animals killed and the impact on affected populations. Indirect effects are mediated through changes in food and cover. While these relationships are generally well understood, the degree to which they are impacted by fire as a specific tool has received much less attention, with the exception of a few of the most prominent game species such as deer, elk, and grouse. Woody debris is an important part of the habitat for a number of nongame wildlife species. Prescribed burning is likely to reduce the availability of this material, and should, therefore, be expected to influence these species, but direct studies are lacking. The use of standing snags by birds is the most extensively studied aspect of debris management. Prescribed burning strategies which minimize impacts on these structures will help minimize the effects of burning on these avian species. Fires are expected to have little effect on large mammalian predators because their range is large and is quite likely to include a mosaic of landscape conditions. The most significant research need in this area is to move beyond the simple local plot study and begin to evaluate effects over broad landscapes.

Public attitudes and regulation of prescribed fire in forest ecosystems

Public perceptions and attitudes are without question the dominant force in the development and implementation of prescribed burning policies and action programs as well as the formalized array of regulations which control them.

Historically, the information on which attitudes about fire were based came from professional resource managers. As the result of a long and intense program of public education about wildfire, the public perception is that fire in the forest is usually undesirable. Public concerns about prescribed burning focus on health effects from smoke inhalation, ecological impacts on the site, aesthetic values, and commercial impacts. Public support is more favorable if prescribed burning is seen to reduce the risk of wildfire, to improve recreational opportunities, or to manage ecological conditions to reflect a more natural state. There are no data to determine public attitudes about the use of fire to promote commercial forestry values. The resistance to burning in managed forests could stem from many factors, including a general aversion to forest harvesting.

The public is increasingly knowledgeable about and supportive of using prescribed fire in recreational areas, although most of this research has been conducted in the Northern Rockies and the Southwest. The degree of public support seems related to the level of knowledge of the individual, with positive benefits recognized most often by those with a natural resource background, although there is wide variation among individuals. Public education can be a powerful tool in the development of future fire management policy.

Air quality is a dominant issue with the public. From studies using standard economic research strategies, it appears the public is quite willing to pay to improve or to assure a high level of air quality. The amount people would be willing to pay varies widely with the individual and the location, but ranges from $2.00 per person per day for wilderness users to $85 annually per household for some park users. Portland area residents were willing to make a one-time payment of $50.00 to assure high visual quality. The present value of aggregated benefits from improved visibility aspects of air quality are reported to be $445 million. These findings may be difficult to interpret because of problems with methodology in this type of research. Nonetheless, it is clear that people place a high value on clean air.

Public perceptions and attitudes do shape policy and regulation. Public acceptance of prescribed burning on managed forest lands requires:
• a strong consensus among managers and most other concerned groups about the correct use and beneficial effects of prescribed fire;

• a long-term effort to educate the public about fire effects and benefits;
• public perception that educational information is scientifically sound and is not coming from groups with vested interests; and
• adequate treatment of the concerns of the public concerning potential health effects, ecological damage, aesthetic impacts (especially impairment of visibility), and the risk of escape of prescribed fires.

Prescribed burning is subjected to a substantial level of regulation, and there are well-institutionalized procedures for making management decisions in this area, including closely controlled permit systems. The broad legislative structure for regulation of prescribed burning in federal programs is embodied in the National Environmental Policy Act (NEPA), the National Forest Management Act (NFMA) for the USDA Forest Service, and the Federal Land Policy and Management Act (FLPMA) for the USDI Bureau of Land Management. There are state statutes which mirror these acts.

Air resource protection is achieved through the Clean Air Act of 1963, as amended. A key provision of this statute is establishment of ambient air quality standards and the requirement that the states implement an EPA approved plan. Oregon and Washington are pioneers in this effort, with the most comprehensively developed and managed plan for regulation of prescribed burning to assure air quality. A complex system of permits is used in the Pacific Northwest for implementation of these programs.

There are at least ten other federal statutes which, while not directly related to prescribed burning or air quality, influence decisions by federal land managers about the use of prescribed burning. They include the following:
• Organic Administration Act: authorizes activities to protect National Forests from destruction by fire.
• National Parks and Recreation Act: authorizes activities to protect National Parks from destruction by fire.
• Wilderness Act: interpreted to mean fire should play its natural role in wilderness.
• National Trails System Act: affects the use of fire and suppression strategies for wildfire.
• Wild and Scenic Rivers Act: increased restric-

tion on activities in riparian zones, including those involving prescribed burning and wildfire.

- Wild Horse and Burros Protection Act: management of habitat may require use of fire.
- National Historic Preservation Act: influences fire management decisions when historic sites may be affected.
- American Indian Religious Freedom Act: influences fire management decisions.
- Endangered Species Act: influences fire management decisions when habitat of endangered or threatened species may be affected.
- Clean Water Act: influences fire management decisions to ensure protection of water quality.

Many states have similar statutes which apply to private and nonfederal public lands.

Integration

Prescribed burning is a tool which in some cases can be useful for accomplishment of resource management objectives. Clear articulation of these objectives is essential in evaluating alternatives for their accomplishment. When fire is determined to be a useful tool (perhaps the best tool) for this purpose, careful site-specific prescriptions are needed to ensure adverse impacts are minimized while the desired effects are obtained. The single most important factor in both cases is the nature and the extent of fuel consumption, which can be controlled or influenced by attention to the nature of the fuels, fuel moisture content, and atmospheric and other site characteristics. There are a number of examples, on both the westside and the eastside of the Cascades in Oregon and Washington, where complex sets of management objectives were accomplished through the use of site-specific prescriptions involving the use of fire.

Many of the decisions concerning prescribed burning involve analysis and balancing of costs and benefits, and the evaluation of risks. While it is often difficult to quantify in common terms various resource values, there are economic methods of analysis for these values. The most common approach to economic analysis is to discount future costs and benefits to a common time base, usually the present, to give a present net worth, or present net value. These are essentially the net difference between costs and benefits, with the effect of discount rates (the time value of money) included. No practice which provides a net worth of less than 0

is rationally acceptable. Alternatively, benefit-cost ratios, or the internal rate of return, can be calculated as a basis for comparison in choosing among alternatives. These approaches can be applied to individual stands or to aggregations of stands across both space and time.

The benefits which need to be included in these economic analyses include reduction in wildfire hazard in the future, improved regeneration effectiveness and efficiency, enhanced stand development, wildlife habitat and range improvement, and possibly some others. There are a large number of factors to be considered within each of these in arriving at the value of the benefit. The cost factor in the economic analysis has many components. These include the direct cost of the operation on a specific site, and the indirect cost of the program allocated across all sites. It also includes the fixed costs which do not vary with the level of activity and the variable costs which do.

The costs vary widely among organizations and are influenced by their operating constraints and objectives. For instance slash burning on the Willamette National Forest ranged from $270 to $450 per acre, while private industry reports costs of about $100 per acre. By contrast, the Fremont National Forest has conducted underburns for $14 to $17 per acre.

Risk is the other factor to be included in economic analysis. Risk includes any event or condition that is uncertain enough for us to worry about the consequences. Some examples of risk are the uncertainty of the probability and magnitude of damage from a wildfire which originated from an escaped prescribed burn. Another example is the uncertainty or risk associated with subsequent regeneration. Other risks which are often difficult to quantify and are not always included in the analysis include uncertainties of health effects, impact on aesthetics, and possible smoke intrusions in sensitive areas. Incorporation of the probability of occurrence (called risk analysis) and the calculation of present net worth across a range of assumptions (called sensitivity analysis) are two approaches used in economic analysis to deal with risk.

Decision analysis is a technique in which alternative approaches to accomplishment of management objectives are subjected to economic analysis, including the more important sources of uncertainty or risk. In this approach each alternative is represented by its expected value (the average value that would be expected if the same choices were made in a large number of similar situations). By adjusting some of the assumptions in the analysis the decision maker can estimate the sensitivity of various choices.

It is exceedingly difficult to include all of the costs, benefits, and risks in these analyses. Most analyses involve only the most fundamental and obvious costs, benefits, and risks—generally those for which there are relatively known values.

The results from economic analysis, and their use in the decision analysis, need to complement, but cannot be the sole basis for, the "final answer." There are often other important factors, either internal or external to the organization. These factors, which may be highly subjective in nature, may cause the manager to select an alternative which provides a lower rate of return than other alternatives. The point is that economic analysis is a powerful tool, but it is only part of the decision-making process.

Synthesis—Fire Management Policy & Programs for the Future

Fire has had a significant impact on Pacific Northwest forests since long before the appearance of the first Native Americans, or any elements of modern civilization. The character of much of the forest as we see it today is a reflection of this important and natural ecological force. Scientists are reasonably sure about such things as the intensity and frequency of these natural fires, and of their consequence in determining forest composition and structure.

In the last 100 years or so there has been a significant new dimension to fire in the forest as a result of the actions of contemporary humans and the practice of forestry. The questions we ask today about fire are not so much about its historical nature as about its role and impact in the forests of today and, more importantly, the forests of tomorrow.

Resource managers are developing policy and action programs, and making day-to-day decisions involving the management of fire in all the forests of the Pacific Northwest, ranging from tree farms to wilderness areas. Regulatory officials, the interested public, and to an increasing degree the legis-lative and judicial branches of government are heavily involved. Sound knowledge of the physical, biological, economic, and social impacts of various strategies for fire management are crucial to the formulation of rational policy and action programs and for making effective day-to-day decisions.

Looking in retrospect to learn about fire in the forest is important and helpful, but the key is to look ahead and to prepare for the future. Our society, the forests, and the environment of the future will surely be different than they are today. Whatever we decide about fire in the forest today must make sense for tomorrow.

Changing character of the forest

In aggregate, the forest of the future will be very different from the forests of the historical Northwest. The key difference is that the forests of the future will all be actively managed to produce an explicit array of values and services. They will fall into four general categories:

Wilderness-like forests. These forests can resemble the historical forest. However, the historical forest was greatly influenced by natural fire. The biological character of wilderness-like forests is certain to change (probably slowly by human standards) if fire is not allowed to play its historical role. Conscious decisions to exclude fire may be perfectly acceptable providing we understand and are prepared to accept the inevitable shifts in vegetation density and species composition, forest structure, and wildlife habitat which are certain to follow in the long run. In addition, lest we forget the lessons from the 1988 Yellowstone fires, it is not humanly possible to exclude all fire, and there is always the possibility of a major conflagration in wilderness forests, despite any policy to the contrary. The challenge is to adopt and carry out policies for the management of fire which will maintain the desired wilderness-like characteristics of these forests in the future.

Long rotation forests. Many of these are publicly owned and will be managed for multiple uses including timber. The intensity of management for timber will be moderate, and significant attention will be given to the active production of nontimber values such as recreation, wildlife, and water. These forests will have a longer rotation age than most intensively managed forests, allowing for longer periods of stabilization and development.

In some instances it will be feasible to manage for an all-aged forest, with selective harvesting of individual trees at periodic intervals on a sustained basis.

Natural fire has been excluded in these forests since the early 1900s, but prescribed fire has played a significant role in fuel reduction and vegetation control during reforestation. As these second-generation forests mature, and as utilization of woody biomass increases, the need for prescribed fire to reduce fuels will decrease.

In some forest types which might be managed on a long rotation basis, the long-term exclusion of both natural and prescribed fire caused significant shifts in vegetation density and species composition. It may be necessary to reintroduce the use of fire in these forests in order to restore the original vegetation type, and to promote species composition and stand densities which minimize stress and subsequent susceptibility to insect attack and disease. Prescribed fire may also continue to be needed in areas where competing vegetation inhibits reforestation.

Short rotation forests. Most of these forests will be privately owned and intensively managed primarily for timber, but with appropriate protection of other values. Intense management combined with a high degree of utilization will greatly reduce fuel loads. Consequently the role of fire in hazard reduction will be less, although it may be quite important in achieving prompt and efficient reforestation in some forest types, and in controlling species composition and stand density in others.

Inactively managed forests. These forests will often be in nonindustrial private ownership where timber was harvested with only minimal attention to reforestation and future timber production. Natural fire has traditionally been excluded and prescribed fire is not used. The active use of fire in these forests in the future under existing ownership is unlikely.

In aggregate these four forest categories provide a spectrum of forest conditions which are quite different from the historical forests of the Pacific Northwest. They differ both at the stand level and the broad landscape level of resolution. The role and impact of fire differs as well. The challenge is to recognize the differences, and to develop appropriate fire management strategies which accommodate them.

Changing character of society

Neither society nor the forest is static, but society is not on a repeating cycle. The early stages of Euro-American society in the western United States focused on human survival and community establishment. Later stages emphasized the formation of institutions and infrastructure which promoted societal welfare and development. Currently, the emphasis is on improving and assuring a high quality of life. Thus the concerns of society are shifting from the more basic requirements essential to short-run survival to those which prolong life (hence much of our concern with health-related issues) and enhance its quality (ergo the increased attention to recreation, aesthetics, and nonconsumptive uses of the forest).

Other changes involve:

- increases in population, life span, level of education, standard of living, and urbanization;
- decreases in the number of individuals involved in basic agriculture, forestry, fisheries, mining, and other natural resource fields;
- decreasing numbers involved in basic manufacture; and
- increases in the numbers involved in professional and service sectors of employment.

The result is a population which is of very different character, and thus has different needs, expectations, and a different base of experience. These changes in our society are manifested by seemingly incompatible demands for increased production of an expanded slate of resource products and values and an increased emphasis on preservation of natural ecosystems. These have resulted in increasing degrees of regulation and public involvement in contemporary forestry matters.

Clearly future policies and programs involving fire in forestry will have to be compatible with the perceptions and wishes of an increasingly concerned and involved public.

Changing character of the environment

In addition to changes in the forest itself and in society, the broader environment is changing as well. Environmental changes will influence how the forest responds to future changes, including those imposed by forest managers—such as the results of fire management strategies.

The changes which draw the most attention because of their potential impacts on the forest involve air quality (particularly acid precipitation), global climate, and long-term forest productivity or sustainability. Fire directly influences each of these parameters. Because these environmental changes affect forest development, future forests can be expected to respond somewhat differently to fire than have the forests of the past.

Thus we are faced with a dynamic situation. Rational fire management in forestry must complement the broader strategies focusing on minimizing environmental change (both locally and globally), and be compatible with the changes in the forest environment which will occur.

Fire management in a changing world

Managers, regulators, the public, and others involved with fire management have an exceedingly complex challenge. It is to formulate policy, action programs, and day-to-day decisions which incorporate our best understanding of the technical information available about fire within a framework of a changing forest, society, and environment. The result must be biologically sound, make sense economically, be socially acceptable, and practically feasible.

Much of the technical information available for this purpose is summarized in section one of this chapter and is presented in detail in the remaining chapters of this book. Other information is needed to incorporate important social and political considerations which are part of the equation. Overview perspectives on fire management for the future are in the two subsections which follow. One is directed at resource managers and regulators, the second at legislators, the judiciary, and the interested public.

Perspective for managers and regulators

Fire management is one tool with which broader resource management objectives can be met. With the greatly increased attention currently focused on fire, it is imperative that fire policy does not direct natural resource management objectives, but rather the reverse. Managers must first establish acceptable objectives for the management of the forest, and *then* evaluate the alternatives for their accomplishment, selecting those which optimize productivity, efficiency, resource protection, and other societal goals. Fire may be one part of the strategy.

Fire management policy needs to have a broad landscape perspective, even though action pro-

grams will be quite site specific. In the last several years forestry has made a quantum jump, as the field of vision has been expanded to include large collections of stands into what is now called the landscape perspective. Just as we have long recognized that individual components of the ecosystem of a stand are interrelated and influence one another, so we now recognize that stands are not independent, but in aggregate they influence on a broader scale such seemingly site-specific things as water, wildlife, microclimate, and forest productivity. We still have a lot to learn about management with a landscape perspective. While the initial research is focused on the biology of these systems, information is also needed on the social and economic aspects such as the flow of timber, efficiency of forest operations, and local and regional economies.

Integrated forest resource management is an important concept that is assuming increasing prominence. It means the active management of the total forest resource to achieve the desired mix of products, services, and amenities. The exact mix of items or the emphasis they receive will be different among ownerships, depending on owners' objectives and constraints, but integrated management means decisions are made with active recognition of the consequences for the full array of resource values. Historically, we often managed for only one or a few values, with the production of other values passively accepted as they happened to occur. In contemporary forestry, various resource specialists work together in developing management strategies to produce the desired mix of values. The outputs are the consequence of active management for their production.

With this broad perspective, forest managers synthesize a tremendous amount of technical, economic, and sociopolitical information to develop resource management objectives, and specifically the strategies for the management of fire which are consistent with them. The key technical elements in this process are:

- Awareness of the historical role of fire in shaping the forest ecosystems of today, and the need for fire or some alternative strategy that accomplishes approximately the same ends if the character of these forests is to be maintained. In some forest types being managed on long rotations, fire plays an essential role in controlling species composition and vegetation density—key factors in minimizing adverse effects from weeds, insects, and disease. These fires can be naturally occurring when managed to accomplish specified objectives. Alternatively, prescribed fire can be used where management policies permit. The key is to make active, intelligent decisions about the management of these forests, including options involving fire or alternatives that emulate its desired effects.

- Awareness of the impacts fire can have on site resources and environmental values. As with any tool or practice, the use of fire has impacts. These include impacts on air quality (aesthetics and human health), site quality (primarily nutrients and organic matter), and wildlife habitat (forage and cover). Strategies for the management of fire must include careful evaluations of these impacts and the methods and cost for their amelioration. In essence this is a cost-benefit analysis, with full recognition of all the costs, both direct and indirect. Comparisons need to be made with alternative techniques and strategies so that tradeoffs are fully understood.
- Awareness of public perceptions (including those of legislators and the judiciary) about forest management and about fire in the forest. Among the various issues faced by managers and regulators, this is by far the most difficult and challenging. It includes a couple of subelements. The most important of these is public education. Unfortunately it has received little attention. Most members of the public have little or no understanding of forest ecology, the ability of professionals to actively manage forest resources in concert with ecological principles for the welfare of society, and the key role of fire in both natural and managed forests. The second subelement is recognition that members of society do not agree on the objectives for forest resource management. The key is to acknowledge these differences, and to chart a path which focusses on topics of common agreement, rather than on topics of dispute. This is an exceedingly difficult task, and one which is made much more difficult because the target is a moving one, since public opinion and desire ebbs and flows in an often unpredictable manner.

Perspectives for the public, legislators, and the judiciary

Five concepts are important in the perspective for the public about fire in the forest:
- The forest is dynamic. Despite its static appearance, the forest is changing, albeit usually slowly by human standards. Efforts to maintain it without enrolling or emulating nature's own processes (including fire) are doomed to fail.
- Forest ecosystems are resilient; that is, they can respond favorably to (or recover from) both natural and human-induced disturbance, including natural and managed fire. They will not instantly recover their former characteristics, but rather will move through the successional pattern dictated by the site, the environment, and the nature of the disturbance. The forest which results is never exactly like the former forest, just as the former forest was never exactly like its predecessor.
- Forests can be managed (including the use of natural or managed fire) in an active and a positive manner to provide a multiplicity of benefits for society. Some of these benefits, such as timber, game, and grazing, are consumptive. Thoughtful and careful management for consumptive uses will ensure their renewability and assure the availability of other values. All values will not always be available at all times on every acre, but across the landscape mosaic of managed forests they may be.
- Forest management practices can be complementary to nature's processes, helping to assure the long-term production of multiple resource values. Natural fire has played an important role historically in shaping the forest, and managed fire can (and probably needs to) play a similar role in contemporary managed forests.
- Forestry is an applied science, with a strong foundation in the basic physical and biological sciences. Perhaps equally important, forests are managed by professionals who use this technical base in the development of both broad policy and site-specific action programs.

Presumably the public wants decisions about forest resources which promote the welfare and development of our society. Towards this end it is essential for the public to understand that the forest is dynamic and resilient, and that it can be actively managed for the benefit of our society, in both the short run and the long. In addition, forestry professionals apply a solid technical base of information in developing strategies for the management of the forest to optimize the mix of values available to society according to the objectives and constraints of the landowner. With these perspectives more firmly in mind, the public can participate more effectively in shaping forest management (including fire) policy.

Research needs

There is a long history of forestry research on the patterns and effects of natural fire, and the use and impacts of prescribed fire. Much of this information is contained in the other chapters of this book, and each author points out the most pressing research needs in their area. These specific research needs are included in the following major categories. Additional research is needed on predicting the behavior of natural fire, techniques for managing natural fire, and quantification of the benefits associated with prescribed fire. The most pressing needs, however, involve the effects of fire on site quality, the contribution of fire to global climate change (e.g., carbon dioxide balance), techniques to minimize emissions from fire, and human health effects from exposure to fire emissions—emerging topics of concern that have not received much research scrutiny. Finally, research is needed which integrates across disciplines and, through a process of synthesis, develops strategies for the management of fire *and* the forest to achieve the general goals of society and the specific goals of landowners and managers.

Making decisions now

There will always be a call for more research, because the more we learn the more we realize how much more there is to learn. The primary motivation for more knowledge is the desire to increase the certainty with which we can draw conclusions, and the confidence we can then place in our decisions. Sometimes there is a tendency to feel that if the information is incomplete, a rational decision is not possible. Fortunately, there is a reasonable base of information which will permit good decisions concerning the use of fire in forest and range management.

Better (or at least more certain) decisions will be possible with the additional information which will come from future research, but the reality is that decisions must be made now, using the best information available. The logical way to proceed in the face of some uncertainty is with caution, using conservative assumptions and building in wide margins of safety. This approach will ensure the decisions can accommodate the unknown, and the possibly unexpected response. This is a common strategy in risk management, and it can be successfully applied to decisions about fire in forestry.

The key is to determine with accuracy the major gaps in knowledge, and the impact of these gaps on the certainty of the decisions which involve them, and the consequence of being wrong. When the gap is significant, the level of certainty is low, and the consequences of being wrong are substantial, then the most conservative approach is warranted. Conversely, if the gap is small, the level of certainty is high, and the consequences of being wrong are minor, a much higher level of risk is acceptable. These extreme positions are easy. The difficulty comes in dealing with the huge middle ground. Developing rational policy and defensible decisions in this area is a challenge for us all.

Once we have reached a decision, there is a danger we may accept it without further serious evaluation. Given that we will never know it all, this complacency can be an insidious danger, causing us to fail to adjust our position or decisions as new information becomes available. The keys to preventing this problem are to assure that foresters and other resource managers carefully observe and evaluate the results of action programs, that researchers focus on the most significant data gaps, and that operations and research workers integrate new information as part of an ongoing program of evaluating past decisions and formulating new ones. Vigilance to the unexpected and new information, combined with thoughtful analysis, are the keys to assuring the long-term success of all forest management decisions, including those involving fire.

II Natural History and Ecology

3 The Historical Role of Fire in Pacific Northwest Forests

James K. Agee

Executive Summary

Fires have burned through Pacific Northwest forests for thousands of years, as evidenced by pollen and charcoal deposits from early forests, fire scars on trees, analysis of stand age classes, and early settler and explorer accounts. Fire is not a uniform process in time or space on the landscape. The frequency, intensity, and extent of fires differ considerably across the Pacific Northwest; these differences can be categorized by the concept of the fire regime. In this chapter, past effects of high-, moderate-, and low-severity fire regimes in natural forests are described, with examples from several forest types in each regime. A comparison of historical and current fires in the Pacific Northwest reveals that modern fire control policies have been effective at reducing acreage burned by free-ranging wildfire. Ironically, success at fire suppression has allowed more uniform and larger fuel loads across the landscape, resulting in more severe fire effects. The objectives of fire management must be broader than simply fire suppression if land management objectives are to be met.

Introduction

Fire has been an important disturbance factor in Pacific Northwest forests for thousands of years. Climatic and cultural changes over these years have affected the distribution of forest types, fire ignition and behavior patterns, and subsequent ecological effects. Fire has played and will continue to play an important role in the development of these forests.

The presence of fire in Pacific Northwest forests can be traced back over many thousands of years through analysis of pollen and charcoal deposited and preserved in bogs (Hansen 1938, Tsukada et al. 1981, Cwynar 1987). Postglacial forest fires were instrumental in changing the course of forest succession, and in replacing certain species on a site by others over time (Hermann 1985). When the first Europeans arrived in the Pacific North-

west, they recorded substantial amounts of burned land. David Douglas, the botanist for whom Douglas-fir was named, remarked often in his journals about the burned-over land in the Willamette Valley. In September 1826, he noted:

> Country undulating; soil rich, light, with beautiful solitary oaks and pines interspersed through it . . . but being all burned. . . . Camped on the side of a low woody stream in the centre of a small plain—which, like the whole of the country I have passed through, is burned (Davies 1980).

Journals of early visitors and settlers to the Puget Sound region of Washington also recorded considerable evidence of fire and smoke in the 1830-60 period (Norton 1979). A history of recent catastrophic fires in western Oregon and Washington (1826-1933) is presented by Morris (1934).

John Muir travelled to Puget Sound in 1918 and was impressed by the fire history of Douglas-fir forests in the Olympic Mountains:

> These last [trees] show plainly enough that they have been devastated by fire, as the black, melancholy monuments rising here and there above the young growth bear witness. Then, with this fiery, suggestive testimony, on examining those sections whose trees are a hundred years old or two hundred, we find the same fire-records, though heavily veiled with mosses and lichens, showing that a century or two ago the forests that stood there had been swept away in some tremendous fire at a time when rare conditions of drought made their burning possible (Weaver 1974).

These early accounts suggest that fires were sometimes infrequent, sometimes common; sometimes killed all the trees, as in Muir's account of Douglas-fir, and sometimes left the mature trees unscathed, as in Douglas' description of pines and oaks. The remainder of this chapter describes these different "fire regimes" and compares historical to current fire in these ecosystems.

Today's fire management strategies in Oregon and Washington are the outgrowth of nine decades of fire management policy evolution. At the turn of the twentieth century, deliberate and accidental fires scoured the western portions of these states, with the 1902 Yacolt fire being the worst in terms of size and lives lost. Fire control organizations began to appear as volunteer groups, and foresters believed that fire control was imperative before forest management could become effective.

In western Oregon and Washington, industrial landowners led the way towards effective fire protection. At the same time, they felt that burning slash fuels on cutover areas would better protect virgin timber supplies. Slash burning was recognized as a legitimate part of forest fire management policy in western Oregon and Washington, where natural fires were generally severe and infrequent.

In eastern Oregon and Washington, where fires of past centuries had been very frequent but of low severity, fire policy was influenced by developments in similar forest types in California. The use of underburning with light surface fires was viewed as a continuation of Indian burning practices, and Piute forestry, as it was called, was declared a challenge to efficient fire management. Total fire suppression was a uniform policy by the late 1920s in these forests.

These views began to be reevaluated in the 1950s, and have eventually resulted in less slash burning on the westside and more underburning on the eastside of Oregon and Washington. Effective fire suppression techniques, fire prevention campaigns, and environmental concerns about smoke have resulted in lower proportions of westside harvested areas being burned. During the same period, fire has been reintroduced as a tool for fire hazard reduction, forest thinning, and wildlife management in the drier forests east of the Cascade Mountains. It is against this cultural history of fire that the following natural history summaries can be compared.

This chapter focuses on the role of fire in "unmanaged," or more descriptively, "natural" forests—those that developed before widespread logging or fire protection existed. Such forests, although described as "natural," did in some areas have significant Indian influence, particularly in relation to fire history. Today, few areas are managed to maintain that primeval influence, and most areas have had these natural fire regimes altered by forest management practices, including too much or too little fire control. The descriptions of natural fire regimes in this chapter are intended to serve as a baseline against which our modern forest practices and management strategies can be compared.

Fire History & Fire Regimes

Fires left impressions not only on early visitors, such as Douglas or Muir, but also on the vegetation. Fire frequency and extent can be deduced from such evidence as stand age class distribution or fire scars on tree stems in natural forests (Fig. 3-1). In some cases, where many smaller trees or only a few large trees have survived, a relative measure of fire severity may also be deduced. Fire scars are most valuable for fire history when fires are frequent but of low severity. Age class analyses of stands across the landscape are most valuable when fire history consists of infrequent but high-severity fires. Both techniques are valuable in studying the fire history of Pacific Northwest forests because both types of fires were dominant in different forest types. Where fires of similar frequency, severity, and extent occur, such forests are said to have a similar fire regime.

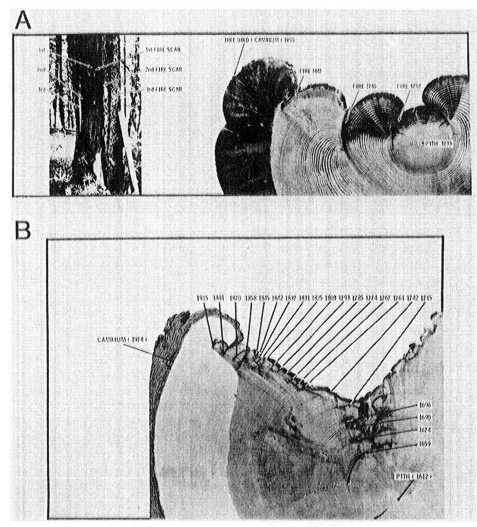

Figure 3-1. Examples of multiple fire scars on (A) lodgepole pine and (B) ponderosa pine. Only part of the cambium is killed by these fires, so the tree slowly heals the wound. The annual growth rings record the number of years of growth since the scar was formed, enabling precise reconstruction of the years of the fires in many cases. (Source: Arno and Sneck 1977)

Fire regimes of the Pacific Northwest have been described by Agee (1981; Fig. 3-2). They are a function of growing environment (temperature and moisture patterns), ignition pattern (lightning, human), and plant species characteristics (fuel accumulation, adaptations to fire; Chapter 4). Effects of forest fires can be more precisely described if effects can be grouped by fire regimes. Fire regimes will be described in this chapter in three broad, artificially grouped categories, which overlap considerably with one another:

High-severity regimes: fires are very infrequent (more than 100 years between fires); they are usually high-intensity, stand-replacement fires.

Moderate-severity regimes: fires are infrequent (25-100 years); they are partial stand-replacement fires, including significant areas of high and low severity.

Low-severity regimes: fires are frequent (1-25 years); they are low-intensity fires with few overstory effects.

These three broad fire regimes can be described by environmental gradients of temperature and moisture (Fig. 3-2). High-severity fire regimes are typically moist and cool; fire occurs under unusual conditions, such as during drought and with dry, hot winds (Pickford et al. 1980). Fires are often of short duration (days to weeks) but of high intensity and severity. Moderate-severity fire regimes occur in areas with typically long summer dry periods and fires will last weeks to months. Periods of intense fire behavior are mixed with periods of moderate- and low-intensity fire behavior; variable weather is associated with variable fire effects. In low-severity fire regimes, nearly continual summer drought exists, and fires are typically frequent and widespread. Frequent fires limit the time for fuel to accumulate, so typical fire intensity is moderate to low.

The Role of Fire in High-Severity Fire Regimes

High-severity fire regimes are common in the coastal mountains of Oregon, the middle to northern Cascades, the Olympic Mountains, and other typical westside forests. The natural fire regime is one of infrequent crown or severe surface fires that usually result in total mortality of trees in the stand. Fires are associated with drought years, east wind synoptic weather types which lower humidity, and an ignition source such as lightning (Huff and Agee 1980, Pickford et al. 1980). Accurate fire return intervals have never been calculated in these forests, because the intervals between fires are long and may not be cyclic (Agee and Flewelling 1983). Three of the common forest types in this fire regime are arranged along a low to high elevational transect: western hemlock/Douglas-fir forests, Pacific silver fir forests, and subalpine forests. Fire in these forest types is an agent of ecosystem instability, as it creates major shifts in forest structure and function. Such shifts include changes in plant species composition, movement of production potential from the tree canopy to the forest floor, significant release of nutrients as ash or into the atmosphere, and both positive and negative changes in wildlife habitat.

Western hemlock/Douglas-fir forests

The western hemlock/Douglas-fir forests are widely distributed across the Pacific Northwest. Fires in this mixed-species forest usually result in almost complete tree mortality (Fig. 3-3). After fire, western hemlock seedlings may outnumber Douglas-fir, but the Douglas-fir are usually more robust. Douglas-fir seedlings are best able to become naturally established in sun (including par-

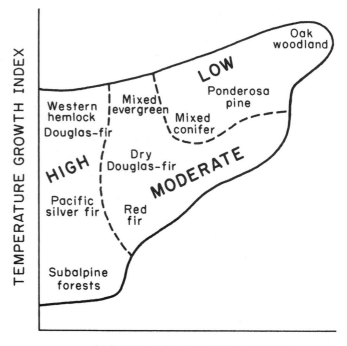

MOISTURE STRESS INDEX

Figure 3-2. The forest types discussed in this chapter are arranged on axes of temperature and moisture along which all the Pacific Northwest forests can be found. The three general natural fire severity regimes (low, moderate, and high) are a function of the general growing environment, fire ignition and intensity patterns, and species adaptations to fire.

tial shading from snags) on shallow forest floors following such disturbances. Douglas-fir establishment in this early postfire environment is critical if it is to later dominate the forest. Understory vegetation is usually similar to that growing in the old-growth, preburn forest: huckleberries, vine maple, sword fern, rhododendron, salal, and Oregon grape.

Twenty years after a fire, much of the new character of the forest has been defined. A thick thatch of berries and bracken fern fronds covers the forest floor and inhibits tree regeneration beyond that already established in the first few years after the fire. Plant and animal diversity is very high at this successional stage of the forest.

As the forest continues to develop, the canopy closes and the natural thinning process accelerates. The lack of light in the understory significantly reduces shrub and herb cover, and the simplified structure of the forest is reflected in lower plant and animal diversity. Many small logs fall to the forest floor, and the overstory trees begin to exhibit some significant diameter variation.

On drier sites, such forests may burn again after 100 to 200 years. Fahnestock and Agee (1983) estimated the regional average at 230 years. Some forests in wetter environments will have even longer fire return intervals. These old-growth forests remain dominated by Douglas-fir, which slowly drop out of the stand, beginning at age 250 and continuing to age 700-1000. By this time all of the tree crown classes are dominated by western hemlock, which quickly occupy any growing space vacated by Douglas-fir. The cycle from Douglas-fir to western hemlock rarely is completed because fires

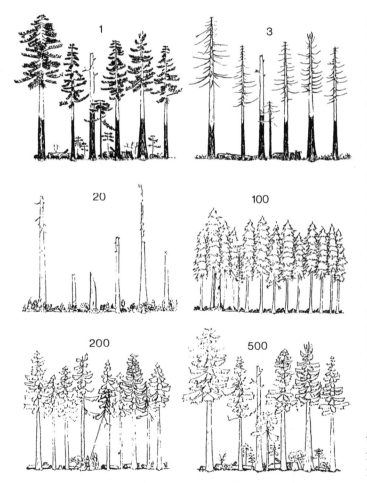

Figure 3-3. A chronosequence of forest development in western hemlock/Douglas-fir forest is schematically presented. Each number above the stand refers to the postfire age of the stand. The typical fire regime is a high-severity fire, and is associated with ecosystem instability. (Adapted from Huff 1984)

usually occur before Douglas-fir disappears from the stand.

Pacific silver fir forests

Pacific silver fir forests are often found in and above the elevation zone of persistent winter snowpack. These forests are cooler and have a shorter growing season than the western hemlock/Douglas-fir forests. Historic fires in lower forest zones have sometimes naturally extinguished themselves upon entering Pacific silver fir forests (Schmidt 1960, Henderson and Peter 1981). Hemstrom and Franklin (1982) estimated fire frequency at 465 years for the Pacific silver fir forests of Mount Rainier, tracing the fire record back to the 13th century. Only a few stands had survived without disturbance since that time. In approximately 1230 A.D. almost half of the forest area burned, while in the 1300s and 1700s less than 5 percent of the forest burned. The record was similarly variable in other centuries. No clear explanation yet exists for such variation, but subtle climatic shifts, such as an increase in lightning fire potential, possibly coupled with drought, may be partially responsible.

Throughout many Pacific silver fir forests, Douglas-fir shares early successional dominance with noble fir and western white pine. The ages of these trees are often used as indicators of a past fire disturbance. As stands become older, Pacific silver fir assumes a more dominant role, similar to that of western hemlock in lower-elevation forests.

Regeneration time after large disturbances may exceed 50 to 75 years in these midelevation forests. At Mount Rainier, some stands that burned near the turn of the century continue to be so open that Douglas-fir is still becoming established (Hemstrom and Franklin 1982).

Subalpine forests

Subalpine forests are, as the name implies, a transitional type between forested and non-forested alpine landscapes. Disturbances such as naturally occurring fire in this ecological tension zone can result in conversion of forest to shrub and herbaceous communities for a century or more. Landscape diversity in subalpine environments depends on the balance between forest and nonforest communities, so that fire has a large role in subalpine landscape maintenance.

Postfire climate has a large effect on forest recovery after fire, by influencing the survival of germinating seedlings. In the Olympic Mountains, tree establishment after fire was related to mild, moist springs and summers and good seed years; even so, large burns will remain meadows for over a century (Agee and Smith 1984; Fig. 3-4). After fire, a wide variety of successional pathways (to huckleberry, heather, or herb communities) is possible (Henderson 1973), depending upon the degree of forest dominance of the site, fire severity, and site factors such as persistence of snowpack into the dry season.

The Role of Fire in Moderate-Severity Fire Regimes

Moderate-severity fire regimes are the most difficult to characterize. Fire frequencies usually range from 25 to 100 years and individual fires often show a wide range of effects, from high to low severity. The overall effect is a patchiness over the landscape as a whole, and individual stands will often consist of two or more age classes.

Dry Douglas-fir forests

Dry Douglas-fir forests may be found in the west-central Cascades, in the San Juan Islands and further south in the Puget Trough, and along the midelevation eastern Cascades. Fire frequency may be in the range of 70 to 100 years (Means 1982, Agee and Dunwiddie 1984, Morrison and

Figure 3-4. Subalpine forest development after high-severity fire can be very slow. (A) A 3-year-old fire in the western Olympic Mountains. (B) The center of a 55-year-old fire in the central Olympic Mountains, essentially treeless after half a century. (C) The edge of the 55-year-old fire. The treeline is slowly advancing upslope adjacent to a seed source. (D) A 90-year-old fire in the western Olympic Mountains. Note the open character of the landscape almost a century after the fire, and the contribution this fire has made to the landscape diversity of the site. (Adapted from Agee and Smith 1984)

Swanson, in press). In these forests, where summer moisture is quite limiting, adequate growing space for regeneration is often linked to forest disturbance which creates sites for tree establishment as a result of overstory mortality. Historically, fire has been the most prominent disturbance in such stands.

Multi-aged forests are common (Fig. 3-5). In Washington's Stehekin Valley, three age classes, each separated from the next by a 90-year fire-free interval, were found in the same stand (Oliver and Larson 1981). In the central Cascades of Oregon, Stewart (1986) documented four fires (approximately 450, 320, 120, and 90 years in the past) associated with various age classes of trees.

Forest development in such forests has been summarized by Means (1982). Fire kills a portion of the canopy trees, and surviving trees often occur in patches. Many small trees are killed because of thin bark and low crowns: some are killed immediately and others die slowly, weakened by decay which enters fire scars on stems and roots. Tree establishment occurs in the newly available growing space, and can continue for decades after fire. Such forests often have an "all-sized" (reverse J-shape) diameter distribution but the age class initiation is not continuous but rather pulsed after fire disturbances.

Mixed-evergreen forests

Tanoak-Douglas-fir forests in southwestern Oregon have a complex disturbance history. Atzet and Wheeler (1982) estimated a 20-year fire return interval for interior stands and perhaps 60 years for stands closer to the coast. A high percentage of natural stands have a history of frequent surface fires, resulting in two- or three-storied stands with each story being even-aged. The layered understory vegetation often contributes to the intensity of the fire: waxy-leaved shrubs and trees can carry flames into the overstory, creating a high-intensity fire.

Following intense fires, which occur in patches on the landscape, tanoak sprouts from the root collar, while Douglas-fir must reestablish from seed. Either species can dominate the stand, or the stands may contain a mixture of both. If tanoak dominates, it will form a solid canopy and exclude Douglas-fir until that canopy begins to break up between age 60 and 100. The eventual stand will be a mix of the two species. If the stand is mixed from

the beginning, Douglas-fir will begin to dominate after 15-30 years because of its faster height growth at and after that time. When the Douglas-fir begins to break up, tanoak established in the understory is released, forming a mix of the two species (Thornburgh 1982).

Examples of such stable, two-story stands are rare because of fire history. Successive intense fires may result in a hardwood-dominated stand, while several less intense fires may result in as many age classes, each dominated by the species best able to take advantage of the environment following the fire.

Red fir forests

Red fir forests occur in southwestern Oregon and in the southern Cascades, and are widespread in the Sierra Nevada of California. They are often

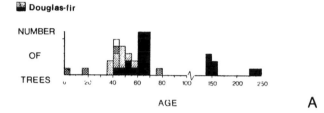

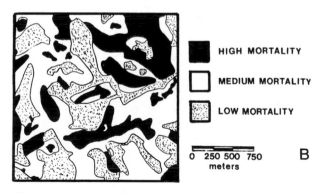

Figure 3-5. (A) Multi-aged forests are a common result of moderate-severity fire regimes. Douglas-fir is found in three age classes: 250, 150, and less than 70 years, all associated with disturbance by fire. The other tree species have established after the most recent disturbance but most or all will be removed by the next fire, leaving Douglas-fir as the major residual species. (Adapted from Agee and Dunwiddie 1984) (B) A mosaic of forest patches is created and maintained by moderate-severity regime fires. This patchy mosaic was created by historic fires in a Douglas-fir forest in the Cascade Mountains of Oregon. (Adapted from Morrison and Swanson, in press)

in a transitional position between lower-elevation and higher-elevation forests which exhibit quite different fire regimes; red fir forests often exhibit a transitional, moderate-severity fire regime.

At Crater Lake National Park, a fire return interval exceeding 40 years was found for low-elevation red fir forests (McNeil and Zobel 1980). A 78-year fire return interval was estimated for red fir forests of Sequoia National Park in California (Pitcher 1987), and the structure of the forest was closely tied to disturbance history. Stands were either one age class (implying an intense fire) or several age classes (implying fires of varying severity).

Recent observations of natural fires at Crater Lake National Park indicate this variable-severity regime is characteristic of fires in red fir forests (Fig. 3-6). Natural fires of this type were allowed to burn in 1978 and in 1986. Fire behavior in much of the area was moderately severe, with some areas of high and low severity. The result will most likely be initiation of new forest age classes in the high- and moderate-severity areas, and very little structural effect in the low-severity area. Fire is associated with increasing landscape diversity in this forest type. A mosaic of even-aged and multi-aged stands is the result of natural disturbance being allowed to create pattern on the landscape.

Climax lodgepole pine forests

The lodgepole pine forests of south-central Oregon are intricately tied to a disturbance pattern including fires, insects, and disease (Gara et al. 1985). They grow on infertile pumice deposits

Figure 3-6. Natural fire in red fir forests at Crater Lake creates a mosaic of fire effects. (A) The Goodbye Fire of 1978 during a period of rapid spread. (B) The Goodbye Fire eight years later, showing the variable severity at a landscape scale. (C) A low-severity patch in the fire, where even some of the small understory trees survived. (D) A moderate-severity patch, where many of the understory trees were killed. The white line is the approximate scorch height of the fire (4 ft). A sheltering overstory of trees remains at this site. (E) A high-severity patch, where all the trees have been killed, after 8 years.

from the eruption of Mount Mazama over 6,000 years ago. They are among the least productive of any forest type in the Pacific Northwest, and litter production is so limited that fires usually cannot spread across the forest floor. Rooting depths are very shallow.

Fires in this forest type usually spread by smoldering along logs that are partially decayed and jackstrawed across the forest floor. Such "cigarette burns" (Fig. 3-7) are a function of dead and down logs, which are created by mountain pine beetle attacks that may have occurred decades earlier. The fires burn slowly and conduct enough heat into the ground that the shallow roots can be killed or scarred; if enough roots are killed, the tree can exhibit stress and be attacked by beetles. Scarred roots are entrance points for decay fungi, which decades later make the tree preferentially attractive to bark beetles. Dead trees, when fallen, are the vectors for another "cigarette burn" (Gara et al. 1985).

The stand structure effects of these linked disturbances are multi-aged stands; neither fires nor bark beetles typically remove all of the trees. The growing space opened up by the death of trees is occupied by new age classes of lodgepole pine (Stuart 1983).

The Role of Fire in Low-Severity Fire Regimes

Low-severity fire regimes are associated with frequent fires of low intensity. Most of the dominant trees are adapted to resist fires of low intensity because of thick bark developed at an early age (Chapter 4). Natural fire frequencies are usually less than 25 years, and limited overstory mortality occurs; most of the structural effects of these fires are on very small trees in the understory. Fires in the low-severity regime are associated with ecosystem stability, as the system is more stable in the presence of fire than in its absence.

Oak woodland

Most oak woodlands in the Pacific Northwest have an extended cultural interaction with native peoples. Indians used acorns, camas, bracken fern, and wildlife in the vicinity of such woodlands (Norton et al. 1984) and often burned the oak woodlands (Thilenius 1968, White 1980). In the Willamette Valley, the burned landscapes that

Figure 3-7. A "cigarette burn" in progress along down and decayed lodgepole pine logs in south-central Oregon. The white lines are ashes left from the logs burning; blackened areas on each side are partially consumed needles. The live trees are all lodgepole pine, growing on infertile pumice soils and with shallow rooting patterns. The burning logs will scar or kill roots, setting up either an immediate attack by mountain pine beetles or root and bole scars which are associated with beetle attack decades later.

Douglas observed were largely in this type. Some oak woodland fires were probably ignited by lightning, but Indian burning was very significant.

Fire frequencies must have been high, although no precise estimates exist. The fires were fast-moving and left the mature oaks undamaged. This is apparent from Douglas's journal and also from Wilkes (1844), who observed fires in northwest Oregon ". . . destroy all the vegetation, except the oak trees, which appear to be uninjured."

The result of these apparently frequent fires was a mosaic of oak openings and oak forest, bordering coniferous forest on the upland edge and treeless prairie on the drier margins. Fires would remove shrub species and kill small oak trees and Douglas-fir trees which would otherwise have turned the savanna into a forest (Habeck 1961).

Oregon white oak is now a declining type, largely due to replacement by Douglas-fir on most sites (Fig. 3-8a; Sprague and Hansen 1946, Thilenius 1968). Oregon white oak can be overtopped by much younger Douglas-fir where fire is no longer an environmental factor (Kertis 1986). This did not occur on a wide scale historically and could only have been prevented by fires killing the Douglas-fir while it was small and more susceptible to fire than Oregon white oak. This would require a fire at least every 5 to 10 years.

Ponderosa pine forests

Ponderosa pine forests are uniquely suited to frequent, low-intensity surface fires. They grow in dry environments with prolonged dry seasons and produce sufficient litter to carry fire almost every year. Fire frequencies range from 5 to 20-25 years on most ponderosa pine sites in the Pacific Northwest (Martin 1982, Bork 1985). Such frequent burning is associated with low-intensity fires (Weaver 1967) because fuel energy on or near the ground is consumed at periodic intervals.

Ponderosa pine typically develops in small, even-aged groups. The forest is a mosaic of many different-aged patches. In mature stands, existing overstory trees limit the survival of understory trees through competition for light and moisture. The understory that survives is usually destroyed by the next low-intensity fire through the area, as it will be only a few feet tall at most. When an old, mature group finally succumbs to insects and disease, succeeding fires burn the debris and create an opening for a new age class. In the opening, fuel accumulates more slowly than under mature tree groups, so the next fire or two will burn very lightly through or skip the opening. The lack of fuel in openings allows the pines to grow large enough that many will survive the fires that eventually will pass through the opening (Biswell et al. 1973).

The most striking effect of low-severity fire regimes in ponderosa pine forests is a pronounced vertical stratification of fuels. The periodic fires consume understory and ground fuels, leaving a large fuel gap between the overstory and the ground. This reduces the probability of crown fire, keeps vistas clear, and yet allows the subsequent reestablishment of conifers, shrubs, and grasses. Most of the shrubs found in ponderosa pine forests resprout after burning or have seeds that require heat to germinate (Chapter 4), so under this periodic fire regime a diverse shrub community is maintained within the reach of browsing animals.

In the absence of fire, ponderosa pine regeneration becomes established under the canopy of the mature trees. High density of reproduction with no thinning results in stagnated two-story stands (Biswell et al. 1973).

Figure 3-8. (A) In the absence of frequent fires, Douglas-fir invades Oregon white oak communities, changing these communities from open, savanna-like stands to closed, dense forest. (B-C) Mixed-conifer forests near Crater Lake. These forests were once kept open and park-like by frequent low-severity fires. Fire suppression has allowed small "tree jungles" to crowd the understory (B). Prescribed fire is being used to kill the understory trees in (C) to help recreate the natural condition.

Mixed-conifer forests

The mixed-conifer forest type is similar to the ponderosa pine type. Both types contain ponderosa pine, but the mixed-conifer type may also contain white fir, Douglas-fir, sugar pine, and perhaps small numbers of other species. Each of the species tends to regenerate in pure clumps (Bonnicksen and Stone 1981, Thomas and Agee 1986). Fire frequency is sometimes higher in mixed-conifer forest (even though it is a more moist type than the ponderosa pine type) because it produces more litter (Martin 1982).

All four commonly occurring species are resistant to fire as mature individuals, but as saplings ponderosa pine are most resistant, followed by sugar pine, Douglas-fir, and white fir. Thus, the major structural effect of fire is on young trees, favoring ponderosa pine as a dominant and white fir as a lesser dominant in this forest type. In the absence of frequent fires, white fir becomes a major dominant, because it is much more tolerant of understory competition than the pines. This species composition change occurred in mixed-conifer forests after fire suppression policies were implemented around 1900 (Fig. 3-8b-c; Parsons and DeBenedetti 1979).

A Comparison of Prehistorical & Current Fires in the Pacific Northwest

The importance of fire as an ecological factor in Pacific Northwest forests is clear from the above examples. The role of fire differs considerably from one forest type to another, but whether the last fire occurred in 1980 or in 1480, that role can be ascertained in the structure of current natural forests. Few of today's forests (except for parks and wilderness areas) are managed for natural conditions such as those created by fires of the past, yet fire can be used to achieve socially desirable conditions for a variety of purposes: commercial forest regeneration, park management, wildlife habitat, range improvement, fuel reduction, etc. A comparison of the prehistorical and current roles of fire can place today's uses of fire in perspective.

One such comparison was done for western Washington in the early 1980s (Fahnestock and Agee 1983). Biomass consumed by current fires, both prescribed fires and wildfires, was compared to that estimated for prehistorical fires over past centuries. Annual prehistoric fuel consumption was estimated from fire return intervals based on forest age class data, and from biomass consumption likely to occur from such fires. Over the prehistoric land base, annual consumption was estimated at 312 lbs per acre. Modern fuel consumption from wildfires and prescribed burning on a smaller modern forestland base was estimated to be 339 lbs per acre. Although these figures are index values rather than precise estimates for any given year, they indicate the amount of biomass consumed by wildland fire has continued at roughly the same rate in western Washington.

Timing of modern fires differs from the prehistoric situation. Prehistoric fires, like modern wildfires, must have occurred largely during the summer dry period from June to October, with most area burned near the end of summer. Burning was extensive during dry years, with much less area burned in wet years. Today most of the area burned in western Washington (over 90 percent) is in prescribed fires. They occur over a much wider span of months than prehistoric fires, and the annual average area burned is much more stable than prehistorically (Chapter 6).

A second comparison can be done for the forests of Oregon. Statistics from an old but comprehensive forest survey of the state (Andrews and Cowlin 1940, Cowlin et al. 1942) were used to summarize the area of different forest types in the state. The average fire frequencies obtained from studies in the state (or in nearby states where the same forest type occurs) were applied to those area statistics. The result was an average fire cycle of 42 years for the state's forests in prehistoric times (Table 3-1).

Table 3-1. Acreage and average fire cycles for forest types in Oregon.

Forest Type	Area in Type[a] (thousand acres)	Fire Cycle (years)	Average Annual Historical Burned Area (thousand acres)
Cedar/spruce/ hemlock	721	400[b]	1.8
Douglas-fir	10,978	150[c]	73.2
Mixed conifer	986	30[d]	32.8
Lodgepole pine	1,870	80[e]	23.3
Woodland	2,473	25[f]	98.9
Subalpine	2,657	800[g]	3.3
Ponderosa pine	7,760	15[h]	517.0
Other	5,921	133[i]	44.5
Total	33,366		794.8

Sources:
[a] Andrews and Cowlin 1940, Cowlin et al. 1942.
[b] Agee (unpublished analysis from Andrews and Cowlin 1940).
[c] Means 1982, Morrison and Swanson, in press.
[d] McNeil and Zobel 1980, Atzet and Wheeler 1982, Agee (unpublished data).
[e] Gara et al. 1985.
[f] Martin and Johnson 1979, Bork 1985, Atzet and Wheeler 1982.
[g] Extrapolated from Fahnestock and Agee 1983.
[h] Weaver 1959, Bork 1985.
[i] A weighted average of other types.

This average fire cycle (33,366,000 total acres of forest type divided by 794,800 acres burned per year equals 42 years) suggests that fire was historically very common, and that the early accounts and descriptions of fire were not aberrations.

A 42-year cycle, applied to the forest land base of Oregon, results in an average annual area burned of 800,000 acres. During 1987, considered the worst year for forest fires in Oregon's history, roughly 153,000 acres burned in wildfires, much of it in southwestern Oregon. An average 90,000-105,000 acres of prescribed slash burning occurs in western Oregon annually (Sandberg et al. 1979, State of Oregon/National Weather Service 1976-86). Added to the above wildfire figure, this totals only 30 percent of the historic annual average area burned. This is primarily because the historic average includes the large area of ponderosa pine that burned with low severity and little fuel consumption each year. If the ponderosa pine area is subtracted from the total, the average historic annual area burned is roughly equivalent to the unusually large 1987 total. On a statewide basis, then, modern fire control has been very effective in reducing free-ranging wildfire, as the 1987 wildfire total is unusually large for Oregon.

Conclusion

The historic role of fire is an important element of baseline information useful in integrating fire strategies with the larger land management picture. It can be helpful in estimating which species are likely to dominate the landscape if fire is eliminated as a management tool, and which species will have a relative advantage in the presence of fire.

In general, fire is less prevalent on today's landscapes than in prehistoric times, due to effective fire control policies. Ironically, success in fire suppression has allowed more uniform and increasing fuel loads across the landscape, shifting forest fire effects that were typically of low and moderate severity in historic fires to more severe fire effects today. Fire management objectives must be broader than simply fire suppression if broader goals are to be met. Prescribed fire, and in some cases natural fires, may be useful strategies to integrate with fire suppression to meet land management objectives.

Literature Cited & Key References

*Agee, J.K. 1981. Fire effects on Pacific Northwest forests: flora, fuels, and fauna, p. 54-66. *In* Proc., Northwest Fire Council 1981.

Agee, J.K., and P.W. Dunwiddie. 1984. Recent forest development on Yellow Island, San Juan County, Washington. Can. J. Bot. 62:2074-2080.

Agee, J.K., and R. Flewelling. 1983. A fire cycle model based on climate for the Olympic Mountains, Washington. Fire For. Meteorol. Conf. 7:32-37.

*Agee, J.K., and L. Smith. 1984. Subalpine tree establishment after fire in the Olympic Mountains, Washington. Ecology 65:810-819.

Andrews, H.J., and R.W. Cowlin. 1940. Forest resources of the Douglas-fir region. USDA Misc. Pub. 389. 169 p.

*Arno, S.F., and K.M. Sneck. 1977. A method for determining fire history in coniferous forests of the mountain west. USDA For. Serv., Intermt. For. Rge. Exp. Sta., Ogden, UT. Gen. Tech. Rep. INT-42. 28 p.

*Atzet, T., and D.L. Wheeler. 1982. Historical and ecological perspectives on fire activity in the Klamath Geological Province of the Rogue River and Siskiyou National Forests. USDA For. Serv., Pac. Northwest Reg., Portland, OR. Pub. R-6-Range-102. 16 p.

*Barrett, S.W. 1988. Fire suppression's effects on forest succession within a central Idaho wilderness. West. J. Appl. For. 3:76-80.

Biswell, H.H., H.R. Kallander, R. Komarek, R.J. Vogl, and H. Weaver. 1973. Ponderosa fire management. Tall Timbers Res. Sta., Tallahassee, FL. Misc. Pub. 2. 49 p.

Bonnicksen, T.M., and E.C. Stone. 1981. The giant sequoia-mixed conifer forest community characterized through pattern analysis as a mosaic of aggregations. For. Ecol. Manage. 3:307-328.

Bork, J. 1985. Fire history in three vegetation types on the east side of the Oregon Cascades. Ph.D. thesis. Oregon State Univ., Corvallis, OR. 94 p.

Cowlin, R.W., P.A. Briegleb, and F.L. Moravets. 1942. Forest resources of the ponderosa pine region of Oregon and Washington. USDA Misc. Pub. 490. 99 p.

*Cwynar, L.C. 1987. Fire and the forest history of the North Cascade Range. Ecology 68:791-802.

Davies, J. 1980. Douglas of the Forests. Univ. Washington Press, Seattle, WA. 188 p.

References marked with an asterisk are recommended for general information.

*Fahnestock, G.R., and J.K. Agee. 1983. Biomass consumption and smoke production by prehistoric and modern forest fires in western Washington. J. For. 81:653-657.

Gara, R.I., W.R. Littke, J.K. Agee, D.R. Geiszler, J.D. Stuart, and C.H. Driver. 1985. Influence of fires, fungi, and mountain pine beetles on development of a lodgepole pine forest in south-central Oregon, p. 153-162. *In* Baumgardner, D.M. et al. (eds.) Lodgepole Pine: The Species and Its Management. Washington State Univ., Pullman, WA. 381 p.

Habeck, J.R. 1961. The original vegetation of the mid-Willamette Valley, Oregon. Northwest Sci. 35:65-77.

Hansen, H.P. 1938. Postglacial forest succession and climate in the Puget Sound region. Ecology 19:528-542.

*Hemstrom, M.A., and J.F. Franklin. 1982. Fire and other disturbances of the forests in Mount Rainier National Park. Quat. Res. 18:32-51.

Henderson, J.A. 1973. Composition, distribution, and succession of subalpine meadows in Mount Rainier National Park, Washington. Ph.D. thesis, Oregon State Univ., Corvallis, OR. 150 p.

Henderson, J.A., and D. Peter. 1981. Preliminary plant associations and habitat types of the Shelton Ranger District, Olympic National Forest. USDA For. Serv., Pac. Northwest Reg., Portland, OR. 53 p.

Hermann, R.K. 1985. The genus *Pseudotsuga*: ancestral history and past distribution. For. Res. Lab., Oregon State Univ., Corvallis, OR. Spec. Pub. 2b. 32 p.

Huff, M.H. 1984. Post-fire succession in the Olympic Mountains, Washington: forest vegetation, fuels, and avifauna. Ph.D. thesis, Univ. Washington, Seattle, WA. 240 p.

*Huff, M.H., and J.K. Agee. 1980. Characteristics of large lightning fires in the Olympic Mountains, Washington. Fire For. Meteorol. Conf. 6:117-123.

Kertis, J. 1986. Vegetation dynamics and disturbance history of Oak Patch Natural Area Preserve, Mason County, Washington. M.S. thesis, Univ. Wash., Seattle, WA. 95 p.

*Martin, R.E. 1982. Fire history and its role in succession, p. 92-99. *In* Means, J.E. (ed.) Forest Succession and Stand Development Research in the Northwest. For. Res. Lab., Oregon State Univ., Corvallis, OR. 170 p.

Martin, R.E., and A.H. Johnson. 1979. Fire management of Lava Beds National Monument, p. 1209-1217. *In* Proc., Conference on Research in National Parks, Vol. 2. Nat. Park Serv., Washington, DC.

*McNeil, R.C., and D.B. Zobel. 1980. Vegetation and fire history of a ponderosa pine-white fir forest in Crater Lake National Park. Northwest Sci. 54:30-46.

*Means, J.E. 1982. Developmental history of dry coniferous forests in the central western Cascade Range of Oregon, p. 142-158. *In* Means, J.E. (ed.) Forest Succession and Stand Development Research in the Northwest. For. Res. Lab., Oregon State Univ., Corvallis, OR. 170 p.

*Morris, W.G. 1934. Forest fires in Oregon and Washington. Oregon Hist. Quart. 35:313-339.

*Morrison, P.H., and F.J. Swanson. In press. Fire history in two forest ecosystems of the central western Cascades of Oregon. USDA For. Serv., Pac. Northwest Res. Sta., Portland, OR. Gen. Tech. Rep.

Norton, H.H. 1979. The association between anthropogenic prairies and important food plants in western Washington. Northwest Anthropol. Res. Notes 13:175-200.

Norton, H.H., E.S. Hunn, C.S. Martinsen, and P.B. Keely. 1984. Vegetable food products of the foraging food economies of the Pacific Northwest. Ecol. Fd. Nutrit. 14:219-228.

Oliver, C.D., and B.C. Larson. 1981. Forest resources survey and related consumptive use of firewood in lower Stehekin Valley, North Cascades National Park Complex. Nat. Park Serv., Pac. Northwest Reg., Seattle, WA. Final Rep., Contract CX-9000-9-E088. 133 p.

*Parsons, D.J., and S.H. DeBenedetti. 1979. Impact of fire suppression on a mixed conifer forest. For. Ecol. Manage. 2:21-33.

Pickford, S.D., G. Fahnestock, and R. Ottmar. 1980. Weather, fuels, and lightning fires in Olympic National Park. Northwest Sci. 54:92-105.

*Pitcher, D.L. 1987. Fire history and age structure in red fir forests of Sequoia National Park, California. Can. J. For. Res. 17:582-587.

*Sandberg, D.V., J.M. Pierovich, D.G. Fox, and E.W. Ross. 1979. Effects of fire on air: a state-of-knowledge review. USDA For. Serv., Washington, D.C. Gen. Tech. Rep. WO-9. 40 p.

Schmidt, R.L. 1960. Factors controlling the distribution of Douglas-fir in coastal British Columbia. Quart. J. For. 54:156-160.

Sprague, F.L., and H.P. Hansen. 1946. Forest succession in the McDonald Forest, Willamette Valley, Oregon. Northwest Sci. 20:89-98.

State of Oregon/National Weather Service 1976-86. Annual Report, Oregon Smoke Management Plan. Salem, OR. Var. pages.

Stewart, G.H. 1986. Population dynamics of a montane conifer forest, western Cascade Range, Oregon, USA. Ecology 67:534-544.

Stuart, J.D. 1983. Stand structure and development of a climax lodgepole pine forest in south-central Oregon. Ph.D. thesis, Univ. Washington, Seattle, WA. 212 p.

Thilenius, J.F. 1968. The *Quercus garryana* forests of the Willamette Valley, Oregon. Ecology 49:1124-1133.

*Thomas, T., and J.K. Agee. 1986. Prescribed fire effects on mixed conifer forest structure at Crater Lake, Oregon. Can. J. For. Res. 16:1082-1087.

*Thornburgh, D.A. 1982. Succession in the mixed evergreen forests of northwestern California, p. 87-91. *In* Means, J.E. (ed.) Forest Succession and Stand Development Research in the Northwest. For. Res. Lab., Oregon State Univ., Corvallis, OR. 170 p.

Tsukada, M., S. Sugita, and D.M. Hibbert. 1981. Paleoecology in the Pacific Northwest. I. Late Quaternary vegetation and climate. Internat. Assoc. Theor. Appl. Limnol. Proc. 21:730-737.

Weaver, H. 1959. Ecological changes in the ponderosa pine forest of the Warm Springs Indian Reservation in Oregon. J. For. 57:15-20.

*Weaver, H. 1967. Fire and its relationship to ponderosa pine. Tall Timbers Fire Ecol. Conf. Proc. 7:127-149.

*Weaver, H. 1974. Effects of fire on temperate forests: western United States, p. 279-319. *In* Kozlowski, T.T. and C.E. Ahlgren (eds.) Fire and Ecosystems. Academic Press, New York, NY. 542 p.

White, R. 1980. Land Use, Environment, and Social Change: The Shaping of Island County, Washington. Univ. Washington Press, Seattle, WA. 227 p.

Wilkes, C. 1844. Narrative of the United States expedition during the years 1838, 1839, 1840, 1841, 1842. Vol. 5. Lea and Blanchard, Philadelphia, PA. 558 p.

4 Ecological Relationships of Vegetation and Fire in Pacific Northwest Forests

J. Boone Kauffman

Executive Summary

Through the millennia, fire has greatly affected the composition, structure, and numerous ecological processes of forest ecosystems in the Pacific Northwest. All forest organisms of the Pacific Northwest are intimately suited for survival in their environment, and this includes specific adaptations to ensure persistence following fire. Adaptations to fire might be best thought of as adaptations to survive within the given fire regime of an ecosystem. Therefore, species adaptations that facilitate survival in one fire regime may not necessarily ensure the same in another.

In general, adaptations to fire can be broadly generalized to include those traits which facilitate survival of the individual, and those traits which facilitate reproduction and, hence, perpetuation of the species. Examples of fire-survival traits include thick bark to protect living tissues or the capacity to sprout from below-ground organs. Thick bark is an effective insulator that can protect cambial tissues from damage by surface fires. Bark can also protect dormant buds on trunks and main branches in epicormically sprouting species. Among sprouters, plant age, phenology, and vigor can affect a species' capacity to sprout following fire. Fire severity (i.e., the level of fire intensity and/or fuel consumption) will greatly influence plant survival. For example, thick bark is an adaptation for survival in regimes of low-intensity surface fires, but of little value in severe, stand-replacement fires.

Numerous seedlings from species which require fire for flower stimulation, seed dispersal, or seed scarification and mineral soil exposure for germination and establishment will be present following fire. However, low-consumption fires may not scarify dormant seeds in the soil or create bare mineral soil conditions required by some species to establish. Conversely, high-consumption fires may kill large numbers of dormant seeds, resulting in decreased seedling densities. These high-severity fires would, however, result in large areas of bare ground, facilitating establishment of windborne seeds with a mineral seedbed requirement.

The functional role of coarse woody debris includes nutrient and carbon storage, sites for plant establishment, the maintenance of soil stability, and the presence of wildlife habitat. In many ecosystems, fire is an important disturbance which influences both input and disappearance of coarse woody debris. In regimes characterized by stand-replacement fires, huge inputs of coarse woody debris occur following fire. In regimes characterized by frequent surface fires, the input may be relatively continuous, with small quantities added with each fire. Consumption by fire may be the primary means of disappearance of coarse woody debris in regimes with frequent fire return intervals, whereas decay or decomposition is more important in forests with long fire return intervals.

Changes in forest structure caused by land-use activities can greatly alter fire regimes, resulting in changes in species composition, ecosystem functions, and successional dynamics. Fire suppression and livestock grazing have effectively eliminated the frequent surface fires that characterized the fire regimes of many ponderosa pine and mixed-conifer forests. As a result, fire-intolerant, shade-tolerant conifers have increased, forest insect outbreaks and fuel loads have increased, and habitat diversity and forage production have decreased. Severe stand-replacement fires now occur. On the other hand, in Douglas-fir and Sitka spruce forests of western Oregon and Washington, clearcut and burn rotations of 60-100 year intervals now occur where the natural fire return intervals were 250-500 years or more. These changes have altered forest structure, ecosystem function, and wildlife habitats.

Prescribed burning can be utilized in a positive manner when resource managers are aware of the historical role and ecological influences of fire in forest ecosystems. Knowledge of the vegetation response and potential effects on forest composition and productivity is necessary in order to improve managerial decisions concerning the use of prescribed fire.

Introduction

Early ecologists and forest land managers considered fire an external disturbance that infrequently occurred in Pacific Northwest forests. This was reflected in traditional successional theory as well as the fire control policies of governmental agencies. Now, there is general acceptance that recurring fires are an integral environmental component of a variety of wildland ecosystems (Chapter 3; Borman 1981).

The presettlement composition and structure of Pacific Northwest forests were greatly influenced by fire. Fire plays a direct role in processes associated with vegetation succession, nutrient cycling, and soil structure and stability. However, fire is a dynamic process. Ecosystem response to fire will vary depending on the amounts of organic matter consumed, season of burn, time lapse since the last burn, and the many variables associated with biotic, physical, climatic, and anthropogenic features of an ecosystem.

To fully understand the effects of fire on forest ecosystems, we must understand the autecological and synecological responses of all species present in an ecosystem (Lotan et al. 1981). Because of complex ecological interactions associated with fire and forests, we currently know little of the response of the dominant species to fire and practically nothing of the subordinate species. To effectively utilize fire in natural resource management, we need to learn how to measure, predict, and interpret the biological and ecological responses to the impacts of prescribed fire and wildfire (Lotan et al. 1981).

In order to successfully establish, grow, and reproduce in a fire-influenced ecosystem, a species must possess certain adaptations to fire. Gill (1981) defined traits adaptive to fire as all of those traits contributing to the successful completion of the life cycle of a species in a fire-prone environment. In general, these traits can be separated into two categories; those which enhance persistence or survival of the individual, and those which ensure persistence or survival of the species. Examples of traits which enhance individual survival include thick bark that protects cambial tissues and sprouting from below-ground plant organs. Traits which enhance species persistence include fire-stimulated flowering, seed storage on the plant (e.g., serotinous cones) and fire-stimulated germination of dormant seeds in the soil. Vegetation adaptations to fire are, in reality, adaptations for survival in certain fire regimes. It should be noted that vegetation adaptations which facilitate survival in a fire regime characterized by frequent surface fires (e.g., thick bark to protect cambial tissues) are of little value in the high-severity regimes characterized by crown fires.

In addition to genetic traits, other factors will influence plant response to fire. Characteristics of the individual plant include age and vigor. Specific adaptations and the capacity to survive a fire often will change with age. Environmental conditions which influence survival include type of fire (surface or crown fire), frequency of recurrence (i.e., the fire return interval), season of burn (during the active growing season or quiescence), fuel consumption, fire intensity, physical site characteristics (slope, aspect, soil), and associated species in the composition.

The closer a forest system is managed in harmony with the natural processes by which it evolved, the more successful that management will be (Lotan et al. 1981). Therefore, it is important for forest managers to understand the natural role of fire in forest systems, vegetation adaptations to survival in fire regimes, and the effects of altering fire regimes on vegetation composition. Alterations of fire regime result from active fire suppression in ecosystems which historically had a frequent fire return interval. Fire regimes are also altered by management activities which shorten fire return intervals (e.g., logging followed by slash burning) or lengthen fire return intervals (e.g., livestock grazing which decreases fire spread in some ecosystems due to removal of herbaceous fuels). It is important to understand how management activities may alter the extent and type of fire inherent in the ecosystem. For example, it must be recognized that the consequences of fire occurring in logging slash where the overstory has been removed and the ground has been disturbed will differ from those of wildfire in natural stands (Lotan et al. 1981).

This chapter is a review of ecosystem adaptations to the fire regimes of Pacific Northwest forests (Table 4-1). An increased knowledge of vegetation response to fire can aid in making managerial decisions that ensure the sustained flow of natural resource values, products, and amenities from Pacific Northwest forests.

Table 4-1. Some ecological adaptations of vegetation to fire in Pacific Northwest forests.

Trait	Function	Example
I. Adaptations which facilitate survival of the individual		
Thick bark	protects cambial tissues from heat damage	ponderosa pine, coast redwood, western larch
Epicormic sprouting	regrowth from dormant buds protected by bark on branches and stems	oaks, Douglas hawthorne, tanoak
Basal sprouting	regrowth from subterranean buds located on roots, rhizomes, or lignotubers	roses, Oregon ash, oaks, tanoak
Protected buds from dense leaf bases	protects buds from heat-induced mortality	sword ferns, many grasses (Idaho fescue, bluebunch, wheatgrass)
II. Adaptations which facilitate survival of the species		
Refractory seed buried in soils	dormant seeds with a capacity to survive for hundreds of years until scarified (stimulated to germinate) by fire	manzanitas, ceanothus, lupines
Fire-stimulated flowering	increased reproductive effort the years following fire	many forbs (sego lily) and grasses (Great Basin wildrye)
Seed storage on plants	long-term seed storage on parent plant released by fire	knobcone pine, lodgepole pine
Windborne seeds	early deposition of post-fire soils	fireweed, woodland groundsel

Traits Which Enhance Persistence or Survival of Individuals

Bark properties

Bark characteristics often reflect a plant's capacity to survive certain types of fire and, therefore, reflect the fire regime as well. For example, thick bark on ponderosa pine and western larch is an adaptation to survival in ecosystems with frequent low-severity surface fires (Fig. 4-1; Chapter 3). Conversely, in areas with fire regimes characterized by stand-replacement fires, many conifer species have thinner bark. Thickness has been thought to be the primary characteristic determining the capacity of bark to insulate underlying cambial and meristematic tissues from lethal temperatures (Martin 1963). However, others have suggested that structure, density, moisture content, and possibly chemical composition also influence the thermal properties of bark (Spalt and Reifsnyder 1962, Hare 1965). These variables, in turn, depend on species, age, and vigor of the tree as well as season and weather at the time of burning (Spalt and Reifsnyder 1962).

Figure 4-1. Thick bark protected the mature trees in this ponderosa pine stand. Even though most of the surface fuels and vegetation were consumed by fire, and scorch heights were up to 20 feet, few mature ponderosa pines were killed.

Starker (1934), Arno (1977), Martin and Dell (1978), and Lotan et al. (1981) have subjectively correlated fire resistance to growth characteristics of forest species in Oregon and Washington. Growth characteristics typified by those resistant to fire include thick bark, deep rooting habits, and self-thinning of crowns. Western larch, Douglas-fir, and ponderosa pine were considered the most resistant; white fir and western redcedar intermediate in resistance; and western hemlock, Engelmann spruce, and Sitka spruce most susceptible to fire. Susceptibility and resistance are interpreted in the context of surface fire severity, as none of these conifers would survive severe crown fires. It is interesting to note that the thickness of the bark of western larch and Douglas-fir as a percentage of the diameter has been measured at 7.4 and 6.7 percent, respectively, while that of Engelmann spruce was 0.7 percent (Spalt and Reifsnyder 1962).

Thermal properties of bark to protect cambial tissues will develop early in the life cycle of many species. In the seedling stage, Hall (1977) found that ponderosa pine developed fire-resistant bark containing a 0.13- to 0.25-inch dead outer layer at 2 inches in diameter; whereas white fir bark remained green and photosynthetically active at sizes up to 4 inches in diameter. In mixed-conifer underburns, Kauffman and Martin (1985) reported large differences in the rates of survival among understory conifers less than 6 feet in height. Almost all incense-cedars were killed while high percentages of ponderosa pine (more than 500 per acre) survived. In the seedling stages, white fir, grand fir, incense-cedar, and even western larch are more susceptible to fire-caused mortality than ponderosa pine (Martin and Dell 1978).

Epicormic sprouting

Survival of an individual after fire will depend on the survival of meristematic tissues with vascular connections to the roots (Gill 1977). If these buds survive a fire when the foliage of the plant is destroyed, they will form shoots. Sprouting which occurs from dormant meristematic tissues located beneath bark on stems and branches is termed *epicormic sprouting*. Sprouting from dormant tissues located on subterranean plant organs is termed *basal sprouting*.

Epicormic sprouting occurs when the dormant buds that are located on trunks and large branches are stimulated to grow as a result of fire-induced mortality of existing foliage. This phenomenon exists for many broad-leaved shrubs and hardwoods in the Pacific Northwest, most notably tanoak, mountain dogwood, Oregon ash, and several oak species. This trait is an advantageous adaptation following fires of low severity where the level of heat release is great enough to kill foliage yet cambial tissues and dormant buds survive.

Sprouting from below-ground plant organs

Soil is an effective insulator from high temperatures experienced during a fire in forested ecosystems. Heat inputs into the soil are minimal compared to the total heat released in a fire. Therefore, only an inch or two of soil is usually sufficient to protect underground buds from heat damage during fires (Rundel 1983). Dormant meristematic tissues may occur on rhizomes, roots, and bulbs on herbaceous and woody perennials. In many plant species, expanded woody root tissues with masses of adventitious buds at their base have developed at or just below ground level. These structures have been referred to as lignotubers, root crowns, or basal burls (Rundel 1983). The lignotuber is regarded as an adaptive trait for recovery and persistence under stresses of many types, including fire (Gill 1981). In the Pacific Northwest, tanoak and many manzanita and ceanothus species possess lignotubers (Fig. 4-2).

There is a tremendous variation in the capacity to sprout among different shrub and hardwood species. Species which depend on sprouting from dormant buds as their sole means of reproduction have been termed obligate sprouters, while those which depend solely on seeds for reproduction have been termed obligate seeders (Wells 1969). Those species with the capacity for reproduction by both seeds and sprouts are facultative sprouters. Big sagebrush is an obligate seeder as are some manzanita and ceanothus species. All Pacific Northwest conifers except coast redwood are obligate seeders. In uplands, quaking aspen could be considered an obligate sprouter. The vast majority of hardwoods and shrubs in the Pacific Northwest are facultative sprouters.

Depending on specific adaptations of species as well as possible differences in phenology and physiology, one species may survive in very high percentages while others may be completely extirpated from a community following fire. In a severe

Figure 4-2. Tanoak sprouting from an exposed lignotuber. The severe fire completely consumed all above-ground biomass of this plant and the litter and duff layers that surrounded its base. Yet some dormant buds survived to produce these sprouts.

northern California underburn, there was a 100 percent mortality of greenleaf manzanita shrubs, while survival of whitethorn ceanothus and golden chinquapin was 40 percent and 27 percent, respectively (Kauffman 1986). Following an underburn in central Oregon, Martin (1982) found that 52 percent of snowbrush ceanothus plants survived and sprouted while only 1 percent of the antelope bitterbrush plants survived.

The quantity of fuel consumed by fire directly influences the heat pulse around the base of plants and is likely the most important variable affecting survival of subterranean tissues. Frequently, the capacity of sprouting is overgeneralized by statements that certain species are "vigorous sprouters" or "invigorated by fire." Even though plant survival is often remarkable following the most severe of fires, it has been shown to decrease with increasing fuel consumption. Tanoak is a species often cited as being very resilient following burning. Greater than 87 percent of tanoak individuals survived spring burns of moderate to low fuel consumption in northern California. However, survival was only 11-21 percent following early fall prescribed burns of high fuel consumption (Kauffman and Martin, in press).

Size or age is likely to influence the capacity of a plant to sprout following fire. In some species the capacity to sprout declines with increasing age because of increased woody growth around potential meristems (Rundel 1983), or decadence associated with senescence. Frequency of stump sprouting decreases as stem size increases in many oaks (Griffin 1980). However, Tappeiner and McDonald (1984) indicated that larger tanoaks sprouted to a greater degree following clipping than smaller individuals. Kauffman and Martin (in press) found that fire tolerance of tanoak, chinquapin, and California black oak increased with individual plant size. For example, following high-consumption burns, mortality in the smallest size classes of tanoak exceeded 97 percent while it was less than 55 percent in the largest size classes.

The season of burn has been reported to be an important factor which influences regrowth of plants following fire (Jones and Laude 1960, Grano 1970). Season of burn relates to distinct combinations of fuel moisture, soil moisture, and plant phenology. With respect to shrub phenology, mortality is higher and regrowth is decreased when the shrub is burned after a period of rapid shoot growth. Mortality of California black oak was 22 percent higher when burned during active aboveground growth than when burned before active growth (Kauffman and Martin 1987). It has been suggested that phenology and fire survival are positively correlated with increasing levels of carbon reserves in roots and the presence or absence of growth-regulating hormones (Jones and Laude 1960, Cremer 1973).

Fuel moisture and its direct relationship with fuel consumption is a factor that fluctuates along seasonal cycles. Soil moisture may greatly affect mortality of subterranean tissues. Frandsen and Ryan (1986) reported that during a fire temperatures in moist soils were depressed due to the absorption of heat of vaporization. They found that the heat load into moist mineral soil was on the average only 20 percent of the heat load into a dry uncovered mineral soil. Soil surface temperature

maxima were 1,256°F in a dry uncovered soil and 176°F in a moist soil with a moist organic horizon. This may help explain why higher mortalities of shrubs occur in areas that are burned when soil moisture is low.

Traits Which Enhance Species Persistence

Soil seed populations and fire-induced germination

In the Pacific Northwest, many species produce seeds with the capacity to remain dormant yet viable in the soil for possibly hundreds of years. Gratkowski (1962) speculated that viable seeds of snowbrush ceanothus were 200-300 years old under an old-growth stand of Douglas-fir in southwestern Oregon. Following fire, these seeds may germinate in extremely high densities (Fig. 4-3).

Figure 4-3. Deerbrush ceanothus seedlings following a fire in mature mixed conifer. Few, if any, were present before the fire. Following the fire, hundreds of thousands of seeds were stimulated to germinate.

Those seeds with a physical barrier to germination requiring a fire or some other scarification treatment for germination are termed refractory seeds or hardseeds. In the Pacific Northwest, this phenomenon is known to occur in the Heath, Pea, Buckthorn, and Saxifrage families—though it probably occurs in many other taxa as well, including leguminous plants and ceanothus and manzanita shrubs.

Soil populations of montane shrub seeds in Pacific Northwest forests have been found in extremely high densities. Anderson (1985) estimated that the soil seed population in the forest floor of a mature, mixed-conifer stand in the northern Sierra Nevada, California was greater than 872,000 per acre of deerbrush ceanothus and 1.46 million per acre of whiteleaf manzanita. The viability of these seeds was 91 and 35 percent, respectively. In a 70-year-old white fir stand in northeastern California, Weatherspoon (1988) estimated there were over 5 million snowbrush seeds per acre in the forest floor. The majority were found in the lower inch of the duff layer and upper 2 inches of the mineral soil surface. Gratkowski (1962) observed similar relationships between seed densities and soil profiles in southwest Oregon. Refractory seeds of shrubs in Pacific Northwest forests are evidently deposited on the soil surface early in the sere, leading to conifer dominance before significant duff layers form, yet after soils have stabilized following disturbance.

These seeds generally do not germinate to any great extent until dormancy is broken by fire or some other scarifying agent (Stone and Juhren 1951, Wells 1969, Gill 1981). This includes disturbance by logging activities, solar insolation following overstory removal, animal digestion, or some other mechanical scarification (Gratkowski 1962, Dyrness 1973, Gill 1981). In the process of scarification by heat, there is a distinct range of tolerance between temperatures too low for scarification and high temperatures resulting in mortality. Typically, few seeds will be scarified at temperatures below 110°F. Optimal temperatures of scarification are generally in the 170-195°F range (4-8 minutes duration), while significant increases in mortality occur when temperatures rise to 250°F or more (Gratkowski 1962, Kauffman 1986). Following treatment within the optimal temperature range, the viability of deerbrush ceanothus seeds ranged from 60 to 90 percent (Kauffman 1986).

Following scarification, seeds of montane ceanothus will not germinate until after they have been stratified (Quick 1959, Gratkowski 1962, Kauffman 1986). This is presumed to be an evolutionary adaptation promoting spring germination when soil moisture is abundant and conditions for growth and establishment are optimal.

Fire effects on the soil seed population will depend on the particular species, season of burn, seed position in the soil and, most importantly, the severity or consumption level of the fire. Anderson (1985) found the density of viable deerbrush seeds in the duff layers to be 169,315 per acre in unburned plots and 12,778 per acre following a high-consumption burn (92 percent reduction in duff biomass). In a northern California true fir stand, Weatherspoon (1988) found that the soil seed bank of snowbrush ceanothus was not significantly reduced by burns of low to moderate consumption, but up to 94 percent were destroyed by high-consumption fires.

In prescribed underburns in mixed-conifer forests, Kauffman (1986) also found a strong relationship between fuel consumption and the density of whitethorn ceanothus and greenleaf manzanita. Few or no seedlings occurred in unburned plots or those with low to moderate consumption. Whitethorn ceanothus densities of 40,000 per acre and greenleaf manzanita densities of 10,100 per acre were measured on plots with 76 percent fuel consumption (37 percent bare ground exposure following fire). In areas of very high duff consumption (94 percent; 60 percent bare ground exposure), densities of whitethorn ceanothus and greenleaf manzanita were much lower: 19,425 per acre and 4,856 per acre, respectively. Because of the relatively narrow range of temperature tolerance between scarification and mortality, seeds must be deep enough to escape destruction from high temperatures, but close enough to the surface to be sufficiently stimulated by fire (Reid and Oechel 1984).

The season of burn may be another important variable that influences the postburn shrub seedling density. Higher densities of ceanothus and manzanita seedlings have been reported following fall burns compared to spring burns (Orme and Leege 1976, Kauffman 1986). Densities of deerbrush ceanothus seedlings in areas burned under spring and fall high-consumption prescriptions (93 percent duff consumption, 60 percent bare ground) were 53,200 per acre and 87,400 per acre, respectively (Kauffman 1986). A similar response was measured for whiteleaf manzanita and sierra goosecurrant. Possibly this is as a result of differences in soil moisture and hence heat transfer into soils. In addition, the length of time between the scarification event and subsequent stratification-germination may be important.

Seedbed conditions as influenced by fire

Requirements for the germination and successful establishment of conifers can provide much insight into the evolutionary relationship of a species and an ecosystem with fire. Species which utilize nurse logs for germination are typically found in ecosystems with extremely long fire return intervals. Conversely, in ecosystems characterized by frequent low-severity surface fires, conifers may require mineral seedbeds in which to germinate.

In pine and mixed-conifer forests of the Pacific Northwest, frequent fires result in mineral seedbeds that facilitate establishment of species such as ponderosa pine, sugar pine, and Douglas-fir. Following a high-consumption fire in a northern California mixed-conifer stand, Douglas-fir increased from 576 to 7,084 seedlings per acre, while ponderosa pine increased from 167 to 1,236 seedlings per acre (Kauffman 1986). Fire suppression or infrequent fires will decrease the abundance of pines and favor species such as true firs and incense-cedar (Chapter 3; Hall 1977, Thomas and Agee 1986). These species are shade tolerant and have the capacity to germinate and establish in well-developed duff layers.

Other species favored by a postfire seedbed include those which originate from windborne seeds from offsite sources. Numerous herbs, in particular willowweeds and woodland groundsel, establish on sites in this way during the first few years following fire (West and Chilcote 1968, Dyrness 1973).

Another seed characteristic which facilitates survival in an ecosystem with frequent light surface fires is cryptogeal germination (germination when seeds remain below ground). This germination strategy has been observed for tanoak and black oak. If the newly emerged cotyledons of these species are killed by a light surface fire, they can produce new sprouts from dormant cotyledons within the protected subterranean acorn.

Other factors that increase seedling success on postfire seedbeds include breakdown of allelopathic compounds, increases in available nutrients, increases in pH, chemical leachates from charred wood which stimulate germination, fewer seed predators and pathogens, and decreased competition (Gill 1981, Rundel 1983, Keeley and Keeley 1987). Keeley and Keeley (1987) found that 42 percent of 57 sampled herbaceous species in California chaparral showed significant enhancement of germination when exposed to charred wood. Parmeter (1977) has suggested that the often observed success of seedlings on burned seedbeds is due to removal by fire of seed decay fungi, damping-off fungi, and seedling root rot fungi.

Fire-stimulated flowering

Fire-stimulated flowering is another phenomenon which increases seedling abundance in burned areas. This increased reproductive effort resulting in a greater abundance of viable seeds is common for both herbaceous and woody plants in many areas of the world (Gill 1981, Rundel 1983) though little information is available for Pacific Northwest plants. Species with fire-induced flowering are primarily monocots of the Grass, Orchid, Iris, and Lily families (Gill 1981). Increased flowering and seed vigor have been observed following fire for grasses in the pine forests and high desert regions east of the Cascades. Gray rabbitbrush, common in low-elevation forests east of the Cascades, is among the few shrubs that sprout flowering culms immediately following a fire. The ecological significance of fire-induced flowering has been little studied, but it likely enhances seedling density following fire (Gill 1981).

Cone serotiny

Another fire adaptive trait to ensure species persistence is long-term storage of seeds in cone scales held shut by resins (Rundel 1983). This trait is termed cone serotiny. Closed-cone morphologies for seed retention are present in many pines and in giant sequoia. Seeds within serotinous cones may remain viable for 30 years or more (Rundel 1983). The best examples of closed-coned pines are the numerous species endemic to California (e.g., Monterey pine, Bishop pine) and lodgepole pine of the northern Rocky Mountains. Cone serotiny on lodgepole pine is uncommon in the Pacific Northwest, with small populations or scattered individuals reported to occur in northeastern Oregon and the southern Cascades. Knobcone pine reaches its northern limit in southern Oregon and is completely dependent on serotinous cones for reproduction. Typically, fires that melt the resins of cones and release the seeds are severe enough to kill the parent plants.

Ecosystem Characteristics That Influence Fire Effects

In addition to these traits that facilitate survival of individuals and species, ecosystem-level traits of many forests may modify fire severity, and hence increase species persistence. These characteristics include both the physical structure and chemical composition of the forest or its species components. Forests in an uneven mosaic of size classes, typical of many old-growth forest ecosystems, are more buffered from catastrophic crown fires than contiguous even-aged stands. Numerous species may possess chemical constituents which act as natural flame retardants (e.g., the acid-insoluble ash or silica-free ash component). High levels of these mineral constituents can depress flame lengths and slow the rate of fire spread. Mutch (1970) found a correlation between fire frequency in ecosystems and the concentration of fire retardants in forest litter.

Fire Effects on Coarse Woody Debris

Coarse woody debris is primarily snags or downed logs and large branches greater than 3 inches in diameter. It is the dead and 1,000-hr timelag fuel (see Chapters 5 and 8). In most forest ecosystems of the Pacific Northwest, fire plays an important role in both the creation and loss of coarse woody debris. Wildfires kill many living trees, thereby creating new coarse woody debris as they consume already existing debris. Coarse woody debris is often a major structural feature, with many crucial ecological functions, including the provision of nurse logs for some conifer species and sites of mycorrhizal activity; influences on soil transport, erosion and retention; and important contributions to energy flow and nutrient cycling (Harmon et al. 1986, Spies et al. 1988). In the forests of western Oregon and Washington, 150 species of wildlife are known to utilize dead

and downed woody material, while 175 species in the Blue Mountains of eastern Oregon and Washington utilize these materials as either primary or secondary components of their habitat requirements (Maser et al. 1979, Bartels et al. 1985). Coarse woody debris is also important in relation to fire behavior, fire effects on existing vegetation, and long-term postfire effects on the ecosystem.

The functional importance of coarse woody debris in both ecosystem function and fire behavior depends on the biomass, size class distribution, spatial arrangement, degree of decay, species, and seral stage of the forest stand. This function will also vary by climatic conditions of the site which affect the agents of breakdown. Harmon et al. (1986) stated that the principal mechanisms of breakdown or decay of coarse woody debris in forest ecosystems are through leaching, fragmentation, transport, collapse, settling, seasoning, respiration, and biological transformation. This is undoubtedly true in forests with long fire return intervals. For example, Spies et al. (1988) measured a gradual decline in coarse woody debris for at least 80-120 years after disturbance in western Oregon and Washington Douglas-fir forests. However, in drier forests or those with a frequent fire return interval (less than 50 years), fire may be the primary agent for the breakdown of coarse woody debris.

In the ponderosa pine and mixed-conifer forests of the Pacific Northwest, wildfires historically occurred during late summer when moisture contents of coarse woody debris were low, resulting in high levels of consumption. Kauffman and Martin (1985) reported up to 85 percent of the downed coarse woody debris (1,000-hr fuels) were consumed by prescribed understory surface fires during September. These burns approximated the effects of natural fires which often occurred at this season.

Fire type as manifested in fire regime will also have a strong effect on rate of input of coarse woody debris into a system. For example, input rates are slow and relatively constant in forests where ponderosa pine are dominant (Avery et al. 1976). Historically, the frequent, low-severity surface fires typical of this forest ecosystem killed only a small percentage of living trees while consuming much of the coarse woody debris. In contrast, huge pulses of coarse woody debris inputs occurred following fires in the high-severity regimes characterized by infrequent, high-consumption, stand-replacement fires (Spies et al. 1988). For example, Agee and Huff (1987) reported a 10-fold increase in standing coarse woody debris (snags) in old-growth western hemlock-Douglas-fir forest following a wildfire. The total biomass of coarse woody debris was 244 tons per acre in an old-growth stand and 565 tons per acre in a recently burned stand.

Ecological Effects of Altering Fire Regimes

The persistence of species in Pacific Northwest forests through the millennia is attributed to the aforementioned vegetation adaptations to fire. Adaptations to fire survival are, in reality, adaptations to a particular ecosystem and its specific fire regime. If the regime is altered, then the capacity for that species to survive in an environment may be eliminated. For example, many closed-cone pine species are relatively short-lived (80-120 years). Fire suppression activities which lengthen the fire cycle to a longer time period than this effectively eliminate the ecological advantage of cone serotiny, and the species may ultimately disappear. Thick bark on conifers such as ponderosa pine, which facilitates survival in regimes with frequent low-severity surface fires, is of little value where fire regimes have been altered to infrequent stand-replacement fires. Short-lived species which depend on sprouting following fire may also be eliminated when fire return intervals are lengthened. Numerous quaking aspen stands in western North American forests are decadent or disappearing as a result of fire suppression. Often, these are being replaced by shade-tolerant conifers, western juniper, or sagebrush. Shortening the fire cycle of an ecosystem may eliminate many species which depend on seeds for reproduction (Keeley 1981).

Fire regimes are simply the manifestation of the biological, physical, climatic, and anthropomorphic components of an ecosystem as reflected in the type, frequency, and size of fires (Pyne 1984). However, this relationship is circular. While the biotic assemblages are an expression of the fire regime, they will in turn influence the pattern and occurrence of fire. If any of the components of the ecosystem are altered, the fire regime will likely change.

Managerial activities associated with logging, grazing, recreation, and fire suppression have altered many ecosystems in the Pacific Northwest. Thomas and Agee (1986) found that fire suppression had effectively eliminated five fire cycles in southwest Oregon mixed-conifer forests. By contrast, clearcut and burn rotations of 60-100 year intervals in western Cascades or Coast range forests represent the addition of four or more fire cycles where the historical return interval was 250-500 or more years. The ecological, managerial, and economic effects of these changes, particularly the long-term implications, are not well understood.

Coarse woody debris, as well as other components of the fuel load, have been modified by harvest and salvage of trees and alteration of natural disturbance regimes. In areas where the fire return interval has been shortened due to harvest and burn rotations, it is likely that levels of coarse woody debris have decreased. Spies and Cline (1988) have predicted that one or two rotations of managed Douglas-fir plantations would result in accumulations of coarse woody debris that were only one-tenth or less of that present in old-growth Douglas-fir forests. Excessive removal of coarse woody debris may decrease long-term site productivity (Harmon et al. 1986).

Activities which lengthen the fire return interval (e.g., fire suppression) have allowed increased accumulations of coarse woody debris to occur. This phenomenon is particularly prevalent in many ponderosa pine and mixed-conifer forests (Parsons and DeBenedetti 1979) and wilderness areas (Barrett 1988). Fire suppression can affect long-term site productivity in complex ways. These include increases in fuel loads and hence fire severity; alterations in nutrient pools; increased stresses on canopy trees and hence increases in insect outbreaks; and numerous alterations in ecosystem structure, function, and succession. All of these effects should be considered in forest planning.

The longest fire-free intervals of many low-elevation forests of the inland Pacific Northwest have occurred since the beginning of the era of active fire suppression (Hall 1977, Bork 1985). The most apparent changes in these forests include succession to fire-intolerant, shade-tolerant conifers (e.g., white fir, grand fir, incense-cedar) and the decrease of species such as ponderosa pine, sugar pine, and western larch. This has resulted in changes in both the horizontal and vertical structure of the forest. Historically, this forest was described as open and parklike. Vegetation patterns resulting from the frequent low-severity fire regime have been described as an uneven-aged stand characterized by a mosaic of even-aged groups (Biswell 1972). Optimal wildlife habitats result when fire creates a mosaic of different age classes of vegetation. This leads to a higher spatial diversity of food and habitat types and creates a maximum of ecotone or edge areas (Nichols and Menke 1984). Fire suppression by humans has resulted in a less distinct patchwork of vegetation and the formation of a dense midstory of shade-tolerant conifers.

In those forested ecosystems which historically had a frequent fire return interval, fire suppression, beginning around the turn of the century, has resulted in dramatic shifts in ground vegetation. Hall (1977) found herbaceous production in Blue Mountain ponderosa pine forests has decreased from 500-600 lbs per acre to 50-100 lbs per acre following canopy closure resulting from fire suppression. He estimated that by 1970, fire suppression and increasing fir cover had resulted in an understory forage loss capable of supporting 40,000 mule deer, 10,000 Rocky Mountain elk, or 10,000 cattle in the Blue Mountains of Oregon alone.

The response of the hardwood component to fire exclusion is variable. Even different species within the same family or genera have different responses to fire suppression. For example, in the Willamette Valley, Oregon white oak has greatly increased in density, changing stand structure from oak savanna to oak forest (Thilenius 1968). In contrast, Parsons and DeBenedetti (1979), Bonnicksen and Stone (1982), and Kauffman and Martin (1987) provided evidence that California black oak has decreased in abundance as a result of fire suppression. As tanoak can successfully germinate and survive under a conifer overstory, fire suppression has probably resulted in an increase in the abundance of this species.

Fire exclusion has also altered the composition and structure of early seral stages of many Pacific Northwest forests. Historic wildfires in many forests killed or scarified many dormant shrub seeds (e.g., ceanothus and manzanita species) in upper soil horizons (Martin 1982, Kauffman and Martin 1985). The frequent surface fires in pine and mixed-conifer forests probably decreased this soil

seed population, resulting in a decreased dominance of these shrub species in early seral stages following overstory loss. After 80-100 years of fire suppression, the early seral stages following timber harvest at many locations are characterized as a much denser and more competitive stand of shrubs and hardwoods.

As a result of vegetation changes in low-elevation pine types, fuel loads have been drastically altered. Vertical separation between surface fuels and the conifer overstory has been eliminated by the formation of a midstory conifer layer. Duff layers and woody debris have increased while the biomass of the herbaceous component has decreased. The overall increase in surface fuels and the laddering effect of the small to medium to tall trees has increased the threat and occurrence of crown fires where historically they were rare (Lotan et al. 1981). In effect, the fire regime has been altered to one of infrequent, stand-replacement fires. These fires may ultimately cost millions of dollars in suppression activities and result in significant losses in forest products, increased soil erosion, loss of human life and property, and long-term damage to the ecosystem. The effects of fire suppression in ponderosa pine forests were voiced by Weaver:

> The great increase in fire hazard is the most ominous change since earlier days. The very success of foresters in suppressing fires has radically changed conditions described by Muir and other early observers. Great advances have been made in fire prevention and suppression, and fewer fires escape control. When they do, however, and they still do and will continue to, they usually are devastating. Uninterrupted fuel accumulations of the past 40-70 years together with development of reproduction and brush thickets have made it extremely difficult to control such fires, and the costs of control may properly be described as fantastic (1974, p. 300).

Conclusion

Fire is a natural ecological factor affecting the structure and function of Pacific Northwest forests. Though fire regimes have been altered by land use, fires still greatly influence the forest ecosystem. The huge conflagrations that burned hundreds of thousands of acres of forest in northeastern Oregon in 1986, southwestern Oregon and northern California in 1987, and Yellowstone National Park in 1988 are a testament to the remarkable influence fire has on forest ecosystems. We must come to a more thorough understanding of natural processes relating to fire. The ecological ramifications of events such as wildfires (and just as importantly the ecological ramifications of suppression policies which affect the eventual behavior of large wildfires) must be evaluated. Knowledge of vegetation and animal adaptations and responses to fire is necessary for this evaluation.

Forest resource managers and the general public must come to view fire and its role in forest ecosystems as a natural environmental component of the ecosystem and not an exogenous factor. Naveh (1974) stated that prejudices and misconceptions about fire have led to its condemnation, instead of an appreciation for its role as a major evolutionary force, and its potential as a tool in enlightened forest management. Utilizing fire as a natural component of the ecosystem to manage fuels, control vegetation succession, manipulate wildlife habitat, and for other purposes may prove to be an environmentally, economically, and socially responsible course to follow. In order to properly utilize fire as a land management tool, it will be necessary to understand the natural role of fire in forest ecosystems and how to properly prescribe and measure the environmental and biological impacts of fire on such systems. The misapplication of fire has led to environmental damage in the past, just as fire exclusion has resulted in environmental damage in other forests. However, with the proper awareness of the dynamic nature of fire and its potential effects on forest composition and productivity, it can be a useful tool in natural resource management.

Literature Cited & Key References

Agee, J.K., and M.H. Huff. 1987. Fuel succession in a western hemlock/Douglas-fir forest. Can. J. For. Res. 17:697-704.

Anderson, J.M. 1985. Effects of prescribed burning on shrub seeds stored in the duff and soil of a Sierra Nevada mixed conifer forest. M.S. Thesis. Univ. California, Berkeley, CA. 39 p.

Arno, S. 1977. Northwest Trees. The Mountaineers, Seattle, WA. 222 p.

*Avery, C.C., F.R. Larson, and G.H. Schubert. 1976. Fifty year records of virgin stand development in southwestern ponderosa pine. USDA For. Serv., Rocky Mt. For. Rge. Exp. Sta., Ft. Collins, CO. Gen. Tech. Rep. RM-22. 71 p.

*Barrett, S.W. 1988. Fire suppression's effects on forest succession within a central Idaho wilderness. West. J. Appl. For. 3:76-80.

Bartels, R., J.D. Dell, R.L. Knight, and G. Shaefer. 1985. Dead and down woody material, p. 171-186. *In* Brown, E.R. (tech. ed.) Management of Wildlife and Fish Habitats in Forests of Western Oregon and Washington. USDA Forest Service, Pac. Northwest Reg., Portland, OR. Pub. R6-F&WL-192-1985.

*Biswell, H.H. 1972. Fire ecology in ponderosa pine-grassland. Tall Timbers Fire Ecol. Conf. Proc. 12:69-96.

Bonnicksen, T.M., and E.C. Stone. 1982. Reconstruction of a presettlement giant sequoia-mixed conifer forest community using the aggregation approach. Ecology 63:1134-1148.

Bork, J.L. 1985. Fire history in three vegetation types on the east side of the Oregon Cascades. Ph.D. thesis. Oregon State Univ., Corvallis, OR. 119 p.

Borman, F.H. 1981. Introduction, p. 1-3. *In* Proc., Conf. on Fire Regimes and Ecosystem Properties. USDA For. Serv., Washington, DC. Gen. Tech. Rep. WO-26. 594 p.

Cremer, K.W. 1973. Ability of *Eucalyptus regnans* and associated evergreen hardwoods to recover from cutting or complete defoliation in different seasons. Aust. For. Res. 6(2):9-22.

*Dyrness, C.T. 1973. Early stages of plant succession following logging and burning in the western Cascades of Oregon. Ecology 54:57-69.

Frandsen, W.H., and K.C. Ryan. 1986. Soil moisture reduces below-ground heat flux and soil temperatures under a burning fuel pile. Can. J. For. Res. 16:244-248.

*Gill, A.M. 1977. Plants' traits adaptive to fires in the Mediterranean land ecosystems, p. 17-26. *In* Mooney, H.A. and C.E. Conrad (tech. coord.) Symp. on the Environmental Consequences of Fire and Fuel Management in Mediterranean Ecosystems. USDA For. Serv., Washington, DC. Gen. Tech. Rep. WO-3. 498 p.

*Gill, A.M. 1981. Fire adaptive traits of vascular plants, p. 208-230. *In* Proc., Conf. on Fire Regimes and Ecosystem Properties. USDA For. Serv., Washington, DC. Gen. Tech. Rep. WO-26. 594 p.

Grano, C.K. 1970. Eradicating understory hardwoods by repeated prescribed burning. USDA For. Serv., Southern For. Exp. Sta., New Orleans, LA. Res. Pap. 50. 11 p.

References marked by an asterisk are recommended for general information.

Gratkowski, H.J. 1962. Heat as a factor in germination of seeds of *Ceanothus velutinus* var. *laevigatus* T. and G. Ph.D. thesis. Oregon State Univ., Corvallis, OR. 122 p.

Griffin, J.R. 1980. Sprouting in fire-damaged valley oaks, Chews Ridge, California, p. 216-219. *In* Plumb, T. (tech. coord.), Symp. on the Ecology and Management and Utilization of California Oaks. USDA For. Serv. Berkeley, CA. Gen. Tech. Rep. PSW-44. 242 p.

*Hall, F.C. 1977. Ecology of natural underburning in the Blue Mountains of Oregon. USDA For. Serv., Pac. Northwest Reg., Portland, OR. R6-ECOL-79-001. 11 p.

Hare, R.C. 1965. Contribution of bark to fire resistance of southern trees. J. For. 63:248-251.

*Harmon, M.E., J.F. Franklin, F.J. Swanson, P. Sollins, S.V. Gregory, G.D. Lattin, N.H. Anderson, S.P. Cline, N.G. Aumen, J.R. Sedell, G.W. Lienkaemper, K. Cromack, Jr., and K.W. Cummins. 1986. Ecology of coarse woody debris in temperate ecosystems. *In* MacFadyen, A. and E.D. Ford (eds.) Advances in Ecological Research 15:133-302.

Jones, M.B., and J.M. Laude. 1960. Relationship between sprouting in chamise and the physiological condition of the plant. J. Rge. Manage. 13:210-214.

Kauffman, J.B. 1986. The ecological response of the shrub component to prescribed burning in mixed conifer ecosystems. Ph.D. thesis. Univ. California, Berkeley, CA. 235 p.

Kauffman, J.B., and R.E. Martin. 1985. A preliminary investigation on the feasibility of preharvest prescribed burning for shrub control, p. 89-114. *In* Proc., 6th Forest Vegetation Management Conf., Redding, CA. 242 p.

Kauffman, J.B., and R.E. Martin. 1987. Effects of fire and fire suppression on mortality and mode of reproduction of California black oak (*Quercus kelloggii* Newb.), p. 122-126. *In* Plumb, T.R., and N.H. Pillsbury (tech. coords.), Proc., Symp. on Multiple Use and Utilization of California's Hardwood Resources. USDA For. Serv., Berkeley, CA. Gen. Tech. Rep. PSW-100. 462 p.

Kauffman, J.B., and R.E. Martin. In press. Sprouting shrub response to varying seasons and fuel consumption levels of prescribed fire in Sierra Nevada mixed conifer ecosystems. For. Sci.

*Keeley, J.E. 1981. Reproductive cycles and fire regimes, p. 231-277. *In* Proc., Conf. on Fire Regimes and Ecosystem Properties. USDA For. Serv., Washington, DC. Gen. Tech. Rep. WO-26. 594 p.

Keeley, J.E., and S.C. Keeley. 1987. Role of fire in the germination of chaparral herbs and suffrutescents. Madrono 34:240-249.

*Lotan, J.E., M.E. Alexander, S.F. Arno, R.E. French, O.G. Langdon, R.M. Loomis, R.A. Norum, R.C. Rothermel, W.C. Schmidt, and J.W. van Wagtendonk. 1981. Effects of fire on flora. USDA For. Serv., Washington, DC. Gen. Tech. Rep. WO-16. 71 p.

Martin, R.E. 1963. A basic approach to fire injury of tree stems. Tall Timbers Fire Ecol. Conf. Proc. 2:151-162.

Martin, R.E. 1982. Shrub control by burning before timber harvest, p. 35-40. *In* Baumgartner, D.M. (ed.) Site Preparation and Fuels Management on Steep Terrain. Symp. Proc., Coop. Ext. Serv., Washington State Univ., Pullman, WA. 179 p.

*Martin, R.E., and J.D. Dell 1978. Planning for prescribed burning in the inland northwest. USDA For. Serv., Pac. Northwest For. Rge. Exp. Sta., Portland, OR. Gen. Tech. Rep. PNW-76. 68 p.

Maser, C., R.G. Anderson, K. Cromack, J.T. Williams, and R.E. Martin. 1979. Dead and down woody material, p. 78-95. *In* Thomas, J.W. (tech. ed.) Wildlife Habitats in Managed Forests: The Blue Mountains of Oregon and Washington. USDA, Washington, DC. Agr. Hbk. 553. 512 p.

*Mutch, R.W. 1970. Wildland fires in ecosystems—a hypothesis. Ecology 51:1046-1051.

Naveh, Z. 1974. The ecology of fire in Israel. Tall Timbers Fire Ecol. Conf. Proc. 13:131-170.

Nichols, R., and J. Menke. 1984. Effects of chaparral shrubland fire on terrestrial wildlife, p. 74-97. *In* DeVries, J.J. (tech. ed.) Shrublands in California: Literature Review and Research Needed for Management. California Water Res. Cent., Univ. California, Davis, CA. Contribution 191. 146 p.

*Noste, N.V., and C.L. Bushey. 1987. Fire response of shrubs of dry forest habitat types in Montana and Idaho. USDA For. Serv., Intermt. For. Rge. Res. Sta. Ogden, UT. Gen. Tech. Rep. INT-239. 22 p.

Orme, M.A., and T.A. Leege. 1976. Emergence and survival of redstem ceanothus (*Ceanothus sanguineus*) following prescribed burning. Tall Timbers Fire Ecol. Conf. Proc. 14:391-420.

Parmeter, J.R. 1977. Effects of fire on pathogens, p. 58-64. *In* Mooney, H.A. and C.E. Conrad (tech. coord.) Symp. on the Environmental Consequences of Fire and Fuel Management in Mediterranean Ecosystems. USDA For., Serv. Washington, DC. Gen. Tech. Rep. WO-3. 498 p.

Parsons, D.J., and S.H. DeBenedetti. 1979. Impact of fire suppression on a mixed conifer forest. For. Ecol. Manage. 2:21-33.

*Pyne, S.J. 1984. Introduction to Wildland Fire Management in the United States. John Wiley and Sons, Inc. New York, NY. 455 p.

Quick, C.R. 1959. *Ceanothus* seeds and seedlings on burns. Madrono 16:23-30.

Quick, C.R., and A.S. Quick. 1961. Germination of *Ceanothus* seeds. Madrono 16:23-30.

Reid, C., and W. Oechel. 1984. Effect of shrubland management on vegetation, p. 25-41. *In* DeVries, J.J. (ed.) Shrublands in California: Literature Review and Research Needed for Management. California Water Res. Cent., Univ. California, Davis, CA. Contribution 191. 146 p.

*Rundel, P.W. 1983. Fire as an ecological factor. Encyclopedia of Plant Physiology 12:501-535.

*Spalt, K.W., and W.E. Reifsnyder. 1962. Bark characteristics and fire resistance: A literature review. USDA For. Serv., Southern For. Exp. Sta., New Orleans, LA. Occ. Pap. S-193. 19 p.

Spies, T.A., J.F. Franklin, and T.B. Thomas. 1988. Coarse woody debris in Douglas-fir forests of western Oregon and Washington. Ecology 69:1689-1702.

Spies, T.A., and S.P. Cline. 1988. Coarse woody debris in manipulated and unmanipulated coastal Oregon forests, p. 5-24. *In* Maser, C., R.F. Tarrant, J.M. Trappe, and J.F. Franklin (tech. eds.) From the Forest to the Sea: A Story of Fallen Trees. USDA For. Serv., Pac. Northwest Res. Sta., Portland, OR. Gen. Tech. Rep. PNW-GTR-229.

Starker, T.J. 1934. Fire resistance in the forest. J. For. 32:462-467.

Stone, E.C., and G. Juhren. 1951. The effect of fire on the germination of seed of *Rhus ovata* Wats. Amer. J. Bot. 38:368-372.

Tappeiner, J.C., and P.M. McDonald. 1984. Development of tanoak understories in conifer stands. Can. J. For. Res. 14:271-277.

Thilenius, J.F. 1968. The *Quercus garryana* forests of the Willamette Valley, Oregon. Ecology 49:1124-1133.

Thomas, T.L., and J.K. Agee. 1986. Prescribed fire effects on mixed conifer forest structure at Crater Lake, Oregon. Can. J. For. Res. 16:1082-1087.

*Volland, L.A., and J.D. Dell. 1981. Fire effects on Pacific Northwest forest and range vegetation. USDA For. Serv., Pac. Northwest Reg., Portland, OR. 23 p.

Weatherspoon, C.P. 1985. Preharvest burning for shrub control in a white fir stand: Preliminary observations, p. 71-88. *In* Proc., 6th Annu. Forest Vegetation Management Conf., Redding, CA. 242 p.

Weatherspoon, C.P. 1988. Preharvest prescribed burning for vegetation management: Effects on *Ceanothus velutinus* seeds in duff and soil, pp. 125-141. *In* Proc., 9th Ann. Veg. Management Conf., Redding, CA. 250 p.

*Weaver, H. 1974. Effects of fire on temperate forests: Western United States, p. 279-320. *In* Kozlowski, T.T. and C.E. Ahlgren (eds.) Fire and Ecosystems. Academic Press, New York, NY. 542 p.

Wells, P.V. 1969. The relation between mode of reproduction and extent of speciation in woody genera of the California chaparral. Evol. 23:254-267.

West, N.E., and W.W. Chilcote. 1968. *Senecio sylvaticus* in relation to Douglas-fir clear-cut succession in the Oregon Coast Range. Ecology 49:1101-1107.

III Application of Prescribed Fire

5 Goals, Methods, and Elements of Prescribed Burning

Robert E. Martin

Executive Summary

Prescribed burning is a valuable technique in the management of natural resources. Use of this technique involves a systematic series of decisions beginning with the overall philosophy and goals of the organization and culminating in a thorough evaluation of burns after they are completed. Intermediate steps in this process include reconnaissance of the proposed burn units, setting objectives for the burns, developing prescriptions, obtaining permits and resources needed, checking weather and fuel conditions, selecting ignition patterns and tools, conducting the burns, mopping up, and documenting the results of the burns.

Introduction

Consideration of the option of using prescribed fire is one of numerous decisions made in the course of managing forest land. If prescribed fire will meet the general land management goals and becomes the treatment of choice, then site-specific prescriptions and conditions must be delineated. This chapter will cover the basic components of prescribed burning: the decision process, objectives and constraints, uses, prescriptions, planning and preparation, ignition patterns and tools, conduct and mop up of burns, and documentation.

Prescribed burning must be considered in a broad context. First, a distinction must be made between an individual burn and a burning program. For any unit of land, each prescribed burn will have particular objectives. However, the objectives of an entire burning program—a series of prescribed burns conducted under a range of conditions at varying intervals—must also be considered. The goals and results of prescribed burning programs are discussed more fully in the chapters on fire use and effects.

The means of igniting fires is a second factor to be considered, and it divides prescribed fires into two groups. The first is the planned ignition, where the manager, basing all decisions on burn objectives and prescriptions, lights the fire in predetermined ignition patterns at a time when appropriate conditions are met. The second is the unplanned ignition, where accidental or lightning-caused fires are permitted to burn under prescription so long as human life, physical improvements, and important resources are not endangered. Most often, the unplanned ignition units are wilderness areas and remote areas in forests and parks. The remainder of this chapter deals primarily with planned and controlled ignitions (Fig. 5-1).

The Decision Process

The decision process begins with the basic philosophy and goals of the organization (Fig. 5-2). Flowing from these are the management plans which define the objectives for successively smaller pieces of land. These may include restoration of natural conditions, maintaining attractive landscapes, ensuring the output of timber, wildlife, livestock, and water, and providing recreational opportunities. If treatment is needed to meet the

Figure 5-1. Methods commonly used to ignite prescribed fires include (A) hand-held driptorches and (B) driptorches suspended from helicopters, known as helitorches. Techniques used to maintain control of prescribed fires include (C) piling debris into discrete piles or windrows prior to burning and (D) igniting broadcast fuels in narrow strips. (Photos A and D courtesy of J.B. Kauffman; photo B courtesy of G.W. Blanchard; photo C courtesy of J.D. Walstad)

objectives for the unit, the manager must consider the methods available, which are commonly grouped under manual, mechanical, fire, chemical, and biological categories. The manager must decide if the use of available techniques with each tool will help meet the objectives specified for the unit. If they will not, then new techniques must be developed or the objectives must be reconsidered. If satisfactory techniques are available, the manager must select the specific treatment or combination of treatments to be used. Each tool has its own capabilities and limitations. Furthermore, individual managers exhibit a range of skills, experience, and preferences for risk taking which may influence the selection. The safe and effective use of prescribed fire requires a high degree of skill and experience, as well as a willingness to assume some level of risk.

Objectives & Constraints

Burn objectives arise from the management goals for the given unit of land. Having observed the condition of the unit, the manager arrives at specific objectives for a treatment. Examples might be to:
- Kill two-thirds of sprouting shrubs
- Reduce understory conifers by 60 percent
- Reduce 1- and 10-hour timelag fuels to 3 tons per acre
- Create 400 planting spots per acre
- Create a 10-foot gap in vertical fuel continuity
- Leave an organic duff layer on at least 80 percent of the site
- Scar no more than 15 percent of ponderosa pine saplings
- Obtain sprouting of 60-80 percent of bitterbrush plants
- Reduce potential shrub seedlings by 60-90 percent.

The more quantitative the objectives, the better a manager can measure the success of a burn or burn program. This not only provides a useful frame of reference for project evaluation, but helps improve future prescriptions as well. A combination of objectives may be used, representing the inputs of several disciplines. Each discipline may have to compromise somewhat; the combined objectives, however, should point toward greater overall good than meeting the narrow objectives of one discipline (Chapter 22).

Waiting for suitable weather conditions is a primary constraint on prescribed burning. Both the fuel and atmospheric conditions must be dry enough to support combustion, yet not so dry that escape of the fire is likely. Atmospheric conditions must also be acceptable from an air quality standpoint (Chapter 16).

Other major constraints include the cost of burning (slash burning, in particular, can be expensive) and the need to avoid adverse impacts on soils and other components of the environment. These are discussed more thoroughly in subsequent chapters.

Uses of Prescribed Burning

Site preparation. One of the best-known uses of prescribed fire is to prepare a site for reforestation (Chapter 6). Burning reduces fuels and competition from other plants, makes planting easier, and prepares planting spots. For natural regeneration, burning may remove organic layers, providing a favorable seedbed for many tree species.

Regulation of stand composition. Prescribed burning can be used to decrease the number of some tree species, where the desirable tree species is fire resistant and the undesirable species is fire prone. For example, when white or grand fir is coming into a stand of ponderosa pine, yet pine is the preferred species, fire can be used to greatly reduce the fir (Chapter 6).

Reducing competition. Competition from non-commercial shrubs and trees in a developing stand can be reduced by burning (Chapter 6). Even though shrubs may sprout, their dominance is reduced, nutrients are recycled, and water consumption is reduced. In overstocked stands, smaller stems can be killed by fire, allowing more growth on the residual trees.

The use of fire before timber harvest as a means of reducing competition with future tree seedlings is also being explored. Burning under the mature stand causes some shrub seeds to germinate. The shrub seedlings cannot compete well under the stand and most will die. Further, the old shrubs under the stand are in a weak condition, and many can be killed by repeated burning, thereby facilitating subsequent reforestation.

Insect and disease reduction. Fire may be important in reducing insect and disease problems, although few studies have been conducted and fire

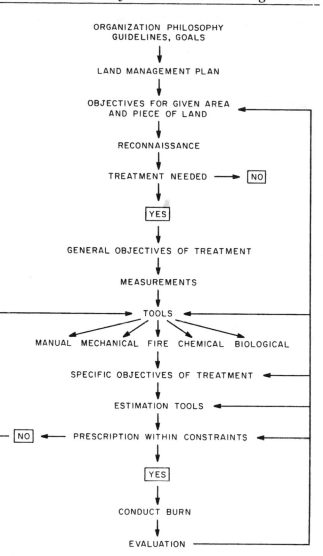

Figure 5-2. The use of prescribed fire is derived from a systematic decision process.

may also increase the incidence of insects or disease under some circumstances (Chapters 10 and 11). Fire could reduce the habitat for pests, enhance the development of organisms antagonistic to them, or remove susceptible host plants.

Fire hazard reduction. One important use of fire is to reduce or modify fuels to lessen the likelihood of wildfires and ensure that those that do occur will be less damaging and easier to control (Chapter 8). Prescribed fire can reduce the amount of fuel as well as its vertical and horizontal continuity, thereby preventing fires from spreading on the surface or climbing into tree crowns.

Wildlife habitat management. Prescribed fire is often used to improve wildlife habitat (Chapter 7). How and where fire is used depends on the species of wildlife desired and the kinds of browse and forage plants available and their response to fire.

Range improvement. Livestock forage is generally improved by fire (Chapter 7). Reductions of organic matter and shrub competition to forage plants, coupled with release of nutrients, can increase the amount of forage and its palatability and nutritional value.

Water management. Prescribed fire can reduce the use of water by plants and increase the amount of water produced by a watershed (Chapter 17). In some situations, water quality can also be increased. Fire often kills or suppresses shrubs and favors shallow-rooted grasses and forbs which use water only part of the year, thereby increasing water yield. The herbs give more complete soil protection than sparsely distributed shrubs, thereby improving water quality. In other situations, certain shrubs are stimulated by fire, thereby rapidly recolonizing areas after burns and protecting water quality.

Prescriptions

Prescribed burning is an art, even though scientific information helps guide the burner in achieving defined objectives. Prescriptions are derived from the objectives and constraints for a burn. Prescriptions contain elements that influence the behavior of the fire: fuels, weather, and topography, collectively referred to as the *fire behavior triangle* (Fig. 5-3). The pattern in which the fire is lighted also influences fire behavior and gives the prescribed burner last-minute control.

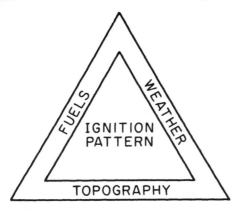

Figure 5-3. Components of the fire behavior triangle.

Prescriptions also include items related to the condition of the vegetation and fauna on the site, as well as off-site factors such as atmospheric conditions. The elements within a prescription are often interactive. It is the sum of the elements within a prescription that produce the overall effects of a burn. Generally, each element has a range of values or conditions which will meet the objectives; the narrower the range and the more elements involved, the smaller is the "window" in which the burn can be conducted. Often, three to five critical elements are all that can be accommodated.

Elements of Prescriptions

Fuels
Fuels are the organic materials on the site which could be burned. They consist of the plant material above, on, and below ground.

Topography
Topography includes slope (how steep the land is), aspect (which way the land faces), and elevation (altitude above sea level). Each influences the weather, vegetation, and fuels at the site.

Slope affects fire behavior, as the true wind and slope combine to make an "effective wind," which will be a major factor in how the fire behaves. As slope increases, the fire will burn faster uphill.

Escape of the fire can occur due to burning cones and logs rolling down a slope. Rolling logs and rocks can also present hazards to personnel and equipment. Slope affects the use of mechanical equipment needed to install and maintain firelines. It also is more difficult for personnel to work on steep slopes.

Slope will affect the vegetation on the site, the development of soil-protective duff layers, and the degree to which soil might be eroded following burning. Thus, prescriptions might include steps to burn less material on steep slopes, especially where soil organic layers are thin (Chapters 12-14, 22).

Aspect affects the microclimate of the site, thereby affecting the vegetation and fuels. These, in turn, affect fire behavior, fuel consumption, and overall effects of the fire. Thus, similar slopes of different aspect often will burn quite differently.

Elevation affects many factors in a prescription. Flora changes with elevation, and use by wildlife also changes. Weather is different at different elevations, varying the days and times of the day suitable for burning.

Weather

Weather factors in a prescription include wind, temperature, humidity, atmospheric stability, precipitation amounts and duration, and time since precipitation or snow melt. Also, daily and seasonal weather patterns are important because of their influence on fuel, and on floral, faunal, and atmospheric conditions.

Wind speed and direction are critical factors in prescribed burning. Wind is often undesirable in situations where large amounts of logging slash (either piled or distributed across the unit) are being burned, because it may carry hot air into adjacent stands, killing or damaging them. Wind also can cause "spotting," the transport of hot embers in convection currents to areas outside the perimeter of the unit being burned. In many rangeland, wetland, and understory burns, on the other hand, wind is necessary to get the fire to spread properly. In underburning within a forest stand, wind also can be advantageous because it leans the flames over, increasing the distance the hot air must travel to the crown, thereby reducing its temperature by the time it reaches the crown and minimizing crown scorch. Although wind will cause a fire to burn more intensely (with larger flames), there are ways to compensate, as discussed below under ignition patterns.

Wind speed and direction can be important in the dispersal of smoke from the area. A strong wind in the wrong direction may carry smoke into urban or recreation areas.

Temperature interacts with humidity to affect fuel moisture and the amount of heat necessary to raise plant tissues to the lethal temperature. Temperature is also important in and of itself as it determines the amount of temperature rise that can be tolerated before living tissues are killed. For example, green pine needles will withstand 120°F for about 1 hour before dying. A fire burning in an ambient temperature of 80°F must heat them only 40°F to reach lethal temperatures, whereas a fire burning in an ambient temperature of 40°F must raise their temperature 80°F. Depending on the objective of the burn, the foliage can be saved or killed by selecting the appropriate temperature conditions.

Humidity affects the moisture content of fuels, the fireline intensity of the fire, and the probability of an ember starting a spot fire.

Atmospheric stability affects the ability of convective gases to move vertically in the atmosphere (Chapter 16). Temperature inversions inhibit such gases and the particulates they contain from rising, creating local air quality problems. Burning may be prohibited at elevations below the inversion but permitted above it.

Time

Time since precipitation or snow melt may be a prescription item, as it will influence the moisture content of larger fuels and duff. This determines how much is consumed, which, in turn, affects residual plants, new germinants, animals, soils, nutrients, and air quality.

Timing of the burn, both diurnally and seasonally, is an important prescription factor. Variable conditions during the course of any given day may affect behavior of the fire and of the smoke in the convection column. Diurnal conditions also influence the effect fire has on vegetation because of the associated temperature regime.

Seasonal timing of burns may be important because of the physiological condition of plants, fuel variations, presence or sensitivity of wildlife, or recreational activity. Plants may be more sensitive to fire damage in the spring or early summer, because they have expended energy to grow, flower, and produce seed. Burning then may catch them with insufficient food reserves to sprout or produce new foliage. Burning before or after seed fall can also be used as a way to regulate the species and densities of plants colonizing an area.

Wildlife may be a crucial consideration in the seasonal timing of burns. If a desirable species is reproducing on the site, then the burn should be conducted at another time. If a particular species of wildlife is considered a pest, then it may be desirable to use burning as a means of controlling the population or reducing its potential for causing damage (Chapter 9).

Fuel loads also vary by season. For example, stands with a high component of deciduous hardwoods have more fuels after leaf fall in the autumn. Burning then may be advantageous if high consumption of material is desired.

Recreational activity is a seasonally variable factor which often influences burning. Smoke may reduce visibility, or make areas uncomfortable or unhealthy (Chapter 16). Freshly burned areas may be aesthetically displeasing and may cause wildlife to move where it cannot be seen or appreciated (Chapter 19).

Ignition patterns

The final factor affecting the behavior and effects of a prescribed burn is the pattern of ignition. As the burn progresses, the pattern may be modified to keep fire behavior within limits. Thus, the ignition pattern is the last element the burner can use to be sure the burn meets objectives.

For units where the slash has been piled or windrowed, the pattern of ignition is usually not critical. Piles or windrows along the downwind or uphill perimeter of the unit are ordinarily burned first to minimize the chance of fire escape. The remaining piles or windrows should then be burned in a safe and efficient manner.

For units slated for broadcast burning, whether in open areas or under forest stands, the pattern of ignition is critically important because it affects not only the duration of the burn, but also the fireline intensity of the flames, the time the fire resides in one place, and fuel consumption. All of these factors can have a significant influence on the relative safety of the burn and environmental impacts.

A brief explanation of fire terminology is necessary to understand the different types of ignition patterns used in broadcast burning. Fires are classified depending on their direction of spread relative to the wind or slope (Fig. 5-4).

Head fires spread with the wind or upslope. They spread fastest and have the longest flames and highest fireline intensity. Head fires are the most difficult to control, particularly if they become wildfires.

Backing fires spread by backing into the wind or downslope. They spread slowly and have the shortest flames and lowest fireline intensity. They are often the gentlest way fire can be used. However, care needs to be exercised if residual trees are to be protected; the relatively long residence time of backing fires can cause more surface organic matter to burn, thus causing more heat damage to root and basal stem tissues.

Flanking fires spread across the wind or slope. They are moderate in rate of spread and have flame lengths and fireline intensities between those of head and backing fires.

A fire starting from a spot ignition will have heading, backing, and flanking components, provided the fuels are satisfactory for spread in all directions (Fig. 5-5). The fire will burn an area which is roughly egg-shaped, with the long axis downwind or uphill. As the strength of the wind or steepness of the hill increases, the length may be large compared to the width of the fire.

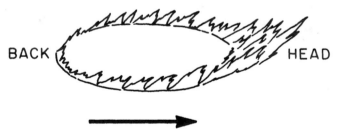

WIND OR UPHILL

Figure 5-5. From a spot ignition, all three types of fire are present.

The type of fire conducted within any given unit is established by the ignition pattern. More than one pattern may be used in the same unit to meet the objectives at different locations.

Head fires may be used where large areas are to be burned, and it is not feasible to light several strips within the unit (Fig. 5-6). Ordinarily, the downwind or uphill fireline is burned first (1) to a

WIND OR UPSLOPE DIRECTION

Small arrows indicate direction of flames

Figure 5-4. Fires are classified as head fires, backing fires, or flanking fires. A head fire spreads with the wind or upslope. A backing fire spreads against the wind or downslope. And a flanking fire spreads across the wind or slope.

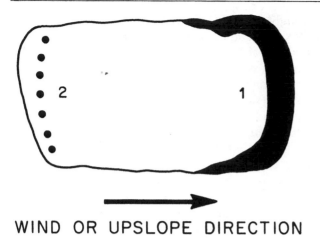

WIND OR UPSLOPE DIRECTION

Figure 5-6. The head fire spreads rapidly, with high fire intensity.

width sufficient to stop the head fire. This may be several hundred feet in a rangeland fire. The head fire is then lighted (2) and allowed to spread across the unit.

The head fire may be inexpensive to use if its fireline intensity is not too high. This ignition pattern is appropriate for some rangeland situations and for broadcast burning of logging slash. Normally, a head fire is not used as an underburn within forest stands until the area has been conditioned by previous fires to reduce fuels.

Backing fires. The backing fire (Fig. 5-7) is lighted at the downwind or uphill end of the unit (1) and allowed to spread into the wind or uphill. Because of its slow rate of spread, it may be necessary to put several firelines across the unit and back fire from each of them, thereby reducing the time of burning. Backing fires are appropriate where flame length (fireline intensity) must be kept to a minimum, such as a forest stand where the fuel load is heavy and fuel ladders to the crown are present.

Flanking fires are intermediate in the rate of spread and fireline intensity between head and backing fires (Fig. 5-8). After a sufficient width has been burned (1), the burners proceed simultaneously into the wind or downhill, lighting as they go (2).

The flanking fire can be used where a moderate rate of spread is desired without incurring the danger of a high-intensity fire. Where fireline intensity is critical, flanking fires can be a problem if the wind is veering by 30° or more. The result could be a series of head fires in close proximity to one another, leading to a high fireline intensity. Indeed, the highest intensity in flanking fires is where two adjacent fires merge, as they are drawn together (3). The width of the "Vs" in comparison to their length is dependent on the ratio of the flanking rate of spread to the rate at which the burners proceed.

A variant of the flanking fire is the *chevron burn*. It consists of a series of flanking fires set by burners proceeding directly downhill from the end of a ridgeline, producing the characteristic chevron shape.

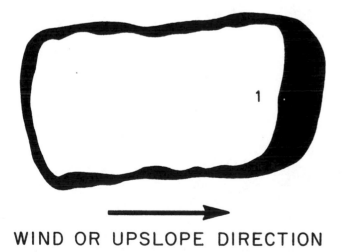

WIND OR UPSLOPE DIRECTION

Figure 5-7. The backing fire spreads slowly, with low intensity.

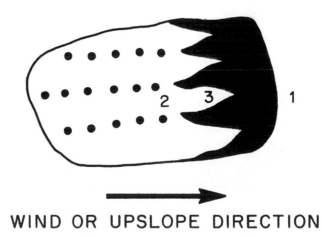

WIND OR UPSLOPE DIRECTION

Figure 5-8. Flanking fires spread at a moderate rate and intensity.

Strip-head fires. Often it is desirable to have fires which spread faster than backing fires and have lower fireline intensities than head fires, or to burn a unit faster than would be possible with a single head fire. *Strip-head fires* can be used in such situations (Fig. 5-9). In this technique, the downwind or uphill line is first burned for a sufficient distance to prevent spotting or jumping over it (1). Then fires are lit successively farther into the wind or downslope (2, 3, 4). The distance between successive strips is determined by the intensity of fire desired, using flame length and rate of spread as a guide. This is based on the time and distance it takes a fire to build up to a steady state (Fig. 5-10).

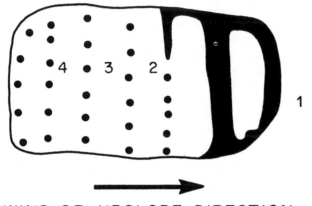

WIND OR UPSLOPE DIRECTION

Figure 5-9. Strip-head fires can be used to facilitate the use of head fire techniques.

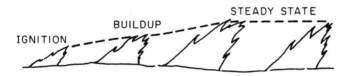

Figure 5-10. A fire, once lighted, builds up to a steady rate of spread, at which it will continue until fuel, weather, or topographic conditions change.

When burning beneath a stand of timber, the width of strips sufficient to achieve a steady-state fire may generate flame lengths too great for the stand to endure. In such cases the strips should be lighted at a closer spacing, thereby preventing build up of flame length to a steady state and keeping the fireline intensity within prescription (Fig. 5-10).

In lighting strip-head fires, no more than two strips should be burning toward the previous strip at one time if fire interaction is to be avoided. The interaction will cause an increase in fireline intensity and may result in excessive damage to the overstory (in the case of underburning) or fire control problems (in the case of both underburning and slash burning). An exception to this is where the strip-head fires at steady state have flames less than 1/50 to 1/100 the distance between them.

If, for some reason, fire interaction is desired, then lighting strip-head fires in rapid succession can produce the same high-intensity fires described below under center firing.

Spot-head fires are similar to strip-head fires, except that fires are lit in spots rather than strips (Fig. 5-11). As with strip-head fires, the downwind or uphill line is first burned (1), then the spots are lighted, progressing into the wind or downhill (2, 3, 4, 5). Spot-head fires allow more manipulation of fireline intensity than do strip-head fires. First, spot-head fires will not achieve the fireline intensity that strip-head fires will attain. Second, by lighting fires in appropriate locations, the higher intensity head fires may be directed at or around specific objects, such as individual trees or thickets. Third, each individual spot will spread with a range of intensities from the back, flank, and head.

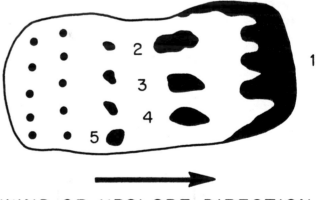

WIND OR UPSLOPE DIRECTION

Figure 5-11. Spot-head fires are another means of controlling the intensity and rate of spread of head fires.

Center firing (also called *ring firing* or *keyhole burning*) is a technique which works best with low wind and flat terrain (Fig. 5-12). The objective of using the technique is generally to get fire interac-

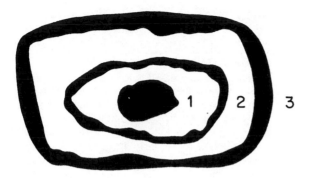

Figure 5-12. Center firing is primarily used on flat terrain to increase fire intensity and disperse smoke.

tion and increase fireline intensity. The burn is started by lighting a fire or ring of fires, usually near the center of the unit (1). As the fireline intensity increases from the first fire ring near the center, an indraft will be generated. As fire rings are lighted farther toward the perimeter (2), the indraft will act as a wind, causing the fire rings to rush inward with high fireline intensity. Finally, the perimeter of the unit is lighted (3), using the indraft to draw the fire into the center and away from the edge.

Center firing is most often used to increase fireline intensity and the updraft in the smoke column, thus lifting the smoke high in the atmosphere and away from the local area. This technique is often used to burn the slash in logging units, particularly those on flat terrain, but it also can be used in rangeland and brushland areas.

Once the techniques of ignition are decided upon, then the specific devices needed to accomplish the ignition can be considered. These vary widely in their cost, versatility, and suitability (Table 5-1).

Planning & Preparation

Resources required

The manager must identify the resources needed to prepare for the burn, conduct the burn, monitor or mop up after the burn, and document the burn and its effects. Resources available may determine whether and how a burn will be conducted.

From past experience, the manager should be able to estimate the funds and requirements for planning and conducting a burn. This will primari-

ly involve personnel time, site reconnaissance, supplies and equipment, and clerical costs. Costs for review and approval should be included. Contingency plans for dealing with potential problems should also be developed.

The unit to be burned may need to have work done on it before burning: piling or windrowing of slash; building firelines; and modifying hazardous conditions by, for instance, felling snags, compacting fuels, breaking fuel ladders, and removing fuels near firelines. This preburn work might also include protecting certain resources such as nesting trees, rare species or habitats, riparian areas, and scenic vistas. Some units may require pretreatment of the vegetation in order to carry the fire: slashing or felling of brush and noncommercial trees is sometimes required and this method is referred to as *slash-and-burn*; another technique, called *brown-and-burn*, involves the use of herbicide desiccants to cure the vegetation prior to burning.

Qualified people to do the burning and to hold the firelines during the burn must be obtained. Training in fire safety, ignition techniques, and fire suppression is essential. Often, it is useful to specify the individuals who will be in charge of the burn well ahead of time.

Permits

The process for obtaining permits varies from state to state (Chapter 20), but usually involves review of the burn plan by a regulatory agency to assess the adequacy of planning and resources. Special provisions for protecting rare and endangered species, site quality, and other values are also involved. Finally, approval by various agencies is required in order to ensure compliance with fire safety and air quality standards.

Public relations

The public is often concerned about resource management and may become involved early during the prescription process. Efforts made to explain the use of prescribed fire and underscore the precautions taken will do much to minimize public concerns (Chapter 19). Advanced notices of burns near populated or sensitive areas should be sent to newspapers and radio and television stations. Notification should also be sent to nearby law enforcement agencies and fire departments to ensure their awareness and preparedness.

Table 5-1. Devices available for ignition of prescribed burns.

Device	Where Used	How Used	Advantages	Disadvantages
Flamethrower	Slash or shrubs; broadcast or jackpot burning	Burner walks firelines or skid trails and ignites fuel combinations	Fastest hand-carried igniter; burner can reach several feet with flame to avoid walking in slash and brush	Somewhat more expensive and complicated than drip torch; heavier to carry and uses more fuel than drip torch
Drip torch *1 part gas* Drag torch *2 parts disel*	Almost any situation	Burner walks firelines, trails, or through fuels, dropping burning fuel	Simple, light, inexpensive, reliable equipment	Slower than flamethrower; burner must often move through heavy fuel
Helitorch	Clearcut slash, shrubs, or "conditioned" stands	Helicopter carries large drip torch in sling; drips burning fuel	Very fast ignition; not committed to predetermined firing plan	Helicopter expensive; safety not yet determined
Electrical ignition (primacord/jellied gasoline)	Clearcuts in west coast states where there is heavy slash	(1) Primacord is wrapped around metal or plastic containers of jellied gasoline; (2) Electrically detonated in desired pattern	Extremely rapid ignition and convective buildup; excellent for smoke dispersal	Expensive to wire; once wired, must burn
Fuses	Anywhere; best used as an auxiliary to other methods when needed	Burner walks fireline, trails, or through fuels; must hold flame to fuel for short period to ensure ignition	Inexpensive, light; can be carried in vest or pocket as an auxiliary tool	Slow; must pause to hold flame to fuel; expensive in labor time to start fire
6-inch igniter cord-safety fuse (DAIDs)	Large or remote areas, from aircraft	(1) Ignited by cigarette lighter; (2) Dropped from plane or helicopter to start spot fires; (3) Flames within 15-20 seconds after ignition	Can ignite remote areas; intermediate expense; can cover large area	Dangerous if mishandled or in crash
Potassium permanganate/ ethylene glycol capsules	*a.* Large or remote areas, from aircraft	(1) Chemicals mixed by liquid injection; (2) Dropped from plane to start spot fires; (3) Ignites within 30-60 seconds	Capsule and contents inexpensive; can cover large areas	Best for large, remote areas
	b. Almost anywhere from helicopter	Same as above but dropped from helicopter	Versatile patterns and fast ignition	Availability and expense of helicopter
Laser/target	Slash, shrubs	Laser used to activate ignition devices in unit	Good control of ignition locations	Relatively expensive unit; needs line-of-sight; target must be preplaced in unit
Laser (in development)	Almost any situation with line-of-sight	High-powered laser ignites fuels directly	Accurate, fast ignition; versatile patterns	Very expensive unit; not yet proven; limited to line-of-sight
Surface-based-remote ignition (in development)	Almost any fuel type	Uses potassium permanganate/ ethylene glycol; capsule fired by compressed gas	Inexpensive unit and capsule could be readily available; light units with difficult or dangerous access	Inaccurate; not appropriate near unit boundaries

Source: Updated from Martin and Dell 1978.

Conducting the Burn

As implementation of the burn approaches, final preparations begin. Resources for the burn are arranged, the unit and permits checked, and the public and key agencies notified. Fuel moisture conditions are determined. Weather predictions for both fire and smoke behavior are obtained. Finally, when all elements are satisfactory, a burn day and time are set.

On burn day, final fuel and weather checks are made, personnel and equipment are assembled, and final notifications are made. The crew is briefed, and a test fire is usually used to check fire behavior. If everything is satisfactory at this point, personnel and equipment are dispersed to their stations and the burn begins.

As the burn progresses, lighting, holding, and suppression procedures are modified by the fire manager to meet changing conditions and exigencies. Important characteristics of the fire are recorded as the burn develops.

Mop Up & Monitoring

After the burn has been conducted, usually there continues to be some flaming and smoldering combustion. As mentioned in Chapters 16 and 22, smoldering combustion can contribute significantly to air pollution. Mop up forces extinguish the smoldering fuels, thus reducing air pollution and eliminating the chances for subsequent escape of the fire should wind and moisture conditions change. For ecological and economic reasons, it is occasionally undesirable to mop up units after burning. In such cases, careful monitoring of burns is important to prevent escape.

When all combustion has been extinguished or ceases, the fire is declared out by the fire manager. Remaining tasks involve evaluation and reporting on the success of the burn vis-à-vis original objectives.

Documentation

The prescribed burn must be documented to have a record of the treatment and its effects. Documentation is important for short-term evaluation to see if objectives were met, to help explain fire effects, and to facilitate prescription modification and improvement for long-term assessment of the benefits of the burning program (Chapters 15 and 21). The degree of documentation will vary, depending on the resources available, the sensitivity of the prescription and results, and the specificity of objectives to be evaluated against.

Documentation of the burn contains many of the initial prescription elements: fuel load and moisture content, soil moisture, temperature, vegetative condition, time since precipitation, season or time of day, wind characteristics, flame length, and pattern of ignition.

Following the burn, observations should be made of site conditions. Within a few weeks, bark and crown scorch, crown consumption, fuel remaining, and the condition of shrub and herbaceous vegetation should be recorded. Fuel remaining gives a means of calculating the amount of fuel consumed and an indication of the amount of heat and smoke released and the degree to which the soil is protected.

Changes in vegetation are important in assessing the long-term effects of burning. Because burning is usually done to favor one or more species, vegetative response, including the performance of trees (Chapters 6 and 15) and other preferred vegetation, is often the real "proof of the pudding" and should be documented.

Conclusion

Prescribed burning is a tool that can help land managers achieve management objectives. Fire may be used alone or in conjunction with other tools—mechanical, manual, chemical, or biological—to achieve desired ends. Prescribed burning is an important tool because of its versatility, usually low cost, and ecological similarity to natural fire in many respects. Prescribed burning may simulate prehistoric fire regimes, or it may be quite distinct from them, depending on the conditions of use.

Knowing the situation in the forest, the manager can arrive at objectives for a burn or burn program. From the situation and objectives flow the prescription conditions and method of fire application. The logistical needs for conducting burns can then be determined. Before, during, and after the burn, documentation helps determine success of the burn and guidelines for future improvements. It is the overall short- and long-term results of prescribed burning that are the measure of its success.

Key References

Allen, M.H., R.W. Berry, D. Gill, et al. 1968. Guide to prescribed fire in the Southwest. Southwest Interagency Fire Counc., Western For. Fire Comm., West. For. Conserv. Assoc., Portland, OR. 58 p.

Barney, R.J., G.R. Fahnestock, W.G. Herbolsheimer, R.K. Miller, C.B. Phillips, and J. Pierovich. 1984. Fire management, p. 189-251. *In* Wenger, K. F. (ed.) Forestry Handbook. 2nd ed. John Wiley & Sons, Inc., New York, N.Y. 1335 p.

Beaufait, W. R. 1966. Prescribed fire planning in the intermountain West. USDA For. Serv., Intermt. For. Rge. Exp. Sta., Ogden, UT. Res. Pap. INT-26. 27 p.

Chandler, C., P. Cheney, P. Thomas, L. Trabaud, and D. Williams. 1983. Fire in Forestry. Vol. II. Forest Fire Management and Organization. Chapt. 9: Managing Fire Use, p. 207-229. John Wiley & Sons, Inc., New York, NY. 298 p.

Dell, J. D. 1976. Fuels and fire management—prescribed fire use on the National Forests in the Pacific Northwest Region. Tall Timbers Fire Ecol. Conf. Proc. 15:119-126.

Fischer, W. C. 1978. Planning and evaluating prescribed fires—a standard procedure. USDA For. Serv., Intermt. For. Rge. Exp. Sta., Ogden, UT. Gen. Tech. Rep. INT-43. 19 p.

Green, R. N., P. J. Courtin, K. Klinka, R. J. Slaco, and C. A. Ray. 1984. Site diagnosis, tree species selection, and slashburning guidelines for the Vancouver Forest Region. Ministry of Forests, Victoria, B.C. Land Manage. Hbk. 8. 143 p.

Hawkes, B. C., and B. D. Lawson. 1986. Prescribed fire decision aids in B.C.: Current status and future developments. Pac. For. Ctr., Can. For. Serv., Victoria, B.C. (Paper presented at Northwest For. Fire Council Annu. Mtg., Olympia, WA, Nov. 18-19, 1986). 16 p.

Kilgore, B. M., and G. A. Curtis. 1987. Guide to understory burning in ponderosa pine-larch-fir forests in the Intermountain West. USDA For. Serv., Intermt. Res. Sta., Ogden, UT. Gen. Tech. Rep. INT-233. 39 p.

Martin, R. E. 1978. Prescribed burning: Decisions, prescriptions, and strategies. Fire For. Meteorol. Proc. 5:94-99.

Martin, R. E., and J. D. Dell. 1978. Planning for prescribed burning in the inland Northwest. USDA For. Serv., Pac. Northwest For. Rge. Exp. Sta., Portland, OR. Gen. Tech. Rep. PNW-76. 68 p.

Mobley, H. E., R. S. Jackson, W. E. Balmer, W.E. Ruziska, and W.A. Hough. 1973. A guide for prescribed fire in southern forests. USDA For. Serv., Southeast Area, State & Priv. For., Atlanta, GA. Southeast Area, State & Priv. For.-2. 40 p.

Norum, R. A. 1977. Preliminary guidelines for prescribed burning under standing timber in western larch/Douglas-fir forests. USDA For. Serv., Intermt. For. Rge. Exp. Sta., Ogden, UT. Res. Note INT-229. 15 p.

Trowbridge, R., B. Hawkes, A. Macadam, and J. Parminter. 1987. Field handbook for prescribed fire assessments in British Columbia: Logging slash fuels. Ministry of Forests and Lands, Victoria, B.C. FRDA Hbk. ISSN 0835-1929; 001. 63 p.

Wright, H. A. 1974. Range burning. J. Rge. Manage. 27(1):5-11.

6 Use and Benefits of Prescribed Fire in Reforestation

John D. Walstad and Kenneth W. Seidel

Executive Summary

Prescribed burning is an important forestry practice which can be used to achieve several management objectives simultaneously: abatement of wildfire hazards, removal of physical obstacles to reforestation, and creation of suitable environmental conditions for seedling establishment and growth. Its utility varies, however, by region, forest type, ownership, and local conditions, thereby making generalizations difficult. Consequently, the best use of prescribed burning for reforestation requires site-specific analysis and careful planning and execution to ensure that the net results will meet management objectives.

Both research studies and operational experience with prescribed burning have yielded conflicting results. Nevertheless, several patterns are consistent:

- Prescribed burning favors conifer regeneration more on moist sites than on dry sites, although many conifers are adapted to periodic burning on dry sites as well.
- Natural regeneration of most conifer species is best on a mineral soil seedbed but is also generally adequate on litter and duff layers not over 1 inch deep. Prescribed fire can be used to create both conditions.
- Slash removal facilitates silvicultural treatments such as planting, trapping of pest animals, surveys of seedling performance, and spot weed control.
- A light amount of slash helps protect seedlings from temperature extremes, drought, and frost heaving on exposed aspects and severe sites.
- Reduction of vegetative competition from burning results in better survival and growth of seedlings.

The objectives of prescribed burning for reforestation are best attained by light to moderate burns that remove some but not all slash, litter, and duff and that kill or retard competing vegetation.

Although the use of prescribed fire for reforestation in the Pacific Northwest is expected to decline over the next several decades as wood utilization and environmental restrictions increase, there will be a continued need for this practice to sustain the efficient management of commercial forests.

Introduction

Reforestation is a critical step in the life cycle of conifer forests in the Pacific Northwest (Fig. 6-1). It influences the course of plant succession. It ensures the renewal of conifer stands and minimizes the time required for their development. It helps protect intrinsic forest values such as water quality, soil productivity, ecological stability, and wildlife habitat. Consequently, reforestation after harvesting, wildfire, or other disturbances is not only good practice, it is required by law.

There are two basic approaches to conifer reforestation: natural and artificial. Natural regeneration, as its name implies, relies on the periodic seedfall from mature trees to furnish the seedlings for the next forest. Artificial regeneration, on the other hand, involves planting seedlings or sowing seed to establish the next forest. The choice of whether to use a natural or artificial means of reforestation depends on a number of biologic and economic factors (cf., Cleary et al. 1978, Burns 1983).

Regardless of which method is used, satisfactory regeneration usually requires preparation of the site (Stewart 1978). Just as the successful establishment of a farm crop requires cultivation, successful reforestation often requires removing excess debris and unwanted vegetation. Prescribed burning is one of the principal methods used, and about 200,000 acres are burned each year in Oregon and Washington.

As described in Chapters 3 and 4, most forest ecotypes in the Pacific Northwest are well adapted to periodic disturbance by fire. Indeed, many of the extensive stands of mature conifers present today originated after fires—most of them catastrophic (Weaver 1974). However, the advent of fire protection in the early 1900s has excluded fire from many areas, changing the pattern of natural fuels and vegetation and altering the resiliency of forests to fire. The judicious use of prescribed burning can avoid many of the destructive consequences of wildfire, yet produce many of the beneficial effects associated with the natural cycle of fire and forest renewal (Walstad et al. 1987). Con-

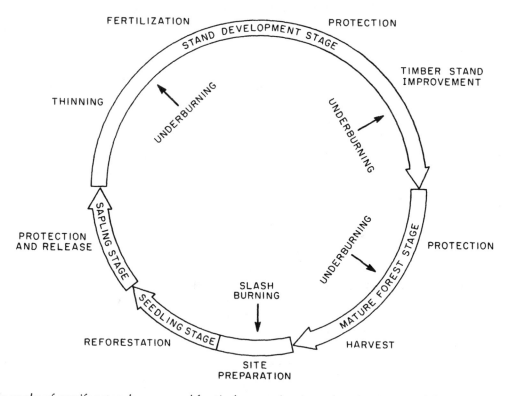

Figure 6-1. *Life cycle of conifer stands managed for timber production, showing stages of development and key forest management practices. Slash burning during site preparation and underburning of developing and mature forests are occasions during the cycle when prescribed fire can be used. (Adapted from Tappeiner and Wagner 1987)*

sequently, prescribed burning has become an important forestry practice in the Pacific Northwest during the past four decades.

The utility of prescribed burning for purposes of reforestation varies by region, forest type, ownership, and local conditions. The most effective use of this practice requires site-specific analysis and careful implementation. To be successful, the prescription and execution of a burn must be specific to the fuel, weather conditions, topography, and management objectives (Beaufait et al. 1975, Chandler et al. 1983).

Uses of Prescribed Burning in Reforestation

Prescribed burning is a multipurpose tool that is used for the following purposes during reforestation:

- Disposal of flammable residues to reduce the risk of subsequent wildfire in the reforested area.
- Removal of logging slash, debris, and vegetation that interfere with efficient reforestation, seedling protection, and stand management activities.
- Creation of suitable environmental conditions for establishment and growth of conifers.
- Manipulation of secondary plant succession to favor the development of preferred species.

Disposal of logging slash and other debris

The disposal of logging slash and other biomass is a key use of prescribed burning (Fig. 6-2). This reduces the chance of, severity of, and liability associated with subsequent wildfire. Ramifications of this use of prescribed fire are discussed in Chapter 8.

Removal of logging slash, brush, and other woody debris also facilitates several other reforestation activities. Access is greatly improved for tree planting, direct seeding, surveys of seedling performance, spot weed control, trapping of pest animals such as mountain beaver, and precommercial thinning. Such work can be done quicker, cheaper, and with higher quality on burned areas. For example, Zasada and Tappeiner (1988) found that both plantability and planting efficiency increased on several burned areas in the Oregon Coast Range. It is no coincidence that many of the well-spaced, uniformly stocked, and rapidly grow-

Figure 6-2. (A) Logging slash, other unmerchantable woody debris, and vegetation are serious obstacles to reforestation activities. (B) Prescribed burning is a key method for disposing of this material.

ing conifer plantations in the Pacific Northwest occur on sites that were prepared by prescribed burning (cf., Keatley 1989) (Fig. 6-3).

Creation of suitable environmental conditions for regeneration

Key coniferous species in the Pacific Northwest (e.g., Douglas-fir, ponderosa pine, lodgepole pine) are adapted to open growing conditions (Fowells 1965). Whether originating from natural seeding, direct seeding, or planting, these species thrive in

Figure 6-3. Full stocking, uniform distribution, and rapid growth are characteristics of many Douglas-fir plantations established after prescribed burning.

full sunlight, provided heat and moisture stress are not excessive. Prescribed burning, either for natural or artificial regeneration, often creates the environment needed to establish a new stand of conifers by providing full sunlight and initial control of competing vegetation.

Manipulation of secondary plant succession

Prescribed burning can be used to manipulate the sequence of plant species colonizing forest areas (Lotan et al. 1981). For example, in the absence of fire, it is common for shade-tolerant species such as true firs and hemlock to invade maturing seral stands, eventually assuming dominance. In areas where early successional species (such as pine and Douglas-fir) have a higher timber value or productivity than true firs and hemlock, prescribed fire can be used to slow or set back the successional process.

Prescribed Burning for Natural Regeneration

Burning is an effective means of preparing seedbeds and obtaining natural regeneration after harvest cutting in many Pacific Northwest forests if properly prescribed and carefully executed. Although natural regeneration can eventually reforest many clearcut areas, planting is generally recommended for most clearcuts to ensure prompt reforestation and obtain desired species and spacing. If natural regeneration is prescribed as the pri-mary means of reforesting clearcuts, then size of the clearcut is critical. Units must be small enough that seed can reach all parts of the clearcut; thus all seedbeds should be within 500 feet of a seed source (Gordon 1970, Roe et al. 1970, Seidel 1979b).

Natural regeneration is the most useful method for reforesting partial-cut or shelterwood units in many forest types because the overstory provides uniform seed distribution and ameliorates harsh microclimatic conditions at the soil surface (Williamson 1973, Seidel 1979a). Underburning can be used to reduce slash, prepare seedbeds, and retard the development of competing vegetation. Where broadcast underburning would kill or damage seed trees and advance regeneration, slash can be piled in open areas and then burned.

Western Oregon and Washington

The effect of broadcast burning on natural regeneration is inherently variable because of differences in fire intensity, variation in microsite conditions (e.g., aspect, slope, forest floor, soil), and other factors. Because of the variability, conflicting evidence results from studies comparing regeneration success in burned versus unburned plots. On clearcut areas in the westside Douglas-fir type, for example, more regeneration was reported on unburned plots in three studies (Munger and Matthews 1941, Isaac 1943, Lavender et al. 1956), but greater stocking was found on burned plots in three other studies (Worthington 1953, Bever 1954, Berntsen 1955), and little difference was found between burned and unburned areas in a region-wide study (Morris 1970). In general, prescribed burning tends to favor conifer regeneration on moist sites (Feller 1982). Prescribed burning also facilitates conifer regeneration on dry sites unless the burn is severe. Burns at high elevations tend to be more detrimental to the process of conifer regeneration (especially true firs and mountain hemlock) than burns at lower elevations.

An examination of seedbeds on which natural regeneration becomes established gives greater insight regarding the critical factors involved. For example, Morris (1970) found that mineral soil occurred on only 25 percent of the surface of unburned plots in the Cascades, whereas 53 percent of the surface of burned plots was mineral soil. In both cases, half or more of the seedlings occurred on mineral soil. Although mineral soil is generally regarded as the most favorable seedbed for seedling establishment and growth (especially for seral species such as Douglas-fir), many seedlings also are found on seedbeds where litter and duff layers are not more than about 1 inch deep. Such layers are often thin enough to have cracks, allowing conifer seeds to gravitate downward and contact the moist mineral soil needed for germination. In any case, it is neither necessary nor desirable to completely remove all litter and duff from an area. Exposure of 30 to 40 percent mineral soil well distributed over a unit as a result of logging and slash treatment is sufficient for most sites. Even less exposure may be required on high-elevation sites.

Another important factor in the success of natural regeneration is the amount of competing vegetation present on the site. Excessive amounts of competing vegetation not only inhibit seedling establishment but also retard their growth. Broadcast burning can eliminate or reduce such vegetation. Isaac (1963) reported that unburned areas had the most Douglas-fir seedlings, but seedlings on burned areas were twice as tall because of less shrub competition.

Although prescribed fire after clearcutting can foster survival and growth of seedlings by reducing vegetative competition, it may also result in more shrubby vegetation because it stimulates dormant seeds of ceanothus and other species to germinate (Fig. 6-4). One way to avoid this problem is to burn in the spring when conditions are relatively moist and cool, thereby minimizing the

germination of shrub seeds. Alternatively, a severe fire that consumes seeds buried throughout the duff and humus layers may be another way to control such species (Pearce 1987). As discussed in later chapters, however, there are potential adverse consequences associated with site productivity and air quality when burns are excessively hot.

The amount of slash present on harvested units also affects natural regeneration. When large amounts of uniformly distributed, deep slash are present, seedbeds suitable for seed germination and seedling establishment are limited, and natural regeneration is poor and sporadic. On the other hand, as with litter and duff, complete slash disposal is not desirable. A light amount of slash provides protection against temperature extremes at the soil surface and increases seedling survival. This is especially true in clearcuts having south-facing aspects.

The available evidence indicates that natural regeneration of Douglas-fir will occur in both burned and unburned units after clearcutting. When broadcast burning is prescribed, a light to medium burn is desirable (McCulloch 1944, Isaac 1963). This kind of burn accomplishes the desired objectives—partial removal of litter, duff, and slash, with some exposure of mineral soil—and it avoids possible soil damage associated with severe burns (Tarrant 1956).

Based on research and experience with broadcast burning in Douglas-fir clearcuts, Isaac (1963) gives general guidelines regarding conditions

Figure 6-4. Prescribed burning of these sites in the Oregon Cascades fostered the germination of (A) snowbrush ceanothus and (B) fireweed, serious competitors of conifer seedlings.

where prescribed fire is or is not recommended to facilitate natural regeneration:

Burn slash when:

- undesirable advance reproduction occupies a site where Douglas-fir regeneration is desired.
- ground is so completely covered with slash, litter, and duff layers that mineral soil seedbed is inadequate for natural regeneration.
- understory vegetation is so dense at time of cutting or immediately after that regeneration cannot become established.
- there are neither seed nor desirable seedlings on the harvested area, but there is a seed crop on nearby trees.

Do not burn slash when:

- an understory or residual stand remains after harvest that has the potential for good future growth and value.
- seed has fallen on the harvested area or seedlings have become established.
- microsite protection provided by light or medium amounts of slash is needed for seedlings to survive on southerly aspects or other severe sites.
- conditions are such as to result in an extremely hot fire that will consume too much slash, litter, and duff, cause soil damage, or kill seed-bearing trees on the timber edge.

Eastern Oregon and Washington

Prescribed fire is also an effective silvicultural tool for obtaining natural regeneration in many forest types in eastern Oregon and Washington. Considerable research on the effect of prescribed burning on natural regeneration has been done in Idaho and Montana in timber types similar to those of eastern Oregon and Washington. The available evidence indicates that the same factors important for natural regeneration in intermountain and westside forests also affect regeneration in eastside forests.

Lodgepole pine regenerates best on mineral soil seedbeds, and broadcast burning can effectively prepare such seedbeds. Work in the intermountain region has shown that prescribed burning of clearcuts resulted in satisfactory regeneration of lodgepole pine, with height growth of the seedlings about twice that for seedlings on unburned areas (Schmidt and Lotan 1980). Another study reported more uniform distribution of lodgepole pine (and hence better stocking) than on unburned or

mechanically treated areas (Alexander 1966). In central Oregon, a prescribed burn that removed about half of the slash from an area resulted in nearly as much lodgepole pine regeneration as in an area moderately disturbed by firewood cutting (personal communication from B. Bonefeld, Winema National Forest, Klamath Falls, OR). Cochran (1973) recommends leaving a light cover of slash to protect lodgepole pine seedlings from temperature extremes and frost heaving. Satisfactory natural regeneration of lodgepole pine can occur on moist sites, provided the duff is not over about 1 inch thick (Tackle 1956).

Prescribed burning also effectively prepares seedbeds for natural regeneration of ponderosa pine (Roe and Squillace 1950, Sackett 1984, Haase 1986).

Western larch requires considerable areas of mineral soil for satisfactory natural regeneration (Schmidt et al. 1976). Studies in Montana have shown that prescribed burns in summer or fall that consumed much of the litter and duff prepared a good seedbed and resulted in successful regeneration in contrast to spring burns that only blackened the surface (Shearer 1976, 1980). Seedling establishment was also better on north- and east-facing aspects than on southerly aspects when protective slash was consumed. Regeneration of larch is better on mineral soil, and growth is greater where burning has reduced vegetative competition (Schmidt 1969).

Another study in Idaho showed that broadcast burning led to acceptable stocking of larch and other species with few excess seedlings, thus reducing future costs for thinning (Boyd and Deitschman 1969). Although mineral soil provides the best seedbed for natural regeneration of both larch and lodgepole pine, dense, overstocked stands of these species can result if complete soil exposure occurs. Therefore a light to medium burn that results in partial soil exposure is desirable.

Prescribed burning for the establishment of natural regeneration is most effective in lower elevation pine, larch, and Douglas-fir communities in eastern Oregon and Washington because of long periods when conditions for burning are suitable. Broadcast burning can also be used for seedbed preparation in higher elevation spruce-fir types, but these communities are so cool and moist that the time when burning conditions are suitable is limited. Thus, timing of the burn is critical. It must be done when moisture content of the duff layer is low enough for most of the duff to be consumed. If only the surface is dry, a blackened organic layer that inhibits seedling establishment will remain (Roe et al. 1970).

The use of broadcast burning for seedbed preparation in shelterwood units requires careful planning and implementation to avoid crown scorch, root kill, and cambial damage. In many old-growth stands (especially ponderosa pine), thick layers of litter and duff are found at the base of the large trees. Severe fires can slowly consume these heavy accumulations, generating enough heat at the root collar to kill the trees. Nevertheless, there are occasions where underburning of shelterwood stands is a viable option, particularly if done during the cooler times of the year or in conjunction with piling operations (Marlega 1981).

As in westside forests, burning in eastside forests can stimulate the germination of fire-adapted shrubs like ceanothus and manzanita, leading to excessive competition for conifer regeneration. Martin (1982) has proposed a sequence of two understory burns prior to harvest to overcome the problem. The first fire top-kills many shrubs, and causes many shrub seeds to germinate. The second fire, about 3 years later, kills new shrub seedlings and greatly reduces sprouting of residual shrubs.

Prescribed Burning for Artificial Regeneration

Numerous studies (cf., Loucks et al. 1987) and over four decades of operational experience attest to the short-term benefits of prescribed fire in enhancing seedling survival and early growth after

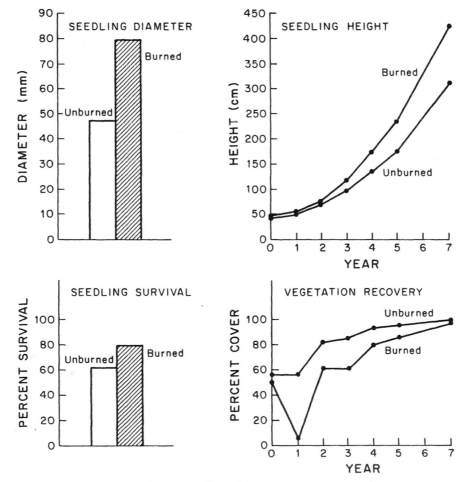

Figure 6-5. Diameter, height, and survival of Douglas-fir and recovery of competing vegetation 7 years after broadcast burning for site preparation in the Oregon Coast Range. (Data from Stein 1986, 1989)

artificial regeneration. As mentioned in the previous section, fire often creates soil conditions conducive to germination of conifer seeds and subsequent development of the seedlings. It also reduces woody debris and competing vegetation that would otherwise shade or sap moisture and nutrients from the seedlings, whether they have germinated from seed or been planted. Consequently, the guidelines for using prescribed burning specified in the previous section on natural regeneration are generally applicable to artificial regeneration as well.

One of the best illustrations of the short-term benefits of prescribed burning in artificial regeneration comes from research underway by the Pacific Northwest Research Station of the USDA Forest Service (Stein 1986, 1989). Six methods of site preparation are being compared at four sites in the Oregon Coast Range. As is evident in Fig. 6-5, broadcast burning has substantially improved the survival and growth of Douglas-fir seedlings during the first 7 years since planting. Survival of seedlings in burned plots was 28 percent greater than in unburned plots. Seedlings in burned plots were also 36 percent taller and 68 percent larger in diameter than seedlings in unburned plots, and the height differences were increasing through the seventh year. Even though the cover of competing vegetation in the burned plots now approaches that in the unburned plots, the initial suppression provided by burning has allowed the seedlings to get a head start.

In another Oregon Coast Range study, Stein (1984) detected a 10 percent improvement in Douglas-fir and western hemlock survival in burned versus unburned plots 5 years after planting. Height growth was improved about 11 percent.

Most of the gains in the aforementioned studies can probably be attributed to the reduction of competing vegetation by burning. However, Stein (1984, 1986, 1989) also detected less damage to seedlings by animals (presumably browsing by black-tailed deer and clipping by mountain beaver) in burned plots. Hooven and Black (1978) recorded a 50 percent reduction in mountain beaver population after broadcast burning, and they recommended this practice as a way to reduce the cost of controlling small mammals that destroy conifer regeneration. On the other hand, Gockerell (1966) encountered more browsing by deer

and elk and less seedling height growth on burned areas than on unburned areas.

Important Considerations When Using Prescribed Burning for Reforestation

Prescribed burning is not always beneficial to conifer regeneration, and, as indicated above, there are cases where seedling survival and growth have been adversely affected in areas prepared by prescribed burning (cf., Loucks et al. 1987). As discussed in later chapters, incorrectly prescribed fires can cause several problems including:

- Destruction of soil structure, soil cover, water permeability, and microbial organisms necessary for adequate seedling survival, growth, and erosion control.
- Excessive loss of nutrients contained in woody debris, duff material, organic matter, and topsoil that are necessary for long-term site productivity.
- Removal of slash needed to protect seedlings from temperature extremes and frost heaving. The darkened soil following burning can also create hot, dry conditions for seedlings, particularly on south-facing slopes.
- Stimulation of germination of fire-adapted shrubs or fostering the invasion of species with wind-borne seed (Fig. 6-4); both groups compete with conifers.
- Death of residual trees left for seed tree and shelterwood purposes.

To avoid or minimize the above problems, the use of fire must be carefully prescribed and implemented. Not all sites are amenable to treatment by burning; conditions have to be suitable with respect to fuel moisture and distribution, weather, vegetation type, and other considerations.

Despite its broad utility, prescribed burning for reforestation is limited by several factors. These include concerns for fire safety (Chapters 5 and 8), health and aesthetics (Chapters 16 through 20), ecology and productivity (Chapters 4 and 12 through 15), and practical considerations such as operational efficiency and economics (Chapter 21). Fortunately an array of burning methods is available which helps maximize opportunities for using fire effectively. As described in Chapter 5, methods range from broadcast burning to burning of piles and windrows. The latter method requires the use of manual labor or machinery to pile the woody debris prior to ignition. The burning of herbicide-treated vegetation (e.g., brown-and-burn) for site preparation is another example where fire is used in conjunction with another forestry treatment.

Prescribed fire can also be used to assist reforestation in place of other forestry treatments such as mechanical scarification, cultivation, herbicide application, and manual cutting. Like fire, these techniques have limitations and disadvantages, too (Walstad et al. 1987). For example, the use of tractors to clear and pile debris can have serious short- and long-term impacts on soil condition, site productivity, and tree growth, particularly if the wrong type blade is used and topsoil is displaced from the site. Although initial seedling establishment may be enhanced by scarification, there may be detrimental effects on seedling growth and stand development. As an illustration of the potential for adverse effects of scarification, Minore (1986) found that Douglas-firs in plantations in southwest Oregon where slash was piled and burned were generally growing well below the original site potential, whereas those in plantations where slash was broadcast burned were growing at rates closely approximating the original potential for the sites. Consequently, there are many occasions where prescribed burning, particularly broadcast burning, is the best choice for preparing sites for reforestation.

Conclusion

Initial work in the management of forest residues primarily focused on the use of prescribed fire as a hazard reduction measure for preventing wildfire (Chapter 8). Little attention was given to effects on regeneration or longer term issues. David M. Smith recognized this problem and summarized the situation:

> Slash disposal has received far more attention as a means of fire protection than as a method of stimulating reproduction. This attitude has sometimes led to the application of methods of slash disposal which are not compatible with the renewal of the forest. The modifications of practice beneficial to reproduction lie in the direction of partial, rather than complete, disposal of slash (Smith 1962, p. 315).

In the future, therefore, it is likely that more attention will be given to the use of prescribed fire for purposes of reforestation—site preparation, weed control, and enhancing the efficiency of planting, tending, and monitoring operations.

These needs notwithstanding, the use of prescribed fire for reforestation in Pacific Northwest forests is expected to decline. Indeed, there are modest trends already in that direction, particularly for the federal sector (Fig. 6-6). The shift from old-growth to second-growth forests will reduce the amount of cull material left on site. The backlog of brushfields and low-value hardwood thick-

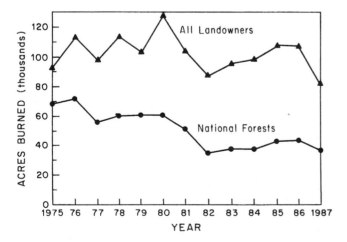

Figure 6-6. *Trends in slash burning in western Oregon, 1975-87. (Source: Forest Protection Division, Oregon Department of Forestry)*

Figure 6-7. *Increased utilization of woody biomass will decrease the need for prescribed burning in the future.*

ets needing rehabilitation or conversion will gradually decline, reducing the need for slash-and-burn treatments. Growing shortages of wood fiber will increase the value of noncommercial tree species and logging residues, thereby increasing utilization of previously unmerchantable material (Fig. 6-7). In other cases, it will be more desirable to leave woody debris on site for purposes of soil protection, nutrient cycling, long-term site productivity, and maintenance of animal habitat. Finally, continued improvements in fire prevention and suppression will reduce the wildfire hazard of logging slash.

Nevertheless, prescribed burning will continue to be an important silvicultural tool for specific situations. Better identification of such situations will be possible as research and experience unfold. The consequences of burning, not burning, or using an alternative practice on a given site will also be better understood as our predictive knowledge improves. Finally, additional ways of ameliorating or mitigating the adverse consequences of fire will be developed (Chapter 22), permitting safer and more ecologically sound application of this important tool.

Literature Cited & Key References

Alexander, R.R. 1966. Establishment of lodgepole pine reproduction after different slash disposal treatments. USDA For. Serv., Rocky Mt. For. Rge. Exp. Sta., Fort Collins, CO. Res. Note RM-62. 4 p.

*Baumgartner, D.M. (ed.) 1982. Site preparation and fuels management on steep terrain. Symp. Proc., Coop. Ext. Serv., Washington State Univ., Pullman, WA. 179 p.

*Baumgartner, D.M., R.G. Krebill, J.T. Arnott, and G.F. Weetman (eds.) 1985. Lodgepole pine—the species and its management. Symp. Proc., Coop. Ext. Serv., Washington State Univ., Pullman, WA. 381 p.

Beaufait, W.R., C.E. Hardy, and W.C. Fischer. 1975. Broadcast burning in larch-fir clearcuts: The Miller Creek-Newman Ridge study. USDA For. Serv., Intermt. For. Rge. Exp. Sta., Ogden, UT. Res. Pap. INT-175. 53 p.

References marked by an asterisk are recommended for general information.

*Benson, R.E. 1982. Management consequences of alternative harvesting and residue treatment practices —lodgepole pine. USDA For. Serv., Intermt. For. Rge. Exp. Sta., Ogden, UT. Gen. Tech. Rep. INT-132. 58 p.

Berntsen, C.M. 1955. Seedling distribution on a spruce-hemlock clearcut. USDA For. Serv., Pac. Northwest For. Rge. Exp. Sta., Portland, OR. Res. Note 119. 7 p.

Bever, D.N. 1954. Evaluation of factors affecting natural reproduction of forest trees in central western Oregon. Oregon State Board For. Res. Bull. 3. 49 p.

Boyd, R.J., and G.H. Deitschman. 1969. Site preparation aids natural regeneration in western larch-Engelmann spruce strip clearcuttings. USDA For. Serv., Intermt. For. Rge. Exp. Sta., Ogden, UT. Res. Pap. INT-64. 10 p.

Burns, R.M. (tech. comp.) 1983. Silvicultural systems for the major forest types of the United States. USDA For. Serv., Washington, DC. Agr. Hbk. 445. 191 p.

*Chandler, C., P. Cheney, P. Thomas, L. Trabaud, and D. Williams. 1983. Fire in Forestry. Vol. 2: Forest Fire Management and Organization. John Wiley & Sons, Inc., New York, NY. 298 p.

Cleary, B.D., R.D. Greaves, and R.K. Hermann (eds.) 1978. Regenerating Oregon's forests. Ext. Serv., Oregon State Univ., Corvallis, OR. 286 p.

Cochran, P.H. 1973. Natural regeneration of lodgepole pine in south- central Oregon. USDA For. Serv., Pac. Northwest For. Rge. Exp. Sta., Portland, OR. Res. Note PNW-204. 18 p.

*Davis, K.P. 1959. Forest Fire: Control and Use. McGraw-Hill Book Co., Inc., New York, NY. 584 p.

*DeByle, N.V. 1981. Clearcutting and fire in the larch/Douglas-fir forests of western Montana—a multifaceted research summary. USDA For. Serv., Intermt. For. Rge. Exp. Sta., Ogden, UT. Gen Tech. Rep. INT-99. 73 p.

*Edgren, J.W., and W.I. Stein. 1974. Artificial regeneration, p. M-1 to M-32. In Cramer, O.P. (org. and tech. ed.) Environmental effects of forest residues management in the Pacific Northwest. A state-of-knowledge compendium. USDA For. Serv., Pac. Northwest For. Rge. Exp. Sta., Portland, OR. Gen Tech. Rep. PNW-24.

*Feller, M.C. 1982. The ecological effects of slashburning with particular reference to British Columbia: A literature review. B.C. Ministry of Forests, Victoria, B.C. Land Manage. Rep. 13. 60 p.

Fowells, H.A. (comp.) 1965. Silvics of Forest Trees of the United States. USDA Forest Serv., Washington, DC. Agr. Hbk. 271. 762 p.

Gockerell, E.C. 1966. Plantations on burned vs. unburned areas. J. For. 64:392-394.

Gordon, D.T. 1970. Natural regeneration of white and red fir— influence of several factors. USDA For. Serv., Pac. Southwest For. Rge. Exp. Sta., Berkeley, CA. Res. Pap. PSW-58. 32 p.

*Gratkowski, H. 1974. Brushfield reclamation and type conversion, p. I-1 to I-31. *In* Cramer, O.P. (org. and tech. ed.) Environmental effects of forest residues management in the Pacific Northwest. A state-of-knowledge compendium. USDA For. Serv., Pac. Northwest For. Rge. Exp. Sta., Portland, OR. Gen Tech. Rep. PNW-24.

Haase, S.M. 1986. Effect of prescribed burning on soil moisture and germination of southwestern ponderosa pine seed on basaltic soils. USDA For Serv., Rocky Mt. For. Rge. Exp. Sta., Fort Collins, CO. Res. Note RM-462. 6 p.

Hooven, E.F., and H.C. Black. 1978. Prescribed burning aids reforestation of Oregon Coast Range brushlands. For. Res. Lab., Oregon State Univ., Corvallis, OR. Res. Pap. 38. 14 p.

Isaac, L.A. 1943. Reproductive habits of Douglas-fir. Charles Lathrop Pack Forestry Foundation, Washington, DC. 107 p.

Isaac, L.A. 1963. Fire—a tool not a blanket rule in Douglas-fir ecology. Tall Timbers Fire Ecol. Conf. Proc. 2:1-17.

Keatley, J.E. 1989. Weyerhaeuser Company's prescribed fire use in Washington, p. 338-340. *In* Hanley, D.P., J.J. Kammenga, and C.D. Oliver (eds.) Proc., The Burning Decision: Regional Perspectives on Slash. Coll. For. Resour., Univ. Washington, Seattle, WA. Inst. For. Resour. Contrib. No. 66. 374 p.

Lavender, D.P., M.H. Bergman, and L.D. Calvin. 1956. Natural regeneration on staggered settings. Oregon State Board For. Res. Bull. 10. 36 p.

*Lotan, J.E., M.E. Alexander, S.F. Arno, R.E. French, O.G. Langdon, R.M. Loomis, R.A. Norum, R.C. Rothermel, W.C. Schmidt, and J.W. van Wagtendonk. 1981. Effects of fire on flora. USDA For. Serv., Washington, DC. Gen. Tech. Rep. WO-16. 71 p.

*Loucks, D.M., S.R. Radosevich, T.B. Harrington, and R.G. Wagner. 1987. Prescribed fire in Pacific Northwest forests: An annotated bibliography. For. Res. Lab., Coll. For., Oregon State Univ., Corvallis, OR. 185 p.

Marlega, R.R. 1981. Operational use of prescribed fire, p. 71-72. *In* Hobbs, S.D. and O.T. Helgerson (eds.) Proc., Workshop on Reforestation of Skeletal Soils. For. Res. Lab., Oregon State Univ., Corvallis, OR. 124 p.

*Martin, R.E. 1976. Prescribed burning for site preparation in the Inland Northwest, p. 134-156. *In* Baumgartner, D.M. and R.J. Boyd (eds.) Tree Planting in the Inland Northwest. Conf. Proc., Coop. Ext. Serv., Washington State Univ., Pullman, WA. 311 p.

Martin, R.E. 1982. Shrub control by burning before timber harvest, p. 35-40. *In* Baumgartner, D.M. (ed.) Site Preparation and Fuels Management on Steep Terrain. Symp. Proc., Coop Ext. Serv., Washington State Univ., Pullman, WA. 179 p.

*Martin, R.E., and A.P. Brackebusch. 1974. Fire hazard and conflagration prevention, p. G-1 to G-30. *In* Cramer, O.P. (org. and tech. ed.) Environmental effects of forest residues management in the Pacific Northwest. A state-of-knowledge compendium. USDA For. Serv., Pac. Northwest For. Rge. Exp. Sta., Portland, OR. Gen Tech. Rep. PNW-24.

*Martin, R.E., and J.D. Dell. 1978. Planning for prescribed burning in the inland northwest. USDA For. Serv., Pac. Northwest For. Rge. Exp. Sta., Portland, OR. Gen. Tech. Rep. PNW-76. 68 p.

McCullough, W.F. 1944. Slash burning. For. Chron. 20:111-118.

*Miller, R.E., R.L. Williamson, and R.R. Silen. 1974. Regeneration and growth of coastal Douglas-fir, p. J-1 to J-41. *In* Cramer, O.P. (org. and tech. ed.) Environmental effects of forest residues management in the Pacific Northwest. A state-of-knowledge compendium. USDA For. Serv., Pac. Northwest For. Rge. Exp. Sta., Portland, OR. Gen Tech. Rep. PNW-24.

Minore, D. 1986. Effects of site preparation on seedling growth: A preliminary comparison of broadcast burning and pile burning. USDA For. Serv., Pac. Northwest Res. Sta., Portland, OR. Res. Note PNW-RN-452. 12 p.

Morris, W.G. 1970. Effects of slash burning in overmature stands of the Douglas-fir region. For. Sci. 16:258-270.

Munger, T.T., and D.N. Matthews. 1941. Slash disposal and forest management after clear cutting in the Douglas-fir region. USDA, Washington, DC. Circ. 586. 56 p.

Pearce, R.B. 1987. Preharvest burning to control postharvest vegetation. USDA For. Serv., Fort Collins, CO. For. Res. West., Dec. 1987. p. 11-14.

*Pierovich, J.M., E.H. Clarke, S.G. Pickford, and F.R. Ward. 1975. Forest residues management guidelines for the Pacific Northwest. USDA For. Serv., Pac. Northwest For. Rge. Exp. Sta., Portland, OR. Gen. Tech. Rep. PNW-33. 273 p.

Roe, A.L., R.R. Alexander, and M.D. Andrews. 1970. Engelmann spruce regeneration practices in the Rocky Mountains. USDA Prod. Res. Rep. 115. 31 p.

Roe, A.L., and A.E. Squillace. 1950. Can we induce prompt regeneration in selectively cut ponderosa pine stands? USDA For. Serv., Northern Rocky Mt. For. Rge. Exp. Sta., Missoula, MT. Res. Note 81. 7 p.

*Ross, D.W., and J.D. Walstad. 1986. Vegetative competition, site preparation and pine performance: A literature review with reference to southcentral Oregon. For. Res. Lab., Oregon State Univ., Corvallis, OR. Res. Bull. 58. 21 p.

*Ruth, R.H. 1974. Regeneration and growth of west-side mixed conifers, p. K-1 to K-21. *In* Cramer, O.P. (org. and tech. ed.) Environmental effects of forest residues management in the Pacific Northwest. A state-of-knowledge compendium. USDA For. Serv., Pac. Northwest For. Rge. Exp. Sta., Portland, OR. Gen Tech. Rep. PNW-24.

Sackett, S.S. 1984. Observations on natural regeneration in ponderosa pine following a prescribed fire in Arizona. USDA For. Serv., Rocky Mt. For. Rge. Exp. Sta., Fort Collins, CO. Res. Note RM-435. 8 p.

Schmidt, W.C. 1969. Seedbed treatments influence seedling development in western larch forests. USDA For. Serv., Intermt. For. Rge. Exp. Sta., Ogden, UT. Res. Note INT-93. 7 p.

Schmidt, W.C., and J.E. Lotan. 1980. Establishment and initial development of lodgepole pine in response to residue management, p. 271-286. *In* Environmental Consequences of Timber Harvesting in Rocky Mountain Coniferous Forests. USDA For. Serv., Intermt. For. Rge. Exp. Sta., Ogden, UT. Gen. Tech. Rep. INT-90. 526 p.

Schmidt, W.C., R.C. Shearer, and A.L. Roe. 1976. Ecology and silviculture of western larch forests. USDA For. Serv., Washington, DC. Tech. Bull. 1520. 96 p.

*Seidel, K.W. 1974. Natural regeneration of east-side conifer forests, p. L-1 to L-25. *In* Cramer, O.P. (org. and tech. ed.) Environmental effects of forest residues management in the Pacific Northwest. A state-of-knowledge compendium. USDA For. Serv., Pac. Northwest For. Rge. Exp. Sta., Portland, OR. Gen Tech. Rep. PNW-24.

Seidel, K.W. 1979a. Regeneration in mixed conifer clearcuts in the Cascade Range and the Blue Mountains of eastern Oregon. USDA For. Serv., Pac. Northwest For. Rge. Exp. Sta., Portland, OR. Res. Pap. PNW-248. 24 p.

Seidel, K.W. 1979b. Regeneration in mixed conifer shelterwood cuttings in the eastern Oregon Cascades. USDA For. Serv., Pac. Northwest For. Rge. Exp. Sta., Portland, OR. Res. Pap. PNW-264. 29 p.

*Seidel, K.W., and P.H. Cochran. 1981. Silviculture of mixed conifer forests in eastern Oregon and Washington. USDA For. Serv., Pac. Northwest For. Rge. Exp. Sta., Portland, OR. Gen. Tech. Rep. PNW-121. 70 p.

Shearer, R.C. 1976. Early establishment of conifers following prescribed broadcast burning in western larch/Douglas-fir forests. Tall Timbers Fire Ecol. Conf. Proc. 14:481-500.

Shearer, R.C. 1980. Regeneration establishment in response to harvesting and residue management in a western larch-Douglas-fir forest, p. 249-290. *In* Environmental Consequences of Timber Harvesting in Rocky Mountain Coniferous Forests. USDA For. Serv., Intermt. For. Rge. Exp. Sta., Ogden, UT. Gen. Tech. Rep. INT-90.

*Smith, D.M. 1962. The Practice of Silviculture. 7th ed. John Wiley & Sons, Inc., New York, NY. 578 p.

Stein, W.I. 1984. The coastal reforestation systems study—five year results. USDA For. Serv., Pac. Northwest For. Rge. Exp. Sta., Portland, OR. Res. Prog. Rep. 10 p.

Stein, W.I. 1986. Comparison of site preparation methods on Coast Range sites. USDA For. Serv., Pac. Northwest Res. Sta., Corvallis, OR. Res. Prog. Rep. 25 p.

Stein, W.I. 1989. Effectiveness and cost of six site preparation methods in the establishment and growth of Douglas-fir. *In* Proc., IUFRO Sympos. on Efficiency of Stand Establishment Operations. New Zealand, Sept. 11-15, 1989.

*Stewart, R.E. 1978. Site preparation, p. 99-129. *In* Cleary, B.D., R.D. Greaves, and R.K. Hermann. Regenerating Oregon's Forests. Ext. Serv., Oregon State Univ., Corvallis, OR. 286 p.

Tackle, D. 1956. Stocking and seedbed distribution on clear-cut lodgepole pine areas in Utah. USDA For. Serv., Intermt. For. Rge. Exp. Sta., Ogden, UT. Res. Note 38. 3 p.

*Tappeiner, J.C. II, and R.G. Wagner. 1987. Principles of silvicultural prescriptions for vegetation management, p. 399-429. *In* Walstad, J.D. and P.J. Kuch (eds.) Forest Vegetation Management for Conifer Production. John Wiley & Sons, Inc., New York, NY. 523 p.

Tarrant, R.F. 1956. Effect of slash burning on some physical soil properties. For. Sci. 2:18-22.

*Walstad, J.D., M. Newton, and D.H. Gjerstad. 1987. Overview of vegetation management alternatives, p. 157-200. *In* Walstad, J.D. and P.J. Kuch (eds.) Forest Vegetation Management for Conifer Production. John Wiley & Sons, Inc., New York, NY. 523 p.

*Weaver, H. 1974. Effects of fire on temperate forests: Western United States, p. 279-319. *In* Kozlowski, T.T. and C.E. Ahlgren (eds.) Fire and Ecosystems. Academic Press, New York, NY. 542 p.

Williamson, R.L. 1973. Results of shelterwood harvesting of Douglas- fir in the Cascades of western Oregon. USDA For. Serv., Pac. Northwest For. Rge. Exp. Sta., Portland, OR. Res. Pap. PNW-161. 13 p.

Worthington, N.P. 1953. Reproduction following small group cuttings in virgin Douglas-fir. USDA For. Serv., Pac. Northwest For. Rge. Exp. Sta., Portland, OR. Res. Note 84. 5 p.

*Wright, H.A., and A.W. Bailey. 1982. Fire Ecology: United States and Southern Canada. John Wiley & Sons, Inc., New York, NY. 501 p.

Zasada, J., and J. Tappeiner. 1988. Effect of slashburning on planting spot availability and planting efficiency. COPE Rep. 1(2):5.

7 Use of Prescribed Fire in Rangeland Ecosystems

Robert G. Clark and Edward E. Starkey

Executive Summary

Rangeland ecosystems, those forested and nonforested areas suitable for extensive management for browsing and grazing animals, evolved under the influence of fire. Natural ignition via lightning, and deliberate or accidental burning by Native Americans, resulted in fire return intervals of a few years to a few centuries. Some plant and animal species are well adapted to repeated rangeland burning, and some species may actually depend on periodic rangeland burning for survival. By contrast, some species do not tolerate fire well and may be, at least temporarily, eradicated by repeated burning. Successful management of fire on rangelands therefore depends on an understanding of the complex role of fire in these ecosystems. Appropriate fire management objectives, derived from the understanding of ecosystem interrelationships and land-use decisions, are used to develop successful fire management programs. In this context, fire is neither bad nor good; it is simply an ecosystem maintenance process used to manage for preferred plant and animal species. In the near future, global warming is likely to alter present fire regimes and provide new challenges to land managers.

Introduction

Rangelands are those lands where the potential natural vegetation is mostly grass, grasslike plants, forbs, or shrubs; where grazing and browsing were important influences during prehistoric time; and that are more suitable for management by ecologic than by agronomic principles (Short 1986). The Pacific Northwest also has forested rangelands that provide food, water, and cover for domestic livestock as well as more traditional forest products. By their nature, rangelands provide essential requirements for game and nongame wildlife species, and can be managed or considered as wildlife habitat. Although much of the rangeland in the region is in federal or state ownership, private lands contribute substantial forage for domestic livestock and habitat for wildlife.

The Region

Rangelands of the Pacific Northwest occur mostly east of the Cascade Mountain chain although forested areas of the Coast and Cascade mountains provide habitat for wildlife. Intermountain valleys, grasslands, and savannas are frequently grazed by livestock and terrestrial wildlife species. Along the Pacific Coast and in western interior valleys, marine influences create a mild, wet climate with long frost-free periods. Precipitation generally increases up the western slope of the Cascades, with many areas receiving 70 to 100 inches annually (Jackson 1985). Above 5,000 feet in elevation, winter precipitation falls as snow instead of rain, and some areas typically receive 20 feet or more. East of the Cascades, precipitation decreases dramatically.

The rainshadow east of the Cascades gives rise to most of the traditional rangeland that is unsuited for forest production, agricultural development or other intensive uses because of inadequate precipitation, steep or rocky slopes, poor soil development, harsh climate, and other restrictions. On these traditional rangelands, average annual precipitation may be as low as 6 inches or less, with much of the total falling as snow outside of the growing season. Cold winters and hot, dry summers typically exclude conifer growth but support grasslands and shrublands that are best suited to use by grazing and browsing animals. The Great Basin, with its saline or alkaline soil influences, reaches north into eastern Oregon, terminating near Burns. Interior mountains in northeastern Oregon, eastern Washington, and northern and central Idaho are cooler and moister than surrounding lowlands, and support much of the forested rangelands in the region.

Historic Role of Fire

Prior to settlement by Europeans, fire was common in forested rangelands, oak-savannas, and shrub-steppes of the Pacific Northwest. Fires resulted from lightning and deliberate or accidental burning by Native Americans. Many early explorers wrote of the use of fire by Indians for such purposes as killing and collecting grasshoppers for food, signaling, as a weapon against enemies, enhancing berry production, and to manage wildlife habitat (Shinn 1980).

Following the arrival of European settlers, fire regimes were greatly altered. Initially much abusive and promiscuous burning occurred which, combined with intensive grazing, degraded rangelands throughout the Northwest. In response to the early uncontrolled use of fire, a broad policy of fire exclusion was subsequently developed. At about the same time livestock reached peak numbers on western rangelands, and fine fuels were greatly reduced by grazing. By the early part of this century, therefore, the influence of fire on rangelands had been diminished.

Thus, native vegetation, which had evolved with fire as a common influence, was greatly altered. As plant communities changed, so did their value as wildlife habitat, particularly for those species such as pronghorn antelope and bighorn sheep, which forage on forbs and grasses. However-

er, factors such as grazing and diseases also influenced native rangeland wildlife species. For example, bighorn sheep populations have been reduced because of competition with livestock for forage, and as a result of domestic livestock diseases (Van Dike et al. 1983).

Plant & Animal Communities

Rangelands include grasslands, shrublands, and forested lands. Pacific Northwest grasslands include the Palouse prairie of southeastern Washington and adjacent areas in Oregon and Idaho. Some estimates place the presettlement size of the Palouse at 30 million acres (Branson 1985). However, much of the original prairie, dominated by bluebunch wheatgrass and Idaho fescue, has been converted to crop production. Other grasslands include the highly productive Willamette Valley, Puget Trough, and Rogue Valley west of the Cascades, and valleys of the Snake River and its tributaries east of the Cascades. There is considerable evidence (e.g., Shinn 1980, Gruell 1985, Boyd 1986) that natural and anthropogenic fires were instrumental in the maintenance, if not the creation, of these grasslands.

Much of the traditional rangeland has been described as shrub-steppe in the Columbia Basin and in central and southeastern Oregon (Franklin and Dyrness 1988), as steppe in eastern Washington (Daubenmire 1970), and as sagebrush-grass habitat types in southern and central Idaho (Hironaka et al. 1983, Tisdale 1985). These rangelands typically include a shrub component and are often dominated by one of the four recognized subspecies (Goodrich et al. 1985) of big sagebrush: mountain, Wyoming, spike, and basin. Together, these four shrubs occur on about 57.6 million acres (West 1983). At least nine other species, subspecies, or forms of sagebrush are important ecologically or economically in the Pacific Northwest (Winward 1980). Associated shrubs commonly include bitterbrush, several species of rabbitbrush, and several species of *Atriplex* (saltbushes).

Bitterbrush, a highly palatable and nutritious winter wildlife browse, is susceptible to fire, although some sprouting occurs (Clark et al. 1982). The rabbitbrushes sprout prolifically after burning and often dominate sites for 30 to 70 years unless chemically controlled. Response of shrubs of the *Atriplex* genus to burning is poorly understood.

Fourwing saltbush usually sprouts vigorously after burning, but exceptions have been noted. Effects of fire on shadscale, another *Atriplex* species, have not been widely reported, probably because it typically occupies sites that lack sufficient fine fuel to carry fire and, therefore, this shrub rarely burns. Other important shrubs include winterfat, which usually sprouts except after extremely intense summer wildfires, and horsebrush, a noxious shrub, which sprouts vigorously and typically increases 2- to 3-fold after burning.

Important grasses associated with shrub-dominated rangelands include bluebunch wheatgrass, bottlebrush squirreltail, and Sandberg bluegrass, all of which usually increase production within 3 to 5 years after spring or fall burning, although recovery may take longer after severe summer wildfires. Idaho fescue, Thurber needlegrass, and prairie junegrass recover more slowly. Cheatgrass, an introduced annual species, readily colonizes many sites in the sagebrush-grass ecosystem. Cheatgrass is highly flammable and shortens the fire return interval.

Ecologically distinct rangelands also occur in commercial forestlands and noncommercial woodlands. Rangelands in commercial forestlands are often dominated by ponderosa pine or lodgepole pine, alone or mixed, and are typically found on moist sites at high elevations such as the eastern slopes of the Cascades, the Blue Mountains of northeastern Oregon, and the mountains of north-central Idaho. Although managed primarily for wood products, these forests often provide valuable forage for domestic livestock and wildlife (Thomas 1979). Rangelands in the noncommercial woodlands of the Pacific Northwest are dominated by western juniper. These woodlands are primarily in central Oregon, though large areas in the Owyhee Mountains of southwestern Idaho and in the southern Cascades of northeastern California are also dominated by western juniper.

Although some investigators (e.g., Burkhardt and Tisdale 1976, Caraher 1978, Eddleman 1987) have suggested that fire control, overgrazing, and other anthropogenic factors have been responsible for large invasions by western juniper during the past century, prehistoric evidence is emerging (Mehringer and Wigand 1987) that western juniper has fluctuated in range and density for millenia. If so, overgrazing, fire suppression, and other human activity could not account for these fluctuations. On some sites juniper communities appear to be stable, with trees more than 300 years old, no evidence of further succession, and sparse understory. These sites do not contain sufficient fine fuels to carry surface fire or dependent crown fire, and crown closure is insufficient to allow independent crown fire. Also, many stands contain numerous fire-scarred snags, suggesting that lightning strikes occurred but that only a single tree was burned. Other juniper sites are clearly undergoing succession, with ample evidence of both range expansion and increase in stand density. Expansion is typically onto grasslands and shrublands, but in at least one instance, on Steens Mountain in southeastern Oregon, western juniper is invading quaking aspen stands.

A large number of wildlife species inhabit Pacific Northwest rangelands. For example, Maser et al. (1984) found 341 species of vertebrates residing in the Great Basin of southeast Oregon. These include important game species (e.g., mule deer, pronghorn antelope, bighorn sheep) as well as a host of nongame species ranging from the tiny calliope hummingbird to the ever-present magpie, and from the Malheur shrew to the ubiquitous coyote.

These wildlife species occupy habitats which provide such basic needs as feeding, reproduction, and protection from predators or weather. Through millenia, wildlife coevolved with rangeland plant communities and adapted to natural processes, including fire. Some wildlife species specialized in early seral communities, such as grasslands, which follow soon after fire. Still others favored climax communities of trees and shrubs. These habitats reflect a complex interaction of environmental variables including soil and climate, but throughout large areas of western rangelands, fire has been an important influence on wildlife populations.

Because their habitat requirements are so diverse, manipulation by fire can be used to change the relative value of habitats for wildlife species. Size and spatial distribution, season of burning, plant communities burned, and fire severity and frequency are examples of important variables which influence the relative suitability of postfire plant communities as habitat for various animal species.

Uses of Prescribed Fire

We know from the reports of early explorers, as discussed above, that Native Americans used fire to manage forested rangelands long before the arrival of European settlers. Thus in many ways contemporary land managers are merely reintroducing a traditional management technique. However, because of changes in vegetation, as well as increased constraints resulting from human development and management objectives, the use of fire is increasingly complex.

Perhaps the single largest obstacle to a successful prescribed fire program on rangelands is the control of livestock. Frequently, prefire rest from grazing is necessary to allow accumulation of adequate fine fuels. But more importantly, postfire livestock control is essential for recovery of plants. Postfire recovery may take 1 to 3 years or longer, depending on environmental and site conditions.

Wright (1974), Vallentine (1980), and Bunting et al. (1987) provide a number of reasons why rangelands are burned. Of these, the four primary purposes for burning Pacific Northwest rangelands are to increase forage quantity for domestic livestock and grazing species of wildlife, control certain species of brush, maintain ecological diversity, and reduce the risk of uncontrollable wildfire.

Burning to improve forage production

Many, but not all, rangeland plant communities increase forage production 2- to 3-fold within 5 years after burning. This dramatic effect results from removal of overstory shrubs which shade understory grasses and forbs, and which use considerable amounts of soil water and nutrients that are typically lacking on rangelands. Although fairly predictable, forage response is not well understood, and specific plant responses appear to depend on the forage species in question, plant physiological status, physical health (vigor), phenological stage, site nutrient status, postburn precipitation, season of burning, land management practices, and other factors related to fuel and weather conditions. For example, Kentucky bluegrass is frequently depressed by spring burning and can be relegated to minor status by repeated application of spring fires. In contrast, we have observed that crested wheatgrass appears unaffected by early spring burning, but will usually initiate growth earlier and increase production during the spring following fall burning. Early initiation of spring growth may be caused by faster warming of the soil due to both removal by fire of the insulating effect of litter, and increased absorption of solar energy by the ash-darkened surface. The increased production usually comes from more growth on existing plants rather than from seedling establishment.

Most annual plant communities, including cheatgrass, appear unaffected by burning because most annuals are prolific seed producers, and large, soil-borne seed reservoirs provide for rapid reestablishment. Any suppression of these annuals by fire is likely to be brief, usually lasting only 1 year. Perennial forbs are usually unaffected by fall burning but may be depressed if burned during the active growth stage. Despite the wide variation in plant responses to fire, and the inherent danger in generalization, some conclusions can be drawn:

- Two wheatgrasses, native bluebunch and the introduced and widely seeded crested complex, almost always increase production following fall burning, although the increase may take 1 to 3 years to develop.
- Some grasses, including Idaho fescue and some needlegrasses, are commonly depressed for 3 years or more after burning and often require special management to maintain their abundance.
- Most other forage grasses respond somewhere between these extremes.

All prescribed burns require carefully planned prescriptions and even more careful postburn management.

Increased forage production results in improved nutrition for game animals, particularly when nutritional status is suboptimum. Not only is the total amount of forage increased, but green forage is available earlier in the spring for 1 to 3 years on burned areas as compared with unburned plant communities. Both bighorn sheep and mule deer typically respond by grazing burned areas more heavily than similar unburned sites (Peek et al. 1979, Hobbs and Spowart 1984). Pronghorn antelope may also be favored by fire, at least on a small scale (Kindschy et al. 1982) because, like bighorn sheep and mule deer, a major portion of their diet consists of grasses and forbs. However, unlike bighorn sheep which feed almost exclusively on grasses and forbs, mule deer browse heavily on shrubs on most western winter ranges and pronghorn antelope may feed on shrubs throughout the year. Thus, prescribed burns to improve forage quality for mule deer or pronghorn antelope should be planned to provide a mosaic of burned and unburned areas to provide an optimum mix of grass-forb and shrub communities. Burns conducted in this manner may also improve brood rearing habitat for sage grouse by increasing the availability of forbs which are important components of the diets of their young (Autenrieth 1981, Call and Maser 1985). However, because sage grouse depend heavily upon sagebrush for cover and food, prescribed burns in sage grouse habitat should result in burned patches no larger than 10-15 acres (Autenrieth 1985).

Burning to control brush species

The second common reason for burning Northwest rangelands is to reduce dominance of certain brush species, most commonly big sagebrush, because increased dominance by brush species usually occurs at the expense of more desirable plant species. The four subspecies of big sagebrush do not sprout, and any fire intense enough to scorch the foliage kills the plant. Sagebrush seeds are relatively heavy and not easily dispersed by the wind, and if the soil-borne reservoir is depleted by repeated burning, big sagebrush can often be eliminated for 20 years or more. Unfortunately, several species of rabbitbrush and horsebrush are often found in big sagebrush plant communities. These two genera are prolific sprouters and rapidly dominate many sites after burning. Rather than solving brush problems, burning these mixed communities often causes more serious management problems than those posed by the preburn community. Detailed preburn investigation and planning are needed to identify those sites that cannot be burned without serious ecological consequences.

Some shrubs, especially those particularly valuable for wildlife, such as bitterbrush, may be killed, with serious implications for wintering animals dependent on browse. These shrubs often provide thermal and escape cover as well as high-protein food for wildlife. During the first 10 to 15 years following a fire, winter browse will be reduced, but the reduction may be partially offset by increased production of herbaceous forage. Cover will also be reduced. Over a much longer period, decadent shrub stands will be rejuvenated and

browse production will increase (Klebenow 1985). Thus, prescribed burning on winter ranges should provide for an optimum mix of various seral stages, so that both forage and cover are provided for wildlife. Thoughtful consideration of the effects on wildlife of burning extensive areas is required to ensure that long-term productivity is enhanced while minimizing short-term negative consequences.

Burning to maintain ecological diversity

Ecological diversity was historically maintained by fire in most rangeland communities (Christensen 1985). Big sagebrush is seldom browsed sufficiently to check its development, and it has few biological controls although snow mold (Nelson and Sturgis 1986) and sporadic infestations of aroga moth (Gates 1964) have been reported. Therefore, fire is the primary agent responsible for periodically reducing sagebrush density. Depending on fire return intervals in specific communities, most rangelands in subclimax condition contain mixtures of shrubs, forbs, and grasses. Although some communities demonstrate remarkable stability in near climax condition, many sagebrush communities do not; they advance progressively toward greater dominance by sagebrush, with corresponding reduction in understory grasses and forbs, and frequently with a reduction in the number of shrub species. These communities, in the climax condition, are essentially big sagebrush monocultures with decreased species diversity, decreased forage and wildlife habitat and quality and, depending on litter accumulation, decreased resistance to surface soil erosion. If burned prior to total dominance (often with cover exceeding 60 percent) by big sagebrush, these communities become more productive and ecologically more diverse. If sagebrush communities achieve the monoculture condition, they become extremely difficult to burn safely, and even if the burn is accomplished, there are few residual understory plants to take advantage of the overstory removal. These sites often must be reseeded.

Wildlife communities are also more diverse when a mosaic of seral stages exists. Many wildlife species utilize edges or ecotones between different plant communities and, therefore, are favored by increased heterogeneity of habitats. Structural diversity can be increased with prescribed burning. For example, a mosaic of burned and unburned areas may contain grass and forb understories, shrub intermediate layers, and climax forest overstories. Tiagwad et al. (1982) found that the variety and numbers of birds were increased by prescribed burning in curlleaf mountain mahogany and sagebrush communities, but that populations decreased and were less diverse on a nearby area which had been burned by an extremely intense wildfire. Vegetation following the wildfire was dominated by grasses which provided little structural diversity.

Although a mosaic of plant communities created by burning can contain a great deal of structural diversity, an important variable is the size of habitat blocks within the mosaic. Very small or very large blocks will result in less wildlife diversity than for some optimum size. Thomas et al. (1979) suggest that average habitat sizes of 200 acres should result in maximum species richness in southeastern Oregon. They emphasize that habitats should be provided that are both larger and smaller than this average. Thus, the relatively small number of wildlife species that require larger habitats will be accommodated, and the smaller habitats will increase the amount of edge.

Burning to reduce wildfire hazard

The fourth major use of fire on rangelands is to reduce wildfire hazard. This use is often employed near buildings, at the urban-wildland interface, near thoroughfares, and where activities such as brush chaining, timber harvest, or natural events create excessive fuel accumulations. Hazard reduction burning is also used to break up large blocks of wildlands where lightning fires are difficult and expensive to control. Hazard reduction fires are prescribed to reduce fuels and usually employ prepared firebreaks, cool air temperatures, low to moderate windspeeds, and elevated relative humidities so that the risk of escape is minimal. In contrast, wildfires in these fuels typically burn with low fuel moistures and relative humidities, high air temperatures and windspeeds, and without firebreaks. There is also evidence that, due to increased fuel consumption, smoke emissions are greater in wildfires than in prescribed fires (Cooper 1976).

From a wildlife perspective, reduction in hazard decreases the likelihood of catastrophic wildfires which are followed by large unbroken blocks of early seral plant communities. Thus, hazard reduction plays an important role in maintaining and enhancing diversity of both plant and wildlife populations.

Fire Effects: Universal Truths or Questionable Assumptions?

Several common assumptions regarding the use of fire on rangelands may not be universally true. Although these assumptions may be based on reports in the fire literature, fire is a complex biological and physical phenomenon, and site-specific conditions rarely duplicate those in the reports.

Questionable Assumption #1: Prescribed fire is cost effective. At least three factors affect cost effectiveness: per acre costs of burning; the value of the benefits of burning; and the duration of the benefits of burning. The costs of burning include not only direct costs, but also those associated with time, such as deferment of grazing for preburn fuel accumulation and postburn plant recovery, and interest on borrowed capital during that interval. For example, a prescribed fire designed to increase forage production from 200 lbs per acre preburn to 400 lbs per acre postburn is probably not cost effective unless per acre costs are held below $5.00 or the increased forage value exceeds $1.50 per animal unit month. Additional benefits, such as reduced soil erosion due to increased postburn plant cover, may accrue; thus, cost effectiveness may vary among landowners with different land-use goals and management objectives.

Questionable Assumption #2: Forage production, and consequently grazing capacity, will double. Some sites do indeed produce remarkable increases in forage after burning. However, some sites have equally remarkable decreases in production, or shifts from preferred plant species to some that are less preferred. In contrast, availability of forage almost always increases, due either to reduction in browse height or removal of the shrub overstory barrier.

Some factors that influence herbaceous production and composition in postburn plant communities include inherent site potential, annual fluctuation in precipitation, tolerance of plants to fire, fire return interval, and preburn and postburn management of livestock. Of these, only the last can be controlled to any degree by the land manager. In addition, if residual herbaceous plants or seed banks are not available to utilize nutrients, soil moisture, and sunlight released by removing a shrub or tree overstory, it is likely that burned plant communities will deteriorate even further. Big sagebrush monocultures, for example, cannot be "improved" by burning.

Sites that may increase production of herbaceous plants after burning are well-managed, inherently productive sites in good condition. Typically, such sites on which sagebrush cover is 15 to 25 percent increase herbaceous production within 3 years after spring or fall burning.

Questionable Assumption #3: Forage quality is improved by burning. Like quantity, forage quality may or may not improve after burning. The literature (e.g., Lyon et al. 1978) suggests that certain nutrients increase due to burning. It is unclear, however, whether specific plant parts have elevated nutrient levels or whether overall quality appears to increase by virtue of a decrease in the dead fraction. Wright and Bailey (1982) suggest that increased succulence of new growth is apparent and is the primary attractant to herbivores. In any case, any increase in forage quality is short-lived, uncertain, and not, of itself, ample justification for burning.

Questionable Assumption #4: Fire, being "natural," should be used in lieu of herbicides and other "artificial" methods of weed control. Many undesirable plants are shrubs that sprout or germinate from seed prolifically after burning. These species, including the rabbitbrushes, horsebrushes, and many annual plants, cannot be eradicated with fire. Burning these plant communities merely trades one brush problem for a second, often more serious, brush problem. Other plants, such as western juniper, often grow on sites which cannot be burned because the natural lack of herbaceous ground cover prevents fire from spreading. Also, some sites cannot be burned because of the threat of fire escape, air quality restrictions, susceptibility of preferred plant species to fire, etc. Thus, some sites either should not, or cannot, be burned.

If some treatment is in order, judicious use of herbicides, mechanical methods or, with a few susceptible species, applied biological control, are options for consideration. Often, a combination of treatments such as burning followed by application of herbicides to control sprouts is required for adequate control. Occasionally, as with western

juniper on some sites, mechanical treatment, followed 3 years later by burning to kill seedlings, will extend the effective life of rangeland treatments.

Questionable Assumption #5: Burning will control exotics. Most exotic plants on rangelands cannot be controlled by burning. Medusahead rye is reportedly reduced by burning under specific circumstances (McKell et al. 1962), but not controlled. Similarly, halogeton, knapweed, and other invaders may be temporarily reduced, unaffected, or enhanced by burning. These annual species are prolific seed producers and well adapted to fire; they either occupy vacant niches or have become established by partially replacing previous tenants. For the most part, they are naturalized and efforts to eliminate them with fire are futile.

Questionable Assumption #6: Western juniper sites are "improved" by burning. Central Oregon, and the Owyhee Mountains in southwest Idaho, have steep, rocky slopes occupied by western juniper; these are sites where the literature suggests that juniper "belongs." However, juniper also occurs in other plant communities.

South-central Oregon, near Fort Rock, has large areas of ancient junipers; many of these trees are at least 200 years old, but precise dating is impossible because the trees are hollow. There is no evidence that this forest ever supported a herbaceous component sufficiently continuous to allow fire to spread. Further, the trees are so widely spaced that an independent crown fire is unlikely. Thus, although many lightning-struck snags are visible, attesting to an ignition source, it is evident that a stand-replacement fire has not occurred for several centuries, if ever. It appears that these sites, which are not on steep, rocky slopes, are climax juniper sites. It is unclear how these sites could be improved by burning, even if fire spread was possible.

In contrast, some grasslands (Caraher 1978) and shrublands (Burkhardt and Tisdale 1976) are transitional, periodically invaded by juniper, then restored by recurring fires. These sites usually can be burned, albeit with difficulty, with resulting increases in herbaceous production. Natural fire return intervals on these sites are not well established but the cycles were probably irregular. Fires probably followed years with large herbaceous fuel accumulation, and occurred often enough that canopy cover had not reduced herbaceous production and the trees had not grown taller than the easily killed 4- to 6-foot height.

Questionable Assumption #7: Fire is good for wildlife. Wildlife species are habitat-dependent, and any event that influences a plant community usually has some effect on associated wildlife. It is clear that fire, under many circumstances, increases the availability of browse and production of herbaceous forage for terrestrial herbivores. Thermal, escape, and hiding cover, however, are also habitat requirements, and cover may be substantially altered by fire. Some rangeland animals require a variety of plant communities; sage grouse, for example, apparently require one type of sagebrush structure for nesting, another type for brood rearing, a third type for mating, and possibly a fourth type for winter occupancy (Autenrieth 1981, Call and Maser 1985). Therefore, it is not clear that fire is equally beneficial to all species of rangeland wildlife, nor is it clear that large, clean burns are beneficial to any species of rangeland wildlife in the short term.

Fire may be good for wildlife, however, depending on habitat requirements for the species in question, on the size, timing, and severity of the fire, and on the mosaic or patchiness of the postburn plant community. It is necessary, therefore, to establish clear management objectives for the plant and animal communities involved, a thorough understanding of habitat requirements of affected animal species, and carefully prepared plans for burning and postburn management.

Questionable Assumption #8: Burning is harmful to rangeland soils. Site-specific effects, usually on forest soils, have erroneously been extrapolated to unrelated rangeland situations. Certainly some effects are nearly universal. Total (but not available) nitrogen and sulfur almost always decrease because both volatilize at relatively low temperatures. However, most of these losses are from above-ground combustion. Thus, although site nutrient budgets decrease, contents in the soil are often unaffected.

Comparatively light fuel loads on rangelands, often less than 1 ton per acre, result in fast-moving fires and little heat penetration into the soil (Wright and Bailey 1982). Thus, soil nitrogen and sulfur are often unaffected on rangelands. Some cations, especially calcium and potassium, increase in soils after burning because they are released from plant material and leach into the soil. However, addi-

tions of the cations are slight (a 1 percent concentration in plant material would add 10 to 20 lbs per acre) and, because these nutrients are seldom limiting to plant growth, the most often observed effect is a slight increase in soil pH.

One effect of fire on soils that warrants further discussion is hydrophobicity, or water repellency. This effect, most noticeable in southern California chaparral communities, occurs only infrequently and is slight and of short duration when it occurs (Salih et al. 1973) on Pacific Northwest rangelands.

Potentially the most serious impact of fire on rangeland soils is erosion. Fall fires, especially on steep slopes, are subject to raindrop impact, and may form crusts or result in soil movement following high-intensity storms. Also, fall burns preclude vegetation recovery until the following spring and, therefore, are subject to wind erosion for an extended period and the alteration or loss of snow retention. Land managers should avoid burning steep slopes or erodible soils and select these sites for emergency rehabilitation following wildfires, especially those that occur too late in the season for natural vegetation recovery to occur prior to winter.

These eight examples illustrate that site-specific effects cannot be generalized to all rangelands, and that fire is not a panacea for all rangeland problems. Although most, if not all, rangeland ecosystems evolved with fire, they are not in a "natural" condition today because of a legacy of grazing, agricultural development, fire suppression, introduction of alien plants, construction of roads and other barriers, alteration of fuel loads, and other factors. It is clear that rangelands have changed; it is unclear what the proper role of fire should be on altered rangelands. For these reasons, fire should be managed carefully so it meets the needs of rangeland plant communities and their occupants.

Future Fire Environments

It seems likely that the climate of the earth is warming as a result of increased concentrations of "greenhouse" gases, such as carbon dioxide, in the atmosphere. Although there is considerable uncertainty over the amount of change expected, various mathematical models suggest an eventual warming of 3.6-9.0°F (Tangley 1988). One of these models, developed by the Goddard Institute for

Space Studies, suggests that warming will be evident during the next 10 years, and predicts that temperatures will warm by 3.6°F by the year 2020. Such an increase would make the earth warmer than at any point in historical time. Projections of temperature extremes for the Pacific Northwest are not available, but to place this increase in perspective consider that under this scenario, Dallas, Texas would experience 78 days above 100°F annually, compared to a current average of 19 such days (Rind 1986). Increases in temperature will not be uniform across North America, and may range from less than 3.6°F on the southern California coast to more than 10.8°F in Arizona, New Mexico, southern Colorado, and southern Utah. Warming will generally increase from west to east and from north to south (Leverenz and Lev 1987).

It is also likely that many areas will become drier, and the frequency and severity of droughts will increase (Tangley 1988). As with temperature, changes in moisture stress for plants will vary among locations and seasons, but much of the western United States will be drier than at present (Leverenz and Lev 1987).

Implications of this climate change are enormous for fire managers. Direct effects would likely include lengthened wildfire seasons, greater frequency and size of wildfires, and changes in the site-specific response of plants to fire. For example, Idaho fescue tends to respond to burning more favorably on moist, fertile sites than on dry, less fertile sites, and more favorably near its geographic center of distribution than near its limits of distribution. In a warmer climate, plants already physiologically stressed may not recover as they did under former conditions.

Accompanying these direct effects would be changes in plant communities. For example, ponderosa pine is projected to increase in California and the Cascades of Oregon, and decrease on the eastern slope of the Washington Cascades, throughout the Rocky Mountains, and in Arizona and New Mexico (Leverenz and Lev 1987). In general plant communities will shift to higher elevations, and some may even disappear from the top of mountains (Peters and Darling 1985).

These changes in climate and plant communities would have a substantial impact on fire management. Budgets for fire suppression will have to be increased, fire prescriptions will require revision, and even objectives will need to be reassessed. For example, control of brush is a common use of fire; but could warming and drying naturally favor grasses over shrubs in some areas, thus reducing the need for prescribed fire?

A great deal of uncertainty exists over the causes, magnitude and impacts of future climatic changes. However, there is substantial consensus that changes are occurring. Furthermore, these changes are likely to influence forests and rangelands in the near future. Research must be initiated to provide a better understanding of the role of fire under various climatic scenarios.

Conclusion

Managing rangelands is complex and involves many trade-offs between competing uses such as livestock, timber, and wildlife production. If objectives are clearly identified during the planning process, fire can be an effective tool in achieving desired outputs from managed rangelands.

A common example of conflicting uses is the dilemma of simultaneously providing for domestic livestock and wildlife. Fire can be used to increase forage production for livestock, and if that were the only objective, relatively large fires could be desirable. However, many wildlife species would be harmed by the exclusion of woody plants from large areas. Thus, land managers often must provide an optimum mix of habitats which include foraging areas for domestic livestock, and habitats which provide food, cover, and edges for wildlife. Fire is in many ways an ideal tool for this task because desired changes in rangelands can be accomplished by carefully prescribing the size, location, and season of burning as well as suitable weather conditions and plant communities to be burned. However, fire management will become increasingly more complex as a result of climatic warming and drying caused by the greenhouse effect. Land managers must soon begin developing alternative strategies to deal with climatically induced changes in fire regimes.

Finally, it should be remembered that fire is but one of many tools available to the land manager. Grazing systems, herbicides, mechanical treatment, biological weed control, and artificial seeding will continue to play important roles in range management. Successful management plans will integrate fire with the full range of techniques needed to accomplish the desired objectives.

Literature Cited & Key References

Autenrieth, R.E. 1981. Sage grouse management in Idaho. Idaho Fish and Game Dept., Boise, ID. Wildl. Bull. 9. 238 p.

Autenrieth, R. 1985. Sage grouse life history and habitat management, p. 52. *In* Rangeland Fire Effects: A Symposium. USDI, Bur. Land Manage. Boise, ID. 124 p.

Boyd, R. 1986. Strategies of Indian burning in the Willamette Valley. Can. J. Anthropol. 5:65-86.

*Branson, F.A. 1985. Vegetation changes on Western rangelands. Soc. Rge. Manage., Denver, CO. Rge. Monogr. 2. 76 p.

*Bunting, S.C., B.M. Kilgore, and C.L. Bushey. 1987. Guidelines for prescribed burning sagebrush-grass rangelands in the northern Great Basin. USDA For. Serv., Intermt. Res. Sta., Ogden, UT. Gen. Tech. Rep. INT-231. 33 p.

Burkhardt, J.W., and E.W. Tisdale. 1976. Causes of juniper invasion in southwestern Idaho. Ecology 57:472-484.

*Call, M.W., and C. Maser. 1985. Wildlife habitats in managed rangelands—the Great Basin of southeastern Oregon. USDA For. Serv., Pac. Northwest For. Rge. Exp. Sta., Portland, OR. Gen. Tech. Rep. PNW-187. 30 p.

Caraher, D.L. 1978. The spread of western juniper in central Oregon, p. 3-7. *In* Martin, R.E., J.E. Dealy, and D.L. Caraher (eds.) Proc., Western Juniper Ecology and Management Workshop. USDA For. Serv., Pac. Northwest For. Rge. Exp. Sta., Portland, OR. Gen. Tech. Rep. PNW-74. 177 p.

*Christensen, N.L. 1985. Shrubland fire regimes and their evolutionary consequences, p. 85-100. *In* Pickett, S.T.A., and P.S. White (eds.) The Ecology of Natural Disturbance and Patch Dynamics. Academic Press, Orlando, FL. 472 p.

Clark, R.G., C.M. Britton, and F.A. Sneva. 1982. Mortality of bitterbrush after burning and clipping in eastern Oregon. J. Rge. Manage. 35:711-714.

Cooper, R.W. 1976. Trade-offs between smoke from wild and prescribed forest fires, p. 19-26. *In* Proc. Internat. Symp. on Air Quality and Smoke from Urban and Forest Fires. Nat. Acad. Sci., Washington, DC.

*Daubenmire, R. 1970. Steppe vegetation of Washington. Washington Agr. Exp. Sta., Washington State Univ., Pullman, WA. Tech. Bull. 62. 131 p.

Eddleman, L.E. 1987. Establishment and stand development of western juniper in central Oregon, p. 155-159. *In* Everett, R.L. (ed.) Proc., Pinyon-Juniper Conference. USDA For. Serv., Intermt. Res. Sta., Ogden, UT. Gen. Tech. Rep. INT-215. 581 p.

*Franklin, J.F., and C.T. Dyrness. 1988. Natural vegetation of Oregon and Washington. Oregon State Univ. Press, Corvallis, OR. 464 p.

Gates, D.H. 1964. Sagebrush infested by leaf defoliating moth. J. Rge. Manage. 17:209-210.

Goodrich, S., E.D. McArthur, and A.H. Winward. 1985. A new combination and a new variety in *Artemisia tridentata*. Great Basin Natur. 45:99-104.

Gruell, G.E. 1985. Fire on the early Western landscape: An annotated record of wildland fires 1776-1900. Northwest Sci. 59:97-107.

Hironaka, M., M.A. Fosberg, and A.H. Winward. 1983. Sagebrush-grass habitat types of southern Idaho. Forest, Wildlife, and Range Exp. Sta., Univ. Idaho, Moscow, ID. Bull. 35. 44 p.

Hobbs, N.T., and R.A. Spowart. 1984. Effects of prescribed fire or nutrition of mountain sheep and mule deer during winter and spring. J. Wildl. Manage. 48:551-560.

Jackson, P.L. 1985. Climate, p. 48-57. *In* Kimerling, A.J. and P.L. Jackson (eds.) Atlas of the Pacific Northwest. 7th ed. Oregon State Univ. Press, Corvallis, OR. 136 p.

Kindschy, R.R., C. Sundstrom, and J.D. Yoakum. 1982. Pronghorns. *In* Wildlife Habitats in Managed Rangelands: The Great Basin of Southeastern Oregon. USDA For. Serv., Pac. Northwest For. Rge. Exp. Sta., Portland, OR. Gen. Tech. Rep. PNW-145. 18 p.

*Klebenow, D.A. 1985. Big game response to fire in sagebrush-grass rangelands, p. 53-57. *In* Rangeland Fire Effects: A Symposium. USDI, Bur. Land Manage. Boise, ID. 124 p.

Leverenz, J.W., and D.J. Lev. 1987. Effects of carbon dioxide-induced climate changes on the natural ranges of six major commercial tree species in the western United States, p. 123-155. *In* Shands, W.E. and J.S. Hoffman (eds.) The Greenhouse Effect, Climate Change, and U.S. Forests. Conserv. Found., Washington, DC. 304 p.

*Lyon, L.J., H.S. Crawford, E. Czuhai, R.L. Fredriksen, R.F. Harlow, L.J. Metz, and H.A. Pearson. 1978. Effects of fire on fauna: A state-of-knowledge review. USDA For. Serv., Washington, DC. Gen. Tech. Rep. WO-6. 22 p.

Maser, C., J.W. Thomas, and R.G. Anderson. 1984. The relationship of terrestrial vertebrates to plant communities and structural conditions. Part I. *In* Wildlife Habitats in Southeastern Oregon. USDA For. Serv., Pac. Northwest For. Rge. Exp. Sta., Portland, OR. Gen. Tech. Rep. PNW-172. 25 p.

References marked by an asterisk are recommended for general information.

McKell, C.M., A.M. Wilson, and B.L. Kay. 1962. Effective burning of rangelands infested with medusahead. Weeds 10:125-131.

Mehringer, P.J., Jr., and P.E. Wigand. 1987. Western juniper in the holocene, p. 109-119. *In* Everett, R.L., (ed.) Proc., Pinyon-Juniper Conference. USDA For. Serv., Intermt. Res. Sta., Ogden, UT. Gen. Tech. Rep. INT-215. 581 p.

Nelson, D.L., and D.L. Sturgis. 1986. A snowmold disease of mountain big sagebrush. Phytopathology 76:946-951.

Peek, J.M., R.A. Riggs, and J.L. Laver. 1979. Evolution of fall burning on bighorn sheep winter range. J. Rge. Manage. 32:430-432.

Peters, R.L., and J.D.S. Darling. 1985. The greenhouse effect and nature reserves. BioScience 35:707-717.

Rind, D. 1986. The greenhouse effect: An explanation. EPA J. 12:12-14.

Salih, M.S.A., F.K.H. Taha, and G.F. Payne. 1973. Water repellency of soils under burned sagebrush. J. Rge. Manage. 26:330-331.

*Shinn, D.A. 1980. Historical perspectives on range burning in the inland Pacific Northwest. J. Rge. Manage. 33:415-422.

*Short, H.A. 1986. Rangelands, p. 93-122. *In* Cooperrider, A.Y., R.J. Boyd, and H.R. Stuart (eds.) Inventory and Monitoring of Wildlife Habitat. U.S. Gov. Print. Off., Washington, DC. 858 p.

Tangley, L. 1988. Preparing for climate change. BioScience 38:14-18.

*Thomas, J.W. (ed.). 1979. Wildlife Habitats in Managed Forests: The Blue Mountains of Oregon and Washington. U.S. Gov. Print. Off., Washington, DC. USDA Agr. Hbk. 553. 512 p.

Thomas, J.W., C. Maser, and J.E. Rodiek. 1979. Edges. *In* Wildlife Habitats in Managed Rangelands: The Great Basin of Southeastern Oregon. USDA For. Serv., Pac. Northwest For. Rge. Exp. Sta., Portland, OR. Gen. Tech. Rep. PNW-85. 17 p.

Tiagwad, T.E., C.M. Olson, and R.E. Martan. 1982. Single-year response of breeding bird populations to fire in a curlleaf mountain mahogany-big sagebrush community, p. 101-110. *In* Starkey, E.E., J.F. Franklin, and J.W. Matthews (eds.) Ecological Research in National Parks of the Pacific Northwest. For. Res. Lab., Oregon State Univ., Corvallis, OR. 142 p.

Tisdale, E.W. 1985. Canyon grasslands and associated shrublands of west-central Idaho and adjacent areas. Forest, Wildlife, and Rge. Exp. Sta., Univ. Idaho, Moscow, ID. Bull. 40. 42 p.

*Vallentine, J.F. 1980. Range Development and Improvements. 2nd ed. Brigham Young Univ. Press, Provo, UT. 545 p.

Van Dyke, W.A., A. Sands, J. Yoakum, A. Polenz, and J. Blasidell. 1983. Bighorn sheep. *In* Wildlife Habitats in Managed Rangelands: The Great Basin of Southeastern Oregon. USDA For. Serv., Pac. Northwest For. Rge. Exp. Sta., Portland, OR. Gen. Tech. Rep. PNW-85. 37 p.

*West, N.E. 1983. Western and intermountain sagebrush steppe, p. 351-374. *In* West, N.E. (ed.) Temperate Deserts and Semi-deserts. Vol. 5: Ecosystems of The World. Elsevier Scientific Publ. Co., Amsterdam, The Netherlands. 522 p.

Winward, A.H. 1980. Taxonomy and ecology of sagebrush in Oregon. Agr. Exp. Sta., Oregon State Univ., Corvallis, OR. Sta. Bull. 642. 15 p.

*Wright, H.A. 1974. Range burning. J. Rge. Manage. 27:5-11.

*Wright, H.A., and A.W. Bailey. 1982. Fire Ecology: United States and Southern Canada. John Wiley & Sons, Inc. New York, NY. 501 p.

IV Interactions of Prescribed Fire with Forest Protection Considerations

8 Effects of Prescribed Fire on Wildfire Occurrence and Severity

John E. Deeming

Executive Summary

Nearly a century of wildfire control and prevention has, paradoxically, increased the threat of large damaging wildfires in some Pacific Northwest forests and rangelands. The accumulation of "natural" fuels over this time-span in the intermediate- and low-elevation forests of the interior Pacific Northwest that would have been consumed by wildfires is one cause; prescribed fire has been touted as an effective means of reducing this "natural" hazard.

The second cause is the large quantities of flammable, spatially continuous slash left in cutover areas—activity fuels. Reducing logging residues is presumed to be an effective means of limiting the damage potential of any subsequent wildfire, or at least making the wildfire easier and less expensive to control. In Oregon and Washington, legislation was passed between 1910 and 1920 requiring landowners to abate the hazard posed by logging slash. Prescribed burning has been an important method of meeting that requirement.

More recently, prescribed burning, utilizing both unplanned natural and planned ignitions, has been advocated to restore and maintain fire-dependent or seral plant communities and ecosystems; and to create vegetation mosaics (Chapters 3 and 4) that serve to confine and otherwise limit the impact of wildfires. Plans have been implemented in selected wildernesses and national parks which allow lightning-set wildfires to burn under close monitoring, the intent being to restore the fuel and vegetation conditions normal before the era of fire suppression and by reestablishing a more natural fire frequency/severity regime in each area.

Unlike other methods of vegetation and slash fuel hazard abatement, prescribed fire can be applied in such a way as to selectively remove only materials less than 1 inch in diameter, the most flammable fuel component.

Prescribed burning will reduce fuel quantity and wildfire potential for a period of time on any particular site. But the argument that prescribed burning is a cost-effective method of reducing the incidence and severity of wildfires is seldom supportable. The prescribed burning cost-effectiveness issue is obscured by the voluminous literature that describes in detail how burning reduces the quantity and breaks up the continuity of fuels. The ameliorating effects of the changes made to the fuel complex on the behavior and severity of any wildfire that may burn over the same ground are implicit. In few instances has an analysis shown that it is cost effective and operationally feasible to burn sufficient area often enough to affect wildfire losses. And those few instances are distinguished by low burning costs, relatively high wildfire threat, and high resource values.

Evidence of the economic soundness of the practice is particularly limited in the Cascades, Olympics, and coastal forests of the Pacific Northwest where there is confounding evidence that escaped prescribed fires cause a significant portion of the wildfire losses. Looking at published experience in the southwestern and southeastern United States where the effects of large-scale prescribed burning on wildfire losses have been studied and found to be beneficial, the case might be made that the practice may be cost effective for similar situations in interior Pacific Northwest rangelands and Douglas-fir and ponderosa pine forests.

Using prescribed fire, as well as any other fuel hazard reduction method, on both project and programmatic scales, requires a systematic assessment of treatment costs (including costs of escaped prescribed fires), wildfire threat, and values at risk. Conventional break-even analysis, decision analysis, and computer-based modeling systems such as the USDA Forest Service's Fuel Appraisal Process, may eventually provide wildland managers with the capability to systematically assess those factors when developing fuel management programs and strategies. However, as of this writing, that time has not come.

Introduction

The Northwest fuel problem

Wilson and Dell (1971) explain why a fuels problem exists in Pacific Northwest forests and rangelands. First, the policy of fire exclusion followed for most of this century has allowed vegetation and vegetative debris to accumulate that otherwise would have been burned by wildfires. This problem is called the "natural fuel hazard." J.R. Swanson (1976) said, "Ironically, this grave fire potential is the result of our own successful efforts to keep wildfire out of the forest environment." It is unlikely that 80 years of fire exclusion has produced unnatural fuel accumulations in westside forests where the fire regimes are characterized by fire return intervals of 200 to 700 years, but the premise is very reasonable for the frequent, low-severity fire regimes characteristic of many eastside, interior range and forest areas (see Chapter 3 for a description of Pacific Northwest fire regimes).

The second reason cited by Wilson and Dell for the Pacific Northwest's fuel problem is the scale of intensive forest management activities. In a typical year in western Oregon and Washington more than 25,000,000 tons of slash fuels are produced—the residues of harvesting and management activities such as timber stand improvement (including thinning and pruning) and right-of-way construction.

Slash hazard ameliorates with time as needle and twigs dry and separate from the branches, slash concentrations settle and become more compact, and decay progresses. Olson and Fahnestock (1955) cite the rates of change of flammability of several species. Douglas-fir, Englemann spruce, and western hemlock lose their needles the first year, while the needles of western white pine and western redcedar persist for several seasons. After only 1 year, the rate of spread of fire in Douglas-fir, Englemann spruce, and western hemlock slash is reduced nearly 70 percent; the rate of spread in white pine and redcedar is reduced only 30 percent. The hazard diminishes rapidly the first few years after harvest, but remains measurable for 10 to 15 years in the moist westside forests and for 20 to 30 years in the drier interior forests.

Laws and regulations

The Pacific Northwest experienced a rash of disastrous fires in 1902 that ranks in the top ten of the most destructive wildfire episodes in United States history (Brown and Davis 1973, Pyne 1982).

The cause was a combination of escaped slash disposal and settler clearing fires. Following the subsequent loss of 3,000,000 acres and 85 lives to wildfires in 1910 in Idaho and Montana caused, in part, by extensive areas of logging slash, the Oregon and Washington legislatures decided that something must be done to manage the accruing slash fuel hazard.

In 1917, both states passed laws making landowners liable for fires originating on their properties from any cause if a hazardous slash condition existed. In Oregon, the Hazard Abatement Law directs the State Forester to ensure that forest lands be maintained to abate any fuel hazard. The Oregon State Department of Forestry regulations approve chemical treatment, mechanical methods, and controlled burning for disposing of slash and vegetation that constitute a hazard.

Washington's Extreme Fire Hazard Law requires the abatement of extreme fuel hazards. Washington defines extreme hazards requiring isolation or reduction to include areas in which there are over 800 acres of continuous forest debris with an average loading greater than 9 tons per acre of material 3 inches or less in diameter. Debris within a defined distance of certain public roads, campgrounds, school grounds, and other specified public areas present a hazard which must be abated by burning, physical removal, or other means (Marcus 1981).

Public agencies such as the USDA Forest Service developed other kinds of standards for treatment. A very common standard until just a few years ago was the "M-M" standard—Moderate rate of spread and Moderate resistance to control. Resistance to control means resistance to fireline building. "Moderate" is a relative term, hence interpretation varied from one agency unit to another. More quantifiable approaches including use of photo series (Maxwell and Ward 1976a, 1976b, and 1980) have been adopted. Commonly, the same hazard abatement standard is applied to areas experiencing 20 fires per million acres per year as to areas with 200 fires per million acres per year; little consideration is given to the seriousness of the wildfire threat.

In short, regulations were adopted that made the management of an activity fuel hazard a virtual requirement for private landowners and public agencies. And, since burning is the most practical method for dealing with the 50 to 200 tons per acre of slash typical of old-growth Douglas-fir and western hemlock clearcuts, slash burning was, for all practical purposes, institutionalized west of the Cascade Crest (Agee 1989).

The hazard abatement requirement has not necessarily imposed a burden on westside timber operators. The heavy loadings of residues common to clearcuts must often be reduced to expedite reforestation. However, there are certainly other situations where the expense and effort are not warranted because of low threat of ignitions and low resource values. Operator interviewees in western Oregon and Washington told Marcus (1981) that fuels reduction is done primarily because it is a legal requirement and reduces their liability. From a practical standpoint, it is more useful for reforestation and silvicultural reasons; hazard reduction is a bonus. East of the Cascades a blanket hazard reduction requirement may be justifiable because of the usual extended high fire danger periods and the ignition risk posed by lightning storms.

Hazard Reduction

A fire occurs when flammable materials (*fuel*) are exposed to an intense heat source (*firebrand*) coincident with conducive weather and fuel conditions (high fire danger). A wildfire loss reduction program can pursue one or both of two strategies: eliminate or reduce the sources of firebrands (risk management); or remove or modify the fuel to reduce its flammability (hazard management).

Risk and hazard are important terms to understand in the context of wildfire prevention. *Risk* is a wildfire causative agent. Examples are: lightning, chainsaws, and campfires. *Hazard* is a rating assigned a fuel complex (defined by kind, arrangement, volume, condition, and location) that reflects its susceptibility to ignition, the wildfire behavior and severity it would support, and/or the suppression difficulty it represents. Hazard ratings are generally subjective, ranging from very low (green grass and conifer litter) to extreme (cured grass and heavy slash).

The prudent fire management planner recognizes the folly of any plan to eliminate all risk. Some level of risk must always be accepted—the acceptable level being determined by the existing level of fuel hazard and the fire destructible values to be protected. Where those values are high and risk cannot be sufficiently reduced, the alternative is to reduce the fuel hazard. In other words, if the effort to reduce wildfire causes to an acceptable level will likely fail (i.e., if there is continuing high risk), the only alternative is to reduce the fuels (i.e., lower the hazard). Hazard reduction can be planned to decrease wildfire incidence and severity, ameliorate rate of spread and/or intensity, and make extinguishment easier and less costly.

Hazard reduction (or *fuel management*) is defined as "the planned treatment or manipulation of naturally growing vegetation or any other flammable material for the purpose of reducing the rate of spread and the output of heat energy from any wildfire occurring in the area treated."

Brown and Davis (1973) list seven hazard reduction *strategies*:

• Remove all ignitable fuels within small, high-risk areas to eliminate ignitions from known sources.

• Remove all fuel in a strip surrounding high-risk areas, to isolate and limit the spread of fires starting inside those areas.

• Remove all fuel in a strip surrounding high-value or high-hazard areas to exclude fires starting outside of those areas.

• Reduce or remove fuels in strategically located blocks to augment natural fire barriers.

• Eliminate fine and intermediate fuels (less than 1 inch in diameter) from extensive areas to reduce wildfire spread rate.

• Eliminate fuels extending from the ground to the tree crowns (ladder fuels) to reduce the danger of crown fires.

• Remove standing dead trees (snags) which can produce embers that can be readily carried across fire control lines.

The fuel treatment *methods* available to the fuel manager include: manual (cutting, scattering, and piling); biological (grazing); chemical (herbicides); mechanical (clearing, crushing, disking, piling); and prescribed burning (broadcast and pile burning).

Using Prescribed Fire To Reduce Fuel Hazard

Removal of the fine and intermediate fuel size classes (elements less than 1 inch in diameter) from a fuel complex effectively eliminates any hazard. Fires start in the fine (less than 1/4 inch in diameter) fuels; the rate at which a fire spreads is determined by the amount, continuity, and moisture contents of fine and intermediate-sized fuels. Fuel moisture conditions can be specified that allow a prescribed fire to consume only those smaller fuels (see Chapters 5 and 22 for a description of appropriate burning methods and prescriptions). Sandberg and Ottmar (1983) have provided fuel moisture guidelines for limiting fuel consumption. Being able to remove only the fine and intermediate fuel classes is an advantage prescribed fire has over other fuel reduction methods.

Activity fuels in clearcuts are broadcast burned in place. Slashings from seed tree and shelterwood cuts and thinnings are typically hand or machine piled and burned during low fire danger periods.

Prescribed burning, specifically broadcast and underburning, is advocated for reducing the abnormal accumulation and limiting the spatial continuity of natural fuels. In the Pacific Northwest, prescribed burning of natural fuels has its greatest application in eastside pine forests (Fahnestock 1973, Martin and Dell 1978). Limited tests of burning for hazard reduction, however, have been conducted in westside forests (Swanson 1976, Marlega 1981); those tests were judged promising.

Prescribed underburning thins or eliminates thickets of saplings and decreases the presence of shade-tolerant trees and shrubs in the understory. In conifer stands, prescribed burning reduces needle drape, the "ladder" that a surface fire can follow into the tree crowns.

In a few wildland preserves—national parks and wildernesses—plans have been implemented which allow for prescribed, planned, and lightning-set fires to burn, the intent being to restore and maintain fire-dependent or seral plant communities and ecosystems. Observations by Saveland (1987) in the Selway-Bitterroot Wilderness in Idaho and Sweaney (1985) in Yellowstone National Park support the thesis that wildfire size and severity are limited by old burns. Although prescribed burning to modify natural fuels is not widely practiced in the Pacific Northwest, particularly west of the Cascade Crest, experience to date shows that fire is the preferred and, indeed, the only means that has the potential for reducing extensive areas of natural fuels.

Impacts of Fuel Hazard Reduction on Wildfire Incidence & Severity

Considerable research has been done to quantify the effects of prescribed burning on the amount and distribution of wildland fuels, both natural and activity. Two excellent state-of-knowledge, summary references are Brown et al. (1985) and Martin et al. (1979). Brown et al. synthesize research done in the Northern Rockies and Pacific Northwest to develop methods for controlling consumption of dead and down woody fuels, litter, and duff. Martin et al. include information from all sections of the country about effects of fire on live as well as dead and down fuels.

In the research surveyed in these two studies, a common goal was to develop guidelines for prescribing burning conditions that would result in specific quantities of fuel being burned (or not burned). Martin et al. (1988) went one step further and modeled the degree to which the fuel reduction from prescribed burning would affect fire behavior. They analyzed postburn fuels in one Washington location, four Oregon locations, and two central California locations. Not too surprisingly, the wildfire potential was reduced in all of the cases studied. Swanson (1976) found that a series of strip head fires applied between mid-July and mid-September in second-growth Douglas-fir greatly reduced half-inch and smaller fuels. According to Swanson, "the trial burns largely eliminated the wildfire problem."

What the authors cited above did not do, and what has been done by only a few authors anywhere in the country, is address the cost effectiveness of the practice, taking into consideration:
- treatment cost (including retreatment and the consequences of escaped prescribed fires);
- historical and projected wildfire occurrence (the threat); and
- values of threatened natural resources and improvements.

The authors cited in the remainder of this section have proposed methods for selecting cost-effective fuel management methods and strategies or have made case studies of the cost effectiveness of prescribed burning on a programmatic scale. Unfortunately for the thrust of this book, few studies of this kind have been done in the Pacific Northwest. Those from other regions are included in the discussion to provide a perspective on the debate over fuel treatment cost effectiveness.

Much of the information that follows is drawn from Wood (1978, 1979, 1982) since he has published extensively on fuel hazard management effectiveness and economic efficiency. Wood references Davis and Cooper (1963), Davis (1965), Zivnuska (1972), and North et al. (1975). Other authors who have studied the utility of various strategies and methods (including prescribed fire) for hazard reduction include: Lyman (1947), Barrows (1951), Biswell et al. (1973), Omi (1977), GEOMET (1978), Marcus (1981), Hardy (1983), Salazar and Gonzalez-Caban (1987), and Saveland (1987). Only Marcus (1981) and Hardy (1983) address fuel management in the Pacific Northwest.

Furthermore, little has been done to quantify wildfire loss reduction benefits. This is true even in California where enormous expenditures have been made to construct and maintain an extensive network of fuel breaks. Zivnuska (1972) attributes the lack of quantified evidence to lack of definition of possible benefits (reduction of losses to wildfires) associated with the various hazard reduction practices and strategies. Nor have considerations of risk and values protected been included in hazard management decisions. Methods have been proposed by Hirsch et al. (1980), Hirsch and Radloff (1981), Cohen et al. (1983), Snell (1986), and Saveland (1987) for this purpose, but only the Fuel Appraisal Process (Snell 1986) is getting any attention at this time. The following paragraphs summarize information from three regions of the United States about the value of prescribed burning (and other methods of hazard management) in reducing wildfire losses.

Southeastern United States

Davis and Cooper (1963) found that treatment of natural fuel hazard strongly affected the occurrence and severity of wildfires in Georgia and Florida. Only 0.03 percent of recently treated areas burned per year compared to 7.0 percent for untreated areas. The benefits were directly related to time since treatment; recently burned areas were the most fire resistant.

For the severe 1985 fire season, the USDA Forest Service, Southeastern Region (1987) determined that hazard reduction efforts were cost effective. On 576,522 acres treated in 1984-86, 282 wildfires burned 5,893 acres; on the remainder of the 4.9-million-acre assessment area, 653 fires burned 32,009 acres. The fires in the treated areas burned an average of 21 acres, whereas fires averaged 49 acres in the untreated areas and areas treated before 1984. The occurrence rate for the treated area was 490 fires per million acres; 1 percent of the area was burned. The fire occurrence rate on the untreated area was 151 fires per million acres; 0.7 percent of the area was burned. Despite the higher occurrence rate and greater percentage of the area burned, the Forest Service analysis showed that there was a savings due to reduced resource damage and lower suppression costs. The savings amounted to $2.8 million after subtracting treatment costs, thereby yielding a 1:2.15 cost/benefit ratio.

Southwestern United States

Davis (1965) calculated the costs of construction and maintenance of fuel breaks in California. He concluded, looking only at estimated acres saved, that the marginal costs of fuel breaks were higher than any estimates of averted damage. Likewise, Omi (1977), after evaluating the effectiveness of the Angeles National Forest fuel break network for the period 1960-75, found that its value was marginal.

North et al. (1975), using loss of life, property and resource damage, and suppression cost criteria, found that fuel breaks in the Santa Monica Mountains would be marginally beneficial only if there was no cost for the land devoted to firebreaks.

Kallander (1969) concluded that understory burning in ponderosa pine stands on the Apache Indian Reservation, Arizona reduced the size of wildfires on treated areas over untreated areas by 60 percent.

Biswell et al. (1973), in a study of the Fort Apache Indian Reservation, showed that prescribed burning an average 84,000 acres per year would be cost effective in reducing the incidence and severity of wildfires. Their assumptions were that wildfire incidence would be reduced 50 to 60 percent (from the 160 fires per million acres per year average of the 1960s); treatment (burning) would be repeated every 6 years; underburning costs would average $0.13 per acre; and wildfire suppression costs would average $45 per acre.

The Pacific Southwest Region of the Forest Service and the California Department of Forestry (1987), in an analysis of the damage caused by wildfires during the 1987 fire season, deduced that selective fuel modification reduced damage and suppression costs for the majority of wildfires. However, they judged that hazard reduction did little to reduce either acreage burned or damage during very severe burning conditions such as were experienced in the fall and late summer of 1987. The team also stated that grass and forb invasion following prescribed burning will increase the potential wildfire rate of spread for several years.

Salazar and Gonzalez-Caban (1987), in a study of the 1985 Wheeler Fire in southern California, examined the effects of fuelbreaks, areas previously burned by wildfires, and an area prescribed burned 1 year preceding the fire on fire spread and severity and suppression effectiveness. They concluded that the reduced fuel loadings found on those areas did significantly affect the final size of the 118,000-acre fire. Improved access and lowered fire rates of spread and burning intensity encountered on those areas by fire fighters were important in determining the final size of the fire. Treatment costs were not provided, nor was an economic analysis attempted.

Northwestern United States

Barrows (1951), looking at nearly 10,000 fires that occurred in western Montana and northern Idaho between 1931 and 1939, found that the per million acre rate of area burned by wildfires in untreated cutover areas was ten times that of green forests.

Lyman (1947), analyzing records for the same period and general area, found that 21 percent of the fires starting in untreated western white pine slash each burned more than 300 acres. In comparison, only 1.7 percent of the wildfires occurring in areas where the slash had been treated (usually piled and burned) reached 300 acres. In the western larch/Douglas-fir forest, none of the fires in treated slash grew to 300 acres, whereas 7 percent of the wildfires in untreated slash burned more than 300 acres. In the ponderosa pine forest, there were negligible differences between treated and untreated areas. Overall, Lyman determined that the number of acres burned by wildfires per million acres in treated areas was only one-seventh of the burned-area rate for untreated harvested areas.

Of the fourteen major wildfires occurring on the Mt. Hood National Forest from 1960 to 1975, all either started or gained momentum in untreated logging slash (Dell 1977).

GEOMET (1978) reported that 44 percent of the wildfires on Washington Department of Natural Resources protected land between 1973 and 1977 started in logging and thinning slash.

Wood (1979) investigated the economics of fuel hazard management in mature timber on the Lolo National Forest in Montana. He found that fuel management, including prescribed burning, could not be justified to protect only timber values because of low expected wildfire occurrence, low timber values, and high treatment costs.

Hardy (1983) determined that even the least intense treatment to reduce fuel hazard was not cost effective in the Illinois Valley on the Siskiyou National Forest in Southwest Oregon. Hardy made his analysis using a modification of the approach developed by Hirsch et al. (1980). He substituted historical wildfire suppression and resource damage costs and large fire experience for the figures that would have been supplied by experts using Hirsch's procedures; Hardy also substituted expected fire size based on historical experience for Hirsch's modeled expected final fire size.

Summary

What emerges from these studies is that the case for hazard reduction as a cost-effective means of reducing wildfire losses depends on the particular circumstances. Where wildfire incidence is high, treatment costs are low, and values protected are high, fuel treatment may be justified; for most other situations, it likely cannot be justified. Evidence of the economic soundness of the practice is particularly limited in the Cascades, Olympics, and coastal forests of the Pacific Northwest. Looking at published experience in the Southwest and Southeast, the case might be made that the practice may be cost effective for similar situations in interior Pacific Northwest rangelands and Douglas-fir and ponderosa pine forests.

Escaped Prescribed Fires

The debate among researchers, landowners, and public agencies over the advisability of widespread slash burning has surfaced periodically over the years. It surfaced anew at a recent symposium sponsored by the University of Washington and Washington State University. Escaped slash fires have been a serious problem since the first decade of this century, accounting for nearly 30 percent of the acreage burned by wildfires in western Oregon and Washington (Agee 1989).

Descamps and Brain (1989) reported a $500,000 per year savings in suppression expenditures when the Mt. Baker-Snoqualmie National Forest slash burning program was reduced by half. McElroy (1989) reported that the role of prescribed burning on 2.1 million acres of trust lands managed by the Washington Department of Natural Resources had been redefined. The risks and benefits of burning to the trust lands had been reassessed, and a new policy of restrained fire use was being implemented. The reason: the damage caused by escaped fires and the high operational costs of prescribed burning made the practice economically inefficient in most situations.

Dissenting viewpoints were offered by Gorman (1989) and Keatley (1989) who reiterated the hazards and liabilities of untreated slash. Their experience with slash burning is that it is cost effective, and that the risk of escapes is tolerable. However, no objective evidence was offered to support their position.

Marcus (1981) invited interviewees from the private sector to provide costs of escaped slash fires —only nine of 27 interviewees responded. The average prorated cost of escaped fires for the nine responses was just under $7 per acre. This contrasts sharply with recent estimates from the Olympic National Forest that the cost of escaped fires per prescribed burned acre nearly equals the direct cost of burning—about $290 per acre (personal interview with Ralph K. Coon, Olympic National Forest, Olympia, WA, October 21, 1988).

Conclusion

For reducing losses to wildfires, there is certainly a role for selective application of fuel reduction, fuel breaks, and other fuel hazard management strategies utilizing prescribed fire. Saveland (1987) states: "There is an opportunity for large financial gains in prescribed burning of natural fuels in critical areas. Further research is needed to determine the effect of prescribed burning on the magnitude of change of the probability of large, severe fires." An excellent example of such a situation is to isolate homes and other improvements adjacent to or within wildlands—the urban interface. Seed orchards, plantations, and intensively managed timber stands are examples of high-value resources where considerable expenditures for fuel hazard reduction in adjacent areas may be warranted.

However, area-wide hazard reduction for most wildland situations is not economically viable. Applications of prescribed fire to reduce fuel hazard in the Southeast and in high fire occurrence areas of the Southwest appear warranted because the costs of treatment (prescribed burning) are low and the resource values and risk of wildfire are both high. Historically, fuel hazard reduction programs have been justified without proper consideration of values protected, wildfire risk, and the risk posed by escaped prescribed fires. With the exception of the Marcus study (1981), none of the studies cited herein included escaped prescribed fires as a cost.

Brackebusch (1973) emphasizes the importance of developing hazard reduction plans for large areas that incorporate a variety of strategies. He suggests that combinations of fuel breaks, vegetation mosaics, and project-level treatment would be more cost effective than project-level treatment alone. It is important that fire management and fuels management specialists refine and utilize objective program-level fuel treatment planning aids such as suggested by Hirsch et al. (1980), Cohen et al. (1983), Snell (1986), and Saveland (1987).

Fuel treatment is a multidimensional issue—determining how much spending is justified for hazard abatement and selecting the hazard abatement strategy (or combination of strategies) and methods that will make the most of the allocated money. Regardless of one's preference for the use of prescribed fire for reducing fuel hazard, any justification of prescribed burning solely for wildfire hazard abatement should be carefully and critically scrutinized.

Literature Cited & Key References

*Agee, J.K. 1989. A history of fire and slash burning in western Oregon and Washington, p. 3-20. *In* Hanley, D.P., J.J. Kammenga, and C.D. Oliver (eds.) Proc., The Burning Decision: Regional Perspectives on Slash. Coll. For. Resour., Univ. Washington, Seattle, WA. Inst. For. Resour. Contrib. No. 66. 374 p.

Barrows, J.S. 1951. Forest fires in the northern Rocky Mountains. USDA For. Serv., North. Rocky Mt. For. Rge. Exp. Sta., Missoula, MT. Sta. Pap. 28. 251 p.

Biswell, H.H., H.R. Kallander, R. Komerek, R.J. Vogl, and H. Weaver. 1973. Ponderosa pine fire management: a task force evaluation of controlled burning of ponderosa pine forests in central Arizona. Tall Timbers Res. Sta. Misc. Pub. 2. Tallahassee, FL. 49 p.

Brackebusch, A.P. 1973. Fuel management—a prerequisite, not an alternative to fire control. J. For. 71:637-639.

*Brown, A.A., and K.P. Davis. 1973. Forest Fire: Control and Use. McGraw-Hill Book Co., Inc., New York, NY. 686 p.

*Brown, J.K., M.A. Marsden, K.C. Ryan, and E. D. Reihardt. 1985. Predicting duff and woody fuel consumed by prescribed fire in the Northern Rocky Mountains. USDA For. Serv., Intermt. For. Rge. Exp. Sta., Ogden, UT. Res. Pap. INT-337. 23 p.

Cohen, D., S. Haas, and P.J. Roussoupolus. 1983. Decision analysis of silvicultural prescriptions and fuel management practices on an intensively managed commercial forest. For. Sci. 29:859-870.

Davis, L.S. 1965. The economics of wildfire protection with emphasis on fuel break systems. Calif. Dept. For., Sacramento, CA. 165 p.

Davis, L.S., and R.W. Cooper. 1963. How prescribed burning affects wildfire occurrence. J. For. 61:915-917.

*Dell, J.D. 1977. Some implications of eliminating prescribed burning as a treatment option in managing forest vegetation and fuels in the Pacific Northwest. USDA For. Serv., Pac. Northwest Reg., Portland, OR. R-6 Fuel Management Notes 5:1-10.

Descamps, V.J. and J. Brain. 1989. Practical efforts to improve air quality in the Pacific Northwest forests, p. 276-284. *In* Hanley, D.P., J.J. Kammenga, and C.D. Oliver (eds.) Proc., The Burning Decision: Regional Perspectives on Slash. Coll. For. Resour., Univ. Washington, Seattle, WA. Inst. For. Resour. Contrib. No. 66. 374 p.

*Fahnestock, G.R. 1973. Use of fire in managing forest vegetation. Trans. Amer. Soc. Agr. Eng. 16:410-413, 419.

References marked by an asterisk are recommended for general information.

GEOMET, Inc. 1978. Impact of forestry burning on air quality. A state-of-the-knowledge characterization of Washington and Oregon. EPA Region 10, Seattle, WA. EPA 910/9-78-052. 253 p.

Gorman, J.F. 1989. Current issues in slash burning: A forest landowner's perspective, p. 21-24. *In* Hanley, D.P., J.J. Kammenga, and C.D. Oliver (eds.) Proc., The Burning Decision: Regional Perspectives on Slash. Coll. For. Resour., Univ. Washington, Seattle, WA. Inst. For. Resour. Contrib. No. 66. 374 p.

Hardy, C.C. 1983. An evaluation of alternative fuel treatments on the Siskiyou National Forest, southwest Oregon. M.F. thesis, Univ. Washington, Seattle, WA. 110 p.

Hirsch, S.N., and D.L. Radloff. 1981. A method for making activity-fuel management decisions. Fire Manage. Notes 42(3):5-9.

Hirsch, S.N., D.L. Radloff, W.S. Schopfer, M.L. Wolfe, and R.F. Yancik. 1980. The activity fuel appraisal process instructions and examples. USDA For. Serv., Rocky Mt. For. Rge. Exp. Sta., Ft. Collins, CO. Gen. Tech. Rep. RM-83.

Kallander, H. 1969. Controlled burning on the Fort Apache Indian Reservation, Arizona. Tall Timbers Fire Ecol. Conf. Proc. 9:241-249.

Keatley, J.E. 1989. Weyerhaeuser Company's prescribed fire use in Washington, p. 338-340. *In* Hanley, D.P., J.J. Kammenga, and C.D. Oliver (eds.) Proc., The Burning Decision: Regional Perspectives on Slash. Coll. For. Resour., Univ. Washington, Seattle, WA. Inst. For. Resour. Contrib. No. 66. 374 p.

Lyman, C.K. 1947. Slash disposal as related to fire control on the National Forests of Montana and northern Idaho. J. For. 47:259-262.

Marcus, A.A. 1981. Improving forest productivity: prescribed burning in the light of the Clean Air Act visibility standards. Battell Human Affairs Res. Cent., Seattle, WA. BHARC-320/81/039. 171 p.

Marlega, R.R. 1981. Operational use of prescribed fire, p. 71-72. *In* Hobbs, S.D. and O.T. Helgerson (eds.), Proc., Workshop on Reforestation of Skeletal Soils. For. Res. Lab., Oregon State Univ., Corvallis, OR. 124 p.

*Martin, R.E., H.E. Anderson, W.D. Boyer, J.H. Dieterich, S.N. Hirsch, V.J. Johnson, and W.H. McNab. 1979. Effects of fire on fuels: A state-of-knowledge review. USDA For. Serv., Washington, DC. Gen. Tech. Rep. WO-13. 64 p.

*Martin, R.E., and J.D. Dell. 1978. Planning for prescribed burning in the inland Northwest. USDA For. Serv., Pac. Northwest For. Rge. Exp. Sta., Portland, OR. Gen. Tech. Rep. PNW-76. 68 p.

*Martin, R.E., J.D. Landsberg, and J.B. Kaufman. 1988. Effectiveness of prescribed burning as a fire prevention measure. *In* Proc., FAO/ECE/ILO/IUFRO Conference on the Use of Prescribed Fire in Fire Prevention. Avignon, France. Mar. 14-18, 1988.

Maxwell, W.G., and F. R. Ward. 1976a. Photo series for quantifying forest residues in: the coastal Douglas-fir-hemlock type, coastal Douglas-fir-hardwood type. USDA For. Serv., Pac. Northwest For. Rge. Exp. Sta., Portland, OR. Gen. Tech. Rep. PNW-51. 101 p.

Maxwell, W.G., and F.R. Ward. 1976b. Photo series for quantifying forest residues in: the ponderosa pine type, ponderosa pine and associated species type, lodgepole pine type. USDA For. Serv., Pac. Northwest For. Rge. Exp. Sta., Portland, OR. Gen. Tech. Rep. PNW-52. 73 p.

Maxwell, W.G., and F.R. Ward. 1980. Photo series for quantifying natural forest residues in common vegetation types of the Pacific Northwest. USDA For. Serv., Pac. Northwest For. Rge. Exp. Sta., Portland, OR. Gen. Tech. Rep. PNW-105. 229 p.

McElroy, P. 1989. Changes for the second hundred years of trust management of Washington's forests, p. 332-337. *In* Hanley, D.P., J.J. Kammenga, and C.D. Oliver (eds.) Proc., The Burning Decision: Regional Perspectives on Slash. Coll. For. Resour., Univ. Washington, Seattle, WA. Inst. For. Resour. Contrib. No. 66. 374 p.

North, D.W., F.L. Offensend, and C.N. Smart. 1975. Planning wildfire protection for the Santa Monica Mountains: an economic analysis of alternatives. Fire J., Jan. 1975:69-78.

Olson, D.S., and G.R. Fahnestock. 1955. Logging slash: a study of the problem in Inland Empire forests. Coll. For.; For., Wildl., Rge. Exp. Sta., Univ. Idaho, Moscow, ID. Bull. 1. 51 p.

Omi, P.N. 1977. A case study of fuel management performance, Angeles National Forest, 1960-1975, p. 404-411. *In* Proc., Symposium on the Environmental Consequences of Fire and Fuel Management in Mediterranean Ecosystems. August, 1977, Palo Alto, CA. USDA For. Serv., Washington, DC. Gen. Tech. Rep. WO-3. 498 p.

*Pierovich, J.M., E.H. Clarke, S.G. Pickford, and F.R. Ward. 1975. Forest residues management guidelines for the Pacific Northwest. USDA For. Serv., Pac. Northwest For. Rge. Exp. Sta., Portland, OR. Gen. Tech. Rep. PNW-33. 273 p.

*Pyne, S.J. 1982. Fire in America: A Cultural History of Wildland and Rural Fire. Princeton Univ. Press, Princeton, NJ. 654 p.

Salazar, L.A., and A. Gonzalez-Caban. 1987. Spatial relationships of a wildfire, fuelbreaks, and a recently burned area. West. J. Appl. For. 2:55-58.

*Sandberg, D.V., and R.D. Ottmar. 1983. Slash burning and fuel consumption in the Douglas-fir subregion. Fire For. Meteorol. Conf. Proc. 7:90-93.

Saveland, J.M. 1987. Using prescribed fire to reduce the risk of large wildfires: a break-even analysis. Fire For. Meteorol. Conf. Proc. 9:119-122.

Salazar, L.A., and A. Gonzalez-Caban. 1987. Spatial relationships of a wildfire, fuelbreaks, and a recently burned area. West. J. Appl. For. 2:55-58.

*Sandberg, D.V., and R.D. Ottmar. 1983. Slash burning and fuel consumption in the Douglas-fir subregion. Fire For. Meteorol. Conf. Proc. 7:90-93.

Saveland, J.M. 1987. Using prescribed fire to reduce the risk of large wildfires: a break-even analysis. Fire For. Meteorol. Conf. Proc. 9:119-122.

Snell, J.A.K. 1986. Determining the most cost efficient fuel treatment strategy for the purpose of fire protection. USDA For. Serv. Region 6 Fuels Notes, Issue 20, Aviation and Fire Management, Pac. Northwest Region, Portland, OR. 6 p.

Swanson, J.R. 1976. Hazard abatement by prescribed underburning in westside Douglas-fir. Tall Timbers Fire Ecol. Conf. Proc. 15:235-238.

Sweaney, J.N. 1985. Old burns limit size of fires, p. 389. *In* Lotan, J.E., B. M. Kilgore, W.C. Fischer, and R.W. Mutch (tech. coords.) Proc., Symposium and Workshop on Wilderness Fire. Nov. 15-18, 1983, Missoula, MT. USDA For. Serv., Intermt. For. Rge. Exp. Sta., Ogden, UT. Gen. Tech. Rep. INT-182. 386 p.

USDA Forest Service, Pacific Southwest Region and the California Department of Forestry. 1987. The effects of chaparral modification on resources and wildfire suppression. Fuels Management Activity Review. San Francisco, CA. (Unpubl.) 21 p.

USDA Forest Service, Southeastern Region. 1987. Fuels treatment assessment, 1985 fire season, Region 8. Administrative Study. Atlanta, GA. (Unpubl.) 18 p.

Wilson, C.C., and J.D. Dell. 1971. The fuels buildup in American forests: a plan of action and research. J. For. 69:471-475.

Wood, D.B. 1978. Economic evaluation of fuel management programs for forestland. Ph.D. thesis, Utah State Univ., Logan, UT. 134 p.

Wood, D.B. 1979. Fuel management opportunities on the Lolo National Forest. USDA For. Serv., Intermt. For. Rge. Exp. Sta., Ogden, UT. Res. Note INT-272. 9 p.

*Wood, D.B. 1982. Fuel management's potential for reducing frequency of large fires in the Northern Rockies. J. For. 80:105-107.

Zivnuska, J.A. 1972. Economic tradeoffs in fire management, p. 69-74. *In* Proc., Fire in the Environment Symposium. U.S. Dept. Agr., Washington, DC.

9 Impact of Prescribed Burning on Damage to Conifers by Wildlife

David S. deCalesta

Executive Summary

Prescribed burning can reduce damage by animals to regenerating conifers directly by reducing numbers of pests and indirectly by altering habitats that pests need for survival. It can potentially provide one to two growing seasons of protection for seedling conifers from some small mammal pests, but usually is not effective in protecting conifer seeds. The effectiveness of other animal damage control techniques can be increased by prescribed burning, though it also may increase the potential for damage to conifer regeneration by mammal pests by creating favorable habitat. Prescribed burning should be carefully integrated with other silvicultural practices, including animal damage control, to provide efficient management of forests and wildlife damage.

Introduction

The cost of damage by wildlife pests to conifer regeneration in the Pacific Northwest reportedly amounts to millions of dollars annually (Borrecco 1976, Anthony et al. 1978, Brodie et al. 1979). Seeds, seedlings, saplings, and sawtimber are vulnerable to damage by an impressive list of pests, including deer, elk, bear, porcupine, hares, rabbits, squirrels, pocket gophers, woodrats, mountain beaver, shrews, mice, and voles.

Fire, including prescribed burning, influences the structure, composition, occurrence, and density of vegetation in woodlands (Chapter 4) and hence wildlife habitat, which directly influences wildlife and determines species composition and abundance (Borrecco 1976, Bruce et al. 1985). Thus, prescribed burning, by directly influencing habitat, indirectly influences types and populations of the wildlife community within a given area (Bendell 1974, Galt et al. 1981). More specifically, prescribed burning can influence the type, welfare, and behavior of wildlife species as these factors relate to prevention and control of damage to

conifers. Timing, intensity, and size of prescribed burns influence their impact on wildlife (Robinson and Bolen 1984) and thus indirectly influence damage. Unfortunately, there are few studies that have measured directly the impact of prescribed burning on damage to conifer regeneration by wildlife pests. Consequently, the impact must be largely inferred from practical experience and professional judgment.

Methods to prevent or control wildlife pest damage to conifer regeneration include:
- repelling pest animals by applying repugnant taste or odor compounds to conifer trees;
- reducing population density of pest species by hunting via more liberalized regulations (e.g., special hunts) or by use of pesticides;
- removing individual animals by shooting or trapping;
- protecting conifers from pest animals via area fencing, tubing, or other exclusion devices; and
- altering vegetative structure, composition, and density in such a way that pest animals cannot obtain required food or cover and subsequently

leave the area, reduce their numbers, or die (Dodge 1968, Anonymous 1978).

The last of these can be achieved through the use of prescribed burning.

Fire also can increase the incidence and intensity of wildlife pest damage to conifers (Anonymous 1978, Galt et al. 1981). Other site disturbances or practices may interact with the effects of burning on wildlife and heighten or lessen the impact of fire on wildlife populations. Determining how fire will influence damage by wildlife pests to conifers requires an understanding of how fire impacts these animals, and how these impacts may be affected by other activities occurring on the site (Chapter 18).

Prescribed Burning as a Tool against Wildlife Damage

Direct reduction in pest numbers

Prescribed burning has been used intentionally to kill pest wildlife on regeneration sites (Krauch 1936, Anonymous 1978, Galt et al. 1981). Hooven (1977) and Motubu (1978) reported up to 50 percent mortality of mountain beaver on sites that were slash burned. Small mammals that live above ground, such as voles, chipmunks, hares, rabbits, and shrews, were eliminated from slash-burned sites and did not reinvade for two or more growing seasons (Cook 1959, Ahlgren 1966, Black and Hooven 1974, Fala 1975).

Large mammal pests of conifer regeneration (deer, elk, and bear) move away from fire (Lyon et al. 1978, Bartels et al. 1985). Prescribed burning of clearcuts of present-day size is unlikely to cause much direct mortality of these animals, and thus has little, if any, positive direct effect on damage by these pests.

Concentrations of predators around actively burning sites have been observed (Stoddard 1963, Komarek 1967, 1969, Motubu 1978). They were reported hunting for small rodents displaced from burrows and protective cover by fire. It is also likely that predators will concentrate around burned sites, preying on remaining unprotected rodents. The intensity of predation by raptors (hawks and owls) on burned clearcut sites likely is greater when some snags are retained as perches. Snags are often removed from clearcut sites prior to or during slash burning, reducing the potential impact of raptor predation on small mammals. Little information is available concerning the number or placement of snags necessary to attract raptors. Hall et al. (1981) found that raptors used artificial perches 8 and 16 feet tall and 300 feet apart in California alfalfa fields. An Oregon study (Schreiber 1987) indicated that 6-8 snags per acre, at least 21 feet tall, provided adequate numbers of nest sites for cavity-nesting birds on clearcuts; snags left purposefully for cavity-nesting birds also should provide adequate numbers of perch sites for raptors.

Indirect reduction in pest numbers or damage

Elimination of grasses and forbs on sites by use of herbicides was associated with significant reduction in numbers of and damage attributable to pocket gophers on conifer regeneration sites (Keith et al. 1959, Tietjen et al. 1967, Black and Hooven 1974, Crouch 1979). It is likely that pocket gopher response to reduction or elimination of forage as an immediate result of prescribed burning would be similar to that caused by use of herbicides, as indicated by Howard and Childs (1959).

However, Volland (1974) stated that pocket gopher populations will increase after logging and burning because of the increase in grass and forb species resulting from site disturbance. In addition, if pocket gophers are not killed by fire, and planted conifer seedlings are the only source of food on burned sites, significant damage could occur. Howard and Childs (1959) and Barnes (1974) noted that pocket gophers rapidly invade cleared sites from adjacent forest openings. DeCalesta and Asman (1987) recommend using prescribed burning to eliminate grasses and forbs for at least the first growing season, followed by other measures (lethal control of pocket gophers or of grasses and forbs) as needed for the second and succeeding growing seasons.

Plants used for food and cover by small mammal pests dwelling above ground (voles, chipmunks, mountain beaver, and woodrats) can be removed by slash-and-burn operations. Sites so treated have been free of these pests for several growing seasons (Gashwiler 1970, Keith and Surrendi 1971, Hooven 1977).

Black bears damage sapling-sized and larger conifers (Maser 1967, Poelker and Hartwell 1973). The damage is thought to be the result of scarcity of preferred foods in spring when bears emerge from denning (Flowers 1987). Applying herbicides to clearcut sites reduces competition by herbaceous and shrubby vegetation with conifer seedlings, but it also reduces vegetation important as spring foods for bears. Prescribed burning, on the other hand, stimulates the growth of grasses, forbs, and fruit-producing plants on clearcuts (Ahlgren and Ahlgren 1960, Daubenmire 1968). Such production of potential bear foods could reduce bear girdling of conifers if prescribed burns are in close proximity to vulnerable stands and of sufficient acreage to provide ready access to large amounts of spring bear foods.

Burning as an enhancement to other damage control tools

Some regeneration sites in western Oregon are seeded with native and domestic grasses and forbs to deter elk from feeding on conifer seedlings; the animals prefer the planted grasses and legumes to seedling conifers (Campbell and Evans 1978, Mereszczak et al. 1981, State of Washington 1983), and damage to conifer seedlings may be reduced (Campbell and Evans 1978). Sites so planted must have a good seedbed prepared, which can include prescribed burning (Taber 1973). Sites planted to grasses and legumes sustain mortality of Douglas-fir seedlings by voles if deer and elk are unable to graze the grasses and legumes sufficiently low to eliminate vole cover (personal communication from S. Smith, USDA Forest Service). Introduction of domestic sheep onto these sites in late summer-early fall when deer and elk grazing pressure is low seems to suppress the grass and legume cover and vole damage to seedlings. This relationship among deer, elk, sheep, and voles demonstrates the need for integration of silvicultural and wildlife management prescriptions as related to prescribed burning.

Registered toxicants may be used to control damage by some wildlife pests (voles, rabbits, mice, pocket gophers, and mountain beaver). Success in the use of pesticides is enhanced when the target pest's natural food supplies are low; the animal will be more apt to feed on a toxic bait when there is little else present to eat. Prescribed burning, by reducing amounts of natural foods, should increase the effectiveness of poison baiting programs. Silvicultural practices such as prescribed burning that remove brush and debris used on

clearcut sites as cover by pests like hares and mountain beaver should also enhance the success of poison baiting by increasing these pests' vulnerability to predation, an additional source of mortality (Hooven 1966).

One of the most effective ways for controlling mountain beaver damage to conifer seedlings is to remove individual animals residing within regeneration sites by kill-trapping (Hooven 1977). Trapping success has been enhanced by preceding trapping with slash burning; freshly excavated soil outside mountain beaver burrows after the fire is readily apparent and helps pinpoint effective placement of traps (Anonymous 1978, Borrecco and Anderson 1980).

Woven plastic tubes can be placed around conifer seedlings to prevent damage by deer, elk, mountain beaver, and pocket gophers (Campbell and Evans 1975, Anthony et al. 1978, Larson et al. 1979). Placement of such tubes is made easier if sites are cleared of slash and debris; prescribed burning performs this function (Hooven 1977).

Prescribed Burning & Increases in Wildlife Damage

Prescribed burning actually may increase rather than diminish wildlife damage to conifer regeneration in some instances. Typically, such cases involve enhancing rather than degrading wildlife habitat, or removing all food sources and replacing them with conifer seed or seedlings before pest numbers have declined.

More mobile wildlife, such as deer and elk, as well as most burrow-dwelling mammals, such as mountain beaver and pocket gopher, survive the small, localized prescribed burns on clearcut sites, and can return to feed after the fire is out. Planted conifer seedlings may be the only food available for these mammals on burned clearcuts. As an example, broadcast burning ponderosa pine sites in northern Idaho resulted in high pocket gopher population density and little conifer regeneration (Green et al. 1987).

Fires of sufficient severity to eliminate small rodent pests from regeneration sites may ultimately result in increased damage by these pests where regeneration by direct seeding is attempted. Deer mice rapidly (within weeks of the prescribed burns) invaded burned sites and attained densities much higher than under preburn conditions

(Moore 1940, Gorman and Orr-Ewing 1949, Tevis 1956, Ahlgren 1966, Gashwiler 1970, Bock and Bock 1983). Burning apparently makes the principal foods of deer mice (seeds and insects) more available. Deer mouse damage to conifer seeds likely will be increased rather than reduced by prescribed burning (Falwells and Schubert 1951, Ahlgren 1966, Sims and Buckner 1972).

Prescribed burning will result in some habitat destruction, leading to emigration of some wildlife pests. Adjacent clearcuts with newly planted seeds or seedlings might exhibit increased levels of damage caused by deer or other animals forced out of adjacent sites by fire (Volland 1974).

Leaving slash on regeneration sites has been associated with a reduction in subsequent deer damage to regeneration; deer cannot feed easily on seedlings growing within slash (Grisez 1960, Allen 1969). Burning of such slash removes the barrier to deer feeding, removes other deer foods, and hence may increase the incidence of browsing on conifer seedlings planted after slash burning.

Integrating Silviculture & Wildlife Pest Control

Planning for site preparation, including prescribed burning, should be integrated with planning for animal damage control to enhance the reduction of damage (Hooven 1966, Borrecco and Anderson 1980) and to avoid increasing animal damage problems (Anonymous 1978). Prescribed burning should be coordinated with other silvicultural practices, such as scarification, slash piling, and herbicide treatment to achieve these ends. Size, placement, intensity, and timing of prescribed burns should be manipulated to work in concert with other silvicultural practices to lessen animal damage.

Conclusion

Prescribed burning can result in reduced damage to conifer seedlings by small mammals by direct reduction of some pests from regeneration sites and also by reducing required food and cover. Effects may persist for two growing seasons or more, providing conifer seedlings with a good start over the development of small mammal pest populations.

Similarly, prescribed burning likely will provide 1-2 years of protection for regeneration by seeding if the principal pests are chipmunks or shrews, though it will provide little, if any, reduction of damage if deer mice are the primary pest.

Prescribed burning, by itself, will not reduce damage to conifer seedlings by large pest mammals such as deer and elk. However, it can help make other animal damage control techniques more effective. Examples include improved seedbeds for forage seeding to reduce deer and elk damage, enhanced efficiency of trapping to control mountain beaver damage, and increased ease of placing protective tubing over seedlings.

Situations in which prescribed burning may result in increased incidence and severity of pest mammal damage to conifer regeneration include the removal of foods mammal pests prefer over conifers; the enhancement of pest mammal habitat; and the removal of slash as a physical barrier to deer and elk.

Prescribed burning should be integrated with other silvicultural practices, including control of animal damage, to ensure that animal damage is managed in a manner to reduce it to an accepted level.

Literature Cited & Key References

*Ahlgren, C.E. 1966. Small mammals and reforestation following prescribed burning. J. For. 64:614-618.

*Ahlgren, I.F., and C.E. Ahlgren. 1960. Ecological effects of forest fires. Bot. Rev. 26:483-533.

Allen, H.H. 1969. The inter-relationships of salmonberry and Douglas-fir in cut over areas. M.S. thesis, Oregon State Univ., Corvallis, OR. 56 p.

*Anonymous. 1978. Animal damage control handbook. USDA For. Serv., Reg. 5-6, Portland, OR. 289 p.

Anthony, R.M., V.G. Barnes, Jr., and J. Evans. 1978. "Vexar" plastic netting to reduce pocket gopher depredation in conifer seedlings. Proc., Vertebrate Pest Conf. 8:138-144.

Barnes, V.G., Jr. 1974. Response of pocket gopher populations to silvicultural practices in central Oregon, p. 167-175. In Black, H.C. (ed.) Proc., Symposium on Wildlife and Forest Management in the Pacific Northwest. Oregon State Univ., Corvallis, OR. 236 p.

References marked by an asterisk are recommended for general information.

*Bartels, R., J.D. Dell, R.L. Knight, and G. Schaefer. 1985. Dead and down woody material, p. 171-197. *In* Brown, E.R. (ed.) Management of Wildlife and Fish Habitats in Forests of Western Oregon and Washington. USDA For. Serv., Portland, OR. Pub. R6-F&W-192-185. 332 p.

*Bendell, J.F. 1974. Effects of fire on birds and animals, p. 73-138. *In* Kozlowski, T.T. and C.E. Ahlgren, (eds.) Fire and Ecosystems. Academic Press, New York, NY. 542 p.

*Black, H.C., and E.F. Hooven. 1974. Response of small-mammal communities to habitat changes in western Oregon, p. 177-188. *In* Black, H.C. (ed.) Proc., Symposium on Wildlife and Forest Management in the Pacific Northwest. Oregon State Univ., Corvallis, OR. 236 p.

Bock, C.E., and J.H. Bock. 1983. Response of birds and deer mice to prescribed burning in ponderosa pine. J. Wildl. Manage. 47:836-840.

*Borrecco, J.E. 1976. Controlling damage by forest rodents and lagomorphs through habitat manipulation. Proc., Vertebrate Pest Conf. 7:203-210.

Borrecco, J.E., and R.J. Anderson. 1980. Mountain beaver problems in the forests of California, Oregon, and Washington. Proc., Vertebrate Pest Conf. 9:135-142.

*Brodie, D., H.C. Black, E.J. Dimock II, J. Evans, C. Kao, and J.A. Rochelle. 1979. Animal damage to coniferous plantations in Oregon and Washington. Part II. An economic evaluation. Sch. For., Oregon State Univ., Corvallis, OR. Res. Bull. 26. 26 p.

*Bruce, C., D. Edwards, K. Mellen, A. McMillan, T. Owens, and H. Sturgis. 1985. Wildlife relationships to plant communities and stand conditions, p. 33-55. *In* Brown, E.R. (ed.) Management of Wildlife and Fish Habitats in Forests of Western Oregon and Washington. USDA For. Serv., Portland, OR. Pub. R6-F&W-192-185. 332 p.

Campbell, D.L., and J. Evans. 1975. "Vexar" seedling protectors to reduce wildlife damage to Douglas-fir. USDA Fish & Wildl. Serv., Washington, DC. Wildl. Leafl. 508. 11 p.

Campbell, D.L., and J. Evans. 1978. Establishing native forbs to reduce black-tailed deer browsing damage to Douglas-fir. Proc., Vertebrate Pest Conf. 8:145-151.

Cook, S.F., Jr. 1959. The effects of fire on a population of small rodents. Ecology 40:102-108.

Crouch, G.L. 1979. Atrazine improves survival and growth of ponderosa pine threatened by vegetative competition and pocket gophers. For. Sci. 25:99-111.

*Daubenmire, R.F. 1968. Ecology of fire in grasslands. Adv. Ecol. Res. 5:209-266.

deCalesta, D.S., and K. Asman. 1987. Controlling pocket gopher damage to conifer seedlings. Oregon State Univ., Corvallis, OR. Ext. Circ. 1255. 8 p.

Dodge, W.E. 1968. Protective measures—a review of chemical, mechanical and other means of controlling damage by animals, p. 60-62. *In* Black, H.C. (ed.) Proc., Symposium on Wildlife and Reforestation in the Pacific Northwest. Sch. For., Oregon State Univ., Corvallis, OR. 92 p.

Fala, R.A. 1975. Effects of prescribed burning on small mammal populations in a mixed-oak clearcut. J. For. 73:586-587.

Falwells, H.A., and G.H. Schubert. 1951. Recent direct seeding trials in the pine region of California. Cal. For. Rge. Exp. Sta., Berkeley, CA. Res. Note 78. 9 p.

Flowers, R.H. 1987. Supplemental feeding of black bear in tree damaged areas of western Washington, p. 147-148. *In* Baumgartner, D.M., R.L. Mahoney, J. Evans, J. Caslick, and D.W. Breuer (co-chairs). Animal Damage Management in Pacific Northwest Forests. Spokane, WA. Coop. Ext., Washington State Univ., Pullman, WA. 164 p.

Galt, D.L., K.L. Eckhouse, and R.N. Stavins. 1981. Management and control of insect, disease and vertebrate pests in commercial forests of the Pacific coast region. Univ. Cal. Coop. Ext. Serv., Berkeley, CA. Proj. Rep. 1. 79 p.

Gashwiler, J.S. 1970. Plant and animal changes on a clearcut in west-central Oregon. Ecology 51:1018-1026.

Gorman, E.H., and A.L. Orr-Ewing. 1949. Direct-seeding experiments in the southern coastal region of British Columbia 1923-1949. B.C. For. Serv. Tech. Pub. T 31.

Green, P., D. Harper, and M. Jensen. 1987. Pocket gopher and successional plant community relationships within the grand fir-wild ginger habitat type of northern Idaho, p. 85. *In* Baumgartner, D.M., R.L. Mahoney, J. Evans, J. Caslick, and D.W. Breuer, (co-chairs). Animal Damage Management in Pacific Northwest Forests. Spokane, WA. Coop. Ext., Washington State Univ., Pullman, WA. 164 p.

Grisez, T.J. 1960. Slash helps protect seedlings from deer browsing. J. For. 58:385-386.

Hall, T.R., W.E. Howard, and R.E. Marsh. 1981. Raptor use of artificial perches. Wildl. Soc. Bull. 9:296-298.

Hooven, E.F. 1966. Pine regeneration in Oregon. Habits and control of seed-eating mammals. For. Res. Lab., Oregon State Univ., Corvallis, OR. Res. Pap. 5. 24 p.

Hooven, E.F. 1977. The mountain beaver in Oregon: its life history and control. For. Res. Lab., Oregon State Univ., Corvallis, OR. Res. Pap. 30. 20 p.

Howard, W.E., and H.E. Childs, Jr. 1959. Ecology of pocket gophers with emphasis on *Thomomys bottae* Mewa. Hilgardia 29:277-358.

Keith, J.D., R.M. Hansen, and A.L. Ward. 1959. Effect of 2-4-D on abundance and foods of pocket gophers. J. Wildl. Manage. 23:137-145.

Keith, L.B., and D.C. Surrendi. 1971. Effects of fire on a snowshoe hare population. J. Wildl. Manage. 35:16-26.

Komarek, E.V. 1967. Fire and the ecology of man. Tall Timbers Fire Ecol. Conf. Proc. 6:143-170.

*Komarek, E.V. 1969. Fire and animal behavior. Tall Timbers Fire Ecol. Conf. Proc. 9:161-207.

Krauch, H. 1936. Some factors influencing Douglas-fir reproduction in the Southwest. J. For. 34:601-608.

Larson, J.E., D.L. Campbell, J. Evans, and G.D. Lindsey. 1979. Plastic tubes for protecting seedlings from browsing wildlife. USDA For. Serv., Proj. Rec. ED&T 2217. 19 p.

*Lyon, L.J., H.S. Crawford, E. Czuhai, R.L. Fredriksen, R.F. Harlow, L.J. Metz, and H.A. Pearson. 1978. Effects of fire on fauna. USDA For. Serv., Washington, D.C. Gen. Tech. Rep. WO-6. 41 p.

Maser, C. 1967. Black bear damage to Douglas-fir in Oregon. Murrelet 48:34-38.

Mereszczak, I.M., W.C. Krueger, and M. Vavra. 1981. Effects of range improvement on Roosevelt elk winter nutrition. J. Range Manage. 34:184-187.

Motubu, D.A. 1978. Effects of controlled slash burning on the mountain beaver (*Aplodondia rufa rufa*). Northwest Sci. 52:92-99.

Moore, A.W. 1940. Wild animal damage to seed and seedlings on cut over Douglas-fir lands of Oregon and Washington. USDA For. Serv., Tech. Bull. 706. 28 p.

Poelker, R.J., and H.D. Hartwell. 1973. Black bear of Washington. Washington State Game Dep., Olympia, WA. Biol. Bull. 14. 108 p.

Robinson, W.L., and E.G. Bolen. 1984. Wildlife Ecology and Management. Macmillan Publ. Co., New York, N.Y. 478 p.

Schreiber, B.P. 1987. Diurnal bird use of snags in clearcuts in central coastal Oregon. M.S. thesis, Oregon State Univ. Corvallis, OR. 63 p.

Sims, H.P., and C.H. Buckner. 1972. The effect of clearcutting and burning in *Pinus banksiana* forests on the populations of small mammals in southeastern Manitoba. Amer. Midl. Natur. 90:228-231.

State of Washington. 1983. The Washington interagency guide for conservation and forage plantings. Washington State Rangeland Comm., Pullman, WA. Misc. Pub. 0058. 70 p.

Stoddard, H.L., Sr. 1963. Bird habitat and fire. Tall Timbers Fire Ecol. Conf. Proc. 2:163-175.

Taber, R.D. 1973. Effects of even-age forest management on big game, p. 59-74. *In* Hermann, R.K. and D.P. Lavender (eds.) Symposium on Even-age Management. Oregon State Univ., Corvallis, OR. 250 p.

Tevis, L., Jr. 1956. Effect of a slash burn on forest mice. J. Wildl. Manage. 20:405-409.

Tietjen, H.P., C.K. Halvorsen, P.L. Hegdal, and A.M. Johnson. 1967. 2-4-D herbicide, vegetation and pocket gopher relationships, Black Mesa, Colorado. Ecology 48:634-643.

Volland, L.A. 1974. Relationship of pocket gophers to plant communities in the pine region of central Oregon, p. 149-166. *In* Black, H.C. (ed.) Proc., Symposium on Wildlife and Forest Management in the Pacific Northwest. Oregon State Univ., Corvallis, OR. 236 p.

10 Effects of Prescribed Fire on Insect Pests

Russel G. Mitchell

Executive Summary

Several insect pests spend part of their life cycle on the forest floor and can be directly affected by underburning the infested forest. Many defoliating insects and most seed and cone insects, for example, are vulnerable to this treatment. Pests associated with logging and thinning slash live under the bark of the slash and are also subject to direct control by fire. However, these kinds of treatment have limitations and must be approached carefully to achieve the control objectives.

Many of the interactions between fire and insects are indirect. For example, trees with more than 50 percent of their crowns scorched by fire usually become attractive to bark beetles, which could be the desired result if the goal of the burn was to remove undesirable tree species or reduce the number of trees in an overstocked stand. Sometimes, however, large trees intended for the final crop are also scorched and attacked by these pests.

Prescribed underburning to maintain stands at some intermediate (seral) level of succession could be the most valuable use of fire in pest management. Wildfire control in the last 75 years—combined with intensive logging of ponderosa pine—has permitted vast acreages of ponderosa pine to be replaced by more shade-tolerant tree species dominated by true firs, a favored host of the Douglas-fir tussock moth and the western spruce budworm. Accordingly, these two pests are now greater problems throughout the West than they were 50 years ago. The status of other insect pests like the mountain pine beetle has also been elevated owing to the effects of wildfire control programs. Because the wildfire control policy will likely continue in most commercial forests, prescribed burning will often be needed to prevent the creation of forests excessively vulnerable to insect pests.

Clearly, the effects of prescribed burning on forest insect pests can be both positive and negative. But it is also clear that most of the negative aspects are trivial and that when prescribed burning is used carefully and intelligently it can be an extremely useful tool in the management of forest insect pests.

Introduction

Prescribed burning is rarely used to manipulate insect populations, but insects are affected by burning, regardless of the intention. And because fire sweeps up everything in its path, it affects beneficial insects, like the scavengers feeding on detritus at the forest floor (mesofauna), as well as pest populations. This chapter addresses just the interactions with insect pests, the results we like, and the ones we would like to forget. Impact of fire on beneficial insects, other than mesofauna, is not specifically addressed in this book; beneficial insects are important but present a level of complexity that would make any discussion extremely speculative. Mesofauna are discussed in the chapter on soil organisms (Chapter 13).

Fire can impact insect pests by killing them directly or by changing the environment they live in. The indirect effect of fire is also seen by looking at the reverse side of the coin—populations can be significantly affected by policies that deliberately avoid fire. Fire has long been a significant ecological force in most forest ecosystems, and there is strong evidence that the wildfire control policies of the last 75 years have greatly increased the problems presented by some well-known forest insect pests.

The interactions of fire and insect pest populations have been tested rarely and then with mixed results. It is hard to control the many variables in the field, and the field is the only place one can test realistic interactions. Also, some relationships are technically and economically impossible to demonstrate—the effects of such policies as fire exclusion, for example, are not evident for decades. Nevertheless, there is considerable empirical evidence for interaction, and a lot of relationships have been defined rather well by plausible inferences (Mitchell and Sartwell 1974, Martin et al. 1976, Lyon et al. 1978, Miller 1979, Martin and Mitchell 1980, Mitchell and Martin 1980).

Killing Insects Directly with Fire

The most obvious effect of fire on insects is the direct one—we can kill insects by burning them up. Many insect pests spend part of their life cycle on the forest floor, providing the opportunity of using light ground fires for control. In the Midwest, for example, Miller (1978) used a prescribed ground fire to control a cone beetle of red pine that overwintered on the forest floor. Also in the Midwest, Simmons et al. (1977) found that prescribed burning in a stand of maple to combat a leaf cutter that pupates on the forest floor was a more effective control measure than insecticide treatments. In the Southwest, an attempt to control a pandora moth population pupating in the soil under ponderosa pine was not too successful (Schmid et al. 1981).

In the Pacific Northwest, several forest insect pests overwinter on the forest floor, either in the duff or in the mineral soil under the duff. This includes many insects affecting seeds and cones, tree defoliators such as several sawflies, and a few pests of regenerating forests such as the western pine shoot borer. Fire can often be used where such pests occur because the forest ecosystems are adapted to fire by trees with thick, heat-protecting bark (Chapter 4). The limitation to this kind of treatment, though, is that it can be applied only periodically; fire, of course, consumes fuel and 4 to 5 years are needed after treatment to accumulate enough fuel to support another fire. Depending on circumstances, this may or may not be an important limitation. Another problem, as noted by Miller and Wagner (1984) for the pandora moth, is that many insect pests have coevolved with fire-resistant tree species and likely developed their own strategies for surviving fires. In the case of the pandora moth, a large percentage of the population pupates in mineral soil and in areas where there is not enough fuel accumulation for a fire to generate lethal temperatures (Schmid and Bennett 1988).

Many insects, including a few pests, breed under the bark of logging slash and can be killed by controlled slash burning. The pine engraver beetle is probably the most significant slash pest in the Pacific Northwest. It is nearly always found in ponderosa pine slash and can be a significant killer of sapling ponderosa pine in the vicinity of logging, particularly the residual trees in precommercial thinnings. It has been demonstrated (unpublished work by the author and R.E. Martin, author of Chapter 5) that a fire in green slash will generate enough heat to kill developing engraver populations under the bark of small-diameter slash. However, the value of destroying bark beetle populations under the bark is yet to be proven; the problem is that it is difficult to show the relationship between treatment and subsequent tree mortality. Bark beetles that kill green trees usually infest those trees about the same time they are attacking the associated slash, not (as commonly believed) when their broods leave the slash. Accordingly, the value of slash burning for bark beetle control must reside in the general effects of population reduction.

It must be remembered that slash does not generate pest problems very often and that those that do occur are usually associated with Douglas-fir and pine slash. Slash from cedar, hemlock, true fir, spruce, and larch rarely present problems (Mitchell and Sartwell 1974). Another feature of slash pests is that nearly all (bark beetles, ambrosia beetles, wood borers, and weevils) require fresh slash for a major portion of their life cycle. Accordingly, burning old slash (more than a year old) accomplishes little in terms of pest control.

One problem with prescribed burning, slash or otherwise, is that it is impossible to anticipate every interaction; sometimes some rather bizarre, untoward results can occur, seemingly on a random basis. For example, a situation was observed by the author in the Coast Range of Oregon where slash burning created a pest out of a rather obscure chrysomelid beetle (*Syneta hamata*) that normally feeds on thimbleberry. In this case, there was a hot slash burn in the fall, one that eliminated nearly all the vegetation on the site. Then, next spring, the beetles emerged from winter hibernation expecting to find thimbleberry but found instead Douglas-fir seedlings that had been planted during the winter; those seedlings were devastated when the hungry beetles opportunistically used them as their principal food supply.

A reverse situation was observed, also in the Oregon Coast Range, when a pest problem was created because logging slash was not burned. A flightless reproduction weevil (*Steremnius carinatus*) used the duff in the unburned slash for an overwintering site and, next spring, emerged and killed the Douglas-fir seedlings that had been planted in the clearcut during the winter. In adjacent, burned clearcuts, there was very little weevil damage; the weevils were either killed directly by the fire or had no duff layer for protection and had to winter elsewhere, some distance from the newly planted seedlings.

Indirect Effects of Fire on Insect Pests

Fire can indirectly have great influence on pest populations by affecting the environment they live in. The relationships can be obvious, such as the association between crown scorch and insect populations, or subtly buried in a complicated web of ecologic trophic levels. The complicated relationship may be something like an insect pest kept at low density levels by a parasite—a parasite that needs the food source of a certain flower that in turn needs the environment produced by repeated light fires. Such complicated relationships are probable but extremely difficult to prove.

The relationship between crown scorch and bark beetles is neither complicated nor difficult to prove. No matter how carefully they are managed, prescribed fires sometimes become too hot and unintentionally scorch the crowns of a few trees, the damage from spring and summer burns being more severe than from fall burns (Harrington 1987). In ponderosa pine, crown scorch exceeding 50 percent invites attacks by engraver beetles, the mountain pine beetle, and the western pine beetle (Mitchell and Martin 1980). When these insects colonize trees, they also produce a perfume-like chemical compound (technically known as an aggregation pheromone) that attracts more beetles, sometimes from considerable distances. When the beetle population in the general area is large, the aggregated beetle population can be so concentrated that several associated green trees and trees with minor scorching can be killed along with the severely scorched trees. In a similar but more subtle relationship, it was found that smoldering fires in rotten logs can scorch the shallow roots of lodgepole pine, providing entry courts for root diseases that, years later, weaken the trees enough to invite attack by the mountain pine beetle and other bark beetles (Gara et al. 1984, Geiszler et al. 1984, Littke and Gara 1986).

Fire-scorch also attracts wood-boring insects, which often invade trees while the fire is still burning (Wickman 1964). Most borers attracted to fires follow the smoke plume, which often provides a rather circuitous path to the fire. One genus of flatheaded borers (Fig. 10-1), though, has a special organ for detecting infrared radiation, allowing the beetles to detect a fire at some distance and then fly directly to the burning trees (Evans 1966). Because wood-boring insects often mine deep into

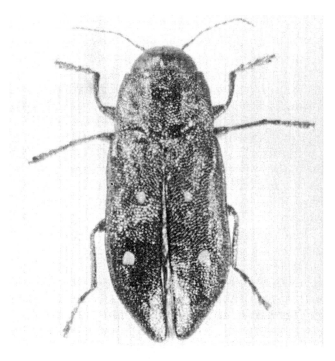

Figure 10-1. Many insects, particularly wood borers, are attracted to forest fires. The flatheaded borer pictured here is one of the first insects to arrive at a fire site.

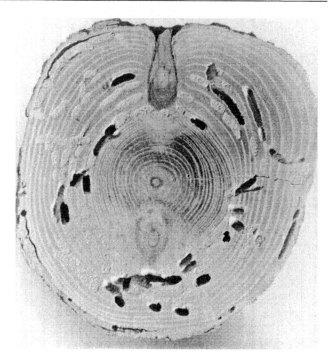

Figure 10-2. Wood-boring insects attracted to fire-scorched trees often mine deeply into the wood. Trees salvaged from fires for commercial use must be processed quickly to avoid significant degrade. The same borers, however, become beneficial insects when the wood is left on site –the deep holes increase the speed with which wood is decomposed and returned to the soil.

the wood, they can be considered either beneficial insects or pests, depending on the plans for the wood. When the goal is to cut the trees into lumber, then borers are pests. When, however, the wood is to be left on the site, the borers become beneficial insects because of their role in accelerating deterioration and nutrient cycling (Fig. 10-2).

Prescribed fires can also be used to thin stands. One effect of thinning is to improve the vigor of the residual stand and reduce infestation rates of bark beetles (Sartwell and Stevens 1975, Larsson et al. 1983). Weaver (1957, 1967) was one of the first to show that fire can be used in ponderosa pine to create thrifty young stands through the effect of thinning thickets of shrubs and trees. Weaver's burns, which included no other treatments, accomplished a degree of growth-release that persisted for many years (Rudnicky and Martin 1979).

Probably the most dramatic example of the effects of fire on pest populations is how fire protection has changed the pattern of species composition in stands over vast areas of the West and how that change has in turn caused some significant pest problems. The increasing size, severity, and frequency of Douglas-fir tussock moth and western spruce budworm outbreaks in the West demonstrates the problem well. As noted by Schmidt (1985), nearly all the forests in the West had "... felt the heat of forest fires sometimes in their past." Before fire control, thousands of acres of ponderosa pine were held in a seral state by repeated light burns (Chapter 3). But, once fire control policies were initiated, the effects of succession (and some high-grade logging) shifted many seral ponderosa pine stands to climax stands of true fir and Douglas-fir—the favored hosts of the tussock moth and the budworm. This pattern was described by Wickman (1978) and Williams et al. (1980) for the tussock moth and Schmidt (1985) for the budworm (Fig. 10-3), each noting that pest outbreaks are more severe in the drier stands where ponderosa pine was once seral than in the cool moist sites always dominated by the spruce-fir type. All tree species, of course, have pests, and changing the forest composition really means replacing one pest complex with another. However, the pest problems associated with ponderosa pine are usually less severe and more easily managed than those associated with true firs and interior Douglas-fir.

A related problem is the invasion of ponderosa pine stands by lodgepole pine. When fire was a regular feature of ponderosa pine forests, the thin-barked lodgepole pine seldom survived. Now, however, stands with both species are common, and they present an increased risk of ponderosa pine being killed by the mountain pine beetle. The threat arises because the beetle prefers lodgepole pine, and its admixture to ponderosa pine stands attracts beetles, sometimes resulting in trees being

Figure 10-3. The western spruce budworm is a notorious insect pest that has become more common in western forests in recent years because the long-term effects of wildfire control policies have greatly expanded its preferred habitat.

killed that would normally be resistant to attack (Mitchell 1989).

Lastly, to show the breadth of the relationship between fire exclusion and pest problems, is a situation found west of the Cascades in Oregon and Washington. There, in the absence of fire and stand disturbance, the shade-tolerant Pacific silver fir has moved downslope in many areas, gradually replacing the seral Douglas-fir. Because silver fir is susceptible to attack by the balsam woolly aphid (an introduced pest from Europe), and because damage by the aphid is most serious at the lower elevations (Mitchell 1966), the effect of fire exclusion has been to increase the impact of the balsam woolly aphid over large areas of the Pacific Northwest.

Conclusion

An evaluation of all possible interactions among insect pests and fire is beyond the scope of this chapter. Instead the goal was to show that prescribed burning presents both problems and opportunities for insect pest management. Another objective was to demonstrate (through selected examples) the nature of the interactions that can be expected among fire and insect pests and to show that there exists some order and predictability in the relationships.

The general conclusion that can be drawn from past experiences is that pest problems generated by prescribed burning are mostly trivial, ephemeral, and usually can be avoided by careful planning and execution. Another conclusion is that prescribed burning can be used in some ecosystems, most notably ponderosa pine, to solve problems posed by insect pests. It is obvious that for the foreseeable future, the policy will be to control destructive wildfires on commercial forest lands as quickly as possible. Accordingly, if we are to counter the untoward effects of that policy, we will almost surely need to utilize prescribed burning in our pest management strategies.

Literature Cited & Key References

Evans, W. G. 1966. Perception of infrared radiation from forest fires by *Melanophila acuminata* DeGeer (Buprestidae: Coleoptera). Ann. Entomol. Soc. Amer. 59:873-877.

Gara, R.I., D.R. Geiszler, and W.R. Littke. 1984. Primary attraction of the mountain pine beetle to lodgepole pine in Oregon. Ann. Entomol. Soc. Amer. 77:333-334.

*Geiszler, D. R., R. I. Gara, and W.R. Littke. 1984. Bark beetle infestations of lodgepole pine following a fire in south-central Oregon. Zeit. angw. Entomol. 39:389-394.

Harrington, M.G. 1987. Ponderosa pine mortality from spring, summer, and fall crown scorching. West. J. Appl. For. 2:14-16

Larsson, S., R. Oren, R.H. Waring, and J.W. Barrett. 1983. Attacks of mountain pine beetle as related to tree vigor of ponderosa pine. For. Sci. 29:395-402.

Littke, W.R., and R.I. Gara. 1986. Decay of fire-damaged lodgepole pine in south-central Oregon. For. Ecol. Manage. 17:279-287.

*Lyon, L.J., H.S. Crawford, E. Czuhai, R.L. Fredriksen, R.F. Harlow, L.J. Metz, and H.A. Pearson. 1978. Effects of fire on fauna: A state- of-knowledge review. Nat. Fire Effects Workshop, Apr. 10-14, 1978, Denver, CO., USDA For. Serv., Washington, DC. Gen. Tech. Rep. WO-6. 41 p.

*Martin, R.E., D.D. Robinson, and W.H. Schaeffer. 1976. Fire in the Pacific Northwest: Perspectives and problems. Tall Timbers Fire Ecol. Conf. Proc. 15:1-23.

*Martin, R.E., and R.G. Mitchell. 1980. Possible, potential, probable, and proven fire-insect interactions, p.138-144. *In* Proc., 1980 Nat. Conv., Soc. Amer. For., Spokane, WA.

Miller, K.K., and M.R. Wagner. 1984. Factors influencing pupal distribution of the pandora moth (Lepidoptera: Saturniidae) and their relationship to prescribed burning. Environ. Entomol. 13:430-431.

Miller, W.E. 1978. Use of prescribed burning in seed production areas to control red pine cone beetle. Environ. Entomol. 7:698-702.

*Miller, W.E. 1979. Fire as an insect management tool. Bull. Entomol. Soc. Amer. 25:137-140.

Mitchell, R.G. 1966. Infestation characteristics of the balsam woolly aphid in the Pacific Northwest. USDA, For. Serv., Pac. Northwest For. Rge. Exp. Sta., Portland, OR. Res. Pap. PNW-35. 18 p.

*Mitchell, R.G. 1989. Mixed host strategies for mountain pine beetle control in Oregon, p.60-63. *In* Amman, G.D. (ed.), Proc., Symp. on the management of lodgepole pine to minimize losses to the mountain pine beetle. Kalispell, MT. July 12-14, 1988. USDA For. Serv., Intermountain Res. Sta., Gen. Tech. Rep. INT-262.

*Mitchell, R.G., and R.E. Martin. 1980. Fire and insects in pine culture of the Pacific Northwest. Fire For. Meteorol. Conf. Proc. 6:182-190.

*Mitchell, R.G., and C. Sartwell. 1974. Insects and other arthropods, p. R-1 to R-22. *In* Cramer, O.P. (ed.) Environmental effects of forest residues management in the Pacific Northwest: A state-of-knowledge compendium. USDA For. Serv., Pac. Northwest For. Rge Exp. Sta. Portland, OR. Gen. Tech. Rep. PNW-24.

Rudnicky, J., and R.E. Martin. 1979. The long-term effects of prescribed burning on a ponderosa pine stand in central Washington. USDA For. Serv., Pac. Northwest For. Rge. Exp. Sta., Bend, OR.

*Sartwell, C., and R.E. Stevens. 1975. Mountain pine beetle in ponderosa pine. J. For. 73:136-140.

Schmid, J.M., and D.D. Bennett. 1988. The North Kaibab pandora moth outbreak, 1978-1984. USDA For. Serv., Rocky Mt. For. Rge. Exp. Sta., Fort Collins, CO. Gen. Tech. Rep. RM-153. 19 p.

Schmid, J. M., L. Thomas, and T. J. Rogers. 1981. Prescribed burning to increase mortality of pandora moth pupae. USDA For. Serv., Rocky Mt. For. Rge Exp. Sta., Fort Collins, CO. Res. Note RM-405. 3p.

*Schmidt, W.C. 1985. Historical Consideration, Chapter l. *In* Brookes, M.H., J.J. Colbert, R.G. Mitchell, and R.W. Stark (eds.) Managing trees and stands susceptible to western spruce budworm. USDA For. Serv., Washington DC. Tech. Bull. 1695. 111 p.

Simmons, G. A., J. Mahar, M. K. Kennedy and J. Ball. 1977. Preliminary test of prescribed burning for control of maple leaf cutter (Lepidoptera: Incurvariidae). The Great Lakes Entomol. 10:209-210.

*Weaver, H. 1957. Effects of prescribed burning in ponderosa pine. J. For. 55:133-138.

*Weaver, H. 1967. Fire as a continuing ecological factor in perpetuation of ponderosa pine forests in western United States. Adv. Front. Plant Sci. 18:137-153.

Wickman, B.E. 1964. Attack habits of *Melanophila consputa* on fire-killed pines. Pan Pac. Entomol. 40:183-186.

Wickman, B.E. 1978. A case study of a Douglas-fir tussock moth outbreak and stand conditions 10 years later. USDA For. Serv., Pac. Northwest For. Rge Exp. Sta., Portland, OR. Res. Pap. PNW-244. 22 p.

Williams, J. T., R.E. Martin, and S.G. Pickford. 1980. Silvicultural and fire implications from a timber type evaluation of tussock moth outbreak areas. Fire For. Meteorol. Conf. Proc. 6:191-196.

References marked by an asterisk are recommended for general information.

11 Effects of Prescribed Fire on Diseases of Conifers

Walter G. Thies

Executive Summary

This chapter summarizes what is known about the interaction of prescribed fire and forest tree diseases in Oregon and Washington. Fire can be used to destroy residual trees infected with dwarf mistletoe after regeneration cuts and to eliminate undesirable advanced regeneration when shifting to a more disease-resistant seral condition. Care should be exercised when underburning to avoid injury to residual trees and the likelihood of infection through fire scars. Additional research is needed to better define fire-disease interactions in the Pacific Northwest, particularly for root disease.

Introduction

There is little doubt that prescribed fire affects the incidence and severity of forest tree diseases. However, only a few limited studies have directly linked fire in the Pacific Northwest to changes in the incidence or severity of diseases. A greater understanding of the interactions between forest diseases and prescribed burning could provide forest managers improved tools to better manage their lands.

To present as complete a picture as possible, the available literature has been examined and many forest pathologists in Washington and Oregon have been consulted in an attempt to distill the collective professional judgments on the matter. The ideas and conclusions presented in this chapter approximate a consensus. While no attempt is made to cite individuals or all references for information presented here, a selected list of pertinent resources is provided. Where lists of references are provided by previous reviewers, only the review papers are cited.

When discussing the impacts of fire on diseases, a distinction should be made between direct effects that influence a particular pathogen (i.e., that establish conditions conducive to the disease process) and indirect effects that act mainly on the host, such as injury or encouraging a shift in plant species.

Root Diseases

Rhizina root rot may be the only documented example of the direct effect of fire on a forest disease in the Pacific Northwest. Spores of the fungus lie dormant in the soil and germinate only after stimulation by high temperatures such as those produced by fire. After spore germination, the fungus colonizes woody debris and may later infect the roots of conifer seedlings. This is primarily a problem with Douglas-fir. Affected seedlings occur in groups, as is typical with root diseases, and may die during periods of moisture stress. In a 1973 survey the fungus was found fruiting (Fig. 11-1, 11-2) on 64 of 277 recently burned Douglas-fir clearcuts on National Forests and state-owned lands in western Washington and Oregon. The disease caused heavy mortality in portions of some burned clearcuts. Frequency of infested clearcuts within the surveyed area increased with increasing

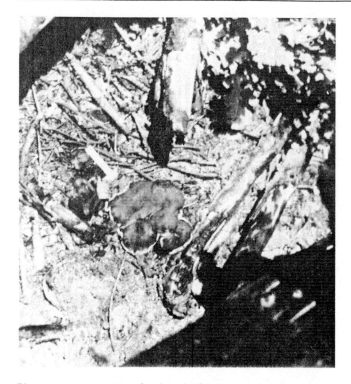

Figure 11-1. Fruiting body of Rhizina undulata, causal agent of rhizina root rot. Pictured is a well-developed fresh specimen, about 4 inches across. Fruiting bodies may be found on or above buried woody debris in areas burned within the previous 3 years. They usually appear 10-16 months after a fire. The fruiting bodies first appear in the spring as small cream-colored buttons. These grow and mature during the early summer, forming a rusty-brown convoluted crust-like structure 2-5 inches in diameter. While actively growing they have a cream-colored margin. (Photo courtesy of USDA Forest Service)

Figure 11-2. Fruiting body of Rhizina undulata at the base of a Douglas-fir seedling. Seedling losses would be expected to occur within 3 years following a burn. Not all seedlings growing near a fruiting body will die. (Photo courtesy of USDA Forest Service)

latitude. On clearcuts where the fungus was found, mortality attributable to rhizina root rot averaged 1.3 seedlings per acre compared with 34.8 seedlings per acre dead from other causes. While the disease may cause spotty but serious seedling mortality, the relatively low overall incidence of loss will not justify consideration of this disease when planning a controlled burn.

Fire does not appear to have a direct effect on major root diseases in the Pacific Northwest. The three major root diseases, laminated root rot, armillaria root disease, and annosus butt rot and root disease, have in common a saprophytic phase during which they occupy stumps and roots. Roots of susceptible trees in the replacement stand may become infected when they contact these pieces of buried inoculum. Normal slash burning, after clearcutting, does not significantly reduce this source of inoculum. Even in hot fires, temperatures adequately high to kill the fungi in a buried piece of wood seldom develop at depths greater than 4 inches below the soil surface. Hollow stumps resulting from laminated root rot may begin burning during a slash fire. This fire could, if allowed to continue, reduce some of the inoculum on the site but such stumps are often considered a hazard and may be extinguished during mop-up procedures. Even if hollow stumps were allowed to burn, the benefit would be slight, since they represent only about 15 percent of the infected stumps and thus contribute relatively little inoculum. There is no evidence that burned sites develop less laminated root rot in the replacement stand than nonburned sites.

Prescribed fire may be used beneficially on some sites with a high incidence of the major root diseases to cause a shift to an earlier seral condition. For example, if the site is a grand fir or white fir habitat type, fire can be used to shift the succession in the understory to an earlier seral condition which often includes larch or pine, which are more resistant to laminated root rot. True firs are thin barked and readily killed with a controlled burn in the understory.

In pine stands in the southeastern United States, annosus root disease has been reduced by underburning prior to thinning operations. This burning reduces the duff layer and thereby sporophore production, reducing the spore load in the stand at the time of thinning. In the Pacific Northwest, where significantly different stand and soil types exist, underburning for control of annosus root disease does not appear to be practical, and tests of this technique have not been reported. When annosus root disease is a management concern for a particular stand, fresh stump tops can be chemically treated with borax to avoid spore infections.

One potentially important indirect effect of underburning may be to predispose some trees to root disease through injury. Live trees which are injured by fire may become so stressed that they are more easily attacked by root pathogens. Stressed trees may attract secondary insects (such as mountain pine beetle to lodgepole pine) which may further encourage root diseases. Windthrown trees resulting from root diseases can also contribute to build-up of insects such as the Douglas-fir bark beetle. Additionally, roots at or close to the soil surface may be killed or injured, providing an entrance for pathogens.

Stem Diseases

Fire may influence the incidence of stem disease in stands where underburning is conducted. If burn conditions result in a hot fire, trees may be fire scarred. A fire scar, especially close to the ground, is an infection court for a variety of fungi capable of causing butt, stem, and heart rots. Examples in the Pacific Northwest are schweinitzii butt rot of Douglas-fir and brown cubical butt and pocket rot of western redcedar. Entrance of fungi

into a tree is a more likely result in nonresinous, thin-barked species but occurs with some regularity in lodgepole pine, a resinous species.

Foliage Diseases

The classic example of using prescribed fire to control a foliage disease is the use of light ground fires to control brown spot needle blight of longleaf pine in the southeastern United States. Light ground fires are used to eliminate inoculum on dry needles near the ground until the seedlings are advanced enough to be out of the "grass" stage, after which the disease has little impact. In the Pacific Northwest, there is not an analogous situation. In general, seedlings do not have a high heat tolerance and will not reliably survive a burn.

Needle diseases are found in all coniferous plant communities and may be locally damaging. They tend to be cyclic, usually building up with wet weather conditions. In general, however, needle diseases do not cause enough economic loss for control procedures such as prescribed fire to be considered. While fire could be used to reduce inoculum produced on needles that have fallen from the trees, this is unlikely to be effective. Needles that fall to the forest floor usually serve as a food base for needle pathogens for a month or two before they are invaded by other saprophytic organisms. Reduction of this inoculum would require yearly light fires. Even so, needles that remain on the trees or catch in bark crevices could provide adequate inoculum for infection of new needles if proper weather conditions exist.

Dwarf Mistletoes

Dwarf mistletoes are endemic, parasitic seed plants that can cause spike tops, witches' brooms, resin-filled stem cankers, growth loss, and death of coniferous trees. The parasitic plants require a live host for their own growth and existence and in general are host specific. In the past, wildfires may have had a sanitizing effect on forests by destroying stands infested by dwarf mistletoe; however, the net effect of periodic fires has probably been to encourage the dwarf mistletoe by maintaining the forests in susceptible seral types. In general, the presence of dwarf mistletoe in a stand is closely tied to the fire history of the area. Used as part of an informed management plan, prescribed burning is unlikely to encourage dwarf mistletoes.

Figure 11-3. Residual lodgepole pine infected by dwarf mistletoe. These trees were left following a harvest cut. The residual mistletoe plants can be expected to infect trees in the replacement stand as they develop. Prescribed fire could be used to kill the trees, thereby eliminating the seed source. (Photo courtesy of the Canadian Forestry Service)

Prescribed burning could be an effective tool in a program to control dwarf mistletoes. Burning the slash from a regeneration cut could serve three control objectives:

• Eliminate the infected residual trees in the cut-over area (Fig. 11-3). This could also be done as an underburning several years before a harvest cut to allow seed from the current stand to germinate and become established before the infected overstory is removed.
• Eliminate residual seedlings or trees to facilitate a species conversion.
• Establish a seedbed when a more resistant seral species is desired.

Under very specific stand and burning conditions, dwarf mistletoe inoculum could be reduced by underburning in a manner that would burn mistletoe brooms in the lower crown of ponderosa pines without causing a crown fire that would kill the trees.

Miscellaneous

The impact that smoke from prescribed fire may have on pathogens is a difficult factor to evaluate. The antimicrobial and preservative effects of smoke are well known. Results have been reported that show that wood smoke has a deleterious effect on spore germination and mycelial growth of several common forest pathogens. Additional work will be needed before this aspect of prescribed fire will become a management consideration.

Conclusion

Relatively little has been written on the effects of prescribed burning on forest diseases, especially those occurring in Washington and Oregon. Based on available data, the important considerations for prescribed burning on forest diseases can be summarized as follows:

• Use fire to destroy residual trees that can carry over dwarf mistletoe into a regenerated stand.
• Use fire to destroy undesirable residual seedlings to accomplish a species conversion in programs to control either dwarf mistletoes or root disease.
• Exercise caution when underburning to avoid injuries that provide infection courts for a variety of pathogens.

In the Pacific Northwest, additional research is needed to clarify the relationships between fire and most forest tree diseases. Information from other regions can help local pathologists and forest managers work with fire interactions with dwarf mistletoes and stem diseases. Foliage diseases are a minor component of the regional disease loss picture and are unlikely to be greatly impacted by prescribed fire. Root diseases, on the other hand, are widespread, economically destructive, and not demonstrably responsive to treatment by prescribed fire.

Key References

Alexander, M.E., and F.G. Hawksworth. 1975. Wildland fires and dwarf mistletoes: A literature review of ecology and prescribed burning. USDA For. Serv., Rocky Mt. For. Rge. Exp. Sta., Fort Collins, CO. Gen. Tech. Rep. RM-14. 12 p.

Boyce, J.S. 1961. Forest Pathology. McGraw Hill Book Co., Inc., New York, NY. 572 p.

Buckland, D.C. 1946. Investigations of decay in western red cedar in British Columbia. Can. J. For. Res. 24:158-181.

Fellin, D.G. 1980. A review of some interactions between harvesting, residue management, fire, and forest insects and diseases, p. 335-414. *In* Symp. Proc., Environmental Consequences of Timber Harvesting in Rocky Mountain Coniferous Forests. September 11-13, 1979, Missoula, MT. USDA For. Serv., Intermt. For. Rge. Exp. Sta., Ogden, UT. Gen. Tech. Rep. INT-90. 526 p.

Froelich, R.C., C.S. Hodges, Jr., and S.S. Sackett. 1978. Prescribed burning reduces severity of annosus root rot in the South. For. Sci. 24:93-100.

Goheen, D.J., G.M. Filip, E. Michaels-Goheen, and S.J. Frankel. 1985. Injuries and potential decay losses in underburned white fir on the Fremont National Forest. Pest Manage. Rep. on file at For. Pest Manage., Pac. Northwest Reg., USDA For. Serv., Portland, OR. 6 p.

Hadfield, J.S., D.J. Goheen, G.M. Filip, C.L. Schmitt, and R.D. Harvey. 1986. Root diseases in Oregon and Washington Conifers. USDA For. Serv., Pac. Northwest Reg., Portland, OR. 27 p.

Hardison, J.R. 1976. Fire and flame for plant disease control. Annu. Rev. Phytopathol. 14:355-379.

Harvey, A.E., M.F. Jurgensen and M, J. Larsen. 1976. Intensive fiber utilization and prescribed fire: Effects on the microbial ecology of forests. USDA For. Serv., Intermt. For. Rge. Exp. Sta., Ogden, UT. Gen. Tech. Rep. INT-28. 46 p.

Littke, W.R., and R.I. Gara. 1986. Decay of fire-damaged lodgepole pine in south central Oregon. For. Ecol. Manage. 17:279-287.

Koonce, A.L., and L.F. Roth. 1980. The effects of prescribed burning on dwarf mistletoe in ponderosa pine. Fire For. Meteorol. Conf. Proc. 6:197-203.

Morgan, P.D., and C.H. Driver. 1972. Rhizina root rot of Douglas-fir seedlings planted on burned sites in Washington. Plant Dis. Rep. 56:407-409.

Nelson, E.E., and G.M. Harvey. 1974. Diseases, p. S-1 to S-11. *In* Cramer, O.P. (ed.) Environmental effects of forest residues management in the Pacific Northwest: A state-of-knowledge compendium. USDA For. Serv., Pac. Northwest For. Rge. Exp. Sta., Portland, OR. Gen. Tech. Rep. PNW-24.

Parmeter, J.R., and B. Uhrenholdt. 1976. Effects of smoke on pathogens and other fungi. Tall Timbers Fire Ecol. Conf. Proc. 14:299-304.

Thies, W.G., K.E. Russell, and L.C. Weir. 1979. Rhizina root rot of little consequence in Washington and Oregon. J. For. 77:22-24.

Wicker, E.F., and C.D. Leaphart. 1976. Fire and dwarf mistletoe (*Arceuthobium spp.*) relationships in the northern Rocky Mountains. Tall Timbers Fire Ecol. Conf. Proc. 14:279-298.

V Effects of Prescribed Fire on Forest Productivity

12 Effects of Prescribed Fire on Nutrients and Soil Productivity

David H. McNabb and Kermit Cromack, Jr.

Executive Summary

All burning, whether wildfire or prescribed, disrupts the cycling of nutrients in forest ecosystems by changing the form, distribution, and amount of nutrients. The combustion of fuels and organic matter most commonly results in the volatilization of elements. Volatilization depends on the temperature at which elements are volatilized, with nitrogen, and to a lesser extent sulfur and phosphorus, being the nutrients most readily volatilized. With increasing fire intensity, these and other nutrients are also lost by convection as ash in the smoke plume.

The loss of nitrogen is of most widespread concern because forests with higher soil nitrogen and organic matter contents are generally more productive, and a majority of the forest stands in the region respond to nitrogen fertilization. Nitrogen is also the nutrient lost in the greatest amounts. Nitrogen losses typically range between 100 and 900 lbs per acre, with wildfires and severe slash fires responsible for the larger losses. Losses of sulfur and phosphorus are a small but proportional fraction of the nitrogen losses; losses of other nutrients are primarily limited to ash transport into the atmosphere.

Wildfires and many fall prescribed burns result in large nutrient losses because these fires are generally more severe and consume large amounts of fuels. Severe wildfires also consume nitrogen in soil organic matter and this can adversely affect other soil properties. Reducing fire intensity decreases nutrient losses from burning. Fire intensity may be reduced by removing some of the available fuels before burning, burning when the forest floor and large fuels are wet, and using burning techniques that reduce fire intensity. Nitrogen losses may be reduced to a quarter to one-half the amount lost in severe slash fires or wildfires by controlling fire intensity and fuel consumption.

The direct effect that prescribed burning has on nutrient cycling and soil productivity depends on the fire regime of the specific site. For example, sites with a history of frequent wildfires have already adapted to repeated cycles of nutrient losses and are less likely affected by prescribed burning. The ultimate effect that prescribed burning has on nutrients and soil productivity, however, cannot be estimated without understanding how the nutrient cycling process, specifically other additions and losses of nutrients from the site, is affected by all forest management practices as a system.

Introduction

Forest ecosystems are dynamic systems that circulate, transform, accumulate, and lose energy and matter. The changes in energy and matter are the result of a large number of biological, chemical, and physical processes varying over both space and time. Although many of these changes occur continuously, others occur periodically, such as daily or seasonal, or irregularly, such as following a drought or wildfire (Waring and Schlesinger 1985).

The difference between the accumulation and loss of matter in the forest is net primary production, one measure of forest productivity (Waring and Schlesinger 1985). Net primary productivity defines the productivity of the entire ecosystem rather than the growth of only one or a few species. While the growth of individual species is important when estimating forest yield or merchantable wood production, the broader definition provides a base for studying changes in ecosystem processes. Both measures of productivity are important, but we will emphasize net primary production because it is the basic productivity on which the yield of managed forests depends.

The structure and productivity of the present forests are an integration of ecosystem processes and their interactions. Although the mature and old-growth forests appear to be in a state of equilibrium, all forests are constantly changing in response to short- and long-term changes in the climate, response to past disturbances, and shifts in species dominance as a result of forest succession. Therefore, estimating how a forest management practice affects forest productivity must not only consider how a practice alters ecosystem processes but also must determine how such changes differ from natural changes and disturbances. This is particularly important with regard to the use of prescribed fire in forest ecosystems because it causes some changes similar to wildfire which has been and remains a principal cause of forest disturbance (Chapter 3; Fahnestock and Agee 1983).

All forest burning, whether wildfire or prescribed burning, changes the form, distribution, and amount of elements or nutrients in the forest ecosystem. The potential for fire to directly affect forest productivity depends on many factors, including but not limited to fire intensity and duration, absolute and relative amounts of organic matter consumed by the fire, the role or elemental cycle of specific nutrients in the forest ecosystem, and the importance of each nutrient to the growth of trees. Indirectly, fire may also affect forest nutrition by changing soil biota (Chapter 13) or increasing erosion (Chapter 14). Finally, estimates of how prescribed fire affects soil nutrition and long-term soil productivity must also consider how fire interacts with other management activities and their combined effects on nutrient cycling and site productivity (McNabb and Campbell 1985, McNabb 1988).

Considerably more information is available on the effects that fire has on soil nutrients immediately after and in the first years following burning (Raison 1979, Wells et al. 1979, Feller 1982) than is available regarding longer-term changes in nutrients and how these changes may affect site productivity (Chapter 15). Our discussion of changes in soil nutrition as a consequence of burning is limited to how the cycling of nutrients is altered by fire and how changes in soil fertility may potentially affect long-term soil productivity. We assume that long-term soil productivity, interacting with climate and topography, sets general limits to net primary plant production in forest ecosystems.

The cycling of nutrients will be discussed in detail as a foundation for understanding the changes occurring in forest nutrition as a consequence of fire. The emphasis will be on the nitrogen budget because nitrogen is the nutrient most often limiting forest growth in the region. Furthermore, our interpretation of changes in nutrient budgets as a consequence of prescribed fire considers the effects of past wildfires, harvesting, and other stand management practices on soil nutrition.

Nutrient Cycling

Nutrient budgets and pathways

Within forest ecosystems, nutrients are primarily cycled within and among the various organic components and the soil, with peripheral additions and losses of nutrients to or from the site. The amount of each nutrient and the rate that nutrients are cycled within the forest, combined with the additions and losses, define a nutrient budget for each element in the forest (Sollins et al. 1980). Figure 12-1 is a simplified example of a nitrogen budget for forests in the western Oregon Cascades.

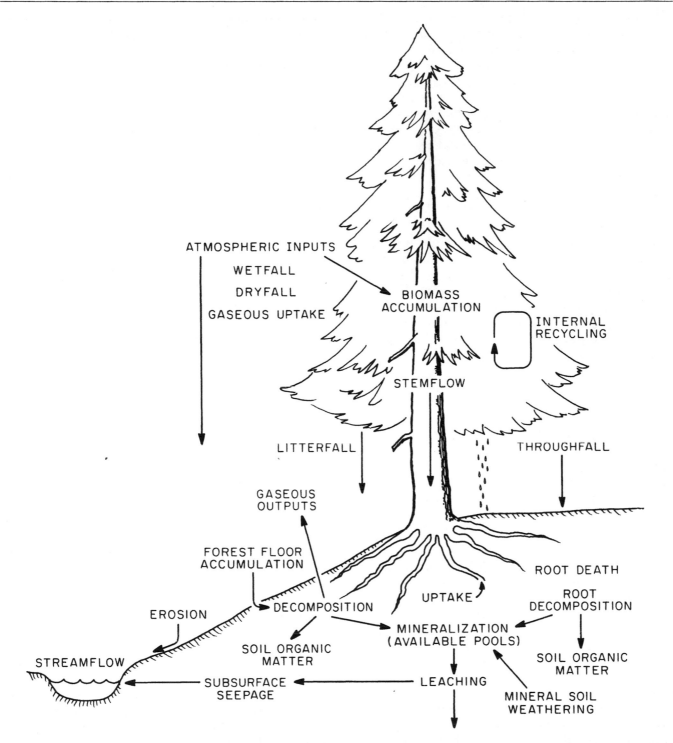

Figure 12-1. A nitrogen budget for a forest includes pools of a nutrient that are stored in the various components of the plants, forest floor, and soil, and move from one pool to another as a result of transformation processes. (Adapted from Binkley 1986) Missing from this generic budget is the input of biologically fixed nitrogen which enters the ecosystem at various locations and times depending on the species (Cromack et al. 1979). Sollins et al. (1980) contains budgets of several specific nutrients for an old-growth forest in western Oregon.

Most nutrients in a forest cycle through living plants. For example, nutrients move from the litter and soil to the roots, up the stem to the needles where some may fall as litter or move back down to produce wood and bark or grow more roots. Some nutrients, particularly in the needles, are transferred to other parts of the plant before it dies but most nutrients are retained in the dead vegetation; this material falls to the ground and accumulates on the forest floor or in the soil as organic matter. Nutrients in this organic matter only become available for plant use again following decomposition of the organic matter. The rates at which nutrients are cycled or accumulated in the plant, forest floor, or soil depend on the amount of and changes in biomass of each component, the demand by vegetation and other organisms, and rates of decomposition.

Losses of nutrients from the forest ecosystem may occur as a result of leaching into the soil or rock below the root zone, removal of litter or surface soil from the site by erosion, and gaseous losses of elements. Losses of nitrogen are typically small in the mature and old-growth forests of the Pacific Northwest; losses of cations are moderate, depending on parent material (Chapter 14; Swanson 1981, Waring and Schlesinger 1985). Losses of all nutrients increase following a disturbance, some several-fold, particularly if major erosion events like landslides are involved (Swanson 1981). Accelerated losses seldom last more than two to three decades; when averaged over the life of a mature forest, these losses normally represent only a small fraction of the total nutrient loss. The volatilization of nitrogen as gaseous compounds, and sulfur and phosphorus in lesser amounts, from the burning of organic matter represent important gaseous losses of elements (Raison et al. 1985). Harvesting and some site preparation practices also remove a significant amount of nutrients from a site (Cromack et al. 1978).

Additions of nutrients occur from deposition in precipitation and dust, weathering of rock, and fixation of atmospheric gases. The weathering of soils and rocks accounts for a substantial portion of most of the nutrients accumulated in forest ecosystems (Sollins et al. 1980) but is an insignificant source of nitrogen because only small amounts occur in rock. Nitrogen is added to Pacific Northwest forests as inorganic compounds in precipitation or dust from the atmosphere but in smaller quantities than is added to eastern forests (Fredriksen 1972, Swank and Waide 1980). The major method of nitrogen accretion in most Pacific Northwest forests is by biological nitrogen fixation (Cromack et al. 1979, Binkley 1986).

Nitrogen

Nitrogen fixation is the conversion of atmospheric nitrogen gas to organic combinations or to forms readily utilized in biological processes. Most forest ecosystems within the region contain several organisms or plant systems capable of biological nitrogen fixation. These include leguminous species, like lupines (McNabb and Geist 1979); actinorrhizal (nonleguminous) hardwoods, such as alder (Binkley 1981) and snowbrush (Youngberg and Wollum 1976, McNabb and Cromack 1983); epiphytic plants, such as lichens in the canopy of old-growth trees (Denison 1973); and bacteria in downed logs (Silvester et al. 1982). Actinorrhizal plants have the greatest potential for adding large amounts of nitrogen to a site quickly. The nitrogen in these plants becomes available to other plants as their parts decompose. On sites with several major sources of biologically fixed nitrogen, a net accretion of nitrogen may occur over several forest generations, resulting in older, residual soils containing large reservoirs of nitrogen (Gessel et al. 1972, Sollins et al. 1980).

Most elements are available in adequate quantities; otherwise, nutrient budgets would show greater retention of elements (i.e., losses would be reduced below the rate of addition) (Sollins et al. 1980). Nitrogen is the only nutrient conserved in old-growth forests where additions are estimated to be several times greater than losses. This accumulation of nitrogen suggests that nitrogen may be the limiting nutrient in forest growth. Stronger evidence that nitrogen is often limiting growth is available from regional fertilizer trials where about 70 percent of the second-growth forests respond to nitrogen fertilization (Miller et al. 1986). Thus, nitrogen is widely regarded as the nutrient most commonly limiting the growth of these forests in the Pacific Northwest (Gessel et al. 1972, Miller et al. 1976).

Nitrogen distribution in the forest ecosystems of the Pacific Northwest varies with the age of the forest and specific site conditions (Table 12-1). Biomass and nitrogen steadily increase in all above-ground components of young forests (except for large, coarse woody debris), with the relative distribution between live crown and stem remaining similar (Turner and Long 1975). Biomass and nitrogen in above-ground components continue to increase in undisturbed stands for centuries, often not reaching a maximum until the forests are 800 to 1,000 years old (Franklin and Waring 1980).

Accumulation of nitrogen and biomass above ground is limited by site quality, rate of decomposition, and wildfire frequency; less productive sites and sites with more frequent wildfire have lower accumulations. In general, the mesic forests of western Oregon and Washington have the potential for the highest accumulations because they are more productive and have a lower frequency of wildfire; the colder, higher-elevation forests have the potential for moderately high accumulations because of slower decomposition; eastern Oregon and Washington forests have moderate accumulations because of lower productivity and more frequent wildfires; and accumulations in the drier forests of southwest Oregon and northern California are primarily limited to standing trees and snags because of lower productivity, rapid decomposition, and frequent wildfires.

Nitrogen becomes available from cycling through soil organisms, oxidation by fire, precipitation, and nitrogen fertilizer. Ammonium, nitrate, and amino acids are the primary forms of available nitrogen. The concentrations present at any one time are much less than the annual requirement of forests and when summed annually the amount is only 1 to 3 percent of the total soil nitrogen (Russell 1973, Brinkley 1986). Even in the Pacific Northwest, where large amounts of nitrogen are found in soil organic matter, only about 2 percent of the nitrogen is considered available (McNabb et al. 1986).

Soil microorganisms must oxidize large amounts of organic matter, lowering the carbon/nitrogen ratio, before the nitrogen becomes available to plants. These same organisms, however, have a high demand for nitrogen to maintain the microbial populations necessary for the task. As a result, soil microorganisms temporarily immobilize nitrogen during their life cycle and reduce the amount of nitrogen available for plants. Therefore, the kinds, amounts, and timing of additions of organic matter to the forest floor and soil have a major effect on the availability of nitrogen.

Table 12-1. Biomass and nitrogen distribution in forest ecosystems of the Pacific Northwest.

Forest type	Age	Vegetation		Forest Floor		Soil	
		Biomass (ton/ac)	Nitrogen (lb/ac)	Biomass (ton/ac)	Nitrogen (lb/ac)	Organic matter (ton/ac)	Nitrogen (lb/ac)
Western Washington Douglas-fir[a]	22	62	131	9	79	—	—
	42	108	153	12	99	—	—
	73	137	164	43	256	—	—
Western Oregon Cascades Douglas-fir dominant[b]	450	320	254	118	288	50	1,650
Western Oregon Cascades[c]							
Joule	—	—	—	98	545	—	1,990
Blackeye	—	—	—	81	439	—	1,000
Western Washington second-growth Douglas-fir[d]	37	92	145	10	78	50	1,250
Central Washington mature, mixed conifer forest[e]	—	—	—	31	374	—	1,030
Southwestern British Columbia western hemlock, western redcedar, and Douglas-fir[f]	70-90	—	—	57	850	—	2,050

Sources:
[a]Turner and Long 1975, Turner 1980.
[b]Grier and Logan 1975, Sollins et al. 1980.
[c]Little and Klock 1985.
[d]Gessel et al. 1972.
[e]Grier 1975.
[f]Feller and Kimmins 1984.

Low availability of nitrogen and accumulation of organic matter in many Pacific Northwest forest ecosystems occurs because decomposition by soil microorganisms is limited by unfavorable moisture and temperature conditions for biological activity and by the high carbon/nitrogen ratio of coarse woody debris (Cromack et al. 1979). Thus, periodically reducing the amount of coarse woody debris by burning often improves the availability of nitrogen as well as other nutrients in forest ecosystems where organic matter tends to accumulate over long periods of time (Van Cleve et al. 1983).

Sulfur and phosphorus

Sulfur and phosphorus may occasionally limit forest growth in the region but the evidence is more site-specific for nitrogen. Where limitations caused by sulfur and phosphorus deficiencies occur, they often result from an interaction with nitrogen deficiencies (Turner et al. 1979, Turner and Lambert 1986). In certain cases the lack of sulfur may reduce Douglas-fir response to nitrogen fertilizer in southwest Oregon (Edmonds and Hsiang 1987) and limit response of ponderosa pine in central Oregon (Cochran 1978). Phosphorus may limit the response of western hemlock in the Coast Range to nitrogen fertilizer (Radwan and Shumway 1984).

Synopsis of current research

Nutrient cycling, soil nutrition, and the response of forests to disturbance and fertilization have been reported for numerous sites in the Pacific Northwest for over 50 years (Isaac and Hopkins 1937). The cycling of nutrients is being intensively studied in several forests of western Oregon and Washington, and detailed nutrient budgets for several elements in old-growth forests have been developed (Sollins et al. 1980). Similar budgets have also been developed for second-growth and old-growth Douglas-fir forests in western Washington (Gessel et al. 1972, Edmonds 1982). Soil fertility and Douglas-fir response to nitrogen fertilization have been reported for over a hundred locations in western Oregon and Washington (Edmonds and Hsiang 1987). This information, coupled with data from other parts of the world, is being used to develop computer models of nutrient cycles to predict forest response to management practices. These models have not been validated (Kimmins

1985), but they are useful in identifying potential changes in the nutrient cycles that may affect forest growth (Kimmins 1987).

Nutrient Losses from Burning

Nutrients are lost from a forest site during or after a fire by convection, volatilization, erosion, and leaching. In this section, the emphasis will be on nitrogen losses because they are generally larger and, as previously discussed, likely to be the most important to the growth of trees. Losses of sulfur and phosphorus will be discussed in less detail while other nutrients will only be discussed when unique factors of burning may affect their cycling.

Convection

Ash (particulate matter) transported into the atmosphere in smoke results in a loss of some nutrients. Ash is the product of nearly complete combustion of organic matter, and it contains small amounts of nitrogen but increased concentrations of cations, silica, and other less volatile elements when compared to the original fuels (Raison 1979, Raison et al. 1985). Except for nitrogen and part of the sulfur and phosphorus, ash contains most of the elements originally present in the fuels before burning. Calcium is present in the highest concentrations because of its high initial concentration and high volatilization temperature. Only during intense burns are the basic cations vaporized (Raison et al. 1985).

The proportion of ash lost to the atmosphere versus that remaining on the forest floor or soil surface depends on the fire intensity and the wind speed near the fire. Winds at the flaming front increase as fire intensity increases; these winds transport the light ash particles upward in the smoke column where surface winds then may carry these materials away from the site. The winds associated with very intense wildfires may remove most of the ash from a site. Reducing fire intensity is an important method of reducing the convective loss of nutrients during prescribed burning.

The effects that nutrients lost by convection during prescribed burning have on soil fertility is assumed to be relatively minor. Part of the ash transported aloft is deposited on adjacent forests. Over time, the loss of nutrients in ash by convection will partially be replaced from adjacent burns, but a net loss of nutrients will occur because some of the ash is transported away from the forests. These transfers of nutrients may not be fully accounted for in estimates of element deposition as dust if forest burning was not common near the collection site. Furthermore, the principal nutrients in ash seldom directly limit forest growth and are normally replenished by the natural weathering of rock (Waring and Schlesinger 1985). The convective loss of nutrients during prescribed burning would generally be much less than the loss during major wildfires; however, the absolute long-term difference would also be dependent on fire frequency.

Volatilization

Volatilization of elements occurs when temperatures are sufficiently high to convert an element into its gaseous forms. Volatilization results in the release of free elements into the atmosphere. Three elements are of primary concern—nitrogen, sulfur, and phosphorus.

Nitrogen is the most easily volatilized element during combustion because most of the nitrogen in organic matter is released as nitrogen gas or nitrogen oxides. Small amounts of ammonia- and nitrate-nitrogen begin to be released when temperatures exceed 210°F, but measurable losses of total nitrogen do not occur until temperatures exceed 400°F (Dunn and DeBano 1977). All nitrogen is lost during total combustion when temperatures remain above 900 to 1,050°F (Dunn and DeBano 1977, DeBano et al. 1979).

Estimates of nitrogen lost from prescribed burning via volatilization are highly variable, ranging from 100 to about 900 lbs per acre (Table 12-2). The higher estimates are for the forests of coastal British Columbia and involve consumption of thick forest floors (Feller et al. 1983, Feller and Kimmins 1984). Current estimates of nitrogen losses from prescribed burning in the western Oregon Cascades are in the 200 to 600 lbs per acre range (Little and Klock 1985, Little and Ohmann 1988). These estimates are for fuel management prescrip-

Table 12-2. Nitrogen mass in forest floors and losses from prescribed burning or wildfire in the Pacific Northwest. Nitrogen percentages are of the total nitrogen in the forest floor and soil.

| Site | Forest Floor | | Soil Nitrogen (0-12 in) (lb/ac) | Proportion Nitrogen Above-ground (%) | Consumed by fire | | |
| | | | | | Mass | Nitrogen Lost | |
	Mass (ton/ac)	Nitrogen (lb/ac)			(ton/ac)	Mass (lb/ac)	Total (%)
Western Oregon[a]							
Joule 11	109	1,300	2,260	36.4	43.4	−465	−13.1
Joule 12	87	890	2,070	30.0	42.1	−175	− 5.9
Blackeye 20	74	860	1,120	43.5	43.5	−380	−19.2
Blackeye 2	89	900	1,070	45.7	58.3	−215	−24.3
Southwestern British Columbia[b]							
Haney[c]	75	2,820	4,150	40.5	—	−875	−31.1
Southwestern Oregon[d]							
Spring-White	20	195	780 +48[e]	18.6	78	−150	−14.8
Western Oregon and Washington[f]							
Average 85 sites[g]	10	185	950	—	—	—	—
Central Washington[h]							
Entiat Wildfire	—	750	1,310 −80[i]	—	97	−810	−39.0

Sources and notes:
[a]Little and Klock 1985.
[b]Feller and Kimmins 1984.
[c]Soil depth was 0-25 in.
[d]McNabb, unpublished.
[e]Soil nitrogen increased significantly following burning.

[f]Edmonds and Hsiang 1987.
[g]Soil depth was 0-6 in.
[h]Grier 1975.
[i]Soil depth was 0-14 in. and a net loss of soil nitrogen was reported.

tions that included removal of coarse woody debris to reduce fire intensity, and burning when the lower part of the forest floor was wet. The smallest nitrogen loss as a consequence of prescribed fire was reported for a site in southwest Oregon where biomass of available fuels was low; hence, the absolute loss of nitrogen was small (McNabb, unpublished).

Nitrogen losses in excess of 1,000 lbs per acre are likely to occur from old-growth forests of the Cascade Mountains and Coast Range during wildfire or fall prescribed burning when the entire forest floor is dry and readily consumed (Table 12-2). Such large losses approach the total amount of nitrogen stored in the top 12 inches of soil. While these losses of nitrogen from the forest floor could change soil fertility and potentially affect site productivity, similar losses of nitrogen have most likely occurred whenever the forest was destroyed by catastrophic wildfire. Thus, when wildfire has been the natural mechanism for stand replacement, site productivity of current old-growth forests reflects periodic, major losses of site nitrogen (McNabb 1988).

Because nitrogen is volatilized at low temperatures, burning of forest fuels results in the release of nitrogen gases in direct proportion to the weight loss of the fuel (Raison et al. 1985). Thus, nitrogen losses from burning can be calculated from information on the nitrogen concentration and biomass of each type of forest fuel consumed. Nitrogen concentration of fuels varies from about 0.10 percent for logs and coarse woody debris to between 0.5 and 1.5 percent for the forest floor (Cromack et al. 1979, Edmonds and Hsiang 1987, Little and Ohmann 1988). Lower forest floor nitrogen concentrations are commonly associated with old-growth forests where the forest floors include a higher percentage of coarse woody debris. Higher nitrogen concentrations tend to occur in the more productive, second-growth forests if most of the original forest floor has been removed. Variation in the nitrogen concentration of forest floor material remains relatively unchanged following burning, however, and losses of nitrogen are generally proportional to the amount of forest floor consumed (Little and Ohmann 1988).

The nitrogen concentration and biomass of forest floor in combination determine the upper limit for nitrogen volatilization by burning of old-growth forests. Although the losses of nitrogen

from harvesting or burning old-growth forests are large, losses of nitrogen following harvesting or burning of younger forests will be much lower because the biomass in trees and forest floor of these stands will most likely be less than that in old-growth forests (Table 12-2).

However, nitrogen losses from burning the thinned forest floors of young forest will be relatively high because consumption of thin forest floors is more difficult to control (Amaranthus and McNabb 1984). The length of rotations will also affect the frequency of nitrogen losses from young stands (McNabb 1988).

Nitrogen losses from wildfires seldom have been reported although an estimate of 809 lbs per acre was made for the nitrogen lost in the 1970 Entiat Fire in central Washington (Grier 1975). This estimate also included an 80 lbs per acre loss from the soil. Some loss of soil nitrogen has been reported from severe slash burns in the past; however, these losses were limited to those portions of a site that were severely burned, generally less than 10 percent of the area (Dyrness and Youngberg 1957, Kraemer and Hermann 1979). When fire intensity is maintained within prescription, soil nitrogen is seldom affected unless the entire forest floor is dry. Thus, volatilization of soil nitrogen is considered an important factor which distinguishes the effect of wildfire on soil fertility from that of most prescribed burns.

Evidence from two sources suggests that nitrogen in woody residues and the forest floor would not be lost by changes in other nutrient cycling processes if it was not volatilized by fire. First, transport of nitrogen in solution from watersheds, including during disturbance, remains low in Pacific Northwest forests (Chapter 17; Fredriksen 1972, Swank and Waide 1980). Second, studies in Oregon have found very low rates of denitrification (the biological conversion of inorganic nitrogen to a gas during decomposition) in mature forests, although the rate may increase in some recently disturbed forests or in riparian zones (Myrold 1986, McClellan 1987). More information is needed on these potential losses of nitrogen from unburned sites to balance the numerous estimated losses from prescribed burning, harvesting, and other silvicultural treatments that may impact the nitrogen budget.

The potential for organic matter and nitrogen mass to increase above natural levels if a site is not burned depends on the ecosystem, the soil, and the natural soil-forming processes (Russell 1973). Nitrogen mass increases naturally in Pacific Northwest ecosystems where alder or ceanothus add large amounts of nitrogen by biological nitrogen fixation; but this may also occur because the soils are relatively young. Less frequent and intense prescribed burning compared to the natural fire regimes of some forest ecosystems also should allow organic residues to accumulate; accumulation on these sites is similar to the addition of organic residues to agricultural lands with a long history of cropping with minimal replacement of organic residues (Russell 1973, Lugo and Brown 1986). Because soil and site organic matter, nitrogen, and the carbon/nitrogen ratio stabilize over time (Jenny 1933, Waring and Schlesinger 1985), changes in the rate that nitrogen is added or lost would change the level at which these properties would stabilize.

Although forest productivity generally increases with site nitrogen and biomass of mesic forest ecosystems of the Pacific Northwest (McNabb 1988), the increase does not always equate to increased productivity on specific sites or other forest ecosystems. The productivity of forests also depends on the availability of that nitrogen. Less than 2 percent of the nitrogen in surface soil of mesic forest types is available in western Oregon (McNabb et al. 1986). The importance of nitrogen availability to forest growth is illustrated by the following:

- higher site qualities are associated with lower soil carbon/nitrogen ratios;
- increased response to nitrogen fertilizer as the carbon/nitrogen ratio of the soil and forest floor increases; and
- the significant response of stands fertilized with 200 lbs per acre nitrogen when the sites contain 10 to 20 times that amount (Peterson et al. 1984, Edmonds and Hsiang 1987).

Fire changes the availability of nitrogen, as well as other nutrients, as a consequence of its effect on the carbon/nitrogen ratio. Burning can decrease the total nitrogen and organic matter biomass on a site while increasing available nitrogen and the growth of young forests (Burger and Pritchett 1988). Disturbance of Pacific Northwest forests generally increases nitrate-nitrogen and ammonium as is evident from stream water chemistry (Fredriksen et al. 1975, Tiedemann et al. 1978,

Wells et al. 1979, Sollins et al. 1981), but direct measures of increased availability of nitrogen following burning are inconsistent (Van Cleve and Dyrness 1983, McNabb unpublished). Burning is most likely to increase nitrogen availability in colder forest types where slow decomposition causes nutrients to accumulate in the forest floor; burning of these forest floors can increase the availability of all nutrients, including nitrogen. In contrast, if a burn consumes the forest floor and portions of the soil organic matter, availability of nitrogen is anticipated to decrease.

Sulfur is volatilized at slightly higher temperatures but in much smaller quantities than nitrogen when forest residues are burned. Some sulfur is retained in the ash, but losses increase from 30 to 70 percent as the temperature of combustion increases (Tiedemann and Anderson 1980). Few estimates of sulfur volatilization from burning have been reported but during underburning of ponderosa pine stands in central Oregon, sulfur losses ranged from 12 to 17 lbs per acre when nitrogen losses averaged about 190 lbs per acre (Nissley et al. 1980, Tiedemann and Anderson 1980). Because sulfur and nitrogen are closely linked in physiological processes, the loss of sulfur relative to the loss of nitrogen is in the same range, between 5 and 9 percent of the nitrogen content.

A detailed nutrient budget for sulfur has not been developed, in part because of the difficulty in developing fast and reliable analytical techniques. In addition, the movement of sulfate through the ecosystem is chemically similar to nitrate, which has been intensively studied, and relatively large amounts of sulfur are specifically adsorbed by soils in unavailable forms. The sulfur cycle differs from the nitrogen cycle with regard to how sulfur accumulates in forest ecosystems. Most important, sulfur, unlike nitrogen, cannot be fixed by biological processes, but is primarily added to sites in precipitation resulting from burning fossil fuels, a component of acid rain, and volcanic eruption.

Sulfur is an important component of gases emitted from volcanoes during an eruption but is present in parent rocks in only small amounts. Sulfur deficiencies have been documented in several of the volcanic soils of eastern Oregon and Washington (Cochran 1978, Tiedemann and Anderson 1980). A lack of sulfur may also be limiting the response of Douglas-fir to nitrogen fertilizer in southwest Oregon (Edmonds and Hsiang 1987), although a significant response to sulfur fertilization in conjunction with nitrogen fertilization has not been observed. If the loss of sulfur does become more limiting of forest growth, the relatively small amounts removed can more easily be replaced with fertilizer than can nutrients such as nitrogen or the basic cations.

Phosphorus is another nutrient which is easily volatilized because of its moderate temperature of volatilization (Raison 1979). Phosphorus is present in concentrations of approximately 20 percent of the nitrogen concentration (Sollins et al. 1980). Burning can remove up to 60 percent of that present in the fuels (Raison et al. 1985). Nutrient budgets have been developed for phosphorus in old-growth Douglas-fir that suggest relatively small additions and losses from the ecosystem (Cole et al. 1967, Sollins et al. 1980). Geochemical additions of phosphorus to the budget appear small, because phosphorus is very insoluble in soil and water.

Phosphorus nutrition of most conifers is not generally considered a serious problem because mycorrihizal fungi are effective at extracting it from soils that are not phosphorus deficient and making it available to trees (Chapter 13; Read 1987), but phosphorus is low in many Coast Range soils (Radwan and Shumway 1984). Results of several fertilization studies indicate that phosphorus may indirectly limit response to nitrogen fertilizers, particularly of western hemlock. Fertilizer response is most often or best correlated to the extractable phosphorus in the forest floor, which supplies a majority of the available phosphorus (Heilman and Ekuan 1980); burning of forest floors may further reduce phosphorus availability on these sites.

Other nutrients. Depending on their vaporization temperatures, some calcium, magnesium, and potassium may be volatilized during high-intensity burns (Raison et al. 1985). The loss of potassium is higher because of a lower vaporization temperature; however, the greatest potential is for convective loss of these nutrients during very intense fires. Grier (1975) estimated losses of calcium, magnesium, and potassium from the Entiat Fire in north central Washington at 67, 30, and 277 lbs per acre, respectively. These were 11, 15, and 39 percent respectively of the total measured on the site. These nutrients were measured as the amount of exchangeable cations in the soil, which is only a few percent of the total amount present in soil minerals. In the case of potassium, exchangeable potassium is generally less than 2 percent of the total present (Russell 1973).

The loss of basic cations is not regarded as a serious consequence of prescribed fire because cations are primarily found in the inorganic soil fraction rather than organic matter. Comparing the amount of cations in organic matter with the exchangeable cations in the soil seriously underestimates the ability of cations to weather from rock. In the Pacific Northwest, the supply of these nutrients from rock is relatively high in young forest soils throughout the region because most rocks, particularly the basic igneous rocks, are high in these minerals and their release by chemical weathering, as opposed to mechanical weathering in colder climates, is more rapid.

Leaching

Leaching of nutrients, fine organic matter, and soil particles in solution downward through the soil and into the groundwater and streams is another process by which nutrients are lost from watersheds. Nutrients leached below the rooting zone or entering streams are unavailable for plant uptake. In the Pacific Northwest, the concentration of nutrients transported in streamflow from undisturbed forest watersheds is substantially less than transported from most other temperate forest ecosystems (Fredriksen et al. 1975, Swank and Waide 1980).

Nutrient leaching is often higher following forest disturbance because nutrient uptake by vegetation is reduced, accelerated decomposition may cause a large release of nutrients, or disturbance by fire releases nutrients in an elemental form (Fredricksen et al. 1975, Swank and Waide 1980, Binkley 1986). For example, the large amounts of cations remaining in ash following a fire are readily soluble or easily transported by water into the soil. The leaching of nitrogen from ash, however, is negligible because most of it was volatilized during the fire (Grier 1975).

While cations are readily transported from ash into the soil, their concentration decreases rapidly as they become attached to clay and organic matter particles (Wells et al. 1979). Over time, cations such as calcium, which are relatively insoluble compounds of oxides and carbonates when entering the soil, are converted to more soluble bicarbonates in acid forest soils. This conversion results in higher concentrations of soluble cations moving deeper into the soil. As a result, losses of cations by leaching following fire may increase several-fold; however, this loss is much smaller than the loss of nitrogen which is less easily attached to soil particles (Grier 1975).

Burning generally increases ammonium in the soil and, to a lesser extent, nitrates; nitrates are the most easily leached form of nitrogen, while ammonium is a cation which is adsorbed onto clay and organic matter particles. The production of nitrates in soil following burning may also be reduced because burning often reduces the population of ammonium-oxidizing *Nitrosomonas* bacteria in the soil; these bacteria are responsible for nitrate production (Chapter 13; Dunn et al. 1979, Wells et al. 1979).

The concentrations and amounts of nutrients leached from the soil following disturbance is several-fold greater than in undisturbed forests, but the total lost remains small because nutrient leaching from undisturbed Pacific Northwest forest soils is very low to begin with (Fredriksen et al. 1975, Swank and Waide 1980, Feller and Kimmins 1984). For example, nitrogen is one of the more mobile nutrients in soil but increases in nitrate-nitrogen in streamflow following a wildfire in eastern Oregon failed to exceed federal standards for municipal use of the water (Tiedemann et al. 1978). The total amount of nitrate-nitrogen lost in solution from watersheds in the Pacific Northwest is less than the amount added in precipitation. The majority of the nitrogen leached from the soil is in the form of soluble organic materials (Fredriksen et al. 1975, Tiedemann et al. 1978, Sollins et al. 1981). Higher amounts of nitrogen may also be lost in eroded sediments transported in streams (Chapter 14; Fredriksen et al. 1975).

Prescribed burning has less effect on leaching of nitrogen than other types of disturbance. Leaching of nitrogen increases with increasing soil depth when the forest floor remains intact but vegetation is killed (Sollins et al. 1981). Harvesting of old-growth forests also increases the transport of nitrogen in streams but the amount of nitrate lost following harvesting and prescribed burning is less than when harvested sites are left unburned (Wells et al. 1979, Martin and Harr 1989).

The potential for nutrients to be lost by leaching is greatly reduced by the rapid revegetation of most burned sites (Gholz et al. 1985). This vegetation is effective in reestablishing the nutrient cycle and establishing a demand for soil nutrients which could otherwise be leached from the soil. Many species are particularly well adapted for this purpose by being prolific seed producers, having vigorous rates of growth, and high demands for nutrients (Chapter 4; Dyrness 1973).

Because nitrogen is conserved in Pacific Northwest forests, leaching losses of nitrogen are consistently less than those reported for temperate forests in other regions (Swank and Waide 1980). The importance of this conservation of nutrients is even more striking given the large losses of nitrogen by fire and additions by biological fixation which can occur in these forest ecosystems over a period of a few years (Table 12-2, Cromack et al. 1978, Youngberg and Wollum 1976, Binkley et al. 1982).

Natural versus Prescribed Fire

Natural wildfires, particularly conflagrations that burn hundreds to thousands of acres, have a far greater potential to seriously affect soil fertility than current prescribed burns or many wildfires caused by humans because the weather is usually more severe and fuel moistures are normally lower. Understanding the effect these fires have had on nutrient budgets and forest growth and development is necessary for interpreting how prescribed burning or the exclusion of fire will affect the growth of future forests (McNabb 1988). Although a few differences between wildfire and prescribed fire have already been mentioned, a more comprehensive discussion of wildfire is needed before the potential of prescribed burning to affect forest productivity can be adequately addressed.

For similar amounts of fuels, natural wildfires often have much higher fire intensities than prescribed fires. The fire duration may be longer during wildfire when the forest floor is dry. Wildfires may also burn through an area, desiccating the vegetation and wetter fuels, and reburn a few hours or days later with greater intensity. Because wildfires generally occur when the soils are driest, soil temperatures will be higher during the fire, causing soil organic matter as well as stumps and roots in the soil to burn. Thus, consumption of soil organic matter is an important distinguishing factor between the effects of natural wildfires on soil fertility and those of most prescribed burns.

Because of the increased fire intensity and the winds which the fire can generate, convective loss of all nutrients is more likely to be higher in wildfires than prescribed burns. Higher fire intensities also increase the vaporization of nutrients. As a result, the proportion of phosphorus and potassium in particulate forms that remain on the site or return to the ground in ashfall increases as fire intensity decreases (Raison et al. 1985).

A wildfire frequency varying from 15 to more than 1,000 years in the Pacific Northwest (Chapter 3) must also be considered when estimating the effect of prescribed burning on soil fertility. Frequent wildfires burn less intensely and may consume the forest floor without destroying the forests, or only portions of the overstory, whereas infrequent wildfire may volatilize a high percentage of the nutrients stored above ground as well as some in the soil. As a result, frequent wildfires are considered less damaging to site productivity than infrequent, more intense, conflagrations (Waring and Schlesinger 1985).

Because wildfire has been an important factor in the periodic replacement of many of the forests in the Pacific Northwest, periodic losses of nutrients from a site by these fires must be considered when establishing the base from which to predict the future effects of prescribed burning on soil fertility and long-term forest productivity (McNabb 1988).

Prescribed Fires & Soil Fertility

Although prescribed fire results in the loss of some nutrients, the potential for these losses to reduce long-term soil fertility and productivity depends on more than whether the site is burned. Factors which must be considered include the current nutrient budget, the effects of past disturbance on the budget, how other management practices affect the nutrient budget, and the magnitude of the losses from prescribed burning and other practices or alternatives. Our emphasis on the nutrient budget provides a basis for understanding the productivity of the present forest and how the forest will most likely respond to disturbance.

Most of the centuries-old forests of the Pacific Northwest are accreting nitrogen mass from the many different sources of biological nitrogen fixation since they were last replaced by a catastrophic disturbance, most often wildfire. Although some fixation occurred coincident with forest regeneration, substantial additions have occurred to all forests after the first 50 to 100 years, which are the common ages for measuring site productivity. Thus, current levels of site nitrogen in old-growth forests are higher than those present when the forest was young. If this accumulated nitrogen would eventually become available to a young forest following only the harvest of old-growth, soil productivity of the young forest would theoretically be higher than presently measured (McNabb 1988).

Because of the amount of nitrogen accumulating in most old-growth forest ecosystems since the forest regenerated, volatilization of nitrogen in a single prescribed burning of old-growth residues is not anticipated to reduce soil and site productivity below that of the harvested old-growth forest. In fact, prescribed burning which leaves a portion of the forest floor intact and protects the soil organic matter should theoretically still have higher site nitrogen than initially present when the old-growth forest became established after wildfire.

The potential for prescribed burning to affect soil fertility and productivity following the harvest of second-growth forests and subsequent rotations depends on the frequency and severity of prescribed burning versus wildfire (McNabb 1988). The severity of prescribed fires in young forests will be lessened because of smaller accumulations of coarse woody debris and other forest floor material. Greater tree utilization and less defective timber will also reduce fire severity. In forests where wildfires are infrequent, such as the more moist areas of western Oregon and Washington, site nitrogen may be reduced by repeated burning on short rotations of 40 to 60 years unless nitrogen-fixing trees or shrubs are part of early plant succession or nitrogen fertilizers are used. In contrast, where wildfires are frequent but rotations longer, such as the drier portions of southwest Oregon, nitrogen and organic matter may begin to accumulate in these forests if some forest floor is left intact, wildfires are excluded, and the frequency of prescribed burning is less than that for historical wildfires.

Nitrogen losses from prescribed burning are but one change in the nitrogen budget of forest ecosystems as they are harvested, reforested, and managed on shorter rotations than old-growth forests. Nitrogen is also lost during harvesting in nearly direct proportion to the weight of the timber harvested. These losses are estimated to range between 100 and 600 lbs per acre, depending on the volume harvested. The higher losses are for old-growth forests while the lower amounts are for less productive sites with smaller volumes available for harvest. Whole-tree harvesting where all above-ground components are utilized would approximately double the amount of nitrogen removed as compared to the amount in the bole; losses of other nutrients would likewise be higher (Kimmins 1987).

Machine piling of slash and other debris before burning can adversely affect site productivity. Because of increased fire intensity, the loss of nutrients, particularly phosphorus, potassium, and sulfur, from burning piles is anticipated to be higher than when the fuels are broadcast burned. Furthermore, the nutrients remaining after burning are no longer uniformly distributed across the site; this causes microsite differences in the nutrient budget and site productivity. Machine piling can also compact and displace soil which may further reduce the productivity of the site (McNabb and Campbell 1985).

Although we have concentrated on nitrogen losses from burning as a means whereby productivity can be reduced, other forest practices can compound or ameliorate the effect of fire on nutrient budgets. Specifically, management practices that increase the frequency of disturbance relative to the frequency of natural disturbance (e.g., shorter rotations) and that reduce additions of nitrogen (e.g., elimination of nitrogen-fixing plants) are most likely to reduce forest productivity. Rotations of about 100 years or less eliminate most of the nitrogen fixation by the epiphytic plant community because of the dense forest canopies and the slow expansion of these life-forms in the canopy. Shorter rotations and "complete" harvesting of timber will also eliminate most of the nitrogen fixation in downed logs and coarse woody debris, although part of the nitrogen added by this process is lost whenever wildfire consumes most or all of the forest floor; the net effect of these changes on the nitrogen budget is uncertain.

The greatest change that forest management may have on nitrogen budgets is how alder, ceanothus, and legumes are treated in those forest eco-systems where they occur (Cromack et al. 1979, McNabb and Geist 1979, Binkley 1986). These species generally only dominate a site following fire and have the potential to add more nitrogen to a site than is lost during burning. In fact, if these species are present every rotation, they potentially are capable of adding more nitrogen to the ecosystem over five rotations of 100 years than the total estimated for a 500-year-old forest from all sources (Cromack et al. 1979). The eradication or severe reduction of alder or ceanothus (because they compete with conifer seedlings) eliminates this potentially important source of nitrogen. Fortunately, vegetation management practices can be used to temporarily suppress these species without jeopardizing their long-term contributions to sustaining ecosystem productivity.

Forest productivity is most likely reduced on those sites where prescribed burning volatilizes large amounts of nitrogen, the rotation is much shorter than the natural disturbance of previous old-growth forests, and seral, nitrogen-fixing plant species are eliminated. These sites are typically of moderate to high productivity and are found in the Coast Range and Western Cascades of Oregon and Washington. Elsewhere, additions and losses of nitrogen from all sources are generally much less, the natural disturbance of the sites more frequent, and the rotations longer. Thus, site-specific interpretations of how all management practices affect nutrient budgets are necessary before the effect of a specific practice, such as prescribed burning, on forest productivity can be determined.

Reducing Nutrient Losses from Prescribed Fire

Managing prescribed burning to reduce nutrient losses is an important goal for limiting its potential adverse effects on soil fertility. Several effective techniques are available for accomplishing this goal. Most of the techniques are also compatible with achieving other resource protection objectives such as reducing the potential for erosion and adverse effects on water and air quality.

The most important criterion for reducing nutrient losses from prescribed burning is to minimize the loss of forest floor. Limiting the consumption of the forest floor is critical because it has the highest nitrogen concentration of any dead fuel. As pointed out previously, nitrogen is lost in direct proportion to the weight loss of the fuel (Raison et al. 1985).

Several techniques are effective in reducing consumption of the forest floor (Chapter 22). Burning when the forest floor is wet and the remaining fuels are dry enough to burn greatly reduces the consumption of the forest floor. A forest floor with a moisture content less than about 30 percent will burn until consumed without addition of heat from other fuels (Sandberg 1980). Thus, burning in the winter, spring, or early summer when the forest floor is wet consumes much less forest floor than late summer or fall burning. In the fall, although the surface of the duff may be moistened by early rains, the underlying duff often remains dry and is readily consumed once it is ignited.

Removing large, unmerchantable logs during harvesting reduces some of the fuels that when burned, dry the forest floor, allowing greater consumption (Sandberg 1983). This condition exists when the forest floor is moist and results in the loss of an additional ton of forest floor for each ton of coarse woody debris consumed during a prescribed burn. Unfortunately, several tons of unmerchantable material must be removed to save a ton of forest floor because generally only the outside of the logs burn. The net loss of nitrogen, however, will often be less because the nitrogen concentration of the forest floor is 5 to 15 times greater than that of the material removed. Removal of coarse woody debris prior to prescribed burning is also an effective technique for reducing particulate emissions (Sandberg 1983); however, it does result in large losses of coarse woody debris that may be important to long-term forest productivity (Chapter 13). Burning in the spring or early summer when the large woody debris is still wet is often the better alternative, reducing consumption while retaining the coarse woody debris.

Nitrogen losses can be reduced by burning within a prescription which limits the fire intensity or uses burning techniques that minimize the preheating and drying of the fuels (Chapters 5 and 22). Our increasing knowledge of fire behavior and ability to control fire intensity have resulted in greater control of fuel consumption and reduced the loss of site nitrogen. Thus, it is generally possible to use prescribed fire to burn only those fuels which represent the greatest hazard without consuming excessive amounts of biomass, including

coarse woody debris. As a result, burning within prescriptions achieving a low to moderate fire intensity results in lower nitrogen losses than are common to wildfires or appear in earlier estimates of losses from less well-controlled prescribed burns (Little and Klock 1985, Little and Ohmann 1988).

Mass ignition techniques, like using the helitorch to rapidly ignite fuels over a large area, can also reduce consumption of forest floor when used to create a low to moderate fire intensity. Mass ignition allows fuels to be burned when they are too wet for hand ignition; this reduces the duration of both the flaming front and the smoldering phase (Chapter 16). As a result, the consumption of wet forest floors can be greatly reduced.

Although burning prescriptions can be prepared that consistently limit the consumption of fuels and consequently conserve site nitrogen, implementation of these prescriptions must also meet air quality objectives as well (Chapter 20). Air quality restrictions with respect to the days available for burning, the distribution and location of units, and the amount of fuels involved are higher priority constraints on prescribed burning than is minimizing the loss of site nitrogen. As a result, prescribed burning to meet silvicultural and air quality objectives often results in a higher loss of site nitrogen than otherwise because burning conditions are less than optimum for achieving the minimum fuel consumption.

Conclusion

Understanding the dynamics and changes in nutrient cycles for each forest site is crucial to managing the forest and soil fertility so as to minimize the loss of nutrients from the site and any consequential effects on long-term soil productivity. Historical estimates of additions and losses, in conjunction with the current nutrient budget of the forest, provide the foundation from which to estimate how forest management activities such as prescribed burning interact with other management practices and change the cycling of nutrients in managed versus natural forest ecosystems.

Nitrogen, and to a lesser extent sulfur and phosphorus, are the elements normally lost during prescribed burning. If consumption is controlled, losses of these nutrients are less in prescribed burns than from wildfire, particularly direct losses from the soil. Nitrogen losses are highest in old-growth forests with thick forest floors; losses from burning second-growth forests and future rotations will be much less because of less time between prescribed burns for forest floor material to accumulate. More information on nitrogen losses from prescribed burning would be useful; however, most losses occur from the forest floor in direct proportion to the amount consumed which can be estimated relatively easily with data on the amount of biomass consumed and the nitrogen concentration of the material. The most serious research question is to determine what becomes of the nitrogen on sites which are not burned and how much of it eventually becomes available to trees.

The greatest changes in the nitrogen budget of the more productive forests of western Oregon and Washington will not come from the losses of nitrogen during prescribed burning but rather from the effects of forest management practices on additions of nitrogen from the various sources of biological nitrogen fixation and removals by harvesting. Managing these forests to reduce nitrogen losses from prescribed burning will become even more important. Reducing nitrogen losses from other forest ecosystems in the Pacific Northwest will also be important because proportionately more of the site nitrogen will accumulate above ground in second and later generation forests.

Past information on long-term changes in soil organic matter and nitrogen has come primarily from agricultural research sites (Russell 1973). Current data for such changes in Pacific Northwest forests range from 10 to 50 years at a few sites, which is not yet enough time to include a complete stand rotation. More reference sites are needed, particularly in managed forests, where the amounts of organic matter and nitrogen in the various components, particularly the soil and forest floor, are documented with statistically sound sampling designs. Both burned and unburned sites should be established. These sites will eventually provide data to validate computer models of changes in nutrient budgets.

The technology for conducting prescribed fires has progressed dramatically in recent years so that the effects of prescribed fire on soil fertility are generally less than previously reported. A prescribed fire in managed forests will typically volatilize fewer nutrients than are lost from old-growth forests. Further reduction of nutrient losses from

prescribed fire will occur regardless of forest type if burning prescriptions and operations continue to use lower fire intensities to achieve other resource objectives. The long-term consequences of nutrient losses from prescribed fire on forest productivity will ultimately depend on frequency and intensity and on how prescribed fire interacts with other silvicultural practices to affect soil fertility.

Literature Cited & Key References

Amaranthus, M., and D.H. McNabb. 1984. Bare soil exposure following logging and prescribed burning in southwest Oregon, p. 234-237. *In* New Forests for a Changing World. Proc., Soc. Amer. Foresters Nat. Conv., Portland, OR. 640 p.

Binkley, D. 1981. Nodule biomass and acetylene reduction rates of red alder and Sitka alder on Vancouver Island. Can. J. For. Res. 5:215-227.

*Binkley, D. 1986. Forest Nutrition Management. John Wiley and Sons, New York. 290 p.

*Binkley, D., K. Cromack, Jr., and R.L. Fredricksen. 1982. Nitrogen accretion and availability in some snowbrush ecosystems. For. Sci. 28:720-724.

Burger, J.A., and W.L. Pritchett. 1988. Site preparation effects on soil moisture and available nutrients in a pine plantation in the Florida flatwoods. For. Sci. 34:77-87.

Cochran, P.H. 1978. Response of pole-size ponderosa pine stand to nitrogen, phosphorus, and sulfur. USDA For. Serv., Pac. Northwest For. Rge. Exp. Sta., Portland, OR. Res. Note PNW-319. 7 p.

Cole, D.W., S.P. Gessel, and S.F. Dice. 1967. Distribution and cycling of nitrogen, phosphorus, potassium and calcium in a second-growth Douglas-fir ecosystem, p. 197-232. *In* Symp., 13 Annu. Mtg., Am. Assoc. Advance. Sci. Univ. of Maine Press, Orono.

Cromack, K., Jr., C.C. Delwiche, and D.H. McNabb. 1979. Prospects and problems of nitrogen management using symbiotic nitrogen fixers, p. 210-223. *In* Gordon, J.C., C.T. Wheeler, and D.A. Perry (eds.) Proc., Workshop on symbiotic nitrogen fixation in the management of temperate forests, April 2-5, 1979. For. Res. Lab., Oregon State Univ., Corvallis, OR. 501 p.

*Cromack, K., Jr., F.J. Swanson, and C.C. Grier. 1978. A comparison of harvesting methods and their impact on soils and environment in the Pacific Northwest, p. 449-515. *In* Youngberg, C.T. (ed.) Forest Soils and Land Use. Proc., Fifth North Amer. Forest Soils Conf., Colorado State Univ., Ft. Collins, CO. 623 p.

References marked by an asterisk are recommended for general information.

DeBano, L.F., R.M. Rice, and C.E. Conrad. 1979. Soil heating in chaparral fires: Effects on soil properties, plant nutrients, and runoff. USDA For. Serv., Pac. Southwest For. Rge. Exp. Sta., Berkeley, CA. Res. Pap. PSW-145. 21 p.

Denison, W.C. 1973. Life in tall trees. Sci. Amer. 228:74-80.

*Dunn, P.H., and L.F. DeBano. 1977. Fire's effect on biological and chemical properties of chaparral soils, p. 75-84. USDA For. Serv., Washington, DC. Gen. Tech. Rep. WO-3.

Dunn, P.H., L.F. DeBano, and G.E. Eberlein. 1979. Effects of burning on chaparral soils. II. Soil microbes and nitrogen mineralization. Soil Sci. Soc. Am. J. 43:509-514.

*Dyrness, C.T. 1973. Early stages of plant succession following logging and burning in the western Cascades of Oregon. Ecol. 54:57-69.

Dyrness, C.T., and C.T. Youngberg. 1957. The effect of logging and slash-burning on soil structure. Soil Sci. Soc. Am. Proc. 21:444-447.

Edmonds, R.L. (ed.). 1982. Analysis of coniferous forest ecosystems in the western United States. US/IBP Synth. Ser. No. 14. Hutchinson Ross Publ. Co., Stroudsburg, PA. 419 p.

Edmonds, R.L., and T. Hsiang. 1987. Forest floor and soil influence on response of Douglas-fir to urea. Soil Sci. Soc. Amer. J. 51:1332-1337.

Fahnestock, G.R., and J.K. Agee. 1983. Biomass consumption and smoke production by prehistoric and modern forest fires in western Washington. J. For. 81:653-657.

*Feller, M.C. 1982. The ecological effects of slashburning with particular reference to British Columbia: A literature review. Ministry of Forests Land Mgmt., Prov. British Columbia, Victoria, B.C. Rep. 13. 60 p.

Feller, M.C., and J.P. Kimmins. 1984. Effects of clearcutting and slash burning on streamwater chemistry and watershed nutrient budgets in southwestern British Columbia. Water Resources Res. 20:29-40.

Feller, M.C., J.P. Kimmins, and K.M. Tsze. 1983. Nutrient losses to the atmosphere during slash burns in southwestern British Columbia. Fire For. Meteorol. Conf. Proc. 7:128-135.

Franklin, J.F., and R.H. Waring. 1980. Distinctive features of the northwestern coniferous forest: Development, structure, and function, p. 59-86. *In* Waring, R.H. (ed.) Forests: Fresh Perspectives from Ecosystem Analysis, Proc., 40th Annu. Biol. Colloq., Oregon State Univ. Press, Corvallis, OR. 199 p.

Fredriksen, R.L. 1972. Nutrient budget of a Douglas-fir forest on an experimental watershed in western Oregon, p. 115-131. *In* Franklin, J.F., L.J. Dempster, and R.H. Waring. (eds.) Proc.—Research on coniferous forest ecosystems—a symp. USDA For. Serv., Pac. Northwest For. Rge. Exp. Sta., Portland, OR. 322 p.

Fredriksen, R.L., D.G. Moore, and L.A. Norris. 1975. The impact of timber harvest, fertilization, and herbicide treatment on streamwater quality in western Oregon and Washington, p. 283-313. *In* Bernier, B., and C.H. Winget (eds.) Proc., Fourth North Amer. Forest Soils Conf. 1973. Laval Univ. Presses, Laval Univ., Quebec. 675 p.

Gessel, S.P., D.W. Cole, and E.C. Steinbrenner. 1972. Nitrogen balances in forest ecosystems of the Pacific Northwest. Soil Biol. Biochem. 5:19-34.

Gholz, H.L., G.M. Hawk, A. Campbell, and K. Cromack, Jr. 1985. Early vegetation recovery and element cycles on a clearcut watershed in western Oregon. Can. J. For. Res. 15:400-409.

*Grier, C.C. 1975. Wildfire effects on nutrient distribution and leaching in a coniferous ecosystem. Can. J. For. Res. 5:599-607.

Grier, C.C., and R.S. Logan. 1975. Old-growth *Pseudotsuga menziesii* communities of a western Oregon watershed: biomass distribution and production budgets. Ecol. Monogr. 47:373-400.

Heilman, P.E., and G. Ekuan. 1980. Phosphorus response of western hemlock seedlings on Pacific coastal soils from Washington. Soil Sci. Soc. Am. J. 44:392-395.

Isaac, L.A., and H.G. Hopkins. 1937. The forest soil of the Douglas-fir region and the changes wrought upon it by logging and slash burning. Ecol. 18:264-279.

Jenny, H. 1933. Soil fertility losses under Missouri conditions. Univ. Missouri, Columbia, MO. College Agri. Agri. Exp. Sta. Bull. 324. 10 p.

Kimmins, J.P. 1985. Future shock in forest yield forecasting: The need for a new approach. For. Chron. 61:503-512.

*Kimmins, J.P. 1987. Forest Ecology. MacMillan Publ. Co., New York. 531 p.

*Kraemer, J.F., and R.K. Hermann. 1979. Broadcast burning: 25-year effects on forest soils in the western flanks of the Cascade Mountains. For. Sci. 25:427-439.

*Little, S.N., and G.O. Klock. 1985. The influence of residue removal and prescribed fire on distributions of forest nutrients. USDA For. Serv., Pac. Northwest For. Rge. Exp. Sta., Portland, OR. Res. Pap. PNW-338. 12 p.

Little, S.N., and I.L. Ohmann. 1988. Estimating nitrogen lost from forest floor during prescribed fires in Douglas-fir/western hemlock clearcuts. For. Sci. 34:152-164.

Lugo, A.E., and S. Brown. 1986. Steady state terrestrial ecosystems and the global carbon cycle. Vegetatio 68:83-90.

Mahendrappa, M.K., N.W. Foster, G.F. Weetman, and H.H. Krause. 1986. Nutrient cycling and availability in forest soils. Can. J. Soil Sci. 66:547-572.

Martin, C.W., and R.D. Harr. 1989. Logging of mature Douglas-fir in western Oregon has little effect on nutrient output budgets. Can. J. For. Res. 19:35-43.

McClellan, M. 1987. Denitrification potentials in the riparian zone of the H.J. Andrews forest. M.S. thesis. Oregon State Univ., Corvallis, OR.

McNabb, D.H. 1988. Interpreting the effects of broadcast burning on forest productivity, p. 89-103. *In* Lousier, D., and G. Stills (eds.) Degradation of Forested Lands—Forest Soils at Risk, Proc., Tenth B.C. Soil Science Workshop, Feb. 20-21, 1986. British Columbia Ministry of Forests, Land Management Report 56, Victoria, B.C. 331 p.

McNabb, D.H., and R.G. Campbell. 1985. Quantifying the impacts of forestry activities on soil productivity, p. 116-120. *In* Foresters' Future: Leaders or Followers? Proc., Soc. Amer. Natl. Conv., Ft. Collins, CO.

McNabb, D.H., and K. Cromack, Jr. 1983. Dinitrogen fixation by a mature *Ceanothus velutinus* (Dougl.) stand in the western Oregon Cascades. Can. J. Microbiol. 29:1014-1021.

McNabb, D.H., and J.M. Geist. 1979. Nitrogen fixation potential of native lupines in western conifer ecosystems, p. 217. Agronomy Abstr., 1979 Annu. Mtg., Amer. Soc. Agron., Fort Collins, CO.

McNabb, D.H., K. Cromack, Jr., and R.L. Fredricksen. 1986. Variability of nitrogen and carbon in surface soils of six forest types in the Oregon Cascades. Soil Sci. Soc. Am. J. 50:1037-1041.

Miller, R.E., G.W. Clendenen, and D. Bruce. 1986. Using nitrogen fertilizers in management of coast Douglas-fir, p. 290-303. *In* Stand Management for the Future, Proc. of the Symp., June 18-20, 1985. Coll. For. Resour. Contrib. 55, Univ. Washington, Seattle, WA.

*Miller, R.E., D.P. Lavender, and C.C. Grier. 1976. Nutrient cycling in the Douglas-fir type—Silvicultural implications, p. 359-390. *In* Proc., 1975 Annu. Conv., Soc. Amer. For., Washington, DC.

Myrold, D. 1986. Relationship between nitrogen cycling and net primary production in the coniferous forest ecosystems of Oregon, p. 39. *In* Abstr. Fourth Int. Symp. Microbiol. Ecol. Syracuse, NY.

Nissley, S.D., R.J. Zasoski, and R.E. Martin. 1980. Nutrient changes after prescribed surface burning of Oregon ponderosa pine stands. Fire For. Meteorol. Conf. Proc. 6:214-219.

Peterson, C.E., P.J. Ryan, and S.P. Gessel. 1984. Response of northwest Douglas-fir stand to urea: Correlations with forest soil properties. Soil Sci. Soc. Am. J. 48:162-169.

Radwan, M.A., and J.S. Shumway. 1984. Site index and selected soil properties in relation to response of Douglas-fir and western hemlock to nitrogen fertilizer, p. 89-104. *In* Stone, E.L. (ed.) Forest Soils and Treatment Impacts. Proc., Sixth North Amer. Forest Soils Conf., June 1983. Univ. of Tennessee, Knoxville, TN. 454 p.

*Raison, R.J. 1979. Modification of the soil environment by vegetation fires, with particular reference to nitrogen transformations: A review. Plant Soil 51:73-108.

Raison, R.J., P.K. Khanna, and P.V. Woods. 1985. Mechanisms of element transfer to the atmosphere during vegetation fires. Can. J. For. Res. 15:132-140.

Read, D.J. 1987. In support of Frank's organic nitrogen theory. Angew. Botanik 61:25-37.

*Russell, E.W. 1973. Soil Conditions and Plant Growth. 10th edition. Longman Group Limited, New York. 849 p.

Sandberg, D.V. 1980. Duff reduction by prescribed underburning in Douglas-fir. USDA For. Serv., Pac. Northwest For. Rge. Exp. Sta., Portland, OR. Res. Pap. PNW-272. 18 p.

Sandberg, D.V. 1983. Research leads to less smoke from prescribed fires, p. 107-121. *In* Proc., 1983 Annual Meeting, Northwest Forest Fire Council, Nov. 21-22, 1983, Olympia, WA. 156 p.

Silvester, W.B., P. Sollins, T. Verhoeven, and S.P. Cline. 1982. Nitrogen fixation and acetylene reduction in decaying conifer boles: Effects of incubation time, aeratona and moisture content. Can. J. For. Res. 12:646-652.

Sollins, P., K. Cromack, Jr., F.M. McCorison, R.H. Waring, and R.D. Harr. 1981. Changes in nitrogen cycling at an old-growth Douglas-fir site after disturbance. J. Environ. Qual. 10:37-42.

*Sollins, P., C.C. Grier, F.M. McCorison, K. Cromack, Jr., and R. Fogel. 1980. The internal element cycles of an old-growth Douglas-fir ecosystem in western Oregon. Ecol. Monogr. 50:261-285.

Swank. W.T., and J.B. Waide. 1980. Interpretation of nutrient cycling research in a management context: Evaluating potential effects of alternative management strategies on site productivity, p. 137-158. *In* Waring, R.H. (ed.) Forests: Fresh Perspectives from Ecosystem Analysis, Proc., 40th Annu. Biol. Colloq., Oregon State Univ. Press, Corvallis, OR. 199 p.

*Swanson, F.J. 1981. Fire and geomorphic processes, p. 401-420. *In* Fire regimes and ecosystems conference, December 11-15, 1979, Honolulu, Hawaii. USDA For. Serv., Washington, DC. Gen. Tech. Rep. WO-26. 594 p.

*Tiedemann, A.R. 1987. Combustion losses of sulfur from forest foliage and litter. For. Sci. 33:216-233.

Tiedemann, A.R., and T.D. Anderson. 1980. Combustion losses of sulfur from native plant materials and forest litter. Fire For. Meteorol. Conf. Proc. 6:220-227.

*Tiedemann, A.R., J.D. Helvey, and T.D. Anderson. 1978. Stream chemistry and watershed nutrient economy following wildfire and fertilization in eastern Washington. J. Environ. Qual. 7:580-588.

Turner, J. 1980. Nutrient cycling in an age sequence of western Washington Douglas-fir stands. Ann. Bot. 48:158-169.

Turner, J., and M.J. Lambert. 1986. Nutrition and nutritional relationships of *Pinus radiata*. Ann. Rev. Ecol. Syst. 17:325-350.

Turner, J., and J.N. Long. 1975. Accumulation of organic matter in a series of Douglas-fir stands. Can. J. For. Res. 5:681-690.

Turner, J., M.J. Lambert, and S.P. Gessel. 1979. Sulphur requirements of nitrogen fertilized Douglas-fir. For. Sci. 25:461-467.

Van Cleve, K., and D.T. Dyrness. 1983. Introduction and overview of a multidisciplinary research project: Structure and function of a black spruce (*Picea mariana*) forest in relation to other fire affected Tiaga ecosystems. Can. J. For. Res. 13:695-702.

Van Cleve, K., R. Barney, and R. Schlentner. 1983. Evidence of temperature control of production and nutrient cycling in two interior Alaska black spruce ecosystems. Can. J. For. Res. 11:258-273.

*Waring, R.H., and W.H. Schlesinger. 1985. Forest Ecosystems Concepts and Management. Academic Press, Inc., New York. 340 p.

*Wells, C.G., R.E. Campbell, L.F. DeBano, C.E. Lewis, R.L. Fredriksen, E.C. Franklin, R.C. Froelich, and P.H. Dunn. 1979. Effects of fire on soil. A state-of-the-art review. USDA For. Serv., Washington, DC. Gen. Tech. Rep. WO-7.

Youngberg, C.T., and A.G. Wollum, II. 1976. Nitrogen accretion in developing *Ceanothus velutinus* stands. Soil Sci. Soc. Am. J. 40:109-112.

13 Effects of Prescribed Fire on Soil Organisms

Jeffrey G. Borchers and David A. Perry

Executive Summary

Life in the soil consists of numerous and diverse groups of organisms, from plant roots to microbes. Members of this community interact with each other and their environment, often in ways that control tree establishment and growth. Prescribed burning influences this community directly by killing or injuring organisms immediately, and indirectly by altering many characteristics of the above- and below-ground environment. Fire also affects microorganisms that associate with tree roots. Beneficial organisms can enhance the ability of trees to take up nutrients and even increase soil fertility, whereas others can cause disease.

Prescribed burning usually leads to short-term reductions in populations of a number of soil organisms, but the effect is not predictable because of variations in fire severity and site factors. Soil invertebrates, intimately involved in nutrient cycling, usually decline in abundance. Of the microorganisms, bacteria generally increase in numbers whereas fungi decrease. Some fungi interact with roots to form mycorrhizae, an association that trees require for sustained growth. Because mycorrhiza formation is so critical to tree survival, researchers have focused on the relationship in managed forest ecosystems that have been burned. Often, declines in mycorrhiza-forming potential of soil have been demonstrated, but this cannot always be attributed solely to fire. Furthermore, only a few studies in the Pacific Northwest have directly linked reductions in mycorrhizae with regeneration problems. On some difficult-to-regenerate sites it appears that mycorrhiza formation is critical to survival and growth of outplanted seedlings.

Introduction

The soil harbors a complex, heterogeneous community of organisms that influences tree growth in one fashion or another. Although soil organisms are affected by fire, by virtue of their location they are also one of the more protected components of the forest community, and often aid survival and growth of regenerating tree seedlings. This chapter explores three parts: the nature of the soil ecosystem and how it influences tree growth; the effects of fire on soil organisms; and how the impacts of fire on soil organisms might influence reforestation success and long-term productivity.

The Soil Ecosystem

The community of soil organisms and the nonliving environment in which they reside make up the soil ecosystem. Solar energy is pumped below ground by plants in several forms, resulting in a diverse assemblage of organisms that interact with each other and their surroundings. The dynamics of this ecosystem are not easily observed, particularly the more complex interactions. Often this hinders our understanding of forest ecosystems.

The organisms

Many animals and plants ranging in size from microscopic bacteria and fungi to large mammals remain below ground during all or part of their life cycle. Our discussion will center on nonmammals that remain predominantly below ground (Fig. 13-1; mammals are treated in Chapter 18). They range in size from the microbiota (e.g., algae, protozoa, fungi, bacteria, and cyanobacteria), to the macrobiota (e.g., insects, earthworms, and plant roots). These organisms not only cycle plant nutrients through the soil, but their biomass may comprise large reservoirs of these nutrients. Thus, bacteria and fungi alone can amount to 4,000 pounds per acre in some forest soils (Bollen 1974). Because

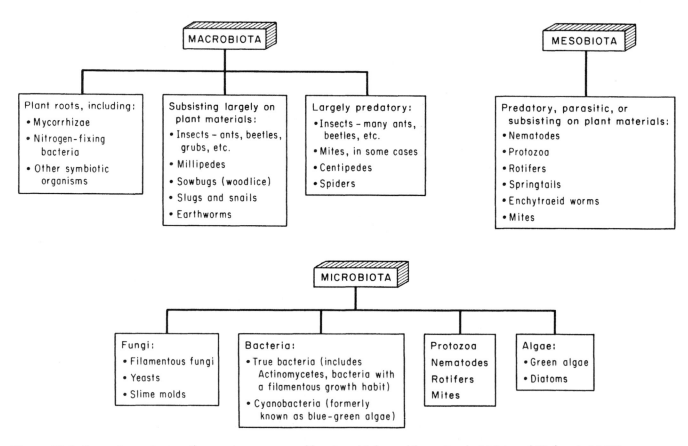

Figure 13-1. Some important soil organisms grouped by size. (Adapted from Brady 1984 and Richards 1987)

soil organisms compete for many of the same resources that plants do, they can affect tree growth.

The environment

Soil organisms occupy a complex matrix of mineral and organic matter, air, and water. Particles of clay and organic matter store nutrients and are sites for root and microbial activity. These materials, as well as the biological activity associated with them, are distributed unevenly below the surface. Over time, organisms and environmental forces produce soil horizons, layers of contrasting temperature, moisture, quantities of mineral and organic matter, nutrients, etc. Generally, surface horizons of forest soils have a greater abundance and diversity of soil organisms, more organic matter, greater acidity, and altered structure. This last feature includes soil aggregates, discrete assemblages of organic and inorganic particles that can influence processes such as erosion and nutrient cycling.

Although soil organisms respond directly to variations in their environment, they also modify their environment chemically and physically; ultimately they are a major factor in soil formation. For this reason the study of soil organisms must encompass a variety of possible interactions within the ecosystem.

Interactions–trees, microbes, and minerals

The effects of fire on soil organisms cannot be understood without an appreciation of the array of possible interactions among plants, animals, and the below-ground environment. Foremost is the rhizosphere, islands of intense biological activity centered at the root surface and adjacent soil. The rhizosphere contains many types of microorganisms that differ from those of the surrounding soil (Hendrickson et al. 1982). But in densely rooted layers, most of the soil may be contained in the rhizosphere. The energy of carbon-rich root exudates and secretions support a proliferation of various bacteria that fix atmospheric nitrogen and release enzymes, growth hormones, antibiotics, or chelators. (Chelators are specialized molecules that bring into solution otherwise insoluble forms of certain nutrients such as iron. In this form they may become available to plants.)

When two organisms interact in close physical association with each other, the result is a symbiosis. Most important commercial tree species form mutually beneficial root symbioses with a wide variety of fungi (Trappe 1962). The resulting root structure, a union of plant and fungal tissue, is termed a mycorrhiza (literally "fungus-root") (Fig. 13-2). Mycorrhizal fungi draw energy from trees and repay their hosts in numerous ways: enhanced water and nutrient uptake, extended root life, and protection against root pathogens (Harley and Smith 1983). Generally, mycorrhizal fungi cannot survive as saprophytes; they must reside on or in a living plant host to complete their life cycle. In a like manner, mycorrhizal fungi are essential for the growth and establishment of most temperate tree species, with the possible exception of forests in highly favorable environments.

Soil fertility on managed forest lands depends to some extent on nutrient inputs from the atmosphere, mainly from nitrogen fixation. Certain shrub and tree species (e.g., red alder, snowbrush, bitterbrush) are symbiotic with actinomycetes, filamentous bacteria that convert nitrogen gas into forms available to plants within specialized root nodules (Akkermans and Houwers 1979). As with mycorrhizal fungi, a nutrient (in this case, nitrogen) is exchanged for energy from the host plant. But the benefits of nitrogen fixation can extend to the whole ecosystem; in Oregon, inputs of nitrogen by nodulated snowbrush may exceed rainfall inputs by 50-100 times (Waring and Schlesinger 1985). The link with forest productivity is more

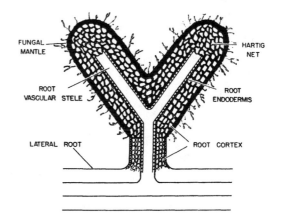

Figure 13-2. Generalized representation of an ectomycorrhizal root, named for its distinct sheath of fungal tissue, the mantle. Forest dominants of temperate and subarctic regions are generally ectomycorrhizal (Harley and Smith 1983), whereas other plants may form mycorrhizae that have little or no fungal mantle. (Diagram courtesy of R. Molina)

elaborate still, because plants like snowbrush form mycorrhizae that may aid in the nutrient requirements of nitrogen fixation (Rose 1985). Still another three-way relationship may exist: there is evidence that some nitrogen-fixing bacteria reside in mycorrhizal root systems of Douglas-fir (Li and Hung 1987). Their significance to tree growth and ecosystem properties is unknown.

Other interactions between soil organisms are equally important in processes that affect plant growth. Many invertebrates consume bacteria and fungi in rhizospheres, and in doing so release nutrients which become available to trees. For example, there are insects that feed on mycorrhizal hyphae in British pine plantations (Shaw 1985). Nutrient fluxes resulting from such grazing can be significant. In three oak woodlands in Great Britain, more than ten times the ammonium nitrogen was released from litter in plots with millipedes than in plots without them (Anderson et al. 1985). In Swedish pine forests, 10 to 50 percent of the nitrogen reduced to plant-available forms was mediated by soil invertebrates (Persson 1983). Earthworms from coastal Vancouver Island forests consumed fungal hyphae while ingesting wood in decaying logs. This substrate may become inoculated with nonsymbiotic nitrogen fixers by passage through the gut (Spiers et al. 1986).

Laboratory microcosms have been useful in studying interactions among select groups of organisms. Ingham et al. (1985) showed that grass grew better with bacteria and bacteria-grazing nematodes than when nematodes were absent. The addition of grazers to this simplified system increased nitrogen availability to the grass. Using a similar approach, Elliott et al. (1980) concluded that when bacteria proliferate in soil pores too small for nematodes to enter, the addition of smaller bacteria-grazing amoebae to the system effectively shuttles energy and nutrients from bacteria in the pores to the nematodes. Nematodes can graze on either bacteria or amoebae, except when soil pore size restricts their entry.

Soil organisms are not only influenced by soil aggregation, but they are largely responsible for it. In a relatively undisturbed soil, individual particles are usually bound into aggregates. Well-aggregated soil ensures a proper balance between air and water content (Brady 1984) which is necessary for root (and tree) survival. Mycorrhizae, their hyphae, and bacteria are major agents of soil aggre-

gation because they release organic "glues" that stabilize mineral particles into aggregates (Lynch and Bragg 1985). Aggregation may also influence soil nutrient cycles by affecting decomposition rates (Anderson and Paul 1984) or loss of nitrogen to the atmosphere (Sexstone et al. 1985). These processes are poorly understood, especially for forest soils. But they occur mainly because aggregated particles form microenvironments distinct from nonaggregated soil, conditions unique for soil organisms.

Influence of Fire on Soil Organisms

Even though soil is an effective insulator from the damage caused by fire (Chapters 4 and 11), there can still be serious effects on soil organisms and the processes they mediate. Fire affects the soil biological community directly by immediately killing or injuring organisms, and indirectly by longer-term influences over such processes as plant succession, soil organic matter transformations, and microclimate (Fig. 13-3). Depending on fire severity, organisms in litter and possibly upper mineral soil layers will be killed outright, while those in deeper soil layers or within protected spots such as logs may survive.

The indirect effects of fire on the soil community are more complex and may alter the ecosystem for years to come (Woodmansee and Wallach 1981). Anything that kills or injures living plants also impacts those organisms that depend on their products for energy, nutrients, or habitat, especially mycorrhizal fungi and rhizosphere dwellers. Similarly, combustion of coarse woody debris, forest floor litter, and soil organic matter may have both immediate and long-term consequences. Changes in the soil environment include decreased acidity, changes in nutrient availabilities (Chapter 12), and altered temperature and moisture regimes (Neal et al. 1965, Raison 1979, Woodmansee and Wallach 1981). In the long term, both direct and indirect effects help orchestrate the succession of plant communities (Volland and Dell 1981). These changes are likely to be reflected in the composition of below-ground communities.

Effect on soil invertebrates

It is difficult to generalize about fire effects on soil invertebrates because fire itself is so variable. Research has been performed world-wide under different regimes of fire severity, frequency, size, and duration, usually on a variety of sites (Lyon et al. 1978). This means that our information is to some extent site specific. Nevertheless, most studies reveal that soil invertebrate activity is decreased by fire anywhere from months to several years (Metz and Dindal 1980). Burning may alter the community structure of soil invertebrates. In South Carolina loblolly pine stands, species of Collembola (common insects that fragment organic matter) were more diverse in burned than in control stands (Metz and Dindal 1975). Overall numbers were reduced immediately following burns, but recovery occurred within several years on less frequently burned areas (Metz and Farrier 1973).

In northern Idaho, a 3-year-old broadcast-burned clearcut supported greater numbers and species of soil arthropods than 1- and 2-year-old burns (Fellin and Kennedy 1972). Although no comparisons with undisturbed forests were made, one can still surmise that the initial impact on organisms (particularly adults) was drastic, but transitory.

In Montana, Fellin (1980) compared soil arthropod populations in undisturbed forests (controls), shelterwood cuts, and clearcuts under two residue management regimes (prescribed burning and mechanical removal). A year after burning, samples of soil, litter, humus, and wood contained significantly fewer arthropods compared to undisturbed forests. About half this effect could be attributed to the burn. Arthropod levels in some shelterwood samples were actually greater than controls, and shelterwood cutting appeared to mitigate the impact of prescribed burning on the organisms. Possibly the benefit of retaining a partial overstory was due to more favorable soil temperature and moisture conditions. In coastal British Columbia, maximum summer soil temperatures were greater after clearcutting, and were further increased by slash burning (Vlug and Borden 1973). Arthropod reductions were greatest in the burned area and less severe where no burning had occurred. This was less noticeable in deeper soil layers; downward migration by arthropods sometimes resulted in increased numbers at depth.

Effects on soil microbes

As with soil invertebrates, it is difficult to generalize about fire effects on microbes. Usually the combined effects of harvesting and burning increase the numbers of bacteria relative to fungi (Smith et al. 1968). Heat affects microbial types differently; fungi are generally the most susceptible, actinomycetes least, and bacteria intermediate (see reviews by Ahlgren 1974, Harvey et al. 1976, Wells et al. 1979, Perry and Rose 1983). There are exceptions to this, however. For example, bacteria that transform nitrogen from ammonium to nitrite and nitrate (called nitrifiers) are less heat tolerant than fungi (Wells et al. 1979), but can still proliferate in the postfire soil environment. This environment generally consists of decreased plant competition for nutrients, less acidity and greater temperature extremes, especially in surface layers where biological activity is so prevalent (e.g., Neal et al. 1965). Other less obvious mechanisms are possible, such as the detrimental effect of smoke on fungal growth observed by Parmeter and Uhrenholdt (1976). These environmental fluctuations can either enhance or decrease overall microbial activity. Of particular significance are the nitrifying bacteria that convert ammonium nitrogen to highly mobile nitrate nitrogen. Should their populations increase, nitrification will result in losses of nitrogen from the ecosystem unless intercepted by regrowing vegetation or immobilized by sorption to soil particles (Vitousek et al. 1979).

Over a 2-year period after clearcutting a lodgepole pine site in Montana, total microbial biomass was reduced more in burned than in unburned areas (Entry et al. 1986). Microbial biomass was controlled to a great extent by soil moisture and temperature. On one unburned site, logging residue inhibited soil freezing and drying in the winter and summer months. This resulted in larger measures of microbial biomass than in undisturbed forests or in clearcuts where residue was burned or removed. Relative to fungi, bacteria proliferated in the burned area, perhaps because their growth and reproduction were favored by decreased soil acidity, optimal temperature and moisture regimes, and nutrient-rich ash.

In Oregon, bacteria increased whereas fungi declined in the year following Douglas-fir slash burns of differing severity (Neal et al. 1965). Burn severity, soil temperature, and moisture appeared to contribute most to the difference. Of the increased bacterial populations, a constant proportion was *Streptomyces*, a group of actinomycetes that produce antibiotics. Some of these compounds depress mycorrhizal and pathogenic fungal growth, an effect more noticeable in soils from clearcut areas, especially when burned (Perry and Rose 1983).

Depending on severity, prescribed burning can remove much of the coarse woody debris from a site. Recent work has focused on the role of decaying wood in forest ecosystems as habitat for nonsymbiotic nitrogen-fixing bacteria (Silvester et al. 1982; see review by Harmon et al. 1986). The amount of nitrogen fixed within coarse woody debris is small relative to symbiotic sources and similar in magnitude to rainfall inputs. In Montana and Idaho less than half a pound per acre was estimated to be fixed in most of the forest types studied (Jurgensen et al. 1987), but the figure may be higher where logging residues are greater (Jurgensen et al. 1982). Although low, these fixation rates can become important to the nitrogen economy of sites that have few nitrogen-fixing plants. The immediate effects of slash burning on this process are not well documented, but severe burns might lead to depletions of coarse woody debris in future rotations.

Effects on mycorrhizae

Because they are an important component of the soil community in terms of tree growth, the remainder of this section is devoted to the effects of fire on roots and mycorrhizal fungi. Since little research has been conducted in forest types where underburning is practiced (e.g., eastern Oregon), the focus will be on clearcuts and broadcast burns.

Generally, mycorrhizal fungi are dependent on their hosts to complete their life cycle, so complete removal of vegetation from a site does not favor their continued presence. Similarly, commercial tree species require fungal partners, especially as seedlings in harsh environments. Various studies have found that trees growing in soils from burned clearcuts have fewer mycorrhizae than trees in soils from unburned clearcuts or undisturbed forests. But in some instances mycorrhiza formation seems to be enhanced by clearcutting and prescribed burning.

Harvey et al. (1980a) sampled soil for active mycorrhizal root tips in Douglas-fir/larch forests of Montana. Partial cuts, either broadcast burned or unburned with residue removed, were compared with an undisturbed site. Two years after the low-consumption burn, numbers of active mycorrhizae were significantly lower in the burned stand than in other treatments. One would expect a reduction only in proportion to the number of trees removed, but these results indicated that postfire changes in soil properties caused a further decline in active mycorrhizae.

In a nearby study, Harvey et al. (1980b) noted even larger reductions in active mycorrhizal roots following clearcutting. After broadcast burning, active mycorrhizae were absent except at the edge of the cut near the undisturbed forest. Tree regeneration may depend on active mycorrhizae in the soil if other fungal sources are lacking. These other sources will be discussed later in some detail.

In the second year after harvesting two sites in Oregon and Washington, fewer mycorrhizae formed on seedlings grown in burned than in unburned areas (Wright and Tarrant 1959). Reductions were greatest on areas most severely burned. Since mycorrhizae tend to proliferate in humus and decayed wood (Harvey et al. 1981), consumption of organic materials by fire probably contributes to decreased mycorrhizal activity (Harvey et al. 1986). In a study encompassing several sites in northern California and southwest Oregon, Douglas-fir and ponderosa pine seedlings grown in soils from logged areas had fewer mycorrhizae than seedlings in undisturbed soil; reductions were greatest in soil from burned clearcuts (Parke et al. 1984). On the other hand, Perry et al. (1982), studying 15-year-old clearcuts in Montana, noted reduced mycorrhiza formation by Douglas-fir, lodgepole pine, and Englemann spruce seedlings regardless of whether slash had been broadcast burned, windrowed, or removed by hand.

In contrast to the above studies, no reductions of Douglas-fir mycorrhizae were detected in burned or unburned clearcuts of the central Cascades (Schoenberger and Perry 1982, Pilz and Perry 1984). Unburned clearcut soil actually stimulated Douglas-fir mycorrhiza formation, but not for western hemlock seedlings (Schoenberger and Perry 1982). In a study of burned clearcuts in three forest types of Oregon, mycorrhiza formation was not significantly affected in the western Cascades Douglas-fir forest. But clearcutting and burning enhanced mycorrhiza activity in soils from a Coast Range Douglas-fir and eastern Cascades ponderosa pine site (Brainerd and Perry 1987). These contrasting results point out that mere enumeration of mycorrhizae without regard for specific organisms tells only part of the story. In most of these cases, burning and clearcutting changed the array of fungal species associated with roots. For instance, mycorrhizal diversity was lower on all clearcut and burned sites in the foregoing study. Unfortunately, few fungal species can be identified when mycorrhizal, yet each may contribute uniquely to the behavior of the host tree. At this point, none of these aspects is well understood.

Why is mycorrhiza formation affected by fire in some instances and not in others? Fire severity may be important, but this has never been tested. The previous studies were, however, conducted on sites that have different natural fire regimes. For example, coastal Oregon forests have infrequent, severe, stand-replacement fires. But fire history in southwest Oregon consists of moderately severe fires at more frequent intervals (Chapter 3). Just as plant communities evolve with the fire regime, so too might their mycorrhizal associates. Conceivably, groups of fungi that evolved in high-severity fire regimes have greater tolerance to conditions on burned clearcuts where stands have also been "replaced."

Fire can influence mycorrhiza formation in a number of ways, with specific mechanisms that should be viewed in the context of Fig. 13-3. Regenerating tree seedlings form mycorrhizae when uninfected roots approach germinating fungal propagules (e.g., spores, hyphae, or active mycorrhizal root tips). After harvest, there are three basic sources for propagules: a local source of propagules near seedling roots; an adjacent source of propagules in undisturbed forests dispersed by animals, wind, or other agents; and refugia, less disturbed areas of soil and vegetation containing propagules.

Local source. The negative impact of heat is most apparent on mycorrhizal propagules present in the upper few inches of soil. In many undisturbed forests, mycorrhizal activity is limited to surface layers of soil and organic matter (Harvey et al. 1986). Hence, they are quite susceptible to disturbance. Fire can cause significant root mortality (Tarrant 1956, Minore 1975, Milne and Grier 1979), and in such a case fungal spores and hyphae will also be killed. However, certain fungi, both

pathogens and mycorrhiza-formers, proliferate in the postfire environment (Egger and Paden 1986).

Summer surface soil temperatures are increased significantly when insulating vegetation and litter have been consumed by prescribed burning (Neal et al. 1965). Mycorrhizae on newly established seedlings are quite vulnerable to the high temperatures of surface soils on many clearcuts (Parke et al. 1983a).

Less immediate in their effect on mycorrhiza formation are the postfire changes in soil chemistry. Forest floor litter layers contain various nutrients and organic compounds that can be leached into the rooting zone by the flow of water. These substances can affect mycorrhizae and plant growth unpredictably. For instance, natural white fir seedlings were larger and had more mycorrhizal root tips when occupying mineral soil without organic layers (Alvarez et al. 1979). Greenhouse results with Douglas-fir demonstrated that water-soluble substances in the litter can inhibit mycorrhiza formation (Schoenberger and Perry 1982), but the picture becomes clouded when the litter type and fungal species are varied: leachates can stimulate fungal growth, depress it, or have no effect (Rose et al. 1983). Stimulation of seedling growth by litter leachates can be attributed not only to the presence of mycorrhiza-forming propagules, but also other beneficial, growth-promoting organisms (Parke et al. 1983b). The effect of partially burned litter and organic matter is not known, but artificially heated soil can produce substances toxic to seedlings, unless they are colonized by mycorrhizal fungi (Zak 1971). In a recent study in New Mexico, ponderosa pine stands were underburned, and less than half the forest floor was consumed. The low fireline intensity nevertheless produced sufficient heat to remove volatile organics from the litter, compounds which were shown to inhibit nitrification. Hence, soil and litter from burned plots produced significantly greater amounts of easily leached nitrate nitrogen than material from unburned areas (White 1986a, 1986b).

Adjacent source. Whereas mycorrhizal fungi that fruit above ground (epigeous) have spores that are readily disseminated by wind, some of the more important mycorrhizal fungi of Northwest conifers fruit below ground (hypogeous). The latter are dispersed by animals, primarily mammals

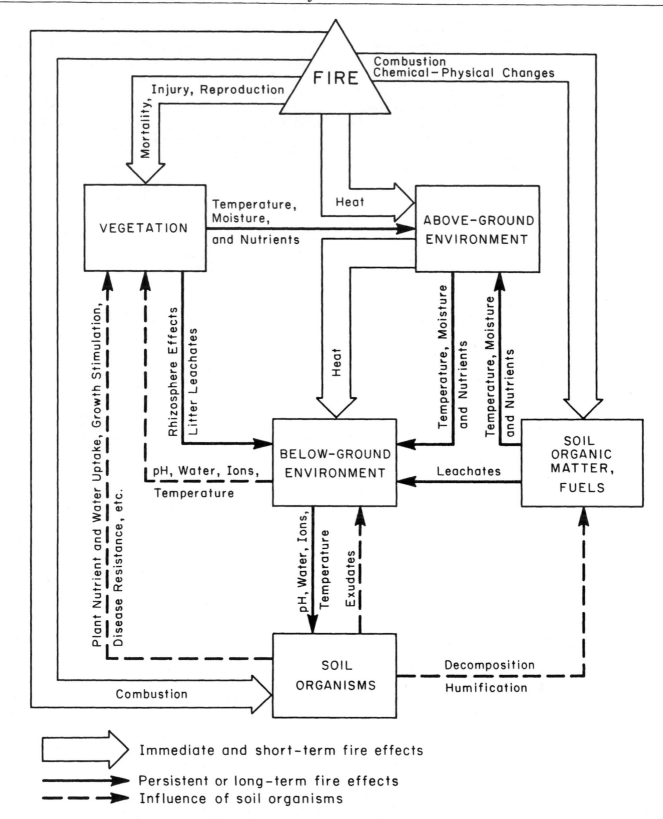

Figure 13-3. Conceptual model of the relationships between fire and soil organisms.

but to some degree by birds and insects. It has been suggested that reinoculation of clearcuts with mycorrhizal fungi depends to some extent on logs and vegetation cover for small mammals which consume and egest hypogeous fungi (Maser et al. 1978). Prescribed burning may decrease the quality of this habitat for mammals that are dependent on slash and shrubs for cover. In southwest Oregon, McIntire (1984) found that mechanical piling and burning of slash in a shelterwood cut decreased the abundance of hypogeous fungi. This was associated with decreased activity of the Siskiyou chipmunk, known for its consumption of hypogeous fungal fruiting bodies. Although the implications for forest regeneration are obvious, the ideas have not yet been adequately tested.

Refugia. Probably the most important factor influencing the postfire survival of mycorrhizal fungi (and other rhizosphere organisms) is how quickly the site is reoccupied by proper host species. Some mycorrhizal fungi can survive in the short term by decomposing dead organic matter, but without living plants of the right species, their numbers will eventually decline. Rapid and successful reforestation is probably the best way to prevent decline of mycorrhizal fungi following fire. However, some nonconiferous plant species can do the same job. This has been most clearly demonstrated in southwest Oregon and northern California, where hardwood shrubs and trees (e.g., Pacific madrone and manzanita) form mycorrhizae with many of the same fungal species as Douglas-fir, true firs, and pines (Molina and Trappe 1982a, 1982b). These hardwoods often reoccupy sites quickly following fire, creating microsites of lower soil temperature and greater soil moisture (Minore 1986). Recent studies show that they also play an important role in stabilizing populations of mycorrhizal fungi and other soil organisms in recently burned areas (Amaranthus and Perry 1987, S. Borchers and Perry 1987), where they serve as sources of fungal propagules for establishing conifer seedlings. Similar studies are underway in other areas of the Pacific Northwest.

Other protected areas may provide refugia for mycorrhizal fungi and soil organisms during fire. The first of these are decomposing logs which are often dense with roots, mycorrhizal hyphae, nitrogen-fixing bacteria, and other organisms. Critical studies are yet to be done, but in all likelihood many organisms survive fire within logs that are

Figure 13-4. (A) Mycorrhizae and fungal hyphae from unconsumed log (B) after stand-replacement fire, southwest Oregon.

not completely burned. For instance, after the southwest Oregon wildfires of 1987, abundant mycorrhizal fungi and hyphae could be found within unconsumed, decomposing logs (Fig. 13-4). These may act as focal points for reinoculation of the burned area, particularly by mammals. Sites lacking logs may lose more fungi during fire than those with logs.

The second possibility for refugia lies in the soil. In Oregon Coast Range Douglas-fir stands, surface soil was disaggregated and organic matter levels reduced following severe burning (Dyrness and Youngberg 1957). Similarly, on nonreforested, burned clearcuts in southwest Oregon most of the larger aggregates have disappeared in the 20 years since harvest and burning. These soils were devoid of the mycorrhizae and fungal hyphae that

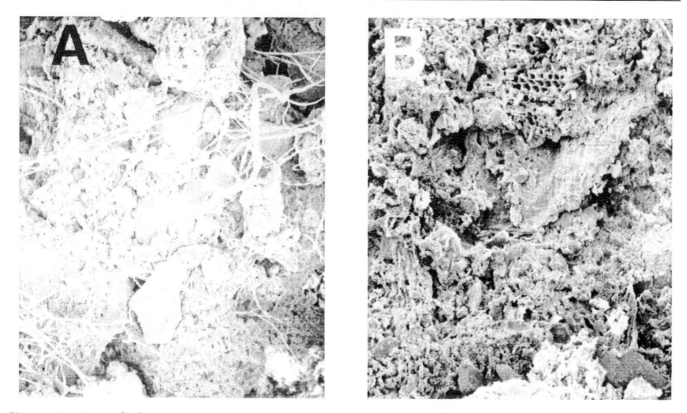

Figure 13-5. Magnified view (X150) of soil aggregate interiors from (A) undisturbed forest and (B) broadcast-burned clearcut. Note abundant fungal hyphae in undisturbed soil.

maintain aggregation in the adjacent undisturbed forest (Fig. 13-5) (Borchers and Perry, in press) and presumably lacked the unique microenvironment associated with soil aggregates. The viability or longevity of mycorrhiza-forming fungal spores appears to be related to the degree of soil aggregation (J. Borchers and Perry 1987), but a direct link to decreased mycorrhiza formation has not been established.

Tree Survival & Growth

Mycorrhizae

The importance of mycorrhizal fungi and other soil organisms to the establishment and growth of trees is still controversial. It appears that at least some level of mycorrhiza formation is necessary for good conifer growth. But at what level do reductions in mycorrhiza formation become detrimental to tree growth? At this point, virtually all of the work in the Pacific Northwest on impacts of

reduced mycorrhizae on tree seedlings has been done in southwest Oregon and northern California. Generally, these studies demonstrate that reduced mycorrhizae negatively impact seedling survival and growth, but the effect varies with site (Perry et al. 1987).

To reinoculate old, unreforested clearcuts with mycorrhizal fungi, Amaranthus and Perry (1987) transferred soil from undisturbed forests and young plantations into planting holes at the time of planting. On one site, a high-elevation clearcut with sandy soils, reinoculation with plantation soil increased mycorrhizal formation, quadrupled seedling basal area growth, and increased first-year seedling survival by nearly 50 percent. On another high-elevation site, but less droughty, reinoculation increased mycorrhiza formation and seedling growth but did not influence survival (which was uniformly high). On a third, low-elevation site, reinoculation influenced the morphological characteristics of seedling mycorrhizae, but otherwise had no effect.

In a second study on a clearcut previously shown to have reduced mycorrhiza formation, seedlings were differentially inoculated with mycorrhizae in a greenhouse by growing them in clearcut and forest soil. All were then outplanted on the clearcut. By the end of the first growing season, seedlings initially grown in the two soil types no longer differed in mycorrhiza numbers. Nevertheless, those started in forest soils—with initially higher levels of mycorrhizae—grew best (M.P. Amaranthus, D.A. Perry, and S.L. Borchers, unpublished manuscript). This suggests that rapidity of mycorrhiza formation is important for seedling growth, a variable rarely considered in studies of this kind.

Many mycorrhizal fungi produce iron chelators (personal communication from S. Miller, University of Wyoming). Perry et al. (1984) showed that iron chelator levels were lower in eight of ten burned clearcuts when compared to undisturbed forest soil. Bioassays conducted in soils from one of the eight sites indicated that growth of Douglas-fir seedlings was iron limited. Recent work from southwest Oregon suggests that iron availability can limit seedling growth in burned clearcuts. Douglas-fir seedlings grew better in soil sampled near hardwood sprouts than in soil from open areas. The size increase was associated with higher iron concentrations in the foliage, but not in the soil (S. Borchers and Perry 1987 and unpublished). It is possible that mycorrhizal fungi and other organisms in the shrub rhizosphere produce chelators that benefit conifer seedlings when iron is limiting growth.

Nitrogen fixation

We previously alluded to associations involving three organisms: tree roots, fungi, and nitrogen-fixing bacteria. The limited research that has been done is intriguing, because it implies that tree growth partly depends on nitrogen fixation within the rhizosphere or mycorrhiza tissues. Conifer vigor on some Vancouver Island sites appeared to be correlated with nitrogen-fixing bacteria that were associated with fungi (Cracknell and Louisier 1986). Douglas-fir mycorrhizae harbor at least two species of nitrogen-fixing bacteria (Li and Hung 1987). In southwest Oregon, outplanted Douglas-fir survival and growth were superior for seedlings exhibiting highest levels of nitrogen fixation (Amaranthus et al. 1987). Such inputs of nitrogen could account for heretofore large, unexplained gains of nitrogen in some forest ecosystems (Richards 1987).

Conclusion

It is natural at this point to lament that so many questions concerning fire and soil organisms remain unanswered. Despite our appreciation for the complexity of fire and the ecosystems where it occurs, our research continues to take a short-term view. But we manage forests on rotations that may exceed our lifespan, hardly aware that vegetation patterns reflect centuries of episodic fire events. Unfortunately, visual observation cannot reveal fire-related patterns for life below ground; for this we have tools. Still, most soil biological investigations are hampered by methodological shortcomings. This predisposes researchers to explore simpler, short-term questions. But the answers often hint at the hidden sequence of cause-and-effect that the fire regime imposes on the soil community. Above ground, patterns of plant succession are easily perceived, but future work must reveal the below-ground events and determine their significance.

What research has confirmed is that the soil ecosystem is exceedingly complex and full of unexpected interactions. The role of soil invertebrates in nutrient cycling is a prime example, as is the partnership between tree and fungus, mycorrhizae. With increasing concern about long-term forest productivity, knowledge about fire and its effects on the soil ecosystem becomes more vital to scientists, managers, and decision makers. The main lesson from research thus far is that no organism lives in isolation. Each is to some extent dependent on others, particularly after fire or other disturbance. Trees are certainly no exception to this, since most are symbiotic. Ultimately, long-term productivity of managed forests depends on the health of the below-ground community.

Literature Cited & Key References

*Ahlgren, I.F. 1974. The effects of fire on soil organisms, p. 47-72. *In* Kozlowski, T.T. and C.E. Ahlgren (eds.) Fire and Ecosystems. Academic Press, New York, NY. 542 p.

Akkermans, A.D.L., and A. Houwers. 1979. Symbiotic nitrogen fixers available for use in temperate forestry, p. 23-35. *In* Gordon, J.C., C.T. Wheeler, and D.A. Perry (eds.) Symbiotic Nitrogen Fixation in the Management of Temperate Forests. For. Res. Lab., Oregon State Univ., Corvallis, OR. 501 p.

Alvarez, I.F., D.L. Rowney, and F.W. Cobb, Jr. 1979. Mycorrhizae and growth of white fir seedlings in mineral soil with and without organic layers in a California forest. Can. J. For. Res. 9:311-315.

Amaranthus, M.P., and D.A. Perry. 1987. Effects of soil transfer on ectomycorrhiza formation and the survival and growth of conifer seedlings on old, non-forested clearcuts. Can J. For. Res. 17:944-950.

Amaranthus, M.P., C.Y. Li, and D.A. Perry. 1987. Nitrogen fixation within mycorrhizae of Douglas-fir seedlings, p.79. *In* Sylvia, D.M., L.L. Hung, and J.H. Graham (eds.) Proc., 7th North American Conference on Mycorrhizae. Institute of Food and Agricultural Sciences, Univ. Florida, Gainesville, FL.

Anderson, D.W., and E.A. Paul. 1984. Organo-mineral complexes and their study by radiocarbon dating. Soil Sci. Soc. Am. J. 48:298-301.

*Anderson, J.A., S.A. Huish, P. Ineson, M.A. Leonard, and P.R. Splatt. 1985. Interactions of invertebrates, micro-organisms and tree roots in nitrogen and mineral element fluxes in deciduous woodland soils, p. 377-392. *In* Fitter, A.H., O. Atkinson, D.J. Read, and M.B. Usher (eds.) Ecological Interactions in Soil, Plants, Microbes and Animals. Blackwell Scientific Publications, Palo Alto, CA.

*Bollen, W.B. 1974. Soil Microbes, p. B-1 to B-30. *In* Cramer, O.P. (ed.) Environmental effects of forest residues management in the Pacific Northwest. A state-of-knowledge compendium. USDA For. Serv., Pac. Northwest For. Rge. Exp. Sta., Portland, OR. Gen. Tech. Rep. PNW-24.

*Borchers, J.G., and D.A. Perry. In press. Organic matter content and aggregation of forest soils with different texture in southwest Oregon clearcuts. *In* Perry, D.A., R. Meurisse, B. Thomas, R. Miller, J. Boyle, J. Means, and P. Sollins (eds.) Maintaining the Long-term Productivity of Pacific Northwest Forest Ecosystems. Timber Press, Portland, OR.

References marked by an asterisk are recommended for general information.

Borchers, J.G., and D.A. Perry. 1987. Effects of soil structure on mycorrhizal inoculum potential of forest soils in southwest Oregon, p. 178. *In* Agronomy Abstracts, Agron. Soc. Amer. Madison, WI.

Borchers, S.L., and D.A. Perry. 1987. Early successional hardwoods as refugia for ectomycorrhizal fungi in clearcut Douglas-fir forests of southwest Oregon, p. 84. *In* Sylvia, D.M., L.L. Hung, and J.H. Graham (eds.) Proc., 7th North American Conference on Mycorrhizae. Institute of Food and Agricultural Sciences, Univ. Florida, Gainesville, FL.

Brady, N.C. 1984. The Nature and Properties of Soils. Macmillan Publ. Co., Inc. New York, NY. 750 p.

Brainerd, R., and D.A. Perry. 1987. Ectomycorrhizal formation in disturbed and undisturbed soils across a moisture elevation gradient in Oregon, p. 144. *In* Sylvia, D.M., L.L. Hung, and J.H. Graham (eds.) Proc., 7th North American Conference on Mycorrhizae. Institute of Food and Agricultural Sciences, Univ. Florida, Gainesville, FL.

Cracknell, P.C., and J.D. Lousier. 1986. N_2-fixing microbial complexes in coniferous seedling establishment. Program abstracts, Roots in Forest Soils: Biology and Symbioses. I.U.F.R.O. Confer., Univ. Victoria, Victoria, B.C., Canada.

*Dyrness, C.T., and C.T. Youngberg. 1957. The effect of logging and slash-burning on soil structure. Soil Sci. Soc. Amer. Proc. 21:444-447.

Egger, K.N., and P.W. Paden. 1986. Biotrophic associations between lodgepole pine seedlings and postfire ascomycetes (Pezizales) in monoxenic culture. Can J. Bot. 64:2719-2725.

Elliott, E.T., R.V. Anderson, D.C. Coleman, and C.V. Cole. 1980. Habitable pore space and microbial trophic interactions. Oikos 35:327-335.

Entry, J.A., N.M. Stark, and H. Loewenstein. 1986. Effect of timber harvesting on microbial biomass fluxes in a northern Rocky Mountain forest soil. Can. J. For. Res. 16:1076-1081.

*Fellin, D.G. 1980. Populations of some forest litter, humus, and soil arthropods as affected by silvicultural practices, residue utilization, and prescribed fire, p. 317-334. *In* Symp. Proc., Environmental Consequences of Timber Harvesting in Rocky Mountain Coniferous Forests. USDA For. Serv., Intermt. For. Rge. Exp. Sta., Ogden, UT. Gen. Tech. Rep. INT-90. 526 p.

*Fellin, D.G., and P.C. Kennedy. 1972. Abundance of arthropods inhabiting duff and soil after prescribed burning on forest clearcuts in northern Idaho. USDA For. Serv., Intermt. For. Rge. Exp. Sta., Ogden, UT. Res. Note INT-162. 8 p.

Harley, J.L., and S.E. Smith. 1983. Mycorrhizal Symbiosis. Academic Press, New York, NY. 483 p.

*Harmon, M.E., J.F. Franklin, F.J. Swanson, P. Sollins, S.V. Gregory, J.D. Lattin, N.H. Anderson, S.P. Cline, N.G. Aumen, J.R. Sedell, G.W. Lienkaemper, K. Cromack, Jr., and K.W. Cummins. 1986. Ecology of coarse woody debris in temperate ecosystems. Adv. Ecol. Res. 15:133-302.

*Harvey, A.E., M.F. Jurgensen, and M.J. Larsen. 1976. Intensive fiber utilization and prescribed fire: Effects on the microbial ecology of forests. USDA For. Serv., Intermt. For. Rge. Exp. Sta., Ogden, UT. Gen. Tech. Rep. INT-28. 46 p.

Harvey, A.E., M.J. Larsen, and M.F. Jurgensen. 1980a. Partial cut harvesting and ectomycorrhizae: Early effects in Douglas-fir—larch forests of western Montana. Can. J. For. Res. 10:436-440.

Harvey, A.E., M.F. Jurgensen, and M.J. Larsen. 1980b. Clearcut harvesting and ectomycorrhizae: Survival of activity on residual roots and influence on a bordering forest stand in western Montana. Can. J. For. Res. 10:300-303.

*Harvey, A.E., M.F. Jurgensen, and M.J. Larsen. 1981. Organic reserves: Importance to ectomycorrhizae in forest soils of western Montana. For. Sci. 27:442-445.

Harvey, A.E., M.F. Jurgensen, M.J. Larsen, and J.A. Schlieter. 1986. Distribution of active ectomycorrhizal short roots in forest soils of the inland Northwest: Effects of site and disturbance. USDA For. Serv., Intermt. For. Rge. Exp. Sta., Ogden, UT. Res. Pap. INT-374. 8 p.

*Hendrickson, O., J.B. Robinson, and L. Chatarpaul. 1982. The microbiology of forest soils: A literature review. Petawawa Nat. For. Inst., Canada. Infor. Rep. PI-X-19. 75 p.

Ingham, R.E., J.A. Trofymow, E.R. Ingham, and D.C. Coleman. 1985. Interactions of bacteria, fungi, and their nematode grazers: Effects on nutrient cycling and plant growth. Ecol. Monogr. 55:119-140.

*Jurgensen, M.F., A.E. Harvey, and M.J. Larsen. 1982. Soil microorganisms, p. 14-18. *In* Benson, R.E. (ed.) Management consequences of alternative harvesting and residue treatment practices—lodgepole pine. USDA For. Serv., Intermt. For. Rge. Exp. Sta., Ogden, UT. Gen. Tech. Rep. INT-132. 58 p.

Jurgensen, M.F., M.J. Larsen, R.T. Graham, and A.E. Harvey. 1987. Nitrogen fixation in woody residue of northern Rocky Mountain conifer forests. Can. J. For. Res. 17:1283-1288.

Li, C.Y., and L.L. Hung. 1987. Nitrogen-fixing (acetylene-reducing) bacteria associated with ectomycorrhizae of Douglas-fir. Plant and Soil 98:425-428.

*Lynch, J.M., and E. Bragg. 1985. Microorganisms and soil aggregate stability. Adv. Soil Sci. 2:133-171.

*Lyon, L.J., H.S. Crawford, E. Czuhal, R.L. Frederiksen, R.F. Harlow, L.J. Metz, and H.A. Pearson. 1978. Effects of fire on fauna. A state-of-knowledge review. USDA For. Serv., Washington, DC. Gen. Tech. Rep. WO-6. 41 p.

Maser, C., J.M. Trappe, and R.A. Nussbaum. 1978. Fungal small-mammal interrelationships with emphasis on Oregon coniferous forests. Ecology 59:799-809.

McIntire, P.W. 1984. Fungus consumption by the Siskiyou chipmunk within a variously treated forest. Ecology 65:137-146.

Metz, L.J., and D.A. Dindal. 1975. Collembola populations and prescribed burning. Environ. Entomol. 4:583-587.

*Metz, L.J., and D.L. Dindal. 1980. Effects of fire on soil fauna in North America, p. 450-459. *In* Dindal, D.L. (ed.) Soil biology as related to land use practices. Office of Pesticide and Toxic Substances, EPA, Washington, DC. EPA-560/13-80-038.

*Metz, L.J., and M.H. Farrier. 1973. Prescribed burning and populations of soil mesofauna. Environ. Entomol. 2:433-440.

Milne, W.A., and C.C. Grier. 1979. Unpublished data, cited in Boyer, D.E., and J.D. Dell. 1980. Fire Effects on Pacific Northwest Forest Soils. Prepared jointly by Watershed Management and Aviation and Fire Management, USDA For. Serv., Reg. 6, Portland, OR.

Minore, D. 1975. Observations on the rhizomes and roots of *Vaccinium membranaceum*. USDA For. Serv., Pac. Northwest For. Rge. Exp. Sta., Portland, OR. Res. Note PNW-261. 5 p.

Minore, D. 1986. Effects of madrone, chinkapin, and tanoak sprouts on light intensity, soil moisture, and soil temperature. Can. J. For. Res. 16:654-658.

Molina, R., and J.M. Trappe. 1982a. Patterns of ectomycorrhizal host specificity and potential amongst Pacific Northwest conifers and fungi. For. Sci. 28:423-457.

Molina, R., and J.M. Trappe. 1982b. Lack of mycorrhizal specificity by the ericaceous hosts *Arbutus menziesii* and *Arctostaphylos uva-ursi*. New Phytol. 90:495-509.

*Neal, J.L., E.W. Wright, and W.B. Bollen. 1965. Burning Douglas-fir slash: Physical, chemical, and microbial effects in the soil. For. Res. Lab., Oregon State Univ., Corvallis, OR. Pap. 1. 32 p.

Parke, J.L., R.G. Linderman, and J.M. Trappe. 1983a. Effect of root zone temperature on ectomycorrhiza and vesicular-arbuscular mycorrhiza formation in disturbed and undisturbed forest soils of southwest Oregon. Can. J. For. Res. 13:657-665.

Parke, J.L., R.G. Linderman, and J.M. Trappe. 1983b. Effects of forest litter on mycorrhiza developments and growth of Douglas-fir and western red cedar seedlings. Can. J. For. Res. 13:666-671.

Parke, J.L., R.G. Linderman, and J.M. Trappe. 1984. Inoculum potential of ectomycorrhizal fungi in forest soils of southwest Oregon and northern California. For. Sci. 30:300-304.

Parmeter, J.R., and B. Uhrenholdt. 1976. Effects of smoke on pathogens and other fungi. Tall Timbers Fire Ecol. Conf. Proc. 14:299-304.

Perry, D.A., M.M. Meyer, D. Egeland, S.L. Rose, and D. Pilz. 1982. Seedling growth and mycorrhizal formation in clearcut and adjacent, undisturbed soils in Montana: A greenhouse bioassay. For. Ecol. Manage. 4:261-273.

*Perry, D.A., R. Molina, and M.P. Amaranthus. 1987. Mycorrhiza, mycorrhizospheres, and reforestation: Current knowledge and research needs. Can J. For. Res. 17:929-940.

*Perry, D.A., and S.L. Rose. 1983. Soil biology and forest productivity: Opportunities and constraints, p. 229-238. *In* Ballard, R. and S.P. Gessel (eds.) I.U.F.R.O. Symp., Forest Site and Continuous Productivity. USDA For. Serv., Pac. Northwest For. Rge. Exp. Sta., Portland, OR. Gen. Tech. Rep. PNW-163. 406 p.

Perry, D.A., S.L. Rose, D. Pilz, and M.M. Schoenberger. 1984. Reduction of natural ferric iron chelators in disturbed forest soils. Soil Sci. Soc. Amer. J. 48:379-382.

Persson, T. 1983. Influence of soil animals on nitrogen mineralization in a northern Scots pine forest, p. 117-126. *In* Lebrun, Ph., H.M. Andre, A. de Medts, C. Gregroire-Wibo, and G. Wauthy (eds.) New Trends in Soil Biology. Dieu-Brichart, Louvain-la-Neuve, France.

*Pilz, D., and D.A. Perry. 1984. Impact of clearcutting and slash burning on ectomycorrhizal associations of Douglas-fir seedlings. Can. J. For. Res. 14:94-100.

*Raison, R.J. 1979. Modification of the soil environment by vegetation fires, with particular reference to nitrogen transformations: A review. Plant and Soil 51:73-108.

*Richards, B.N. 1987. The Microbiology of Terrestrial Ecosystems. John Wiley & Sons, New York, NY. 400 p.

Rose, S.L. 1985. Tripartite associations: A carbon-nitrogen-phosphorus give and take, p. 125-127. *In* Molina, R. (ed.) Proc., 6th North American Conference on Mycorrhizae. For. Res. Lab., Oregon State Univ., Corvallis, OR. 471 p.

Rose, S.L., D.A. Perry, D. Pilz, and M.M. Schoenberger. 1983. Allelopathic effects of litter on the growth and colonization of mycorrhizal fungi. J. Chem. Ecol. 9:1153-1162.

Schoenberger, M.M., and D.A. Perry. 1982. The effect of soil disturbance on growth and ectomycorrhizae on Douglas-fir and western hemlock seedlings: A greenhouse bioassay. Can. J. For. Res. 12:343-353.

Sexstone, A.J., N.P. Revsbech, T.B. Parkin, and J.M. Tiedje. 1985. Direct measurement of oxygen profiles and denitrification rates in soil aggregates. Soil Sci. Soc. Amer. J. 49:645-651.

Shaw, P.J.A. 1985. Grazing preferences of *Onychiurus armatus* (Insecta:Collembola) for mycorrhizal and saprophytic fungi of pine plantations, p. 377-392. *In* Fitter, A.H., O. Atkinson, D.J. Read, and M.B. Usher (eds.) Ecological Interactions in the Soil Environment. Blackwell Scientific Publications, Palo Alto, CA. 400 p.

Silvester, W.B., P. Sollins, and T. Verhoeven. 1982. Nitrogen fixation and acetylene reduction in decaying conifer boles: Effects of incubation time, aeration, and moisture content. Can. J. For. Res. 12:646-652.

Smith, W.H., F.H. Bormann, and G.E. Likens. 1968. Responses of chemautotrophic nitrifiers to forest cutting. Soil Sci. 106:471-473.

Spiers, G.A., D. Gagnon, G.E. Nason, E.C. Packee, and J.D. Louisier. 1986. Effects and importance of indigenous earthworms on decomposition and nutrient cycling in coastal forest ecosystems. Can. J. For. Res. 16:983-989.

Tarrant, R.F. 1956. Changes in some physical soil properties after a prescribed burn in young ponderosa pine. J. For. 54:439-441.

Trappe, J.M. 1962. Fungus associates of ectotrophic mycorrhizae. Bot. Rev. 28:588-606.

Vitousek, P.M., J.R. Gosz, C.C. Grier, J.M. Melillo, W.A. Reiners and R.L. Todd. 1979. Nitrate losses from disturbed ecosystems. Science 204:469-474.

Vlug, H., and J.H. Borden. 1973. Soil Acari and Collembola populations affected by logging and slash burning in a coastal British Columbia coniferous forest. Environ. Entomol. 2:1016-1023.

*Volland, L.A., and J.D. Dell. 1981. Fire effects on Pacific Northwest forest and range vegetation. Prepared jointly by Watershed Management and Aviation and Fire Management, USDA For. Serv., Reg. 6, Portland, OR.

*Waring, R.H., and W.H. Schlesinger. 1985. Forest Ecosystems. Concepts and Management. Academic Press, New York, NY. 340 p.

*Wells, C.G., R.E. Campbell, L.F. DeBano, C.E. Lewis, R.L. Frederiksen, E.C. Franklin, R.C. Froelich, and P.H. Dunn. 1979. Effects of fire on soil. A state-of-knowledge review. USDA For. Serv., Washington, DC. Gen. Tech. Rep. WO-7. 34 p.

White, C.S. 1986a. Effects of prescribed fire on rates of decomposition and nitrogen mineralization in a ponderosa pine ecosystem. Biol. Fertil. Soils 2:87-95.

White, C.S. 1986b. Volatile and water-soluble inhibitors of nitrogen mineral and nitrification in a ponderosa pine ecosystem. Biol. Fertil. Soils 2:97-104.

*Woodmansee, R.G., and L.S. Wallach. 1981. Effects of fire regimes on biogeochemical cycles, p. 379-400. *In* Fire Regimes and Ecosystem Properties. Confer. Proc., USDA For. Serv., Washington, DC. Gen. Tech. Rep. WO-26. 594 p.

*Wright, E., and R.F. Tarrant. 1959. Occurrence of mycorrhizae after logging and slash burning in the Douglas-fir type. USDA For. Serv., Pac. Northwest For. Rge Exp. Sta., Portland, OR. Pap. 160. 7 p.

Zak, B. 1971. Detoxication of autoclaved soil by a mycorrhizal fungus. USDA For. Serv., Pac. Northwest For. Rge. Exp. Sta., Portland, OR. Res. Note PNW-159. 4 p.

14 Effects of Fire on Soil Erosion

David H. McNabb and Frederick J. Swanson

Executive Summary

Erosion is the product of complex interactions among geomorphic processes, climate, vegetation, soils, and landforms. The energy derived from falling or flowing water and gravity dominates erosion processes in Pacific Northwest forests. Rainfall causes splash erosion of exposed soil, and flowing water may cause sheet, rill, and gully erosion. Freezing water occasionally loosens soil by frost heaving for subsequent transport by water. Gravity causes soil and rocks to move down steep slopes as ravel, the slow creep of the soil mantle downslope; and mass wasting includes various types of landslides. Channel erosion adds material directly to streams.

Disturbance of Pacific Northwest forest ecosystems generally accelerates erosion processes, alters the transport and storage of sediment within watersheds, and increases export of material from watersheds relative to undisturbed forested lands. The frequency and severity of wildfire, a major forest disturbance, affects the magnitude of accelerated erosion. Prescribed fire in managed forests can also accelerate erosion and alter the dominant forms of erosion.

Fire increases the potential for accelerated erosion primarily through its effects on vegetation and soil. As fire increases in severity, more vegetation is killed, more forest floor is consumed, and it becomes more likely that the physical properties of the soil and watershed are changed. These changes increase the potential for erosion by exposing mineral soil to erosion processes.

The potential for prescribed fire to increase erosion increases with fire severity, soil erodibility, steepness of slope, and intensity or amount of precipitation. The magnitude of fire-accelerated soil loss from forest land in the Pacific Northwest is usually minor because the times and situations when these four factors occur concurrently are rare.

Hydrologic and other soil physical properties are particularly important factors affecting the potential for surface erosion. Coarse-textured soils low in organic matter are most susceptible to surface erosion; these soils are much less common in the Pacific Northwest than elsewhere in the western United States. Most undisturbed forest soils in the region have a high porosity which, coupled with the low intensity of most rainfall events, seldom result in overland flow. Prescribed fire can increase soil movement by ravel on steep slopes, but has a negligible effect on mass wasting.

Accelerated erosion from prescribed fire usually has a minor effect on long-term forest productivity in the Pacific Northwest. The potential for prescribed fire to affect productivity, however, increases if fires are severe, soils are highly erodible, and prescribed fires are more frequent than past wildfires. The potential for prescribed fire to cause accelerated erosion decreases with the severity and frequency of its use.

Introduction

Fire changes forest ecosystems and interacts with geomorphic processes, climate, and landform in a variety of ways to alter the landscape and temporarily increase the potential for erosion (Fig. 14-1). Soil erosion in Pacific Northwest forests is typically low when the soil is protected by litter and the site is covered by a closed forest canopy. Disturbance of forests by wildfire, harvesting, road construction, and site preparation (including prescribed burning) increases the potential for erosion.

Fire affects erosion processes by exposing readily erodible material and in some cases, increasing hydrologic energy available to move it. Exposure of erodible material depends on how the severity of fire affects vegetative cover, the organic forest floor, and soil. Following a fire, landform, soil properties, and climate interact to determine the dominant geomorphic processes that move material downslope and into stream channels. The hydrologic characteristics of the soil and drainage network control many erosional processes, but on steeper slopes gravitational processes become increasingly important.

In presettlement time, wildfire was an important factor affecting geomorphic processes and forest communities in the Pacific Northwest (Chapter 3; Swanson 1981). In many respects, the effects of prescribed burning on geomorphic processes are similar to wildfire, although the severity of prescribed fires is often less than that of wildfires. However, the effect of harvesting and road construction either supercede or dominate many erosion processes in managed forests, particularly when prescribed burns are not severe.

This chapter begins with a discussion of fire-induced changes in vegetation, soil physical properties, and hydrology that may alter geomorphic processes and accelerate erosion. The direct effects of fire are followed by a discussion of the three types of accelerated erosion which may follow—surface erosion, mass wasting, and stream channel erosion. Where appropriate, changes following prescribed burning are contrasted with

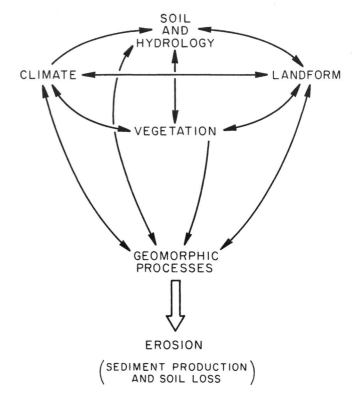

Figure 14-1. Fire and other disturbances interact with climate, landform, and vegetation to shape the landscape by a variety of geomorphic processes. The interaction of these factors determines the type and rate of soil loss by erosion.

those following a wildfire or the interactions of prescribed burning with other management practices. Finally, the potential for erosion from prescribed burning to affect forest productivity is addressed.

Fire Effects on Vegetation

A combination of harvesting and prescribed burning in managed forests temporarily leaves most sites with little, if any, vegetative cover. The temporary removal of vegetation detrimental to reforestation efforts is an important objective of using prescribed burning for site preparation (Chapter 6); however, several species that aggressively invade newly burned sites or require fire for germination may ultimately become more competitive with newly planted seedlings than existing vegetation (Chapter 4). In contrast to prescribed fire, the effect of a wildfire on vegetation is often more dependent on fire severity. Low-severity wildfires generally burn slowly through the understory and have little direct effect on overstory vegetation. At higher fire severities, trees may be killed by heat. Under the most severe conditions, entire crowns and portions of the stem may be burned. If the crowns do not burn, dead foliage often falls to the ground and covers some of the exposed soil (Megahan and Molitor 1975).

Pioneer species or sprouts of residual species that have adapted to disturbance by fire rapidly occupy most burned sites (Chapter 4; Dyrness 1973, Gholz et al. 1985). Although the cover provided by vegetation is not as effective at protecting the soil as that provided by the forest floor, newly established vegetation produces litter to replace that burned.

Fire Effects on Soils

Depending on severity, fire may change several forest floor and soil properties which affect the movement of water into or over the soil surface and the susceptibility of exposed soil to erosion processes. The forest floor is the organic horizons covering soil and comprises litter, duff (partially and completely decomposed organic material), and woody debris. Retention of a portion of the forest floor generally protects the soil from the adverse effects of fire.

Forest floor

The forest floor buffers the soil from extremes in temperature and moisture and protects it from surface erosion. The bulk density of forest floors is typically 20 percent or less of the underlying soil horizons (Wooldridge 1970). The low bulk density results from the lower particle density of organic particles; the high porosity of these layers causes the forest floor to have much higher hydraulic conductivities than soil.

The thickness and natural variation in density of forest floors depend on the age and type of forest ecosystem (Gessel and Balci 1965). Forest floors are often less than an inch thick in drier climates and young forests (Amaranthus and McNabb 1984, Edmonds and Hsiang 1987), but are much

thicker in more mesic or older forests (Little and Ohmann 1988).

The thickness and density of forest floors also affect physical properties, such as temperature and moisture gradients, that limit or slow their consumption by fire (Sandberg 1980). Thin forest floors dry quickly and are most susceptible to consumption by fire (Amaranthus and McNabb 1984). Forest floors greater than about 2 inches in thickness typically dry from the surface downward, resulting in a dry surface layer over a much wetter layer (Little and Ohmann 1988). While the dry surface layer may be readily consumed by a fire, the wet layer is much less susceptible to consumption (Sandberg 1980, Little and Ohmann 1988). As more of the surface layer dries in late summer, more of the forest floor may be consumed by a fire.

Moisture content of the forest floor also affects its ability to change temperature; high moisture contents slow changes in temperature and help limit the consumption of forest floor materials. Forest floors with a high moisture content are difficult to burn without an external source of heat, such as the burning of woody fuels (Sandberg 1980). Dry forest floors, however, are often consumed during a fire because less water must be evaporated before the temperature for combustion is reached; this condition is most likely to occur during a severe late summer wildfire or an early fall prescribed fire.

Water repellency and infiltration capacity

When forest floors burn, some of the organic compounds may be partially volatilized (Chapter 16). Most of these are lost to the atmosphere in smoke, but some move downward into the soil by convection where they condense on the surfaces of cooler soil particles. Compounds of long-chain aliphatic hydrocarbons are believed to cause water repellency when they condense on soil particles (DeBano 1981). The development of a water-repellent layer reduces the infiltration capacity of the soil and increases the potential for overland flow. The infiltration capacity is the potential maximum rate at which water enters soil. The infiltration capacity of soil is not constant but decreases as soil becomes wetter and the wetting front moves deeper into the soil. Some water repellency of soil is a natural phenomenon in unburned soils of the Pacific Northwest (Singer and Ugolini 1976, Johnson and Beschta 1980, McNabb et al. 1989).

An increase in water repellency of soil following prescribed burning or wildfire has been reported for several locations in the Pacific Northwest (Megahan and Molitor 1975, Dyrness 1976, Johnson and Beschta 1980, McNabb et al. 1989). Water repellency induced by a low-to-moderate-severity prescribed fire is usually of short duration. In southwest Oregon, repellency resulting from a late spring prescribed burn returned to near natural levels soon after the fall rains began (McNabb et al. 1989). Following a late summer wildfire in the Oregon Cascade mountains, however, repellency of volcanic ash soils did not return to nonburn levels for about 6 years (Dyrness 1976).

Water repellency and its persistence are affected by differences in soil moisture, soil texture, severity of the fire, and quantity and composition of the litter (DeBano 1981). Water repellency is more common in coarse-textured soils because the soil temperature gradients that affect volatilization and condensation during burning are often greater and the soil has less surface area on which volatilized compounds may condense. Coarse-textured soils include soils derived from pumice and other volcanic ash, glacial till, and granite. Fortunately, these soils are generally less common in the high-precipitation zones of western Oregon and Washington, have high porosities, or tend to weather to finer-textured soils.

Water repellency at the soil surface is most likely to occur when fire severity and duration cause moderate increases in soil temperatures (DeBano 1981). Severe fires producing high soil temperatures force the water-repellent layer to form deeper in the soil. Reducing the severity of prescribed burns, retaining forest floor, and burning when soil moisture is high are effective techniques for keeping soil temperatures low and minimizing water repellency.

Water repellency is less likely to cause surface erosion if the reduced infiltration capacity of the soil is higher than precipitation intensity. In southwest Oregon, an increase in water repellency reduced the infiltration capacity of the surface soil from greater than 4 inches per hour to an average of 3.5 inches per hour following a late spring prescribed burn; the lowest infiltration capacity measured was 2 inches per hour (McNabb et al. 1989). Despite this decrease, the lowest capacity still exceeded, by a factor of two, the maximum storm intensity expected in a 25-year period.

A water-repellent layer forming below the soil surface is likely to cause more erosion than such a layer at the surface. The infiltration capacity of the soil over a water-repellent layer is much higher than the hydraulic conductivity of the underlying water-repellent layer. As a consequence, the surface soil is easily saturated by even low-intensity rainfall events, which can cause overland flow or loss of the surface soil in a shallow debris flow above the water-repellent layer (DeBano 1981).

Water repellency has been measured in numerous studies, but only a few have also measured the infiltration capacity of the soil (Megahan and Molitor 1975, McNabb et al. 1989). The high porosity of most forest soils in the Pacific Northwest (Dyrness 1969, Harr 1977), coupled with the low to moderate intensity of most rain events, normally preclude overland flow except immediately after a severe fire or other site disturbance. Overland flow is more likely to occur because the lower hydraulic conductivity of subsoil horizons and underlying rock causes the upper soil horizons to become saturated during large storms; this can cause overland flow unrelated to fire (Dyrness 1969, Beasley 1976). The hydrologic properties of the subsoil are not affected by fire.

Porosity and soil structure

Only the most severe fires are likely to alter soil properties sufficiently to directly affect soil porosity and structure (Dyrness and Youngberg 1957). These conditions may occur where large concentrations of dry fuel are burned over a dry forest floor and soil.

Soil structure improves the macroporosity of soil responsible for the high infiltration capacity typical of forest soils of the Pacific Northwest (Dyrness 1969, Harr 1977). It is altered when fire burns the organic matter that helps bind soil particles together (Dyrness and Youngberg 1957). The breakdown of soil structure frees individual soil particles, making them more susceptible to transport by raindrop splash and overland flow. Smaller soil particles may also move downward into the macropores of the underlying aggregated soils, effectively blocking the macropores, sealing the soil surface, and reducing the infiltration capacity.

Following a severe fall prescribed burn, soil structure was affected over less than 8 percent of a severely burned site in the Oregon Coast Range (Dyrness and Youngberg 1957). But further destruction of soil aggregates may occur from raindrops falling on exposed soil (Packer and Williams 1973).

The most severe fires may occasionally raise soil temperatures enough to alter clay mineralogy and fuse silicate minerals together into cinder-like rocks (Dyrness and Youngberg 1957). Fusion of soil particles is less common than the loss of soil structure and is generally confined to areas with the highest concentration of woody debris, such as near landings. Current burning prescriptions, more complete utilization, and removal of other woody debris generally prevent the high fire severities that cause fusion of soil particles.

Soil temperature

All fire may cause some changes in the thermal properties of soil, but large changes in soil temperature usually result from the loss of vegetation and forest floor. The forest floor is a heat sink when wet and acts as an insulator when dry; both attributes help minimize soil temperature fluctuations.

Burning can alter soil color and the ability of the soil to absorb heat. Charred or blackened surfaces absorb more heat than unburned litter layers or lighter colored soil. As a consequence, burning often results in higher soil temperatures, and greater diurnal temperature fluctuations and extremes (Isaac and Hopkins 1937, Neal et al. 1965). These changes may slow the rate at which vegetation is reestablished and increase the period when soil is more susceptible to erosion processes.

Increased frequencies of low temperatures can cause repeated freezing and thawing of soil exposed following burning of the forest floor. Ice layers forming in soil may destroy soil structure, separate soil aggregates, and uproot shallow-rooted plants as the surface soil is heaved upward. A single frost heave cycle may temporarily raise the surface soil by several inches. Heaving of soil is accomplished by the transfer of soil water from deeper in the soil profile to the freezing front (Chalmers and Jackson 1970, Heidmann 1976). Maximum heaving occurs when the heat lost from freezing water is balanced by the transfer of warmer water deeper in the soil profile to the freezing front. Frost heaving is most severe in moist, medium-textured soils with relatively high rates of unsaturated hydraulic conductivities.

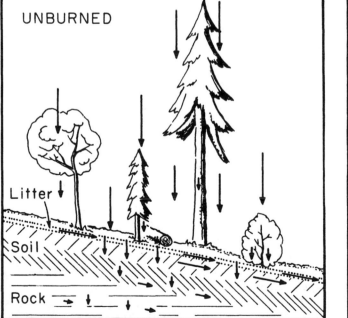
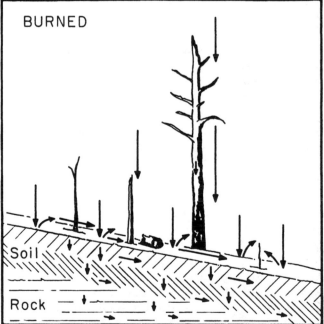

Figure 14-2. Vegetation and the forest floor reduce the energy of water flowing through the litter and reaching the soil. Length of the shaft on the arrow suggests the relative energy of the raindrop or flowing water. A severe burn increases the energy of rain striking the ground and of flow across exposed soil. The flow of water into and through the surface may also be reduced.

Fire Effects on Hydrology

Fire-induced changes in vegetation, forest floor, and soil properties may alter the movement of water over as well as into the soil. The reduction or loss of the forest floor has the greatest potential for altering hillslope hydrology but is often confounded by the concurrent loss of vegetation by fire and harvesting. The largest changes in hillslope hydrology are likely to occur following changes in soil properties but are generally limited to small areas where fire was severe. Changes in hillslope hydrology will ultimately cause some changes in channel hydrology and erosion processes.

Hillslope hydrology

Vegetation intercepts precipitation and alters the energy of falling raindrops striking the ground (Fig. 14-2). Although some intercepted precipitation may evaporate or flow down the stems of plants to the soil surface, the changes in the energy of droplets striking the ground have a major impact on erosion of surface soil.

Vegetation killed by fire no longer transpires soil water, resulting in reduced on-site storage of water during subsequent precipitation events. Changes in soil moisture are least during the winter when transpirational rates are low but low transpiration causes soil moisture to be higher for a longer period of the year and increases the annual yield of water (Chapter 17; Harr 1976, Klock and Helvey 1976, McNabb et al. 1989).

The loss of tree cover following a severe wildfire may increase snow depths and affect melt rates. Changes are similar to those following clearcut harvesting. Snowpacks in openings will melt faster as a result of direct radiation and contact with a more turbulent, warm air mass. In the Pacific Northwest, heat exchange and air turbulence during rain events accelerate the melt of thin snowpacks; this is most likely to occur on middle elevation sites with intermittent snowpacks (Harr 1981, Berris and Harr 1987). Increased melt rate increases the potential for surface erosion, mass wasting, and stream channel changes.

The loss of vegetation will have minimal effect on erosion of surface soil if the forest floor remains relatively undisturbed, because the forest floor is more effective at adsorbing the impact of falling raindrops. In addition, the forest floor stores water, slows the flow of water over the soil surface, helps maintain the porosity of the surface soil, and reduces the transport of sediment by surface water.

Depending on thickness, the forest floor may hold up to 2 inches of water (Gessel and Balci 1965); however, the amount of water that can be stored in the forest floor during a precipitation event will depend on the initial water content. Following a severe slash fire in the Oregon Coast Range, Dyrness et al. (1957) estimated that the destruction of a 2-inch-thick forest floor reduced soil water storage by 0.75 inch of water. More importantly, the forest floor temporarily detains precipitation for later infiltration into the soil or slows the flow of water over the surface (Dyrness 1969). The forest floor protects the soil from raindrop splash that decreases porosity and increases the potential for overland flow (Packer and Williams 1973).

Fire has a minor effect on the ability of the soil profile to hold water. The water storage capacity of the surface 2 inches of soil was reduced by 0.25 inch following a severe broadcast burn in the Oregon Coast Range but the loss was observed to occur only over a small percentage of the site (Dyrness et al. 1957). The importance of this loss is minor compared to the overall water-holding capacity of soils capable of holding 6 or more inches of water and temporarily detaining nearly an equal amount (Dyrness 1969).

Deeper soil horizons, with lower permeabilities, can cause a temporary rise in the water table during rainfall/snowmelt (Harr 1977). The water table may eventually reach the soil surface during storms of moderate to high intensity and long duration; this condition may produce overland flow, increasing the potential for surface erosion. Fire may cause overland flow on sites where it normally does not occur by reducing the permeability of the surface soil that would normally be adequate to transport water throughout the slope (Packer and Williams 1973). This is the most likely cause of overland flow on sites having thin surface soil horizons, well-developed subsurface horizons of low permeability, high percentage of coarse fragments, or a shallow soil over bedrock.

Overland flow is also less likely on undisturbed forest slopes of the Pacific Northwest coast because most winter storms are of low intensity. Summer thunderstorms over the high mountains of the region, however, may produce higher-intensity storm events of shorter duration (1.5 inches in

30 minutes) than winter storms (Helvey 1973). These storms are generally local events whose frequency of occurrence has not been measured. In contrast, much higher rates of sustained precipitation occur in Midwest and Eastern forests where large thunderstorms are common (Orr 1973, Patric 1981).

The potential for overland flow also increases for a specific rainfall intensity if the soil profile is nearly saturated from a previous storm event or results in rapid melt of snowpack (Meeuwig 1971, Harr 1981, Berris and Harr 1987). This is an important factor increasing runoff from small watersheds in the Pacific Northwest where rain-free periods are often short during the wettest months of the year (Istok and Boersma 1987).

Channel hydrology

The reduction in transpiration increases annual water yield from a few inches in forests east of the Cascade crest to approximately 20 inches in western Oregon forests (Chapter 17; Helvey 1972, Harr 1976, Klock and Helvey 1976). Increases in flow are most noticeable in early fall, although flow also remains higher through the summer months; these increases have little effect on channel erosion west of the Cascade crest because the flows generally remain below those necessary for significant sediment transport. Changes in spring snowmelt following wildfire in high elevation and eastside forests, however, may result in increased peak flows (Helvey et al. 1976). Winter peak flows in westside forests seldom are affected by fire unless it changes soil physical properties sufficiently to cause overland flow (Chapter 17; Harr 1976). Although overland flow can speed the movement of surface water to streams, thereby increasing peak flows, it is not known to what extent higher sediment yields may be attributed to such changes in flow.

Fire Effects on Erosion Processes

Erosion is an important factor shaping the landscape of the Pacific Northwest and, historically, disturbance of forest ecosystems by fire has been a major factor affecting geomorphic processes. As a result of disturbance, geomorphic processes and accompanying erosion vary both temporally and spatially (Swanson 1981). In addition to the complex factors affecting natural rates of erosion (Fig. 14-1), forest operations such as road construction,

harvesting, and site preparation also influence erosion, making it more difficult to allocate erosion to a specific type of disturbance, such as prescribed fire.

Although the literature on the direct effects of fire on vegetation and soil is voluminous (Chapters 4, 12, and 13; Wells et al. 1979, Feller 1982), a conceptual framework for estimating erosion has not been formulated for all types of erosion processes affected by fire. Several watershed studies have been installed in the past few decades that provide valuable information as to the direct effects of fire on larger areas, but the complexity of the erosion processes involved requires careful review before extrapolating to other sites. Studies of erosion at the level of forest ecosystems and on the timescale of repeated disturbances are extremely rare because of their greater complexity and the longer periods of time necessary to observe changes (Swanson 1981).

The following is an overview of soil erosion processes—surface erosion, mass wasting, and channel erosion. Changes in hillslope and channel hydrology dominate most forms of erosion but gravity becomes increasingly important on steeper slopes. Erosion processes and transport of sediment are seldom constant but typically accelerate in response to ecosystem disturbance.

Surface erosion

Vegetation and soil properties altered by fire affect surface erosion in a variety of ways. Splash, sheet, rill, and gully erosion caused by changes in hillslope hydrology, frost heaving caused by changes in the soil temperature regime, and ravel from the gravitational movement of material downslope all contribute to surface erosion. The interaction of geomorphic processes, soil and hydrologic properties, climate, and landform determine the relative importance and magnitude of these processes on a specific site.

Splash erosion occurs when raindrops strike exposed mineral soil with sufficient force to dislodge soil particles and small aggregates. Vegetation and the forest floor generally protect the soil from splash erosion. Splash erosion on exposed soil is least under low shrubs, forbs, and grasses because of the short distance intercepted raindrops must travel to the soil. Interception of raindrops by foliage and stems of tall trees, including fire-killed trees without needles or leaves, generally increases drop size and subsequent splash erosion (Herwitz 1987).

Precipitation intensity and slope steepness affect splash erosion less than the size of the soil particles or aggregates (Farmer 1973, Yamamoto and Anderson 1973). Fine sand-sized particles (less than 0.004 to 0.01 inch diameter) are most easily transported in droplet splash; larger particles of single-grained soils are more easily displaced than those in clayey soils (Farmer 1973).

When soils are saturated, splash erosion increases markedly; part of the increase is from a 2-fold increase in the size of material susceptible to detachment by raindrop impact (Farmer 1973). In addition, when raindrops strike saturated soil they cause positive hydrostatic pressures in the surface soil from the soil deforming under their impact. These positive pressures are transmitted outward and upward from the point of impact, aiding particle detachment (Al-Durrah and Bradford 1982). This process is an important factor responsible for a significant increase in splash erosion of finer-textured, single-grained soils.

Splash erosion is an underrated and often misdiagnosed surface erosion process in the Pacific Northwest. It has not been measured in this region as it has elsewhere (Farmer and Van Haveren 1971). It is often confused with sheet erosion because the saturated soil conditions most conducive to splash erosion often cause the overland flow responsible for sheet erosion. Splash erosion is generally uniform across a slope but sheet erosion results in more variable loss of soil and produces deposits of sediments in depressions and behind obstructions.

Splash erosion generally occurs whenever soil is exposed; however, exposure of rock fragments in some soils will eventually protect the underlying soil from raindrop impact. Partial retention of the forest floor during prescribed burning is critical to reducing splash erosion. The relative importance of splash erosion as a geomorphic process increases if prescribed fires that expose soil become more frequent than past wildfires.

Sheet and rill erosion. Once soil particles are detached by splash erosion, they are more easily transported in overland flow. The hydraulic energy of water flowing over the soil also has the ability to detach soil particles. Transport is often as sheet erosion where water flow is not concentrated into small channels (Meeuwig 1970).

Sheet erosion increases exponentially with increasing slope steepness and as the clay content of the soil increases (Meeuwig 1970). Organic matter has a variable effect on sheet erosion; coarse-textured soils become more erodible as organic matter increases while fine-textured soils become less erodible. In general, soils with a relatively high percentage of sand particles (0.002 to 0.08 inches in diameter) are the most erodible. These include many soils derived from granite, sandstone, and volcanic ash.

Sheet and splash erosion are most severe immediately following exposure of the soil to rain or snowmelt. These forms of erosion decrease rapidly after the first year, primarily because of reestablishment of vegetative cover, but also because of "armoring" of the surface by larger particles and aggregates (Megahan 1974). Armoring may be the dominant process reducing erosion of gravelly surface soils (soils with greater than 35 percent rock fragments). Reports of sheet erosion following prescribed burning are rare. Some transport of sediment in overland flow on burned sites occurred during snowmelt in western Montana, but the rate was less than 200 pounds per acre per year and only lasted 2 years (DeByle and Packer 1972).

Rill and gully erosion are less common in forest soils than in agricultural soils because of greater surface roughness, more rock fragments, and absence of tillage that regularly mixes and loosens soil horizons. Rill erosion has been reported on erodible soils following a severe wildfire in unburned logging slash, although rilling was not evident in adjacent uncut timber killed by the wildfire (Megahan and Molitor 1975). Gullies are uncommon in undisturbed forest ecosystems (Heede 1975).

Frost heaving increases the downslope movement of soil when the ice lenses supporting soil particles melt, allowing the soil to drop vertically to the surface. Rapid warming or rain also can cause frost-heaved material to slide or flow down the slope, particularly if the underlying soil remains frozen. Furthermore, the loosening of soil particles by frost heaving makes the individual particles more susceptible to transport by other surface erosion processes.

Fire increases the potential for accelerated erosion by frost heaving when it consumes the forest floor and exposes mineral soil. The contribution of frost heaving to accelerated surface erosion, however, depends on the texture of the soil, landform, and climate. Daily, or periodic, freeze-thaw cycles in temperate climates are most likely to increase erosion from frost heaving. Frost heaving is generally less in cold climates because the freezing front moves progressively deeper into the soil, and thawing is infrequent or snow cover insulates the soil.

Ravel. The movement of soil particles and organic debris down steep slopes in response to gravity is a geomorphic process accelerated by fire. This process is often referred to as "dry ravel," but movement may occur during any season (Anderson et al. 1959); referring to surface erosion by gravity as ravel is a more encompassing term. The material moving may include soil, gravel, cobbles, boulders, and organic debris (Figure 14-3). Detachment can occur by drying and shrinking of the soil particles, frost heaving, animal disturbance, and decomposition or burning of supporting organic debris. Because transport is by gravity, substantial ravel occurs only on slopes exceeding the angle of repose—approximately 35 degrees (Mersereau and Dyrness 1972, Bennett 1982).

Ravel is a natural process occurring on steep forest slopes, but rates are often low because vegetation, forest floor, and other woody debris slow or stop the movement. Burning initially disturbs or eliminates many of the organic structures holding loose material on the slope. As a result, large increases in ravel are observed during and immediately following a burn. In the Oregon Coast Range, two-thirds of the ravel measured the first year following prescribed burning occurred in the first 24 hours (Bennett 1982). Part of the accelerated ravel from burning of harvested sites, however, may be material initially dislodged by movement of logs and equipment over the soil surface during harvesting (McNabb and Crawford 1984). Slash and other woody debris remaining after harvesting trap loose material that is released by burning.

Locally, ravel is an important geomorphic process that is responsible for talus slopes and scree (gravel layers) that may bury soil horizons on steep slopes. Rates of ravel following prescribed burning are several hundred times greater on slopes greater than 60 percent than on less steep slopes (Mersereau and Dyrness 1972, Bennett 1982). Also, vegetation is established more slowly on slopes with high ravel; consequently, ravel continues at elevated rates for a longer time (more than a decade). Ravel deposited directly in streams is readily transported from the watershed by fluvial processes (DeBano and Conrad 1976).

Mass wasting

Rain, snow, and rain-on-snow events may trigger the downslope movement of one or more soil horizons, parent material, and sometimes the underlying rock, by mass wasting. Mass wasting includes debris flows, debris slides, debris avalanches, earthflows, slumps, and creep, depending on the landform, and the depth, rate, and properties of the material moving (Burroughs et al. 1976). In the Pacific Northwest, steep slopes, high rainfall, a history of tectonic uplift, and rapid weathering of weak rocks combine to make mass wasting a dominant erosion process.

Fire leads to an apparent reduction in soil strength following the decay of root systems of fire-killed vegetation (Burroughs and Thomas 1977). Live roots increase the stability of shallow soils on steep slopes by binding the soil mantle across potential failure surfaces (Ziemer and Swanston 1977). The root component of soil strength is less significant in deeper soils where the root zone occupies a smaller percentage of a landslide zone of failure.

The potential for shallow mass wasting increases for several years during the period when dead roots decay and before the roots of new vegetation become fully established (Burroughs and

Figure 14-3. Ravel is the downslope movement of surface soil, rock fragments, and organic debris. Rates increase exponentially as slopes exceed 60 percent.

Thomas 1977). Soil strength is reduced more when conifers are killed because most conifers cannot sprout and maintain a viable root system, as do many hardwood tree and shrub species.

Soil creep is generally a slow process in which the soil mantle may move downslope only a few hundredths of an inch to a few inches annually. The rate is thought to be affected by the length of time a soil remains wet (Gray 1973, Harr et al. 1979). Soil creep contributes to accelerated erosion along stream banks as the banks encroach on stream channels. Devegetation lengthens the seasonal period when soil moisture is high (Chapter 17; Rothacher 1973), which may increase the annual rate of soil creep.

On steep slopes at high elevations, fires may kill vegetation and consume organic debris that help anchor snowpacks and prevent or limit the extent of snow avalanches (Swanson 1981). The loss of vegetation may also increase snow accumulation and hence the risk of avalanches. Avalanches may entrain soil and rocks by scour and uproot trees, including unburned vegetation in the runout area. Avalanche tracks can be slow to revegetate because of repeated avalanches.

Of the several forestry operations that can affect mass wasting, the effect of prescribed burning is usually minor. Most of the potential for the root systems of trees to reduce the risk of mass wasting is lost when the trees are harvested. Road construction and harvesting, rather than prescribed burning, are the dominant factors contributing to increased mass wasting in managed forests (Swanston and Swanson 1976). Wildfires that kill vegetation can have an equivalent or greater effect on mass wasting than harvesting, but the amount of road constructed to harvest fire-killed timber will have an important effect on the overall rate of erosion.

Channel erosion

Fluvial transport is the main mechanism moving soil and nutrients from watersheds. This process is discussed in Chapter 17 but part of the fluvial transport process involves channel erosion, which is relevant here.

Streambank cutting is primarily aided by encroachment of streambanks into channels from creep and other mass wasting processes (Fig. 14-4). Of lesser importance are effects due to increases in peak flow. Changes in hillslope hydrolo-

Figure 14-4. Material which encroaches upon stream channels by surface erosion, creep, or mass wasting may become unstable when supporting vegetation or debris is consumed by fire.

gy often result in an expanded network of perennial and intermittent streams which transport water only following major forest disturbances or extreme peak flows (Fig. 14-5). Seldom used and intermittent stream channels are susceptible to erosion because they are less likely to be armored with rock (Helvey et al. 1985).

Fire increases channel erosion as a result of altered hydrology and sediment availability (Chapter 17; Helvey et al. 1985, Berris and Harr 1987). These conditions may occur when loss of cover affects snow accumulation or melt, water yield is a small percentage of the total precipitation, or loss of transpiring vegetation temporarily increases stream flow.

Wildfires are far more likely than prescribed burning to increase channel erosion. Prescribed fires, in addition to typically being less severe, are generally separated from larger channels by an uncut, unburned buffer strip. Wildfires generally consume all the vegetation and fuels along streams, and the topography along intermittent streams is likely to cause the most severe fire.

Accelerated erosion

Erosion is the consequence of numerous geomorphic processes. Much of the material moving on hillslopes in Pacific Northwest forests is temporarily stored on slopes or in stream channels. Some material is stored for very long periods of time, sometimes centuries in small watersheds

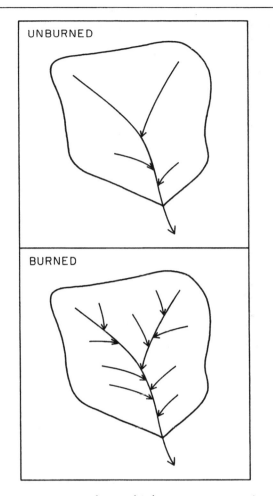

UNBURNED

BURNED

Figure 14-5. Severe fires which remove vegetation and alter soil properties may increase runoff and expand the stream network into smaller, less frequently used channels. Fluvial transport of sediment from the new channels may be high because organic debris which stored sediment was consumed by fire, and the channels generally are not armored.

and longer in larger basins. Noticeable movement generally awaits severe disturbances. The frequency and severity of disturbance such as wildfire, windthrow, road construction, harvesting, and site preparation can affect the balance between the relatively low baseline erosion of the undisturbed forest and the accelerated erosion triggered by disturbance of vegetation (Swanson 1981).

Although the baseline rate of erosion provides a reference for measuring accelerated erosion from

natural forest disturbances, the average long-term rate of erosion is an integration of the baseline and accelerated rates of erosion. The long-term rate of erosion is higher than baseline and can only be estimated over a timescale of multiple disturbances. In many forest ecosystems of the Pacific Northwest, the historical frequency of vegetation disturbance resulting in accelerated erosion is presumed to be closely associated with the frequency of wildfire. In regions with a long interval between fires, accelerated erosion is a smaller percentage of the long-term average rate of erosion than in regions where natural disturbance is more frequent (Swanson 1981).

Forest management affects both the frequency and severity of disturbance that, in turn, may alter the accelerated, baseline, and average rates of sediment production. The effects of prescribed burning on these rates can only be assessed by knowing how forest management practices affect the frequency of fire and how fires in managed forests affect erosion. In general, prescribed fire increases erosion less than associated forest practices or severe wildfire in the Pacific Northwest, particularly when burning results in partial retention of the forest floor. The risk of detrimental erosion increases when burning fails to leave some of the forest floor.

Soil Loss Following Fire

In a hypothetical analysis, Swanson (1981) suggests that accelerated erosion following a major forest disturbance in a small watershed in the western Oregon Cascades may persist as long as two to three decades and account for 25 percent of the total long-term sediment yield, assuming major disturbances occur at an average interval of 200 years. Accelerated erosion accounts for a higher percentage of the total long-term erosion when disturbances are more frequent. More frequent disturbances are likely to increase surface erosion and mass wasting because mineral soil is exposed and root contribution to soil strength is reduced for a larger percentage of the time. Increased erosion is likely because of the greater probability that a site may be susceptible when a storm capable of causing major erosion occurs.

Estimates of accelerated erosion are highly variable because of the complex interaction of various factors that affect erosion processes (Fig. 14-

| Erosion Process | Major Factors Affecting Erosion Processes | |
	Amplitude of Peak	Timing of Peak
Splash	Soil exposure Soil texture Slope Amount of rainfall Intensity of rainfall Loss of vegetation	Formation of forest floor Rate of revegetation
Sheet	Soil exposure Infiltration capacity Armoring of soil surface Amount of rainfall Intensity of rainfall Antecedent precipitation	Armoring of soil surface Formation of new forest floor Timing of major storm events
Ravel	Soil exposure Slope steepness Type of material exposed Position on slope Removal of supporting organic debris Other disturbances	Rate of revegetation Other disturbances
Mass Wasting	Slope Amount of rainfall Antecedent precipitation Loss and importance of root strength Road construction/harvesting	Major storm events Revegetation (root strength)
Channel	Size and stability of channel Armoring of channel Amount of rainfall Antecedent precipitation Rain or snow Removal of organic debris	Major storm events Mass wasting Revegetation

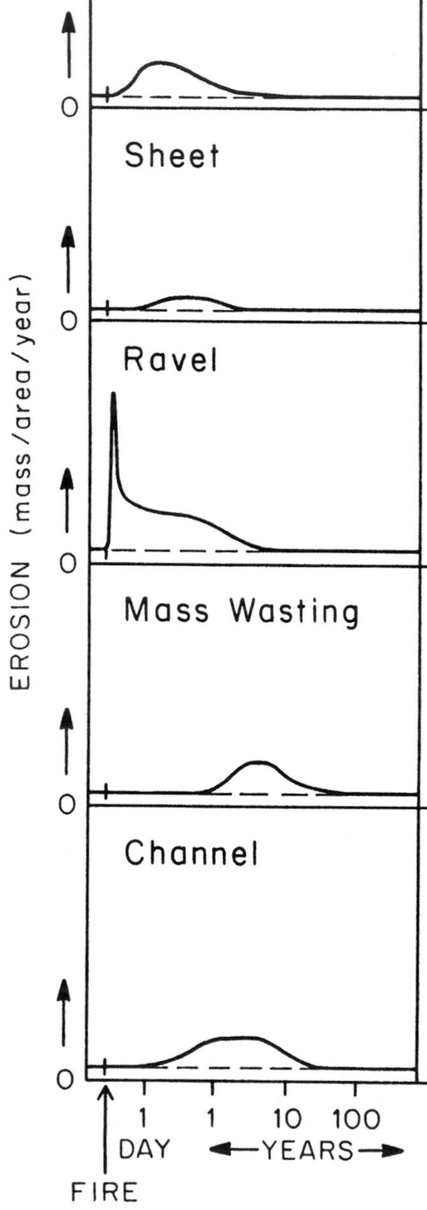

EROSION (mass/area/year)

1 DAY   1   10   100   ◄—YEARS—►

FIRE

Figure 14-6. *The interaction of numerous factors affects erosion processes. Important factors which affect both the amplitude and timing of specific types of erosion are listed in conjunction with the relative effect on erosion rate: inherent to all factors is the effect of fire.*

6). For example, ravel is high immediately following a prescribed burn (Bennett 1982), but also includes ravel dislodged by harvesting and stored in slash (McNabb and Crawford 1984), and elevated rates of ravel can persist for years on steep slopes if revegetation is slow (Mersereau and Dyrness 1972). Other forms of surface erosion will most likely be greatest during the first few years following a fire, depending on how quickly the site is revegetated and the surface becomes armored. The potential for severe mass wasting is generally highest 4 to 7 years after disturbance (Burroughs and Thomas 1977, Ziemer and Swanston 1977), but can occur sooner or later depending on precipitation events and rates of decomposition and reestablishment of root systems.

Erosion directly attributable to prescribed burning is rarely considered a serious problem in the Pacific Northwest (Swanston and Swanson 1976, Wells et al. 1979, Helvey et al. 1985). Where fire-related erosion has been observed, the prescribed fires were locally severe or were confounded by harvesting disturbance (Fredriksen et al. 1975, Beschta 1978, Bennett 1982). Direct measurements of erosion specifically resulting from prescribed fires are invariably confounded by erosion from road construction and harvesting (Swanston and Swanson 1976).

The potential for increased erosion from prescribed fire in a managed forest is primarily a function of the frequency and severity of prescribed fire relative to that of past wildfires. The greater the difference in frequency or severity, the more likely that rates of erosion will differ between natural and managed forest conditions. Surface erosion will likely increase in managed forests unless the intensity of prescribed burning is such that a portion of the forest floor is retained. On the other hand, managed forests will most likely have lower fuel loads which should result in less severe burns.

Erosion following prescribed burning in the Pacific Northwest is different from other regions in the United States where burning may be as frequent as every other year, soils are more erodible, or burning vegetation releases compounds which cause the soil to be water repellent (Ralston and Hatchell 1971, Megahan 1974, DeBano and Conrad 1976). A combination of thick forest floors, high soil infiltration capacities and hydraulic conductivities, complex slope configurations, and low-intensity precipitation events results in fewer opportunities for serious erosion in the Pacific Northwest.

Effects of Soil Loss on Forest Productivity

Soil erosion decreases forest productivity when the rate at which that soil is lost exceeds the rate of soil formation (Swanson et al. 1989), but forest productivity may be affected by other fire-induced changes in soil than erosion (Chapter 12 and 13). A net soil loss can reduce the volume of soil available for root occupancy, soil moisture storage, and availability of nutrients. The ratio of soil loss to soil formation by weathering provides a relative index of the sensitivity of forest ecosystems to the effects of forestry practices on productivity. For a number of reasons, such tolerance indices (the amount of soil loss a site can withstand without having productivity impaired) either have not been developed or are highly speculative estimates for Pacific Northwest forest ecosystems (Wischmeier 1974, Pierce et al. 1984). Furthermore, existing tolerance indices are based on soil lost by sheet and rill erosion, which are relatively minor forms of erosion in forests of the Pacific Northwest, except on severely disturbed sites (Swanson et al. 1989).

Loss of soil from some forest ecosystems is more critical than others (Klock 1982, Swanson et al. 1989), and the history of past site disturbance is important to interpreting these differences among sites (McNabb 1988). Losses of forest floor and soil are more critical on sites where the potential for transpiration by vegetation is high, precipitation is low, and evaporation of water from exposed soil is significant (Flint and Childs 1987). Increased plant moisture stress caused by excessive evaporative and transpirational losses generally have greater influence on revegetation and plant growth than the direct loss of soil water-holding capacity.

Locally, mass wasting may substantially reduce the productivity of the failed portion of a site (Miles et al. 1984), but prescribed burning has a minor effect on mass wasting. Reduced forest productivity from soil loss following sheet or rill erosion has not been measured; but where soil has been removed mechanically, forest growth has been reduced significantly (Glass 1976). Surface erosion rarely causes a critical loss of soil in Pacific Northwest forests because of high infiltration rates and relatively low precipitation intensities (Wells et al. 1979). With the possible exception of highly erodible soils such as granitic soils, or the possible formation of a water-repellent layer below the soil surface following an unusually severe fire, surface erosion is unlikely to reduce forest productivity in the region (Swanson et al. 1989). Prescribed burns which leave a portion of the forest floor covering the soil can minimize all forms of surface erosion.

The loss of nutrients during a fire is much more likely to reduce the productivity of Pacific Northwest forests than is erosion of surface soil (Chapter 12). Significant reductions in site nutrients and the associated forest floor and woody debris, however, can reduce soil organic matter and affect soil biology over an extended period of time (several rotations). Reduced soil organic matter will cause detrimental changes in soil physical properties that could substantially increase surface erosion. Thus, using prescribed burning techniques which minimize the loss of nutrients will lessen the risk of future soil erosion.

Managing Prescribed Burning to Reduce Erosion

Based on the few studies of wildfires and severe prescribed burns, accelerated erosion is greatest on sites with steep slopes and highly erodible soils prone to overland flow (Megahan and Molitor 1975, Helvey et al. 1985). Retention of some forest floor over all soil until postfire vegetation begins to replace lost forest floor materials, particularly in the riparian zone, is an important method of reducing surface erosion (Brown and Krygier 1971). The thickness of forest floor which should be left to achieve this objective varies by forest ecosystem because of differences in decomposition rate and hydrology. In addition, maintaining some vegetation in intermittent stream courses with poorly defined channels may also be an effective technique for reducing erosion when the stream network expands during major storm events.

Using prescribed burning techniques which leave a portion of the forest floor covering the soil (Chapter 22) prevents detrimental changes in soil properties. Of the many burning techniques available, burning when the forest floor is moist is particularly effective for retaining some forest floor. Retention of a portion of the forest floor is least likely to occur during late summer and fall burns because the forest floor remains dry even after several inches of precipitation.

Grass seeding sometimes speeds revegetation of severely burned sites after a late summer wildfire. Seeding generally has minimal impact on deterring surface erosion in the Pacific Northwest because most soils are generally well aggregated, seldom subject to overland flow, and revegetate quickly (Dyrness et al. 1957, Helvey and Fowler 1979, Wells et al. 1979). Grass seeding may successfully reduce the immediate risk of surface erosion in riparian zones, soil disturbed by construction of fire lines, and areas with particularly steep slopes and erodible soils. Grass seeding for erosion should be used judiciously, however, to avoid jeopardizing the reforestation and natural revegetation of burned sites. Grass seeding may hinder the establishment of native vegetation on burned sites (Taskey et al. 1989) and increase the risk of mass failures on steep slopes in later years.

All prescribed burning practices that minimize nutrient losses and protect soil biota are compatible with reducing the potential for soil erosion. Practices that burn fuels when the forest floor is dry are incompatible with minimizing impacts on soil erosion and forest productivity.

Conclusion

Severe wildfires have been, and potentially remain, a dominant factor that temporarily accelerates several erosion processes, including mass wasting, surface erosion, and ravel, in the forest ecosystems of the Pacific Northwest. Wildfires increase erosion by removing part or all of the vegetation canopy, consuming the forest floor, and causing detrimental changes in surface soil properties. In contrast, prescribed fire alone is less likely to cause as much erosion, because harvesting rather than fire removes most of the vegetation, and the intensity of the burn can be controlled to reduce its severity. It is possible, and common, to prescribe burn a site while leaving a portion of the forest floor covering the soil and not to affect soil physical properties.

Retention of some forest floor covering the mineral soil and rapid revegetation of burned sites effectively prevent or limit most accelerated surface erosion. Therefore, the thickness and areal coverage of forest floor remaining after a prescribed burn is the most important measure of the potential for surface erosion. Protection of the forest floor is more difficult in the managed forests of northwestern Oregon and western Washington because the planned rotation length in these forests is less than the natural fire frequency. Increased frequency of burning results in thinner forest floors that will require greater adherence to burning prescriptions designed to minimize consumption of the forest floor. Elsewhere in the region, retention of the forest floor is no less important. Although rotations may be longer than the interval between wildfires, slower forest growth and slower production of a new forest floor will require greater retention of forest floor to sustain its protective role.

Surface erosion caused by prescribed burning has seldom been measured in the Pacific Northwest because it is not perceived to be a major cause of erosion from forested lands. Road construction and harvesting are more serious causes of erosion, particularly mass wasting on steeper slopes. Furthermore, erosion by these practices often obscures erosion caused by prescribed burning. Measurement of surface erosion processes, however, will become more important in the future because forest floors in managed forests will be thinner and more difficult to protect from burning, particularly if other constraints such as concern for air quality or fire hazard reduction result in burning when fuels and forest floor are dry.

The judicious use of prescribed burning in most forest ecosystems of the Pacific Northwest is not anticipated to cause sufficient erosion to adversely affect long-term forest productivity, although the productivity of a few highly erodible soils may be reduced if burned frequently or severely.

Literature Cited & Key References

Al-Durrah, M.M., and J.M. Bradford. 1982. Parameters for describing soil detachment due to single waterdrop impact. Soil Sci. Soc. Am. J. 46:836-840.

*Amaranthus, M., and D.H. McNabb. 1984. Bare soil exposure following logging and prescribed burning in southwest Oregon, p. 234-237. *In* New Forests For A Changing World. Proc., 1983 Soc. Amer. For. Nat. Conv., Portland, OR. 640 p.

Anderson, H.W., G.B. Coleman, and P.J. Zinke. 1959. Summer slides and winter scour . . . dry-wet erosion in southern California mountains. USDA For. Serv. Pac. Southwest For. Rge. Exp. Sta., Berkeley, CA. Tech. Pap. PSW-36. 12 p.

Beasley, R.S. 1976. Contribution of subsurface flow from the upper slopes of forested watersheds to channel flow. Soil Sci. Soc. Am. J. 40:955-957.

Bennett, K.A. 1982. Effects of slash burning on surface soil erosion rates in the Oregon Coast Range. M.S. thesis, Oregon State Univ., Corvallis, OR. 70 p.

Berris, S.N., and R.D. Harr. 1987. Comparative snow accumulation and melt during rainfall in forested and clear-cut plots in the Western Cascades of Oregon. Water Resour. Res. 23:135-142.

Beschta, R.L. 1978. Long-term patterns of sediment production following road construction and logging in the Oregon Coast Range. Water Resour. Res. 14:1011-016.

Brown, G.W., and J.T. Krygier. 1971. Clear-cut logging and sediment production in the Oregon Coast Range. Water Resour. Res. 7:1198-1198.

*Burroughs, E.R., Jr., and B.R. Thomas. 1977. Declining root strength in Douglas-fir after felling as a factor in slope stability. USDA For. Serv. Intermt. For. Rge. Exp. Sta., Ogden, UT. Res. Pap. INT-190. 27 p.

Burroughs, E.R., Jr., G.R. Chalfant, and M.A. Townsend. 1976. Slope stability in road construction, a guide to the construction of stable roads in western Oregon and northern California. USDI Bur. Land Manage., Portland, OR. 102 p.

Chalmers, B., and K.A. Jackson. 1970. Experimental and theoretical studies of the mechanism of frost heaving. U.S. Army, Cold Regions Res. and Engr. Lab., Hanover, NH. Res. Rep. 199. 23 p.

*DeBano, L.F. 1981. Water repellent soils: a state-of-the-art. USDA For. Serv., Pac. Southwest For. Rge. Exp. Sta., Berkeley, CA. Gen. Tech. Rep. PSW-46. 21 p.

References marked by an asterisk are recommended for general information.

DeBano, L.F., and C.E. Conrad. 1976. Nutrients lost in debris and runoff water from a burned chaparral watershed, p.3:13-27. *In* Proc., 3rd Fed. Inter-Agency Sediment Conf., Denver, CO. U.S. Water Resources Council, Washington, DC.

*DeByle, N.V., and P.E. Packer. 1972. Plant nutrient and soil losses in overland flow from burned forest clearcuts, p. 296-307. Nat. Symp. Watersheds in Transition, Amer. Water Resour. Assoc., Colorado State Univ., Ft. Collins, CO. 405 p.

Dyrness, C.T. 1969. Hydrologic properties of soils on three small watersheds in the Western Cascades of Oregon. USDA For. Serv. Pac. Northwest For. Rge. Exp. Sta., Portland, OR. Res. Note PNW-111. 17 p.

Dyrness, C.T. 1973. Early stages of plant succession following logging and burning in the western Cascades of Oregon. Ecol. 54:57-69.

Dyrness, C.T. 1976. Effect of wildfire on soil wettability in the High Cascades of Oregon. USDA For. Serv. Pac. Northwest For. Rge. Exp. Sta., Portland, OR. Res. Pap. PNW-202. 18 p.

*Dyrness, C.T., and C.T. Youngberg. 1957. The effect of logging and slash-burning on soil structure. Soil Sci. Soc. Amer. Proc. 21:444-447.

Dyrness, C.T., C.T. Youngberg, and R.H. Ruth. 1957. Some effects of logging and slash burning on physical soil properties in the Corvallis watershed. USDA For. Serv. Pac. For. Rge. Exp. Sta., Portland, OR. Res. Pap. PNW-19. 15 p.

Edmonds, R.L., and T. Hsiang. 1987. Forest floor and soil influence on response of Douglas-fir to urea. Soil Sci. Soc. Amer. J. 51:1332-1337.

Farmer, E.E. 1973. Relative detachability of soil particles by simulated rainfall. Soil Sci. Soc. Amer. Proc. 37:629-633.

Farmer, E.E., and B.P. Van Haveren. 1971. Soil erosion by overland flow and raindrop splash on three mountain soils. USDA For. Serv., Intermt. For. Rge. Exp. Sta., Ogden, UT. Res. Pap. INT-100. 14 p.

*Feller, M.C. 1982. The ecological effects of slashburning with particular reference to British Columbia: a literature review. British Columbia Ministry of Forests, Univ. of British Columbia, Vancouver, B.C. Land Manage. Rep. 13. 60 p.

Flint, L.E., and S.W. Childs. 1987. Effect of shading, mulching and vegetation control on Douglas-fir seedling growth and soil water supply. For. Ecol. Manage. 18:189-203.

*Fredriksen, R.L., D.G. Moore, and L.A. Norris. 1975. The impact of timber harvest, fertilization, and herbicide treatment on streamwater quality in western Oregon and Washington, p. 283-313. *In* Bernier, B., and C.H. Winget, (eds.) Forest Soils and Forest Land Management. Proc., 4th North Amer. For. Soils Conf., Laval Univ., Quebec. 675 p.

Gessel, S.P., and A.N. Balci. 1965. Amount and composition of forest floors under Washington coniferous forests, p. 11-23. *In*: Youngberg, C.T. (ed.) Forest-Soil Relationships North America. Proc., 2nd North Amer. For. Soils Conf., Oregon State Univ., Corvallis. 532 p.

Gholz, H.L., G.M. Hawk, A. Campbell, K. Cromack, Jr., and A.T. Brown. 1985. Early vegetation recovery and element cycles on a clear-cut watershed in western Oregon. Can. J. For. Res. 15:400-409.

Glass, G.G., Jr. 1976. The effects from rootraking on an upland piedmont loblolly pine (*Pinus taeda* L.) site. Sch. Forest Resour., North Carolina State Univ., Raleigh, NC. Tech. Rep. 56. 44 p.

Gray, D.H. 1973. Effects of forest clearcutting on the stability of natural slopes—results of field studies. Report for National Science Foundation GK-24747. Dept. Civil Eng., Univ. Michigan, Ann Arbor.

*Harr, R.D. 1976. Forest practices and streamflow in western Oregon. USDA For. Serv., Pac. Northwest For. Rge. Exp. Sta., Portland, OR. Gen. Tech. Rep. PNW-49. 18 p.

Harr, R.D. 1977. Water flux in soil and subsoil on a steep forested slope. J. Hydrol. 33:37-58.

Harr, R.D. 1981. Some characteristics and consequences of snowmelt during rainfall in western Oregon. J. Hydrol. 53:277-304.

Harr, R.D., R.L. Fredriksen, and J. Rothacher. 1979. Changes in streamflow following timber harvest in southwestern Oregon. USDA For. Serv. Pac. Northwest For. Rge. Exp. Sta., Portland, OR. Res. Pap. PNW-249. 22 p.

Heede, B.H. 1975. Stages of development of gullies in the west, p. 155-161. *In* Present and Prospective Technology For Predicting Sediment Yields and Sources. Proc., Sediment-Yield Workshop, USDA Agr. Res. Serv., Oxford, MS. ARS-S-40, 1972. 285 p.

Heidmann, L.J. 1976. Frost heaving of tree seedlings: A literature review of causes and possible control. USDA For. Serv., Rocky Mt. For. Rge. Exp. Sta., Ft. Collins, CO. Gen. Tech. Rep. RM-21.

Helvey, J.E. 1972. First-year effects of wildfire on water yield and stream temperature in north-central Washington, p. 308-312. *In* Nat. Symp. on Watersheds in Transition, Amer. Water Resour. Assoc., Colorado State Univ., Ft. Collins, CO. 405 p.

Helvey, J.D. 1973. Watershed behavior after forest fire in Washington, p. 403-422. *In* Proc., Irrigation and Drainage Division Specialty Conf. Amer. Soc. Civil Engr., New York, NY. 808 p.

Helvey, J.D., and W.B. Fowler. 1979. Grass seeding and soil erosion in a steep, logged area in northeastern Oregon. USDA For. Serv., Pac. Northwest For. Rge. Exp. Sta., Portland, OR. Res. Note PNW-343. 11 p.

*Helvey, J.D., A.R. Tiedemann, and T.D. Anderson. 1985. Plant nutrient losses by soil erosion and mass movement after wildfire. J. Soil Water Conserv. 40:168-173.

*Helvey, J.D., A.R. Tiedemann, and W.B. Fowler. 1976. Some climatic and hydrologic effects of wildfire in Washington State. Tall Timbers Fire Ecol. Conf. Proc. 15:201-222.

Herwitz, S.R. 1987. Raindrop impact and water flow on the vegetative surfaces of trees and the effects on streamflow and throughfall generation. Earth Surf. Processes Landf. 12:425-432.

Isaac, L.A., and H.G. Hopkins. 1937. The forest soil of the Douglas-fir region and the changes wrought upon it by logging and slash burning. Ecol. 18:264-279.

Istok, J.D., and L. Boersma. 1987. Effect of antecedent rainfall on runoff during low-intensity rainfall. J. Hydrol. 88:329-342.

*Johnson, M.G., and R.L. Beschta. 1980. Logging, infiltration capacity, and surface erodibility in western Oregon. J. For. 78:334-337.

Klock, G.O. 1982. Some soil erosion effects on forest soil productivity, p. 53-66. *In* Determinants of Soil Loss Tolerance. Proc., Symp. Soil Sci. Soc. Amer., Aug. 5-10, 1979, Am. Soc. Agron. Fort Collins, CO. Spec. Pub. 45. 153 p.

Klock, G.O., and J.D. Helvey. 1976. Soil-water trends following wildfire on the Entiat Experimental Forest. Tall Timbers Fire Ecol. Conf. Proc. 15:193-200.

Little, S.N., and J.L. Ohmann. 1988. Estimating nitrogen lost from forest floor during prescribed fires in Douglas-fir/western hemlock clearcuts. For. Sci. 34:152-164.

McNabb, D.H. 1988. Interpreting the effects of broadcast burning on forest productivity, p. 89-103. *In* Lousier, D., and G.Stills (eds.) Degradation of Forest Lands—Forest Soils at Risk, Proc., Tenth British Columbia Soil Sci. Workshop, Feb. 20-21, 1986. British Columbia Ministry of Forests and Lands, Land Management Report 56. Victoria, B.C. 331 p.

McNabb, D.H., and M.S. Crawford. 1984. Ravel movement on steep slopes caused by logging and broadcast burning, p. 263. *In* Agron. Abstr., 76th Annu. Mtg. Amer. Soc. Agron., November 25-30, 1984, Las Vegas, NV. 285 p.

McNabb, D.H., F. Gaweda, and H.A. Froehlich. 1989. Infiltration, water repellency, and soil moisture content after broadcast burning of forest site in southwest Oregon. J. Soil Water Conserv. 44:87-90.

Meeuwig, R.O. 1970. Sheet erosion on intermountain summer ranges. USDA For. Serv. Intermt. For. Rge. Exp. Sta., Ogden, UT. Res. Pap. INT-85. 25 p.

Meeuwig, R.O. 1971. Soil stability on high-elevation rangeland in the intermountain area. USDA For. Serv. Intermt. For. Rge. Exp. Sta., Ogden, UT. Res. Pap. INT-94. 10 p.

Megahan, W.F. 1974. Erosion over time on severely disturbed granitic soils: a model. USDA For. Serv. Intermt. For. Rge. Exp. Sta., Ogden, U. Res. Pap. INT.156. 14 p.

*Megahan, W.F., and D.C. Molitor. 1975. Erosional effects of wildfire and logging in Idaho, p. 423-444. *In* Watershed Management Symp., Aug. 11-13, 1975. Irrig. Drainage Div., Amer. Soc. Civil Engr., Logan, UT.

*Mersereau, R.C., and C.T. Dyrness. 1972. Accelerated mass wasting after logging and slash burning in Western Oregon. J. Soil Water Conserv. 27:112-114.

*Miles, D.W.R., F.J. Swanson, and C.T. Youngberg. 1984. Effects of landslide erosion on subsequent Douglas-fir growth and stocking levels in the western Cascades, Oregon. Soil Soc. Amer. J. 48:667-671.

Neal, J.L., E. Wright, and W.B. Bolen. 1965. Burning Douglas-fir slash: physical, chemical, and microbial effects in the soil. For. Res. Lab. Res. Pap. 1. Oregon State Univ., Corvallis. 32 p.

Orr, H.K. 1973. The Black Hills (South Dakota) flood of June 1972: impacts and implications. USDA For. Serv. Rocky Mt. For. Rge. Exp. Sta., Fort Collins, CO. Gen. Tech. Rep. RM-2. 12 p.

*Packer, P.E., and B.D. Williams. 1973. Logging and prescribed burning effects on the hydrologic and soil stability behavior of larch/Douglas-fir forests in the northern Rocky Mountains. Tall Timbers Fire Ecol. Conf. Proc. 14:465-479.

Patric, J.H. 1981. Soil-water relations of shallow forested soils during flash floods in West Virginia. USDA For. Serv. Northeastern For. Exp. Sta., Broomall, PA. Res. Pap. NE-469. 20 p.

Pierce, F.J., W.E. Larson, and R.H. Dowdy. 1984. Soil loss tolerance: Maintenance of long-term soil productivity. J. Soil Water Cons. 39:136-139.

*Ralston, C.W., and G.E. Hatchell. 1971. Effects of prescribed burning on physical properties of soil, p. 68-85. *In* Proc. Prescribed Burning Symp. USDA For. Serv., Southeast For. Exp. Sta., Asheville, NC. 160 p.

Rothacher, J. 1973. Does harvest in west slope Douglas-fir increase peak flow in small forest streams? USDA For. Serv. Pac. Northwest For. Rge. Exp. Sta., Portland, OR. Res. Pap. PNW-163. 13 p.

Sandberg, D.V. 1980. Duff reduction by prescribed underburning in Douglas-fir. USDA For. Serv. Pac. Northwest For. Rge. Exp. Sta., Portland, OR. Res. Pap. PNW-272. 18 p.

Singer, M.J., and F.C. Ugolini. 1976. Hydrophobicity in the soils of Findley Lake, Washington. For. Sci. 22:54-58.

*Swanson, F.J. 1981. Fire and geomorphic processes, p. 401-420. *In* Proc., Fire Regimes and Ecosystems Conf., December 11-15, 1979, Honolulu, HI. USDA For. Serv., Washington, DC. Gen. Tech. Rep. WO-26. 594 p.

*Swanson, F.J., R.L. Fredriksen, and F.M. McCorison. 1982. Material transfer in a western Oregon forested watershed, p. 233-266. *In* Edmonds, R.L. (ed.), Analysis of coniferous forest ecosystems in the western United States. US/IBP Synth. Ser. No 14. Hutchinson Ross Publ. Co., Stroudsburg, PA. 419 p.

*Swanson, F.J., J.L. Clayton, W.F. Megahan, and G. Bush. 1989. Erosional processes and long-term site productivity, p. 67-81. *In* Perry, D.A., R. Meurisse, B. Thomas, R. Miller, J. Boyle, J. Means, C.R. Perry, and R.F. Powers (eds.), Maintaining the Long-term Productivity of Pacific Northwest Forest Ecosystems. Timber Press, Portland, OR. 257 p.

*Swanston, D.N., and F.J. Swanson. 1976. Timber harvesting, mass erosion, and steepland forest geomorphology in the Pacific Northwest, p. 199-211. *In* Coates, D.R. (ed.) Geomorphology and Engineering. Hutchinson Ross Publ. Co., Stroudsburg, PA. 360 p.

Taskey, R.D., C.L. Curtis, and J. Stone. 1989. Wildfire, ryegrass seeding, and watershed rehabilitation, p. 115-124. *In* Symp., Fire and Watershed Management. USDA For. Serv. Pac. Southwest Res. Sta., Berkeley, CA. Gen. Tech. Rep. PSW-109. 164 p.

*Wells, C.G., R.E. Campbell, L.F. DeBano, C.E. Lewis, R.L. Fredriksen, E.C. Franklin, R.C. Froelich, and P.H. Dunn. 1979. Effects of fire on soil. USDA For. Serv. Washington, DC. Gen. Tech. Rep. WO-7. 34 p.

Wischmeier, W.H. 1974. New developments in estimating water erosion, p. 179-186. *In*: Land Use: Persuasion or Regulation. Proc., 29th Annu. Mtg. Soil Conserv. Soc. Amer., Aug. 11-14, 1974, Syracuse, New York.

Wooldridge, D.D. 1970. Chemical and physical properties of forest litter layers in central Washington, p. 151-166. *In*: Youngberg ,C.T., and C.B. Davey (eds.) Tree Growth and Forest Soils. Oregon State Univ. Press, Corvallis, OR.

Yamamoto, T., and H.W. Anderson. 1973. Splash erosion related to soil erodibility indexes and other forest soil properties in Hawaii. Water Resour. Res. 9:336-345.

Ziemer, R.R., and D.H. Swanston. 1977. Root strength changes after logging in southeast Alaska. USDA For. Serv. Pac. Northwest For. Rge. Exp. Sta., Portland, OR. Res. Note PNW-306. 10 p.

15 Effects of Prescribed Fire on Timber Growth and Yield

Richard E. Miller and Kenneth W. Seidel

Executive Summary

Forest practices are undertaken when they appear to have benefits that exceed immediate or long-term costs. Decisions to use or not use some practices are often made without critical information because their effects on tree growth are inadequately quantified.

In this chapter we show that the effect of prescribed burning on timber yields has been measured at relatively few locations, and the results evidently depend on local conditions. Consequently, decisions to burn or how to burn must recognize that predictions of subsequent timber yield and costs of production are uncertain; the effect can range from positive to negative. Like most forest practices, slash burning has potential benefits and costs with respect to timber yields in both the immediate and the long term. Prescribed fires—and the wildfires they attempt to reduce—can affect trees directly and also indirectly through factors that influence tree growth. When growth of individual trees and stands is aggregated, forest and regional productivities are affected. Site-to-site variation and a paucity of reliable information about tree growth after prescribed burning in both eastside and westside forests requires that interim decisions be made on judgment and experience. Uncertainty will continue until long-term data and reliable predictions are available.

Monitoring programs should be established to document response of trees and site factors to prescribed slash burning and underburning. Data from long-term monitoring plots could be used to evaluate current practices and to construct reliable predictive models that quantify effects of fire and other forest practices on stand and forest productivity.

Introduction

Forest practices are undertaken when they appear to have benefits that exceed immediate or long-term costs. Effects of some practices on tree growth are poorly quantified, so current forest management decisions are often made without potentially critical information. Predicting the net effect of most practices on forest productivity is difficult given the change in practices and environmental conditions over time; the different mix of practices that may be used, and the interactions among them; the difference in expertise with which practices are carried out; the variability of sites and stands; and the scarcity of appropriate, long-term sample plots where effects on tree growth can be isolated and measured. These variations and uncertainties provide ample room for divergent results and viewpoints of forest practices on timber growth and yield.

Fire is commonly prescribed after timber harvest in the Pacific Northwest to reduce risk of wildfire in logging slash and to prepare harvested areas for regenerating a new crop (Chapters 6 and 8). Yet slash fires, like wildfires, present a risk to nearby trees and other resources. Slash fires usually have high burning intensity and can affect growth and species composition of the new forest through fire's effects on residual seedlings and shrubs, soil properties, microclimate, and subsequent plant establishment and succession.

East of the Cascade Range, low-severity fires are increasingly prescribed for established stands to reduce the fire hazard created by accumulations of organic matter on the soil, or control the number or species composition of trees and other vegetation (Chapter 6). Although these controlled underburns generally consume much less organic matter than do slash burns or the wildfires they replace, they too can affect subsequent yield of merchantable timber from the current stand and perhaps from future stands. The lower inherent productivity of eastside sites suggests a greater susceptibility of eastside forests to nutrient and organic matter losses. This justifies concern about the effects of repeated underburning on long-term site productivity, especially in the absence of corrective measures like fertilization.

In this chapter, we present evidence that the effects of prescribed burning on timber yields are poorly quantified and depend on local site and stand conditions. Consequently, decisions to burn or how to burn must recognize that net effects of prescribed fire on subsequent timber yield, timber value, and costs of timber production are uncertain and apparently range from positive to negative.

Growth & Yield After Slash Fires in Westside Forests

Effects of slash burning on early survival and growth of natural and planted seedlings were discussed in Chapter 6. Subsequent growth of established stands is controlled strongly by inherent productivity of the soil, which can be changed by previous harvest and site preparation (Chapters 12, 13, and 14). Because tree growth frequently can be increased by control of competing vegetation, by thinning, and by fertilization, such silvicultural practices may offset impairments of inherent site productivity that may occur on some sites from physical impacts of machinery or nutrient losses.

The westside experience

Valid comparisons of long-term growth and yield on burned and unburned sites that are otherwise identical would provide direct proof of slash burning effects. Unfortunately, current data are limited in amount, geographic distribution, reliability, and period of measurement. Long-term data are not available, even for one rotation of 50 or more years. Moreover, comparisons at numerous locations are necessary because of large variability in stand growth and yield caused by soil and climatic differences and by harvest and management activities.

Morris (1958) started the most extensive, long-term study on effects of slash burning in the Pacific Northwest. Recent measurement of trees on the burned and the adjacent unburned plot at 44 of his original locations in the Cascade Range of western Oregon and Washington provides growth comparisons over the longest period available to quantify and explain the net effects of slash burning in this area (Fig. 15-1). The stands on these 0.12- to 0.58-acre plots were measured 35 to 42 years after clearcutting.

Burning old-growth slash at these 44 locations resulted in a mosaic of microsite conditions depending on local fire severity. Small areas of unburned slash were observed in almost all burned plots, as were severely burned patches with ab-

Figure 15-1. Burning logging slash after harvest can remove large quantities of above-ground organic matter. (A) Unburned plot and (B) burned plot at Location 18 near Blue River, OR.

sence of the duff layer and reddening of the soil (Morris 1970). Unburned and severely burned patches have been observed in other locations in the Cascade Range (Tarrant 1956) and the Oregon Coast Range (Dyrness et al. 1957). Young seedlings survived harvesting activities at some locations. This advance regeneration on unburned plots was a potential component of the subsequent stand. Few seedlings survived the slash fire on burned plots. This elimination or reduction of advance regeneration is a direct effect of fire which can affect subsequent species composition, stand density, tree size, and stand volume at some locations.

Results and interpretations

Effects on site quality. Height growth is a measure of site quality; trees grow taller on good quality sites. A difference in height of same-age crop trees on burned and unburned areas, therefore, can indicate a change in site quality. To compare site quality between areas where crop trees are not equal-aged, however, foresters relate height/age measurements to the height at a standard age (usually 25, 50, or 100 years). This height is called site index. For example, site index$_{50}$ 110 indicates that the largest trees in a stand average 110 feet tall when their breast-high age is 50 years; site index 110 is about average site quality for coast Douglas-fir. Younger trees on this quality land will average 54 feet at 20 years breast-high age and 95 feet at 40 years (King 1966).

Current analysis of the data from Morris's 44 test plots indicated that the average difference in site quality between burned and unburned plots was not statistically significant. Although 10 or more percent differences in site index between the two plots were measured at some locations, no consistent pattern related to burning is evident (Fig. 15-2). Moreover, no consistent difference in site index existed between burned and unburned plots at locations that had been planted instead of naturally regenerated. Future analyses may provide bases for predicting where slash burning may have the greatest impact. Clearly, these data must be supplemented by additional site index and growth data collected in planted stands because planting is the conventional method of regenerating Douglas-fir forest.

Effects on species composition. Twenty-eight locations were regenerated naturally; 16 were planted, but frequently with limited success. Subsequent species composition differed among the 44 locations and differed between the burned and unburned plot at most locations. In general, Douglas-fir was more abundant in numbers on burned plots, whereas western hemlock, western redcedar, and true fir species were more abundant on unburned plots. Advance regeneration of these

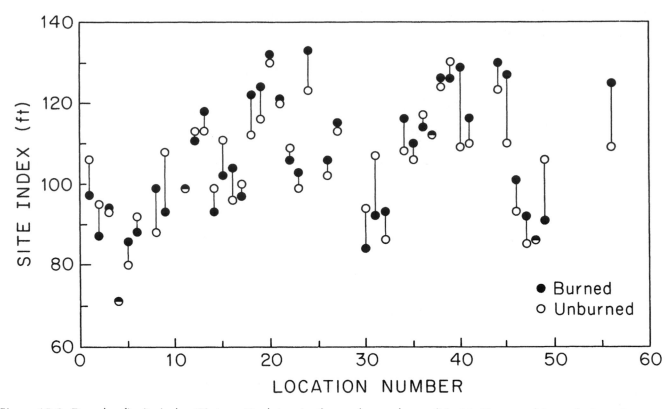

Figure 15-2. Douglas-fir site index (SI₅₀) on 42 plot-pairs (burned vs. unburned) in 35-42-year-old stands. Locations are numbered in ascending order from the most northerly near Enumclaw, WA, to the most southerly near Roseburg, OR. (Source: unpublished manuscript on file at USDA Forest Service, Forestry Sciences Laboratory, Olympia, WA.)

more shade-tolerant conifers survived on unburned areas, whereas the greater extent of exposed mineral soil on burned areas initially favored Douglas-fir establishment (Morris 1970). Species composition by cubic volume (Fig. 15-3) corresponds to these differences in tree numbers.

Effects on volume growth. Tree size and number differed on burned and unburned plots depending on the cumulative effects of initial harvest, slash fire (or lack of it), and subsequent silvicultural activities. At each location, the same activities were applied to both plots; however the same activities did not occur at all locations. For example, both plots at some locations were thinned to concentrate growth on fewer trees, but thinning was not done at all locations.

For the combined species (including hardwoods), mean annual volume production since harvest of the previous stand was greater on burned plots at some locations and on unburned at others (Fig. 15-4). Average total volume produc-

tion, in trees 1.6 and 7.6 inches diameter at breast height (dbh) and larger for all species combined, on the burned and unburned plots at 44 locations is shown in Table 15-1. The average difference in cumulative growth (live, cut, dead volume) between burned and unburned plots was not statistically significant either for the total stand (1.6 inches dbh and larger) or for the near-merchantable stand (7.6 inches dbh and larger). Douglas-fir volume production, however, averaged greater on burned plots and, conversely, that of other conifers averaged greater on unburned plots (Fig. 15-3).

At seven locations, cumulative volume growth on a burned and planted plot could be compared to that on an adjacent burned and naturally regenerated plot (Fig. 15-4). Volume production on the planted plots averaged 892 ft³ per acre or 34 percent more than on naturally regenerated plots. No long-term data are available from this or other studies to compare validly the performance of planted stands on burned vs. unburned areas.

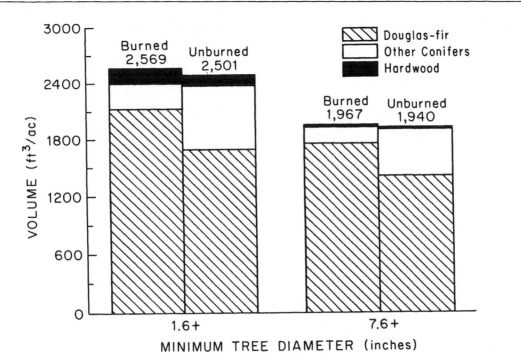

Figure 15-3. *Average cumulative gross volume production on burned and unburned plots since harvest, by species and minimum tree size.*

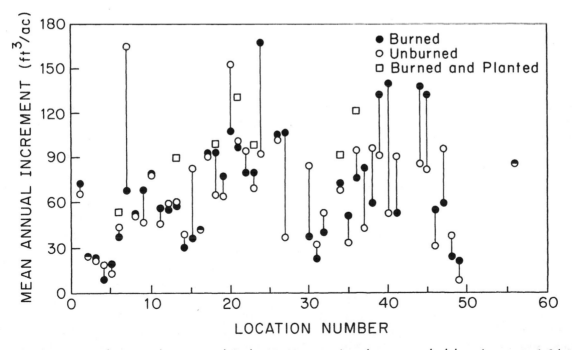

Figure 15-4. *Average annual gross volume growth in the 35-42 years since harvest or slash burning; trees 1.6 inches and larger in diameter at breast height of all species on 44 plot-pairs (burned vs. unburned). Locations are numbered in ascending order from the most northerly near Enumclaw, WA, to the most southerly near Roseburg, OR. At seven locations, a third plot was established next to the existing burned plot to compare growth on the burned, planted plot vs. that on the burned, naturally regenerated plot. (Source: unpublished manuscript on file at USDA Forest Service, Forestry Sciences Laboratory, Olympia, WA.)*

Interpretations. Current analyses indicate that the net effect of slash burning on site index and stand productivity varied among these 44 locations in the western Cascade Range. Slash burning affected future stand productivity directly, by killing advance regeneration, and indirectly, by reducing or enhancing competing vegetation, creating or destroying seedbeds and changing microclimate. Consequently, the effects of slash burning on growth and yield can be positive, negative, or neutral, depending on location and tree species of interest. Gains in coast Douglas-fir yield can be expected at most locations because fire creates additional mineral soil seedbeds and reduces cover of shrub species (except *Ceanothus* spp.). Advance regeneration of other conifers is also destroyed or damaged by slash fires and this also increases the Douglas-fir component. Conversely, reduced growth can be expected where forest regeneration is strongly dependent on advance regeneration and where fire stimulates cover of *Ceanothus* spp. and this is not controlled in other ways. We have no direct evidence that slash fires reduce tree growth by affecting inherent physical, chemical, or biological properties of soils in the western Cascade Range. Pending analyses will attempt to define characteristics of locations that show the greatest and least effects of burning. Data from a planted versus naturally regenerated plot at seven of these locations indicate substantial benefits of planting on burned areas to avoid delays in natural regeneration and to gain uniform stocking.

Long-term implications and projections

Like most forest practices, slash burning has potential benefits and costs with respect to timber production in both the immediate and the long term. Prescribed fire—and the wildfires they attempt to reduce—can affect many factors that in turn affect stand growth and, when growth of many stands is aggregated, forest and regional productivity. Both slash fires and wildfires kill or damage standing timber and they, or measures to control them, may damage soil or other resources.

Projections by computer models. Because only short-term tree response information is available to indicate treatment effects, other means for making reasonable predictions are needed. Current short-term data on yields of coast Douglas-fir after slash burning can be extrapolated by existing em-

Table 15-1. *Average total volume production on burned and unburned plots at 44 locations 35 to 42 years after clearcutting.*

Stand Component	Treatment	Cumulative Gross Volume (ft₃/acre)
Trees 1.6 in. dbh and larger	Burned	2,568
	Unburned	2,501
	Difference ± S.E.	67 ± 197 (3%)
Trees 7.6 in. dbh and larger	Burned	1,967
	Unburned	1,940
	Difference ± S.E.	27 ± 175 (1%)

pirical growth and yield models, such as DFSIM (Curtis et al. 1981) or by the biologically based model, FORCYTE (Kimmins and Scoullar 1984). The accuracy of these projections is unknown, however, because no longer-term data are available to check against them. Nonetheless, such projections of yields from burned versus unburned plot data at 35 to 40 years to the end of an assumed 80- to 100-year rotation should at least provide an indication of future trends in yields.

We used DFSIM to project current stand statistics of burned and unburned plots. Of the original 44 pairs, 17 pairs contained 80 or more percent of the current basal area in Douglas-fir and were thus suitable for DFSIM projections. In this subset of locations, current volume of combined species averaged 20 percent greater on burned plots (Fig. 15-5); this difference was statistically significant for the total stand (trees 1.6 inches dbh and larger; $p = 0.10$) and for trees 7.6 inches dbh and larger ($p = 0.06$). Future volume in these alternative size classes was estimated for stand age 60, 80, and 100 years (Fig. 15-5). These simulations indicated that the current difference in volume (and number of trees) of all species between burned and unburned plots would gradually diminish in future decades. By stand age 100, projected volume on burned plots averaged only 5 percent more than on unburned plots. Average tree size (diameter and volume) was about the same for burned and unburned plots in both current and projected stands. Thus, the greater number of trees on burned plots accounted for the greater observed and projected volume. Depending on merchantability standards, these estimated gains in volume yield on burned areas might be recovered by intermediate thinnings and final harvests.

No FORCYTE simulation was attempted because the current model (Kimmins and Scoullar 1984) is not calibrated for use in western Washington and Oregon, and because some of the site-descriptive data necessary to make projections specific to each pair of burned-unburned plots were not available. Because FORCYTE yield projections are strongly conditioned by estimated amounts of nitrogen supply and demand, we anticipate that major losses of nitrogen from slash burning would result in FORCYTE projections of reduced future yields on burned plots, at least on poor quality sites with relatively small amounts of nitrogen.

Growth & Yield After Prescribed Underburning in Eastside Forests

Major objectives of underburning

Prescribed underburning has been used to reduce fire hazard in mature stands; to reduce competition from understory shrubs in open stands; to improve quality of forage, particularly bitterbrush; and to reduce numbers of trees in young, overstocked coniferous stands. If successfully accomplished, weeding- and thinning-by-fire suppresses understory shrubs and kills surplus trees; such fires could increase site resources available for crop trees and increase merchantable yields. Because of greater risk of crown fire, however, application of underburning in overstocked stands is less controllable and results are less predictable

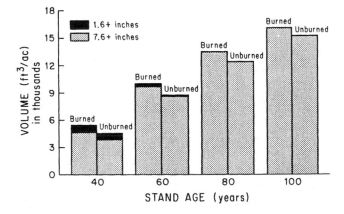

Figure 15-5. Average current volume of 17 Douglas-fir stands at average age 40 years and their simulated volume through stand age 100 years, by treatment and size class.

than underburning in open or previously thinned stands.

Reduction of forest residues and competing vegetation are the two major objectives of most underburning in the United States. Underburning has been a standard forestry practice in the Southeast and Southwest for many decades. East of the Cascade Crest in the Pacific Northwest, underburning has progressed in the last decade from experimental to operational. In westside forests, underburning has been applied experimentally in previously thinned stands of Douglas-fir to reduce fire hazard from slash (Sandberg 1980). No evaluation of the effects of such underburning on Douglas-fir growth has been published; therefore, further discussion is limited to the eastside experience.

At issue are the potential trade-offs between immediate and long-term benefits and costs of underburning. Potential benefits include reduced fuel and thus hazard of wildfire, increased forage production and thus improved animal habitat, maintenance of fire-adapted species, and reduced density in overstocked stands and thus increased growth of crop trees. Besides the treatment cost, potential costs include damage from escaped fire and from smoke, consequences of nutrient losses, and net effects on short- and long-term tree growth and timber yields.

Data available in the South and Southwest

Only limited and relatively short-term data are available for quantifying the effects of prescribed underburning on growth and yield of forests; information is available from the South (Clason 1978, Waldrop and Van Lear 1984, Cain 1985, Wade and Johansen 1986, Boyer 1987, Waldrop et al. 1987) and the Southwest (Lindenmuth 1962). Underburning can be extremely variable in its severity. Consequently, the direct effects of underburning on trees and indirect effects on site factors that influence tree growth produce conflicting information and results.

Before summarizing current information for eastside forests, general results of prescribed burning and their interpretation are presented.

Direct effects of underburning on trees

As discussed in Chapter 4, tree size, stand condition, and fire severity (largely determined by fuel, weather, soil moisture) generally determine the extent to which the bole cambium is damaged; needles and buds are scorched or killed; roots are scorched or killed; and trees are killed directly by fire or later by insects or disease. Young, short, and shallow-rooted trees are most vulnerable to direct damage by fire. At least short-term reductions in growth, if not outright tree mortality, are likely from damage. If damage and mortality are restricted to noncrop trees, then improved growth and yield of underburned stands can be expected —at least in the short term.

Experiences in the Southeast (Ferguson 1955, Hodgkins and Whipple 1963, Waldrop and Van Lear 1984, Cain 1985, Wade and Johansen 1986) and Southwest (Lindenmuth 1962) and in Idaho from wildfires (Lynch 1959) indicate that tree damage and potential reductions in tree growth and yield can be minimized by reducing burn severity and avoiding crown fires. Yet this presents a dilemma because the greater the fire severity, the greater percentage of fuel is consumed and the larger the percentage of released trees. Cooler burns are more likely with winter (cool, wet conditions) than with summer burns, on level than on steep topography, with backing fires than with head fires, in open stands than in dense stands, and with light rather than heavy accumulations of forest residues and duff (Lindenmuth 1962). Wade and Johansen (1986) suggest numerous ways to avoid fire damage to trees during prescribed burns. See Chapter 5 in this book for a description of underburning techniques.

Indirect effects of underburning on trees

Underburning also can affect tree growth by affecting factors that influence tree growth; these indirect effects can increase or decrease tree growth and timber yields. For example, fire temporarily increases amounts of available nutrients for trees, vegetation, and microorganisms (Klemmedson 1976, Ryan and Covington 1986). However, ash losses in convective air movement and volatilization of nitrogen, sulfur, and phosphorus during burning reduce the total amount of nutrient elements in the ecosystem unless they are subsequently replaced by nitrogen-fixing organisms, atmospheric deposition, mineral weathering (of sulfur and phosphorus), or fertilization. The frequent response of conifer stands to nitrogen fertilization in the Pacific Northwest suggests that this nutrient commonly limits growth (Miller et al.

1986, Powers et al. 1988); therefore, it is especially prudent to conserve nitrogen or attempt to replace losses by fertilization. Published (Cochran 1978) and unpublished data from fertilization trials in eastside lodgepole pine and ponderosa pine stands suggest that sulfur losses should be also avoided, especially on soils derived from pumice.

The eastside experience

Underburning to thin overstocked coniferous stands. Extensive acreage of naturally regenerated, overstocked stands exists in the western United States. These stands usually occur on poor quality land where returns from silvicultural investments are marginal. Although costs of prescribed underburning can be much less than thinning with power saws, the comparative effects of these two thinning tools on tree growth have not been investigated. Risk of stand damage is clearly greater with underburning than with mechanical thinning. Thinning with fire is feasible only at early stand ages and with low-severity fires (personal communication from the late George Fahnestock, forest fire consultant, Seattle, WA). Several investigators have described general effects of underburning pine thickets in the western United States, but growth data are only available from two stands in northeast Washington.

Underburning open or previously thinned stands. Landsberg et al. (1984) and J.D. Landsberg and P.H. Cochran (unpublished manuscript [Ponderosa pine tree growth after prescribed underburning] on file at USDA Forest Service, Pacific Northwest Research Station, Bend, OR) provide growth data for underburning at a location in central Oregon (Table 15-2). Lindenmuth (1962) provides descriptive information from a systematic survey of prescribed fire on about 27,000 acres intensively burned in Arizona. The information describes burning severity, fuel consumption, and percentage of potential crop trees that were released, damaged, or killed in a wide variety of initial stand conditions.

Results and interpretation

Underburning to thin overstocked coniferous stands. Effects of underburning to thin two overstocked, ponderosa pine stands are summarized in Table 15-2. Evaluations made 6-15 years after the fire showed that the total number of trees per acre was reduced by 67 percent at Coyote Creek and 86 percent at Pe-Ell, while the diameter and height growth of predesignated crop trees was increased at Coyote Creek, but not at Pe-Ell (Wooldridge and Weaver 1965). The analyses at Coyote Creek indicated that fire-induced reductions in competing trees explained most but not all of the increases in crop tree growth; increased availability of water and nutrients also may have contributed to increased growth at this location. Although crown scorch and fire scars adversely affected height growth, negative effects on diameter growth were offset apparently by a concurrent reduction in competition (Morris and Mowat 1958). Unfortunately, effects on per acre growth and yield were not reported for either study area.

Underburning open or previously thinned stands. Landsberg et al. (1984) and Landsberg and Cochran (1980 and unpublished manuscript on file at USDA Forest Service, Pacific Northwest Research Station, Bend, OR) describe stand growth after moderate and after severe fuel consumption in a 45-year-old ponderosa pine stand near Bend, Oregon (Table 15-2). The stand had been thinned about 20 years before the burn. Initial effects of the more severe underburning were as follows:

- 88 percent of the duff layer was consumed;
- "most of the fine feeding roots located near the surface of the soil were destroyed";
- needle weight and nitrogen content were reduced by crown scorch; and
- 4 percent of the initial trees were killed.

Effects of the moderate burn were much less severe. In the 4 years after the severe burn, needle mass and nitrogen content declined to even lower levels, and in the 8 years after burning height, diameter, and volume growth were significantly reduced. Landsberg et al. (1984) concluded: "Prescribed burning needs further evaluation in larger studies conducted over a longer time in a variety of ponderosa pine communities to determine long-term effects on tree growth" (p. 12).

Table 15-2. Results of underburning experiments in ponderosa pine, per acre basis.

	Northeast Washington[a]		Bend, Oregon[b]	
	Coyote Creek[c]	Pe-Ell[d]	Moderate burn	Severe burn
Initial stand				
Total stems	2,550	2,032	240	240
Crop stems	95	140	240	240
Age (years)	20	mixed	45	45
Fire characteristics				
Fuel reduction				
Wood (%)	86	—	35	69
Duff (%)	—	—	49	88
Scorch (%)	46	—	—	—
Needle loss (%)	—	—	4	20
Postfire data				
After fire (yrs)	1-7 7-15	1-6	1-8	1-8
Surviving stems				
Total	830 820	294	237	231
Crop	83 80	—	—	—
Crop tree growth				
Burned vs. unburned % change				
Diameter	+37	+27	-12	-16
		0		
Height	+ 7[e]	+23	-10	-20
		-14		
Volume	—	—	-14	-22

Sources and notes:
[a]Objective: to reduce stocking.
[b]Objective: to reduce fire hazard. Source: Landsberg and Cochran, unpublished manuscript.
[c]Morris and Mowat 1958 (years 1-7); Weaver 1967 (years 7-15).
[d]Wooldridge and Weaver 1965.
[e]Height growth was reduced in 20% of surviving crop trees that were fire scarred.

Long-term implications for overstocked and open stands

The limited data available on the effects of prescribed underburning in eastside forests precludes meaningful estimation or even speculation about effects on growth and yield.

A general consensus exists among foresters and fire ecologists that prescribed fire is generally necessary to reduce risk of wildfires that are frequent in areas of low rainfall. In discussing the extensive mixed-conifer-pinegrass community in eastern Oregon, Hall (1976) concluded that successful fire prevention and control have created an increased hazard in a known fire environment. This has changed a naturally fire-resistant community to a fire-susceptible one. "We may not have a choice about burning—only a choice of how to burn; prescribed fire or wildfire" (p. 168-9). A similar conclusion was made for ponderosa pine forests of Central Arizona (Biswell et al. 1973). The periodic outbreak of extensive wildfires in western states further supports the apparent necessity of prescribed fire to protect forests in specific environments. See also chapters 3 and 4 of this book.

Lindenmuth concluded:

> Intentional burning of ponderosa pine timberlands to treat fuels and timber stands presents many unsolved complex problems. More control over the intensity of fire will be necessary for consistently accomplishing specific objectives. More knowledge of desired fire intensities and practical techniques for controlling fire intensity is urgently needed (1962, p. 810).

Since that time, techniques for controlling intensity and area of prescribed burning have improved (Chapter 5). Yet the paucity of data to quantify effects of prescribed underburning on forest growth justifies concern and action to secure more information about short- and long-term effects.

Conclusion

Biologically sound forest management requires that factors controlling tree growth be maintained in suitable quantities and balance for sustained, high levels of forest productivity. In the Pacific Northwest—as in most forest regions—reliable and long-term quantitative data about the relative contribution of inherent site factors and of management practices to long-term stand productivity are not available to either support or reject most current practices. This paucity of reliable information requires that interim decisions be made on judgment and experience. Uncertainty will continue to prevail until long-term data or reliable predictions are available.

Forest productivity is determined by many factors including soil, climate, species, management practices, disease, insects, time, and the interactions among these factors. Maintenance of or even increases in timber production may be possible by substituting intensive silvicultural practices for some losses of inherent site productivity caused by prescribed burning or other practices. In the final analysis, however, the comparative biological and economic benefits and costs of soil conservation versus replenishment or substitutions must be evaluated. Reliable economic analyses require direct, quantitative evidence, including measured or reliably predicted tree growth or yield.

Long-term effects of prescribed fire on factors of site productivity are not easily predicted because sufficient investigations have not been made. The research is complex because prescribed fire varies in severity, and sites differ in their tolerance to initial effects and in their capacity to recover over time. Apparent negative effects on soil properties do not always result in reduced tree growth. Forest growth is a complex process necessitating well-designed experiments to isolate the effects of treatment. Currently, we can state with confidence only that predicting consequences is uncertain; that tree response information is needed to improve predictions; and that, therefore, forestry techniques or practices should be prescribed prudently and specifically to fit the local situation.

Monitoring programs should be established to document the response of trees and site factors to prescribed slash burning and underburning. Long-term plots must be established, and reliable predictive models must be constructed to evaluate forest practices.

Literature Cited & Key References

Biswell, H.H., H.R. Kallander, R. Komarek, R.J. Vogl, and H. Weaver. 1973. Ponderosa fire management, a task force evaluation of controlled burning in ponderosa pine forests of central Arizona. Tall Timbers Res. Sta. Tallahassee, FL. Misc. Pub. 2. 49 p.

Boyer, W.D. 1987. Volume growth loss: A hidden cost of periodic prescribed burning in longleaf pine? South. J. Appl. For. 11:154-157.

Cain, M.D. 1985. Prescribed winter burns can reduce the growth of nine-year-old loblolly pines. USDA For. Serv., South. For. Exp. Sta., New Orleans, LA. Res. Note SO-312. 4 p.

Clason, T.R. 1978. Removal of hardwood vegetation increases growth and yield of a young loblolly pine stand. South. J. Appl. For. 2:96-97.

Cochran, P.H. 1978. Response of a pole-size ponderosa pine stand to nitrogen, phosphorus, and sulfur. USDA For. Serv., Pac. Northwest For. Rge. Exp. Sta., Portland, OR. Res. Note PNW-319. 8 p.

Curtis, R.O., G.W. Clendenen, and D.J. Demars. 1981. A new stand simulator for coast Douglas-fir: DFSIM user's guide. USDA, For. Serv., Pac. Northwest For. Rge. Exp. Sta., Portland, OR. Gen. Tech. Rep. PNW-128. 79 p.

Dyrness, C.T., C.T. Youngberg, and R.H. Ruth. 1957. Some effects of logging and slash burning on physical soil properties in the Corvallis watershed. USDA For. Serv., Pac. Northwest For. Rge. Exp. Sta., Portland, OR. Res. Pap. 19. 15 p.

Ferguson, E.R. 1955. Fire-scorched trees—will they live or die? p. 102-113. *In* Proc., 4th Annu. Forest Symp., Louisiana State Univ., Baton Rouge, LA.

Hall, F.C. 1976. Fire and vegetation in the Blue Mountains—implications for land managers. Tall Timbers Fire Ecol. Conf. Proc. 15:155-170.

Hodgkins, E.J., and S.D. Whipple. 1963. Changes in stand structure following prescribed burning in a loblolly-shortleaf pine forest. J. For. 61:498-502.

Kimmins, J.P., and K.A. Scoullar. 1984. FORCYTE-11: A flexible modelling framework with which to analyze the long-term consequences for yield, economic returns and energy efficiency of alternative forest and agro-forest crop production strategies, p. 1-5. *In* Proc., 5th Canadian Bioenergy R & D Seminar. Nat. Res. Counc., Ottawa, Canada.

King, J.E. 1966. Site index curves for Douglas-fir in the Pacific Northwest. Forestry Research Center, Weyerhaeuser Co., Centralia, WA. Weyerhaeuser For. Pap. 8. 49 p.

Klemmedson, J.O. 1976. Effect of thinning and slash burning on nitrogen and carbon in ecosystems of young dense ponderosa pine. For. Sci. 22:45-53.

Landsberg, J.D., and P.H. Cochran. 1980. Prescribed burning effects on foliar nitrogen content in ponderosa pine. Fire For. Meteorol. Conf. Proc. 6:209-213.

*Landsberg, J.D., P.H. Cochran, M.M. Finck, and R.E. Martin. 1984. Foliar nitrogen content and tree growth after prescribed fire in ponderosa pine. USDA For. Serv., Pac. Northwest Res. Sta., Portland, OR. Res. Note PNW-412. 15 p.

*Lindenmuth, A.W., Jr. 1962. Effects on fuels and trees of a large intentional burn in ponderosa pine. J. For. 60:804-810.

Lynch, D.W. 1959. Effects of a wildfire on mortality and growth of young ponderosa pine trees. USDA For. Serv., Intermt. For. Rge. Exp. Sta., Ogden, UT. Res. Note 66. 8 p.

Miller, R.E., P.R. Barker, C.E. Peterson, and S.R. Webster. 1986. Using nitrogen fertilizers in management of coast Douglas-fir: Regional trends of response, p. 290-303. *In* Douglas-fir: Stand Management for the Future. Univ. Washington, Seattle, WA. 388 p.

Morris, W.G. 1958. Influence of slash burning on regeneration, other plant cover, and fire hazard in the Douglas-fir Region. USDA For. Serv., Pac. Northwest For. Rge. Exp. Sta., Portland, OR. Res. Pap. PNW-29. 49 p.

*Morris, W.G. 1970. Effects of slash burning in overmature stands of the Douglas-fir region. For. Sci. 16:258-270.

Morris, W.G., and E.L. Mowat. 1958. Some effects of thinning a ponderosa pine thicket with a prescribed fire. J. For. 56:203-209.

Powers, R.F., S.R. Webster, and P.H. Cochran. 1988. Estimating the response of ponderosa pine forests to fertilization, p. 219-225. *In* Proc., Symp. on Future Forests of the Mountain West, Sept. 29-Oct. 3, 1986. Univ. of Montana, Missoula, MT. USDA For. Serv. Intermt. Res. Sta., Ogden, UT.

Ryan, M.G., and W.W. Covington. 1986. Effect of a prescribed burn in ponderosa pine on inorganic nitrogen concentrations of mineral soil. USDA For. Serv., Rocky Mt. For. Rge. Exp. Sta., Fort Collins, CO. Res. Note RM-464. 5 p.

Sandberg, D. 1980. Duff reduction by prescribed underburning in Douglas-fir. USDA For. Serv., Pac. Northwest For. Rge. Exp. Sta., Portland, OR. Res. Paper PNW-272. 19 p.

Tarrant, R.F. 1956. Effects of slash burning on some soils of the Douglas-fir region. Soil Sci. Soc. Amer. Proc. 20:408-411.

References marked by an asterisk are recommended for general information.

Wade, D.D., and R.W. Johansen. 1986. Effects of fire on southern pine: Observations and recommendations. USDA For. Serv., Southeastern For. Exp. Sta., Asheville, NC. Gen. Tech. Rep. SE-41. 14 p.

Waldrop, T.A., and D.H. Van Lear. 1984. Effect of crown scorch on survival and growth of young loblolly pine. South. J. Appl. For. 8:35-40.

*Waldrop, T.A., D.H. Van Lear, F.T. Lloyd, and W.R. Harms. 1987. Long-term studies of prescribed burning in loblolly pine forests of the southeastern coastal plain. USDA For. Serv., Southeastern Res. Sta., Asheville, NC. Gen. Tech. Rep. SE-45. 23 p.

*Weaver, H. 1967. Some effects of prescribed burning on the Coyote Creek test area, Colville Indian Reservation. J. For. 65:552-558.

Wooldridge, D.D., and H. Weaver. 1965. Some effects of thinning a ponderosa pine thicket with a prescribed fire, II. J. For. 63:92-95.

VI Effects of Prescribed Fire on Nontimber Resources

16 Effects of Prescribed Fire on Air Quality and Human Health

David V. Sandberg and Frank N. Dost

Executive Summary

Fire is used to treat more than 200,000 acres of forest land per year in Oregon and Washington. Although smoke emissions have decreased by 30 to 50 percent in the last decade, concern is growing that exposure to smoke from prescribed fire may present a health hazard to fireline workers and to the public. This chapter discusses prescribed fire as a source of air pollution in Oregon and Washington, examining concepts of air resource management, biomass consumption, combustion products, mitigating measures for prescribed fire smoke, and assessment of risk to human health.

Air resource management involves determining public policy regarding air pollution and establishing the legal strategies for executing that policy; setting goals and standards for ambient air quality and human exposures to air pollution; assessing air quality and exposures with respect to those goals; and implementing control techniques.

The Clean Air Act, passed in 1963 and amended several times, is the primary legal instrument for air resource management. It establishes a strategy of managing widespread air pollution to maintain standards for ambient air quality. It also establishes the strategy of imposing emission standards for hazardous air pollutants from stationary sources or for applying risk management tactics, such as work rules, to limit exposures to hazardous pollutants from temporary sources (de Nevers et al. 1986).

National Ambient Air Quality Standards have been established by the Environmental Protection Agency (EPA) for six pollutants. These standards apply nationwide and are revised periodically. New standards pertain to smaller particles than in the past. Because smoke from prescribed fire is dominated by fine particles, each new standard results in a larger share of monitored pollution being apportioned to these fires.

In response to the Clean Air Act, Oregon and Washington have been among the first states to implement strategies to protect visibility, emphasizing annual reduction in emissions and restrictions on slash burning in the summer. Oregon and Washington also monitor the air for concentrations of pollutants, as do all states. If a standard is violated, source-oriented models and receptor models are used to apportion the sources of pollution. In 1984, a case study using receptor models concluded that 44 percent of the reduction in visibility during late summer was caused by slash burning.

The primary National Ambient Air Quality Standards are health standards for criteria pollutants. In addition, the EPA maintains a list of toxic substances found in air and threshold exposure values. The Occupational Safety and Health Administration also regulates worker exposure to several compounds. Risk assessment estimates consequences to the health of individuals or populations exposed to harmful agents, but assessment of health risks from prescribed fires is marked by uncertainty, such as in quantifying the amount of toxic compounds emitted by fires.

Although it is known that a few hundred substances are formed, liberated, or modified during combustion of vegetation, little information exists about the quantities of these substances. Ninety percent of the total mass emitted from wildland fires is water and carbon dioxide, neither of which is classified as a pollutant. The more efficient the combustion, the more carbon is converted to carbon dioxide. The portion of carbon not converted to carbon dioxide is converted to carbon monoxide, particulate matter, or to volatile organic compounds.

Particulate matter is the most important category of pollutants from prescribed fire; it is the major cause of reduced visibility, and serves as sorption surfaces for harmful gases. Particulate matter is the primary index for evaluating smoke movement. No specific health effects of these complex organic chemicals have yet been identified. In urban environments, particulate loads have been related to health impacts, including mortality, but no methods exist for isolating particulate effects from other chemicals in the air.

Certain volatile organic compounds (VOCs) may be important to human health. Polynuclear aromatic hydrocarbons (PAHs) are best known of these because some members of the class are carcinogenic. Risk associated with PAH emissions from prescribed fire appears trivial from early evidence, but more research is needed.

The aldehydes may be important. Of these, formaldehyde has been extensively studied, is known to cause cancer in laboratory animals, and is regulated as a human carcinogen. It is an irritant and is allergenic at low concentrations. Estimating exposures to formaldehydes is tenuous but it is quite likely that formaldehyde may be responsible for some of the eye and upper respiratory irritation near fires. Measurements of formaldehyde emission from forestry burning are not considered reliable, although order-of-magnitude estimates can be constructed. Measurements of emissions from fireplaces and stoves have been reported but must be used with care because of differences in estimates from prescribed burning.

Combustion of herbicides applied to vegetation before prescribed or accidental burning is of public interest. No residues from herbicides have yet been found in smoke, although only limited study has been made in the field. Estimates based on smoke distribution and volume of distribution of herbicides and related products show that exposures to any products, or to the parent chemical, would be trivial even in dense smoke.

Smoke management programs have depended on meteorological scheduling to avoid smoke-sensitive areas, on dispersion of pollutants to achieve acceptable concentration and duration, and on emission reduction. Washington has established a goal for reducing emissions from prescribed burning by 35 percent before 1990. Oregon expects a reduction in emissions of 50 percent by the year 2000. As yet, emission-reduction goals have not depended on information from health-risk assessments. In a sense, risk management has preceded risk assessment.

Biomass consumption in prescribed fires has become much better understood in recent years. Predictive algorithms are available for large fuel consumption and duff consumption during prescribed fires. Large fuel consumption depends primarily on moisture content. Duff consumption depends mainly on the mass consumed or fire duration, except during very dry periods. Biomass-consumption equations and updated emission factors have been combined into a model that predicts emission from prescribed fires. The model can be used to decide what combinations of residue utilization, burn scheduling, and ignition techniques will provide the needed site preparation and minimize smoke production. The model has also been used to verify and predict regional success in meeting emission-reduction goals. A new system to inventory emissions from forest burning in Oregon uses inventories of slash quantities, an upgraded smoke management reporting system, a national fire-weather library, and an emission production model. The system has been used to compare emissions for 1976-79 with emissions for 1984-85. Emissions appear to have declined as a result of improved utilization and other factors.

The health effects from emissions of prescribed fires are studied to determine whether exposure to fire products can reach harmful levels. The extent and nature of the emission mix determine exposure at the site of concern. Data describing the adverse effects of the chemical in question and its dose-response relationship are also needed.

Some of the known emissions in smoke, particularly PAHs and formaldehyde, are known to be carcinogens on the basis of laboratory assays. However, using maximizing assumptions of emission and exposure, it seems clear that exposure to smoke from prescribed burns does not represent a significant carcinogenic risk. Respiratory irritation and allergic responses are the most important short-term consequences of smoke exposure. It appears that formaldehyde, formic acid, and acrolein may be significant contributors to the respiratory effect, but as yet it is not possible to establish their respective roles. There may also be other important substances or interactions with other chemicals or conditions that are not yet recognized.

It is difficult to imagine a significant toxicologic impact on the general population for most of the enormous variety of emission products from prescribed fire, including the combustion of vegetation treated with herbicide. Even those combustion products with significant toxicity are diluted so extensively that most human exposures are very small and have no expected impact. Control strategies and measures to reduce particulate emissions and avoid human exposures are also directly beneficial in reducing exposure.

Even when the general population is not at risk, there will be unusual circumstances or sensitive populations that must be protected. Certain locations are particularly prone to smoke accumulation because of topography, climatology, or fuel conditions. Certain individuals are allergic or otherwise especially prone to injury from exposure to low concentrations of pollutants. Smoke management and risk management strategies must recognize and protect against these unusual events as well as manage for the general case.

Smoke management programs in the Pacific Northwest have been effective in minimizing intrusions of smoke from prescribed fires into designated smoke-sensitive areas, but there is room for improvement. Since 1984, smoke management has reduced the use of fire as a tool for the management of wildland resources. Smoke management programs must now allocate what sites can be burned at all, in addition to assuming the traditional role of determining when they can be burned during the year. An evaluation of needs or an incentive system for reducing emissions should be added to the decision matrix. Improved systems for information management and dispersion modeling are available that could also improve the effectiveness of smoke management.

Risk assessment for firefighter safety and public exposure to hazardous air pollutants has hardly begun. There is an urgent need for new research to identify hazardous compounds, quantitatively assess human exposures, and assess risk.

Introduction

Prescribed fire is a large source of atmospheric emissions in the Pacific Northwest. Fire is used to treat more than 200,000 acres per year in Oregon and Washington forests, emitting about 110,000 tons of smoke (Cook et al. 1978, Sandberg and Peterson 1987). The smoke is of concern because of possible violation of National Ambient Air Quality Standards (or more stringent local standards), because it degrades visibility, and because it may present a health hazard to fireline workers or to the public (Breysee 1984, Morgan 1989).

Prior to 1970, air quality considerations had little effect on the practice of prescribed burning. Smoke from fires was considered natural, local, and innocuous (Komarek 1970, Hall 1972). Most burning in the Pacific Northwest was done in the fall, when fire control was easiest but atmospheric dispersion was often poor. No attempt was made to reduce emissions.

From 1970 to 1984, smoke management programs were used effectively to avoid intrusions of smoke into designated (primarily urban) areas. The area burned each year actually increased during that period, even though smoke management restrictions made burning harder to schedule and consequently much more expensive (Sandberg and Schmidt 1982). More of the burning was shifted into the summer to improve dispersion. Pollutant emissions per acre burned were reduced by 30 percent from 1979 emissions by using improved harvesting and burning practices (Sandberg 1987).

Since 1984, protection of visibility in National Parks and Wilderness has increased as required by the 1977 Clean Air Act Amendments [1977 Clean Air Act Amendments (PL 95-95)]. Smoke management programs were extended to protect those areas, especially during the summer months. With the need to protect both urban areas and wilderness, the opportunities to burn were again much reduced. The combination of increased regulation and unusually high fire danger has resulted in approximately a one-third decrease in the area burned per year, compared to 1984.

Smoke management efforts to date have focused on general improvements in air quality and the avoidance of general pollution events. However, there is growing recognition that individuals must also be protected from degraded air quality. Residents of rural areas near forestry operations deserve clean air, and the Oregon and Washington air quality agencies are now devising strategies to improve their protection from smoke intrusions (Core 1989).

There is growing public concern over the possible health effects from exposure to smoke from prescribed fires (Turpin 1989). Public exposure to smoke from residential wood heating and from wildfires has increased in recent years, and that has naturally heightened public awareness of potential health hazards (Morgan 1989).

The degree of risk to firefighters and workers from exposures to smoke during prescribed fires has also not been adequately assessed, but is of increasing concern. Numerous studies of worker exposures and physical reactions to exposures have been made during recent major wildfire episodes, but the results are too preliminary to review here.

This chapter examines prescribed fire as a source of air pollution in Oregon and Washington. Some important air resource management concepts and definitions are presented first, then the magnitude of biomass consumption and the pollutant source are discussed. The combustion products from prescribed burning and their health effects are described. A preliminary assessment of health risk is presented. Finally, mitigation measures and trends are discussed.

Air Resource Management

Air resource management involves determining public policy regarding air pollution and establishing the legal strategies for executing that policy; setting goals and standards for ambient air quality and human exposures to air pollution; assessing air quality and exposures with respect to those goals; and implementing control techniques.

Each of these steps will be discussed in its relation to prescribed fire. The first two steps will be introduced briefly in this chapter, then covered in greater detail in Chapter 20. The third step, assessing air quality impacts and exposures, will be presented entirely in this chapter. The final step, implementing control techniques, will be covered partly in this chapter and partly in Chapter 22.

Other reviews of the subject have been presented by the Southern Forest Fire Laboratory (1976), Sandberg et al. (1979), the National Wildfire Coordinating Group (1985), and Hanley et al. (1989).

Public policy and the Clean Air Act

Public policy with regard to air pollution shifted dramatically in the 1970s. Prior to the adoption of the Clean Air Act (PL 88-206, 1963) and its amendments [The Clean Air Act Amendments of 1966 (PL 89-675), the Clean Air Amendments of 1970 (PL 91-604), the Clean Air Act Amendments of 1977 (PL 95-95), and the 1981 Amendments (PL 97-23)], the only control over air pollution was through nuisance statutes or private litigation. In either case, the burden of proof of discomfort, inconvenience, damage, or injury rested with the complainant; for a complaint to be successful, the

damage had to be clearly linked to the pollutants emitted by the defendant. Such actions were only applicable to single, clearly identifiable sources—and only after the fact.

The Clean Air Act generally shifts the burden of proof to the polluter. It also establishes two air resource management strategies. *Air quality management* is the regulation of the amount, location, and time of pollutant emissions for achieving some clearly defined set of air quality goals or standards. This strategy is the predominant strategy used to improve ambient air quality. A second strategy of imposing *emission standards* for stationary pollutant sources is the predominant means to control hazardous air pollutants and to ensure the best practical control technology is used for new sources. As an alternative to enforcing emission standards for hazardous air pollutants, risk management procedures may be used.

The air quality management strategy is applied to prescribed burning primarily to control visible intrusions of smoke into sensitive areas or to reduce visibility impairment in national parks and wilderness areas. Emission standards, in the form of a general requirement to use the best practical technology to reduce emissions, are also part of the strategy in Oregon to reduce visibility impairment. Risk management, in the form of rotating work schedules and the use of respirators, is being used increasingly by land managers to limit hazardous exposures, albeit with a currently inadequate technological basis for setting work rules.

Air quality goals and standards

Air pollution is defined as "the presence in the atmosphere of one or more contaminants in such quantities, of characteristics, and of durations such as to be injurious to human, plant, or animal life or to property, or which unreasonably interferes with the comfortable enjoyment of life and property" (Rossano 1969). Other definitions can be found, but the important feature of pollution is that an effect or injury must occur before pollution occurs.

A *contaminant* is "anything added to the environment that causes a deviation from the geochemical mean composition" (Williamson 1973). A contaminant does not necessarily have the potential to do harm. A *pollutant* is a contaminant that has physical or chemical characteristics that give it the potential for harm. *Criteria pollutants* are those pollutants for which ambient air quality standards have been established. The term *hazardous air pollutant* (or *air toxic*) means an air pollutant that is reasonably anticipated to result in mortality or in an increase of serious irreversible or incapacitating illnesses. Emission standards for stationary sources, rather than ambient standards, are applicable to hazardous pollutants.

Statements of what degree of quality for ambient air would insure that the public health and welfare would be protected are called *air quality criteria*. They are determined on the basis of known or suspected adverse effects: toxic effects in humans or animals, damage to vegetation or materials, and degradation of aesthetic aspects of the environment. An air quality criterion indicates the threshold concentration, dosage, and exposure time above which a pollutant or combination of pollutants is considered to have an adverse effect. It is a technical statement that prescribes no legal standard on its own.

The desired levels of air quality are stated as *air quality goals* that include practical considerations, such as public opinion and economic impacts, as well as the air quality criteria.

National Ambient Air Quality Standards (NAAQS) are a set of goals established by the Environmental Protection Agency (EPA) for six ubiquitous air pollutants including inhalable particulate matter, oxides of sulfur, oxides of nitrogen, carbon monoxide, ozone, and lead.[1] The ambient standards are of two types: primary standards at levels designed to protect human health, and secondary standards designed to protect public welfare. NAAQS are subject to periodic revision.

Ambient standards and prescribed fire

Standards set for ambient particles in air visibility have had the most impact on prescribed fire.

In setting standards for air quality, *inhalable particles*, a category of particles having an aerodynamic diameter smaller than 10 micrometers, or PM10, has replaced the earlier category of total suspended particulate matter (TSP).[2] Inhalable particulates are more closely related to health effects. The annual standard for average PM10 con-

---

[1] A standard for hydrocarbons as a class of compounds has been rescinded.

[2] The airborne material sampled by a standard high-volume device that limits the size of particles sampled to about 40-45 micrometers.

centration in ambient air is now 50 micrograms per cubic meter. The new 24-hour standard is 150 micrograms per cubic meter, with an allowance that permits one expected exceedance per year. The primary and secondary standards for PM10 are identical.

Fine particles having an aerodynamic diameter smaller than 2.5 micrometers, or PM2.5, are most closely related to visibility impairment. Standards for PM2.5 may be promulgated in 1989 or 1990.

The PM10 standard and the anticipated PM2.5 standard are significant to forest burning because fine particles are abundant in wood smoke when compared to noncombustion sources. Several areas that did not exceed the TSP standard may exceed the PM10 standard, primarily because of residential wood combustion. When an area exceeds the PM10 standard regardless of the cause, control of prescribed fire may be part of the strategy for compliance. For example, LaGrande, Oregon, may exceed PM10 standards and that may affect future smoke management restrictions in the area.

The 1977 Clean Air Act Amendments also establish a national goal for "the prevention of any future and the remedying of any existing impairment of visibility in mandatory Class I federal areas which impairment results from manmade air pollution" [1977 Clean Air Act Amendments (PL 95-95)]. The regulations require states to consider strategies for reducing visibility impairment from prescribed burning. Revisions to the Oregon and Washington smoke management programs since 1980 have responded to this goal.

Standards for exposure

The primary NAAQS are health standards for criteria pollutants, based primarily on controlled human exposures and epidemiological evidence of risk (i.e., data derived from statistical surveys of the incidence of disease). In addition, the EPA maintains a list of hazardous pollutants found in air, with threshold exposure values defined for each. The EPA encourages risk assessment and risk management where possible exposure exists.

The Occupational Safety and Health Administration (OSHA) also sets regulations for worker exposure to several compounds, including carbon monoxide and formaldehyde, which are produced in abundance by prescribed fires, but few studies have assessed this risk on fireline workers in either prescribed or wild fire. There is no evidence yet that these emissions impose a risk. This is an area of growing concern, and a major effort has been proposed by the National Wildfire Coordinating Group to better assess the risk and to evaluate ways to manage the work environment (National Wildfire Coordinating Group 1989).

Assessment of Ambient Air Pollution

Prescribed fires are a difficult source to describe because several thousand burns are conducted annually in the Pacific Northwest. Each is somehow unique with respect to the amount and chemistry of combustible material present, and with respect to the combustion environment that determines the amount and chemistry of pollutants emitted. It is difficult to estimate total emissions because there is no typical case that can be used to generalize pollutant production. It is necessary to characterize each burn separately, then sum the result in order to compile an emission inventory.

Because of the complexity of the source and receptors, a considerable technology has developed to predict and mitigate the effects of fire on air quality.

Quantifying emission production

An emission production model has been developed through cooperative research that enables quantitative estimates of smoke production to be made for individually prescribed fires in many important fuel types. The emission production model is frequently used by foresters to compare fuel modification or to schedule options before burning. Iterative use of the model helps design specific slash treatments that meet land management objectives with a minimum of pollutant production.

Emission inventory

A new system to inventory air pollutant emissions from forest burning is in place in Oregon as of 1987 and has been used to retrospectively estimate emissions for western Oregon and Washington as far back as 1976 (Sandberg and Peterson 1987). The system relies on periodic region-wide inventories of slash quantities (Howard 1981, Sandberg et al. 1988), an upgraded smoke management reporting system (Oregon Department of Forestry 1987), a National Fire-weather Library (Furman and Brink 1975), and an Emission Pro-

duction Model (Sandberg and Peterson 1985) to compute emissions of TSP, PM10, and carbon monoxide on a daily basis (Fig. 16-1, 16-2).

Emission baseline

The average annual emissions for the period 1976-79 are considered the baseline values for measuring emission reduction in Oregon and Washington. That period is used as the baseline because reliable input data for the inventory system were available then, and it predates the cooperative and mandatory programs for emission reduction that are now in place. Emission estimates for the period are thought to be accurate within 15 percent in western Oregon and Washington. However, emission estimates for eastern Oregon and Washington are considered accurate only within a factor of 2.

Emissions of total suspended particulate matter averaged 40,000 tons per year for the period in western Washington. Emissions of TSP were 82,000 tons in western Oregon, 9,000 tons in eastern Oregon, and 30,000 tons in eastern Washington. PM10 emissions are thought to comprise about 80 percent of TSP.

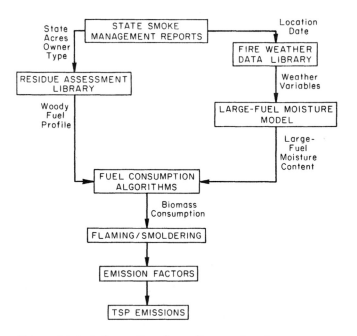

Figure 16-1. Information-flow diagram for the computation of emissions for prescribed burning when the only specific information known is the area burned. Site-specific values, when known, replace the value inferred from regional inventories and meteorological models.

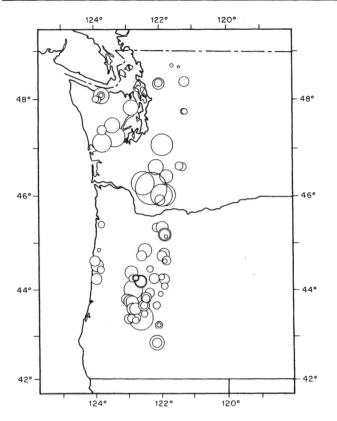

Figure 16-2. Example of the daily computation of particulate emissions for prescribed fire in western Oregon and Washington: The symbol size is proportional to the smoke emitted. Estimates are based on the emission-production model diagrammed in Figure 16-1.

Air quality monitoring

Air quality is measured and assessed by the states under delegated authority from the EPA. The states operate extensive monitoring networks that periodically assess the concentration of pollutants. The network is augmented by monitors installed and operated by federal land management agencies and others.

Source apportionment

If a standard is violated, the next step is to apportion the relative contribution from each contributing source to the monitored pollution episode. Two approaches are used to apportion the sources of pollution: source-oriented models and receptor models.

Source-oriented models begin with an inventory of emission sources and meteorological conditions, and use atmospheric dispersion models to estimate impacts. In contrast, receptor models begin with ambient aerosol measurements at points of concern, and differentiate the relative contribution of sources with combinations of properties uniquely associated with each source.

Dispersion models have been used in a few instances to anticipate and prevent intrusions from planned burn operations, but have not been used in any meaningful way to explain the relative contribution of prescribed burning to pollution in the Northwest. Compiling an emission inventory is the first step in source apportionment when using a source-oriented approach. However, not all sources have the same potential to contribute to pollution events because of differences in their locations relative to the receptor. Dispersion models can be used to model the probable effect of pollutants emitted from distant sources.

Receptor modeling

Receptor modeling is a statistical technique that compares the chemistry and morphology of monitored pollution to characteristic profiles of the possible sources of the pollutants. The possible combination of sources that best explains the monitored pollution is accepted as an estimate of the relative contribution of source categories.

An assessment was made in late summer 1984 of the visibility impairment in the Pacific Northwest states (Beck and Associates 1986) using receptor models. The case study showed that 44 percent of the visibility impairment in that period was caused by slash burning. Because of that conclusion, prescribed fire has been emphasized in the drafting of regulations to remedy visibility impairment.

Receptor modeling has become an increasingly useful, and increasingly used, tool for source apportionment. However, very substantial inaccuracies still abound in the procedure, especially when applied to sources that are more than a few miles from the receptor. Additional analysis of the usefulness of receptor modeling results is underway, and continued research and development are expected to improve its performance. In the meantime, the reader is cautioned to at least determine the statistical uncertainty associated with any conclusion about prescribed fires drawn from receptor modeling, especially in comparison to collinear sources such as field burning.

Biomass Consumption

Pollutants are formed when biomass is consumed by fire. Prescribed fire in western Oregon and Washington consumes an average of about 43 tons of biomass per acre. The high average values are evidence that the preponderance of prescribed burning is in logging slash fuelbeds. About half of the biomass consumed is litter and duff material; one-quarter is large (greater than 3-inch diameter) woody residues; and the remainder is made up of small woody pieces, hardwood foliage, conifer needles, herbaceous and shrubby vegetation, and rotted wood (Fig. 16-3). East of the Cascades, about 25 tons per acre are consumed in slash fuelbeds, and about 5 tons per acre are burned in natural fuelbeds to improve range and wildlife habitat.

Forest fuels are consumed in a complex combustion process that adds to the variety of combustion products. Approximately half of the biomass consumed in broadcast burns occurs during the flaming combustion stage, with the remainder occurring in the glowing and smoldering stages. The flaming and glowing stages are most efficient; that is, they tend to emit the least pollutants relative to the mass of fuel consumed.

Biomass consumption varies widely between individual fires, depending on the fuelbed condi-

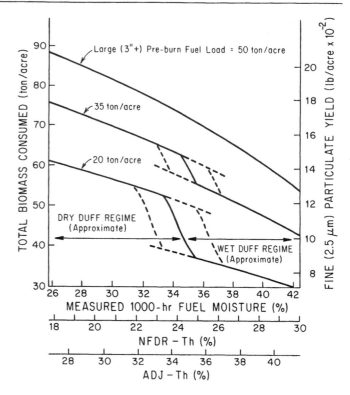

Figure 16-4. Equations for predicting biomass consumed in broadcast burning are available in several forms, including nomographs. This figure can be used to estimate the total consumed biomass based on the loading of large fuels (greater than 3-inch diameter), large-fuel moisture, and duff moisture.

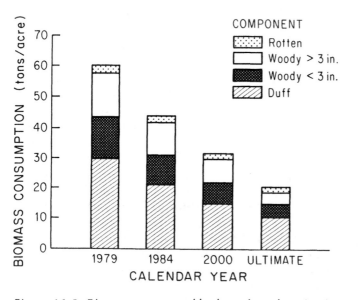

Figure 16-3. Biomass consumed by broadcast burning in western Oregon and Washington. Approximately half of the consumed biomass is litter and duff material.

tion and the way that fire is applied. It is necessary to predict consumption for specific cases in order to consider options for mitigating effects. Biomass consumption in prescribed fires has become much better understood in recent years. Predictive algorithms are available for large fuel consumption and duff consumption during broadcast burns for the common fuel types in the Pacific Northwest (Ottmar 1983). Large fuel consumption depends primarily on moisture content. Duff consumption depends mainly on the mass consumed or fire duration in the woody fuels, except during very dry periods.

Consumption of litter and duff is the least understood component of biomass consumption in broadcast burning. Consumption occurs primarily during the flaming stage, and is probably controlled by the moisture content in the duff layer. The proportion of woody fuel and duff consumed during the flaming and smoldering stages is also predictable. The flaming period is usually sustained as long as the surface litter and small surface fuels are available to sustain flaming, so flaming consumption depends primarily on the abundance of 1- to 3-inch-diameter fuels. A backing fire in small fuels consumes a greater share during the flaming stage, increasing overall combustion efficiency.

Fuel consumption in piled slash has not been modeled, but it is assumed that about 90 to 95 percent of the woody fuels are consumed, along with the duff layer directly covered by the piles. Probably 80 percent or more of the combustion takes place in the flaming stage, so the process is relatively efficient.

Equations for predicting biomass consumption are now widely available in several forms (Fig. 16-4). Nomograph solutions, such as those contained in the Oregon State Smoke Management Operating Instructions (Oregon Department of Forestry 1987) are available to all burners in that state. Many USDA Forest Service fire managers also have access to interactive computer programs that predict fuel consumption.

The biomass consumption equations and updated emission factors have been combined into a model that also predicts pollutant production from prescribed fires (Sandberg and Peterson 1985). Particulate matter and carbon monoxide emission rates are predicted from a set of up to 18 inputs that describe weather and fuelbed conditions. The program can be run repeatedly with different combinations of inputs. The outputs can be used to decide what combinations of fire use, scheduling, and ignition techniques will provide the needed site preparation and minimize smoke production.

Combustion Products

Combustion of biomass is one of the most common of all environmental chemical reactions, and its products are virtually ubiquitous in air. At the same time, our knowledge of the products of combustion is limited. We are aware qualitatively of a few hundred substances formed, liberated, or modified during combustion of vegetation, but little information exists about quantities and only for a few products.

Emissions from prescribed fires include a diverse group of contaminants. Some, like water vapor, carbon dioxide, and hundreds of trace-gas compounds, have no potential to pollute the atmosphere. Others, like carbon monoxide and sulphur dioxide, are criteria pollutants released in insufficient quantities to threaten ambient air quality, although carbon monoxide concentrations may temporarily exceed safe levels at the fireline. Others, like the aldehydes and benzopyrenes, are hazardous pollutants for which no ambient standards exist. Still others, especially particulate matter, are criteria pollutants sometimes emitted in sufficient quantity and duration to cause widespread air pollution.

An *emission factor* is the mass of a contaminant emitted to the atmosphere divided by the level of that activity (e.g., pounds of contaminant per ton of fuel burned). An emission factor can be calculated for a single burn or a single combustion stage of one burn, or it can be a statistical average for a geographical area or a set of similar activities. Statistical emission factors are published in an EPA reference document known as AP-42 (U.S. Environmental Protection Agency 1983). The document is frequently revised to include new information and supplements are added to include newly developed emission factors. The section on prescribed burning was revised in 1988. Emission factors for prescribed burning were also summarized at an EPA conference (Ward et al. 1988).

Carbon dioxide and water

Carbon dioxide and water make up over 90 percent of the total mass emitted from wildland fires. If the combustion process was perfectly complete, 1 ton of wood would yield 3,670 pounds of carbon dioxide and 1,080 pounds of water. In this process, all of the carbon in the fuel would be converted to carbon dioxide, so the combustion process would be defined as 100 percent efficient. Combustion efficiency in prescribed fires actually ranges from 60 to 95 percent (Ward and Hardy 1984); therefore, the emission factor for carbon dioxide ranges from 2,200 to 3,500 pounds per ton of fuel consumed. The portion of carbon that is not converted to carbon dioxide is converted to particulate matter, carbon monoxide, or to volatile organic matter.

Carbon dioxide is not considered a pollutant, although it may soon be classified as a pollutant because of its effect on the global radiation budget (the greenhouse effect). Carbon dioxide emissions from prescribed fires may be exempted from such classification because emission occurs whether biomass decays or is burned, and carbon dioxide emissions may be offset during photosynthesis.

Criteria pollutants and health effects

Particulate matter (PM) is the most important category of pollutants from prescribed fire. Particulates are the major cause of reduced visibility and serve as sorption surfaces for harmful gases. Particles vary in size and chemical composition, depending on fire intensity as well as fuelbed character.

The majority of particles are condensed droplets, with diameters of about 0.1 to 0.3 micrometers, consisting of organic hydrocarbons that have intermediate vapor pressures. These sizes are capable of intercepting visible light, thus their efficiency in reducing visibility. High-intensity fires contribute larger particles composed mostly of solid graphitic carbon, so the proportion of PM2.5 in smoke may range from 50 to 90 percent.

Emission factors for particulate matter, without regard to size, range from 18 to 50 pounds per ton for broadcast burning and 14 to 30 pounds per ton for piled slash, averaging about 34 pounds per ton for both methods. Emission factors for PM2.5 range from 9 to 32 pounds per ton and average about 22 pounds per ton for prescribed burning in

the Pacific Northwest. Emission factors are highest during the inefficient smoldering combustion stage and lowest during flaming combustion (Fig. 16-5). Emission factors for PM10 fall between those for total PM and PM2.5. Almost 2 percent of the carbon released in forest burning is contained with the particles.

Particles themselves have unknown toxicological properties even though they are the primary index for evaluating smoke movement. These complex accumulations of organic chemicals might have specific health effects, but such effects have not been identified. There is an allusion to an absence of particulate effects in a report by Kensler and Battista (1966) on tobacco smoke that introduced a charcoal filter into the smoke stream, stopping the gases and allowing particulate matter to pass. Most of the depression in ciliary activity in the upper respiratory tract was caused by substances in the gas phase, and particulates passing into the tract were not very active. Because much of the particulate fraction is temperature related, the fine condensation droplets may then trap other toxicologically significant compounds.

Little is known about the role of particulates in either adsorbing and stabilizing other compounds, or conversely, in promoting degradation of other chemicals. The effect of fine ash, by itself or as an adsorption surface for organic material, is unknown.

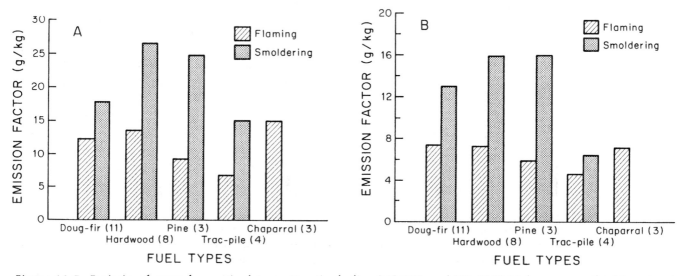

Figure 16-5. Emission factors for particulate matter (including [A] TSP and [B] PM2.5) from prescribed burning in several western fuel types. Note the relatively high emission factors during the smoldering combustion phase. The emission factor representative of a specific fire or group of fires is the average of smoldering and flaming emission factors, weighted by the amount of fuel consumed in each phase.

In urban environments, particulate concentrations in the atmosphere have been related epidemiologically to health impacts, including mortality, but no methods have been developed for isolating the effects of particles from the effects of other pollutants emitted from the same source.

Much of smoke related regulatory activity is based on the amount of particulate material of respirable size in the air, not on any discrete health effects of the visible material. The weakness of the data has led to such exercises as assuming that air into which a single smoke type has intruded has the same health impact as urban air with the same particulate level. Urban pollution and pollution derived from single sources of vegetation smoke are clearly different. Ozone and nitrogen oxide concentration are much higher in an urban atmosphere and they in turn lead to a variety of reaction products not seen in rural smokes. Ketone and nitro derivatives of the polynuclear aromatics scarcely appear in vegetative smoke. Similarly, the various chlorodioxins and furans, when found, are usually from urban combustion sources. The character of the nonvolatile components, such as soil, masonry dust, fly ash, asbestos, machinery wear products, bacteria, and so on, is also much different in the urban matrix. This issue is given considerable attention in a review and discussion by Matanoski et al. (1986).

Carbon monoxide is the most abundant pollutant from forest burning. It is a criteria pollutant. Emission factors range from 70 pounds per ton from flames to 800 pounds per ton for some smoldering fires and average about 150 pounds per ton for all fires. On the average, 6.4 percent of the carbon in forest fuels is converted to carbon monoxide.

Carbon monoxide could represent a direct hazard to human health at the fireline, depending on the concentration, duration, and level of physical activity during exposure. A small number of measurements have been made of carbon monoxide and blood carboxyhemoglobin during wildfire control work that suggests some firefighters have significant carbon monoxide exposures, while most do not. Concentrations of carbon monoxide higher than 200 parts per million (ppm) have been recorded close to flames, but dilute very rapidly beyond 100 feet from a fire. Carbon monoxide from prescribed fires probably poses no risk to community air quality.

Oxides of sulfur and nitrogen are criteria pollutants that do not contain carbon and are of limited interest in regard to environmental or health risks from prescribed fire. Most forest fuels contain less than 0.2 percent sulfur, so oxides of sulfur are probably produced only in negligible quantities. Elevated levels of oxides of sulfur have never been measured near fires.

Formation of oxides of nitrogen (a criteria pollutant) normally occurs through fixation of atmospheric nitrogen at temperatures above normal flame temperatures in open burning. However, a small amount of oxides of nitrogen is produced at lower temperatures from nitrogenous compounds in forest fuels. Oxides of nitrogen are important in the complex atmospheric chemistry involving aldehydes and ozone, but the amounts formed in forest burning are not sufficient to contribute significantly to those reactions.

Small amounts of lead have been measured in slash fire smoke by Ward and Hardy (1986), who presumed that it consists of secondary emission of lead previously deposited from transportation sources. Lead is often used as a key element in receptor modeling, so reentrainment of lead by prescribed fires could confound source apportionment efforts in some cases.

Ozone is not found in the vicinity of fire, but it has been shown to form by photochemical reactions in the tops of plumes from prescribed fires and wildfires. Formation of ozone appears to be limited by penetration of light into the plume; as the plume becomes less dense, ozone concentrations become greater relative to smoke density. As a result, a fire may contribute a significant fraction of the total ozone load; if the plume comes to ground, it may carry photochemically formed ozone with it. Because ozone is a significant pulmonary and vegetative toxicant, this source needs examination as a possible contributor to human health effects.

Noncriteria pollutants, including hazardous pollutants

The most important potential for health effects is from exposure to organic hydrocarbons. Several hundred compounds are emitted in smoke from prescribed fires. The compounds may remain in the air as gases, termed volatile organic compounds (VOCs), may condense into droplets (alone or in association with water or other hydrocarbons), or may be adsorbed onto carbon or ash particles. Two of the important classes of compounds are polynuclear aromatic hydrocarbons, and the aldehydes.

Volatile organic compounds are a diverse class of compounds containing hydrogen, carbon, and sometimes oxygen. Methane constitutes about half of this class. Emission factors range from about 4 to 50 pounds per ton, and average about 20 pounds per ton. They account for 1.5 percent of the carbon in the consumed biomass.

As a class, VOCs are no longer a criteria pollutant because the majority have no biological effect except at very high concentrations. However, a few constituents of the hydrocarbon fraction are important in photochemical smog formation and may be important to human health.

Polynuclear aromatic hydrocarbons (PAHs) are a well-known component of smoke. PAHs are not free in the environment as vapor, but are incorporated in fine particulates that are respirable. They are assumed to follow the smoke plume. There has been concern that fires burning in slash and grass-straw smoke may produce enough PAHs to be a significant cancer risk. Emissions from residential wood combustion have been extensively measured, but less information is available about smoke from prescribed burning, though enough data exist to provisionally estimate the risk associated with PAHs from prescribed fire.

Cancer is the most important of the potential health impacts of PAH compounds. These substances also have some potential for causing mutation, but the probability of mutation will be well represented by estimates of carcinogenic effects. PAH compounds known to be carcinogenic and known to be produced when biomass fuels are burned include benzo-c-phenanthrene, the benzo-fluoranthrenes, 3-methylcholanthrene, dimethyl-benzanthracene, and benzo-a-pyrene (BaP). Benzo-a-pyrene (Fig. 16-6) has been studied in more detail as an air pollutant than any of the others. It can serve generally as a baseline PAH in estimating the risk associated with the class. As will be shown later in this chapter, risk associated with PAH emissions from prescribed fire is apparently trivial.

Nitro derivatives of PAHs do not appear to be produced in significant amounts by prescribed fires because they are only formed significantly in the presence of ambient oxides of nitrogen. The

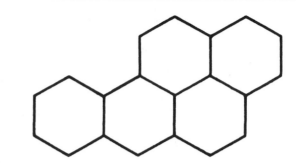

Figure 16-6. Chemical structure of benzo-a-pyrene (BaP).

extent to which highly diluted PAHs in smoke will react with the higher concentrations of oxides of nitrogen or other reactive chemicals in polluted urban areas is unclear. The concentration of PAHs in plumes from prescribed fires will likely be diluted to low enough concentrations that the necessary reactions will not proceed, but firm evidence for this conclusion is not yet available.

Of the aldehydes and related substances produced in combustion, formaldehyde is the most extensively studied because of its wide use as a process chemical and as a component of adhesive resins in wood products. It is known to cause cancer in laboratory animals and is regulated as a human carcinogen. It is an irritant and is allergenic at low concentrations. These latter effects of formaldehyde are probably much more important in consideration of smoke effects than its carcinogenicity.

Formaldehyde is present in the atmosphere as a gas and as a solute in aqueous aerosols. There is an equilibrium between formaldehyde and formic acid in cloud water (Adewuyl et al. 1984), and such an equilibrium may exist in the moist environment near a fire. Irritancy may derive from both compounds, or the equilibrium may favor one strongly enough so the other is insignificant.

Acetaldehyde, acrolein, and other aldehydes are emitted from combustion of biomass. With its great irritant potential, acrolein may even have a greater role than formaldehyde as an irritant in smoke. Acetaldehyde has far less irritant potential and is probably not an important factor in acute effects of smoke exposures.

Measurements of formaldehyde emission from forestry burning are not considered reliable, although order-of-magnitude estimates can be constructed from the scant data that exist. The only measurements in the field have been those of Ward and Hardy (1986), who found acetaldehyde outputs of 3.11 grams per kilogram in the flaming phase of one fire and 2.62 grams per kilogram in the smoldering phase. In another fire, however, the acetaldehyde/fuel ratios were 5 grams per kilogram and 0.45 grams per kilogram. Formaldehyde was not measured but must be expected to be present in greater amounts than acetaldehyde. Several reports have given measurements of aldehyde emissions from fireplaces and stoves, which must be used with care because of differences in fuel and fire characteristics from prescribed burning.

It appears that an estimate of between 1 and 7 grams of formaldehyde per kilogram of consumed biomass is reasonable, with accompanying estimates of 0.5-1 grams per kilogram of acetaldehyde and 0.05-0.1 grams per kilogram of acrolein. We will use the upper estimate in the risk assessment exercise presented later in this chapter.

For regulatory purposes, a potency factor has been established by the EPA for formaldehyde. Definition of exposures resulting from prescribed fire, however, is tenuous. Apparently a small amount of formaldehyde is produced naturally through photo-oxidation of methane, resulting in a background concentration in remote areas of about 0.4 parts per billion (ppb), according to Singh et al. (1982). Urban air contains 10 to 20 ppb formaldehyde, according to measurements by Singh et al. (1982).[3]

The same series of studies has shown that degradation of formaldehyde in the atmosphere approaches 90 percent per day; unlike most small volatiles, photolysis (the breakdown of chemicals by sunlight) is an important process in removal of formaldehyde.

Evidence, as yet not absolutely established, shows that combustion of wood and other materials that do not contain chlorophenol may still form various chlorinated dioxins and related compounds. The concentrations formed are very low, if they do occur, and represent an insignificant contribution.

Combustion of herbicides applied to vegetation before prescribed (brown-and-burn) or accidental burning should be considered because of great public interest. Factors that enter into the exposure calculations are the rate of degradation of the chemicals and the products that might be formed. No residues from herbicides have yet been found in smoke from prescribed fires (Lande 1987), although we cannot conclude that there is none because relatively little study has been made in the field. Estimates based on maximum available amounts of herbicides and all related products in smoke, fuel conversion to smoke, and smoke density show that exposures to the parent chemicals or to any product will be trivial even in dense smoke.

Assessment of Risk to Human Health

General principles of risk assessment

Risk assessment estimates consequences to the health of individuals or populations exposed to hazardous air pollutants. It begins with hazard identification; that is, a qualitative identification of the kind of hazard from exposure to a pollutant and quantitative assessment of the amount of pollutant emitted by a source. This is followed by an exposure assessment to quantify the magnitude and duration of exposure; an assessment of the toxicology, or dose-response relationship with respect to pertinent biological effects; and a risk assessment, which brings these steps together to characterize the probability of an adverse effect (Sullivan 1988).

Uncertainties are encountered at every step in the assessment: in quantifying the amount of hazardous pollutants emitted by fires; in selecting the appropriate dose-response relationship to use; and in characterizing the exposure of workers or the public to smoke. These uncertainties need research; however, in the absence of more precise data, risk assessments for some hypothetical cases will be developed later in this chapter.

Hazard identification. The limited knowledge regarding production of hazardous pollutants by fires was reviewed in an earlier section on combustion products. Smoke contains hundreds and perhaps thousands of chemicals in several classes of compounds, and in proportions that vary from case to case. It is not unreasonable to suggest that no two fires are exactly alike. There is little knowledge about the behavior of most of these substances in sunlight, when adsorbed onto particles

---

[3]The EPA Health Risk Assessment for Formaldehyde generalizes by considering levels below 0.05 ppm (50 ppb) as ambient.

of various kinds, or in any other mode of environmental behavior. Hazard identification deals with this aspect of the subject.

Exposure assessment. In evaluating the health impact of combustion products, we utilize the same principles that apply to every other study of toxicology. Exposure is the amount and nature of material that will reach a body surface from which it can be absorbed—in this case, predominantly the respiratory tract. The extent and nature of the emission mix, and its environmental movement and reactions, determine the exposure at the site of concern.

Estimates or measurements of atmospheric concentrations of combustion products will help estimate respiratory exposure which, in turn, will help estimate the dose of the chemical in question over time. When coupled with projections from laboratory toxicological data, a reasonable idea of the risk associated with the exposure is possible.

Exposure, of course, is only part of the information we must have. It is also necessary to have sound toxicological information—that is, good data describing the adverse effects of the chemical in question. It is of no value to have information only about the amounts of the chemical in the atmosphere, or data only about the toxicology of the chemical. Even the most toxic substance poses no threat if the exposure is low enough; conversely, chemicals of limited toxicity represent a significant hazard when exposures are excessive.

Dose-response relationship. The dose-response relationship applies to air pollutants, just as it does to other chemicals. With every chemical, as the dose changes, the effect changes in the same direction (Fig. 16-7). There are no exceptions to this orderly relationship. When we discuss risk assessment, which is the process of learning the probability that given exposures to chemicals will cause harm, the essential nature of the dose-response curve is obvious.

The great variety of substances formed in smoke suggests the possibility of physiological interaction. If such interactions occur, the combined effects of mixtures of chemicals may be additive, synergistic, or potentiating. Chemicals that are synergistic have similar effects alone and produce responses together that are greater than the sum of the effect of the individual chemicals $(1 + 1 = 3)$. A potentiator is a chemical that produces no response alone, but increases the effect

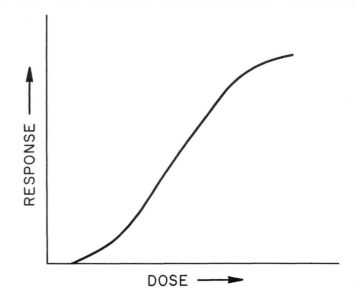

Figure 16-7. *Typical dose-response curve.*

of another $(1 + 0 = 2)$. Such effects are not large and are threshold dependent. Irritating substances are usually additive and should not produce multiplied effects. The greatest potential for amplified effects will be in increased absorption of other kinds of smoke constituents through mucous membranes inflamed by the irritating components. Based on extensive studies of therapeutic drugs, interactions of any kind are not likely to cause more than a few-fold difference.

As we study health effects of emissions from prescribed fires, our objectives are no different from those considered for any other toxic substance. We need to determine whether exposures to specific fire products can reach a level that either too closely approaches a threshold of reversible or nongenetic effect or represents more than a *de minimis* carcinogenic risk. When that is accomplished, the findings should guide policy development that includes risk/benefit considerations, fire management research, changes in burning techniques, or development of fire-free alternatives.

Knowledge of health effects of smoke from wood and foliage combustion is limited to clinical observation of a few people who suffer from acute smoke inhalation at fire sites, and to a few more who experience respiratory distress under lesser exposure. Others show clinical symptoms when slash or field burning smoke intrudes into urban areas, possibly suffering effects from combined pollutants. The role of intruding smoke alone, however, is impossible to gauge in most cases.

Which data on health effects are applicable? Good human-health observations in the field and exposure data may be more informative than data derived from laboratory animals, but it is easy to use the wrong data. For example, findings associated with urban air pollution, with its multitude of sources, cannot be used as an index of the impact of a single source that does not include the components of the urban sample. A finding of illness associated with a broad-scale, undefined component like "particulates" in the urban context does not indicate the risk associated with particulates from a single source such as field or slash burning.

Whether using laboratory or field data, we may also be burdened with a mass of assumptions that reflect our best judgment, because real knowledge may be lacking. In other words, projection of the health impacts of smoke is sometimes rather like computing the volume of a room by measuring one dimension exactly, estimating the other two from a distance by eye, then calculating the product to three decimal places. We need to be cautious about our assumptions because they may lead to a false sense of security.

Risk analysis. A major practical problem confronts us when we study smoke. A risk analysis for a single chemical can employ the toxicology data specific to that chemical, and in most cases an exposure estimate can be made that is, say, within an order of magnitude of reality.

How do we obtain data about the impact of smoke constituents when neither their nature nor their toxicology has been fully studied? There are a variety of approaches, of every degree of reliability. Many of the known products of combustion are not unique to combustion and have been studied in some other context. If exposures to a substance can be determined, and if there is reasonable knowledge of its toxicology, we are a long way toward being able to estimate the risk associated with the substance.

Formaldehyde is a good example of the kind of problem that can be solved in this way. We have a lot of good information, but there are gaps that must be filled with estimates and assumptions. The data base on toxicology of formaldehyde is extensive. We know that formaldehyde forms in fires. There is a serious question about the

amounts, but some data from wood stoves might give us a crude estimate to apply to the emissions from a slash fire. At this point, however, an obstacle arises. Does formaldehyde remain intact in the atmosphere? Does it degrade in the presence of other chemicals in the air? Does it attach to the surface of particulates, or go into solution within particulates and stabilize, or does it break down on particle surfaces? With all the information we do have, we may not have certain critical items that would permit us to estimate risk with some certitude.

Because of the complexity of smoke, there is a tendency to seek common denominators to represent the entire emission pattern, thus saving the labor of learning about each part of the pattern and its variations. Sometimes, it is assumed that the easily measurable components of a given smoke, usually particulates, represent the distribution of all components of the emission. However, the behavior of both ozone and nitrogen dioxide have been shown to change differently from the change in particulate concentration, probably because of increased penetration of light into the plume. Even with those known discrepancies, the premise is at least usable. An unworkable premise is the assignment of some common and proportional magnitude of health impact to all atmospheres containing particulates, regardless of source and accompanying compounds. A more exhaustive treatment of this subject is provided by Matanoski et al. (1985), Graedel and Weschler (1981), Moller and Altheim (1982), and de Wiest et al. (1982).

In the following discussion, we have chosen to examine the risk issues that are uppermost in the public consciousness or that are scientifically considered to be most important.

Risk assessment for exposure to polynuclear aromatic hydrocarbons

Some of the classes of materials present in smoke have received considerable public attention, sometimes based on real experience, sometimes on the strength of speculation. A consequence is often excessive worry and a loss of attention to possibly more important substances. A good example is the polynuclear aromatic hydrocarbons, of which benzo-a-pyrene (BaP) is the best known (Fig. 16-6).

Many of these compounds are carcinogenic in certain kinds of assays, and it is not unreasonable to wonder whether they represent a significant hazard in smoke from prescribed fire. Dost (1986) estimated risks associated with a group of the PAHs for which sufficient toxicological data are available, and which are significant components of smoke. As will be seen below, it is unlikely that this group, to the extent that it arises from prescribed burning, represents a cancer risk because exposures are so low. It must be kept in mind that there are many uncertainties in these estimates, but maximizing assumptions are used to compensate.

A large number of PAHs have been detected as wood combustion products, but few of these have been quantified. In addition, it is clear that combustion conditions and fuel type have considerable influence on this class of emissions. For example, PAH production increases with the amount of green vegetation, and decreases as the rate of burn increases. Even with wide variation in output, however, there is enough information available that reasonable estimates of PAH production from prescribed burning may be made.

There is a further complication, however, in that the atmospheric chemistry of these compounds is poorly understood. It is possible to interpret various data as suggesting that PAHs survive extended periods or that they are interconverted to other substances in the atmosphere. For the present, and for this discussion, they will be assumed to follow the smoke distribution, intact, with change in concentration due only to dilution.

BaP concentrations in air can be most easily estimated if there is some idea of the ratio between particulates and BaP. This makes it possible to visualize them, literally, by relating particulate levels arising from smoke to visibility distances. This, of course, is unsatisfactory if other impairment of visibility occurs. There is some direct information on atmospheric particulate/PAH ratios. Measurements of ratios between fuel consumption versus particulate production, and fuel consumption versus PAH production, also lead to estimates of PAH levels in smoke. The latter approach has provided an estimated ratio of 0.30 micrograms (μg) BaP per mg of particulate, which represents the highest BaP and lowest particulate outputs (Dost 1986). The use of those extremes leads to the maximum estimate of BaP concentration. Direct measurement of BaP/particulate ratios leads to estimates about 10-fold lower.

The next problem is: How much particulate is there, and will that tell us how much BaP is present? Smoke will obstruct light when there is about 0.5 grams of particulate per square meter. In other words, a square column, 1 meter on a side, containing 0.5 grams of smoke particulate will block light when viewed through its length. The length of the column does not matter; if that amount were to be distributed uniformly on a glass plate 1 meter square, it would presumably obstruct light. If the distance is 100 meters, the volume of the column would be 100 m³, and the 0.5 grams of particles would then be at a concentration of 0.005 grams, or 5.0 mg per m³. Thus, if the visibility in a smoky area is 100 meters, one can presume that the concentration of particulates is about 5 mg per m³.

If the respiratory ventilation of a human is 20 m³ per day, a 70-kg individual exposed to an atmosphere containing 5 mg particulate per m³ would acquire 100 mg of particulate daily, accompanied by 30 μg of BaP. The dose would be expressed as 30 μg per 70 kg per day, or 0.43 μg per kg per day. Table 16-1 gives an estimate of BaP doses at different smoke densities (derived from visibility distances), using the convention just described.

A straightforward and simple risk estimate for PAH carcinogenicity associated with smoke can be developed from the relation between cancer po-

Table 16-1. The relation between visibility and benzo-a-pyrene (BaP) concentration at various densities.

Visibility	Particulate/m³ (mg)	BaP/m³ (μg)	24-hr dose (μg)	Dose/kg/day (μg)
100 meters	5.0	1.5	30	0.43
1,000 meters	0.5	0.15	3	0.043
1 mile	0.31	0.093	1.86	0.027
2 miles	0.155	0.046	0.93	0.013
5 miles	0.062	0.018	0.372	0.0053

Table 16-2. Concentration of polynuclear aromatic hydrocarbons (PAH) at various atmospheric particulate (smoke) loadings.[a]

	100 m		1,000 m		1 mile		2 miles		5 miles	
Visibility limit:										
Particulate/m³:	5 mg		0.5 mg		0.31 mg		0.115 mg		0.062 mg	
					$\mu g/m^3$					
	A[b]	B[c]	A	B	A	B	A	B	A	B
Benzo-a-pyrene (BaP)	1.5	0.12	0.15	0.012	0.093	0.007	0.046	0.004	0.018	0.001
Pyrene	8.69	0.69	0.87	0.07	0.54	0.043	0.27	0.021	0.108	0.009
Benzo-c-phenanthrene	3.80	0.3	0.38	0.03	0.24	0.019	0.12	0.01	0.148	0.004
Benzo fluoranthenes	0.52	0.042	0.052	0.0042	0.032	0.002	0.016	0.001	0.006	0.0003
Fluoranthene	6.05	0.48	0.6	0.05	0.37	0.03	0.18	0.014	0.074	0.006
Perylene	1.0	0.08	0.1	0.008	0.06	0.005	0.031	0.002	0.012	0.001
Benzo-g,h,i-perylene	3.15	0.25	0.3	0.025	0.19	0.015	0.096	0.008	0.038	0.003

Sources and notes:
[a]Concentrations of all PAHs calculated from relative outputs measured by Ryan and McMahon (1976).
[b]Column A assumes 300 μg BaP/mg particulate based on assumption of 2500 μg BaP/kg fuel and 8.5 g particulate/kg fuel.
[c]Column B assumes 24 μg BaP/mg particulate based on direct measurement by White (1985, 1987).

tency and the concentration of a carcinogen in the atmosphere. The procedure has been discussed in detail in a report to the USDI Bureau of Land Management (Dost 1986). The cancer risk can be estimated by using a potency figure calculated by the Cancer Assessment Group of EPA to be 3.3×10^{-3}. This number means that a person exposed to 1 μg BaP per m³ per day for a 70-year lifetime would be subjected to an *increased* risk, or probability of cancer, of 3.3 chances in 1,000. The incidence of cancer in the general population is more than one case in four lifetimes.

For substances acquired by other than air intake, the potency is expressed as the added probability of cancer per mg per kg per day of intake. For shorter periods, the exposure is averaged over a lifetime, which is appropriate according to our current understanding of cancer mechanisms. For example, exposure to 1.0 μg per m³ daily for 7 years would result in an estimated added risk 10-fold less, or 3.3×10^{-4} (3.3 chances in 10,000).

If BaP were the PAH of concern, a rough risk estimate would derive directly from the smoke density as determined by visibility limits. There are many other PAHs in smoke, however, and some way must be found to estimate their contribution. Although the primary concern is for lung cancer, the only laboratory data usable for comparison come from studies in which the materials are painted on the skin, which is a standard research technique but is of questionable use in estimating the risk of pulmonary disease. An assumption is made that the relative potencies for lung cancer and skin tumors are similar among species, which enables a provisional comparison.

In Table 16-2, the estimated concentrations of various PAHs are shown for several visibility limits, using two different methods for estimating PAH/particulate ratios.

Cancer risk as estimated for twenty 6-hour exposures per year at 2-mile visibility for 10 years is shown in Table 16-3. These risks, which are one in a million to one in a billion or lower, are probably extreme because of the several maximizing assumptions. As shown in Dost (1986), the risks associated with living in a wood-burning community are no less, and living in a home heated by wood carries a greater risk.

It must be emphasized that these are estimates only, with no solid basis in data. However, we believe they represent the high range of values that would be found in the field. As more reliable data become available, the estimates of risk can be improved by simple arithmetic.

Risk assessment for exposure to aldehydes

The output numbers for estimating aldehyde exposure can be related to the concentrations at various smoke densities in the same way they were used in estimating PAH exposure.

If formaldehyde output is 7 grams per kg fuel consumed, compared with 8.5 grams of particulate, the information in Table 16-2 can be converted by the ratio 7/8.5, giving formaldehyde concentrations at 100 meters visibility of 5 mg per m³ × 7/8.5 = 4.12 mg formaldehyde per m³, which trans-

Table 16-3. Risk associated with various polynuclear aromatic hydrocarbons (PAH) at smoke density characterized by 2-mile visibility, assuming twenty 6-hour exposure days/year over 10 years of residence, normalized to continuous average exposure over a 70-year lifetime.[a,b]

Chemical	Potency[c]	Concentration ($\mu g/m^3$)	Concentration norm to 70-yr ($\mu g/m^3$)	Risk if BaP-300 $\mu g/g$ particulate[f]	Risk if BaP-24 $\mu g/g$ particulate
Benzo-a-pyrene (BaP)	3.3×10^{-3}	0.046	0.00009	3.0×10^{-7}	2.4×10^{-8}
Pyrene	0	0.27	0.00053	0	0
Benzo-c-phenanthrene	$3.3 \times 10^{-3[d]}$	0.12	0.00023	7.6×10^{-7}	6.1×10^{-8}
Benzo fluoranthenes	$3.3 \times 10^{-4[d]}$	0.016	0.000031	1.0×10^{-8}	8.0×10^{-10}
Fluoranthene	0	0.18	0.00035	0	0
Perylene	$3.3 \times 10^{-4[e]}$	0.031	0.000061	2.0×10^{-8}	5.0×10^{-9}
Benzo-g,h,i-perylene	$3.3 \times 10^{-4[e]}$	0.096	0.00019	6.27×10^{-8}	5.0×10^{-9}
Total risk[g]				1.1×10^{-6}	8.8×10^{-8}

Sources and notes:
[a] Visibility is related to particulate density by use of extinction factor of 0.5 g particulate/m^2.
[b] A constant ratio of BaP to other PAHs at 0.1 lb/ft^2 fuel loading is assumed.
[c] Potency is estimated by comparison of cancer resulting from 70 years inhalation exposure to 1 $\mu g/m^3$.
[d] Potency is estimated by comparison of skin painting data for PAHs with data from similar experiments with BaP, and assuming that pulmonary carcinogenic potency will bear a similar relation to potency of 3.3×10^{-3} for BaP estimated by EPA-CAG.
[e] Where evidence is insufficient to determine whether a compound is/is not carcinogenic, potency is assumed as 10% of BaP potency.
[f] 300 μg BaP/g particulate, based on assumption of 2500 μg BaP/kg fuel; 8.5 g particulate/kg fuel based on direct measurement by White (1985).
[g] Total risk is assumed to be sum of risks ascribed to individual PAHs.

lates to 3.08 ppm, if formaldehyde is assumed to be an ideal gas. Estimated concentrations of formaldehyde at the distances used in Table 16-2 would, therefore, be as indicated in Table 16-4 if there are no atmospheric reactions of formaldehyde.

Some humans experience eye irritation after a few minutes of exposure to 0.1 ppm of formaldehyde, although this is not usual. Most people will feel eye irritation at 1.0 ppm, sometimes in a few minutes. If the concentrations estimated above are realistic, it is quite likely that formaldehyde may be responsible for some of the eye and upper respiratory response at or near the fireline. For a few sensitive individuals, there may be enough formaldehyde in the plume to evoke a response at a mile from the source.

The same figures may be used in estimating cancer risks associated with formaldehyde exposure. The model exposure used above to estimate risk associated with PAHs above was twenty 6-hour exposures per year at 2-mile visibility for 10 years. The relation for formaldehyde, which has an upperbound unit risk of 1.3×10^{-5} or 1.3 chances per 100,000 lifetimes per μg per m^3 (U.S. Environmental Protection Agency 1987), is linear when normalized over a lifetime. Twenty $\times$ 6 hours per year $\times$ 10 years is 1,200 hours of exposure, compared to 613,200 hours in 70 years. The nominal

concentration in this exercise is 0.127 mg (127 μg) per m^3, compared to that at unit risk of 1.0 μg per m^3. The added risk would therefore be $1.3 \times 10^{-5} \times (1200/613,200) \times (127/1.0) = 3.23 \times 10^{-6}$, or 3.23 chances in one million. Regulatory agencies consider a risk of 1 in a million to be the practical equivalent of zero.

The real risk would undoubtedly be much lower, given the maximizing assumptions of 7 grams of formaldehyde emitted per kg of fuel, exclusive of the 90 percent per day reduction of formaldehyde (Singh et al. 1982), the very large exposure period used in the estimate, and the fact that the unit risk is the 95 percent upperbound estimate.

Measurements of acrolein concentrations or emissions are even less well established than those for formaldehyde. Our estimates are that acrolein outputs will be from 1 to 10 percent of the formaldehyde production, which would lead to an expected concentration of acrolein at 100-meter visibility of 0.04 to 0.4 mg per m^3. These figures are equivalent to 1.6 and 0.16 ppm, on a volume/volume basis.

Studies with human volunteers indicate that 1 ppm is capable of causing possible severe eye irritation in 5 minutes, 0.3 ppm can cause some eye and nose irritation, and that the odor threshold is about 0.03 ppm. The concentrations expected at and near the fireline under our assumptions should clearly result in at least part of the effects experienced close to a fire. It is not likely, however, that acrolein has effects at a distance of a mile.

Acrolein is not considered carcinogenic, and no attempt is made to judge such risk.

We caution again that much of the basis for these estimates is hypothetical and must be brought into the realm of reality when better data become available.

Risk assessment for exposure to herbicide combustion products

The perception is widespread that when chemicals burn, products of extraordinary toxicity may be produced. This belief also applies to herbicides or insecticides that have been used on forest land that is later burned, whether intentionally or by accident. There is enough information on combustion of organic compounds in general, and on herbicides in particular, from which worst-imaginable-case estimates of combustion products can be prepared. It is clear that the amounts in the atmosphere do not approach levels sufficient to produce responses.

In a report to the Bonneville Power Administration, Dost (1982) considered whether combustion of applied herbicides might produce substances with significant potential for health impacts. Several studies had shown a limited number of terminal combustion products of herbicides, of which carbon dioxide and carbon monoxide predominate, as would be expected. Almost all of the chlorine in such chemicals will be oxidized to hydrogen chloride. Very small amounts of chlorine gas and phosgene can be produced under forced laboratory conditions, so it was assumed (for purpose of the analysis) that these were also possible products in the field. It was also assumed that ammonia and cyanide, and in some cases acetonitrile, could arise from nitrogenous herbicide compounds. In the case of the herbicide, glyphosate, the phosphorus present was known to form some phosphorus pentoxide, which then formed phosphoric acid.

By calculating the amount of herbicide assumed to be present, a relation was established with fuel loading, which in turn related to smoke production, visibility limits, and a volume of distribution, which therefore defined atmospheric concentration. This approach to estimation was described earlier with the discussion of polynuclear aromatic hydrocarbons. Typical adult respiratory rates were used to estimate intake, as in the examples already discussed.

The calculations showed that even when it was assumed that all of the chlorine in a herbicide formed phosgene, chlorine gas, or hydrogen chloride, the amounts were trivial when compared with known toxicology or with established federal workplace standards. The same conclusion was reached with respect to herbicides containing nitrogen or phosphorus. All of the potential products are common industrial chemicals with well-established allowable levels for workplace exposure. When it was assumed that the herbicides simply volatilized and distributed in the smoke cloud, exposures were again well below no-effect levels.

There is frequent concern about possible formation of some kind of chlorodioxin during combustion of chlorinated organics. Very small quantities of 2,7-dichlorodibenzo-p-dioxin might arise from combustion of 2,4-D, although measurements have never been made. 2,7-DCDD is of relatively limited toxicity, and at the low levels that could be produced should not be of consequence. No production of 2,3,7,8-TCDD, the most toxic form of dioxin, should occur.

Mitigating Measures for Prescribed Fire Smoke

The pollutants emitted by fires may or may not cause air pollution, depending on the success of mitigating measures and the relative importance of other polluting sources. It is difficult to describe the relative contribution of burning to pollution events because fires are remote from most receptors, and are both variable and temporary.

Similarly, the potential to mitigate pollutant production at the source is difficult to generalize.

Table 16.4. Estimated concentrations of formaldehyde in air following burning.

	100 m	1,000 m	1 mile	2 miles	5 miles
ppm	3.08	0.31	0.19	0.095	0.038
mg/m$^{3[a]}$	4.12	0.41	0.25	0.127	0.051

Note:
[a] Volume:volume basis

Forest managers evaluate each potential site of a prescribed burn before burning. Less than one-fourth of the harvested areas are burned, after considering the costs and benefits on each site. When a site is to be burned, managers consider several options to reduce emissions, and smoke management coordinators judge whether the expected air quality result is permissible. The improvement in air quality and the progress toward air quality goals are the cumulative result of these many thousand decisions.

Mitigation methods

Avoidance, dilution, and emission reduction are all used to reduce polluting ambient air from prescribed burning. Avoidance is a strategy of considering meteorological conditions when scheduling fires in order to avoid incursions of prescribed burning smoke into smoke-sensitive areas; for example, a populated area where any noticeable impact is objectionable. Dilution involves controlling the rate of emissions or scheduling for dispersion to assure a tolerable concentration of smoke in designated areas. Emission reduction techniques minimize the emission of pollutants per unit area treated.

Smoke management

Smoke from prescribed burning has been managed in Oregon and Washington under cooperative smoke management programs since 1970 (Chapter 20). The Oregon Department of Environmental Quality and the Washington Department of Ecology establish air quality standards and work with the forestry agencies (the Oregon Department of Forestry and the Washington Department of Natural Resources) to regulate burning. The state forestry agencies issue burning permits and coordinate the daily operation of the plans.

For nearly two decades, the smoke management systems have been used to nearly eliminate objectionable intrusions of smoke into designated smoke-sensitive areas. The systems rely on trained foresters and meteorologists to make swift go/no-go decisions based on burn reports and weather forecasts. We are fortunate to have such experts in the Pacific Northwest states. Each state publishes annual reports detailing the successes and failures of the programs (e.g., Carnine 1984, Oregon Department of Forestry 1984).

The Washington Smoke Management Plan was extensively revised in January 1984 (Weaver and Droege 1984), and the Oregon Plan was revised in December 1986, to provide visibility in Class I areas as required by changes in the Clean Air Act.

The purposes of the Oregon and Washington programs are similar. Both recognize the importance of allowing prescribed burning, but also provide for the protection of ambient air quality and visibility. For example, the objective of the Oregon Smoke Management Program is:

> To prevent smoke, resulting from burning on forest lands, from being carried to or accumulating in designated areas and other areas sensitive to smoke; to provide maximum opportunity for essential forest land burning while minimizing emissions; to coordinate with other smoke management programs; to conform with state and federal air quality and visibility requirements; to protect public health; and to encourage the reduction of emissions.

Smoke management plans relied exclusively on avoidance and dilution during the 1970s to achieve air quality objectives. Those techniques are still important features of smoke management, but reducing emissions has become a prominent technique in the 1980s.

Visibility improvement

Oregon and Washington have been among the first states to implement visibility protection strategies, and both emphasize annual reduction in emissions and place additional restrictions on slash burning from July 4 to Labor Day. Both states have also scheduled annual reviews of the success of the strategies and a major review after 3 years (scheduled for 1989). Substantial revision of the regulations is possible at that time, provided that visibility is protected to at least the same degree as under current regulations.

Burn allocation

Prior to 1985, no evidence could be found that smoke management restrictions significantly reduced the number of acres treated by fire (Sandberg and Schmidt 1982). The restrictions caused changes in burn plans and numerous schedule changes that increased burn costs, but almost all planned burns were accomplished. However, the combination of increased regulation since 1984 and the recent series of unusually large wildfires has now resulted in an approximate 30 percent decrease in the use of prescribed fire.

Current smoke management programs are effective for rescheduling burns during the year, but are not structured effectively to allocate the absolute opportunity to burn. No consideration is given to the relative need to burn individual units and no incentive is given to individual land managers to reduce their volume of burning. In addition, smoke management coordinators do not make use of the best available dispersion models and decision models that might increase the number of opportunities to burn without causing air pollution.

Emission reduction

The State of Washington was first to establish a goal of reducing emissions from prescribed burning. The goal was set at a 35 percent reduction by 1990, compared to emissions in the baseline period 1976-79. The State of Oregon expects a reduction of emissions of 50 percent by the year 2000. The goals provide some flexibility in the manner of attainment. Forest managers can choose between a reduction in the use of fire, a decrease in the mass of fuel consumed by fire, or an increase in combustion efficiency (i.e., cleaner burning).

Effective techniques to reduce emissions from prescribed fires have been developed over the last 7 years through a cooperative research and development effort. A series of more than 150 field experiments showed that smoke emissions could be reduced by 18 to 35 percent by increasing the removal and utilization of residues, compared to current standard practices typified by the removal of pieces larger than 8 inches in diameter and 10 feet in length (Fig. 16-8). Rescheduling broadcast slash burns from a dry fall period to a wet spring period was also shown to reduce emissions by more than 50 percent by reducing biomass consumption (Fig. 16-9). Emission reduction techniques are developed further in Chapter 22.

An emission inventory of western Oregon and western Washington for 1984-85 was completed and compared to the 1976-79 baseline period (Sandberg 1987). If the inventory is correct, particulate matter emissions declined by about 29 percent to 60,000 tons per year in western Oregon and 26,000 tons in western Washington. The reduction in emissions appears to have resulted about half

Figure 16-8. Smoke emissions can be reduced by 18 to 35 percent by removing and utilizing smaller residue pieces before broadcast burning, according to results of several demonstration projects in western Oregon and Washington.

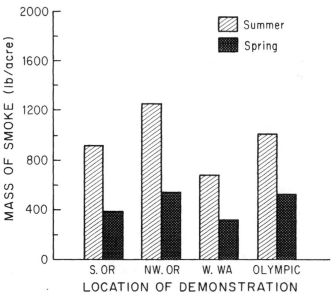

Figure 16-9. Spring burns emitted an average of 54 percent less smoke than did fall burns in a series of demonstration projects in broadcast burning of logging slash west of the Cascades.

from improved utilization and half from other factors. The conclusion is somewhat in doubt because of the uncertainty in characterizing the timber utilization standards in recent years. That uncertainty is currently under investigation by the USDA Forest Service, Pacific Northwest Research Station, and by the U.S. Department of Energy. The area treated with fire annually changed by less than 1 percent from the baseline period until 1984.

Future emission reductions

Federal agencies are required by law to anticipate the environmental impacts of major management decisions. For example, the USDA Forest Service's Pacific Northwest Region has released a Final Environmental Impact Statement (EIS) for vegetation management (USDA Forest Service, Pacific Northwest Region 1988) projecting emissions from prescribed burning through the year 2000 on lands managed by the Forest Service. Emissions from prescribed burning on national forests are expected to decline by at least 23 to 49 percent by the year 2000 from 1986-87 levels (Fig. 16-10). Added to the reduction that has already taken place since the baseline period (1976 through 1979), the total emission reduction will be at least 55 percent. The area burned by the Forest Service is expected to decline by 12 percent from current levels, and the rest of the reduction will come through improved utilization and a change to spring burning.

State and private landowners are not required to follow the federal Environmental Impact Statement (EIS) process, so there is no detailed way of knowing what the nonfederal sector expects in the way of utilization standards or in the size of future prescribed burning programs.

Risk management

Risk management is the process of using the information gained in a health-risk assessment in light of regulatory, technical, political, and socioeconomic considerations to diminish risk from exposure to hazardous pollutants. It is too early to say whether risk assessments for prescribed burning will result in any significant change of work schedules or other protective measures for fireline workers, or whether smoke management procedures will be further stiffened to protect public health. Some managers are intuitively applying risk management procedures in advance of any proven health risk, sometimes in response to employee union requests. In a sense, risk management procedures are being invoked in advance of an adequate risk assessment.

Conclusion

Prescribed fires in the Pacific Northwest represent a substantial source of air pollutants. They are the predominant source of anthropogenic particulate matter in the Northwest, and the abundance of fine particles in smoke increases their importance to visibility impairment and potential health risk. More than 100,000 tons of inhalable particulates are emitted annually from prescribed fires. In one study, 44 percent of visibility impairment was shown to result from slash burning. Goals have been set in Oregon and Washington to reduce emissions substantially before the year 2000, thus reducing visibility impairment.

Wildfires also contribute substantially to air pollution in the Pacific Northwest. For example, the 1987 wildfire episode in southwest Oregon probably emitted more pollutants than all prescribed burning that year. The pollutants were concentrated by a stagnant weather system, so the pollution was much greater than from managed smoke. Prescribed fires can obviously be used to reduce potential wildfire severity. However, the production of smoke from wildfires is considered natural and exceptional by air resource managers, so does not influence the regulation of prescribed fire emissions.

A consistent theme at a recent symposium on slash burning (Hanley et al. 1989) was that no blanket rules apply to the decision of whether and how to burn slash. Several speakers at the symposium lamented the inadequate knowledge base for evaluating the various costs and benefits of prescribed fire, and for evaluating the cost of mitigation measures when fire is used. We recommend continued research and development of information to specifically evaluate the costs and benefits of alternative residue treatments.

The smoke management systems in Oregon and Washington are highly effective systems without equal in other states. For nearly two decades, they have been used to nearly eliminate objectionable intrusions of smoke into designated smoke-sensitive areas. The systems rely on trained foresters and meteorologists to make swift go/no-go decisions based on burn reports and weather forecasts.

Improvements in the smoke management programs are still necessary. Air quality protection should be extended to rural areas, where residents are finding smoke increasingly objectionable. Also, unusual and local intrusions due to poor dispersion conditions are not always preventable. The needs of especially sensitive or allergic indi-

viduals must also somehow be considered. Finally, smoke managers can now allocate the absolute opportunity to burn as well as schedule opportunities and can add efficiency by utilizing better dispersion models, optimization techniques models, and decision rules to provide new burn opportunities.

Considerable technology has also evolved to support air quality management decisions. Quantitative models are available for many important fuel types to predict biomass consumption and

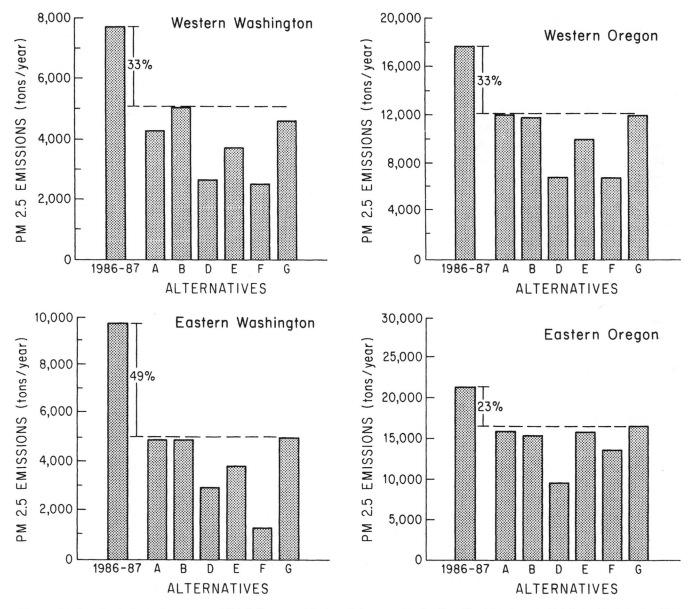

Figure 16-10. Emissions from prescribed fires on National Forests in the Pacific Northwest Region are expected to decrease by at least 23 to 49 percent before the year 2000 according to a Draft Environmental Impact Statement. Each bar represents an alternative vegetation management strategy.

emission production. The models form the basis for the revised Oregon Smoke Management reporting system, are used by forest managers to evaluate emission reduction options, and are used to plan for and verify programmatic success in reducing emissions.

However, development and application of the emission production model are incomplete. For example, fuel consumption during very wet burning conditions and consumption of ponderosa pine duff are two conditions that are poorly understood. Additional research is needed to extend the range of conditions where the model is reliable. Also, the model is not packaged well enough for widespread use. We recommend accelerated completion of the research components of the emission production model, including the development of user-friendly software.

Two methods are used to assess the contribution of smoke from prescribed fires relative to other pollution sources. One uses dispersion modeling in conjunction with an emission inventory to predict the trajectory of smoke. That method has never been used in a serious way in the Pacific Northwest because of the lack of available technology to model dispersion. Another uses receptor models to compare ambient air chemistry to the effluent chemistry of possible sources. This technique is becoming more useful as the technology advances. However, enormous errors remain in the conclusions drawn from such models, owing to the lack of certainty in the chemical profile of emissions and the difficulty in interpreting the statistical results of the modeling.

Dispersion models are becoming increasingly available and conveniently packaged on small computers, so we recommend evaluation of their use to improve source apportionment. We also recommend continued research and development of receptor modeling techniques, with better reporting of the uncertainty of conclusions in the interim.

Concern is also increasing over the risk of exposure to carbon monoxide and certain aldehydes by firefighters, as well as over the exposure to substances that could conceivably contribute to the incidence of cancer in the general population. The difficult process of identifying hazardous pollutants and assessing the risk to either group has just begun. Forest managers have a clear responsibility to anticipate and mitigate possible human exposures to smoke from prescribed burning. There is a low probability that public health is at risk, but a rigorous risk assessment is needed to address this increasingly sensitive issue. Fireline workers more likely are occasionally at risk, so a better assessment is needed to prevent or manage that risk.

Production of potentially hazardous pollutants is very poorly understood. A few measurements of polynuclear aromatic hydrocarbons and aldehydes are available from fires, but hazard identification for the most part must be inferred from measurements in the laboratory or from wood stoves that may differ greatly from prescribed fires. We recommend accelerated research on the production and fate of hazardous air pollutants from burning, especially in describing their relationship to easily measured components such as particulate matter.

Approaches to risk assessment and risk management for exposures to hazardous air pollutants are now well defined and have been used in this text by example. However, we are seriously lacking in the basic inputs for making an adequate assessment. In addition to the lack of information about the production of hazardous pollutants, there is inadequate knowledge of the exposure of populations to known concentrations and durations of the pollutants and an inadequate knowledge of the relevant toxicology.

We urge the forest management community to consider health risks from exposure to prescribed-fire smoke as our highest priority air quality issue.

Literature Cited & Key References

Adewuyl, Y.G., S.-Y. Cho [and others]. 1984. Importance of formaldehyde in cloud chemistry. Atmos. Environ. 18:2413-2420.

Beck, R.W., and Associates. 1986. Panoramas. Vol. 1. Washington Dept. Ecol., Olympia, WA. DOE Final Rep., Contract C86-044.

*Breysse, P.A. 1984. Health hazards of smoke. J. For. 82:89.

Carnine, G. 1984. Prescribed burning activities conducted under Washington Smoke Management Plan. Washington Dept. Natur. Resour., Div. Fire Control, Olympia, WA. Annu. Rep. 70 p.

References marked by an asterisk are recommended for general information.

*Cook, J.D., J.H. Himel, and R.H. Moyer. 1978. Impact of forestry burning upon air quality: A state-of-the-knowledge characterization in Washington and Oregon. U.S. Environ. Prot. Agency, Seattle, WA.

*Core, J.E. 1989. Air quality and forest burning: Public policy issues, p. 237-245. *In* Hanley, D.P., J.J. Kammenga, and C.D. Oliver (eds.) Proc., The Burning Decision: Regional Perspectives on Slash. Coll. For. Resour., Univ. Washington, Seattle, WA. Inst. For. Resour. Contrib. No. 66. 374 p.

de Nevers, N.H., R.E. Neligan, and H.H. Slater. 1986. Air quality management, pollution control strategies, modeling, and evaluation, Chapter 1. *In* Stern, A.C. (ed.) Air Pollution (3rd ed.). Academic Press, New York, NY. References marked by an asterisk are recommended for general information.

de Wiest, F., D. Rondia, R. Gol-Winkler, and J. Gielen. 1982. Mutagenic activity of non-volatile organic matter associated with suspended matter in urban air. Mutation Res. 104:201-207.

Dost, F.N. 1982. Combustion of herbicides. Special Report to the Bonneville Power Administration, Portland, OR.

Dost, F.N. 1986. An estimate of carcinogenic risk associated with polynuclear aromatic hydrocarbons in smoke from prescribed burns in forests. Special Report to the Bureau of Land Management. USDI, Bur. Land Manage., Portland, OR. 16 p.

Furman, W.R., and G.E. Brink. 1975. The national fire-weather data library: What it is and how to use it. USDA For. Serv., Rocky Mt. For. Rge. Exp. Sta., Ft. Collins, Co. Gen. Tech. Rep. PM-19. 8 p.

Graedel, T.E., and C.J. Weschler. 1981. Chemistry within aqueous atmospheric aerosols and raindrops. Rev. Geophys. Space Phys. 19(4):505-539.

*Hall, J.A. 1972. Forest fuels, prescribed fire, and air quality. USDA For. Serv., Pac. Northwest For. Rge. Exp. Sta., Portland, OR. 44 p.

*Hanley, D.P., J.J. Kammenga, and C.D. Oliver (eds.) 1989. Proc., The Burning Decision: Regional Perspectives on Slash. Coll. For. Resour., Univ. Washington, Seattle, WA. Inst. For. Resour. Contrib. No. 66. 374 p.

Howard, J.O. 1981. Logging residue in the Pacific Northwest: Characteristics affecting utilization. USDA For. Serv., Pac. Northwest For. Rge. Exp. Sta., Portland, OR. Res. Pap. PNW-289. 41 p.

Kensler, C.J., and S.P. Battista. 1966. Chemical and physical factors affecting mammalian ciliary activity. Amer. Rev. Respir. Dis. 93:93-102.

*Komarek, E.V., Sr. 1970. Controlled burning and air pollution: An ecological review. Tall Timbers Fire Ecol. Conf. Proc. 10:141-173.

Lande, G.E. 1987. A study of air quality sampling during prescribed burning for forest sites treated with desiccants and pesticides. Paper presented at NCASI West Coast Reg. Mtg., Nov. 11, 1987. Portland, OR. [Unpublished].

*Matanoski, G., and L. Fishbein. 1986. Contribution of organic particulates to respiratory cancer. Environ. Health Perspect. 70:37-49.

Moller, M., and I. Altheim. 1982. Mutagenicity of airborne particles in relation to traffic and air pollution parameters. Environ. Sci. Technol. 16:221-225.

*Morgan, M. 1989. Health risks from slash fire smoke, p. 226-236. *In* Hanley, D.P., J.J. Kammenga, and C.D. Oliver (eds.) Proc., The Burning Decision: Regional Perspectives on Slash. Coll. For. Resour., Univ. Washington, Seattle, WA. Inst. For. Resour. Contrib. No. 66. 374 p.

*National Wildfire Coordinating Group. 1985. Smoke management objectives and regulatory requirements, Chapter 1. *In* Prescribed Fire—Smoke Management Guide. Boise Interagency Fire Center, Boise, ID. Bur. Land Manage. NFES NO. 1279 PMS 420-1.

National Wildfire Coordinating Group. 1989. The Effects of Forest Fire Smoke on Firefighters—a Comprehensive Study Plan. Prepared for Congressional Committee on Appropriations Title II [not numbered]. Available from: U.S. Dept. of Agriculture, Intermountain Research Station, Missoula, MT.

Oregon Department of Forestry. 1987. Operational Guidance for the Oregon Smoke Management Program. State Dept. For., Salem, OR. Protection 12/86 —PN No.750, Directive 1-4-1-601. p.1.

Oregon Department of Forestry, Forest Protection Division. 1984. Oregon smoke management annual report. State Dept. For., Forest Prot. Div., Salem, OR. 19 p.

Ottmar, R.D. 1983. Predicting fuel consumption by fire stages to reduce smoke from slash fires, p. 87-106. *In* Proc., Annu. Mtg. Northwest Fire Council, Nov. 21-22, 1983, Olympia, WA. Northwest Fire Council, Portland, OR.

Rossano, A.T., Jr. (ed.) 1969. Air Pollution Control Guidebook for Management. Environ. Sci. Serv. Div., E.R.A. Inc., Stamford, CT. 214 p.

Ryan, P.W., and C.K. McMahon. 1976. Some chemical and physical characteristics of emissions from forest fires. *In* Proc., 1976 Air Pollution Control Assoc. Mtg., Air Pollution Control Assoc., Pittsburgh, PA. 76-2.3

*Sandberg, D.V. 1987. Progress in reducing emissions from prescribed forest burning in western Washington and western Oregon. *In* Proc., 23rd Annu. Mtg. Air Pollution Control Assoc., Nov. 19-21, 1986, Portland, OR. Air Pollution Control Assoc., Pac. Northwest Internat. Sect., Pittsburgh, PA. 13 p.

Sandberg, D.V., and J. Peterson. 1985. A source strength model for prescribed fires in coniferous logging slash. *In* Proc., 1985 Air Pollution Control Assoc., Nov. 12-14, 1984, Portland, OR. Air Pollution Control Assoc., Pac. Northwest Internat. Sect., Portland, OR. 10 p.

Sandberg, D.V., and J.L. Peterson. 1987. Daily slash burn emissions inventory design part II. U.S. Environ. Prot. Agency, Off. Air Prog.—Reg. X. Seattle, WA. Fin. Rep. EPA Contract IAG EPA 83-291.

Sandberg, D., and R.G. Schmidt. 1982. Smoke-management costs for forest burning. *In* Proc., Air Pollution Control Assoc. Annu. Mtg., Nov. 15-17, 1982, Vancouver, B.C., Canada. Air Pollution Control Assoc., Pittsburgh, PA. 4A-3.1-4A-3.10.

Sandberg, D.V., J.L. Peterson [and others]. 1988. Regional reduction in air pollutant emissions as a result of increased forest residue recovery. U.S. Dept. Energy, Bonneville Power Admin., Portland, OR. Fin. Rep. Contract DE-RP79-85B22323, IAG DE-A179 86BP60175 (PNW-86-472).

*Sandberg, D.V., J.M. Pierovich, D.G. Fox, and E.W. Ross. 1979. Effects of fire on air. USDA For. Serv., Washington, DC. Gen. Tech. Rep. WO-9. 40 p.

Schulam, P., R. Newbold, and L.A. Hull. 1985. Urban and rural ambient air aldehyde levels in Schenectady, New York, and on Whiteface Mountain, New York. Atmos. Environ. 19(4):623-626.

Singh, H.B., L.J. Salas, and R.E. Stiles. 1982. Distribution of selected gaseous organic mutagens and suspect carcinogens in ambient air. Environ. Sci. Technol. 16:872-880.

*Southern Forest Fire Laboratory. 1976. Southern Forestry Smoke Management Guidebook. USDA For. Serv., Southeastern For. Exp. Sta., Asheville, NC. Gen. Tech. Rep. SE-10. 140 p.

Sullivan, M.J. 1988. Understanding risk assessment for environmental health protection. *In* Proc., 1987 West Coast Reg. Mtg. Nat. Counc. Air Stream Improve., Nov. 10-11, 1987, Portland, OR. NCASI, New York, NY. NCASI:GS-9.

*Turpin, J.C. 1989. Current issues in slash burning: An environmental perspective, p. 25-30. Hanley, D.P., J.J. Kammenga, and C.D. Oliver (eds.) The Burning Decision: Regional Perspectives on Slash. Coll. For. Resour., Univ. Washington, Seattle, WA. Inst. For. Resour. Contrib. No. 66. 374 p.

USDA Forest Service, Pacific Northwest Region. 1988. Managing competitive and unwanted vegetation. Final Environmental Impact Statement. USDA For. Serv., Pac. Northwest Reg., Portland, OR [not numbered]. *In* cooperation with the Environmental Protection Agency.

U.S. Environmental Protection Agency. 1983. Supplement 14 for compilation of air pollutant emission factors. 3rd ed. (including supplements 1-7), AP-42 Supplement 14.

U.S. Environmental Protection Agency, Office of Pesticides and Toxic Substances. 1987. Assessment of Health Risks to Garment Workers and Certain Home Residents from Exposure to Formaldehyde. U.S. Environmental Protection Agency, Washington, DC.

Ward, D.E. 1988. Organic and elemental profiles for smoke from prescribed fires. *In* Receptor Models in Air Resources Management: Trans. APCA/EPA Spec. Conf., Feb. 24-26, 1988, San Francisco, CA. Air Pollution Control Assoc., Pac. Northwest Internat. Sect., Pittsburgh, PA. 31 p.

Ward, D.E., and C.C. Hardy. 1984. Advances in the characterization and control of emissions from prescribed fires. *In* Proc., 77th Annu. Mtg. Air Pollution Control Assoc., June 24-29, 1984, San Francisco, CA. Air Pollution Control Assoc., Pittsburgh, PA. 32 p.

Ward, D.E., and C.C. Hardy. 1986. Advances in the characterization and control of emissions from prescribed broadcast fires of coniferous species logging slash on clearcut units. U.S. Environ. Prot. Agency., Seattle, WA. Final Rep., Contract IAG EPA DW12930110-01-3, DOE DE-A179-83BP12869.

Ward, D.E., C.C. Hardy, and D.V. Sandberg. 1988. Emission factors for particles from prescribed fires by region in the United States, p. 372-386. *In* Mathai, C.V., and D.H. Stonefield, (eds.) PM-10: Implementation of Standards. Trans., APCA/EPA Internat. Spec. Conf., Feb. 23-25, 1988, San Francisco, CA. Air Pollution Control Assoc., Pittsburgh, PA.

Weaver, D., and H.F. Droege. 1984. Washington State smoke management plan: Objectives, operations, and results. *In* Proc., 77th Annu. Mtg. Air Pollution Control Assoc., June 24-29, 1984, San Francisco, CA. Washington Dept. Ecol., Olympia, WA.

White, J.D. 1985. Validating a simplified determination of benzo(a)pyrene in particulate matter from prescribed forestry burning. Amer. Ind. Hygiene Assoc. J. 46:229-302.

*White, J.D. 1987. Emission rates of carbon monoxide, particulate matter, and benzo(a)pyrene from prescribed burning of fine southern fuels. USDA For. Serv., Southeastern For. Exp. Sta., Asheville, NC. Res. Note SE-346. 8 p.

Williamson, S.J. 1973. Fundamentals of Air Pollution. Addison-Wesley Pub. Co., Reading, MA. 472 p.

17 Effects of Fire on Water Quantity and Quality

Robert L. Beschta

Executive Summary

The effects of fire on the hydrology and water quality of forested watersheds are varied in time and space. Wildfires that destroy overstory forest vegetation will generally increase annual water yields; this increase will decrease with time as regrowth of forest vegetation occurs. Short-term increases in base flow may also occur. Prescribed burning will generally have little impact upon water yields.

Catastrophic wildfires and hot slash burns can cause undesirable impacts to the water quality of forested mountain watersheds. Accelerated erosion represents one of the primary problems associated with these types of burns. Erosional effects become increasingly greater as terrain steepness increases. Where logging slash is machine piled and burned, the piling operation is more likely to cause accelerated surface erosion than either the burning of scattered slash piles or broadcast burning without piling.

Where low-severity burns occur, much of the organic matter comprising the forest floor may remain following burning. In these situations, the effects of burning are generally insignificant with regard to a wide range of hydrologic and water-quality variables.

In a few studies of small watersheds, increased concentrations of selected ions have been measured for several days following a burn or during the first couple of rainfall events after the burn. However, in most studies, either no change or relatively small changes in nutrient export have been found within the first several years following burning. A concurrent increase in water yield due to the loss of overstory vegetation by wildfire or harvesting may limit concentration increases (because of dilution effects) of many nutrients.

Introduction

The hydrology of forested watersheds is strongly influenced by the direct and indirect effects of overstory vegetation, and conditions of the soil and forest floor. Hydrologic processes such as interception, evapotranspiration, infiltration, soil moisture storage and subsurface flow can often be modified by altering forest vegetation and the soil/atmosphere interface through the use of fire. Weathering rates, the production and mineralization of organic matter, nutrient cycling, and surface erosion processes can also be influenced. In turn, these processes alter the quantity and quality of streamflow at the mouth of a watershed. From a water-resources perspective, the effects of fire in forest ecosystems can range from disastrous to essentially none at all.

Prescribed burning represents one of several management practices (e.g., felling and yarding operations, road construction and maintenance, mechanical site preparation, release, and thinning) that influence the hydrology of forested watersheds. Thus, where the effects of fire upon a watershed's hydrology have been studied and evaluated, the results usually incorporate the effects of several management activities and it is often difficult to isolate the effects of fire. This may even be true with wildfire, because soil exposure and compaction often occur when heavy machinery is used for access development and fire-suppression activities. Salvage operations that remove fire-damaged timber create additional impacts that are difficult to isolate.

The existing literature on the effects of fire has developed from widely scattered studies. Individually, these studies provide a series of case histories related to the hydrologic effects of fire. Collectively, they provide a general framework from which to view the role of fire upon the water quantity and quality of streams draining forested watersheds.

The unpredictability of many fire effects upon water resources relates, in part, to the wide range of topographic conditions, site differences in soil characteristics and moisture content, variations in fuel moisture and fuel loads, density of vegetation, various microclimates associated with a given slope, aspect and topographic position, and variability in weather patterns before, during, and after the occurrence of a fire. The result is a mosaic of fire severity and effects across a hillside or landscape, even from the "same" fire. In similar fashion, hydrologic processes across the landscape are affected to various degrees. Yet, at the mouth of a given watershed, the stream system provides an integrated response that can be used to identify and assess hydrologic impacts. It is in the stream that this chapter will concentrate.

General Hydrologic Responses

The hydrologic effects of fire are typically greatest for severe burns. These are often encountered during major wildfires; they can also occur during slash disposal operations. In contrast, low-severity burns that do not entirely consume the organic matter comprising the forest floor may have little or no effect on the hydrologic output of a watershed. As an increasing proportion of a watershed is burned, there is usually a concomitant increase in the hydrologic response. Where fire occurs close to a channel or its adjacent "variable source areas," the effects of a burn may be somewhat

magnified. Furthermore, as watershed slope increases, so does the potential for accelerating the entry of rock, soil, and organic debris into a channel system. The effects of management activities (roading, logging, burning, etc.) upon sediment yields are often amplified as slopes steepen. Certain soils, particularly noncohesive soils of granitic origin, seem particularly susceptible to accelerated erosion following fire. Hence, the hydrologic responses from burning, measured at the mouth of a watershed, are typically related to several major factors:

- The severity of a burn.
- The proportion of the watershed burned.
- The relative proximity of the burned area to the stream channel.
- General slope of the watershed.
- Soil type.

The first three factors are strongly influenced by operational aspects of a prescribed burn. The fourth and fifth factors are site properties and are particularly important with regard to potential changes in erosion and sedimentation rates (Rothacher and Lopushinsky 1974, Swanson et al. 1987).

Where measurable hydrologic responses occur following burning, they are typically greatest within the first year or two and then return or "decay" toward prefire levels. The time necessary for recovery often depends upon the severity of the initial fire effects and the rate of vegetation recovery following burning. Recovery is generally longer for forested areas with relatively dry climates (e.g., eastern Oregon and Washington).

Water Quantity & Timing

Water yield

In most forested areas of the Pacific Northwest, the removal of trees by logging or the death of forest vegetation from wildfire greatly reduces evapotranspiration and causes an increase in annual water yield. Initial increases in annual yields range from a high of approximately 20 acre-inches for watersheds in the Coast Range and the west slopes of the Cascades (Rothacher 1970, Harr 1983) to a low of approximately 3 to 5 acre-inches for forested watersheds on the east side of the Cascades (Helvey 1980); increases are generally proportional to annual precipitation. Increases in water yield from the Trask and Wilson watersheds in the central Oregon Coast Range averaged 9 acre-inches over a 15-year period following the 1933 Tillamook Burn (Anderson 1976). Initial increases in water yield decline to prefire levels within 20 to 40 years as regeneration and growth of forest vegetation occur.

Where overstory forest removal by clearcutting occurs, and prescribed burning is utilized for slash disposal and site preparation, the control of understory vegetation by fire probably accounts for only a small percentage (less than 10 percent) of the overall increase in water yield. Prescribed burning of understory vegetation by itself is not an effective mechanism for increasing annual water yields.

Summer flow

Clearcut harvesting, clearcut harvesting and burning, and wildfire often cause an increase in summer flow for several years (Rothacher 1970, Harr and Krygier 1972, Helvey 1973). Anderson (1976) reported that the July-through-September flow from the Trask and Wilson watersheds increased 16 and 20 percent (0.5 and 0.7 inches), respectively, for the 16 years following the 1933 Tillamook Burn.

Prescribed burning probably has little influence on summer flows. Where increases do occur, they are caused primarily by the harvesting of overstory vegetation.

Peakflow

The effect of fire on peakflow is usually dependent upon changes in physical properties, if any, that occur at the soil surface. During rainfall or snowmelt on forested watersheds, moisture typically infiltrates the soil and moves as subsurface flow to a stream. Thus, reduced infiltration rates following burning can conceivably cause water to reach a channel more rapidly via overland flow. Reduced infiltration rates following burning can occur from the formation of a hydrophobic layer, removal of protective vegetative cover and forest floor materials, a breakdown in soil structure, or a reduction in soil porosity (Feller 1982, Gaweda 1983, McNabb and Froehlich 1988).

The areal extent, continuity, and persistence of water-repellent conditions following fire differ widely. Although hydrophobic conditions have been found for a wide variety of soil and vegeta-

tion types outside the Pacific Northwest (DeBano 1981), the extent to which water-repellent soils occur following fire is not known for much of the Pacific Northwest. Dyrness (1976) found water-repellent conditions associated with lodgepole pine stands in the Cascade Mountains of Oregon to persist for approximately 5 years following wildfire, but it is not known to what extent, if any, the repellency limited overall infiltration. Water-repellent soils also have been identified following prescribed burning and wildfires in southwest Oregon, but the water-repellent layer was thin and discontinuous, as were areas of reduced infiltration capacity (McNabb and Froehlich 1988). In general, water-repellent conditions following fire may be largely ameliorated during the first few fall rains and are not considered a major hydrologic concern in the Pacific Northwest, except for soils of granitic origin. When bare soil occurs after burning, this conditions tends to largely disappear within several years or less in the Pacific Northwest when vegetation reoccupies the site and provides a protective cover of litter.

The destruction of the forest floor by fire is an important factor influencing erosion processes. For example, raindrop impact can break down exposed soil aggregates and rearrange soil particles. Smaller particles can clog soil macropores and reduce infiltration rates. Instead of water percolating through a soil and moving to a stream as subsurface flow, rainfall or snowmelt may instead become overland flow. The occurrence of overland flow is of particular concern during periods of relatively high-intensity rainfall or rapid snowmelt, and may lead to increased peakflows. More importantly, as slope steepness increases, the potential for overland flow to cause accelerated surface erosion and sediment transport is enhanced.

Wildfires in particular have the capability to alter peakflows and other hydrologic characteristics of mountain watersheds. In the central Oregon Coast Range, the Trask and Wilson watersheds experienced 45 percent increases in annual peakflow the first year following the 1933 Tillamook Burn; the increases in peakflow disappeared within 8 years (Anderson 1976). Helvey et al. (1976) reported an increased snowmelt peakflow of 50 percent the first year following wildfire in north-central Washington. The increase in the snowmelt peakflow was even greater the second year when conditions of relatively high autumn soil moisture and high snow accumulation occurred. Forested watersheds in other parts of the United States often have shown an increase in peakflow following hot slash burns or wildfire (Tiedemann et al. 1979).

Research in the Pacific Northwest has generally indicated that harvesting trees, followed by broadcast burning, probably does not affect the magnitude of peakflows. For example, Rothacher (1971) found that major peakflows were not significantly changed for a watershed that was clearcut and burned in the Oregon Cascades. A similar conclusion was reached by Brown (1972) after evaluating the effects of clearcut logging and burning for several Oregon Coast Range watersheds. More recently, Harr (1976, 1986) has indicated that increases in peakflows from forested watersheds can sometimes occur following management activities. Whether such increases are caused by soil compaction during logging or slash piling, the effects of roads, or altered snowmelt rates during rain-on-snow conditions is not known.

Table 17-1. Effects of fire and associated treatments on sediment and nitrogen yields from forested watersheds in the western United States and Canada.

Vegetation	Location	Land use, experimental treatment	Sediment yield		Maximum nitrate-nitrogen concentrations		Solution transport of nitrate-nitrogen		Nitrogen export associated with sediment transport		Source
			Pretreatment or control	Post treatment	Pretreatment or control	Post treatment	Pretreatment or control	Post treatment	Pretreatment or control	Post treatment	
			–tons/square mile/year–		mg/l		lbs/acre/year		lbs/acre/year		
Douglas-fir	Northern Oregon Cascades	25% Clearcut, roaded, broadcast burned	6	9	<0.1	0.1	<0.3	1.1	—	—	Fredriksen 1971 Fredriksen et al. 1975 Larson & Sidle 1980
Douglas-fir	Central Oregon Cascades	25% Clearcut, roaded, broadcast burned	31	1,300	—	—	—	—	—	—	Larson & Sidle 1980
Douglas-fir	Central Oregon Cascades	Clearcut, broadcast burned	23	520	<0.1	0.6	<0.1	1.9	0.3	5.0	Fredriksen 1971 Fredriksen et al. 1975 Larson & Sidle 1980
Douglas-fir	Central Oregon Cascades	Clearcut, roaded, broadcast burned	31	37	—	—	—	—	—	—	Larson & Sidle 1980
Douglas-fir	Southern Oregon Cascades	90% Clearcut, piled & broadcast burned	130	520	—	—	—	—	—	—	Larson & Sidle 1980
Douglas-fir, red alder	Central Oregon Coast Range	25% Clearcut, roaded, broadcast burned	280	390	3.2	2.7	25.3	23.6	—	—	Brown et al. 1973 Beschta 1978
Douglas-fir, red alder	Central Oregon Coast Range	82% Clearcut, broadcast burned	150	420	0.7	2.1	3.5	13.7	—	—	Brown et al. 1973 Beschta 1978
Douglas-fir, pinegrass	Eastern Washington	Wildfire	—	—	<0.1	0.6	<0.1	2.7	—	—	Tiedemann et al. 1978
Ponderosa pine, Douglas-fir	Eastern Washington	Wildfire	18	320	—	—	—	—	—	—	Helvey et al. 1985
Ponderosa pine, Douglas-fir	Eastern Washington	Wildfire, salvage logged, grass seeded	2	96	—	—	—	—	—	—	Helvey et al. 1985

Continued on next page

Physical Water Quality

Sediment and turbidity

Sediment and turbidity are perhaps the most significant water-quality responses associated with fire. Turbidity is an optical property of a water-quality sample and typically increases directly with suspended sediment. These variables require different measurement techniques, but either can be used to index the relative magnitude of in-stream sediment following fire or other management activities. Although an increase in sediment can degrade water quality and affect a wide range of aquatic organisms, undesirable effects on fisheries are not always noted (Chapman and McLeod 1987, Everest et al. 1987).

Table 17-1 indicates the regional variability of sediment yields where fire represents at least part of the overall watershed treatment. In most cases, cause-and-effect responses due to fire alone cannot be clearly delineated because most results were also influenced by other management prac-

Table 17-1 continued. Effects of fire and associated treatments on sediment and nitrogen yields from forested watersheds in the western United States and Canada.

Vegetation	Location	Land use, experimental treatment	Sediment yield (–tons/square mile/year–)		Maximum nitrate-nitrogen concentrations (mg/l)		Solution transport of nitrate-nitrogen (lbs/acre/year)		Nitrogen export associated with sediment transport (lbs/acre/year)		Source
			Pretreatment or control	Post treatment	Pretreatment or control	Post treatment	Pretreatment or control	Post treatment	Pretreatment or control	Post treatment	
Ponderosa pine, Douglas-fir	Eastern Washington	Wildfire, salvage logged, grass seeded, fertilized	3	170	—	—	—	—	—	—	Helvey et al. 1985
Ponderosa pine	Northern Arizona	Wildfire (moderate burn)	<1	1	—	—	—	—	—	—	Campbell et al. 1977
Ponderosa pine	Northern Arizona	Wildfire (severe burn)	<1	111	—	—	—	—	—	—	Campbell et al. 1977
Ponderosa pine	California	Understory burn	0	0	—	—	—	—	—	—	Biswell & Schultz 1957
Spruce-fir	N.E. Oregon	Selection harvest, hand piled, burned	—	—	—	—	<0.1	<0.1	—	—	Tiedemann et al. 1988
Spruce-fir	N.E. Oregon	17% Clearcut, machine piled, burned	—	—	—	—	<0.1	0.3	—	—	Tiedemann et al. 1988
Spruce-fir	N.E. Oregon	41% Clearcut, machine piled, burned	—	—	—	—	0.2	1.2	—	—	Tiedemann et al. 1988
W. hemlock, w. redcedar	Vancouver Is., B.C.	Clearcut, broadcast burned	—	—	4.9	4.5	<0.6	<1.3	—	—	Feller & Kimmins 1984
W. hemlock, Sitka spruce	S.E. Alaska	Clearcut, broadcast burned	—	—	<0.1[a]	<0.1[a]	—	—	—	—	Stednick et al. 1982
W. white pine, w. redcedar	Northern Idaho	Clearcut, broadcast burned	—	—	0.8	7.6	—	—	—	—	Snyder et al. 1975
White-fir, ponderosa pine	Central California	Wildfire	—	—	<0.1	<0.1	—	—	—	—	Johnson & Needham 1966
Mixed conifer, shrub	Central Sierra Nevada, California	Wildfire	—	—	<0.1	0.3	—	—	—	—	Hoffman & Ferreira 1976
W. larch, Douglas-fir	Western Montana	Clearcut, slash burned	0	34	—	—	—	—	0	8.5	DeByle & Packer 1972

Note:
[a] Average values

tices, such as harvesting and roading. Nevertheless, these results generally indicate that where terrain is steep and a hot burn occurs (either from natural wildfire or slash disposal), substantial increases in sediment yields can occur. Results from the Needle Branch Watershed in the central Oregon Coast Range provide an example of sediment yield increases that can occur on a moderately steep (35 percent slope) watershed following clearcut harvesting and a hot burn, where a buffer strip of unburned vegetation was not left along the channel (Fig. 17-1). Clearing the channel of woody debris also released an unknown amount of stored sediment that probably contributed to the increased sediment loads. After burning, there was an initial 5-fold increase in annual sediment yields, followed by a return to pretreatment levels within 7 years.

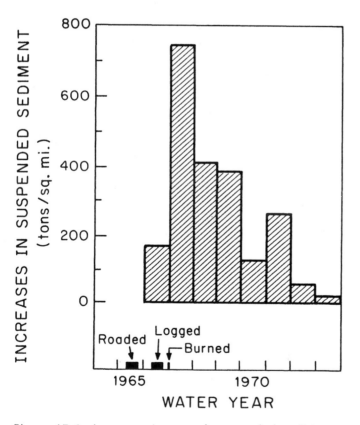

Figure 17-1. *Increases in annual suspended sediment load after careful roading, clearcutting, and severe broadcast burning in the Oregon Coast Range. Pretreatment loads averaged 151 tons/square mile/year. (Source: Beschta, R.L. Water Resources Research 14:1013. 1978. Copyright by the American Geophysical Union)*

Sediment yields for the Wilson River watershed, burned during the 1933 Tillamook Fire, were 252 tons per square mile per year, or 5.7 times higher than for a comparable unburned watershed. The number of days that the river was too turbid to fish (i.e., sediment concentrations greater than 27 mg per liter) increased from 18 to 102 days per year (Anderson 1976). It is not known to what extent salvage operations in the burned area contributed to these changes in sedimentation. Similarly, increased sediment yields were found after a wildfire burned three relatively steep (average slopes of 50 percent) watersheds in the central Washington Cascades (Helvey 1980, Helvey et al. 1985). An increased susceptibility to debris torrents was noted following the fire and was an important factor in causing increased sediment yields.

It is important to note that overland flow following fire is not a prerequisite for accelerated onsite erosion. For example, Bennett (1982) observed that soil movement occurring as dry ravel averaged 475 cubic yards per acre during the first 24 hours following a slash burn associated with steep (slopes greater than 60 percent) clearcut areas in the Oregon Coast Range. Although actual stream sedimentation was not determined, the study clearly demonstrated the unstable nature of steep slopes that are exposed by fire.

The effects of prescribed burning on soil erosion and sedimentation in streams can be minimized in several ways. Where watershed slopes average approximately 30 percent or more, burning needs to be carefully controlled. In particular, hot burns should be avoided either through fuel management or burning at a time when there is sufficient fuel and soil moisture to prevent total consumption of organic matter at the soil surface. Although bare mineral soil sometimes may be a desirable management objective for the planting and establishment of forest trees, bare soil and sloping terrain are also conducive to accelerated surface erosion. Where organic matter comprising the forest floor is only partially consumed by fire, the effects of fire upon surface erosion processes may be minimal. Providing an unburned buffer strip along streams may also help minimize the direct entry of sediment into a channel from riparian areas and channel banks (Heede et al. 1988). In many headwater watersheds, however, sediment is often delivered to channels by mass soil movements, and unburned vegetation along a channel may do little to prevent the entry of sediment into streams. Management practices that prevent the occur-rence of hot slash burns and encourage rapid re-vegetation will help minimize potential increases in fire-related sedimentation from upslope sourc-es. Relatively "cool" burns should have little im-pact on erosion and sedimentation, regardless of general watershed slope.

A live plant canopy reduces the potential for surface erosion from raindrop splash and overland flow. Canopies temporarily intercept raindrops, reducing the velocity at which they strike the ground. More importantly, plants also produce lit-ter to cover an exposed soil. This litter effectively prevents the mechanical breakdown of soil aggre-gates and sealing from raindrop impact, and re-duces the velocity of any overland flow. Where an adequate cover of grass can be established, the blades and fibrous root systems will assist in re-ducing surface erosion. Of particular importance with regard to hillslope erosion are fire trails, skid trails, and roads in burned areas. These can con-centrate overland flow and become a significant source of erosion. In addition to grass seeding, functional water bars and other drainage struc-tures are often needed for diverting surface flow off these roads and trails (McNabb and Froehlich 1988).

From 1963 to 1972 there was a trend toward in-creased pile-and-burn treatments on National For-ests of the Pacific Northwest (Cramer 1974), in-creasing the potential for undesirable impacts on water quality from the effects of heavy machinery used during piling operations. For the period 1976 to 1985, approximately 105,000 acres were pre-scribed burned on an annual basis in western Ore-gon, of which over one-half involved piling opera-tions. Little research has been undertaken in the Pacific Northwest to evaluate the effects of pile-and-burn practices upon hydrology and water quality, but studies from other areas indicate this practice can have severe detrimental effects upon the suspended sediment loads and turbidity of streams (Packer 1971, Beasley 1979, VanLear et al. 1985). Soil exposure and compaction effects of a machine/tractor piling operation are more likely to impact onsite hydrology and erosion than the burning of scattered slash piles. The potential for accelerated erosion from machine piling generally increases rapidly with increased slope.

Stream temperature

Daily temperature fluctuations of forest streams are largely regulated by the amount of solar radia-tion they receive (Brown 1972); the removal of a forest canopy by fire or harvesting can thereby cause an increase in water temperatures. For ex-ample, maximum daily stream temperatures in-creased up to 10°F in late summer following a se-vere wildfire on the Entiat Experimental Forest in north-central Washington (Helvey 1972).

A wide range of studies has demonstrated that increases in stream temperature can result when harvesting removes overstory vegetation along small streams (Beschta et al. 1987). Although the harvest operation is generally considered to have the major effect on stream temperatures, the re-moval of slash and streamside vegetation through burning may cause an added increase in the maxi-mum water temperature of small streams. For ex-ample, in the central Oregon Cascades, clearcut harvesting along a stream increased summertime maximum temperatures by 4°F, but the next sum-mer, following burning, maximum temperatures were 14°F above those measured in an undis-turbed forest watershed (Levno and Rothacher 1969). In the central Oregon Coast Range, clearcut harvesting along a stream increased maximum summer temperatures by 17°F; after a hot slash burn, an additional increase of 10°F was measured the following summer (Brown 1972). These two examples clearly indicate that burning along small streams can cause additional temperature in-creases above those expected from harvesting alone.

The rate of reestablishment of streamside vege-tation, which provides shade to the stream, is the major factor influencing the return of increased summertime temperatures to pretreatment levels. These rates of recovery vary from less than 10 years for small streams in the Oregon Coast Range to several decades in the higher elevation Cas-cades (Fig. 17-2).

The potential biological impacts from altered water temperatures following fire are not easy to predict (Beschta et al. 1987). For example, some streams may be too small to support a fishery; in other cases the temperature increases are within an optimum range for biological populations. Al-though stream temperature is clearly an important component of the habitat of many stream organ-isms, it is only one of several closely interconnected physical factors affecting stream biota that can be simultaneously influenced by fire, land-use activities, and other environmental factors.

Chemical Water Quality & Nutrients

Plant communities accumulate and cycle substantial quantities of nutrients and provide a biological continuum linking soil, water, and the atmosphere (Tiedemann et al. 1979). Nutrients are cycled in a relatively orderly manner unless management activities or natural disturbances alter their form or distribution. Fire can exert profound effects on the nutrient status of plant communities and soils when plant- and litter-incorporated nutrients are volatilized or lost from the system (Chapter 12). Reductions in plant cover and surface organic matter by fire increase the susceptibility of nutrients to erosional losses. Opportunities for nutrient uptake by plants are also reduced, which further increases the potential for nutrient loss by leaching. Although some increase in nutrient losses might normally be expected from harvesting alone (for example, due to increased nutrient availability from the decomposition of logging slash), fire can accentuate the export of some nutrients.

Changes in the water chemistry of mountain streams following fire can vary among watersheds because of differing amounts of plant biomass and litter, differential fire severity, the ion exchange/retention capacity of humus and soil, moisture flux and timing, and other factors. Where debris torrents occur, major amounts of nutrients may be transported out of a watershed to be deposited elsewhere (Helvey et al. 1985). However, most studies show relatively small increases, if any, in nutrient concentrations and export following fire (Tiedemann et al. 1979, Richter et al. 1982). Because many streams in the Pacific Northwest have relatively low nutrient levels, additional nutrient inputs may provide a basis for increased aquatic productivity.

Initial postburn responses

Immediately after burning, there may be a brief flush of certain nutrients. For example, elevated ammonia-nitrogen and manganese concentrations in streamflow occurred for a period of 12 days after burning in the central Cascades of Oregon (Fredriksen et al. 1975). Similarly, in a watershed study

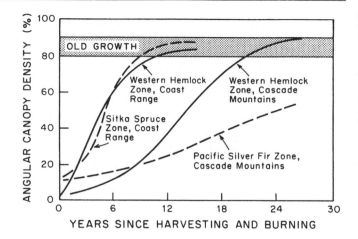

Figure 17-2. Relationship between angular canopy density (a direct measure of vegetation shading) and stand age for selected vegetation zones in western Oregon. (Source: Summers 1983)

in the central Oregon Coast Range, potassium concentrations increased to a peak of 4.4 mg per liter during the first major rainfall after burning and then immediately returned to prelogging levels of 0.6 to 1.2 mg per liter (Brown et al. 1973). These relatively transitory pulses of nutrient export have not always been reported, perhaps because of infrequent sampling, rapid immobilization by aquatic organisms, or sediment adsorption.

Nitrogen responses

Several forms of nitrogen occur naturally in stream systems, but nitrate-nitrogen has typically been studied because it is one of the most mobile ions in soil-water systems and is one of two forms of nitrogen commonly used by plants (Tiedemann et al. 1979). Nitrate usually moves with moisture through the soil profile to streams. The maximum recommended concentration of nitrate-nitrogen in drinking water is 10 mg per liter.

Nitrate concentrations are normally low in streams draining undisturbed forested watersheds. Maximum reported nitrate-nitrogen concentrations range from less than 0.1 mg per liter to a high of 4.9 mg per liter for forested watersheds in the western United States (Table 17-1). Most reported maximum concentrations are less than 1 mg per liter. Average concentrations are typically at least an order of magnitude smaller than the reported maximum concentrations.

A substantial increase (from 0.8 to 7.6 mg per liter) in maximum nitrate-nitrogen concentrations was reported following forest harvesting and burning in northern Idaho (Snyder et al. 1975), but most studies have shown essentially no change or relatively small increases (Table 17-1). Over one-half of the reported studies show maximum concentrations remaining less than 1 mg per liter following fire or harvesting and fire.

The total nitrogen export from a watershed is influenced by both concentration and flow. If either or both of these factors are increased following fire, then increased nitrogen losses may be expected. Natural yields of nitrate-nitrogen for streams in the western United States vary from less than 1 to approximately 25 lbs per acre per year (Table 17-1). Although increases have occurred following management disturbances in some studies, these increases are generally small. Even where losses increased from 3.5 to 13.7 lbs per acre per year following harvesting and prescribed burning on a watershed in the central Oregon Coast Range, a nearby undisturbed watershed had nitrate-nitrogen losses of over 25 lbs per acre per year (Brown et al. 1973).

The loss of nutrients attached to sediment particles is an integral part of the overall nutrient loss from watersheds. The few watershed studies that have attempted to quantify nitrogen export associated with sediment losses (Table 17-1) indicate that this may be an important mechanism for the transport of nitrogen, as well as other nutrients (Tiedemann et al. 1978, Helvey et al. 1985).

A detailed nutrient budget conducted in southwestern British Columbia (Feller and Kimmins 1984) provides an important perspective on total nitrogen capital in relation to losses associated with harvesting and fire (Table 17-2). The overall effects of prescribed burning (primarily atmospheric export) substantially reduced nitrogen storage. Feller and Kimmins indicate it is unlikely that the nitrogen lost from this clearcut and burned watershed will be replaced within 80 years. Furthermore, much of the remaining nitrogen is tied up in compounds that are not easily decomposed and is relatively unavailable for plant growth. Although streamwater export of nitrogen increased following clearcutting and burning, the magnitude of loss was less than from clearcutting alone (Table 17-2). In both cases, however, the increases in streamwater export of nitrogen were small.

In general, the export of nitrogen (in solution and attached to sediment) from harvested and burned watersheds is generally low, and maximum nitrate-nitrogen concentrations in streams rarely exceed 1 mg per liter. Small increases in nitrogen export following burning may occur, but this response is not universal. Changes in nitrogen concentrations or yields, if any, following prescribed burning should not significantly alter stream productivity or water quality. In comparison to total watershed reserves, nitrogen export by streams is a relatively insignificant loss. Nitrogen export by streams is also small in comparison to atmospheric losses that occur during a burn (Table 17-2). It is not clear from the results of various watershed studies whether burn severity affects stream concentrations and export of nitrogen.

Phosphorus responses

Phosphorus in stream water is mainly present in two forms—orthophosphate (inorganic) and organic phosphate. Phosphate anions are not as readily leached as nitrate anions because they complex readily with organic compounds in the soil (Tiedemann et al. 1979).

Phosphorus export in stream water may increase following burning, but losses are generally small. Mean annual orthophosphate-P concentra-

Table 17-2. Nitrogen storage, inputs, and losses from three experimental watersheds in southwestern British Columbia, during the first 2 years following treatment.

	Watershed		
	Forested (Control)	Clearcut	Clearcut/ broadcast burned
	——— lbs/acre ———		
Nitrogen storage			
Forest floor	1,490	1,630	2,180
Mineral soil	3,920	4,570	4,650
Total	5,410	6,200	6,830
Nitrogen inputs and export	——— lbs/acre/year ———		
Precipitation input	4	4	4
Log export from harvesting	—	117	154
Atmospheric export from burning	—	—	491
Streamwater export	<1	6	2
Net gain (+) or loss (−)	+3	−119	−643

Source: Feller and Kimmins 1984.

tions of 0.02 mg per liter increased to 0.04 mg per liter for the first several years following slash burning in the central Oregon Cascades (Fredriksen et al. 1975). Total phosphorus concentrations of 0.02 mg per liter increased to 0.03 mg per liter following slash burning in southeast Alaska, but no changes from preburn orthophosphate levels (which averaged approximately 0.01 mg per liter) were found (Stednick et al. 1982). Total phosphate concentrations, which ranged from 0.01 to 0.10 mg per liter for several watersheds in the central Oregon Coast Range, remained unchanged following harvesting and burning (Brown et al. 1973). Similarly, phosphorus export in streamwater remained unchanged following harvesting and burning in southwestern British Columbia (Feller and Kimmins 1984) and following wildfire in southeastern British Columbia (Gluns and Toews 1989).

Bicarbonate responses

Concomitant fluctuations of bicarbonate and cation concentrations indicate that the bicarbonate anion may provide a general index of cation loss. Studies throughout the western United States indicate that bicarbonate concentrations are generally increased as a consequence of burning (Tiedemann et al. 1978).

Cation responses

A wide variety of elements can be affected by the occurrence of prescribed burning or wildfire. These include potassium, calcium, magnesium, copper, iron, manganese, zinc, and others. Metallic elements such as calcium, magnesium, and potassium are converted to oxides and remain as ash. These oxides are relatively insoluble until they react with carbon dioxide and water to form cations; they then become more vulnerable to loss via surface runoff and leaching or become incorporated in plant tissues and litter (Tiedemann et al. 1979).

From a water-quality perspective, studies in Pacific Northwest forest ecosystems have typically not found major changes in cation concentrations following burning. Although total cation export may be increased following burning, these increases do not necessarily translate directly into higher concentrations. For example, if concentrations remain unchanged and water yield increases, net export will increase. Furthermore, a number of studies have observed that concentrations of major cations are inversely proportional to flow

(Tiedemann et al. 1979). Thus, increased streamflow resulting from transpiration reduction may limit concentration increases.

Following wildfire in the central Washington Cascades, cation losses the first 2 years increased 2.5 times in comparison to prefire losses of 17 lbs per acre per year. A substantial portion of this additional export was associated with increased water yields following the fire. For calcium, magnesium, potassium, and sodium, the cumulative solution loss over the first 5 postfire years comprised 17, 13, 14, and 39 percent, respectively, of the available capital in the upper 14 inches of soil (Tiedemann et al. 1978).

In the central Oregon Cascades, cation losses following harvesting and burning increased 1.6 to 3.0 times the loss from the undisturbed watershed (Fredriksen 1971). In southwestern British Columbia, cation losses for a control watershed (unharvested) and a clearcut and burned watershed averaged 3 and 8 lbs per acre per year for potassium, 8 and 9 lbs/acre/year for magnesium, and 49 and 49 lbs per acre per year for calcium, respectively, during the first 2 years following treatment (Feller and Kimmins 1984).

Although the literature is not conclusive, the effects of wildfire on cation release to streams may be greater than that from prescribed burns due to larger quantities of organic matter being mineralized. Because the solubility, mobility, and other characteristics of individual cations are highly variable, it is difficult to predict specific instream responses to fire. Furthermore, because of the increased water yields that typically occur after wildfire and also after harvesting and prescribed burning, elevated cation concentrations have not always been found. Changes in cation concentrations following burning have not been identified as a major fisheries concern for streams draining forest watersheds in the Pacific Northwest (Gregory et al. 1987).

Cumulative Effects

In recent years, the issue of the cumulative effects of forest management practices has often been raised in the context of water quality and other environmental concerns (Geppert et al. 1984). Where concentration criteria have been established for water-quality variables, the major concern following burning will be for those stream reaches immediately below the treated area. Significant changes in water quality will be most easily detected at these locations. Farther downstream, our ability to isolate the effects of fire on water quality is reduced because of the mixing that occurs with tributary and groundwater inflow, changing environmental conditions, and the effects of other management activities. Furthermore, temporal concentration "spikes" associated with a particular water-quality variable tend to become less pronounced in a downstream direction. If the prescribed burning of small watersheds, where the burning is spatially and temporally separated, is not causing significant hydrologic or water-quality impacts onsite or immediately downstream, the potential for significant cumulative effects farther downstream has probably been minimized.

Conclusion

Research results from a variety of forest ecosystems in the western United States have provided an important basis from which to view changes in hydrology and water quality associated with fire. However, the effects of fire are often imbedded within those of other forest operations that typically precede or follow prescribed burning. Thus, although general hydrologic and water-quality responses can be identified, our capability to predict site-specific responses is limited.

Fire has a great potential to alter the water quality of streams draining forested watersheds. Whether such changes become manifest depends upon a large number of site-specific factors. Perhaps of most concern is the potential to accelerate surface erosion on steep slopes. Prescribing low-severity broadcast burns should minimize potential adverse impacts. Similarly, providing an unburned buffer along channels may reduce potential erosion along stream channels and riparian areas. This latter practice represents current USDA Forest Service policy and has been specified as a forest practices rule (e.g., Oregon Department of Forestry 1987). Leaving an unburned buffer of vegetation along streams will also reduce the potential for increasing summertime stream temperatures. Prompt reseeding of bare ground in erosion-prone areas with grass may assist in preventing significant soil losses (Klock et al. 1975, Barro and Conard 1987, Soil Conservation Service

1988). Functional water bars on abandoned roads, skid trails, and fire trails are also an essential part of minimizing accelerated soil delivery to stream systems. On some sites, broadcast burning instead of machine piling and burning may prevent major increases in erosion and sedimentation.

The effects of accelerated surface erosion upon water quality are usually most pronounced during rainfall/snowmelt periods. Increases in either sediment or temperature can have important effects (either beneficial or adverse, depending upon local conditions) for a wide range of aquatic organisms and fish species (Beschta et al. 1987, Everest et al. 1987). Increases are generally considered to represent undesirable effects on overall water quality and impacts to downstream water users. State water-quality standards and forest practices rules are formulated to minimize or prevent significant increases in either of these two important water-quality variables.

Nutrient concentrations and export can be influenced by fire, but the effects are often relatively small. Nitrogen, because of its importance in the biological productivity of forest and stream ecosystems, has been the most widely studied. Instream nitrogen responses following fire have ranged from none to a several-fold increase in total yield. Although changes in selected nutrient levels have been measured that exceed drinking standards for short periods of time (several days to several weeks) following fire, the water quality of such streams often returns to pretreatment levels relatively quickly. Concentrations of a particular nutrient are usually reduced as the stream mixes with tributary and groundwater inflow.

Increased nutrient levels in forest streams may locally benefit aquatic organisms and increase stream productivity. However, because aquatic organisms and fish respond to a wide range of environmental factors, changes in nitrogen and other nutrients are not always accompanied by greater biological productivity.

Although wildfires and/or hot slash fires can affect stream conditions and water quality, research results indicate that prescribed burning, judiciously applied with an awareness of potential onsite and offsite impacts, can be used without causing significant changes to the water quality of streams draining forested ecosystems in the Pacific Northwest. For those advocating prescribed burning as a necessary and important forest management tool, the hydrologic challenge is quite simple. Fire prescriptions should be planned and implemented to prevent the occurrence of severe burns. In doing so, any potentially adverse impacts to the hydrology and water quality of forested watersheds will generally be minimized.

Literature Cited & Key References

Anderson, H.W. 1976. Fire effects on water supply, floods, and sedimentation. Tall Timbers Fire Ecol. Conf. Proc. 15:249-260.

Barro, S.C., and S.G. Conard. 1987. Use of ryegrass seeding as an emergency revegetation measure in chaparral ecosystems. USDA For. Serv., Pac. Southwest For. Rge. Exp. Sta., Berkeley, CA. Gen. Tech. Rep. PSW-102. 12 p.

Beasley, R.S. 1979. Intensive site preparation and sediment losses on steep watersheds in the Gulf Coastal Plain. J. Soil Sci. Soc. Amer. 43:412-417.

Bennett, K.A. 1982. Effects of slash burning on surface erosion rates in the Oregon Coast Range. M.S. thesis, Oregon State Univ., Corvallis, OR. 70 p.

Beschta, R.L. 1978. Long-term patterns of sediment production following road construction and logging in the Oregon Coast Range. Water Resour. Res. 14:1011-1016.

*Beschta, R.L., R.E. Bilby, G.W. Brown, L.B. Holtby, and T.D. Hofstra. 1987. Stream temperature and aquatic habitat: Fisheries and forestry interactions, p. 191-232. *In* Salo, E.O., and T.W. Cundy (eds.) Streamside Management: Forestry and Fishery Interactions. Inst. For. Resour., Univ. Washington, Seattle, WA. Contrib. 57. 471 p.

Biswell, H.H., and A.M. Schultz. 1957. Surface runoff and erosion as related to prescribed burning. J. For. 55:372-374.

Brown, G.W. 1972. The Alsea Watershed Study. Pac. Logging Cong. Loggers Hbk. Vol. 32. 6 p.

Brown, G.W., A.R. Gahler, and R.B. Marston. 1973. Nutrient losses after clear-cut logging and slash burning in the Oregon Coast Range. Water Resour. Res. 9:1450-1453.

Campbell, R.E., M.B. Baker, Jr., P.F. Ffolliott, F.R. Larsen, and C.C. Avery. 1977. Wildfire effects on a ponderosa pine ecosystem: An Arizona case study. USDA For. Serv., Rocky Mt. For. Rge. Exp. Sta., Fort Collins, CO. Res. Pap. RM-191. 12 p.

Chapman, D.W., and K.P. McLeod. 1987. Development of criteria for fine sediments in the Northern Rockies Ecoregion. U.S. Environ. Prot. Agency, Seattle, WA. 910/987-162. 279 p.

Cramer, O.P. 1974. Annual slash status report. USDA For. Serv., Reg. 6, Portland, OR.

*DeBano, L.F. 1981. Water repellent soils: A state-of-the-art. USDA For. Serv., Pac. Southwest For. Rge. Exp. Sta., Berkeley, CA. Gen. Tech. Rep. PSW-46. 21 p.

DeByle, N.V., and P.E. Packer. 1972. Plant nutrient and soil losses in overland flow from burned forest clearcuts, p. 296-307. *In* Csallany, S.C., T.G. McLaughlin, and W.D. Striffler (eds.) Nat. Symp. on Watersheds in Transition. Proc., Amer. Water Resour. Assoc. 14. 405 p.

Dyrness, C.T. 1976. Effect of wildfire on soil wettability in the High Cascades of Oregon. USDA For. Serv., Pac. Northwest For. Rge. Exp. Sta., Portland, OR. Res. Pap. PNW-202. 18 p.

Everest, F.H., R.L. Beschta, J.C. Scrivner, K.V. Koski, J.R. Sedell, and C.J. Cederholm. 1987. Fine sediment and salmonid production: A paradox, p. 98-142. *In* Salo, E.O., and T.W. Cundy (eds.) Streamside Management: Forestry and Fishery Interactions. Inst. For. Resour., Univ. Washington, Seattle, WA. Contrib. 57. 471 p.

*Feller, M.C. 1982. The ecological effects of slashburning with particular reference to British Columbia: A literature review. B.C. Ministry of Forests, Victoria, B.C. Land Manage. Rep. 13. 60 p.

Feller, M.C., and J.P. Kimmins. 1984. Effects of clearcutting and slash burning on streamwater chemistry and watershed nutrient budgets in southwestern British Columbia. Water Resour. Res. 20:29-40.

Fredriksen, R.L. 1971. Cooperative water quality—natural and disturbed streams, p. 125-137. *In* Krygier, J.D., and J.D. Hall (eds.) Forest Land Uses and Stream Environment. Oregon State Univ., Corvallis, OR. 252 p.

*Fredriksen, R.L., D.G. Moore, and L.A. Norris. 1975. The impact of timber harvest, fertilization, and herbicide treatment on streamwater quality in western Oregon and Washington, p. 283-313. *In* Bernier, B., and C.H. Winget (eds.) Forest Soils and Forest Land Management. Les Presses De L'Universite Laval, Quebec. 675 p.

Gaweda, F.M. 1983. First-year effects of broadcast burning on soil infiltration and wettability in southwest Oregon. M.S. thesis, Oregon State Univ., Corvallis, OR. 110 p.

Geppert, R.R., C.W. Lorenz, and A.G. Larson. 1984. Cumulative Effects of Forest Practices on the Environment: A State of the Knowledge. Ecosystems, Inc., Olympia, WA. 208 p. plus appendices.

References marked by an asterisk are recommended for general information.

Gluns, D.R., and D.A.A. Toews. 1989. Effect of a major wildfire on water quality in southeastern British Columbia, p. 487-499. *In* Woessner, W.W., and D.F. Potts (eds.) Symp. Proc. on Headwaters Hydrology. Amer. Water Resour. Tech. Publ. Series, TPS-89-2. 708 p.

Gregory, S.V., G.A. Lamberti, D.C. Erman, K V. Koski, M.L. Murphy, and J.R. Sedell. 1987. Influence of forest practices on aquatic production, p. 233-255. *In* Salo, E.O., and T.W. Cundy (eds.) Streamside Management: Forestry and Fishery Interactions. Inst. For. Resour., Univ. Washington, Seattle, WA. Contrib. 57. 471 p.

Harr, R.D. 1976. Forest practices and streamflow in western Oregon. USDA For. Ser., Pac. Northwest For. Rge. Exp. Sta., Portland OR. Gen. Tech. Rep. PNW-49. 18 p.

Harr, R.D. 1983. Potential for augmenting water yield through forest practices in western Washington and western Oregon. Water Resour. Bull. 9:383-393.

Harr, R.D. 1986. Effects of clearcutting on rain-on-snow runoff in western Oregon: a new look at old studies. Water Resour. Res. 22(7):1095-1100.

Harr, R.D., and J.T. Krygier. 1972. Clearcut logging and low stream flows in Oregon coastal watersheds. For. Res. Lab., Oregon State Univ., Corvallis, OR. Res. Note 54. 3 p.

Heede, B.H., M.D. Harvey, and J.R. Laird. 1988. Sediment delivery linkages in a chaparral watershed following a wildfire. Environ. Mgt. 12(3):349-358.

Helvey, J.D. 1972. First-year effects of wildfire on water yield and stream temperature in north-central Washington, p. 308-312. *In* Csallany, S.C., T.G. McLaughlin, and W.D. Striffler (eds.) Nat. Symp. on Watersheds in Transition. Proc., Amer. Water Resour. Assoc. 14. 405 p.

Helvey, J.D. 1973. Watershed behavior after forest fire in Washington, p. 403-422. *In* Agricultural and Urban Considerations in Irrigation and Drainage. Proc., Irrigation & Drainage Division Specialty Conference, Amer. Soc. Civil Engr., New York, NY. 808 p.

Helvey, J.D. 1980. Effects of a north central Washington wildfire on runoff and sediment production. Water Resour. Bull. 16:627-634.

Helvey, J.D., A.R. Tiedemann, and T.D. Anderson. 1985. Plant nutrient losses by soil movement after wildfire. J. Soil Water Conserv. 40:168-173.

Helvey, J.D., A.R. Tiedemann, and W.B. Fowler. 1976. Some climatic and hydrologic effects of wildfire in Washington State. Tall Timbers Fire Ecol. Conf. Proc. 15:201-222.

Hoffman, R.J., and R.F. Ferreira. 1976. A reconnaissance of effects of forest fire on water quality in Kings Canyon National Park. USDI Geol. Surv., Menlo Park, CA. Open-file Rep. 76-497. 17 p.

Johnson, C.M., and P.R. Needham. 1966. Ionic composition of Sagehen Creek, California, following an adjacent fire. Ecology 47:636-639.

Klock, G.O., A.R. Tiedemann, and W. Lopushinsky. 1975. Seeding recommendations for disturbed mountain slopes in north central Washington. USDA For. Serv., Pac. Northwest For. Rge. Exp. Sta., Portland, OR, Res. Note. PNW-244. 8 p.

Larson, K.R., and R.C. Sidle. 1980. Erosion and sedimentation data catalog of the Pacific Northwest. USDA For. Serv., Pac. Northwest Reg., Portland, OR. R6-WM-050-1981. 64 p.

Levno, A., and J. Rothacher. 1969. Increases in maximum stream temperatures after slash burning in a small experimental watershed. USDA For. Serv., Pac. Northwest For. Rge. Exp. Sta., Portland, OR. Res. Note PNW-110. 7 p.

*Loucks, D.M., S.R. Radosevich, T.B. Harrington, and R.G. Wagner. 1987. Prescribed fire in the Pacific Northwest: An annotated bibliography. For. Res. Lab., College For., Oregon State Univ., Corvallis, OR. 185 p.

McNabb, D.H., and H.A. Froehlich. 1988. Soils and watershed protection. FIR Report 9(4):8-9, Oreg. State Univ., Medford, OR.

Oregon Department of Forestry. 1987. Oregon Forest Practice Rules. Oreg. Dept. For., Salem, OR.

Packer, P. E. 1971. Site preparation in relation to environmental quality, p. 23-28 *In* Proc., 1971 Annu. Mtg., West. Reforestation Coord. Comm., West. For. Conserv. Assoc., Portland, OR. 73 p.

Richter, D.D., C.W. Ralston, and W.R. Harms. 1982. Prescribed fire: Effects on water quality and forest nutrient cycling. Science 215:661-662.

Rothacher, J. 1970. Increase in water yield following clear-cut logging in the Pacific Northwest. Water Resour. Res. 6:653-658.

Rothacher, J. 1971. Regimes of streamflow and their modification by logging, p. 40-54. *In* Krygier, J.D., and J.D. Hall (eds.) Forest Land Uses and Stream Environment. Oregon State Univ., Corvallis, OR. 252 p.

Rothacher, J., and W. Lopushinsky. 1974. Soil stability and water yield quantity, p. D-1 to D-23. *In* Cramer, O.P. (org. and tech. ed.) Environmental Effects of Forest Residues Management in the Pacific Northwest. USDA For. Serv., Pac. Northwest For. Rge. Exp. Sta., Portland, OR. Gen. Tech. Rep. PNW-24. 517 p.

Snyder, G.G., H.F. Haupt and G.H. Belt, Jr. 1975. Clearcutting and burning slash alter quality of stream water in northern Idaho. USDA For. Serv., Intermt. For. Rge. Exp. Sta., Ogden, UT. Res. Pap. INT-168. 34 p.

Soil Conservation Service. 1988. Oregon Interagency Seeding Guide. USDA Soil Conserv. Serv, Portland, OR. 53 p.

Stednick, J.D., L.N. Tripp, and R.J. McDonald. 1982. Slash burning effects on soil and water chemistry in southeastern Alaska. J. Soil Water Conserv. 37:126-128.

Summers, R.P. 1983. Trends in riparian vegetation regrowth following timber harvesting in western Oregon watersheds. M.S. thesis, Oregon State Univ., Corvallis, OR. 151 p.

Swanson, F.J., L.E. Benda, S.H. Duncan, G.E. Grant, W.F. Megahan, L.M. Reid, and R.R. Ziemer. 1987. Mass failures and other processes of sediment production in Pacific Northwest forest landscapes, p. 9-38. *In* Salo, E.O., and T.W. Cundy (eds.) Streamside Management: Forestry and Fishery Interactions. Inst. For. Resour., Univ. Washington. Seattle, WA. Contrib. 57. 471 p.

*Tiedemann, A.R., C.E. Conrad, J.H. Dieterich, J.W. Hornbeck, W.F. Megahan, L.A. Viereck, and D.D. Wade. 1979. Effects of fire on water. USDA For. Serv., Washington, D.C. Gen. Tech. Rep. WO-10. 28 p.

Tiedemann, A.R., J.D. Helvey, and T.D. Anderson. 1978. Stream chemistry and watershed nutrient economy following wildfire and fertilization in eastern Washington. J. Environ. Qual. 7:580-588.

Tiedemann, A.R., T.M. Quigley, and T.D. Anderson. 1988. Effects of timber harvest on stream chemistry and dissolved nutrient losses in northeast Oregon. For. Sci. 34:344-358.

VanLear, D.H., J.E. Douglass, S.K. Cox, and M.K. Augspurger. 1985. Sediment and nutrient export in runoff from burned and harvested pine watersheds in the South Carolina Piedmont. J. Environ. Qual. 14:169-174.

18 Effects of Fire on Fish and Wildlife

Thomas E. McMahon and David S. deCalesta

Executive Summary

Fire has the potential to accentuate impacts to fish and wildlife associated with timber harvesting, roadbuilding, and other forest management practices. For fish, the primary concerns relative to fire are increases in water temperature and sediment and the long-term loss of woody debris from stream channels. The most long-lasting and severe effects on fish habitat from fire—whether prescribed or wild—occur when it is associated with the loss of the streamside forest.

The major impacts of fire on wildlife center on its influence on vegetation structure and composition, down and dead woody material, and snags. In particular, the loss of down and dead woody material and snags during a prescribed burn removes essential structural habitat components for a variety of wildlife and reduces species diversity.

Use of cool burns in spring when the ground is moist, providing an unburned buffer along stream channels, maintaining integrity of the soil surface, and leaving and protecting snags during burning, should help prevent or limit undesirable impacts to fish and wildlife. Staggering prescribed fires over time, and spacing of burns across the landscape will minimize impacts on small wildlife that occupy areas of prescribed burn size or smaller. For larger wildlife species, such placement could maximize potential benefits by providing a relatively continuous (through space and time) distribution of forage areas. Of concern are the effects of burning in or near headwater channels which facilitate the transport of sediment and logging slash downslope into fish-bearing streams when stream networks expand during periods of high runoff. More detailed monitoring studies are needed to fully evaluate the effectiveness of burning prescriptions to limit impacts to fish and wildlife.

Introduction

Consideration of potential impacts to fish and wildlife from prescribed fire is an important factor in decisions of when and how to burn. Forests of the Pacific Northwest are home to 66 freshwater fish and 460 wildlife species (Brown and Curtis 1985, Everest et al. 1985), a number of which have considerable commercial and recreational value. Legislation and public opinion over the past 20 years also have increasingly recognized the "non-consumptive" or amenity values of fish and wildlife as integral components of Pacific Northwest forest ecosystems.

Fire can directly affect fish and wildlife populations by causing mortality or avoidance of an area during and after burning (Chandler et al. 1983). Of greater importance, though, are the long-term consequences of fire on fish and wildlife habitats. Fire may impact the abundance and diversity of fish habitat and populations in streams by affecting the composition and structure of riparian vegetation and influencing water quality and quantity in a stream. For wildlife, important habitat alterations from fire include changes in the structure and composition of forest vegetation in the understory and overstory, and microclimate within and adjacent to burned areas (Bendell 1974, Martin and Dell 1978). These habitat changes in turn determine wildlife species composition and abundance (Chapter 6).

Despite a large number of studies conducted throughout the Pacific Northwest on the potential impacts to fish and wildlife habitats associated with timber harvesting and reforestation (e.g., Salo and Cundy 1987, Raedeke 1988), relatively little information is available on the direct and indirect effects of fire. As discussed in previous chapters, the effects of prescribed burning on fish and wildlife are often difficult to identify, since it typically precedes or follows other forest management practices and is subject to site-specific variation (Lyon et al. 1978).

As a result, a combination of approaches was used to assess the impacts of prescribed fire on fish and wildlife. In addition to synthesizing what is known, potential impacts were inferred by linking data on the effects of fire on particular watershed functions or characteristics as summarized in previous chapters[1] with information from other, non-fire-related studies that showed relationships between these particular watershed or vegetative processes and fish and wildlife populations or communities (e.g., effects of sedimentation on fish; effects of stand composition on wildlife abundance and diversity). Since use of prescribed fire has changed over the past 10 years, resource managers in the region were also consulted to document the observations of practicing professionals and to describe and evaluate practices currently used to minimize undesirable impacts. Where possible, responses of fish and wildlife to prescribed fire were compared to those from wildfires.

Fish and wildlife exist in significantly different environments, so their responses to prescribed fire will be treated separately. Mortality directly resulting from fire, habitat relationships as they are affected by burning, resultant fish and wildlife

responses, management implications and ways to minimize undesirable impacts, and research needed to fill information voids will be addressed in this chapter.

Effects of Fire on Fish

In the forested regions of the Pacific Northwest, the term "fish" is generally equated with salmon and trout (salmonids). Twelve native and four non-native salmonid species occur throughout the region, many of which support highly prized sport and commercial fisheries (Everest et al. 1985). In this section, we will focus on the effects of fire on this group of fishes. Although differing in their habitat preferences and residence time in freshwater, salmonids share a number of common requirements: cool, flowing waters; clean gravel substrate for reproduction; invertebrates for food; low turbidity (necessary for sight feeding); instream cover; and, if anadromous, free migratory access to and from the sea (Reiser and Bjornn 1979, McMahon 1983, Everest et al. 1985).

Fire can modify the quantity, quality, and use of salmonid habitat by altering water temperatures, sedimentation rates, riparian vegetation, nutrient availability and food resources, and woody debris in forest streams. The potential of fire to harm production of salmonids is perhaps greatest for those species (e.g., coho and chinook salmon; cutthroat and steelhead trout) that spawn or rear in small-to-medium-size streams draining forested lands. Because of the narrow valley floors, steep hillslopes, and abundant rainfall common to this region, the terrestrial and aquatic components of these watersheds are closely linked. Hence, riparian zones and fish populations are strongly influenced by fire and associated forest management activities occurring upslope as well as along the stream (Swanson et al., in press).

Temperature

Temperature is a major factor affecting fish survival, distribution, production, and community composition in forest streams of the Pacific Northwest (Beschta et al. 1987). One of the most direct effects of fire along streams is the potential to elevate water temperatures above upper thermal tolerance limits of salmonids during burning. Yet, only two studies have measured water temperatures during prescribed burns or wildfires, and only one

---

[1]For example, effects of fire on accelerated hillslope erosion and sedimentation in streams—Chapters 14 and 17; effects of fire on forest succession and wildlife forage—Chapters 4 and 7.

study has monitored fish mortality (Hall and Lantz 1969). Feller (1981) noted an immediate rise in temperature from 55° to 61°F within 6 hours after slash burning along a small stream in southwest British Columbia; temperatures returned to near prefire levels 13 hours later. During a hot slash burn in the Needle Branch watershed, Oregon, temperatures in the upper reaches of this small stream rose rapidly from 55° to 82°F, causing high mortalities of juvenile coho salmon, cutthroat trout, and sculpins (Hall and Lantz 1969). By contrast, in the lower, less constrained portion of the watershed, the fire was less intense, and no fish mortality was observed. In the nearby patch-cut Deer Creek watershed, where the slash burn was separated from the stream by a buffer strip of vegetation, there was no increase in temperature during burning.

As noted in Chapter 17, the large increases in stream temperature associated with streamside timber harvest are further accentuated when followed by additional removal of streambank vegetation by slash burning (Levno and Rothacher 1969, Feller 1981, Holtby and Newcombe 1982). Depending on location, aspect, and stream size, temperature increases may persist for a few years to several decades until shading returns to prelogging levels (Fig. 17-2; Moring 1975, Andrus and Froehlich 1988).

Though water temperatures are rarely elevated sufficiently by fire to cause direct mortality, significant indirect and longer lasting effects on fish populations may occur (Beschta et al. 1987). Numerous studies have documented increased summer production of salmonids following streamside logging and slash burning from the combination of increased light and higher temperatures (leading to higher primary and secondary production) (Beschta et al. 1987, Gregory et al. 1987). However, the small (1.8°-3.6°F) attendant increases in winter and spring temperatures which also occur (Feller 1981, Holtby and Newcombe 1982) may largely offset any positive effects of elevated summer temperatures by altering the timing of critical life history events such as emergence of fry from spawning beds and smolt migration (Ringler and Hall 1975, Holtby 1988a). Persistent, sublethal temperature increases following logging and slash burning may also result in shifts in fish species composition. For example, Reeves et al. (1987a) found evidence that steelhead trout in western

Oregon streams are less aggressive, more susceptible to disease, and commonly replaced by their more tolerant competitor, the redside shiner, in stream sections with elevated summer temperatures. Similarly, Barton et al. (1985) suggested that sublethal temperature increases (maximum summer temperature greater than 71.6°F) following streamside clearing were one possible cause of the observed shifts from cold water salmonids to warm water fishes in Ontario streams over several decades. Since warmed stream waters lose little of their heat as they move downstream unless diluted by cooler water sources, elevated water temperatures from the upper parts of a watershed can affect salmonid populations in lower reaches (Beschta et al. 1987). Hence, cumulative and basin-scale perspectives are needed to fully evaluate the impacts of temperature alterations due to fire and logging (Beschta and Taylor 1988).

One potential impact of slash burning that has perhaps been overlooked is its effect on groundwater temperatures. Groundwater inflows from springs into streams can greatly moderate stream temperature alterations associated with logging (Swift and Messer 1971). Such inflows also serve as important sites for salmonid spawning and as summer and winter thermal refugia for juveniles and for adult steelhead trout and chinook salmon returning upstream to spawn (Bilby 1984a, Cunjak and Power 1986, Shepherd et al. 1986). Following slash burning, increased solar heating of blackened soils and wood debris could lead to increases in soil water temperatures in clearcuts (Chandler et al. 1983). Some researchers have speculated that increases in soil and groundwater temperatures following logging and slash burning may in turn lead to stream temperature increases (Hewlett and Fortson 1982, Hartman et al. 1984). However, such effects may be small and/or short-lived, particularly in coastal areas of the Pacific Northwest where revegetation commonly occurs within 1-2 years after logging and slash burning. Further research is needed to better define the extent and magnitude of this possible influence.

Nutrients and food resources

In Northwest forest streams, the type and quantity of the food base for fish is governed by the combined interaction of light, nutrients, substrate, and organic matter inputs (leaves, needles, twigs) from the surrounding riparian vegetation (Sedell and Swanson 1984, Gregory et al. 1987). Few studies have examined in detail the response of fish populations or fish food resources to the increases in nutrients that commonly occur in streams following wildfires or logging and slash burning (Chapter 17). However, because nutrient increases are usually small or of short duration (Chapter 17; Brown et al. 1973, Scrivener 1982), their effects on food resources and fish populations are probably negligible in most cases. Commonly, nutrient spikes following fires are most pronounced during storm events in the autumn, after the summer period of maximum algal production and fish growth (Scrivener 1982). Also, studies of the response of stream biota to wildfire in forests in Alaska (Lotspeich et al. 1970), California (Hoffman and Ferreira 1976), and Washington (Wood 1977) did not detect significant changes in either algal production or aquatic insects.

Pacific Northwest streams are generally light- rather than nutrient-limited. The higher primary and secondary production that is observed in streams for about 10 years following streamside logging and slash burning is primarily attributed to the changes in type and quantity of available food associated with canopy removal over the stream rather than to increased nutrient concentrations (Sedell and Swanson 1984, Wilzbach et al. 1986, Gregory et al. 1987). Similarly, in a comparison of burned and unburned watersheds in Yellowstone National Park, Albin (1978) found similar nutrient levels but lower stream shading, higher (by 2.7°F) summer stream temperatures, and greater abundance of aquatic insects in the stream draining the watershed burned previously by wildfire. Some instances where nutrients or ash from fires exceeded federal water pollution standards (Fredriksen 1971) or caused fish kills (Leopold 1923) have been reported, but nutrient levels generally do not reach toxic or very high levels unless hot, severe burns occur either directly within the stream channel or are immediately followed by a heavy rainfall (Fredriksen 1971).

Since streamside logging and burning initiate a sequence of changes in the composition, structure, and density of riparian vegetation (Agee 1988, Andrus and Froehlich 1988), how these changes affect the food base of forest streams must also be considered. Along small coastal streams, the removal of trees in riparian zones and the exposure of bare soil through yarding and slash burning tends to favor the rapid establishment of alder, salmonberry, and other deciduous vegetation which then may dominate riparian stands for at least 80 years prior to the reestablishment of conifers (Fig. 18-1; Sedell and Swanson 1984, Agee 1988, Andrus and Froehlich 1988). These vegetation changes cause a shift in the food base from the diverse mixture of deciduous and conifer litter and algae characteristic of unmanaged streamside forests to a simpler food base with algae as the chief energy source during the time period prior to canopy closure over the stream (Fig. 17-2). Later, the food base shifts to one primarily driven by deciduous litter derived from the dense corridors of alder bordering the stream (Fig. 18-1; Sedell and Swanson 1984, Gregory et al. 1987, Bilby and Bisson 1989). Higher biomass but lower diversity of aquatic invertebrates are associated with these food base shifts (Newbold et al. 1980, Murphy et al. 1981, Gregory et al. 1987). The response of fish populations to this changing food web is variable, with biomass increasing markedly during the open canopy phase (Bilby and Bisson 1989) and then declining as the alder canopy closes over the stream (Chapman and Knudsen 1980, Murphy et al. 1981, Gregory et al. 1987).

Woody debris

Potentially one of the most important and long-term impacts to fish habitat following streamside logging and burning is the loss of large woody debris. Historically, infrequent stand-replacement wildfires in Douglas-fir forests were the source of large inputs of large wood into streams and on hillslopes (Chapters 3 and 4). However, clearcut and burn rotations of 60- to 100-year intervals in western Cascades or Coast Range forests have resulted in much lower levels of woody debris compared to unmanaged forests (Spies et al. 1988). Surveys of various streams flowing through second-growth stands in western Oregon and Washington show an overall decline in large coniferous woody debris compared to unmanaged systems (Sedell et al. 1984, Grette 1985, Bisson et al. 1987, Andrus et al. 1988, Heimann 1988). Woody debris in streams plays a dominant and complex role in the physical and biological processes that affect production of salmonids (Bryant 1983, Bisson et al. 1987). Without management regulations or prescriptions for maintaining and establishing conifers in riparian zones as a source of large

Old-growth forest

Intensively managed, short-rotation forest

Managed forest – no active streamside management

Forest streamside managed for multiple resources

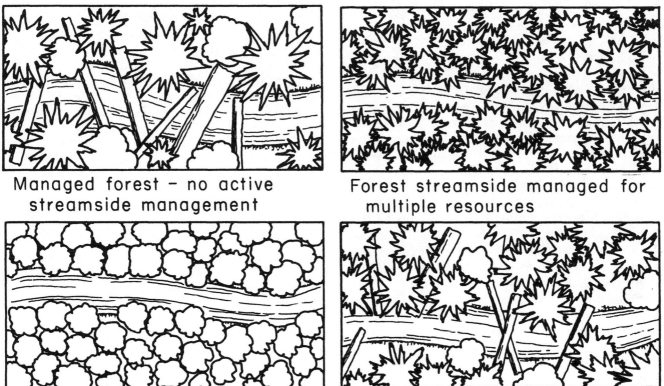

Figure 18-1. Schematic representation of changes in riparian vegetation and large woody debris in streams under different riparian management scenarios. (Adapted from Sedell and Swanson 1984)

woody debris, over time streams that flow through intensively managed (short rotation) or alder-dominated riparian zones lose much of the sediment and organic matter storage capacity and fish habitat provided by large downed conifers in the stream channel (Fig. 18-1; Bisson et al. 1987, Andrus et al. 1988). As a result, stream channels become simpler and less stable, and lose much of the habitat complexity important for providing the diversity of stream velocities and cover used as feeding and resting sites by salmonids (Sedell and Swanson 1984, Tripp and Poulin 1986a,b). Consequently, marked changes in abundance of salmonid fishes and aquatic insects have been observed following the removal or loss of debris from streams (Bryant 1983, Dolloff 1986, Elliott 1986, Murphy et al. 1986). The effects of this loss are particularly acute during winter when large woody debris provides fish refuge from high stream veloc-

ities during the frequent and at times severe freshets common to Northwest streams (Tschaplinski and Hartman 1983, McMahon and Hartman, in press); this loss of winter habitat may nullify the beneficial effects of increased fish production associated with canopy removal that has often been observed in streams after streamside logging and slash burning (Heifetz et al. 1986, Murphy et al. 1986).

The loss of large coniferous wood can have a long-term effect on the productivity of salmonid streams (Holtby 1988b). Second-growth conifer stands do not produce appreciable amounts of the large stems and rootwads necessary to form stable and complex debris accumulations for at least 50 years after harvesting (Grette 1985, Bisson et al. 1987, Heimann 1988). Although alder contributes to woody debris in streams, its value as large woody debris is much less than that of cedar, spruce, and Douglas-fir because of its relatively small stem size and rapid decomposition (Bisson et al. 1987).

Streamside logging and overzealous removal of debris from stream channels under the auspices of protecting roads, bridges, water quality, or fish passage (Bilby 1984b, House and Boehne 1987) have likely had a greater effect than slash burning on the loss of much of the present and future sources of large wood from streams. However, by creating more bare soil and a more uniform soil environment in riparian areas, slash burning along streams may reduce the establishment, growth, and future recruitment of conifers as woody debris into streams by creating an even more favorable environment for the formation of dense and uniform stands of deciduous trees and shrubs than would logging alone (Fig. 18-1; Agee 1988). Conversely, judicious use of prescribed fire in riparian zones in conjunction with thinning or conifer planting may be a useful site preparation tool for reestablishing conifers in brush-dominated riparian zones to insure a future supply of large wood and snags (Fig. 18-1; Hibbs 1987, Andrus et al. 1988).

Logging commonly creates large quantities of slash and one of the key purposes of prescribed burning is to decrease the amount of this material to meet site preparation and fire hazard reduction objectives (Chapters 6 and 8). One possible side effect of burning, particularly severe burns on steep slopes, is to decrease the stability of existing debris; burning logs and other slash rolling downhill are not an uncommon sight during a fire. Due to the effects of water and gravity, large quantities of logging slash may accumulate in streams, especially steep draws and headwater channels (Brown 1974, Bryant 1983). During large storm events, this small, floatable material can then be transported downstream in the form of debris torrents, where it builds up and causes failure of formerly stable natural debris jams (Swanson and Lienkaemper 1978, Toews and Moore 1982, Bryant 1983, Hartman et al. 1987). Large deposits of small, unstable slash and debris may also form barriers to upstream fish passage (Bisson et al. 1987). Proposed guidelines for the removal of slash that has a high likelihood of moving during storm flows while protecting the integrity of stable debris have been offered by Bryant (1983), Bilby (1984b), and Dolloff (1986).

Sediment and turbidity

Despite widespread concern over the potential effects of fire-related sedimentation on fish and aquatic habitats (Lyon et al. 1978, Chandler et al. 1983), questions about how much sediment is delivered to streams following prescribed burning and what effects this has on fish habitat are difficult to answer definitively. Relatively few studies have measured sediment or turbidity during and after fires. And, in the sediment yield studies that have been done (Chapter 17), it is difficult to clearly identify burning as the source of sediment input into streams since several other potentially sediment-producing management activities occur concurrently with the use of fire.

Salmonids in the Pacific Northwest have evolved in steep, highly erosive, sediment-rich watersheds with highly variable streamflow; but too much sediment can adversely impact salmonid habitat in a number of ways (Everest et al. 1985, 1987). Excessive sediment reduces suitable spawning and rearing habitat by increasing scouring and intrusion of fine sediments into spawning gravels. In low-gradient stream sections, where fish production is often concentrated and sediment deposition occurs (Reeves et al. 1987b), the filling of pools and the creation of wide, shallow, unstable stream channels prone to dewatering during periods of low flow in summer may also result from high sediment inputs (Swanson and Lienkaemper 1978, Tripp and Poulin 1986a,b). The net effect of these changes is a reduction in the survival of salmonid eggs and fry (Cederholm and Reid 1987, Hartman et al. 1987) and a shift in the species and age composition of the fish community from one dominated by pool-dwelling species such as coho salmon and older steelhead and cutthroat trout to one dominated by riffle-dwelling species such as young steelhead and cutthroat trout (Bisson and Sedell 1984). Even relatively small but chronic increases in suspended sediment or turbidity may negatively influence fish populations by decreasing food production, feeding rate, and growth and by increasing avoidance of the affected area (Bisson and Bilby 1982, Sigler et al. 1984, Lloyd et al. 1987). Reduced angler effort and success may be an additional side effect of high turbidity, even at relatively low levels (Chapter 17; Everest and Harr 1982).

In most instances, however, roads or soil and bank disturbances associated with timber harvesting along streams are the dominant factors contributing to increased sediment delivery to streams via increased surface soil erosion or mass wasting (Chapter 14; Brown and Krygier 1971, Swanston and Swanson 1976). A sediment budget developed for various management practices in the South Fork Salmon River, Idaho, watershed estimated that sedimentation due to fire contributed less than 1 percent of the total annual sediment to the river; 85 percent of the total yield was due to roads (Nobel and Lundeen 1971; see also Cederholm and Reid 1987). However, as indicated in Chapters 14 and 17, several-fold increases in sediment yield can be expected after clearcutting and a hot burn on steep slopes (see also Mersereau and Dyrness 1972, Rothacher and Lopushinsky 1974). These chapters also discussed several ways to minimize accelerated soil erosion and increased sedimentation of streams draining steep watersheds through well-planned and supervised logging operations and site preparation that limit the exposure of bare soils and maintain soil and root strength. These practices include avoidance of hot burns or use of alternative methods for slash removal; minimizing consumption of the organic duff layer by use of cool burns; providing an unburned buffer along stream channels; rapid revegetation of bare soil; and maintaining vegetation in small headwater channels.

Maintaining large woody debris in streams and on hillslopes is also crucial for moderating the input and adverse effects of increased stream sediment associated with burning. By dissipating stream energy and erosive power during storm events, large woody debris in streams greatly increases the capacity of a channel to deposit and store sediment, and thus reduces levels of bedload and suspended sediment and turbidity (Beschta 1979, Bisson et al. 1987). In a similar fashion, woody debris on hillslopes, terraces, and in headwater stream channels serves as erosion barriers, trapping fine sediments and small debris, and hence helping buffer downstream fish habitats against rapid pulses of sediment (Mersereau and Dyrness 1972, Wilford 1984, Bisson et al. 1987).

Other considerations

The importance of offchannel, floodplain habitats (minor tributaries, beaver ponds, ephemeral swamps, sidechannels) to the overall production of juvenile salmon (primarily coho salmon) and steelhead and cutthroat trout has become increasingly recognized (Bustard and Narver 1975, Cederholm and Scarlett 1982, Peterson 1982, Hartman and Brown 1988). Representing only a small fraction of the total stream area and in some places situated several hundred yards from the main stream channel, these protected sites nevertheless can provide overwintering habitat for a significant portion of the smolts produced in a stream basin (Cederholm and Scarlett 1982, Brown and McMahon 1988). However, these sites are small and often dry during the summer, and thus are commonly overlooked during forestry operations. Although relatively invulnerable to direct impact of fire due to their wetland-type characteristics, these areas are very susceptible to sediment and slash deposition from upslope harvesting, roads, and prescribed burning because of their position in the watershed. Ways to identify and protect the quantity, quality, and use of these sensitive and important floodplain habitats during logging and site preparation are discussed by Hartman and Brown (1988).

Wildfire versus prescribed fire

Fire has been a relatively common occurrence in Pacific Northwest forests for at least the past 10,000 years (Chapter 3). The adaptations or responses of fish and stream ecosystems to the effects of historical fires provide an important context from which to view modern-day uses and impacts of prescribed fire on fish in managed forests (Sedell and Swanson 1984).

The catastrophic stand-replacement wildfires that occurred throughout western Oregon and Washington on the average of every 100-250 years (Chapter 3) undoubtedly had large impacts on fish habitat via the introduction of large pulses of sediment and debris. The impacts of such large-scale and severe events, however, were probably ameliorated when riparian zones remained intact. Studies by Hemstrom and Franklin (1982) in Mount Rainier National Park and Teensma (1987) in the central Oregon Cascades revealed that the oldest forest stands often occur along streams, indicating that historic stand-replacement fires less commonly extended down to the moist valley floors and streamside areas.

In addition, Sedell and Swanson (1984) suggest that even where fires did burn across riparian areas the remaining structural influence of the forest from snags and large woody debris in the stream served to minimize sedimentation and hasten recovery of disturbed stream areas. In studies of streams previously burned by major wildfires in western Oregon, Swanson and Lienkaemper (1978) and Andrus et al. (1988) found that large wood in streams may persist for many decades after fires, continuing to provide the majority of the structure for fish habitat in streams until the postfire stand begins to produce large wood.

Despite the many large and well-publicized wildfires that have occurred throughout the Pacific Northwest during the past 100 years, monitoring of fish population responses to these disturbances has been limited. The effects of the Mt. St. Helens volcanic eruption in 1980 were analogous in their impacts to stream ecosystems to a very large and severe wildfire. In the blast zone, riparian forests were buried, streams were inundated with massive amounts of ash and fine sediment, and most of the fish populations were eliminated (Martin et al. 1986). However, in stream channels where structural features provided by large quantities of wood remained both from the preblast forest and from blowdown during the blast, there was little channel widening, pools were maintained, and recovery of the channel and riparian vegetation has been rapid due to the large quantities of ash and fine sediment being either transported downstream or deposited onto the floodplain within a few years after the blast (Sedell and Dahm 1984). By contrast, in areas where downed trees and riparian forests were either buried by mudflows or removed during salvage logging, streams lacked such structural features and had wide, shallow, highly unstable channels and few pools and side channels, and carried high sediment loads of fine sand (Sedell and Dahm 1984). Due to a combination of high summer water temperatures and a lack of large wood for winter refuge, coho salmon reintroduced into streams throughout the blast area within 1-2 years after the eruption exhibited their lowest survival in stream sections exhibiting these latter characteristics (Martin et al. 1986).

Compared to historic or modern-day wildfires, prescribed burns are generally much less severe and much smaller in areal extent; hence, the impacts on fish populations can be expected to be much less severe as well. The above information on wildfires or wildfire-like events suggests that potentially the most long-lasting and severe ef-

fects of fire—whether prescribed or wild—will be when results include the loss of the streamside forest and its mediating influence on stream temperature, sediment, and woody debris.

Management implications

Table 18-1 summarizes various approaches to minimizing undesirable impacts to fish habitat during and after prescribed fire. The recent shift in the Pacific Northwest to the use of more cool burns, coupled with leaving riparian buffers along fish-bearing streams, should help alleviate many of the potential impacts of fire on fish and stream ecosystems. As noted in Chapters 14 and 17, burning when the forest floor is moist is a particularly effective way to minimize sedimentation by limiting

Table 18-1. Management prescriptions for minimizing potential impacts of fire on fish habitats.

Potential Impact	Prescriptions
Increased water temperature	Maintain stream shading via riparian buffer strip; promote rapid revegetation of charred hillslopes.
Nutrient increases/altered food resources	Avoid hot burns especially prior to high rainfall in the fall; maintain riparian buffer with mix of coniferous and deciduous vegetation.
Loss of large woody debris	Maintain riparian buffer strip with large conifers; prevent input of large quantities of slash into streams.
Sedimentation	Use cool or spring burns; promote rapid revegetation of burned sites; avoid stream bank disturbance; maintain or enhance sediment storage capacity by leaving large wood in streams and on hillslopes and by leaving vegetation in and along headwater channels.
	Use alternative methods for slash removal (e.g., cable yarding) on steep (>80%), unstable slopes.
Floodplain habitat damage	Maintain fish access; minimize disturbance from sediment and slash deposition; protect vegetative cover.

the exposure of bare soil and the loss of large wood pieces on hillslopes and headwater or intermittent stream channels that serve as effective sites for deposition and storage of sediment.

Riparian buffer strips, too, serve an important and multipurpose role in protecting the integrity of fish habitat during and after fire and associated management activities (Hall and Lantz 1969, Froehlich 1973, Barton et al. 1985, Beschta et al. 1987, Bisson et al. 1987, Hartman et al. 1987). Recent changes in forest practice regulations in the Pacific Northwest reflect increasing awareness of the important role of streamside vegetation in providing fish and wildlife habitat over the long term by requiring the leaving of live conifers as a future supply of large wood for snags and instream woody debris (Adams et al. 1988).

A concern during the planning and operational phases of a prescribed burn is how to protect riparian buffer strips during a fire. A recent survey of 45 buffer strips in the Siuslaw National Forest revealed that nine (20 percent) had been damaged by prescribed fires, with four of these sites moderately to severely damaged (defined as having more than 40 percent of total area affected) (Swanson and Roach 1987). Use of sprinklers, fire lines, removal of slash from buffers, burning when buffer strips are moist, and erection of sheet metal barriers to prevent rolling embers from entering buffers are some of the ways used to minimize fire damage to these sensitive areas. Prompt reseeding of fire lines constructed to protect buffers will help ensure that these areas do not act as a sediment source for nearby streams.

A continuing challenge for prescribed fire management is to minimize downstream effects from burning in or near intermittent or headwater stream channels. Commonly, buffers are not left along these channels because they usually do not support fish. Nevertheless, they represent the majority of stream miles within a basin; for example, intermittent tributaries comprise about 70 percent of the total stream miles in the Mount Hood National Forest (personal communication from D. Heller, Mount Hood National Forest). Fire severity and accumulation of small, floatable slash tend to be higher in these steep, narrow sites; hence, they can be important contributors of sediment and small debris to fish-bearing waters downstream when stream networks expand during major storm events (Chapter 14). More information is

needed to evaluate to what extent and under what conditions downstream impacts on fish habitat occur due to burning in or near headwater channels, and to identify and assess prescriptions for minimizing these impacts.

Effects of Fire on Wildlife

Direct effects

Although the literature is somewhat divided on the magnitude of wildlife mortality resulting directly from fire, the consensus is that this mortality is insignificant in terms of number of animals killed and impact on affected populations (Bendell 1974, Wright and Bailey 1982). Death of small mammals with small home ranges, such as voles, deer mice, shrews, chipmunks, tree squirrels, woodrats, and rabbits, has been documented for prescribed burns (Tevis 1956, Chew et al. 1958, Cook 1959, Ahlgren 1966, Komarek 1969, Gashwiler 1970, Black and Hooven 1974, Fala 1975). Mortality of small mammals is related to uniformity, severity, size, and duration of the burn (Buech et al. 1977). Ground-dwelling mammals can avoid the intense heat of fires simply by going underground (Chandler et al. 1983); soil temperature just inches below the surface stays within normal ranges (Kahn 1960, Lawrence 1966). Komarek (1963) observed no mortality of marked cottonrats following a small prescribed burn.

Even when individual small mammals are killed during prescribed burns, the impact on the population may be ephemeral, at least for some species. Tevis (1956), Tester (1965), and Simms and Buckner (1973) noted that mice and voles colonized areas that had been prescribed burned within weeks.

There is little documentation of avian mortality resulting from fire. Chew et al. (1958) found two passerine bird carcasses following a wildfire in California chaparral. Obviously, prescribed burns conducted during nesting season will destroy ground-nesting bird nests. Doerr et al. (1970) reported failure of grouse to nest in an area following a fire; notably, no adult grouse carcasses were found.

Medium-to-large mammals usually move rapidly enough to escape fire. Members of a raccoon family left a 24-acre prescribed burn, returning afterwards to resume normal activities (Sunquist 1967). Deer and other larger mammals rarely are found in burned areas, unless the burn is of sufficient size and severity that they are trapped; such characteristics are not typical of prescribed burns. Chew et al. (1958) did find one dead black-tailed deer following a chaparral fire. Cause of death among wildlife in fires seems due mostly to asphyxiation, rather than to burning (Chew et al. 1958, Lawrence 1966).

It is reasonable to expect that by manipulating prescribed burns (size, season, location) there will be little direct wildlife mortality of consequence.

Indirect effects

Mechanism of indirect effects. Providing food and cover (for protection from environmental extremes and predators) are basic tenets of wildlife management (Dasmann 1981, Robinson and Bolen 1984). Food, cover, and water and their arrangement are essential components of wildlife habitat (Thomas 1979). Each wildlife species is adapted to a specific arrangement and amount of these habitat components, collectively called "habitat." The greater the diversity of these habitats, the greater, in turn, the diversity of wildlife species (Odum 1971). The structure (arrangement of vegetative layers—grasses and forbs, shrubs, saplings, maturing and mature trees) and composition (by species) of vegetation provide diversity of food (for herbivorous wildlife) and cover.

In addition to quantity, the quality condition of foods influences abundance and welfare of wildlife. Wildlife provided good nutrition are better able to withstand severe weather conditions and generally exhibit higher reproductive rates (Robinson and Bolen 1984). Fire is presumed to improve the quality of foods by release of such nutrients as nitrogen, calcium, and phosphorous, but other factors related to burning, such as greater exposure of plants to sunlight, and removal of litter, may also influence forage quality. Bendell (1974) noted that there is not a simple relationship among burning, release and uptake of nutrients, and use by wildlife. He noted that the level of nutrients in plants after burning may increase, decrease, or not change, depending on season, soil, weather, nature of fuel and fire, and other factors.

The size and arrangement in space and time of habitat components also influence wildlife abundance and diversity. Generally speaking, the smaller the wildlife species, the smaller the area within which it seeks its habitat needs. Mouse or vole habitat may include an area of less than 1 acre, whereas mountain lions and eagles usually include thousands of acres in their habitats. Larger wildlife species usually include more than one kind of vegetative structure/plant community in the list of habitat components they require. For these animals, the proximity (called juxtaposition) of these different, required habitat components determines animal presence and welfare; components in close proximity require less travel to get from one to the other, which results in less exposure to predation and weather extremes. If components are sufficiently far apart, they cease to be available to some animals, the animals' habitat needs are not met, and some will cease to exist.

Because of plant succession, those wildlife habitats that include seral plant communities phase in and out as determined by factors that control succession. The degree to which prescribed burning advances, retards, or maintains seral plant communities influences habitats and wildlife. Anything forest managers do that affects structure or composition of vegetation influences habitats and, in turn, wildlife species residing within those habitats. Because prescribed burning affects plant structure, composition, and succession (Chapter 4), it has the potential to alter the composition and abundance of the wildlife community existing in the vicinity of the burn.

Prescribed burning may impact none, a few, many, or all of the multitude of habitat components that determine the abundance and composition of wildlife communities in the vicinity of the burn. The impact(s) may be beneficial, detrimental, or innocuous, depending on timing, scope, severity, and placement of the burn, site characteristics (soil type and depth, slope, moisture, exposure), and on the wildlife species under consideration (Neitro et al. 1985).

Impacts of prescribed burning on groups of wildlife. Much is known of habitat requirements for such game species as deer, elk, and grouse. The management strategy for game animals usually is to optimize their abundance, and it includes management practices like burning and seeding to improve quality and quantity of foods.

Swanson (1970) noted that availability of forage for elk in western Oregon was determined by amount and distribution of slash and residual vegetation, which was reduced by prescribed burning. Bunnell and Eastman (1976) and Taber et al.

(1981) indicated that prescribed burning improves forage productivity of clearcut sites and extends the length of time preferred forages are available.

Orme and Leege (1976) noted that prescribed burning in fall resulted in successful germination, seedling growth, and survival of redstem ceanothus, an important elk winter browse food in Idaho. Spring prescribed burning was less expensive and resulted in a higher rate of sprouting of preferred winter browse species (Leege 1968). Prescribed burning reduces the height of existing browse, making it more available to elk, increases palatability of browse, and adds new browse plants via enhanced seed germination (Nelson 1976).

Prescribed burning has long been recognized as an important factor in management of bobwhite quail in the South (Stoddard 1963) for provision of nesting habitat and seed and insect foods. However, the impact of prescribed burning on upland game birds in the Pacific Northwest is unclear. Marshall (1946) stated that regeneration of preferred foods of ruffed grouse in Idaho is stimulated by fire, but Doerr et al. (1970) found little change in grouse numbers, mortality, and reproductive success before and after a wildfire in Alberta. Wright and Bailey (1982) stated that fire enhances spring, summer, and fall blue grouse habitat, but Redfield et al. (1970) stated that clearcut logging alone seemed to provide increases in blue grouse numbers.

Nongame wildlife includes such diverse groups as small rodents (mice and voles), sciurids (chipmunks and squirrels), birds of prey (hawks, owls, eagles, and vultures), and reptiles and amphibians. Until the last decade, there was little interest in nongame wildlife species unless they were categorized as threatened or endangered. Wildlife species so classified were accorded special status, including protection under federal laws from alteration of habitats which might result in reductions of their numbers or have other adverse effects upon them. Now, in addition to the protection afforded threatened and endangered species, nongame wildlife are receiving more attention, including manipulation of habitat for their benefit.

A number of reptiles, amphibians, small mammals, and birds use clearcuts and other forest openings. A required structural component within forest openings for these animals is down and dead woody material, such as logs and downed branches (Maser et al. 1979). These animals seek prey under logs, dig and nest in burrows in and under logs, store pine cones inside them and feed on fungi growing on and within logs. Some use logs as lookout posts. Larger mammals (snowshoe hares, skunks, and raccoons) use hollow logs for protection from weather extremes and predators (Maser et al. 1979).

Removing slash by prescribed burning or other methods eliminates this essential habitat component. Several years are required before chipmunks and voles colonize prescribed burned sites (Cook 1959, Ahlgren 1966, Fala 1975). These and other small mammals (ground squirrels and deer mice) have been identified as carrying spores of mycorrhizal fungi from adjacent forest lands onto clearcut sites (McIntire 1985). The fungi form a symbiotic relationship with commercially valuable conifers, enhancing uptake of soil nutrients, which is crucial on harsh, stressful sites (Chapter 13; Mikola 1970, Molina and Trappe 1982). Prescribed burning, by negatively impacting these small mammals, could conceivably have a deleterious effect on growth of conifers, especially on droughty sites. Maser et al. (1979) outlined procedures whereby prescribed burns would have least negative impacts on down and dead woody materials (e.g., burn in spring before logs dry out, or after recent precipitation has occurred; rake combustible materials away from logs prior to burning).

Some small mammals (bats, flying squirrels, and chipmunks) use cavities in snags, as do cavity-nesting birds (woodpeckers, flickers, bluebirds, swallows, sparrowhawks), for nest sites and protection from weather extremes and predators (Thomas et al. 1979, Neitro et al. 1985). Insectivorous birds like woodpeckers, nuthatches, and creepers obtain their prey primarily from snags. Other, noncavity-nesting birds nevertheless use snags as perching sites and hunting platforms.

Standard practice for prescribed burns has been either to: fell snags prior to the burn and burn them with other slash, or ensure that they are burned during the prescribed burn (Martin and Dell 1978). This practice eliminates nesting and roosting sites for the above-mentioned mammals and birds as well as a primary source of food. Studies have shown clearly that without snags on or near clearcut sites, the cavity-dwelling birds and mammals are lost from the wildlife community, reducing animal species diversity by about one-third (Mannan et al. 1980, Morrison and Meslow 1983, Schreiber 1987).

Several practices may be employed to protect snags during prescribed burning, including conducting the burn in early spring before snags lose much moisture, treating the base of snags and surrounding flammable material with fire-retardant material, and removing flammable material from the base of snags prior to the burn, via hand or machine piling of slash (Maser et al. 1979, Neitro et al. 1985, Schreiber 1987).

Larger mammalian predators (fishers, martens, foxes, coyotes, bobcats, mountain lions, bear) and avian predators or raptors (hawks, owls, vultures, and eagles) have such large home ranges that areas impacted by prescribed burning usually comprise but a small proportion of the total. Impact on the cover component of habitat is likely to be negligible. Predators congregate on burned areas, presumably because of the vulnerability and availability of prey species (Stoddard 1963, Komarek 1967, 1969, Bendell 1974). Thus, prescribed burning likely will increase short-term quantity of food available to predators.

Impact of prescribed burning on damage caused by wildlife to forest regeneration is slight and is discussed in Chapter 9. The use of prescribed fire to enhance wildlife habitat is discussed in Chapter 7.

Impacts of prescribed burning on wildlife communities. Like other forest perturbations, fire (at least fire contained within areas of the size representative of prescribed burns) seems to have negligible impacts on species abundance and diversity (Bendell 1974). Some species disappear from burned areas, while others appear which were absent prior to fire. Except in the case of endangered or threatened species, for which an area under consideration for burning might constitute a significant portion of the species' known distribution, prescribed burning should have a minimal effect on individual species.

As the proportion of prescribed burned lands in an area under consideration increases, the potential for impact on the wildlife community increases. Timing and placement of prescribed burned areas also influence impact. Staggering the conduct of prescribed burns over time, and distributing the burns evenly over the landscape will minimize impact on small wildlife species that occupy areas of prescribed burn size or smaller. For

larger wildlife species, such placement could maximize potential benefits by providing a more even (through time and space) distribution of enhanced forage areas of the size likely to be fully utilized. (Note: Above a certain size of opening, deer and elk utilization of forage areas declines.)

If larger areas are prescribed burned, or a series of burns is conducted over a short time frame on contiguous areas, the overall effect is to create one large prescribed burn, which will result in increased negative impacts on small mammals (because they cannot escape the direct effects of fire), and reduced use by small animals (especially "edge-effect" animals) and larger animals (if the area is larger than typical foraging area). Again, however, the effects of prescribed burning must be separated from those caused by clearcutting and thinning, which may have a greater impact on wildlife use of an area than fire.

Management implications

Maximizing positive effects and minimizing negative effects of prescribed burning on wildlife requires careful comparison of its impacts on wildlife resident within the area considered for burning. Needs of, and areas inhabited by, threatened and endangered species must be evaluated in light of responses of these species to the characteristics of the proposed burn. Of even greater importance may be evaluation of the impact of practices proposed to precede (e.g., clearcutting, thinning) or follow (e.g., seeding of exotic forage plants; planting single species of conifer) the burn.

Where prescribed burning as a procedure by itself may result in negative impacts, mitigation measures may be called for, such as removing flammable material around logs or snags to prevent their consumption during the burn (Chapter 22). Careful timing and placement of the burn will avoid many potential negative effects as well as optimize potential beneficial effects. Planning for a sequence of prescribed burns during a burn season, or even over a period of years, will assure that benefits are optimized and detrimental effects are minimized.

Conclusion

For fish, the major habitat impacts associated with fire are increases in water temperature and sediment and the long-term loss of large woody debris from stream channels. Current information suggests that the use of cool burns and riparian buffers along streams should effectively prevent or limit these impacts in most cases, but more before-and-after monitoring studies of the effectiveness of these management practices are needed. This is particularly the case for fires on steep slopes and in headwater stream channels where the potential for downstream transport of sediment and slash is high. Expanded use by land management agencies of site-specific prescribed burn plans that mesh reforestation goals with soils, fish, and wildlife considerations should also help minimize stream impacts associated with prescribed fire. A future research and management challenge will be to evaluate the use of fire along selected portions of brush-dominated riparian zones as a means to reestablish conifers for snags and woody debris.

For wildlife, it seems likely that impacts from prescribed fire should not differ substantially from those of wildfire on wildlife. Indeed, because prescribed burns likely are of lesser severity, cover much smaller areas, and can be controlled concerning season, slope, moisture content of fuel, and other factors that impact wildlife, it would seem that negative impacts of fire posed by prescribed burning could be minimized, and positive impacts optimized.

In the future, for managers to make more definitive statements about the implications of prescribed fire on wildlife, there is a need, too, for monitoring studies of fire effects under various management scenarios. For example, rather than infer that wildlife welfare and abundance will automatically increase with increases in the quantity and nutritional quality of forage resulting from prescribed burning, it would be helpful if wildlife responses were monitored directly. The same could be said for inferred detrimental effects, such as the destruction of ground-dwelling bird nests, snags, and dead and down woody debris.

For both fish and wildlife, separation of the impacts of prescribed fire from those of clearcutting, thinning, and other management practices is also a valid research goal. Similarly, the response of fish and wildlife to the pattern of prescribed burns over large landscapes, such as watersheds, through time intervals spanning several to many seasons, would be valuable information for managers.

Literature Cited & Key References

*Adams, P.W., R.L. Beschta, and H.A. Froehlich. 1988. Mountain logging near streams: Opportunities and challenges, p. 153-162. *In* Proc., Internat. Mountain Logging and Pacific Northwest Skyline Symp., Coll. For., Oregon State Univ., Corvallis, OR. 193 p.

Agee, J.K. 1988. Successional dynamics in forest riparian zones, p. 31-43. *In* Raedeke, K.J. (ed.) Streamside Management: Riparian Wildlife and Forestry Interactions. Coll. For. Resour., Univ. Washington, Seattle, WA. Inst. For. Resour. Contrib. 59.

Ahlgren, C.E. 1966. Small mammals and reforestation following prescribed burning. J. For. 64:614-618.

Albin, D.P. 1978. Some effects of forest fires on selected streams in Yellowstone National Park. M.S. thesis, Humboldt State Univ., Arcata, CA.

Andrus, C. and H.A. Froehlich. 1988. Riparian forest development after logging or fire in the Oregon Coast Range: Wildlife habitat and timber value, p. 139-152. *In* Raedeke, K.J. (ed.) Streamside Management: Riparian Wildlife and Forestry Interactions. Coll. For. Resour., Univ. Washington, Seattle, WA. Inst. For. Resour. Contrib. 59. 277 p.

Andrus, C., B.A. Long, and H.A. Froehlich. 1988. Woody debris and its contribution to pool formation in a coastal stream 50 years after logging. Can. J. Fish. Aquat. Sci. 45:2080-2086.

Barton, D.R., W.D. Taylor, and R.M. Biette. 1985. Dimensions of riparian buffer strips required to maintain trout habitat in southern Ontario streams. North Amer. J. Fish. Manage. 5:364-378.

*Bendell, J.F. 1974. Effects of fire on birds and mammals, p. 73-138. *In* Kozlowski, T.T., and C.E. Ahlgren (eds.) Fire and Ecosystems. Academic Press, New York, NY. 542 p.

Beschta, R.L. 1979. Debris removal and its effect on sedimentation in an Oregon Coast Range stream. Northwest Sci. 53:71-77.

*Beschta, R.L., R.E. Bilby, G.W. Brown, L.B. Holtby, and T.D. Hofstra. 1987. Stream temperature and aquatic habitat: Fisheries and forestry interactions, p. 191-232. *In* Salo, E.O., and T.W. Cundy (eds.) Streamside management: Forestry and Fishery Interactions. Coll. For. Resour., Univ. Washington, Seattle, WA. Inst. For. Resour. Contrib. 57. 471 p.

Beschta, R.L., and R.L. Taylor. 1988. Stream temperature increases and land use in a forested Oregon watershed. Water Resour. Bull. 24:19-25.

Bilby, R.E. 1984a. Characteristics and frequency of cool-water areas in a western Washington stream. J. Freshwater Ecol. 2:593-602.

References marked by an asterisk are recommended for general information.

Bilby, R.E. 1984b. Post-logging removal of woody debris affects stream channel stability. J. For. 82:609-613.

Bilby, R.E., and P.A. Bisson. 1989. Relative importance of allochthonous vs. autochthonous carbon sources as factors limiting coho production in streams, p. 123-135. *In* Proc., 1988 Coho and chinook workshop. No. Pac. Inter. Chap., Amer. Fish. Soc. 284 p.

Bisson, P.A., and R.E. Bilby. 1982. Avoidance of suspended sediment by juvenile coho salmon. North Amer. J. Fish. Manage. 4:371-374.

*Bisson, P.A., R.E. Bilby, M.D. Bryant, C.A. Dolloff, G.B. Grette, R.A. House, M.L. Murphy, K V. Koski, and J.R. Sedell. 1987. Large woody debris in forested streams in the Pacific Northwest: Past, present, and future, p. 143-190. *In* Salo, E.O., and T.W. Cundy (eds.) Streamside Management: Forestry and Fishery Interactions. Coll. For. Resour., Univ. Washington, Seattle, WA. Inst. For. Resour. Contrib. 57. 471 p.

Bisson, P.A., and J.R. Sedell. 1984. Salmonid populations in streams in clearcut vs. old-growth forests of western Washington, p. 121-129. *In* Meehan, W.R., T.R. Merrell, Jr., and T.A. Hanley (eds.) Fish and Wildlife Relationships in Old-growth Forests: Proc. Symp., Amer. Inst. Fish. Res. Biol., Moorehead City, NC. 425 p.

Black, H.C., and E.F. Hooven. 1974. Response of small-mammal communities to habitat changes in western Oregon, p. 177-188. *In* Black, H.C. (ed.) Proc., Symp. Wildlife and Forest Management in the Pacific Northwest. Oregon State Univ., Corvallis, OR. 236 p.

Brown, E.R., and A.B. Curtis. 1985. Introduction, p. 1-15. *In* Brown, E.R. (ed.) Management of Wildlife and Fish Habitats in Forests of Western Oregon and Washington. Part 1: Chapter narratives. USDA For. Serv., Pac. Northwest Reg., Portland, OR.

Brown, G.W. 1974. Fish habitat, p. E-1—E-15. *In* Cramer, O.P. (ed.) Environmental effects of forest residues management in the Pacific Northwest: A state-of-knowledge compendium. USDA For. Serv., Pac. Northwest For. Rge. Exp. Sta., Portland, OR. Gen. Tech. Rep. PNW-24.

Brown, G.W., A.R. Gahler, and R.B. Marston. 1973. Nutrient losses after clear-cut logging and slash burning in the Oregon Coast Range. Water Resour. Res. 9:1450-1453.

Brown, G.W., and J.T. Krygier. 1971. Clear-cut logging and sediment production in the Oregon Coast Range. Water Resour. Res. 7:1189-1198.

Brown, T.G., and T. McMahon. 1988. Winter ecology of juvenile coho salmon in Carnation Creek: Summary of findings and management implications, p. 108-117. *In* Chamberlin, T. (ed.) Proc., Workshop: Applying 15 Years of Carnation Creek Results. Pac. Biol. Sta., Nanaimo, B.C. 239 p.

Bryant, M.D. 1983. The role and management of woody debris in west coast salmonid nursery streams. North Amer. J. Fish. Manage. 3:322-330.

Buech, R.R., K. Siderits, R.E. Radtke, H.L. Sheldon, and D. Elsing. 1977. Small mammal populations after a wildlfire in northeast Minnesota. USDA For. Serv., North Central For. Exp. Sta., St. Paul, MN. Res. Pap. NC-151. 8 p.

*Bunnell, F.L., and D.S. Eastman. 1976. Effects of forest management practices on wildlife in the forests of British Columbia, p. 631-6898. *In* Proc., Div. 1, XVII IUFRO World Cong., Oslo, Norway.

Bustard, D.R., and D.W. Narver. 1975. Aspects of the winter ecology of juvenile coho salmon (*Oncorhynchus kisutch*) and steelhead trout (*Salmo gairdneri*). J. Fish. Res. Bd. Can. 32:667-680.

Cederholm, C.J., and L.M. Reid. 1987. Impact of forest management on coho salmon (*Oncorhynchus kisutch*) populations of the Clearwater River, Washington: A project summary, p. 373-398. *In* Salo, E.O., and T.W. Cundy (eds.) Streamside Management: Forestry and Fishery Interactions. Coll. For. Resour., Univ. Washington, Seattle, WA. Inst. For. Resour. Contrib. 57. 471 p.

Cederholm, C.J., and W.J. Scarlett. 1982. Seasonal immigrations of juvenile salmonids into four small tributaries of the Clearwater River, Washington, 1977-1981, p. 98-110. *In* Brannon, E.L., and E.O. Salo (eds.) Salmon and Trout Migratory Behavior Symp. Coll. Fisheries, Univ. Washington, Seattle, WA. 309 p.

Chandler, C., P. Cheney, P. Thomas, L. Trabaud, and D. Williams. 1983. Fire in Forestry. Volume I. Forest Fire Behavior and Effects. John Wiley & Sons, Inc., New York, NY. 450 p.

Chapman, D.W., and E. Knudsen. 1980. Channelization and livestock impacts on salmonid habitat and biomass in western Washington. Trans. Amer. Fish. Soc. 109:357-363.

Chew, R.M., B.B. Butterworth, and R. Grechman. 1958. The effects of fire on the small mammal populations of chaparral. J. Mammal. 40:253.

Cook, S.F., Jr. 1959. The effects of fire on a population of small rodents. Ecology 40:102-108.

Cunjak, R.A., and G. Power. 1986. Winter habitat utilization by stream resident brook trout (*Salvelinus fontinalis*) and brown trout (*Salmo trutta*). Can. J. Fish. Aquat. Sci. 43:1970-1981.

Dasmann, R.F. 1981. Wildlife Biology. 2nd ed. John Wiley & Sons, Inc. New York, NY. 212 p.

Doerr, P.D., L.B. Keith, and D.H. Rusch. 1970. Effects of fire on a ruffed grouse population. Tall Timbers Fire Ecol. Conf. Proc. 10:25-46.

Dolloff, C.A. 1986. Effects of stream cleaning on juvenile coho salmon and Dolly Varden in southeast Alaska. Trans. Amer. Fish. Soc. 115:743-755.

Elliott, S.T. 1985. Reduction of a Dolly Varden population and macrobenthos after removal of logging debris. Trans. Amer. Fish. Soc. 115:392-400.

*Everest, F.H., N.B. Armantrout, S.M. Keller, W.D. Parante, J.R. Sedell, T.N. Nickelson, J.M. Johnson, and G.N. Haugen. 1985. Salmonids, p. 199-230. *In* Brown, E.R. (ed.) Management of Wildlife and Fish Habitats in Forests of Western Oregon and Washington. Part 1: Chapter narratives. USDA For. Serv., Pac. Northwest Reg., Portland, OR. 332 p.

*Everest, F.H., R.L. Beschta, J.C. Scrivener, K V. Koski, J.R. Sedell, and C.J. Cederholm. 1987. Fine sediment and salmonid production: A paradox, p. 98-102. *In* Salo, E.O., and T.W. Cundy (eds.) Streamside Management: Forestry and Fishery Interactions. Coll. For. Resour., Univ. Washington, Seattle, WA. Inst. For. Resour. Contrib. 57. 471 p.

Everest, F.H., and R.D. Harr. 1982. Silvicultural treatments. *In* Meehan, W.R. (ed.) Influence of forest and rangeland management on anadromous fish habitat in western North America. USDA For. Serv., Pac. Northwest For. Rge. Exp. Sta., Portland, OR. Gen. Tech. Rep. PNW-96. 19 p.

Fala, R.A. 1975. Effects of prescribed burning on small mammal populations in a mixed-oak clearcut. J. For. 73:586-587.

Feller, M.C. 1981. Effects of clearcutting and slashburning on stream temperature in southwestern British Columbia. Water Resour. Bull. 17:863-867.

Feller, M.C. 1982. The ecological effects of slashburning with particular reference to British Columbia: A literature review. B.C. Min. For. Land Manage. Rep. 13. 60 p.

Fredriksen, R.L. 1971. Comparative water quality—natural and disturbed streams, p. 125-137. *In* Krygier, J.D., and J.D. Hall (eds.) Forest Land Uses and Stream Environment. Oregon State Univ., Corvallis, OR.

Froehlich, H.A. 1973. Natural and man-caused slash in headwater streams. Pac. Logging Conf., Vancouver, B.C. Loggers Hbk. 33:15-17, 66-70, 82-86.

Gashwiler, J.S. 1970. Plant and animal changes on a clearcut in west-central Oregon. Ecology 51:1018-1026.

*Gregory, S.V., G.A. Lamberti, D.C. Erman, K V. Koski, M.L. Murphy, and J.R. Sedell. 1987. Influence of forest practices on aquatic production, p. 233-255. *In* Salo, E.O., and T.W. Cundy (eds.) Streamside Management: Forestry and Fishery Interactions. Coll. For. Resour., Univ. Washington, Seattle, WA. Inst. For. Resour. Contrib. 57. 471 p.

Grette, G.B. 1985. The role of large organic debris in juvenile salmonid rearing habitat in small streams. M.S. thesis, Univ. Washington, Seattle, WA.

Hall, J.D., and R.L. Lantz. 1969. Effects of logging on the habitat of coho salmon and cutthroat trout in coastal streams, p. 335-375. *In* Northcote, T.G. (ed.) Symposium on Salmon and Trout in Streams. H.R. MacMillan Lectures in Fisheries. Univ. British Columbia, Vancouver, B.C. 388 p.

Hartman, G.F., and T.G. Brown. 1988. Forestry-fisheries planning considerations on coastal floodplains. For. Chron. 64:47-51.

Hartman, G.F., L.B. Holtby, and J.C. Scrivener. 1984. Some effects of natural and logging-related winter stream temperatures on the early life history of coho salmon (*Oncorhynchus kisutch*) in Carnation Creek, British Columbia, p. 141-149. *In* Meehan, W.R., T.R. Merrell, Jr., and T.A. Hanley (eds.) Fish and Wildlife Relationships in Old-growth Forests. Amer. Inst. Fish. Res. Biol. Morehead City, NC. 425 p.

Hartman, G.F., J.C. Scrivener, L.B. Holtby, and L.A. Powell. 1987. Some effects of different stream-side treatments on physical conditions and fish population processes in Carnation Creek, a coastal rainforest stream in British Columbia, p. 330-372. *In* Salo, E.O., and T.W. Cundy (eds.) Streamside Management: Forestry and Fishery Interactions. Coll. For. Resour., Univ. Washington, Seattle, WA. Inst. For. Resour. Contrib. 57. 471 p.

Heifetz, J., M.L. Murphy, and K V. Koski. 1986. Effects of logging on winter habitat of juvenile salmonids in Alaskan streams. North Amer. J. Fish. Manage. 6:52-58.

Heimann, D.C. 1988. Recruitment trends and physical characteristics of coarse woody debris in Oregon Coast Range streams. M.S. Thesis, Oregon State Univ., Corvallis, OR.

Hemstrom, M.A., and J.F. Franklin. 1982. Fire and other disturbances of the forests in Mount Rainier National Park. Quaternary Res. 18:32-51.

Hewlett, J.D., and J.C. Fortson. 1982. Stream temperature under an inadequate buffer strip in the southeast Piedmont. Water Resour. Bull. 18:983-988.

Hibbs, D.E. 1987. Management of riparian zone vegetation in western Oregon, p. 57-63. *In* Managing Oregon's Riparian Zone for Timber, Fish, and Wildlife. Nat. Counc. Air Stream Improve. Tech. Bull. 514. 96 p.

Hoffman, R.J., and R.F. Ferreira. 1976. A reconnaissance of effects of a forest fire on water quality in Kings Canyon National Park. USDI, Geol. Surv. Open File Rep. 76-497.

Holtby, L.B. 1988a. Effects of logging on stream temperatures in Carnation Creek, British Columbia, and associated impacts on the coho salmon (*Oncorhynchus kisutch*). Can. J. Fish. Aquat. Sci. 45:502-515.

Holtby, L.B. 1988b. The effects of logging on the coho salmon of Carnation Creek, British Columbia, p. 159-174. *In* Chamberlin, T. (ed.) Proc., Workshop: Applying 15 Years of Carnation Creek Results. Pac. Biol. Sta., Nanaimo, B.C.

Holtby, L.B., and C.P. Newcombe. 1982. A preliminary analysis of logging-related temperature changes in Carnation Creek, British Columbia, p. 81-99. *In* Hartman, G.F. (ed.) Proc., Carnation Creek Workshop: A 10-year review. Pac. Biol. Sta., Nanaimo, B.C. 239 p.

House, R.A., and P.L. Boehne. 1987. The effect of stream cleaning on salmonid habitat and populations in a coastal Oregon drainage. West. J. Appl. For. 2:84-87.

Kahn, W.C. 1960. Observations on the effect of a burn on a population of *Sceloporus occidentalis*. Ecology 41:358-359.

Komarek, E.V. 1963. Fire, research, and education. Tall Timbers Fire Ecol. Conf. Proc. 2:181-187.

Komarek, E.V. 1967. Fire and the ecology of man. Tall Timbers Fire Ecol. Conf. Proc. 6:143-170.

Komarek, E.V. 1969. Fire and animal behavior. Tall Timbers Fire Ecol. Conf. Proc. 9:161-207.

Lawrence, G.E. 1966. Ecology of vertebrate animals in relation to chaparral fire in the Sierral Nevada foothills. Ecology 47:278-291.

Leege, T.A. 1968. Prescribed burning for elk in northern Idaho. Tall Timbers Fire Ecol. Conf. Proc. 8:235-253.

Leopold, A. 1923. Wild followers of the forest—the effects of fires on fish and game. Amer. For. 515-519, 566.

Levno, A., and J. Rothacher. 1969. Increases in maximum stream temperatures after slash burning in a small experimental watershed. USDA For. Serv., Pac. Northwest For. Rge. Exp. Sta., Portland, OR. Res. Note PNW-110. 7 p.

Lloyd, D.S., J.P. Koenings, and J.D. LaPerriere. 1987. Effects of turbidity in fresh waters of Alaska. North Amer. J. Fish. Manage. 7:18-33.

Lotspeich, F.B., E.W. Mueller, and P.J. Frey. 1970. Effects of large scale forest fires on water quality in interior Alaska. USDI, Fed. Water Poll. Contr. Admin, Alaska Water Lab, College, AK.

*Lyon, L.J., H.S. Crawford, E. Czuhai, R.L. Fredriksen, R.F. Harlow, L.J. Metz, and H. A. Pearson. 1978. Effects of fire on fauna: A state-of-knowledge review. USDA For. Serv., Washington, DC. Gen. Tech. Rep. WO-6. 41 p.

Mannan, R.W., E.C. Meslow, and H.M. Wight. 1980. Use of snags by birds in Douglas-fir forests, western Oregon. J. Wildl. Manage. 44:787-797.

Marshall, W.H. 1946. Cover preferences, seasonal movements, and food habits of Richardson's grouse and ruffed grouse in southern Idaho. Wilson Bull. 58:42-52.

Martin, D.J., L.J. Wasserman, and V.H. Dale. 1986. Influence of riparian vegetation on posteruption survival of coho salmon fingerlings on the west-side streams of Mount St. Helens, Washington. North Amer. J. Fish. Manage. 6:1-8.

Martin, R.E., and J.D. Dell. 1978. Planning for prescribed burning in the inland northwest. USDA For. Serv., Pac. Northwest For. Rge. Exp. Sta., Portland, OR. Gen. Tech. Rep. PNW-76. 67 p.

Maser, C., R.G. Anderson, K. Cromack,, Jr., J.T. Williams, and R.E. Martin. 1979. Chapter 6: Dead and down woody material, p. 78-95. *In* Thomas, J.W. (tech. ed.) Wildlife Habitats in Managed Forests of the Blue Mountains of Oregon and Washington. USDA For. Serv., Washington, DC. Agr. Hbk. 553. 512 p.

McIntire, P.W. 1985. The role of small mammals as dispersers of mycorrhizal fungal spores within variously managed forests and clearcuts. Ph.D. thesis, Coll. For., Oregon State Univ., Corvallis, OR. 142 p.

McMahon, T.E. 1983. Habitat suitability index models: Coho salmon. USDI, Fish Wildl. Serv., Washington, DC. FWS/OBS-82/10.49. 29 p.

McMahon, T.E., and G.F. Hartman. In press. Influence of cover complexity and current velocity on winter habitat use by juvenile Coho salmon. Can. J. Fish. Aquat. Sci. 49.

Mersereau, R.C., and C.T. Dyrness. 1972. Accelerated mass wasting after logging and slash burning in western Oregon. J. Soil Water Conserv. 27:112-114.

Mikola, P. 1970. Mycorrhizal inoculation in afforestation. Internat. Rev. For. Res. 3:123-196.

Molina, R., and J.M. Trappe. 1982. Patterns of ectomycorrhizal host specificity and potential among Pacific Northwest conifers and fungi. For. Sci. 28:423-458.

Moring, J.R. 1975. The Alsea Watershed Study: Effects of logging on the aquatic resources of three headwater streams of the Alsea River, Oregon. Part II—Changes in environmental conditions. Oregon Dep. Fish Wildl., Salem, OR. Fish. Res. Rep. 9.

Morrison, M.L., and E.C. Meslow. 1983. Avifauna associated with early growth vegetation on clearcuts in the Oregon Coast ranges. USDA For. Serv., Pac. Northwest For. Rge. Exp. Sta., Portland, OR. Res. Pap. PNW-305. 12 p.

Murphy, M.L., C.P. Hawkins, and N.H. Anderson. 1981. Effects of canopy modification and accumulated sediment on stream communities. Trans. Amer. Fish. Soc. 110:469-478.

*Murphy, M.L., J. Heifetz, S.W. Johnson, KV. Koski, and J.F. Thedinga. 1986. Effects of clear-cut logging with and without buffer strips on juvenile salmonids in Alaskan streams. Can. J. Fish. Aquat. Sci. 43:1521-1533.

Neitro, W.A., R.W. Mannan, D. Taylor, V.G. Binkley, B.G. Marcot, F.W. Wagner, and S.P. Cline. 1985. Chapter 7: Snags. *In* Brown, E.R. (tech ed.) Management of Wildlife and Fish Habitats in Forests of Western Oregon and Washington. USDA For. Serv., Pac. Northwest For. Rge. Exp. Sta., Portland, OR. PNW Pub. R6-F&WL-192. 332 p.

*Nelson, J.R. 1976. Forest fire and big game in the Pacific Northwest. Tall Timbers Fire Ecol. Conf. Proc. 15:85-102.

Newbold, J.D., D.C. Erman, and K.B. Roby. 1980. Effects of logging on macroinvertebrates in streams with and without buffer strips. Can. J. Fish. Aquat. Sci. 37:1076-1085.

Nobel, E.L., and L.J. Lundeen. 1971. Analysis of rehabilitation treatment alternatives for sediment control, p. 86-96. *In* Krygier, J.T., and J.D. Hall (eds.) Forest Land Uses and Stream Environment. Oregon State Univ., Corvallis, OR.

Odum, E.P. 1971. Fundamentals of Ecology. 3rd. ed. W.B. Saunders Co., Philadelphia, PA. 574 p.

Orme, M.L., and T.A. Leege. 1976. Emergence and survival of redstem (*Ceanothus sanguineus*) following prescribed burning. Tall Timbers Fire Ecol. Conf. Proc. 14:391-420.

Peterson, N.P. 1982. Immigration of juvenile coho salmon (*Oncorhynchus kisutch*) into riverine ponds. Can. J. Fish. Aquat. Sci. 39:1308-1310.

Raedeke, K.J. (ed.) 1988. Streamside management: Riparian wildlife and forestry interactions. Coll. For. Resour., Univ. Washington, Seattle, WA. Inst. For. Resour. Contrib. 59.

Redfield, J.A., F.C. Zwickel, and J.F. Bendell. 1970. Effects of fire on numbers of blue grouse. Tall Timbers Fire Ecol. Conf. Proc. 10:63-83.

Reeves, G.H., F.H. Everest, and J.D. Hall. 1987a. Interactions between the redside shiner (*Richardsonius balteatus*) and the steelhead trout (*Salmo gairdneri*) in western Oregon: The influence of water temperature. Can. J. Fish. Aquat. Sci. 44:1603-1613.

Reeves, G.H., R.L. Beschta, F.J. Swanson, M.H. McHugh, and M.D. McSwain. 1987b. The Elk River basin: an integrated investigation of forest management impacts on fish habitat, p. 47-51. *In* Managing Oregon's riparian zone for timber, fish, and wildlife. Nat. Counc. Air Stream Improve. Tech. Bull. 514. 96 p.

Reiser, D.W., and T.C. Bjornn. 1979. Influence of forest and rangeland management of anadromous fish habitat in the western United States and Canada. 1. Habitat requirements of anadromous salmonids. USDA For. Serv., Pac. Northwest For. Rge. Exp. Sta., Portland, OR. Gen. Tech. Rep. PNW-96. 54 p.

Ringler, N.H., and J.D. Hall. 1975. Effects of logging on water temperature and dissolved oxygen in spawning beds. Trans. Amer. Fish. Soc. 104:111-121.

Robinson, W.L., and E.G. Bolen. 1984. Wildlife Ecology and Management. Macmillan Pub. Co., New York, NY. 478 p.

Rothacher, J.S., and W. Lopushinsky. 1974. Soil stability and water yield and quality, p. D-1—D-23. *In* Cramer, O.P. (ed.) Environmental effects of forest residues management in the Pacific Northwest: A state-of-knowledge compendium. USDA For. Serv., Pac. Northwest For. Rge. Exp. Sta., Portland, OR. Gen. Tech. Rep. PNW-24.

Salo, E.O., and T.W. Cundy (eds.) 1987. Streamside Management: Forestry and Fishery Interactions. Coll. For. Resour., Univ. Washington, Seattle, WA. Inst. For. Resour. Contrib. 57. 471 p.

Schreiber, B.P. 1987. Diurnal bird use of snags on clearcuts in central coastal Oregon. M.S. thesis, Oregon State Univ., Corvallis, OR. 63 p.

Scrivener, J.C. 1982. Logging impacts on the concentration patterns of dissolved ions in Carnation Creek, p. 64-80. *In* Hartman, G.F. (ed.) Proc., Carnation Creek Workshop: A 10-year review. Pac. Biol. Sta., Nanaimo, B.C.

Sedell, J.R., and C.N. Dahm. 1984. Catastrophic disturbances to stream ecosystems: Volcanism and clear-cut logging, p. 531-539. *In* Klug, M.J., and C.A. Reddy (eds.) Current Perspectives in Microbial Ecology. Amer. Soc. Microbiol., Washington, DC.

*Sedell, J.R., and F.J. Swanson. 1984. Ecological characteristics of streams in old-growth forests of the Pacific Northwest, p. 9-16. *In* Meehan, W.R., T.R. Merrell, Jr., and T.A. Hanley (eds.) Fish and Wildlife Relationships in Old-growth Forests. Amer. Inst. Fish. Res. Biol., Moorehead City, NC. 425 p.

Sedell, J.R., F.J. Swanson, and S.V. Gregory. 1985. Evaluating fish response to woody debris, p. 222-245. *In* Hassler, T.J. (ed.) Proc., Pacific Northwest Stream Habitat Management Workshop. Humboldt State Univ., Arcata, CA. 329 p.

Shepherd, B.G., G.F. Hartman, and W.J. Wilson. 1986. Relationships between stream and intragravel temperatures in coastal drainages, and some implications for fisheries workers. Can. J. Fish. Aquat. Sci. 43:1818-1822.

Sigler, J.W., T.C. Bjornn, and F.H. Everest. 1984. Effects of chronic turbidity on density and growth of steelhead and coho salmon. Trans. Amer. Fish. Soc. 113:142-150.

Simms, H.P., and C.H. Buckner. 1973. The effect of clearcutting and burning in *Pinus banksiana* forests on the populations of small mammals in southeastern Manitoba. Amer. Midl. Natur. 9:228-231.

Spies, T.A., J.F. Franklin, and T.B. Thomas. 1988. Coarse woody debris in Douglas-fir forests of western Oregon and Washington. Ecology 69:1689-1702.

Stoddard, H.L. 1963. Bird habitat and fire. Tall Timbers Fire Ecol. Conf. Proc. 2:163-175.

Sunquist, M.E. 1967. Effects of fire on raccoon behavior. J. Mammal. 48:673-674.

Swanson, D.O. 1970. Roosevelt elk-forest relationships in the Douglas-fir region of the southern Oregon Coast Range. Ph.D. thesis, Univ. Michigan, Ann Arbor, MI. 186 p.

Swanson, F.J., J.F. Franklin, and J.R. Sedell. In press. Landscape patterns, disturbance, and management in the Pacific Northwest, USA. *In* Zonneveld, I.F., and R.T.T. Forman (eds.) Landscapes in Flux: An Ecological Perspective. Springer-Verlag.

Swanson, F.J., and G.W. Lienkaemper. 1978. Physical consequences of large organic debris in Pacific Northwest streams. USDA For. Serv., Pac. Northwest For. Rge. Exp. Sta., Portland, OR. Gen. Tech. Rep. PNW-69. 12 p.

Swanson, F.J., and C.J. Roach. 1987. Administrative report of the Mapleton Leave Area study. USDA For. Serv., Pac. Northwest Res. Sta., Corvallis, OR.

Swanston, D.N., and F.J. Swanson. 1976. Timber harvesting, mass erosion and steepland forest geomorphology in the Pacific Northwest, p. 199-221. *In* Coates, D.R. (ed.) Geomorphology and Engineering. Dowden, Hutchinson, and Ross, Inc., Stroudsburg, PA.

Swift, L.W., and J.B. Messer. 1971. Forest cuttings raise temperatures of small streams in the southern Appalachians. J. Soil Water Conserv. 26:111-116.

Taber, R.D., D. Manuwal, and S.D. West. 1981. Wildlife management in the mesic-temperate forest of Washington and Oregon, p. 575-589. *In* Proc., Div. I, XVII IUFRO World Cong., Oslo, Norway.

Teensma, P.D.A. 1987. Fire history and fire regimes of the central western Cascades of Oregon. Ph.D. thesis, Univ. Oregon, Eugene, OR.

Tester, J.R. 1965. Effects of a controlled burn on small mammals in a Minnesota oak-savanna. Amer. Midl. Natur. 74:240-243.

Tevis, L., Jr. 1956. Effect of a slash burn on forest mice. J. Wildl. Manage. 20:405-409.

Thomas. J.W. 1979. Chapt. 1: Introduction. *In* Thomas, J.W. (tech. ed.) Wildlife Habitats in Managed Forests of the Blue Mountains of Oregon and Washington. USDA For. Serv., Washington, DC. Agr. Hbk. 553. 512 p.

Thomas, J.W., R.G. Anderson, C. Maser, and E.L. Bull. 1979. Chapt. 5: Snags. *In* Thomas, J.W. (tech. ed.) Wildlife Habitats in Managed Forests of the Blue Mountains of Oregon and Washington. USDA For. Serv., Washington, DC. Agr. Hbk. 553. 512 p.

Toews, D.A.A., and M.K. Moore. 1982. The effects of streamside logging on large organic debris in Carnation Creek. B.C. Min. For., Land Manage. Rep. 11. 29 p.

Tripp, D.B., and V.A. Poulin. 1986a. The effects of mass wasting on juvenile fish habitats in Queen Charlotte Island streams. B.C. Min. For., Land Manage. Rep. 45. 48 p.

Tripp, D.B., and V.A. Poulin. 1986b. The effects of logging and mass wasting on salmonid spawning habitat in streams on the Queen Charlotte Islands. B.C. Min. For., Land Manage. Rep. 50. 29 p.

Tschaplinski, P.J., and G.F. Hartman. 1983. Winter distribution of juvenile coho salmon (*Oncorhyncus kisutch*) before and after logging in Carnation Creek, British Columbia, and some implications for over-winter survival. Can. J. Fish. Aquat. Sci. 40:452-461.

Wilford, D.J. 1984. The sediment-storage function of large organic debris at the base of unstable slopes, p. 115-119. *In* Meehan, W.R., T.R. Merrell, Jr., and T.A. Hanley (eds.) Fish and Wildlife Relationships in Old-growth Forests. Amer. Inst. Fish. Res. Biol. Morehead City, NC. 425 p.

Wilzbach, M.A., K.W. Cummins, and J.D. Hall. 1986. Influence of habitat manipulations on interactions between cutthroat trout and invertebrate drift. Ecology 67:898-911.

Wood, J.F. 1977. The aquatic insects of Rainy Creek with special reference to caddisflies (Trichoptera). M.S. thesis, Central Washington Univ., Ellensburg, WA.

Wright, H.A., and A.W. Bailey. 1982. Fire Ecology: United States and Southern Canada. John Wiley & Sons, Inc., New York, NY. 501 p.

VII Public Attitudes and Regulation of Prescribed Fire in Forest Ecosystems

19 Public Attitudes and Perceptions about Prescribed Burning

Bo Shelby and Robert W. Speaker

Executive Summary

Public attitudes about the use of fire as a management tool depend largely on perceptions of the reason for a prescribed burn and knowledge about its probable impacts on air and water quality, public health, ecological conditions, and nearby resources with commercial or aesthetic value. Many people have concerns about the negative impacts of fire on public health and ecological and aesthetic conditions, despite increasing recognition that some fires may have beneficial effects. Public acceptance of the shift in policy from immediate suppression of all fires to the use of fire as a management tool has been slow because of the effectiveness of earlier campaigns in convincing the public that all fires should be immediately suppressed, public concerns about air quality, and the lack of a consensus about the use of fire. People also place a high value on air quality.

Public support for the use of prescribed burning in forested recreation lands has increased greatly in the last 20 years through a long-term effort to inform people about the natural role of fire in undisturbed ecosystems. However, many people oppose prescribed burning for removal of logging slash and site preparation in commercially managed forests. Some of this opposition may be related to the belief that current levels of timber harvests are too high. Increasing support for slash burning will probably require consensus about the use and effects of fire, a long-term information effort, perception of information as objective and scientifically sound, and adequate treatment of specific public concerns such as safety, health, ecological integrity, and air quality.

Introduction

Public attitudes and perceptions about fires in forested lands have historically depended on information provided by professional forest managers. Shortly after its inception in 1905 the USDA Forest Service adopted and aggressively pursued a policy of immediately extinguishing all forest fires, a policy that received almost unanimous public support (Hendee et al. 1968, Folkman 1979). In 1977, this basic policy changed from strict control to the use of wildfire as a management tool. One of the specific aims of this policy was to use prescribed fires (ignited either naturally or by humans) to protect, maintain, and enhance forest resources (Taylor and Daniel 1985). This change in policy resulted from recognition of the fact that fire can have many beneficial effects on forests and from the rapidly increasing costs of fighting all fires.

Public understanding and acceptance of this change in fire policy have lagged behind its implementation because of:

- an over-generalized interpretation of the "Smokey Bear" message that all forest fires have detrimental effects;
- public concern about and subsequent legislation related to air quality; and
- the lack of a consensus among forest managers on the use of fire (Omi and Laven 1982).

The environmental movement of the 1960s and 1970s gave rise to the widespread view that humans, including forest managers, cannot improve a natural ecosystem (Baas et al. 1985). This preference for naturalness has been found in many studies, and some people will overlook, expect, or even wish to encounter debris from natural causes in forested wildlands (Wagar 1974). Slash and debris from commercial timber management operations do not receive the same level of acceptance, however, even though their net effect may be the same. Residues from timber management have a strong negative impact on recreation use and public perceptions of the naturalness of an area (Benson 1974, Wagar 1974, Daniel and Boster 1976).

Public attitudes toward prescribed burning are largely focused on concerns about the health, ecological, aesthetic, and commercial impacts of these fires. Health concerns focus on the effects of smoke (especially from chemically treated sites) on air quality, and the effects of burning on water quality. Ecological concerns are directed toward the effects of burning on vegetation, wildlife communities, water quality, and animal mortality. Aesthetic concerns focus on visibility impairment from smoke and the effects of burning on the scenic quality and recreation acceptability of a site. Concerns about losses of commercially valuable timber caused by prescribed burning in wilderness areas and the added risk to timber when prescribed burning is not used to dispose of flammable logging slash are more often voiced by individuals associated with the wood products industry than by the public in general.

Public attitudes about fire depend on how the fire started and knowledge of its probable impacts on air and water quality, public health, ecological conditions, and nearby resources with commercial or aesthetic value. Public support may be high if a prescribed burn is used to reduce the risk of severe wildfire, to manage ecological conditions by simulating the historic fire regime, or to improve recreation potential (Zwolinski et al. 1983, Gardner et al. 1985, Taylor and Daniel 1985). Less

support is likely if people perceive that there is a potential health or visibility problem from smoke, that a reduction in water quality is likely to result, that there is a high risk of the fire getting out of control, or that the aesthetic quality or recreational acceptability of the site will be degraded. No surveys have been conducted to determine public attitudes toward prescribed burning of logging slash for management of commercial timber stands. Testimony received at public hearings on Oregon's proposed Visibility Protection and Smoke Management Plan indicates that public reaction to prescribed burning of logging slash is usually mixed, with individuals associated with commercial wood products industries generally in support of the use of fire and many people outside this group opposed (Oregon Department of Environmental Quality 1986).

Public Testimony on Burning in Western Oregon

Several concerns regarding prescribed burning of logging residues and agricultural fields in western Oregon were expressed during public testimony on the Department of Environmental Quality's proposed Visibility Protection and Smoke Management Plan (Oregon Department of Environmental Quality 1986). The plan proposed:

- limiting agricultural field burning between July 4 and Labor Day to weekdays (since 80 percent of the visitation to Oregon's National Parks and wilderness areas takes place on weekends between these dates);
- prohibiting burning in the Cascades during this period (except when natural visibility impairment is high, for conversion from hardwoods to conifers, or for research);
- further reductions in agricultural field burning in the future; and
- further reductions in prescribed forest burning in the future through more efficient utilization of logging residues.

Concerns expressed during the hearings centered on:

- the effects of smoke on air quality and public health, especially (but not limited to) smoke from areas that had been treated with herbicides;
- the effects of reduced visibility on scenic and aesthetic quality;

- the waste of resources resulting from the burning of logging residues; and
- the economic impacts of the proposed restrictions on commercial forestry and agriculture.

Public hearing testimony from individuals associated with the wood products industries was about equally divided between support for the proposed plan (assuming no further restrictions), and opposition to the plan on the grounds that it was already too restrictive. Many people associated with these industries as well as some private woodland owners and local chambers of commerce felt that the proposed restrictions were unnecessary and would have unreasonably harsh economic impacts. Many people in this group voiced the view that prescribed burning was necessary for site preparation and cost-effective reforestation.

Individuals representing the Oregon Environmental Council, Oregon Natural Resources Council, Sierra Club, and Oregon Chapter of the American Lung Association opposed the proposed plan on the grounds that it permitted too much burning. Environmental groups felt that the enforcement provisions of the plan were inadequate and that year-round protection should be provided, as they felt was mandated in the federal Clean Air Act.

The 76 members of the public who testified but did not identify themselves with any advocacy group held varying attitudes toward the plan and the use of prescribed burning on forest and agricultural lands (Table 19-1). Forty-three percent were opposed to the plan because it did not sufficiently restrict burning (one-third of these individuals felt that burning should be prohibited at all times). Eleven percent favored adoption of the plan, stating that it provided the minimum amount of restriction they would be willing to accept; another 11 percent said that the restrictions were a good compromise; and 14 percent approved of the plan but felt that it contained the maximum amount of restriction acceptable to them. Twenty-one percent were opposed to the plan because it restricted burning too much.

The proposed Visibility Protection and Smoke Management Plan was adopted in March 1986. An emergency escape clause that allows agricultural field burning in the Willamette Valley in the event of unusual conditions that may result in undue economic hardship was added to the plan after the public hearings. The plan was implemented on a

Table 19-1. Public reaction to the Oregon Visibility Protection and Smoke Management Plan.[a]

Position	Individuals not identified with an advocacy group (%)
Opposed—Provides insufficient restrictions on burning	43
Supported—Provides minimum acceptable level of visibility protection	11
Supported—Proposed restrictions are a good compromise	11
Supported—If no further restrictions on burning are imposed	14
Opposed—Plan restricts burning too much	21

Source: Oregon Department of Environmental Quality 1986
[a]Views expressed by the 76 individuals who were not identified with the forest products industry or an environmental group at the 1986 public hearing on the proposed Visibility Protection and Smoke Management Plan.

trial basis with the condition that the entire plan will be reviewed after 3 years. A new plan that provides equal or greater visibility protection will be implemented after the review process.

Attitudes toward Prescribed Burning on Recreation Lands

Public knowledge about and support for the use of prescribed burning as a management tool in National Parks, Wilderness Areas, and on other forested recreation lands has increased in the last 20 years. Most of the research in this area has been conducted in the southwestern United States and northern Rocky Mountains. In general, public support for the use of fire has increased much more rapidly than understanding of its specific uses and effects. Since 1968 prescribed burning in National Parks and wildlands has become more common, and the public has gradually become aware that fire can be a valuable management tool, even though they may not know the specific reasons for its use (Omi and Laven 1982). Visitors to the Selway-Bitterroot Wilderness area in Idaho in 1984 knew only slightly more about the effects of fire on natural ecosystems than 1971 visitors, but opinion had shifted from majority (56 percent) support for fire suppression in 1971 to majority (73 percent) support for the use of fire as a management tool in 1984 (Stankey 1976, McCool and Stankey 1986). In 1984, 50 percent of the visitors felt that even human-ignited fires could have beneficial effects on the ecosystem.

The level of acceptance of prescribed burning in wildlands is related to an individual's knowledge of the uses and impacts of fire (Gardner et al. 1985, Taylor and Daniel 1985). Public knowledge and acceptance of the use of fire as a management tool in mature ponderosa pine forests in Arizona was increased by informing people of the beneficial effects of fire (Taylor and Daniel 1985). Individuals given information on fire effects in short brochures and graduate students who had taken a course in fire ecology were significantly more knowledgeable about the effects of fire and more supportive of its use than individuals who did not receive information beforehand.

In a nationwide survey of diverse groups of forest users, Gardner et al. (1985) found that most people were willing to support the use of fire as a management tool, but there were significant differences in knowledge, attitudes, and beliefs based on education, training, and reasons for using an area. Knowledge about the effect of fire was related to the individual's educational background, with professional foresters being the most knowledgeable and off-road vehicle users the least. Most people believed that fire could have beneficial effects on the ecosystem, and this feeling was nearly universal among foresters. Several other groups, however, were more divided in their views. Off-road vehicle users and hunters were the most skeptical about the positive effects of fire on forests, and members of conservation organizations also expressed doubts. With the exception of professional foresters, there was considerable disagreement among members of each group, with some members holding extreme viewpoints on both sides of the issue.

The perceived risk of a fire getting out of control was an important factor in determining an individual's level of support for the use of prescribed burning. Foresters were willing to accept a much greater risk than all other groups, while members of conservation groups were most strongly opposed to such risks.

Public awareness and acceptance of prescribed burning of understory vegetation in mature ponderosa pine stands was high in the area around Tucson, Arizona (Cortner et al. 1984). More than 67 percent of the people surveyed felt that fires could have a beneficial effect on forests and that it was acceptable to use prescribed burning as a management tool. In response to an open-ended question, 60 percent correctly identified several of the benefits that could be expected. Eighty-four percent were familiar with the concept of prescribed burning and 80 percent of this group approved of its use. The authors feel that these unusually high awareness and acceptance levels may have been due to the extensive public information programs in the area. Whenever visible fires were planned, news media were notified and people were informed of burning schedules and the reasons for the burns by local television and newspapers. Despite the high level of awareness, people were generally uninformed about specific details of the local fire management policy (e.g., effects on animals, acreages burned, fire intensity, and vegetative reestablishment patterns). Some of the most frequently voiced concerns were:

- High animal mortality rates (animal mortality was perceived to be much higher than it often is).
- Fear that the fire may get out of control.
- Concern that fires cause damage to natural ecosystems.
- The belief that natural systems are too complex to be fully understood and should be left alone.
- The belief that fires should be aggressively suppressed at all times.

Public concerns about the use of prescribed burning are not always easily put to rest. Information about the use of fire given to visitors to Grand Canyon National Park failed to significantly increase their knowledge about fire effects or support for its use (Baas et al. 1985).

Public attitudes about prescribed burning, then, reflect both the long-held view that all fires should be suppressed immediately, and our growing knowledge about the natural role of fire. This dichotomy is particularly evident in views expressed by Olympic National Park visitors and area residents (Rauw 1980). Both groups generally supported the use of prescribed fire for fuel reduction and restoration of natural vegetation, and many knew that some fires were impossible to control. Despite this understanding, 65 percent of the people surveyed felt that all fires should be controlled at any cost.

The research summarized here indicates that education on the uses and effects of prescribed burning in wildlands is potentially a powerful tool in shaping public attitudes. A high level of support for the use of prescribed burning in wildlands currently exists because of a widespread, long-term effort to make people aware of the beneficial uses of fire. These programs were successful because they stressed information about the general effects and site-specific consequences of prescribed fires, thus building support for flexible fire suppression policies while preserving the fire prevention ethic necessary to deter destructive, uncontrolled wildfires. It appears that the key elements of the successful information and education programs were:

• A long-term effort to inform the public about the natural role of fire in undisturbed ecosystems. The favorable shift in attitudes toward prescribed burning in wildlands occurred gradually over the last 20 years.
• A strong consensus among managers and local user groups about the correct use and beneficial effects of prescribed burning.
• Public perception that the information provided was scientifically sound and not coming from a particular interest group.
• Adequate treatment of specific public concerns related to the use of fire (e.g., the risk of prescribed fires getting out of control or smoke intrusion into inhabited areas).

Willingness to Pay for Maintenance or Improvement of Air Quality

Economic value assessment techniques attempt to quantify attitudes and behaviors associated with changes in air quality by measuring the trade-offs people are willing to make in order to enjoy cleaner air. These methods provide a technique for estimating how much people value air quality and how much protection is desirable (Rowe and Chestnut 1983). The majority of studies to date have been done around several National Parks in the southwestern United States. They attempt to assess how much residents and visitors are willing to pay to ensure that high air quality is maintained in the region. The impetus for these studies was the proposed construction of several new power facilities that would significantly reduce visual air quality near some parks.

These studies found that both residents and park visitors were willing to pay between $50 and $85 annually per household for significant improvements in air quality. The forms of payment suggested in the studies were increases in recreational user fees, sales taxes, and utility bills. The present values of aggregate benefits were estimated at $12 million to $19 million, based on a 30-35 year period and a 10 percent discount rate (Randall et al. 1975, Brookshire et al. 1976, Blank et al. 1978, Rowe et al. 1980, Schulze et al. 1981). Several of these studies found that people were willing to pay substantially more for maintaining or improving air quality in pristine areas, or in areas that were perceived to be unique national treasures such as the Grand Canyon, than in natural areas where the environment is perceived as having already been degraded to some extent.

A contingent valuation study in the Portland/ Willamette Valley area in Oregon was commissioned to provide information to be used in the development of Oregon's Visibility Protection and Smoke Management Plan. It was found that Central Oregon Cascades wilderness users would be willing to pay an additional user fee of about $2 per day to assure high visual quality in the area (Crocker 1986). Portland area residents were willing to make a one-time payment of about $50 to assure high visual quality. Crocker estimated that assurance of a 50-mile summer visual range in the Willamette Valley would annually generate $24.4 million in additional benefits. The present value of aggregate benefits from this assurance would be $445 million. Assurance of high visual range in the Central Oregon Cascade wilderness areas would produce $6.4 million in benefits annually, with a present value of aggregate benefits of $116 million.

The applicability of results from these economic value assessments is limited by problems with the methodologies used. Nevertheless, they clearly show that people place a high value on the health and visibility benefits of clean air.

Conclusion

Public attitudes toward fires in forested lands have historically depended on information provided by professional forest managers. Prior to 1977, the USDA Forest Service's policy of immediately suppressing all forest fires received nearly unanimous public support, due largely to an aggressive public education campaign. In the late 1970s, fire policy changed from immediate suppression to the use of fire as a tool in managing forests. The campaign to gain public support in preventing forest fires had been so effective, however, that public acceptance of this new policy lagged behind its implementation. Attempts to inform people about beneficial uses of fire have been met with concerns about its impacts on air and water quality, public health, ecological conditions, and nearby resources with commercial or aesthetic value.

A shift toward public acceptance of the use of prescribed burning in National Parks, Wilderness Areas, and other forested recreation lands occurred gradually over the last 20 years as people came to realize that periodic fires could substantially reduce the potential for catastrophic, uncontrolled wildfires and could have many other beneficial effects on forest ecosystems. As a consensus among managers and forest users developed, the general public began to accept prescribed burning as a tool in managing forests. This has resulted in public acceptance of prescribed burning in wildland areas. Forest managers have found that providing the public with specific information about the reasons, location, time, and effects of a prescribed burn can result in a high level of acceptance, even for highly visible fires.

Prescribed burning for removal of logging slash and site preparation in commercially managed forests may not receive the same level of public support as the use of fire in wildlands. It is difficult to determine how much of the opposition to slash burning stems from the view that too much timber is being harvested and that restrictions on burning are one means of reducing harvest levels. Some people feel that the impacts of prescribed burning on air quality, water quality, and visibility, as well as the waste of resources from burning logging residues, outweigh the benefits of reduced wildfire hazard, more rapid reforestation, and increased productivity. Numerous studies have shown that, for a variety of reasons, many people place a high value on environmental quality.

For a significant change in public acceptance of the use of prescribed burning in commercially managed forests to occur, the public must be convinced that the benefits from burning are large relative to any perceived environmental degradation. Experience from the response to changes in fire policy in wildlands indicates that public accept-

ance of prescribed burning for forest management requires:

- A strong consensus among forest managers and most other concerned groups about the correct use and beneficial effects of prescribed burning.
- A long-term effort to determine the existing level of knowledge and educate the public about effects and benefits of which they are unaware.
- Public perception that educational information is scientifically sound and not coming from a group with a vested interest.
- Adequate treatment of specific public concerns related to the use of prescribed burning. Some of the specific concerns that must be addressed are: effects on public health, especially smoke intrusion into populated areas and problems from burning chemically treated sites; ecological damage; aesthetic impacts, especially visibility impairment; and the risk of prescribed fires getting out of control.

Public attitudes toward prescribed burning of commercially managed forests will probably remain divided until the public in general, and environmental and recreation groups in particular, are convinced that it is necessary and beneficial and specific concerns about the use of fire are adequately addressed.

Public interest in fire and fire management is here to stay. The need for public support of fire policies will become even more important as recreation use and interest in resource management continue to increase. Resource managers will thus have to work with public opinion; the important question is whether they will do so from a defensive position, or whether they will help create a well-educated public that can have a positive role in shaping resource policy.

Managers must work to avoid the types of catastrophic fires that galvanize public opinion and may take policy formation out of the arena of rational decision making. But such events often uncover issues that have been smoldering without proper resolution, and it is here that managers and researchers can join forces to constructively work with public opinion on an ongoing basis. We offer the following suggestions on areas in which research about public attitudes and perceptions could be helpful to resource managers in the Northwest.

Most of the work reported here has been done in the Southwest or Rocky Mountain states. Although there is no need to replicate all of it, it makes sense to consider gathering similar information with specific application to concerns unique to the Pacific Northwest. For example, there may be important differences in public attitudes about field burning (which is unique to the Pacific Northwest) and prescribed burning in forests. It would be helpful to sort out public perceptions related to these two management programs, perhaps utilizing the approaches developed in other regions.

The work reviewed here identifies public concerns about air and water quality, public health, ecological conditions, and nearby resources with commercial or aesthetic value. It would be helpful to use survey work to analyze generalized public concern about prescribed burning into these specific components, thereby targeting areas in which informational and educational efforts might best be spent.

There is a considerable body of work in political science and social psychology related to public opinion, interest groups, attitudes, and attitude change. These theoretical perspectives could be applied to provide greater leverage in understanding attitudes toward prescribed burning. Such efforts might help differentiate deeply held values, which are probably resistant to change, from more specific beliefs, which are perhaps more amenable to change in response to information. There are also opportunities here to use experimental work to see which types of educational approaches might be most successful for particular problem areas.

Taken together, these areas offer numerous opportunities for research which could help managers do a better job of understanding public opinion and working to create enlightened public interest groups which can become effective allies to the policy-making process.

Literature Cited & Key References

*Baas, J.M., G.E. Haas, D.M. Ross, and R.J. Loomis. 1985. A pilot study of visitor knowledge and support for prescribed burning at Grand Canyon National Park, p. 310-314. *In* Proc., Symp. and Workshop on Wilderness Fire. USDA For. Serv., Intermt. For. Rge. Exp. Sta., Ogden, UT. Gen. Tech. Rep. INT-182. 434 p.

Benson, R.E. 1974. Lodgepole pine logging residues: Management alternatives. USDA For. Serv., Intermt. For. Rge. Exp. Sta., Ogden, UT. Res. Pap. INT-160. 28 p.

Blank, F., D. Brookshire, T. Crocker, R. d'Arge, R. Horst, and R. Rowe. 1978. Valuation of aesthetic preferences: A case study of the economic value of visibility. Final Res. Rep. to Electric Power Res. Inst., Resour. and Environ. Econ. Lab., Univ. Wyoming, Laramie, WY.

Brookshire, D.S., B.C. Ives, and W.D. Schulze. 1976. The valuation of aesthetic preferences. J. Environ. Econ. Manage. 11:325-346.

Brookshire, D., R. d'Arge, W. Schulze, and M. Thayer. 1979. Methods development for assessing air pollution control benefits. Vol. 2: Experiments in valuing nonmarket goods. A case study of alternative benefit measures of air pollution control in the South Coast Air Basin of Southern California. U.S. Environ. Prot. Agency, Washington, DC. EPA-600/6-79-0016.

Cortner, H.J., M.J. Zwolinski, E.H. Carpenter, and J.G. Taylor. 1984. Public support for fire-management policies. J. For. 82:359-361.

Crocker, T.D. 1986. Economic benefits of visibility in Oregon's urban and wilderness areas. Rep. to Oregon Dep. Environ. Qual., Air Qual. Div., Portland, OR. 47 p.

Daniel, T.C., and R.S. Boster. 1976. Measuring landscape esthetics: The scenic beauty estimation method. USDA For. Serv., Rocky Mt. For. Rge. Exp. Sta., Fort Collins, CO. Res. Pap. RM-167. 66 p.

Folkman, W.S. 1979. Urban users of wildland areas as forest fire risk. USDA For. Serv., Pac. Southwest For. Rge. Exp. Sta., Berkeley, CA. Res. Pap. PSW-137. 23 p.

*Gardner, P.D., H.J. Cortner, K.F. Widaman, and K.J. Stenberg. 1985. Forest-user attitudes toward alternative fire-management policies. Environ. Manage. 9:303-313.

Hendee, J.C., W.R. Catton, Jr., L.D. Marlow and C.F. Brockman. 1968. Wilderness users in the Pacific Northwest: Their characteristics, values and management preferences. USDA For. Serv., Pac. Northwest For. Rge. Exp. Sta., Portland, OR. Res. Pap. PNW-61. 92 p.

References marked by an asterisk are recommended for general information.

*McCool, S.F., and G.H. Stankey. 1986. Visitor attitudes toward wilderness fire management policy—1971-1984. USDA For. Serv., Intermt. For. Rge. Exp. Sta., Ogden, UT. Res. Pap. INT-357. 7 p.

*Omi, P.N., and R.D. Laven. 1982. Prescribed fire impacts on recreational wildlands: A status review and assessment of research need. Colorado State Univ. and USDA For. Serv., Rocky Mt. For. Rge. Exp. Sta., Eisenhower Consortium Bull. 11. 18 p.

*Oregon Department of Environmental Quality. 1986. Summary of public hearing testimony on proposed Visibility Protection and Smoke Management Plan. Agenda Item No. E., Oct. 24, 1986, Environ. Qual. Comm. Meeting, Oregon Dep. Environ. Qual., Air Qual. Div., Portland, OR.

Randall, A., B. Ives, and C. Eastman. 1975. Benefits of abating aesthetic environmental damage from the Four Corners power plant, Fruitland, New Mexico. Agric. Exp. Sta., New Mexico State Univ., Las Cruces, NM. Bull. 618.

Rauw, D.M. 1980. Interpreting the natural role of fire: Implications for fire management policy. Fire For. Meterol. Conf. Proc. 6:228-233.

Rowe, R.D., D.S. Brookshire, and R.C. d'Arge. 1980. An experiment on the economic value of visibility. J. Environ. Econ. Manage. 7:1-19.

Rowe, R.D., and L.D. Chestnut. 1983. Managing Air Quality and Scenic Resources at National Parks and Wilderness Areas. Westview Press, Boulder, CO. 314 p.

Schulze, W.D., R.C. d'Arge, and D.S. Brookshire. 1981. Valuing environmental commodities: Some recent experiments. J. Environ. Econ. Manage. 57:151-172.

Stankey, G.H. 1976. Wilderness fire policy: An investigation of visitor knowledge and beliefs. USDA For. Serv., Intermt. For. Rge. Exp. Sta., Ogden, UT. Res. Pap. INT-180. 17 p.

Taylor, J.G., and T.C. Daniel. 1985. Perceived scenic and recreational quality of forest burn areas, p. 398-406. *In* Proc., Symp. and Workshop on Wilderness Fire. USDA For. Serv., Intermt. For. Rge. Exp. Sta., Ogden, UT. Gen. Tech. Rep. INT-182. 434 p.

*Taylor, J.G., H.J. Cortner, P.D. Gardner, T.C. Daniel, M.J. Zwolinski, and E.H. Carpenter. 1986. Recreation and fire management: Public concerns, attitudes, and perceptions. Leisure Sci. 8:167-187.

Wagar, J.A. 1974. Recreational and esthetic considerations, p. H-1 to H-15. *In* Environmental effects of forest residues management in the Pacific Northwest: A state-of-knowledge compendium. USDA For. Serv., Pac. Northwest For. Rge. Exp. Sta., Portland, OR. Gen. Tech. Rep. PNW-24.

Zwolinski, M.J., H.J. Cortner, E.H. Carpenter, and J.G. Taylor. 1983. Public support for fire management policies in recreation land management. Final Report to the Eisenhower Consortium, Rocky Mt. For. Exp. Sta., Fort Collins, CO. 160 p. Res. Rep. to Electric Power Res. Inst., Resour. and Environ. Econ. Lab., Univ. Wyoming, Laramie, WY.

20 Regulation of Prescribed Fire

James N. Craig

Executive Summary

Federal and state laws and regulations influence the users of prescribed fire in California, Oregon, and Washington. The regulatory structure attempts to deal with public concerns about air quality, protection from wildfire, liability for damages, and potential effects on other resources. Requirements for federal land managers differ from those for nonfederal entities. Permits are required for most open burning in the region. Oregon, Washington, and the federal agencies require prescribed burning plans for most projects. The regulatory structure dealing with prescribed fire in each of these states is usually developed and administered cooperatively. Increasing public concern about the effects of prescribed fire, especially of logging slash, is expected to lead to increasingly sophisticated rules.

Introduction

Federal, state, and local legislation, regulations, and rules influence the use of prescribed fire. Public land managers must operate within the mandate of the legal authorizations and limitations that apply to their agency. Both public and private wildland managers are expected to comply with applicable laws and regulations.

Regulatory requirements are normally designed to protect the public health and welfare from potentially adverse effects of prescribed fire. Health concerns in the Pacific Northwest primarily involve exposure of people to smoke (Chapter 16). Inhalation of both fine particulates and toxic combustion products from herbicides and pesticides are frequently mentioned. Secondary concerns involve traffic safety and the potential for direct injury by fire. Potential adverse effects on public welfare include impairment of visibility by smoke, potential damage to the property of others, and potential adverse effects that can occur on- or off-site if an area is too severely burned.

Legislation is usually a response to public demands or court actions; it most often deals with policies, desired objectives, and planning requirements. Statutes directed at public health, welfare (including visibility), and economic liability objectives can affect the use of prescribed fire. Legislation has also created the regulatory agencies and authorized their activities.

Regulations most often deal with burning plans, permit requirements, air resource protection, and liability for damages. Specific requirements and standards in these areas provide a basis for site-specific agreements between regulatory agencies and prescribed fire users. Figure 20-1 diagrammatically displays the regulatory process.

Cooperation between regulatory agencies is a key element in meeting public objectives. Private organizations or individuals are also frequently involved in cooperative efforts. Cooperation or coordination may be a legal requirement, or it may simply be the expedient way to do a job. Cooperation is particularly appropriate in the use of prescribed fire, because neither escaped fires nor smoke are limited in their spread by property boundaries or land management jurisdiction.

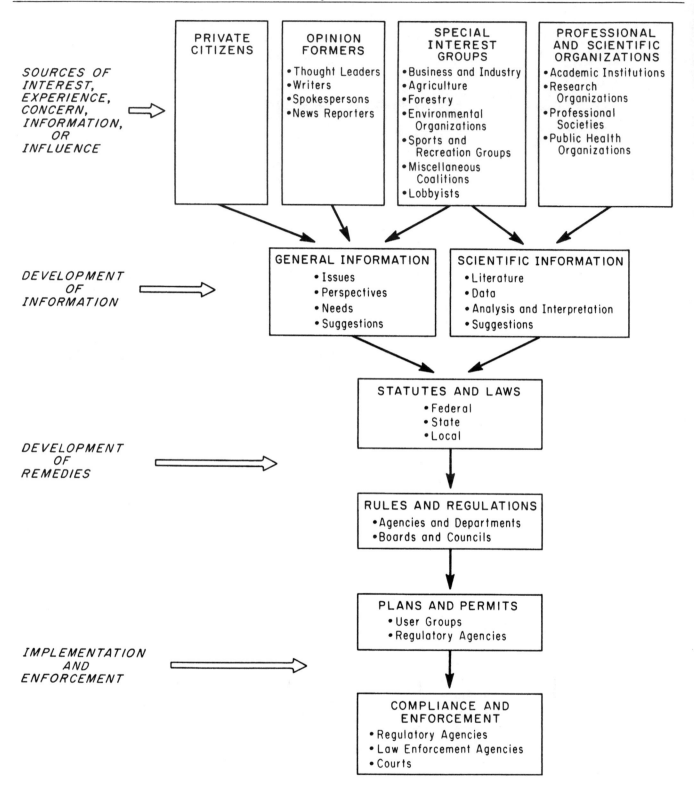

Figure 20-1. Process for initiation, development, implementation, and enforcement of regulations concerning prescribed burning.

Broad Planning Statutes

Federal land management agencies are required to use systematic, interdisciplinary approaches to all planning. The National Environmental Policy Act (NEPA) is the broadest statute, because it applies to all agencies of the federal government. States may also have statutes similar in intent to NEPA. California and Washington are examples. National Forest planning is guided by the National Forest Management Act (NFMA). Planning for public lands managed by the Bureau of Land Management is guided by the Federal Land Policy and Management Act (FLPMA). State and private land managers are not required to meet these provisions (Table 20-1).

The federal statutes (FLPMA and NFMA) that require the Bureau of Land Management and the USDA Forest Service to prepare land-use plans include requirements for consistency:

> Land use plans of the Secretary under this section shall be consistent with state and local plans to the maximum extent he finds consistent with federal law and the purposes of this Act [43 United States Code (U.S.C.) 1711].
> The Secretary of Agriculture shall develop, maintain and, as appropriate, revise land and resource management plans for units of the National Forest System, coordinated with the land and resource management planning processes of state and local governments and other federal agencies (16 U.S.C. 1604).

These unit or forest plans may prescribe or exclude the use of fire in some areas. Frequently, specific purposes for which prescribed fire may or may not be used are described. Normally, these land management plans provide the objectives, and sometimes additional information, for preparation of burning plans.

Air Resource Protection

The Clean Air Act of 1963, as amended (42 U.S.C. 7401 et. seq.), provides the federal statutory basis for air resource protection. The Environmental Protection Agency (EPA) has issued implementing regulations [40 CFR 1-87 (Code of Federal Regulations)]. One of the key provisions of the Act is the establishment of ambient air quality standards and the requirement that the states develop and obtain EPA approval for State Implementation Plans (SIP) to meet or exceed national standards. These plans set air quality standards and establish the means by which the states will maintain or improve air quality (Yoho et al. 1980). Disapproval of a SIP, in whole or in part, by the EPA may result in the substitution of federal regulations.

Pioneers in the field, Oregon and Washington developed smoke management plans to deal with ambient air quality concerns about prescribed fire in 1969. These were cooperatively developed plans involving state, local, and federal agencies

Table 20-1. Planning statutes and regulations impose unique requirements on activities of various land management organizations.

Statutes & Rules	Organizations Affected	Requirements	Lands Affected
NEPA	All federal agencies	Environmental Analysis or Environmental Impact Statement	Any on which a federal action affecting the environment occurs
NFMA	USDA Forest Service	Forest land & resource plan	National Forests
FLPMA	USDI Bureau of Land Management	Land use plan	Federal public lands
State Environmental Policy Acts	State agencies	Environmental Analysis	Nonfederal land on which a state action affecting the environment occurs
State Forest Practices Rules	State agencies	Hazard reduction, burning permits	Nonfederal forest land
State Air Quality Implementation Plans, Smoke Management Plans	All land managers	Smoke management instructions	All forest lands

and industry representatives (Ayer and Kirkpatrick 1970, Williams 1984). The plans were originally voluntary agreements, but they were soon incorporated into state statutes and administrative rules. In Oregon this was required by the Oregon Forest Practices Act, passed in 1971 (Patterson 1976). The early plans focused on total suspended particulates in heavily populated areas, but protection was soon extended to other, "smoke sensitive," areas (Hoover 1983). Chapter 16 discusses the effects of prescribed fire on air quality.

The 1977 amendments to the Clean Air Act require, among other things, protection of air quality related values (AQRV) in Class I areas. AQRVs may include visibility, odor, flora, fauna, water, soil, climate, geological features, and cultural resources. Mandatory Class I areas are defined in the Act as all international parks, national wilderness areas, and memorial parks which exceed 5,000 acres, and national parks which exceed 6,000 acres and which were in existence on the date of enactment of the 1977 amendments. Processes by which the states and Indian tribes can designate additional Class I areas are also established in the Act.

Oregon and Washington have completed visibility amendments to the SIPs and have revised their smoke management plans to protect visibility in the Class I areas. Both plans have been approved by the EPA. Although specific rules differ, both smoke management plans are meteorologically based systems designed to prevent smoke intrusions into areas of concern (Ayer and Kirkpatrick 1970, Williams 1984). Forestry prescribed burning elements of both plans are administered by the respective state forestry agency. Planned burning is screened daily, and instructions are issued identifying the number of tons of fuel that can be burned by location or area. The Washington plan applies statewide. The Oregon plan covers western Oregon and the area around Bend in eastern Oregon.

California uses a more decentralized approach. The State Air Resource Board issues daily notices as to whether the following day is a burn day or a no-burn day for each district or airshed. Sometimes the notice is delayed until the following morning. The notices are based on meteorological criteria. County or Air Quality Management District plans are then the basis for issuing permits.

On July 1, 1987, EPA issued regulations setting standards for fine particulate matter 10 microns and smaller in diameter (40 CFR 50-53 and 58). The states are directed to develop plans to meet the standard. These regulations may affect burning plans since fine particulates are abundant in smoke from prescribed fire (Chapter 16).

Review and revision of regulations and administrative rules to protect air quality and AQRVs is a continuous process. EPA requires each SIP visibility protection plan to be reviewed and updated every third year. Oregon has begun the review of existing wilderness areas which are not mandatory Class I areas. A recommendation as to redesignation as Class I areas is expected in conjunction with the 1989 review of the visibility amendment to the SIP. EPA also proposes to develop regulations setting standards for finer particulate matter, perhaps 2.5 microns and smaller.

Burning Plans

Burning plans, also called prescribed fire plans, are documents that describe how the work on the treatment area is to be completed. Their purpose is to ensure consideration and protection for all forest land values. The most detailed plans describe the unit to be treated, the objectives to be achieved, pre- and postburn monitoring requirements, fuel and weather conditions needed to meet objectives, funding sources and limitations, burning and containment procedures, personnel and equipment for all phases of the operation, coordination and public involvement needs, consideration for air quality and visibility, contingency plans if the weather changes or the fire escapes, and an assessment of the risk of escape and the consequent damage. Some of these elements are required by all forest fire protection agencies in the Pacific Northwest, but most are not. The amount of information required also depends on the size, complexity, and risk of the project (Chapter 5).

Except in California, burning plans are required for nearly all prescribed burning on forest lands in the Pacific Northwest. Federal agency requirements are contained in agency policy and procedural guides. State requirements are in administrative rules. In Oregon, plans are required for all prescribed burning on forest land during the closed fire season (T. Lorensen, Office of State Forester, Oregon, personal correspondence, 1987). In Washington, plans are required for all burns in excess of 100 tons of fuel. In California, minimum legal requirements for equipment, relative humidity, or other applicable items are included in permits for forestry burning. Federal land managers are required to meet or exceed state requirements.

Permit Requirements

Fire protection agencies need to know when, where, and how open burning is being done within areas they protect. The state forestry agencies of the Pacific Northwest states have statutory authority to require that burning permits be obtained for all open burning on nonfederal lands for which they have fire protection responsibilities (Mobley 1976). Permitting agencies differ in the way this authority is exercised. Anyone contemplating the use of prescribed fire should contact the local wildland fire protection agency well in advance of the date planned for ignition to obtain permit rules.

Federal agency managers are not required to obtain state burning permits for operations on federal land. The Clean Air Act (CAA), however, requires compliance with state and local requirements:

> Each department, agency, and instrumentality of executive, legislative, and judicial branches of the Federal Government (1) having jurisdiction over any property or facility, or (2) engaging in any activity resulting, or which may result, in the discharge of air pollutants, and each officer, agent, or employee thereof, shall be subject to, and comply with, all Federal, State, interstate, and local requirements, administrative authority, and process and sanctions respecting the control and abatement of air pollution in the same manner and to the same extent as any nongovernmental entity (42 U.S.C. 7418).

To improve control over smoke emissions, Oregon and Washington do sometimes approve specific burns on federal lands for air resource protection even though state burning permits have not been issued to the federal land managers. Washington regulates specific burns, with emphasis on protection of air quality and visibility during summer weekends. Oregon regulates by broad land areas, with emphasis on protection during July and August.

The California Air Resources Board requires permits for open burning in order to control air pollution. The USDA Forest Service and the California Department of Forestry are designated by the Board as having authority to issue permits within their respective areas of jurisdiction. In addition, permits may be issued by counties or by an Air Quality Management District. The Northern Sierra Air Quality Management District recently set a national precedent by establishing a schedule of fees for burning in order to finance regulatory operations. In some cases, permits must be obtained from two agencies. Furthermore, private parties burning for improvement of wildlife or game habitat must obtain a certified written statement from the California Department of Fish and Game. Annual operating permits may also be required in California.

Liability

Variation in state laws precludes anything other than a very general statement on liability in this chapter. The general rule is that a person who ignites a fire, even if for lawful reasons, may be held liable if negligent in igniting or controlling the fire. Liability for nonnegligent fires varies depending on the circumstances. Such factors as location, size of the area, and ownership may influence the extent of liability. Failure to abate a hazard as defined by state law can also create liability. When prescribed fire is chosen for hazard abatement, the landowner has the risk of liability for an escaped fire even though the fire may have been set to avoid the liability for maintaining a hazard.

The United States is generally liable for tort claims in the same manner and to the same extent as a private individual under like circumstances.

Liability is more likely when there is no burning plan; there is an inadequate burning plan; or the burning plan is not followed.

Other Legal Requirements

Legal requirements not directly related to prescribed burning or air quality also influence the way federal land managers use prescribed fire. Examples not discussed in this chapter are (Anon. 1983):

- Organic Administration Act (16 U.S.C. 551). Activities to protect the National Forests from destruction by fire are authorized.
- National Parks and Recreation Act (16 U.S.C. 1). Activities to protect the National Parks from fire are authorized.

- Wilderness Act (16 U.S.C. 1131-36). Direction to maintain natural ecological systems is interpreted to mean that fire should play its natural role in wilderness.
- National Trails System Act (16 U.S.C. 1241-49). Maintenance and protection standards for the system sometimes affect the use or suppression of fire.
- Wild and Scenic Rivers Act (16 U.S.C. 1271-85a). More restrictions are placed on riparian management than on general forest zones, affecting both wildfire and prescribed fire.
- Wild Horses and Burros Protection Act (16 U.S.C. 1331-40). Protection and management of wild horses and their habitat sometimes requires modified fire management.
- National Historic Preservation Act (16 U.S.C. 470). The potential for damage to sites listed or potentially eligible for listing in the National Register must be considered in fire management decision making.
- American Indian Religious Freedom Act (42 U.S.C. 1996). The potential for impacts on American Indian religious practices must be considered by federal land managers using prescribed fire.
- Endangered Species Act (16 U.S.C. 1531-40). Federal agencies are required to ensure that no agency action adversely affects the habitat of an endangered or threatened species.
- Clean Water Act (33 U.S.C. 1288). The use of prescribed fire is affected by the requirement that best management practices be applied to protect water quality.

The states often have similar laws with which public agencies or private persons must be able to demonstrate compliance.

Coordination

Frequently, various categories of landownership (tribal, federal, state, and private) are intermingled or adjoin each other for considerable distances. Together with the fact that escaped fires may cross property boundaries and smoke may disperse widely, this makes coordination between all parties involved with use of prescribed fire important. Coordination and cooperation take many forms in the Pacific Northwest.

Coordination of federal resource management planning has been discussed. Where different landownerships are intermingled, fire management plans and burning plans may be jointly prepared and approved. Fire protection agencies frequently trade protection responsibilities in the interest of efficiency. When this has been done, the agency which has jurisdiction nearly always retains responsibility for the use of prescribed fire and the issuance of burning permits. The states frequently use their authority to appoint others in addition to full-time employees to issue and administer burning permits. Federal employees are sometimes appointed to do this in California. Because of concerns about liability, this is not now being done in Oregon or Washington.

Reference was made to cooperation in smoke management planning in the section covering air resource protection. There are additional cooperative efforts in this field. The Washington smoke management plan establishes several cooperative committees to monitor, guide, and implement the plan. Visibility and smoke management monitoring are cooperative efforts throughout the region. The strong role of counties and Air Quality Management Districts in California adds a level of complexity that is lacking in smoke management in the other states. Numerous research and development efforts have multiple support.

Conclusion

A complex web of legislation and regulation influences the use of prescribed fire in the Pacific Northwest. Oregon and Washington are among the national leaders in development of smoke management plans. In the area of visibility protection, as in several other air quality areas, the region is a model for other states and for EPA.

More sophisticated regulations affecting use of prescribed fire are expected. Concern about public health impacts is increasing the number of people and organizations that wish to influence the regulatory process. Public concern about logging on public lands and about fire risk in the urban/wildland interface areas may also lead to rule changes.

Regulatory requirements are sometimes cited as a cause for increased costs of prescribed burning. Practitioners, however, realize that mitigation of effects on long-term site productivity, riparian area protection, wildlife habitat maintenance, and other forest values would have contributed to increased costs whether or not the need for them had been expressed in the form of statutes and regulations. The challenge is to find positive ways to deal with all of these concerns.

Literature Cited & Key References

*Anon. 1983. The Principal Laws Relating to Forest Service Activities. USDA For. Serv., Washington, D.C. Agr. Hbk. 453. 591 p.

Ayer, H., and R. Kirkpatrick. 1970. Where there is smoke. ESSA, Rockville 5(4):16-19.

*Ferry, G. et al. 1985. Prescribed fire smoke management guide. Nat. Wildfire Coord. Group, Boise, ID. NFES 1279.

Fox, D.G., J.C. Bernabo, and B. Hood. 1987. Guidelines for measuring the physical, chemical, and biological condition of wilderness ecosystems. USDA For. Serv., Rocky Mt. For. Rge. Exp. Sta., Fort Collins, CO. Gen. Tech. Rep. RM-146. 48 p.

Hoover, K. 1983. The amended Washington State Smoke Management Plan. Unpublished speech. Washington State Forestry Conference. November 4, 1983. 3 p.

*Hoover, K. 1989. Working with the rules and regulations governing slash burning in Washington State, p. 171-220. *In* Hanley, D.P., J.J. Kammenga, and C.D. Oliver (eds.) Proc., The Burning Decision: Regional Perspectives on Slash. Coll. For. Resour., Univ. Washington, Seattle, WA. Inst. For. Resour. Contrib. No. 66. 374 p.

Mobley, H.E. 1974. Air pollution regulations and their effect on forest management, p. 29-38. *In* Proc., Control Technology for Agricultural Air Pollutants. Air Pollution Control Assoc., Pittsburgh, PA.

*Mobley, H.E. 1976. Summary of state regulations as they affect open burning, p. 206-212. *In* Air Quality and Smoke from Urban and Forest Fires Proc., Internat. Symp., Fort Collins, CO. Nat. Acad. Sci., Nat. Res. Counc., Washington, DC.

*Patterson, H.M. 1976. Laws, standards, and regulations for smoke abatement in Oregon, p. 183-197. *In* Air Quality and Smoke from Urban and Forest Fires. Proc., Internat. Symp., Fort Collins, CO. Nat. Acad. Sciences, Nat. Res. Counc., Washington, DC.

*Robinson, F. 1989. Rules and regulations governing slash burning in Oregon, p. 135-150. *In* Hanley, D.P., J.J. Kammenga, and C.D. Oliver (eds.) Proc., The Burning Decision: Regional Perspectives on Slash. Coll. For. Resour., Univ. Washington, Seattle, WA. Inst. For. Resour. Contrib. No. 66. 374 p.

Williams, B. 1984. Smoke management improvements in Washington since 1972 and SIP. Unpub. presentation to Pac. Northwest Internat. Sec., Air Pollution Control Assoc., Nov. 1984. 6 p.

Yoho, N.S., N.R. Paulson, D.B. Botts, R.O. Cornelius, J.N. Graff, H.K. Mikell, S.R. Miller, J.M. Pierovich, J.H. Richardson, and R.D. Day, Jr. 1980. Wildland fires, air quality, and smoke management. J. For. 78:688-697.

References marked by an asterisk are recommended for general information.

VIII Integration

21 Economic Analysis of Prescribed Burning

David A. Cleaves and J. Douglas Brodie

Executive Summary

Prescribed burning in its various forms offers an array of benefits, costs, and risks. Economic analysis provides a structured approach for converting these elements to dollar terms and evaluating them in a common time frame, i.e., discounting them to the present. Burning can be compared with nonburning options in achieving financial return. Alternative strategies for applying the prescribed burning program can also be compared either at the stand level or across the aggregations of stands at the ownership level.

Some of the benefits amenable to economic analysis include hazard reduction, regeneration effectiveness, reforestation efficiency, animal damage reduction, and overall growth and yield enhancement. However, economic results are limited by the state of knowledge about biological and physical relationships and by the validity of human judgments used in constructing the analyses. Research is needed to further quantify these effects and to evaluate operational practices if we are to improve the ability of economic analyses to guide prescribed burning decisions.

Two elements are especially critical to economic results because they occur early in the analysis time stream: burning costs and the probabilities of accidental prescribed fire damage (either to the stand being treated or to adjacent stands). High costs associated with either of these can strongly decrease the value of prescribed burning. If we can better understand how these elements influence economic feasibility, we can make wiser prescribed burning decisions.

Economic analysis is no panacea. The analytical requirement of converting benefits and costs to dollar values may leave out important preferences not determined in the market place. Human preferences for such intangibles as clean air or freedom from risk might be better handled with other analytical techniques. Finally, the act of discounting, by definition, places more importance on today's than tomorrow's costs and benefits. This may be unacceptable in some decision situations and organizational contexts.

Much work remains to be done in fine-tuning economic analysis methods for prescribed burning. Unsolved methodological issues include: how to allocate costs based on the interactive benefits of burning; how to determine premiums for insuring against losses caused by prescribed fire escapes that may be substantial but rarely occur; and how to evaluate the impact of regulatory constraints and multiple-use objectives. Decision analysis, a collection of techniques to formally integrate economics and professional judgment, can provide a way to focus on important uncertainties and describe the decision process. The result is a clear definition of costs, benefits, and risks, thereby leading to decisions that more efficiently use the information that is available.

Introduction

Decisions about prescribed burning are many and varied. When to burn, how to burn, what objectives to pursue, and what resources to use are four important categories of decisions commonly faced by the forest and fire manager. A more central question may be whether to burn at all. Might there be an alternative practice that delivers more of the attributes desired and fewer of the risks feared by the manager and the public? Answering these questions requires consideration of biological, social, and economic factors. The economic dimension is best handled with an analysis that incorporates a fair assessment of the dollar values of the benefits and the costs of all alternatives. A complete analysis will attempt to evaluate the effects of the practice not only at the level of the individual forest stand but also on the resource values and flows of goods and services from the collection of stands as a forest unit (cf. Brodie et al. 1987).

Economic analysis takes different forms and includes different components, depending on the purpose it is intended to serve. Nonetheless, every analysis should employ generally accepted techniques and principles. Where some kind of benefit has been established beforehand as a target objective, the analysis can identify the least costly alternatives. Most analyses, however, use criteria that compare the financial benefits from a practice or sequence of practices with its costs. Because these benefits and costs are distributed through time, meaningful comparison requires that they all be discounted to a common point in time, usually the present. Hence, the "present value" of the benefits can be compared to the "present value" of the costs. This is most commonly calculated in the form of the present value of net benefits, known as present net value (PNV) or present net worth (PNW). Essentially, it represents the difference between benefits and costs, with the effect of discount rates factored in. In equation form, PNW (or PNV) can be expressed as:

$$PNW = \sum_{t=1}^{n} \frac{B_t}{(1+r)^t} - \sum_{t=1}^{n} \frac{C_t}{(1+r)^t} \quad (1)$$

Where:
Σ = mathematical symbol for a summation; in this case the sum of the benefits minus the sum of the costs for a time period running from year 1 to year n.
B_t = benefits received in year t
C_t = costs incurred in year t
r = chosen discount rate
t = time in years; t = 1 means beginning at year 1
n = the time horizon (years) of the investments or returns

No practice that results in PNW less than zero is acceptable. Of two or more available options, each having PNW of zero or greater, the one with the largest PNW is usually preferred. Validity of the comparison between two or more options requires that the time horizon of the investments and returns be made comparable; hence the importance of including the discount rate and time factors in the analysis.

Alternatively, the analysis can be done using the benefit-cost ratio (B/C) or the internal rate of return (IRR):

$$B/C = \sum_{t=1}^{n} \frac{B_t}{(1+r)^t} \Big/ \sum_{t=1}^{n} \frac{C_t}{(1+r)^t} \quad (2)$$

$$IRR = r, \text{ where } \sum_{t=1}^{n} \frac{B_t}{(1+r)^t} = \sum_{t=1}^{n} \frac{C_t}{(1+r)^t} \quad (3)$$

The internal rate of return is the rate of discount which makes the present value of the benefits exactly equal to the present value of the costs. In other words, it is the rate of discount which makes the present value of benefits and costs exactly equal to zero (Mishan 1976). Compared with

PNW, B/C and IRR will maximize the return per dollar spent but will not necessarily maximize the return to the total land investment. Some practices that require little investment may yield high return per dollar. The return per acre, however, may be relatively low compared to that from an alternative practice.

The discount rate (r) used in Equations 1, 2, and 3 represents the "opportunity cost" of funds relevant to the decision-making entity; that is, what the funds to be expended could earn in alternative investments. For forest products firms, this might be the real or net-of-inflation rate of interest they could earn from buying bonds with maturities equal to stand rotations. For public land management agencies, the appropriate discount rate might be the real cost of public debt. Because future inflation rates are so difficult to predict, "real" or net-of-inflation values are normally used in the measurement of benefits and costs. Generally, a real rate of interest should be used for the discount rate.

Prescribed burning and other treatments may change the optimal rotation length and the desirability of subsequent regeneration and other silvicultural treatments. It is conventional in forestry to use the PNW of an infinite series of rotations, known as the soil expectation value (SEV), when comparing silvicultural regimes of different lengths. The economic objective of forest managers should be to choose the regime that maximizes the value of the site in producing future crops. Generally this comparison is made at year 0 and is often referred to as "bare land analysis." The optimal treatment for a stand already established may differ from what should be done at the bare ground stage.

The question now arises as to what should be included in the benefits (B_t) and the costs (C_t). This is a difficult judgment because prescribed fire is typically employed to produce a number of kinds of benefits on each unit burned. These benefits are often so interrelated that it is difficult to separate them out for the purpose of assigning values. Another complexity is the uncertainty about when in the future these benefits might accrue. Customarily, the benefits are the market values of the additional products expected to result from the practice. The costs are the labor, materials, equipment, and overhead used in the practice. A broader definition of benefits could include increases in the level of output of products, services, and environmental amenities. Any increases in risks to public health and safety could be viewed as costs. These more broadly defined benefits and costs are very difficult to measure and more subject to biases in subjective estimation and conflicting stakeholder values. For these reasons, they are omitted in many analyses.

Benefits of Prescribed Burning

Many uses of prescribed burning have been described in earlier chapters, each of which presupposes benefits. Benefits that may be amenable to an economic evaluation include:
- reduction in wildfire hazard in the future;
- improvement in regeneration effectiveness;
- improvement in the efficiency of conducting regeneration activities;
- control of competing vegetation; and
- wildlife habitat and range improvement.

Hazard reduction

The economic benefit from wildfire hazard reduction can be measured in savings in future suppression costs and decreased resource losses either in the stand to be prescribed burned or in adjacent stands. The difference between the future cost-plus-loss in stands or forests without prescribed burning and the cost-plus-loss in the same stands or forests with prescribed burning is the expected savings, or benefit, attributed to the prescribed burning program. This difference should then be compared with the difference in present costs of implementing the burn and no burn treatments.

Prescribed fire changes the fuel type and reduces fuel volumes. This fuel modification may lower wildfire impacts by moderating the fire behavior of wildfires that do occur and by making control efforts easier and less expensive. These modifications apply to logging slash as well as natural fuels. Because of the overriding influence of uncertain factors such as weather and ignition sources and the great variation in burning sites, accurate estimates of wildfire hazard reduction due to fuel modification are difficult to obtain. A few agencies have developed such estimates (Chapter 8). In other words, it is not always certain that an economic gain can be registered solely from the hazard reduction effects of prescribed burning. It is even possible that the conversion from heavy slash to light, flashy fuels could actually increase vulnerability to fire in the prescribed burned stand.

Suppression costs can be estimated for the with- and without-prescribed burning cases. These estimates are based on an assumed response of people and equipment to wildfires in the two differently treated stands over a chosen period into the future. These costs are estimated under an assumed level of availability for fire fighting resources over the time in which the hazard reduction effect will last. Region 6 of the USDA Forest Service has implemented an analysis and planning process, the Fuel Analysis Process (FAP) that uses this approach (Snell 1986).

Losses other than suppression costs include damage to timber and other resources. Resource losses are measured by the difference between the PNW of the stand without prescribed burning and the PNW with prescribed burning. This analysis may be extended to adjacent stands since prescribed burning may influence future fire behavior there. Potential timber losses depend on the age and condition of the trees at the time of the wildfire and on assumptions made by the analyst about rehabilitation costs, replacement costs, salvage values, and recovery potential. Nontimber losses such as siltation and predisposition to floods, recreational impairment, and structural damage may also become important parts of the analysis.

The potential wildfire may actually have beneficial effects, or negative costs. Examples of wildfire-induced benefits include improvements in forage production and palatability and in habitat for certain wildlife species. The greater the possible benefit from wildfire, all else being equal, the lower is the net loss from wildfire and the less valuable is the prescribed burning program or project in reducing wildfire.

Hazard reduction benefits should be confined to the reduction in potential loss values that occurs as one fuel type is changed to another via prescribed burning. Hazard reduction is one of several economic effects that are combined to produce the net benefit. Separation of hazard reduction from the other benefits is difficult. Several previous economic studies (Wood 1978, Radloff 1984) have shown positive but not overwhelming hazard reduction benefits. Recently, National Forests in the Pacific Northwest have developed estimates of cost-plus-loss (i.e., wildfire suppression costs plus the loss in value of timber consumed) in different fuel profiles (combinations of fuel depths and weight) which are useful in isolating the hazard reduction effect. Changing the fuel from one type (at e.g., $700 per acre cost-plus-loss) to another type (at $500 per acre) using prescribed burning would constitute a benefit (or potential loss reduction) of $200 per acre. For example, underburning in natural fuels in ponderosa pine type was estimated to reduce wildfire acreage burned by 86 percent and loss per acre by $519 (personal communication from T. Tyree, USDA Forest Service, Fremont National Forest, Lakeview, Oregon, 1987).

Regeneration effectiveness

Prescribed burning can enhance seedling establishment and improve early growth. Improving uniformity in seedling distribution is another benefit noted by forest managers but it is more difficult to measure in economic terms. Regeneration improvements can be carried forward in the analysis time frame in the form of additional volumes available for commercial thinning and final harvest, or in the opportunity to harvest on shorter rotations. These incremental yields or differences in rotation lengths are then discounted as explained earlier.

Another aspect of increasing regeneration effectiveness and efficiency is in controlling damaging animal populations, especially mountain beavers and pocket gophers (Chapter 9). Less damage can result in improved seedling survival and reduce the need for replanting. Less damage also enhances the likelihood of a stand carrying full stocking, thereby achieving planned thinning and final harvest volumes. Managers' estimates of mountain beaver population reduction are as high as 50 percent. Population reductions and increased accessibility for trapping also translate to lower costs for trapping, tubing, and other protection measures. Informal estimates of these savings range up to $150 per acre, depending on the initial population and the effectiveness of the burn.

Planting efficiency

Fire can reduce brush and other obstacles to planting, allowing planters to cover ground faster and more efficiently. Estimates of planting cost reduction are quite varied, however. Vyse and Muraro (1973) projected planting cost savings of from $9 to $30 per acre in coastal British Columbia depending on the planting method used. An informal survey by the authors of private landowners in the Coast Range produced subjective estimates of $40 per acre in reduced planting costs. On the Mt. Hood National Forest, however, A. Webber (personal communication from USDA Forest Service, Mt. Hood National Forest, Gresham, Oregon, 1988) observed little reduction in contract planting costs from prescribed burning.

Planting cost savings occur early in the rotation. Consequently, their effect is less diluted than later cash flows by the discounting process and may be more directly felt in the financial outcome. On some sites, prescribed burning may make natural regeneration a biologically feasible, low-cost alternative to planting. For example, underburning in eastern Washington National Forests was estimated to contribute to a success level of 75 percent in naturally regenerating stands that would otherwise have had to be planted. Savings were estimated at $146 for each acre so regenerated (Petersen and Mohr 1984).

The dollar estimates above relate to benefits only. They do not include the costs of producing the benefit. Both benefits and costs are difficult to estimate without uniform and stable cost accounting practices. Increased emphasis on economic efficiency in the last decade has encouraged many organizations to improve collection of these data. These improvements should make economic evaluations easier in the future.

Control of competing vegetation

Few long-term studies are available on which to base estimates of the economic effect of vegetation control. Total growth and yield effects are composed of many interacting influences on survival, early growth, and spatial distribution. Separate estimates of the vegetation control components are difficult to obtain. Any such estimates should be tested across a wide range of possible values.

Some estimates of timber yield effects have been attempted. The recent draft environmental impact statement for vegetation management in National Forests in the Pacific Northwest estimated 2.5 to 3 percent reduction in annual long-term sustained yields under a program of no prescribed burning (USDA Forest Service 1987). Research-based estimates are more difficult to find (Chapter 15). Research started by Morris (1970) and contin-

ued by Miller (1989; see also Chapter 15) showed both increases and decreases in projected volume under prescribed burning, depending on understory and overstory composition and other factors. Prescribed burning's growth-and-yield effects obviously depend on many biological, physical, and managerial variables. It is important to identify the significant variables at the site and to understand and quantify their interrelationships. Concepts and procedures of economic analysis must be focused on units of analysis that are meaningful to the decision.

Costs of Prescribed Burning

The total cost of prescribed burning has many components. *Direct costs* are expenses created by actually preparing the site and doing the burning; *indirect costs* are associated with support functions and are allocated across the burning program as a whole. *Fixed costs* are those that do not vary with the level of activity, as measured by the number of acres burned or the area to be burned in a single treatment. *Variable costs*, on the other hand, increase or decrease as the size of the burning operation becomes larger or smaller. Indirect costs are usually fixed in nature, while direct costs can be fixed or variable, depending on the type of activity being analyzed.

An important distinction in deciding what costs to include in an analysis is relevance. Relevant costs, regardless of their physical basis, are those components of total cost that are used to compare alternatives. To be relevant to a particular decision, a cost must meet two criteria: it must be an expected future cost, and it must be an element of difference between alternatives in the decision to be made. Overhead, for example, is sometimes not a relevant cost if all the practices are assessed for overhead costs at the same level. Costs that are already borne by the stand and cannot be changed are "sunk" costs and, by definition, are not relevant in comparing future prescribed burning alternatives.

On-the-ground costs of burning (costs excluding overhead) are incurred during four different stages: planning and layout; line-building and other burn preparation; ignition; and mop up. Each of these components may vary considerably from stand to stand in response to topography, weather conditions, and the fuels to be treated. Different burning objectives, expressed in specific levels of fuel removal, will also cause the amount of planning, people, precautions, and equipment, and thus the costs, to vary. For example, on-the-ground cost of slash burning in 1987 on the Willamette National Forest ranged from $270 to $450 per acre (personal communication from H. Mapes, USDA Forest Service, Willamette National Forest, Eugene, Oregon, 1987). A recent cost figure quoted by private industry for slash burning is around $100 per acre (Gorman 1989). In contrast, underburning on the Fremont National Forest in Southeastern Oregon cost $14 to $17 per acre (including overhead) (Nesbit et al. n.d.). The large differences in cost reflect the differences in the timber types and fuels treated, the precautions required to conduct a safe burn, the objectives of the burn program, the overall efficiency of the operation, and different cost collection methods (Gonzalez-Caban et al. 1984, McKetta and Gonzalez-Caban 1985).

Size of the stand to be burned is one of the most important factors influencing cost per acre. It often takes as many people and as much equipment to treat small areas as it does to treat larger units. Consequently, the larger units often have much smaller costs on a per acre basis. The relationships shown in Table 21-1 demonstrate the impact of unit size on contract burning on the Mt. Hood National Forest. A similar effect exists because of shape; irregularly shaped units are more difficult to monitor for escapes during burning and require more resources. Tract size and shape effects are a factor of the trade-offs that are generated between low-cost practices and the environmental and aesthetic values sometimes sought with small and irregularly shaped parcels. The increased per-acre cost of executing and monitoring a burn is, in effect, the opportunity cost of whatever other resource needs dictated the unit's small size and high perimeter ratio.

Risks in Prescribed Burning

A strong influence on prescribed burning cost comes from the risk of escape and the burn manager's perception of that risk. This perception varies widely from one manager to the next, even if burning conditions are similar. Some managers will use more people and equipment to guard against the probable consequences of an escape, thereby in-

curring higher costs. Gonzalez-Caban and McKetta (1986) believe that most of the total variation noted in costs may be due to managerial perceptions and organizational policies toward risk.

The risk of escape is only one type associated with prescribed burning. Risk refers to any event or condition that is uncertain enough for us to worry about potential consequences as well as the probabilities of those consequences. Most economic analyses are done under an assumption of certainty; i.e., the expected results will be forthcoming and no unforeseen events will interfere to change either the benefits or the costs. Although this assumption is unrealistic, it works in many cases because the sources of uncertainty are not strong enough to sway the relative outcome of the alternatives or because potential positive and negative influences tend to cancel each other out. Forest managers, however, must deal with several well-defined sources of uncertainty, any one of which may have profound impacts on present net worth.

The escape of fire from the burn perimeter is probably the most well-known risk in prescribed burning. Unfortunately, much data on escaped fires is so broadly aggregated that it is not helpful in giving site-specific prognoses. The seriousness of the resulting escape can range from minor "slopover" to full-scale conflagration. Inability to conduct a burn after preparations have been made is another risk in prescribed burning. Inside the burn perimeter, the fire may damage the residual stand or impair the productivity of the site. The fire may fail to accomplish burn plan objectives, requiring a costly reburn or other treatment. Possible smoke intrusion into surrounding areas is an-

Table 21-1. Cost of slash disposal for prescribed burning.[a]

Unit Size Class (acres)	Unit Cost ($/acre)[b]
0- 4	1,280
5-14	704
15-29	531
30-60	418
60+	398

Source: Carlton 1987.
[a] Figures are for spring contract burning; contracts include costs of ignition, mop up, and contractor overhead and profit.
[b] Includes line building cost of $0.66 per foot of fireline using area/perimeter ratios that increase as area increases.

other risk, with implications for human health, aesthetics, and traffic safety.

Each source of uncertainty has a range of probabilities and consequences, many of which have not been experienced or recorded. *Risk analysis*, or the incorporation of probability estimates in the PNW computation, and *sensitivity analysis*, which is the calculation of PNW results across a broad range of assumptions, are two approaches to dealing with risk. These procedures tend to make the risks more explicit to the decision maker so that decisions can be made on how much to spend to avoid or mitigate them. Without an explicit expression of risk, more may be spent than necessary to compensate for a relatively rare occurrence.

Economic Analysis of Prescribed Burning at the Stand Level

The principles and techniques of conducting an economic analysis of prescribed burning can be illustrated with a hypothetical example. The analysis is a partial one in that it does not incorporate all the benefits described above. Our purpose is to illustrate fundamental technique with the understanding that a complete analysis would be much more complex. The (regeneration effectiveness) benefits selected here are more easily quantifiable than those omitted. Ironically, a more complete analysis may involve more uncertainty than a par-

tial one. The danger in becoming too realistic is in creating complexities that actually hamper rather than enhance the decision maker's understanding of the decision.

The type of analysis we will illustrate is known as stand-level analysis, and it looks at the value of successive forest crops on an acre of bare land with and without prescribed burning of logging slash. The soil expectation value (SEV), which is the value of an infinite series of forest crops, is compared, and the difference in value indicates the long-run value of the practice.

To examine the economics of prescribed burning at the stand level, DFSIM, a growth and yield model for Douglas-fir (Curtis et al. 1981), was used. The yield tables with prescribed burning were derived for site $index_{50}$ 135 (King 1966), precommercially thinned to 300 trees per acre at age 10, and commercially thinned to 200 trees per acre at age 30. Final harvest was at age 60. The assumptions for no prescribed burning were the same silviculturally, but the stand at age 30 was projected to have 15 percent fewer trees, 10 percent smaller in diameter. Our assumption was that prescribed fire, through enhancements in plantation survival and control of competing vegetation, allowed the stand to support more crop trees which grew faster. The theoretical stand regenerated without prescribed fire could not support a thinning at age 30, whereas the treated stand could. Projected volumes and tree size were larger in the

Table 21-2. Diameters at breast height, yields,[a] and harvest values with and without prescribed slash burning for a hypothetical Douglas-fir stand.

| Age (years) | With Prescribed Burn | | | Without Prescribed Burn | | |
	Diameter (inches)	Volume (cubic feet/acre)	Value ($/acre)	Diameter (inches)	Volume (cubic feet/acre)	Value ($/acre)
10		—				
20		—				
30	10.3	3,578		9.3	3,149	
	9.3	1,066	435			
40	13.8	7,419		11.9	6,201	
50	16.0	11,106		14.4	9,220	
60	18.1	14,419	12,977	16.5	12,100	9,535
70	20.1	16,952		18.5	14,768	
80	21.9	19,014		20.3	17,195	
90	23.6	20,794		21.9	19,333	
100	25.2	22,338		23.5	21,103	

Note:
[a]Generated with DFSIM; site index at base age 50 years is 135. Precommercial thin at age 10; thin to 200 trees at age 30 for burning alternative only. Trees are 15% fewer with 10% less diameter at age 30 if there is no prescribed burn.

treated stand at every stage. The projected difference in yields is provided in Table 21-2, and the economic assumptions are listed in Table 21-3. To simplify our example, we did not incorporate estimates of changes in long-term fire hazard or the risks of escape. A wildfire in this stand could prevent it from reaching a full rotation and dictate an adjustment in the management strategy. The economic influence of prescribed burning on this set of events would require more space and analytical complexity than this chapter allows.

The assumed cost for prescribed burning was $350 per acre and for planting was $300 per acre, for a total initial cost of $650 per acre. The untreated stand cost only $350 per acre, reflecting a higher planting cost because of obstructions to planting.

The SEV of a treated acre was $664 versus $500 for an untreated acre, if a 4 percent discount rate was used. This result indicates a $164 per acre net gain for prescribed burning. The results of such an analysis are sensitive to the discount rate, however. At 5 percent a treated stand has SEV of $12, whereas an untreated stand is worth $83, indicating a net gain of $71 for *not* burning. The large difference in initial cost and long (60 year) discounting period contribute to this sensitivity. Obviously, the selection of a discount rate is a critical factor that should be deliberated fully by the decision-making organization. Discount rate selection is a complex topic and is introduced in Davis and Johnson (1987). The economic information is summarized in Table 21-3.

From the stand-level analysis we can conclude that under the assumptions of our example, the incremental real rate of return (net of inflation) for prescribed burning is greater than 4 percent and less than 5 percent. This analysis reflects only the impacts on yields, tree size, and treatment costs of burning and planting. Additional benefits such as wildfire hazard reduction, reduced animal trapping costs, and increased effectiveness of animal damage control or wildlife forage enhancement would enhance the present net worth from the burn prescription, as they are early rotation benefits that offset some of the increased costs. These benefits could be incorporated if estimates of physical/biological response and dollar values are available. Resources that are not assigned values in a distinct market (for example, recreation) can be valued with techniques such as contingent valu-

Table 21-3. Costs, revenues, and soil expectation values for the prescribed burning alternatives.

Item	Prescribed Burn ($/acre)	No Prescribed Burn ($/acre)
Burning cost	350	0
Planting cost	300	350
Precommercial thinning cost at age 10	100	100
Commercial thinning return at age 30	435	0
Harvest value at age 60	12,977	9,535
Soil expectation value, 60-year rotation, 4% discount rate	664	500
Soil expectation value, 60-year rotation, 5% discount rate	12	83

ation (Mitchell and Carson 1989). These techniques would have to be estimated for with- and without-fire treatments, but so far little applied research has tackled this problem.

Decision Analysis

Deciding to use prescribed burning means considering a number of alternatives. For stand establishment, the options may include no site preparation, burning, chemical spraying, mechanical scarification or crushing, or any of a number of combinations such as spray-and-burn or spray-pile-burn. Each option presents its own array of costs, benefits, and risks. An example of a typical decision is given in Table 21-4 and Fig. 21-1. Note that this is a different example than the one described in the previous section, and involves different cost assumptions and three treatment options.

Decision analysis is a helpful tool for structuring options and displaying the economic results of each alternative as well as the more important sources of uncertainty. A decision tree such as the one displayed in Fig. 21-1 is composed of choice nodes (squares) representing decision options (major branches) and event nodes (circles) representing events (sub-branches) whose consequences are out of the decision makers' control. The likelihood of events is described with probabilities. The sum of probabilities at each event node equals 1. The estimates of probabilities can be developed from data or be estimated by professional judgment. The end points of the decision tree are the outcomes of the various interplays of controllable actions and uncontrollable events, measured in economic terms such as PNW, SEV, B/C, and IRR.

In decision analysis, each alternative can be represented by its *expected value*, or the probability-weighted average of all the outcomes possible from that alternative. Expected value can be calculated for economic outcomes or for physical outcomes such as trees per acre or acres burned. Some criteria such as SEV require selection of the alternative with the highest expected value, while others, such as total cost, dictate that the alterna-

tive with the lowest expected value be selected. The decision maker does not expect each selection to return exactly the expected value. Expected value represents the average value that would be obtained if the same choice was made over a large number of similar decisions.

Figure 21-1 displays a choice of site preparation techniques. Two types of risks are incorporated: escape from the broadcast burn, and the uncertainty of different survival levels of the planted stock. The probability of escape is very low (0.05) but if it does occur, an escape adds a very high suppression cost and resource loss component to the broadcast burn alternative. The pile-and-burn and no burn option are assumed to present no chance of fire escape. Seedling survival uncertainty is part of every site preparation option, but note that the probabilities across the three levels of success differ from option to option. The pile-and-burn option gives a somewhat higher probability

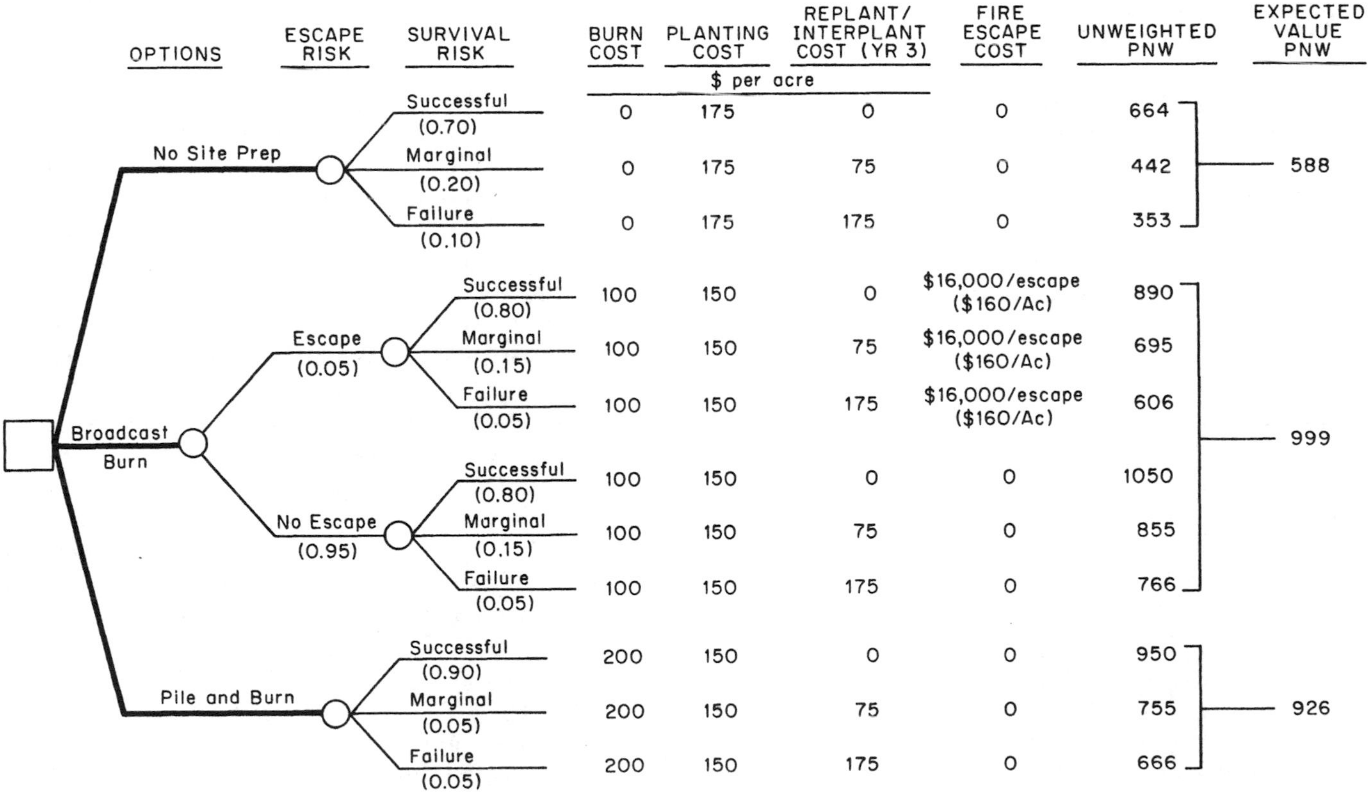

Figure 21-1. Decision tree analysis of three alternative methods of site preparation for a hypothetical 100-acre stand.

(Note: Expected values of PNW shown in the right-hand column are derived by multiplying the unweighted PNW for each outcome by its respective probability and then summing the values for each management option. For example, the Expected Value PNW for the pile-and-burn option is calculated as follows: (950 × 0.9) + (755 x 0.05) + (666 x 0.05) = 926.)

Table 21-4. Assumptions for decision analysis example in Fig. 21-1.

Assumption	Assumed value
Douglas-fir 1+1 hand-planted (300 trees/acre)	$150 per acre ($175 per acre in absence of site preparation)
Broadcast burning site preparation	$100 per acre
Pile-and-burn site preparation	$175 per acre
Replanting cost (includes repreparing site)	$175 per acre at year 3
Interplanting cost (on marginal stocking)	$75 per acre at year 3
Precommercial thinning cost	$100 at year 10
Discount rate	4 per cent
Total fire escape cost (average escape fire size of 40 acres × $400 per acre burned cost-plus-loss)	$16,000
Assume the unit under consideration is 100 acres and the total cost of the escape is allocated to the prescribed burn	$160 per acre
Growth and yield bases (for DFSIM simulations)	Assumptions from previous analysis (Table 21-2)
No site preparation—no commercial thinning at age 30; 15 percent fewer trees; 10 percent smaller in diameter than the burn-related alternatives below. See Table 21-2.	
Broadcast burn—See Table 21-2.	
Pile-and-burn—Same as broadcast burn.	
All sites 135 site index at base age of 50 years; precommercial thin to 300 trees/acre at age 10; to 200 trees/acre at age 30. Final harvest at age 60.	
Criterion for regeneration success (live seedlings/acre)	
success ≥250 marginal 150-250 failure <150	

for full survival than the broadcast burn option and a much higher success than the no preparation option. The consequences of marginal success or failure are additional costs in the form of interplanting or replanting, respectively.

The expected value Present Net Worths are shown to the right of the decision branches for each option. In this example, the broadcast burn option displays the highest expected value and would be preferred. Note, however, that by varying either the probabilities or some of the costs (Table 21-4), the results of this analysis can change. The unweighted PNWs are such that the no site preparation alternative is inferior to the other two options at all levels of survival, even if the $25 additional planting cost (from burnable obstructions) is deleted. Therefore, even a 100 percent successful program without site preparation would not be preferred to the other options. A $73 increase in broadcast burning costs would shift the preferred option to pile-and-burn, as would an increase in the probability of escape to 0.48 (under Table 21-4 assumptions). Increases in the predicted size or cost-plus-loss of the average escape fire would also tilt the analysis toward the "safer" pile-and-burn option. Other cost/return and probability assumptions could be tested across ranges of values to give the decision maker a feel for the "sensitivity" of various choices. The economic analysis and its decision analysis complement are not the final answers to the questions of "which is best." A decision maker may justifiably select options of lower expected value because of important influences external to the analyses. For example, he or she may not be willing to accept the chances of an escape or may wish to favor an alternative that delivers more of some nonmarket amenity not included in the economic analysis. The analyses are merely tools to help guide the decision maker and test the economic boundaries of the consequences being faced.

Conclusion

Economic analysis can help compare prescribed burning with alternative practices or plan burning strategies. The analysis exercise can help decision makers in structuring and communicating the complexities of the decision, focusing on especially troublesome aspects, and in identifying options that might escape notice in less formal approaches. Economic analysis can also display the relative importance of missing pieces of information, which can act as a guide to future research.

The results of economic analysis are only as good as the level of quantification of biological and physical relationships on which it is built. From a timber management perspective, much uncertainty exists about the influence of prescribed fire on wildfire hazard, growth and yield, and animal damage. To recognize that these effects depend greatly on the situation is not enough. Additional research must be done to define such situations and to develop reliable predictive relationships so that economic analysis can better help in refining decisions.

Good records on costs and results are needed for future analyses. They are also important guides for current decision making and for communicating the "art" of prescribed burning to novice forest managers and the public. The influence of cost on variability of economic return is strong because of its early position in the time stream. In addition, effects such as planting cost savings, stocking levels, and fire escapes are important in making analyses realistic. Many public and private organizations have begun to keep better records of these and other factors. Only with good cost data and documentation of results can the multiple objectives of burning be achieved within the framework of financial and environmental constraints.

Economic analysis can be used to evaluate policy options. For example, limitations on burning from smoke management regulations can be included in an analysis by reducing the availability of burning as an option at certain places or times. Increased costs or the replacement of fire and smoke risks with risks associated with other practices then become part of the "opportunity cost" of the regulation. In a similar fashion, forest management influences that dictate small or irregularly shaped units can be modeled.

Economic analysis does not evaluate alternatives as good or bad. If done correctly, it points out more clearly the trade-offs that are to be made in the decision at hand.

Literature Cited & Key References

*Brodie, J.D., P.J. Kuch, and C. Row. 1987. Economic analyses of the silvicultural effects of vegetation management at the stand and forest levels, p. 365-395. *In* Walstad, J.D., and P.J. Kuch (eds.) Forest Vegetation Management for Conifer Production. John Wiley & Sons, Inc., New York, NY. 523 p.

Carlton, D. 1987. Summary of multi-year contract order. Internal document on file at USDA For. Serv., Mt. Hood Nat. For., Gresham, OR.

Curtis, R.O., G.W. Clendenen, and D.J. Demars. 1981. A new stand simulator for Douglas-fir: DFSIM user's guide. USDA For. Serv., Pac. Northwest For. Rge. Exp. Sta., Portland, OR. Gen. Tech. Rep. PNW-128. 79 p.

Davis, L.S., and K.N. Johnson. 1987. Forest Management. Third Edition. McGraw-Hill Book Co., New York, NY. 790 p.

*Gonzalez-Caban, A., and C.W. McKetta. 1986. Analyzing fuel treatment costs. West. J. Appl. For. 1:116-121.

Gonzalez-Caban, A., C.W. McKetta, and T.J. Mills. 1984. Costs of fire suppression forces based on cost-aggregation approach. USDA For. Serv., Pac. Southwest For. Rge. Exp. Sta., Berkeley, CA. Res. Pap. PSW-171. 16 p.

*Gorman, J.F. 1989. Current issues in slash burning—A forest landowner's perspective, p. 21-24. *In* Hanley, D.P., J.J. Kammenga, and C.D. Oliver (eds.) Proc., The Burning Decision: Regional Perspectives on Slash. Coll. For. Resour., Univ. Washington, Seattle, WA. Inst. For. Resour. Contrib. No. 66. 374 p.

King, J.E. 1966. Site index curves for Douglas-fir in the Pacific Northwest. Weyerhaeuser Co., West. For. Res. Cent., Centralia, WA. Weyerhaeuser For. Pap. 8. 49 p.

McKetta, C.W., and A. Gonzalez-Caban. 1985. Economic cost of fire-suppression forces. J. For. 83:429-432.

Miller, R.E. 1989. Effects of slash burning or subsequent site index and volume in midrotation-aged stands, p. 69-80. *In* Hanley, D.P., J.J. Kammenga, and C.D. Oliver (eds.) Proc., The Burning Decision: Regional Perspectives on Slash. Coll. For. Resour., Univ. Washington, Seattle, WA. Inst. For. Resour. Contrib. No. 66. 374 p.

Mishan, E.J. 1976. Cost-benefit Analysis. Praeger Publishers, Holt, Rinehart, and Winston, CBS, Inc., New York, NY. 454 p.

Mitchell, R.C., and R.T. Carson. 1989. Using Surveys to Value Public Goods: The Contingent Valuation Method. Resources for the Future. Washington, DC. 463 p.

References marked by an asterisk are recommended for general information.

Morris, W.G. 1970. Effects of slash burning in overmature stands of the Douglas-fir region. For. Sci. 16:258-270.

Nesbit, J., B. Nichols, and T. Tyree. (no date). Fuel appraisal process. USDA For. Serv., Fremont Nat. For., Lakeview, OR.

Petersen, G.J., and F.R. Mohr. 1984. Underburning on white fir sites to induce natural regeneration and sanitation. Fire Manage. Notes 45(2):17-20.

*Radloff, D.L. 1984. Using decision analysis to evaluate fire hazard effects of timber harvesting. Fire Manage. Notes 45(1):10-16.

*Snell, J.A.K. 1986. Determining the most cost efficient fuel treatment strategy for the purposes of fire protection. USDA For. Serv., Pac. Northwest Reg., Portland, OR. 1986 R-6 Fuels Management Notes: 20 (December).

USDA Forest Service. 1987. Managing competing and unwanted vegetation. Draft Environmental Impact Statement. USDA For. Serv., Pac. Northwest Reg., Portland, OR.

Vyse, A.H., and S.J. Muraro. 1973. Reduced planting cost . . . a prescribed fire benefit. Can. For. Serv., Pac. For. Res. Cent., Victoria, B.C. Infor. Rep. BC-X-84.

Wood, D.B. 1978. Economic evaluation of fuel management programs for forestlands. Ph.D. thesis, Utah State Univ., Logan, UT. (Diss. Abst. 39:20363).

22 Conserving Resources and Ameliorating Losses from Prescribed Burning

Susan N. Little

Executive Summary

Many of the potentially adverse effects traditionally associated with fire can be avoided through careful prescriptions. Loss of organic matter and nutrients, increased susceptibility to erosion, and impacts on air quality all result, in large part, from the consumption of forest floor. This consumption is controlled by the moisture content of the forest floor and the amount and duration of heat provided by the burning of large woody fuels (larger than 3 inches in diameter) to drive off that moisture. Forest floor consumption can be reduced by burning under moist conditions (e.g., spring burns) and by removing large fuels prior to burning. In the case of timber harvests, this removal can be done during the initial harvest, or can be part of a second harvest, most often as firewood. Reducing the amount of large fuels broadens the range of moisture conditions under which the unit can be burned while still retaining a desired amount of forest floor.

Reducing competing vegetation or enhancing desired vegetation depends on the requirements of the species in question. Some species benefit from exposure of mineral soil, others from retention of forest floor. Prescriptions written with the desired end results in mind for all resources to be affected by the burn are most successful.

This chapter discusses the factors that influence consumption and the effects of that consumption on specific forest resources. Examples are given to illustrate the process of developing prescriptions when more than one resource objective is of concern. Methods for ameliorating negative effects of burning are also discussed.

Introduction

This chapter ties together the objectives and mechanics of prescribed fire, as outlined in Chapters 5, 6 and 7, with the effects of fire on forest resources as discussed in Chapters 8 through 18. In most cases, the use of fire to achieve forest management objectives is not in direct conflict with the production or maintenance of nontimber resources. Fire can be used without appreciable loss of resource values, and in some cases nontimber resource qualities can be enhanced. There are situations, however, where the use of fire has an undesirable effect on a resource. This chapter will discuss first the manager's ability to conserve resources through appropriate prescriptions, and then the methods of ameliorating potential resource losses. But first, a few comments on the decisions involved are in order.

Making Decisions

As discussed in Chapters 5 through 7, prescribed fire is used to meet many objectives. Some of the more common objectives are:

- to facilitate planting by reducing debris generated from thinning or timber harvest;
- to reduce wildfire hazard;
- to enhance habitat or browse for wildlife or livestock;
- to reduce incidence of disease or insect infestation; and
- to favor the development of desired plant species.

The decision to use fire to achieve a management objective is often made in conjunction with several other decisions. For example, the question of whether or not to underburn a stand of pine to promote browse is considered in light of the broader management objectives for the stand. Is the stand to be thinned? How will thinning slash be treated? Are there insect or disease considerations? Is an underburn the most cost-effective way to promote browse in light of these other considerations?

The most common use of prescribed fire in the Pacific Northwest is to treat fuels resulting from harvest activities. Fuels created from thinning activities are burned to reduce fire hazard, promote browse, and to sanitize the area with regard to insect or disease infestation. Fuels created after clearcut harvests are burned to reduce impedi-

ments to planting, to reduce competing vegetation, and to reduce fire hazard in the next stand.

The first decision to burn or not to burn for silvicultural purposes should occur during the initial planning of the harvest. The decision is based on what end results are desired for the unit (e.g., target species, available planting spaces, limitations of soil resource, protection of key nontimber resources). Although fire may be the most cost-effective means of site preparation, its use may be precluded by other resource concerns. Air quality constraints may reduce the days available to burn under prescription to the point where costs and time constraints are prohibitive. On sites where erosion hazard is high, use of fire may be precluded by a concern for maintaining forest floor cover and protecting soil and water resources (Chapters 14 and 17). If these trade-offs are anticipated prior to harvest, an appropriate method of removing unwanted debris can be made part of the timber sale process. Harvest practices, in terms of the amount and size of wood to be removed or left on site and the method of harvest, can be set to reduce site treatment costs and negative effects of burning on resources. Likewise, the boundaries of harvest units and the layout of roads may be designed in such a way as to facilitate burning by providing adequate access, facilitate holding and mopping up the fire, and reduce the likelihood of an escape.

In some cases, burning may not be the most cost-effective means of site preparation. When faced with increased costs for equipment and labor, or unacceptable risk of escape (necessitating high control costs), managers may decide not to burn, but to invest in other means of site preparation and spend more time and effort in planting.

The decision to burn or not to burn should be reevaluated during and after harvest by all who are responsible for the resources affected. Reviews are often done by an interdisciplinary team for each harvest area. These reviews are used to alter current management prescriptions for the area in question, and as input to the development of future prescriptions on similar sites with similar objectives and constraints. A similar process is followed for burns conducted to influence wildlife habitat, range forage, and sanitation of insect or disease problems.

The management of wilderness often includes fire (Lotan et al. 1985). Wildfire has played a critical role in the establishment and development of many wilderness ecosystems. To exclude all fire might mean a shift in ecosystem dynamics away from those intended to be preserved by wilderness designation. The decision to suppress unplanned fires (usually resulting from lightning) or to let fires run their natural course in wilderness depends on many things, but is part of the overall management plan for each wilderness. The plan sets prescriptions (fuel and weather conditions) that will result in a burn that is typical for the ecosystem, and will preserve or enhance resource values. The plan contains not only conditions for allowing natural fires to burn, but conditions which warrant containment or suppression. Decisions to suppress or contain fire usually depend on whether or not the fire meets the management prescription, and whether or not it poses unacceptable threats to property, water resources, or human life.

The frequency and severity of wildfires in wilderness areas and National Parks in 1987-88 prompted a thorough review of wilderness fire policy on federal lands (Philpot et al. 1988). The interagency review team found that the principles behind fire policy on these lands were sound and that fire, when properly managed, can play a constructive role in maintaining wilderness values. Inconsistent implementation of policy and lack of coordination between public agencies resulted in unacceptable threats and damage to property and resource values as wilderness fires escalated into wildfires in Yellowstone and elsewhere during those years of extreme drought.

Conserving Resources through Viable Prescriptions

As discussed in Chapter 5, there are four basic categories of fuel: large woody fuel (3 inches in diameter or larger), fine woody fuel (smaller than 3 inches in diameter), forest floor, and live vegetation. We distinguish between these categories because they influence resource values and influence and respond to fire behavior differently. Any effect from fire on a forest resource results from the consumption of one or more of these fuels. Controlling that consumption is the key to conserving resources. The relation between the various resources and fuel types is outlined below, followed by a discussion of how prescriptions are written to influence the consumption of each type.

Influencing resource quantity and quality

Timber production is dependent on adequate reforestation and on sufficient supply of light, water, air, and nutrients throughout the life of the stand (Chapters 6 and 15). Reforestation is aided by removal of small fuels. Planting and seeding can be facilitated by exposure of mineral soil (through reduction of the forest floor). Seedling growth and survival, on the other hand, depend on adequate moisture and shading; stand growth depends on adequate nutrient reserves and favorable soil conditions. These are enhanced by the retention of forest floor and large, rotten logs. Maintaining forest floor and large, rotten logs also helps maintain beneficial soil organisms (Chapter 13) and prevents erosion (Chapter 14).

Competing vegetation can be either reduced or encouraged by burning (Chapters 4, 6, and 15). Pioneer brush species, both competitors and nitrogen fixers, often benefit from exposure of mineral soil. The heat needed to kill woody brush or their seed, such as ceanothus and vine maple, may preclude retention of forest floor. The same often holds true for areas infected with dwarf mistletoe where the prescription is to eliminate infected seedlings and saplings with fire. Avoiding injury to residual trees in these stands through appropriate specification and implementation of prescriptions is important when underburning.

In summary, the key fuels of concern relative to timber production are the fine fuels (which may impede planting), large rotten logs, and forest floor. The decision to reduce or retain forest floor depends on many factors, including the local conditions of erosion hazard, nutrient supplies in the soil, and presence or potential for competing vegetation, disease, or insect infestations.

Air quality impairment results from the consumption of fuels (Chapter 16). In many cases, the greatest contributor to smoke is the emissions from smoldering forest floor. By reducing the smoldering of forest floor, emissions may be greatly reduced. The same techniques for reducing smoldering of forest floor also reduce smoldering emissions from large fuels. Live fuels burn inefficiently and can contribute harmful chemicals to the atmosphere though, in most cases, this contribution is relatively small.

Water quality, as discussed in Chapter 17, is adversely affected by inputs from erosion and by increased temperatures resulting from removal of shade along streams. Erosion hazard is dependent on soil type and rainfall patterns, but it is proportional to the slope of the land and is controlled by the covering of the soil by forest floor, root mats, and large logs which help hold soil on site. Shade, of course, is provided by live vegetation along riparian zones.

Wildlife habitat comes in many shapes and sizes (Chapters 4, 7, and 18). Live vegetation on site may be desirable for habitat, or it may need to be altered to promote more palatable browse. Downed logs and standing snags provide habitat for many species of insects, birds, and mammals. In general, protection of large, decaying logs and snags is desirable.

Controlling consumption

Prescriptions, as discussed in Chapter 5, define the conditions and efforts needed to achieve the end results desired from a burn. If the objective is to reduce forest floor cover and expose mineral soil, the prescription outlines how much forest floor is to be consumed, and how this is to be achieved while meeting any management constraints arising from concerns for other resources (for example, protecting standing snags for habitat or not exceeding standards for erosion hazard). The fuel manager, through the burn plan, then defines the specific conditions desired at time of ignition, the method of burning, and mop up needed to achieve the prescription. These instructions focus on controlling ignition patterns, fire spread, and the amount of fuels consumed during the fire. The following paragraphs provide a general discussion of how consumption is controlled by fuel moisture and loading. For a discussion of how lighting techniques and mop up influence fire behavior, see Chapter 5. Schroeder and Buck (1970) discuss

how weather patterns influence fuel moisture. For more detailed information on fuel consumption, see Pierovich et al. (1975), Sandberg (1980), Sandberg and Ottmar (1983), Little et al. (1986), Harrington (1987), and Little and Ohmann (1988).

Fuel moisture at time of ignition is determined by the size and shape of the fuel, the amount and duration of rainfall, and the weather pattern prior to ignition. Typically, the smaller the fuel and the larger surface-to-volume ratio it has, the quicker it will respond to changes in relative humidity. Thus, a twig will dry out quicker, and absorb moisture faster, than a large log. A mat of forest floor on top of saturated soil will dry more slowly than branches suspended above the ground. In spring, after fuels have been saturated from winter rains and snow, it takes long periods without rain to dry out the larger fuels. After a long, dry summer, an occasional rain may moisten the fine fuels, but may not have much influence on the moisture content of large fuels.

The moisture content of a fuel determines if the fuel will ignite and how it will burn (Table 22-1). Dry fuels ignite readily and burn efficiently. Fire intensity (in units of Btu per ft per second) is a rate of the amount of heat production at the flaming front of the fire. High intensity, resulting from efficient combustion, indicates high temperatures. Temperature thresholds are critical for killing living tissue (e.g., unwanted vegetation or seed) and chemical reactions (e.g., volatilizing nutrients). Low intensities result from scant fuel loadings or inefficient combustion of moist fuels. Inefficient combustion can extend fire duration. Fuels which are too moist to ignite on their own may dry out as surrounding, drier fuels provide heat to drive off that moisture. How quickly the moist fuels dry controls duration. Tables 22-2 through 22-4 sum-

Table 22-1. Fuel loading and moisture content necessary to achieve desired fire intensity and duration.

| Fuel | High Intensity | | Low Intensity | |
	Long Duration	Short Duration	Long Duration	Short Duration
	Fuel loading/moisture content			
Large fuels	Heavy/moist-dry	Light/dry or heavy/moist	Heavy/moist	Light or heavy/wet
Fine fuels	Heavy/dry	Moderate/dry	Moderate/dry	Light/dry
Forest floor	Moist	Very wet underlying drier large fuels, or very dry	Moist or dry	Wet

Table 22-2. Effects of fire intensity and duration on achieving burn objectives.

| Objective | High Intensity | | Low Intensity | |
	Long Duration	Short Duration	Long Duration	Short Duration
Consumption of fine fuels	Nearly complete.	Nearly complete.	Incomplete.	Incomplete.
Consumption of large fuels	High consumption; with smoldering.	Low consumption; little smoldering.	Consumption varies; occurs mostly as smoldering.	Little consumption; little smoldering.
Consumption of forest floor	High consumption; long smoldering.	Consumes only dry forest floor.	Mostly smoldering consumption.	Very little consumption.
Mortality and consumption of live shrubs and trees	High mortality; high consumption.	High mortality; some consumption.	Some mortality; low consumption.	Some defoliation.
Exposure of mineral soil	High exposure; some damage to chemical and physical properties.	Depends on forest floor moisture.	Some exposure.	Little exposure.

marize the influence of fire intensity and duration on consumption and the subsequent effects on resource values.

Fine fuels (smaller than 3 inches in diameter) are the first to ignite during a fire. They act as kindling, burning rapidly because of their low moisture content and high surface-to-volume ratio. Fuel managers prescribe moisture contents of the fine fuels low enough to allow the spread of the fire throughout the area intended to be burned. These low fuel moistures ensure nearly complete consumption of the fine fuels (Fig. 22-1).

In general, large fuels (greater than 3 inches in diameter) burn according to their moisture content, provided that the small fuels are dry enough to consume and ignite the larger material. During the flaming stage of the fire, fine fuels are consumed. The heat generated from this consumption serves to ignite and sustain the consumption of larger logs. After the flaming front has passed, large logs continue to smolder until the moisture within them quenches the fire. If fine fuels are dry enough to be totally consumed during the fire, the percent of large fuels consumed is proportional to the moisture content of those large fuels. Hence, reducing the total amount of large fuel consumed depends on reducing the amount of large fuels prior to burning, or burning when their moisture content is high.

Large, decaying logs are usually slow to ignite because of their relatively high moisture content.

Consequently, once lit, they burn primarily during the smoldering phase of the fire. Reduction of the smoldering phase of the burn, either through scheduling during periods of high large-fuel moisture, removing large fuels prior to ignition, or through diligent mop up, reduces consumption of this resource.

Which factors control the consumption of forest floor depend on the moisture content of the forest

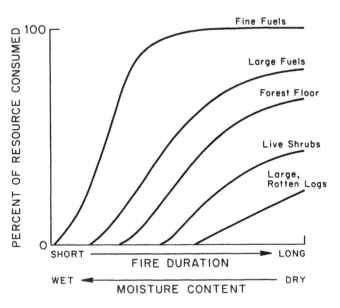

Figure 22-1. Relationship of fire duration and moisture content to the amount of resources consumed.

Table 22-3. Effects of fire intensity and duration on timber resource values.

| Objective | High Intensity | | Low Intensity | |
	Long Duration	Short Duration	Long Duration	Short Duration
Reforestation:				
Natural seeding	Favors species that require exposed soil and are intolerant of competition.	Depends on amount of soil exposed. May aid opening of serotinous cones.	Depends on amount of soil exposed and reduction of competing vegetation.	Favors tolerant, moist-site conifers (e.g., hemlock).
Planting	———————— Improves access and quality of planting. ————————			If fine fuel not consumed, may leave impediments to planting.
Initial stand development	Some loss of nutrients to be expected. Loss of forest floor may expose soil and seedlings to temperature and moisture extremes. Amount of competing vegetation depends on the species typical of the area (see below).			Because woody fuel and forest floor are lightly consumed, initial stand development will be similar to areas not burned.
Vegetation management:				
Shrubs	Kills shrubs and trees. May stimulate germination of ceanothus seed.		Kills shrubs and trees with shallow root systems or thin bark.	Least effect on shrubs. May defoliate shrubs under moisture stress.
Herbs, forbs, and grasses.	Stimulates those species that benefit from soil exposure. This may cause competition for soil moisture on dry sites.		Depends on amount of soil exposed.	May not kill seeds or roots of plants in forest floor. Retention of duff layer may prevent invasion by light-seeded species.
Forest protection:				
Wildfire hazard	———————— Reduced by removal of fine fuels. ————————			May leave patches of fine fuels and poorly consumed shrubs.
Chance of escape	Requires diligent mop up.	Moderate.	Requires diligent mop up.	Low.
Animal pests	Removes cover for pest species (e.g., porcupine). Improves access for elk and deer. Presence of palatable browse (grasses and shrubs) may divert grazers from seedlings. Facilitates trapping and other direct control measures.			Little effect.
Insect pests	May reduce populations overwintering in the forest floor (depending on time of burn). May cause mortality of some species. In cases of underburning, crown and bark scorch may weaken trees, leaving them more susceptible to insect damage.			Little effect.
Diseases	Can be effective tool for eradicating mistletoe. Fire scars can provide infection courts for disease and decay fungi.			Little effect.
Logistics and economics	Smoldering logs, stumps and forest floor require diligent mop up.	Rapid ignition to achieve this may reduce costs for lighting. Smoldering and mop up will be reduced.	Smoldering logs, stumps, and forest floor require diligent mop up.	Fewer personnel needed to light, hold, and mop up the fire.

Table 22-4. Effects of fire intensity and duration on nontimber resource values.

Objective	High Intensity		Low Intensity	
	Long Duration	Short Duration	Long Duration	Short Duration
Air quality	High emissions from long, smoldering combustion.	Reduced, efficient combustion with good smoke dispersion.	Moderate emissions from smoldering; poor column development.	Moderate emissions; poor smoke dispersion.
Water quantity and quality	Water quality and quantity are affected by the increased erosion and run-off on slopes where vegetation and forest floor are removed. Typically, burns of longer duration expose the most soil. The time needed to recover from these impacts will depend on the ability of planted and natural species to invade and occupy the site.			Little effect.
Wildlife	Promotes herbaceous forage. Removes cover.		Minimizes damage to shrubs used for browse. May stimulate sprouting of some browse species. High retention of snags and decaying logs.	
Natural fire ecology	Mimics infrequent, high-severity wildfire (moist climates).		Mimics frequent, low-severity wildfire (dry climates).	
Aesthetics	Presents uniform landscape and relatively homogeneous stands. Smoke column is highly visible during burning.		Leaves a patchwork of burned and unburned areas which can result in a more diversified stand structure. Smoke appears more diffuse within burned areas.	

floor (Fig. 22-2). If the forest floor is dry, it will behave like the fine woody fuels and burn independently once ignited. If the forest floor is moist, external heat from the consumption of large fuels is necessary to drive off enough moisture for the forest floor to ignite. Typically, this drying is a slow and gradual process, as heat from the large fuels penetrates downward. After it dries, the top layer of forest floor ignites and burns, providing an additional source of heat to dry the layers below. After the external input of heat from the burning of large fuels has ceased, the forest floor will smolder and consumption will stop when the fire reaches a layer where the moisture content is too high to sustain combustion (Fig. 22-3). When the forest floor is wet, it behaves like the large, rotten logs, requiring tremendous heat to drive off excess moisture to the point where it can ignite. The most reduction in forest floor, with the worst effect on air quality and nutrients, occurs during long, hot, smoldering fires.

Live vegetation is normally killed by destruction of the cambium at or near the root collar. Fire can also kill vegetation by scorching the crown of nonsprouting species and by injuring the roots of shallow-rooted species. The amount of mortality depends on species characteristics, particularly bark thickness (for instance, it is harder to kill a

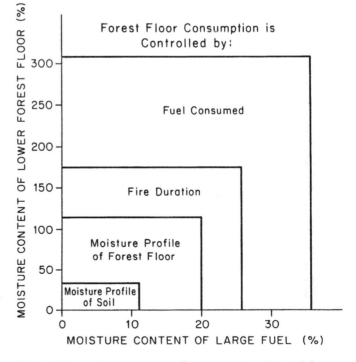

Figure 22-2. Factors controlling consumption of forest floor under different large fuel and forest floor moisture contents. (Source: R.D. Ottmar, USDA Forest Service, Pacific Northwest Research Station, Seattle, WA)

vine maple than a sword fern); the moisture content of the vegetation; the amount of heat available from woody fuels being consumed; and the moisture of the surrounding forest floor and soil (which will control soil temperature during the burn). Quick burns generally do not consume live shrubs; long, hot burns do.

High-intensity, long duration burns which consume large amounts of forest floor will also eliminate the seed of some species stored either in the forest floor or in the top layers of soil. A less consumptive burn, however, may actually stimulate the germination of such seed. Ceanothus and manzanita are two such shrub genera on which prescribed fire can have either a positive or negative effect.

Putting it all Together: Examples of Prescriptions

Protecting water quality, air quality, and soil nutrients depends on retention of forest floor and low consumption of large, decaying logs. Creating planting spots and seedbeds depends on reducing fine to small fuels and exposing mineral soil by reducing forest floor. Reducing competing vegetation depends on providing enough heat to kill the seeds, roots, cambium, or crown; the amount

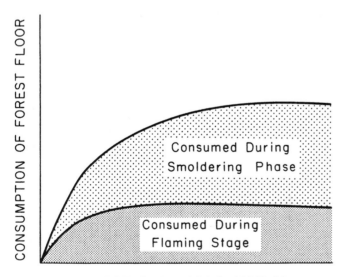

Figure 22-3. Relationship of forest floor consumption to consumption of large fuels. (Source: R.D. Ottmar, USDA Forest Service, Pacific Northwest Research Station, Seattle, WA)

needed depends on the species and its condition. Thus, some resource objectives benefit from the same prescription; some are in conflict with each other. The following examples illustrate how conflicts between resource objectives, or between burn objectives and other resource constraints, can be resolved in the process of developing prescriptions.

Example 1: The use of fire for timber stand improvement.
Nick II Sale, Tonasket Ranger District, Okanogan National Forest, Washington

The Nick II Sale area is on the eastern slopes of the Cascade Range in Washington. Stand composition consisted mostly of Douglas-fir and western larch, with small amounts of lodgepole pine and Englemann spruce. The first entry into the area was a commercial timber harvest in the 1950s, which left a shelterwood system of regeneration. The regeneration, 30 years old at the time of the sale, was overstocked and heavily infected with mistletoe. The sale was intended to remove the overstory shelterwood (approximately 7 million board feet). Thinning and sanitation of the understory would then follow to enhance long-term yields.

Because of the relatively low value, the timber could only be harvested economically by tractor. The Environmental Analysis originally called for mechanical thinning following the commercial harvest and piling and burning of all slash. Prescriptions such as this were considered standard operating procedure when the sale was originally planned.

Following the harvest, the site was visited by the post-sale and fuels management personnel to reevaluate the initial prescription. The field review focused on two areas of concern: ecology (long-term site productivity, soil compaction, erosion control, and thermal cover), and costs. Four fuels treatment options were discussed within that framework:

- No treatment.
- Minimize probabilities of fire started by human activities by creating a fuel break above the road (natural lightning starts are uncommon in this area).
- Underburn following the thinning operations.
- Burn fuels resulting from overstory harvest (activity fuels) prior to thinning.

Option 1 was considered but not recommended because the fuel loadings following thinning would exceed tolerable limits for fire hazard. It was felt that handpiling a buffer strip adjacent to the road would only serve as a cosmetic quick fix and would not contribute to long-term management goals. Burning the combined thinning and activity fuels would create too hot a burn, causing adverse effects on the stand. Burning activity fuels before thinning would be compatible with resource objectives while satisfying cost considerations.

This last alternative would contribute the most good with the smallest dollar investment. Thinning costs would be reduced (because of easier access and any thinning caused by the fire). Machine piling would be eliminated because fuels would be burned in place, thereby avoiding any soil compaction. The fuel loads after thinning would not be sufficient to require further treatment. The underburn would also promote natural regeneration.

Because the use of fire under these conditions was relatively untested on the District, a trial burn was conducted on 55 acres representative of the total 107-acre unit. A moderate-severity burn designed to provide enough heat to eliminate the fire hazard and to ensure some mortality of the infected trees and trees less than 6 inches in diameter was prescribed. A spring burn was chosen, since large diameter fuels would be too moist to burn while small diameter fuels would burn completely. Because of the high moisture content of the forest floor, blacklines (previously burned strips) could be used to hold the fire within the prescribed boundaries instead of having to construct more expensive machine firelines.

The treatment objectives for the prescription included: hazard reduction; wildlife enhancement by protecting logs and snags and by promoting sprouting of wild rose, snowberry, and ninebark; thinning; and removal of infected trees.

The trial burn was conducted on May 28, 1986. Heat intensities observed were moderate, with flame lengths ranging from 2 to 4 feet. Thermal cover for wildlife was not adversely affected as the overstory was not burned. Hazard reduction goals were met by reducing the fine fuels by 90 percent or more. The larger diameter fuels still remained, providing niches for wildlife. Tree mortality was patchy, thinning out some areas and leaving some areas unchanged. Although thinning objectives were not met on every acre, the burn was considered a success because additional thinning would only be needed in a few isolated areas. In some areas mineral soil was exposed, providing sites for natural regeneration. A similar prescription was successfully followed for the remainder of the sale.

Example 2: Use of fire for slash reduction under wildlife constraints.
Dugout Timber Sale, Tonasket Ranger District, Okanogan National Forest, Washington.

The Dugout Timber Sale was an entry into a previously unroaded area. The management of the area stressed wildlife objectives, the foremost concern being maintenance or enhancement of several species of huckleberry. The area also contained heavy infestations of dwarf mistletoe and root rot, and so it was important from a silvicultural standpoint to sanitize some of the stands.

The units were to be tractor logged. Although machine piling of slash would have been cheaper than broadcast burning, the interdisciplinary team decided to broadcast burn so that physical disturbance of the huckleberry would be minimized.

Because site-specific data for huckleberry response to fire was lacking or inconclusive, fuel specialists established several plots on a similar site and experimented with fuel loadings and fire intensities to develop guidelines for the Dugout prescription. These trials indicated that a spring burn (with sufficient moisture levels in the large fuels and soil) should protect huckleberry under the fuel loads predicted for the area. In order to get adequate site preparation for planting, some reduction of forest floor and exposure of mineral soil would be necessary. The final prescription was for a broadcast burn that would be cool enough to protect the huckleberry but hot enough to meet hazard reduction and site preparation objectives.

Two preparation needs aside from firelining were identified to protect and conserve resources on the site. One was to conduct an inventory to determine how many and what types of snags should be protected, then to clear areas around these wildlife snags, thereby excluding them from the burn (Fig. 22-4). The area also contained an abundance of large logs. Although these logs could contribute to long-term site productivity, they also could provide firewood. Removal of some of the logs could reduce fire effects on the huckleberry by reducing the duration of the burn. In the winter

Figure 22-4. To protect snags for wildlife habitat, accumulation of slash near the base of snags as illustrated here should be pulled away. Hosing with water to increase local moisture content prior to ignition may also reduce consumption. (Source: Tonasket Ranger District, Okanogan National Forest, Washington)

of 1986-87 a contract was awarded for removal of the logs. Yarding was undertaken with sufficient snow on the ground to avoid soil disturbance. This operation provided nearly 200 cords of firewood for public use and still maintained sufficient large woody material on site to address concerns for long-term site productivity.

The burn was undertaken in the spring of 1987 with protection of the huckleberry resource, hazard reduction, and site preparation as the major objectives. A follow-up field review that summer with the district silviculturist, wildlife biologist, timber management assistant, ranger, fuels specialist, and forest timber staff was conducted. From a fuels standpoint, sufficient slash was removed (mainly in the 0- to 3-inch diameter fuels) to

meet protection needs. From the biologist's standpoint, the various species of huckleberry were already sprouting and, although there was some setback in areas with heavy fuel concentrations, wildlife objectives were generally met. Site preparation was marginally sufficient; competition from shrubs would likely hinder seedling performance the following spring.

Although the silviculturist would have preferred a burn with lower large fuel moistures to expose more mineral soil and set back the competition, it was decided that similar spring burns would be preferred for the remainder of the Dugout units to favor the wildlife objectives. Planting the same spring as the burn might eliminate some of the problems of competition as well as reduce the need for extra scalping.

Example 3: Reducing slash in clearcuts to facilitate planting while complying with water quality constraints.
Smith Whittaker Units 3 and 4, Eugene District, BLM, Oregon.

The Whittaker units are on the east side of the Coast Range, between Florence and Eugene, Oregon. The units were clearcut, and broadcast burning was prescribed to facilitate planting, reduce mountain beaver habitat, and forestall competition from unwanted brush. Units 3 and 4 are separated by a stream (Fig. 22-5A). Constraints on the burn included a desire to retain a riparian buffer strip, retain one-half inch of forest floor to prevent erosion, and keep residual smoke at a minimum. Untreated slash in an adjoining young stand could pose a threat of escape. Fuel loads averaged 10 tons per acre of fuels less than 3 inches and 38 tons per acre of fuels larger than 3 inches in diameter. Objectives called for burning 90 percent of the area and reducing fine fuels by 75 to 90 percent.

To meet the objectives and constraints, the following conditions at time of ignition were prescribed and met, except for 1,000 hr moisture:

	Prescribed	*Actual*
Temperature	55-80°F	64F
Relative humidity	45-80%	52%
Wind speed (mid flame)	2-10 mph	0-3 mph
Wind direction	NE-NW	N
Fuel moistures:		
1 hr	8-14%	(not measured)
10 hr	10-16%	10-14%
100 hr	12-18%	12-16%
1,000 hr	18-24%	32%

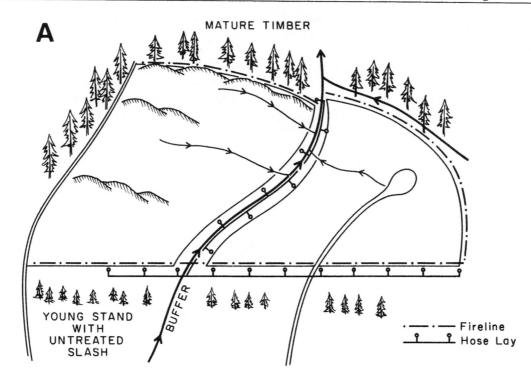

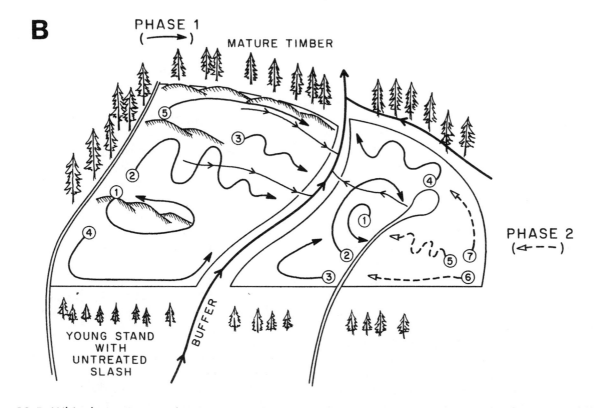

Figure 22-5. Whittaker units 3 and 4. (A) Active hose lines were strung along buffer and adjacent young stand for protection. (B) Lighting pattern to draw heat away from adjacent stands and buffer while providing good plume development.

The burn was conducted on the morning of July 30, 1987. A rapid lighting pattern (Fig. 22-5B) ensured a quick fire, minimizing residual smoke. Firelines along the buffer and boundaries with adjacent young stands were kept wet, with hot spots hosed down as they occurred. Although the burn covered the entire area, only 10 percent of the mineral soil was exposed. Fuel loadings were reduced to approximately 3 tons per acre of fine fuels and 8 tons per acre of large fuels. Thus, even under the narrow constraints necessary to meet the objectives of this burn, it was successfully accomplished due to careful planning and implementation.

Ameliorating Losses

Prescriptions are designed to achieve the primary objective of the burn without adversely impacting other resources. In some cases, other resources may be enhanced (e.g., browse). Occasionally, this is not the case (e.g., burning to control unwanted shrubs may dictate hot fires of long duration which reduce browse and forest floor cover below acceptable levels). For some resources, there are measures, however costly, which can be taken before or after burning to ameliorate unwanted losses. For others, notably air quality, there is no postburn solution. Increased incidence of insect pests or disease may not show up for years to come.

The causes of failures to achieve objectives or meet minimum standards for a resource should be assessed after the burn. The results of such analyses can be used as input to future prescriptions and burn plans. It is this long-term accumulation of knowledge through thorough documentation, monitoring, and review that enables forest managers to improve their skills to achieve desired results on a site-specific basis.

It may become desirable to ameliorate losses when:
- a burn was conducted out of prescription (perhaps due to air quality constraints);
- conflicting objectives and constraints resulted in a burn that compromised one resource for the protection or enhancement of another; or
- a postburn shift in management emphasis makes enhancement of impacted resources desirable or feasible.

Lost nutrients can be replaced through fertilization (Chapter 12; for a thorough discussion of forest fertilization, see Binkley 1986). Lost organic matter, important to soil structure, soil nutrient availability, and water-holding capacity, cannot be replaced as readily. Interplanting or short rotations of nitrogen-fixing species can be used to replace nitrogen, help reduce erosion hazard, and provide inputs of organic matter over time (Gordon et al. 1979, Binkley and Greene 1983, Murray and Miller 1986).

As noted in Chapter 13, restocking the site with seedlings soon after the burn will help retain resident populations of soil biota. Inoculating seedlings at the nursery or planting seedlings with a bit of inoculated soil from other areas can be successful in restoring populations of mycorrhizal fungi.

Erosion hazard can be abated by placing water bars in skid roads and fire lines. Seeding with grass or other vegetative cover can help hold soil in place until the next stand is established. However, this vegetation may later compete with seedlings on sites where soil moisture or nutrient availability is limiting (Chapters 6 and 12).

When undesirable species are promoted by fire, they can be physically removed by machine or hand, or chemically controlled with herbicides. Physical removal can be costly, and the use of herbicides may be precluded by regulation or other concerns. Insect and disease infestations promoted by fire are most often dealt with by removing the affected trees during salvage cuts. The trees are either harvested or burned on site.

Wildfire within wilderness boundaries is considered, in most cases, as part of the natural cycle of events. Suppression activities within wilderness boundaries are usually directed at protecting forest, water, and human resources adjacent to the wilderness. In some cases, no rehabilitation is planned after wildfire; in others, it may be desirable to reestablish vegetative cover as quickly as possible to protect soil and water resources, and to provide forage. The Silver Fire of 1987 provides a recent example.

Example 4: Unplanned ignition in the Kalmiopsis Wilderness.
Silver Fire, Siskiyou National Forest, Oregon.

Of the 96,540 acres burned in the Silver Fire in September and October of 1987, 51,540 acres were in the Kalmiopsis Wilderness. The fire was suppressed because of threats to life and property outside the wilderness boundaries. The fire itself was deemed "natural," and postfire activities focused on removing evidence of the suppression activities. No land-based rehabilitation work, such as grass seeding, was done on the burned area in the wilderness. The following is a summary of rehabilitation treatments used:

Firelines: All firelines in the wilderness were waterbarred to prevent gullies from developing. Where firelines intersected recreation trails, brush was pulled across the lines to hide their presence as much as possible. Waterbars were designed to avoid channelling water onto the trails.

Recreation trails used as firelines: All stumps adjacent to the trails were cut flush and covered with dirt. Stumps were scattered out of sight of the trails. Brush along the trails was lopped to 18 inches in height and the residue scattered. Burms were removed and treads leveled where cup trenching was done on the trail. Finally, drainage was reestablished on the trails where needed.

Helispots: Brush removed to create the helispots was scattered. All cut material was removed from natural meadows and openings.

Spike camps were returned to natural grade where areas were leveled for sleeping areas.

In all cases, evidence of human presence was removed as much as possible, including the removal of all trash and flagging. All of the work listed above required an estimated 350 work days to complete. In addition to wages, a large amount of helicopter time was used to shuttle crews in and out of the wilderness. Personnel costs were approximately $35,000; flight costs were $15,000. A total of 18 miles of handlines and recreation trails and 22 helispots were rehabilitated.

Conclusion

The effects of fire on forest resources result from the consumption of fuel, whether it be wood, forest floor, or live vegetation. Managing this consumption is the key to achieving burn objectives and avoiding unwanted loss of resource values. Reducing fine fuels reduces fire hazard and improves access for planting and thinning crews and wildlife, but reduces cover for small mammals and birds. The smoldering of large fuels and forest floor contributes to losses of nutrients and reduction in the quality of air, water, and habitat. On the other hand, reduction of forest floor might be desired to facilitate natural regeneration of preferred species. Heat generated from the combustion of large fuels may be necessary to kill unwanted brush.

In general, consideration of all management objectives and constraints prior to a decision to burn will lead to the most successful prescriptions. Incorporating this analysis into the design of harvest activities will allow greater flexibility in developing prescriptions. It is cheaper and easier to control the effects of prescribed fire through appropriate prescriptions rather than to mitigate any losses incurred. Trial burns, as described in examples 1 and 2, are useful for developing site-specific prescriptions that will meet desired objectives under local conditions and constraints.

Literature Cited & Key References

*Binkley, D. 1986. Forest Nutrition Management. John Wiley & Sons, Inc., New York, NY. 290 p.

Binkley, D., and S. Greene. 1983. Production in mixtures of conifers and red alder; the importance of site fertility and stand age, p. 112-117. *In* Ballard, R., and S.P. Gessel (eds.) I.U.F.R.O. Symposium on Forest Site and Continuous Productivity. USDA For. Serv., Pac. Northwest For. Rge. Exp. Sta., Portland, OR. Gen. Tech. Rep. PNW-163. 406 p.

Gordon, J.C., C.T. Wheeler, and D.A. Perry (eds.). 1979. Symbiotic Nitrogen Fixation in the Management of Temperate Forests. Workshop Proc., February 5, 1979. Oregon State Univ., For. Res. Lab. Corvallis, OR. 501 p.

Harrington, M.G. 1987. Predicting reduction of natural fuels by prescribed burning under ponderosa pine in southeast Arizona. USDA For. Serv., Rocky Mt. For. Exp. Sta., Ft. Collins, CO. Res. Note RM-472. 4 p.

Little, S.N., and J.L. Ohmann. 1988. Estimating nitrogen lost from forest floor during prescribed fires in Douglas-fir/western hemlock clearcuts. For. Sci. 34:152-164.

*Little, S.N., R.D. Ottmar, and J.L. Ohmann. 1986. Predicting duff consumption from prescribed burns on conifer clearcuts in western Oregon and western Washington. USDA For. Serv., Pac. Northwest Res. Sta., Portland, OR. Res. Pap. PNW-362. 29 p.

References marked by an asterisk are recommended for general information.

*Lotan, J.E., B.M. Kilgore, W.C. Fischer, and R.W. Mutch. 1985. Proc., Symposium and Workshop on Wilderness Fire. USDA For. Serv., Intermt. For. Rge. Exp. Sta., Ogden, UT. Gen. Tech. Rep. INT-182. 434 p.

Murray, M., and R.E. Miller. 1986. Early survival and growth of planted Douglas-fir with red alder in four mixed regimes. USDA For. Serv., Pac. Northwest Res. Sta., Portland, OR. Res. Pap. PNW-336. 13 p.

Philpot, C., B. Leonard. 1988. Report on Fire Management Policy. Conducted by the U.S. Departments of Agriculture and Interior. Report submitted for public review 12/14/88. Final report is expected to be published in the Federal Register in summer, 1989.

*Pierovich, J.M., E.H. Clarke, S.G. Pickford, and F.R. Ward. 1975. Forest residues management guidelines for the Pacific Northwest. USDA For. Serv., Pac. Northwest For. Rge. Exp. Sta., Portland, OR. Gen. Tech. Rep. PNW-33. 273 p.

Sandberg, D.V. 1980. Duff reduction by prescribed underburning in Douglas-fir. USDA For. Serv., Pac. Northwest Res. Sta., Portland, OR. Res. Pap. PNW-272. 18 p.

*Sandberg, D.V., and R.D. Ottmar. 1983. Slash burning and fuel consumption in the Douglas-fir subregion. Fire For. Meteorol. Conf. Proc. 7:90-93.

*Schroeder, M.J., and C.C. Buck. 1970. Fire weather . . . a guide for application of meteorological information to forest fire control operations. USDA For. Serv., Washington D.C. Agr. Hbk. 360. 229 p.

Appendix 1

List of Common and Scientific Names

Birds

Bluebird	*Sialia* spp.
Creeper	*Certhia* spp.
Eagle	
Bald	*Haliaetus leucocephalus*
Golden	*Aquila chrysaetos*
Flicker	*Colaptes* spp.
Grouse	
Blue	*Dendragapus obscurus*
Ruffed	*Bonasa umbellus*
Sage	*Centrocercus urophasianus*
Hawk	*Accipiter, Buteo, & Circus* spp.
Hummingbird, calliope	*Stellula calliope*
Magpie	*Pica* spp.
Nuthatch	*Sitta* spp.
Owl	Many genera
Quail, bobwhite	*Colinus virginianus*
Sparrowhawk	*Falco sparverius*
Swallow	Many genera
Vulture, turkey	*Cathartes aura*
Woodpecker	*Dendrocopos, Dryocopus, & Picoides* spp.

Fishes

Dace	*Rhinichthys* spp.
Salmon	
Chinook	*Oncorhynchus tshawytscha*
Coho	*O. kisutch*
Sculpin	*Cottus* spp.
Shiner, redside	*Richardsonius balteatus*
Trout	
cutthroat	*Salmo clarki*
steelhead	*S. gairdneri*

Insects

Aphid, balsam woolly	*Adelges piceae*
Beetle	
Ambrosia	Many genera
Bark	Many genera
Chrysomelid	*Syneta hamata*
Cone	*Conophthorus* spp.
Douglas-fir bark	*Dendroctonus pseudotsugae*
Engraver	*Ips & Scolytus* spp.
Mountain pine	*D. ponderosae*
Pine engraver	*Ips pini*
Western pine	*D. brevicomis*
Borer	
Flatheaded	Many genera
Western pineshoot	*Eucosma sonomana*
Wood	Many genera
Budworm, western spruce	*Choristoneura occidentalis*
Collembola (springtails)	Many genera
Leaf cutter	Many genera
Moth	
Aroga	*Aroga websterii*
Douglas-fir tussock	*Orgyia pseudotsugata*
Pandora	*Coloradia pandora*
Sawfly	Many genera
Weevil, reproduction	*Steremnius carinatus*

Mammals

Antelope, pronghorn	*Antelocapra americana*
Bat	Many genera
Bear	*Ursus* spp.
Black	*U. americanus*
Beaver, mountain	*Aplodontia rufa*
Bobcat	*Lynx rufus*
Cattle	*Bos* spp.
Chipmunk	*Eutamias & Tamias* spp.
Siskiyou	*T. siskiyou*
Cottonrat	*Sigmodon* spp.
Coyote	*Canis latrans*
Deer	*Odocoileus* spp.
Black-tailed	*O. hemionus hemionus*
Mule	*O. hemionus*
Elk	*Cervus* spp.
Rocky Mountain	*C. elaphus*
Fisher	*Martes pennanti*
Fox	*Urocyon & Vulpes* spp.
Gopher, pocket	*Thomomys & Geomys* spp.
Hare	*Lepus* spp.
Snowshoe	*L. americanus*
Lion, mountain	*Felis concolor*
Marten	*Martes americana*

Mice	*Peromyscus* spp.
Deer	*P. maniculatus*
Porcupine	*Erithrizon dorsatum*
Rabbit	*Sylivilagus* spp.
Raccoon	*Procyon lotor*
Sheep, bighorn	
(mountain)	*Ovis canadensis*
Shrew	*Sorex* spp.
Malheur	*S. preblei*
Skunk	*Mephitis & Spilogale* spp.
Squirrel	
Flying	*Glaucomys* spp.
Ground	*Spermophilus* spp.
Tree	*Sciurus* spp.
Vole	*Microtus* spp.
Woodrat	*Neotoma* spp.

Herbs

Alfalfa	*Medicago sativa*
Buckthorn family	Rhamnaceae
Fern	
Bracken	*Pteridium aquilinum*
Sword	*Polystichum munitum*
Grass family	Graminae, Poaceae
Grass	
Bluegrass, Kentucky	*Poa pratensis*
Sandberg	*P. secunda*
Bottlebrush squirreltail	*Sitanion hystrix*
Fescue, Idaho	*Festuca idahoensis*
June grass, prairie	*Koeleria cristata*
Needlegrass	*Stipa* spp.
Wheatgrass, western	*Agropyron smithii*
Bluebunch (bunch)	*Agropyron spicatum*
Crested	*A. desertorum*
Wildrye, medusahead	*Elymus caput-medusae*
Groundsel, woodland	*Senecio sylvaticus*
Halogeton	*Halogeton* spp.
Heath family	Ericaceae
Iris family	Iridaceae
Knapweed	*Centaurea* spp.
Lily family	Liliaceae
Lupine	*Lupinus* spp.
Orchid family	Orchidaceae
Pea family	Fabaceae
Saxifrage family	Saxifragaceae
Willoweed	*Epilobium* spp.

Shrubs

Bitterbrush, antelope	*Purshia tridentata*
Ceanothus	
Deerbrush	*Ceanothus integerrimus*
Redstem	*C. sanguineus*

Snowbrush	*C. velutinus* var. *velutinus*
Whitethorn	*C. cordulatus*
Goosecurrant, Sierra	*Ribes roezlii*
Hawthorn, Douglas	*Crataegus douglassii*
Huckleberry	*Vaccinium* spp.
Mahogany, curlleaf mountain	*Cercocarpus ledifolius*
Manzanita	
Greenleaf	*Arctostaphylos patula*
Whiteleaf	*A. viscida*
Maple, vine	*Acer circinatum*
Ninebark	*Physocarpus* spp.
Oregon grape	*Berberis repens*
Rabbitbrush, gray	*Chrysothamnus nauseosus*
Rhododendron	*Rhododendron* spp.
Rose, wild	*Rosa* spp.
Sagebrush	
basin big	*Artemisia tridentata tridentata*
mountain big	*A. tridentata vaseyana*
Wyoming big	*A. tridentata wyomingensis*
Salal	*Gaultheria shallon*
Saltbrush	
Fourwing	*Atriplex canescens*
Shadscale	*A. confertifolia*
Snowberry	*Symphoricarpos* spp.
Thimbleberry	*Rubus parviflorus*
Winterfat	*Eurotia* spp.

Trees

Alder	*Alnus* spp.
Ash, Oregon	*Fraxinus latifolia*
Aspen, quaking	*Populus tremuloides*
Cedar	*Chamaeocyparis, Libocedrus & Thuja* spp.
Chinkapin, golden	*Castanopsis chrysophylla*
Dogwood, mountain	*Cornus nuttalli*
Douglas-fir	*Pseudotsuga menziesii*
Fir	
Grand	*Abies grandis*
Noble	*A. procera*
Pacific silver	*A. amabalis*
Red	*A. magnifica*
White	*A. concolor*
Hemlock, western	*Tsuga heterophylla*
Incense-cedar	*Libocedrus decurrens*
Juniper, western	*Juniperus occidentalis*
Larch, western	*Larix occidentalis*
Maple	*Acer* spp.

Oak
  California black   *Quercus kelloggii*
  Oregon white   *Q. garryana*
Pine
  Bishop   *Pinus muricata*
  Coulter   *P. coulteri*
  Knobcone   *P. attenuata*
  Loblolly   *P. taeda*
  Longleaf   *P. palustris*
  Monterey   *P. radiata*
  Ponderosa   *P. ponderosa*
  Red   *P. resinosa*
  Sugar   *P. lambertiana*
  Western white   *P. monticola*
Redcedar, western   *Thuja plicata*
Redwood   *Sequoia sempervirens*
Sequoia, giant   *Sequoia giganteum*
Spruce
  Engelmann   *Picea engelmannii*
  Sitka   *P. sitchensis*
Tanoak   *Lithocarpus densiflorus*

Tree Disease Pathogens

Blight, brown spot needle   *Scirrhia acicola*
Butt rot
  Brown cubical butt and
    pocket rot of cedar   *Poria asiatica*
  Schweinitzii   *Phaeolus schweinitzii*
Mistletoe, dwarf   *Arceuthobium* spp.
Root rot (disease)
  Annosus   *Heterobasidion annosum*
  Armillaria   *Armillaria ostoyae*
  Laminated   *Phellinus weirii*
  Rhizina   *Rhizina undulata*

Appendix 2
English-to-Metric Conversion Factors

Length
in × 2.54 = cm
ft × 0.305 = m
breast height (4.5 ft) = 1.4 m
mi × 1.61 = km
mph × 1.61 = km/h

Area
in² × 6.45 = cm²
ft² × 0.093 = m²
ft²/acre × 0.23 = m²/ha
acre × 0.405 = ha

Volume–solid
in³ × 16.4 = cm³
ft³ (CF) × 0.0283 = m³
ft³/acre × 0.07 = m³/ha
bd ft* (BF) × 0.00236 = m³
thousand bd ft* (MBF) × 2.36 = m³
bd ft*/acre × 0.0058 = m³/ha
thousand bd ft* (MBF)/acre × 5.8 = m³/ha

Volume–liquid
fl oz × 28.4 = ml
qt × 0.95 = liter
U.S. gal × 3.785 = liter

Mass
oz × 31.1 = g
lb × 0.454 = kg
lb/acre × 1.12 = kg/ha
ton × 0.9 = metric ton
ton/acre × 2.24 = metric ton/ha
lb/ton × 0.5 = kg/metric ton

Miscellaneous
bar × 100 = kPa
degree Fahrenheit (°F): 0.555 (°F−32) = degree Celsius (°C)
British thermal unit (Btu) × 1.056 = kilojoule (kJ)
Btu/ft/sec × 6.23 = kilowatt (kW)/m/sec

Costs and values
$/acre × 2.47 = $/ha
$/ft³ × 35.3 = $/m³

*Based on nominal measurement (1 in × 1 ft × 1 ft), not actual measurement derived from scaling.

Appendix 3
Glossary

actinomycetes. A special group of bacteria frequently associated with *nitrogen fixation* in species such as red alder and snowbrush ceanothus.

actinorrhizal hardwood. Hardwood such as red alder which bears *nodules* containing nitrogen-fixing *actinomycetes* on its roots.

activity fuels. *Fuels* resulting from or altered by forestry practices such as timber harvesting, *thinning*, etc., as opposed to naturally created fuels.

adsorption. The adherence of particles of a substance to the surface of another substance.

advance regeneration. Young trees that become established before a *regeneration cutting*.

adventitious bud. Bud that arises from any part of a stem, leaf or root, but lacks vascular connection with the pith.

aerosol. An air-suspension (i.e., a mist or fog) of extremely fine, dry or liquid particles, of less than 4 *microns* diameter.

airshed. The geographic area covered by an air supply.

aggradation. Generally, the building up of land surfaces by deposition. More particularly, the filling up of the bed of a watercourse by deposition of detritus, in contrast to scouring by abrasion.

aggregates (soil). A collection of mineral and organic particles bound into a coherent whole.

algorithm. Any particular procedure for solving a certain type of problem, as the rule for finding the greatest common denominator.

aliphatic hydrocarbon. Open-chain or cyclic (non-benzene ring) compound containing hydrogen and carbon; e.g., methane.

allelopathy. The influence of plants, other than microorganisms, upon each other, arising from the products of their metabolism such as exudates and *leachates*.

allergenic. Capable of causing an allergic reaction due to hypersensitivity to a particular substance.

ambrosia beetles. A group of pin-hole borers in wood which culture fungi in their galleries.

anadromous. Species of fish (e.g., salmon, steelhead trout) that migrate from ocean to freshwater rivers and streams to spawn.

angle of repose. Maximum angle of inclination at which a given slope is considered stable.

angular canopy density. The density of a *canopy* in relation to the path of incoming solar radiation measured at an angle to vertical.

animal-unit month (AUM). A measure of rangeland carrying capacity expressed in terms of the number of animals (usually a breeding cow or bull) a given parcel of land will support for 30 days.

anion. Negatively charged *ion*.

annosus root disease (or *rot*). A root rot disease of certain conifers caused by *Heterobasidion annosum* (formerly *Fomes annosus*).

anthropogenic fires. Fires caused by humans, esp. fire caused in antiquity by native Indians.

armillaria root disease (or *rot*). A root rot disease of certain conifers and hardwoods caused by *Armillaria* spp.

arthropods. Small animals with jointed legs (e.g., spiders, mites, and insects).

artificial regeneration. Regeneration of forest stands by planting or direct seeding.

aspect. The direction a slope is facing (e.g., north, east, south, or west).

atmospheric stability. A meteorological term for the degree to which the atmosphere resists turbulence and vertical motion.

AUM. See *animal-unit month*.

autecology. The study of the ecology of individual organisms or species.

axil. The notch at the base of a *cotyledon*, leaf, or branch from which buds and subsequent leaves or branches arise.

bark beetles. A group of beetles that can kill live trees by boring galleries in the inner bark, thereby girdling them.

basal area. The cross-sectional area of the trunk of a tree or *stand* of trees at *breast height* (4.5 ft).

basal burl. A dome-shaped growth at the base of the trunk of certain trees (e.g., tanoak, Pacific madrone).

basal sprouting. The emergence of shoots from *adventitious buds* located at the base of certain trees (e.g., tanoak, Pacific madrone).

basalt soils. Soils derived from the *weathering* of basalt extruded in lava flows from the earth's crust.

bedload. Nonsuspended *sediment* and gravel moved by the flow of water along the bottom of stream channels.

bioassay. The use of living material (e.g., plants or animals) to determine the effect or potency of a substance such as a chemical.

biomass. The mass or weight of material in a *habitat* derived from living organisms.

Words and phrases in italics in the definitions are themselves defined in the glossary. Many of the definitions contained in this glossary were derived from sources listed at the end.

blackline. Fire control line created by preburning *fuels* adjacent to areas to be *prescribed burned.*

board foot. A unit for measuring wood volumes equalling 144 cu in.

bole. The main tree trunk.

breast height. 4.5 ft. above ground.

breast high age. The age of a tree when it reaches *breast height.*

broadcast burn. Intentional burning of debris on a designated unit of land, where the *fuel* has not been *piled* or *windrowed*, by allowing fire to spread freely over the entire area.

brown-and-burn. A method of *prescribed burning* in which a *herbicide* is used to desiccate living vegetation prior to burning.

brown cubical butt rot. Characteristic stem decay of conifers caused by *Phaeolus schweinitzii* (formerly *Polyporus schweinitzii*) and *Poria asiatica.*

burn window. The seasonal period available for conducting a burn within *prescription.*

cambium. The *meristematic* layer of cells beneath the bark of a tree that produces diameter growth through the process of cell division.

canopy. The tree crowns in a *stand.*

carcinogen. A substance capable of causing cancer.

cation. Positively charged *ion.*

cation exchange. The replacement of one *cation* by another in soil (e.g., passing a dilute solution of ammonium sulfate through a soil yields calcium sulfate in the *leachate*).

cation exchange capacity. The sum total of exchangeable *cations* that a soil can *adsorb.*

cavity-nesting birds. Bird species which construct nests in cavities in the trunk of a tree or *snag.*

channel erosion. Rearrangement and transport of material from the banks and streamsides of a defined stream or river channel.

chaparral. Scrubby broad-leaved evergreen shrubs characteristic of dry, fire-prone climates.

chelator. Nonmetallic chemical compound capable of binding strongly with metallic *ions.*

chemosynthesis. The process whereby certain bacteria capture energy from inorganic nutrients, creating new organic nutrients (foods) out of carbon dioxide and water. It differs from *photosynthesis* in that the source of energy is derived from chemical reactions involving inorganic materials such as sulfur, iron, and nitrogen, rather than sunlight.

chrysomelid beetles. A family of beetles which feed on foliage; commonly known as leaf beetles.

Class I area. Zone where air quality is expected to be pristine or void of impairments of visibility from human-caused pollution (e.g., National Parks and Wilderness).

clay mineralogy. The physical and chemical properties of inorganic soil material with particles less than 0.0008 inch in diameter.

clearcut. Removal of the entire standing crop of trees at one time.

climax. The final or mature stage in *secondary plant succession* which persists for an indefinite period of time if no major disturbances occur.

closed fire season. Period of the year during which permits are required for open burning if it is allowed at all. Special fire suppression precautions are required for industrial operations (e.g., harvesting, road construction) on forest land.

coarse woody debris. Snags, fallen trees, and decaying logs and large limbs distributed across the *forest floor* that are larger than 4 inches in diameter.

Collembola. An order of minute insects usually found in damp soil and decaying logs; commonly known as springtails.

colloids (soil). Small particles generally less than several *microns* in diameter. The name refers to the bulk behavior of many such particles which is determined by their surface properties.

cone beetles. Small species of beetles that damage pine cones, sometimes causing heavy seed losses.

contingent valuation. A survey technique for estimating the market value of a traditionally nonmarket resource (e.g., clean air, aesthetics), by determining an individual's willingness to pay for or to accept compensation for foregoing the item or experience.

controlled burn (or *fire*). The planned application of a fire to forest or rangeland *fuels* with the intent to confine it to a predetermined area.

convection. 1) In meteorology, vertical atmospheric motion (upward) in a predominantly unstable atmosphere. 2) In fire physics, the transfer of heat by the movement of masses of hot air; the natural direction is upwards in the absence of any appreciable wind speed and/or *slope.*

cool burn. A qualitative term, usually referring to a *prescribed burn* conducted during the spring when the *forest floor* and *large fuels* are relatively moist, thereby reducing *duff* and *fuel* consumption.

cotyledon. Temporary food storage leaf of a germinating plant.

cover. Vegetation which provides protection of animals from weather extremes and predators.

creep. The slow, downslope movement of a soil mass, generally from a few hundredths of an inch to a few inches per year.

crown fire. A fire that advances through the *canopy* of a forest.

cryptogeal germination. Germination hidden from view.

cull material. Nonmerchantable trees and logs that are left on site.

culm. A stem or stalk, especially the jointed, hollow stem of certain grasses.

cumulative effects. The collective influence of a number of land management practices on a watershed or downstream conditions.

cup trenching. Trenching across a *slope* to create a berm to catch falling debris.

damping off. The inhibition of seed germination or the wilting of the emerging shoots due to fungal infection of the radicle (emerging root) or fungal attack at the base of the shoots.

dbh. Diameter of a tree at *breast height*.

debris flow (or *avalanche, slide, torrent*). The sudden movement and transport of a liquified matrix of logs, limbs, and other woody debris down a stream or river channel.

debris jam. A matrix of logs, limbs, and other woody debris blocking a stream or river channel; a log jam.

deciduous. A plant which loses all its leaves or needles during the fall and winter.

decomposers. Microorganisms responsible for the decay of organic material.

defoliators. Insects, usually caterpillars, that feed on the foliage of plants, often defoliating them.

denitrification. The process, involving soil microorganisms, whereby nitrate and nitrite bound in soil are reduced and returned back to the air as nitrogen gas or nitrous oxide.

density (in forestry). The number of trees per unit area.

dependent crown fire. A *crown fire* that depends on a *surface fire* to sustain itself.

downed logs. Fallen trees and large logs lying on the *forest floor*.

driptorch. An incendiary device (aerial or hand-held) that releases slow-burning flaming *fuel* at a predetermined rate.

duff. The layer of partially and fully decomposed organic materials lying below the *litter* and immediately above the *mineral soil*. It corresponds to the *fermentation* and *humus layers* of the *forest floor*.

dwarf mistletoe. *Parasitic plant* which infects certain conifers, often causing characteristic "witches' brooms" and reducing growth. ·

earthflow. The slow or incremental downhill flow of soil or soil layers saturated with water.

ecosystem. Any complex of living organisms with their environment.

ecotone. The transition zone between two adjoining communities.

ecotype. A locally adapted variant of a species (biotype) resulting from natural selection by the special conditions of a particular *habitat*.

edge. The more or less well-defined boundary between two or more elements of the environment, e.g., field/woodland.

engraver beetles. Small species of *bark beetles* that carve characteristic galleries in the inner bark of mostly weakened, injured, dying, or recently killed trees.

epicormic sprouting. Shoots arising spontaneously from *adventitious buds* on the stem or branch of a woody plant.

epidemiology. The science of studying disease in populations.

epigeous fungi. Fungi fruiting above ground.

epiphytic plant. Plant (e.g., lichens, moss) growing on, but not nourished by, another plant; in contrast to *parasitic plant*.

equilibrium moisture content. The moisture content that *fuels* will attain if exposed for an infinite period in an environment of specified constant temperature and humidity; when fuels have reached their equilibrium moisture content, the net exchange of moisture between them and their environment is zero.

evapotranspiration. The conversion of water, whether open or as soil moisture (both by evaporation) or within plants (by *transpiration*), into water vapor that is released to the atmosphere.

exchange capacity. See *cation exchange capacity*.

exudate. Excretions of chemical substances by plant roots.

facultative sprouters. Plants which have the capacity to reproduce by either seeding or sprouting, depending on the situation (e.g., most shrubs and hardwoods).

felling. The practice of cutting timber.

fermentation layer (or *horizon*). The layer near the surface of forest soils where decomposition of the *litter* by microorganisms first takes place. The litter is still recognizable in this layer, in contrast to the *humus layer* directly beneath it.

fine fuels. *Fuels* that ignite readily and are consumed rapidly by fire (e.g., cured grass, fallen leaves, needles, small twigs less than 1/4-inch in diameter).

fire intensity. See *fireline intensity*.

fire interaction. A situation where two or more separate fires interact, often resulting in increased *fireline intensity* or extreme fire behavior.

fire return interval. The average time between wildfires in a given *ecosystem*.

fire scar. A healing or healed-over injury, caused or aggravated by fire, on a woody plant.

fire severity. A qualitative term used to describe the relative effect of fire on an *ecosystem*, especially the degree of *organic matter* consumption and soil heating. Thus, fires are commonly classed as low, moderate, and high severity. Fire severity may or may not be closely related to *fireline intensity*.

firebrand. Any burning material such as leaves, wood, glowing charcoal, and sparks, that could start a forest fire.

fireline intensity. The rate of heat energy release per unit time per unit length of fire front. Usually expressed as Btu/sec/ft or kW/sec/m.

flash point. The lowest temperature at which a solid or liquid first gives off flammable vapor at a sufficient rate to produce a flash in still air on applying a small flame.

flatheaded borers. Beetles in the family Buprestidae, the inner bark-boring larvae of which have flattened heads invaginated somewhat into the prothorax.

foliage disease. Abnormal physiological condition of the leaves or needles of plants, usually caused by *pathogenic* microorganisms.

food web. The complex and frequently interlocking pattern of different *trophic levels* in an *ecosystem*.

forb. Broadleaved herbaceous plant.

forest floor. The surface organic-matter layer of forest soil types.

forest productivity. See *site productivity*.

forest succession. See *secondary succession*.

frost heaving. Upward displacement of normal soil levels as a result of expansion due to ice formation in frozen soil.

fry. The young of fishes.

fuel. Any substance or composite mixture susceptible to ignition and combustion.

fuel break. Any natural or constructed barrier utilized to segregate, stop, and control the spread of fire or to provide a control line from which to work.

fuel ladder. A vertical continuity in *fuel* between the ground and crown of a forest *stand*.

fuel load. The dry weight of combustible materials per unit area; usually expressed as t/ac.

fuel management. The planned manipulation and/or reduction of living or dead forest *fuels* for forest management and other land-use objectives.

gasification. The process whereby heat is used to convert solids or liquids to gases.

geomorphic processes. The geological and environmental processes whereby *landforms* are created.

granitics. Soils derived from granite.

grass stage (of pine). The seedling stage of longleaf pine, sometimes lasting several years, before height growth begins.

greenhouse effect. The hypothesized gradual warming of the earth due to the accumulation of carbon dioxide and other gases in the atmosphere that trap *infrared radiation*.

gross volume. The total volume of wood in a tree, whether merchantable or not.

growth (of timber). The increase in size, quality, or volume of individual trees or *stands* during a given period of time.

gully erosion. A form of erosion resulting from continued incision of steep-walled channels by water.

habitat type. A distinct assemblage of plants and animals occupying a given area that can be distinguished from surrounding areas on the basis of certain identifiable characteristics, including environmental conditions.

hack-and-squirt. A method of applying *herbicides* that involves making a notch or frill in the lower *bole* of target trees and then treating the cut surface with a systemic herbicide.

hazard. 1) In *toxicology*: The capability of a chemical to cause an adverse health effect. 2) In *fuel management*: The existence of a *fuel* complex that constitutes a threat of wildfire ignition, unacceptable fire behavior and severity, or suppression difficulty.

hazard reduction (or *abatement*). In *fuel management*: The planned treatment or manipulation of naturally growing vegetation or any other flammable material for the purpose of reducing the rate of spread and the output of heat energy from any wildfire occurring in the area treated.

heat capacity. The ability of a substance to absorb heat; specifically, the heat (or energy) required to raise the temperature of a unit volume or mass of a given substance 1°C. For example, the heat required to raise one gram of water 1°C is one calorie, and the specific heat capacity for water is, therefore, 1 cal/g·°C.

heat of vaporization. The quantity of heat per unit mass that must be supplied to a material at its boiling point to convert it completely to a gas at the same temperature. For example, the heat of vaporization of water at 100°C is 539 cal/g.

heart rot. A decay characteristically confined to the heartwood. It usually originates in the living tree.

helispot. A temporary area prepared to facilitate helicopter landings.

helitorch. A specialized *driptorch*, using a gelled *fuel*, slung beneath and activated from a helicopter.

herbicide. A chemical capable of killing plants or suppressing their growth and development.

herbivore. An animal that feeds on plants (e.g., insects, deer, cattle).

high-grading. A harvesting technique that removes only the best trees to obtain high, short-term financial returns at the long-term expense of remaining *stand* growth potential.

hot burn. A qualitative term used to describe a burn conducted under dry conditions (usually in summer or early fall), leading to a high degree of *fuel* consumption (sometimes including the *duff* layer of soil).

humus. A general term for the more or less decomposed plant and animal residues in the soil. Specifically, the more or less stable fraction from the decomposed soil organic material; generally amorphous, *colloidal*, and dark colored.

hydraulic conductivity. A proportionality factor describing the viscous flow of water in soil.

hydrology. The study of the circulation of water in and between the atmosphere and the earth's crust, with particular emphasis on the phases initiated by precipitation and ending with *evapotranspiration*.

hydrophobic soil. A soil condition in which the *infiltration* of water into the soil profile is impeded by the presence of a layer of *colloids* that have little attraction for water.

hydrophobicity. The property of repelling the *infiltration* of water into a soil profile.

hydrostatic pressure. The pressure created by the presence of a fluid (specifically water in *ecosystem* situations).

hyphae. The filamentous strands that form the mycelium (vegetative network) of fungi.

hypogeous fungi. Fungi fruiting below ground.

igneous rock. Rock of volcanic origin or crystallized from molten magma or other sources of intense heat (e.g., granite).

independent crown fire. A fire that advances only in the crown *fuel* layer or *canopy* of a forest.

indraft. The inward movement of air toward a fire. It is caused by the reduced air pressure as flames, smoke, and heated gases rise. Creating an indraft can be useful in *prescribed burning* patterns such as center firing, as well as in fire control.

infection court. The site of infection by a *pathogen*, often a wound or damaged area on the plant.

infiltration. The penetration of still, clear water downwards into a soil.

infiltration capacity. The rate of penetration of still, clear water downwards into a soil.

infrared radiation. Longwave radiation or radiation from the infrared portion of the electromagnetic spectrum; usually detectable as sensible heat.

inoculum. A quantity of infectious agent.

intermediate fuels. Fuels too large to be ignited until after the leading edge of the fire front passes, but small enough to be completely consumed.

interplanting. The practice of setting young trees among existing forest growth, planted or natural.

inversion. The meteorological phenomenon of increase of air temperature with vertical height. It is associated with minimal air movement or stagnation.

invertebrates. Animals lacking a backbone or vertebrae (e.g., insects, spiders, worms).

ions. Electrically charged atoms or groups of atoms.

jackstrawed. Fallen trees and logs scattered in a random fashion like "pick-up sticks."

kill-trapping. The practice of trapping pest animals using lethal traps.

ladder fuels, laddering. Fuels that provide vertical continuity between the surface fuels and crown fuels in a forest *stand*, thus contributing to the ease of torching and crowning.

laminated root rot. A root disease of conifers caused by *Phellinus weirii* that, in advanced stages, causes laminated decay of the wood.

landform. Geographic and topographic patterns of a particular landscape (e.g., mountains, plateaus, capes).

leach, leaching. The removal of soluble substances from soil by percolating water.

leachate. The solution containing leached substances.

leaf cutter. A category of insects that cut leaves for nest-building and nourishment (e.g., leaf-cutting ants).

legume, leguminous. A family of plants characterized by possessing seed pods; many species are noted for *nitrogen-fixing* properties (e.g., locust, vetch, pea).

lignotuber. A woody storage structure, forming a swelling more or less at ground level, that originates from the *axils* of *cotyledons* or, less commonly, from one or more pairs of the earliest seedling-leaves, and from whose concealed, dormant buds a new tree can develop following severe injury to the old one.

litter layer (or *horizon*). The uppermost layer of organic debris on a *forest floor*; essentially the freshly fallen or only slightly decomposed vegetable material, mainly foliate but also bark fragments, twigs, flowers, fruits, etc. Note: This and the less decomposed portion of *humus* are together often termed *duff*.

mass ignition. The setting of a number of individual fires throughout an area either simultaneously (usually with explosives) or in quick succession (usually with a *helitorch*) and so spaced that they soon coalesce, influence, and support each other to produce a hot, fast-spreading fire throughout the area.

mass soil failure (or *mass movement, mass wasting*). The sudden movement of soil and above-ground material downslope.

meristem, meristematic. Plant tissue primarily concerned with protoplasmic synthesis and formation of new cells by division (e.g., buds, *cambium*).

mesofauna. Insects, mites, spiders, and other small animals inhabiting the soil.

microclimate. Generally, the climate of small areas (e.g., around a seedling), especially insofar as it differs from the general climate of the region. More particularly, the climate under a plant or other *cover*, differing, for example, in extremes of temperature and moisture from the climate outside that cover.

micrometer, micron. One-millionth of a meter.

mineral soil. The layer of soil beneath the *duff*.

mineralization. The conversion of an element from an organic form to an inorganic state as a result of microbial decomposition.

mistletoe. See *dwarf mistletoe*.

monocot. Plant derived from a seed embryo with only one *cotyledon* (e.g., grass).

mop up. The act of extinguishing a fire after it has been brought under control.

mortality (in a *stand*). The number or volume of trees that died because of fire, insects, disease, climatic factors, or competition from other trees or vegetation. Some mortality volume can be salvaged and thus contribute to total *yield*.

mudflow. The slow, downhill flow of soil or soil layers saturated with water.

mycorrhizae. 1) Literally "fungal-roots"; the phenomenon of the probably *symbiotic*, or at least non*parasitic*, association between the root or *rhizome* of a green plant and a fungus. 2) The structure so produced by the combination of the modified rootlet with fungal tissue.

natural regeneration. The renewal of a tree crop by natural seeding or sprouting.

nematode. Microscopic eelworm that feeds in the intercellular spaces of plant tissue, causing disintegration of the cells.

net primary production. The accumulation of organic matter in plant tissues (through *photosynthesis* and *chemosynthesis*) in excess of the respiratory utilization by plants during the period of measurement.

niche. The specific spot or role occupied by an individual organism in its environment.

nitrification. A two-step process whereby ammonia is oxidized to nitrite and then to nitrate.

nitrifiers. Microorganisms (primarily bacteria) in the soil capable of oxidizing ammonia and nitrite to nitrate.

nitrogen fixation. The conversion of elemental nitrogen from the atmosphere to organic combinations or to forms readily utilizable in biological processes. Usually accomplished by *nodule* bacteria in *legumes*, by other microorganisms in certain nodulated nonlegumes, and by blue-green algae in some lichens.

Nitrosomonas. A genus of bacteria capable of oxidizing nitrite to nitrate.

nodule. Swollen excrescence on the outside of roots of certain plants (e.g., *legumes*, alder, ceanothus) that contain *nitrogen-fixing* bacteria in a *symbiotic* relationship with the plants.

nonresinous species. Coniferous species lacking normal resin canals in their wood (e.g., hemlocks, true firs).

noxious plants (or *weeds*). Weeds legally classified as a particular threat to agricultural crops or livestock (e.g., Canada thistle, tansy ragwort, Russian knapweed).

nurse log. A decaying log which provides a perch for the establishment of tree seedlings such as hemlock and western redcedar.

nutrient budget. The amount and rate of a given nutrient or collection of nutrients as they cycle in and through an *ecosystem*.

nutrient cycle. The path which nutrients follow as they flow through an *ecosystem*.

obligate seeder. A plant which reproduces solely by seed (e.g., most conifers).

obligate sprouter. A plant which reproduces solely by vegetative means, specifically sprouting from dormant buds (e.g., aspen in some upland settings).

old-growth forest. Forest *ecosystem* that has developed over a long period essentially free of catastrophic (including human) disturbance. In the Pacific Northwest, an old-growth forest generally ranges in age from 200 to 750 years or more and contains the following structural features: 1) large, live old-growth trees, 2) *snags*, and 3) large logs on the *forest floor* and in streams.

1-hr timelag fuels. *Fuels* consisting of dead herbaceous plants and roundwood less than about one-fourth inch in diameter. Also included is the uppermost layer of needles or leaves on the *forest floor*. See *timelag*.

organic compound. Chemical substance derived from living matter that contains carbon as an integral component.

organic matter. Material consisting of or derived from living organisms. In soil, organic matter is the more or less decomposed residue of plants and animals, commonly referred to as *humus*.

overland flow. See *runoff*.

oxide. Chemical compound formed by the reaction of oxygen combining with another element (e.g., carbon dioxide).

parasitic plant. Plant (e.g., mistletoe) that grows on and is nourished by another plant; in contrast to *epiphytic plant*.

partial cut. Any cutting method that removes less than the total tree *stand* at any one time.

particulates. A component of polluted air consisting of any liquid or solid particles suspended in or falling through the atmosphere. Particulates are responsible for the visible forms of air pollution.

passerine birds. Birds belonging to the order *Passeriformes*, characterized by feet adapted for perching (e.g., sparrows, finches).

pathogen. An organism, usually microscopic, or virus, directly capable of causing disease.

pH. A measure of acidity. Technically, the negative logarithm of the hydrogen *ion* concentration of a solution.

phenology. The study or pattern of the time of appearance of characteristic periodic phenomena in the lifecycle of organisms in nature (e.g., migration of birds, flowering and leaf-fall in plants), particularly as these phenomena are influenced by local environmental factors.

pheromone. A substance secreted by an animal (particularly certain insects) or produced synthetically that influences the behavior of other members of the same species. Some pheromones attract females, some attract males, and some are anti-aggregating.

photolysis. The splitting of a chemical compound by light, leading to its degradation.

photosynthesis. The building up of *organic compounds* in green plant cells from carbon dioxide in the presence of water and light.

pile-and-burn. A *controlled burn* where *slash* is concentrated, usually by machinery, before burning.

PNV. See *present net value*.

PNW. See *present net value*.

pocket rot. In wood, any rot localized in small areas, generally forming rounded or lens-shaped cavities; variants, according to appearance, are honeycomb rot and pitted (sap) rot.

ppb. Parts per billion.

ppm. Parts per million.

precipitation intensity. The amount of rainfall per unit time.

prescribed burn (or *fire*). The controlled application of fire to wildland *fuels* in either their natural or modified state, under such conditions of weather, fuel moisture, soil moisture, etc. as allow the fire to be confined to a predetermined area and at the same time to produce the intensity of heat and rate of spread required to further certain planned objectives of *silviculture*, wildlife management, grazing, *hazard reduction*, etc. The intention is to employ fire scientifically so as to realize maximum net benefits with minimum damage and at acceptable cost.

present net value (or *worth*). The net value at one point in time of a series of benefits and costs arising at subsequent points of time. Discounting procedures are used to equate the values at a single point in time, the present.

primary production. The storage of energy by *photosynthetic* and *chemosynthetic* organisms (chiefly green plants) in the form of organic material which can be used as food by other organisms.

propagules. Plant parts, such as buds, tubers, roots, or shoots used to propagate an individual vegetatively.

protoplasmic synthesis. The formation of living matter.

protozoa. Animals consisting of one cell or of a colony of like or similar cells.

quiescence. A state of rest or suspended activity in plants, usually associated with unfavorable environmental conditions for growth.

raptor. Bird of prey (e.g., hawk, eagle, owl, falcon).

ravel, raveling. The downslope movement of the unstable mantle of soil, gravel, rocks, and organic debris covering certain soil types on steep terrain.

reach. In logging, the distance a *yarding* system can traverse to retrieve logs.

refractory seed. Seed in which it is difficult to induce germination due to strong dormancy controls (e.g., ceanothus seed that require *scarification* by heat from fire before they germinate).

regeneration cut. Any removal of trees intended to assist regeneration already present or to make regeneration possible.

residues. The *slash* and other unmerchantable woody debris left after logging operations.

resinous species. Conifer species with distinct resin canal systems (e.g., pines, spruces, larches, and Douglas-fir).

rhizome. A stem, generally modified (particularly for storing food materials), that grows along but below the ground surface and produces adventitious roots, scale leaves, and suckers irregularly along its length, not just at nodes (e.g., certain ferns and berry plants).

rhizosphere. The microenvironment of roots.

rill erosion. Mild water erosion producing very small and numerous channels.

riparian zone. The zone of vegetation growing adjacent or in close proximity to a watercourse, lake, swamp or spring, and often dependent on its roots reaching the water table.

risk. 1) In *toxicology*: The probability of an adverse effect occurring from exposure to a chemical. 2) In *fuel management*: A source of or causative agent for wildfire.

root collar. On a tree, the transition zone between stem and root. Usually recognizable in trees and seedlings by a slight swelling.

root crown. Expanded root tissue near the base of certain woody plants that contains *adventitious buds* capable of sprouting.

root disease. Deterioration or abnormal physiological functioning of root systems caused by various species of root rot fungi.

root strength. The ability of plant roots to bind soil particles together or to underlying rock, thereby increasing *soil strength*.

root throw. See *windthrow*.

rotation. The planned number of years between the formation or regeneration of a crop or *stand* and its final cutting at a specified stage of maturity.

runoff. The natural drainage of water away from an area. Conventionally, the stream flow that represents the collected drainage water from an area. It includes both surface and *subsurface flow* and is generally measured in cubic feet or acre-feet of water.

salmonid. A family of fishes, most of which spend part of their life cycle in freshwater and part in saltwater (e.g., salmon, steelhead trout).

sanitize. In *silviculture*, the practice of removing dead, damaged or susceptible trees, essentially to prevent the spread of pests or *pathogens* and so promote forest hygiene.

saprophyte, saprophytic. A plant organism that is incapable of synthesizing its nutrient requirements from purely inorganic sources, and feeds on dead organic material, commonly assisting its decay.

sawflies. A group of insects, the larvae of which are noted for their ability to *defoliate* trees, particularly conifers. The name is derived from the serrate, sawlike ovipositor of the females.

scalping. Physically removing the sod or surface layer of debris, exposing *mineral soil* for tree planting.

scarification. 1) Of seed: Wearing down, by abrasion, heat, or chemical (generally acid) treatment, the outer coats of hard seed, essentially so as to improve their germinability. 2) Of soil: Disturbing the *forest floor* and topsoil in preparation for *natural regeneration*, direct seeding or planting.

schweinitzii butt rot. Brown rot decay of the lower *bole* of conifers caused by the fungus *Phaeolus schweinitzii* (formerly *Polyporus schweinitzii*).

sciurids. Chipmunks and squirrels.

scree. A mantle of rocks and gravel, generally void of soil material, that can cover soils on steep slopes.

sculpin. Fresh- and saltwater fish characterized by a large head with one or more spines on each side.

second-growth forest. Forest that originated naturally or was planted on the site of a previous *stand* (usually virgin) which was removed by cutting, fire, or other disturbance.

secondary production. The accumulation of energy by consumer and decomposer organisms in the food chain.

secondary succession. The gradual replacement of one plant community by another until ecological stability occurs or disturbance reinitiates the cycle. In contrast to *primary succession* which involves the colonization of sites that have previously not borne vegetation.

sedimentation. The accumulation of soil in stream channels, estuaries, and lake bottoms as a result of upland erosion.

seral stage. A distinct but transitory community in the process of plant *succession*.

sere. The sequence of communities in the process of plant *succession*.

serotiny, serotinous. Referring to cones of certain species of conifers (e.g., lodgepole and knobcone pines) that remain closed on the tree after maturity, awaiting events such as a fire before opening and shedding their seed.

SEV. See *soil expectation value*.

shear strength. In soil physics, the capacity of a soil mass to resist shearing deformation.

sheet erosion. Erosion of a fairly homogeneous layer of material; may be imperceptible, particularly when caused by wind, or else evidenced by numerous fine *rills*.

shelterwood. A situation in which new seedlings grow and become established in the partial shade and protection of older trees left after partial cutting. Subsequent harvest(s) are usually 5 to 10 years later, yielding an even-aged *stand*.

shrub-steppe. An extensive plain or rolling grassland containing intermittent shrubs such as sagebrush.

silica. The dioxide form of silicon found in quartz, sand flint, and agate.

silicate minerals. Minerals containing *silica*.

silviculture. The art, science, and practice of establishing, tending, and reproducing forest *stands* with desired characteristics, based on knowledge of species characteristics and environmental requirements.

site index. A particular measure of site class (*soil productivity*), based on the height of the dominant trees in a *stand* at an arbitrarily chosen age (usually 25, 50, or 100 years).

site preparation. Preparing an area of land for forest establishment. Methods used may involve clearing of debris, vegetation control, and soil treatment.

site productivity. The inherent capacity of a site to produce biomass. In forestry it is commonly expressed as site class or *site index*.

skidroad. Any way, more or less prepared, over which logs are dragged, usually from their point of harvest to a loading area.

slash. The unmerchantable residue left on the ground after logging, *thinning*, or other forest operations. This includes tree tops, branches, defective logs, bark, chips, uprooted stumps, and felled shrubs and noncommercial trees.

slash-and-burn. The *felling* and burning of nonmerchantable shrubs or trees on a site to prepare the site for establishment of a new *stand* of trees.

slash burn. A *prescribed burn* to dispose of unmerchantable residue left after logging or *site preparation* operations.

slope. The degree of incline of a land surface in relation to a horizontal plane. It is usually expressed as a percentage equal to the vertical rise or fall in elevation divided by the horizontal distance and then multiplied by 100.

slope stability. The inherent resistance of a soil and underlying layers to downward movement by gravity.

slopover. A fire that crosses a control line intended to confine the original fire.

slump. The sagging or subtle downslope shifting of a soil mass due to unstable soil structural conditions.

smolt. Young silvery salmon migrating to the sea.

snag. A standing dead tree from which the leaves and most of the branches have fallen.

soil biota. The collection of living organisms (e.g., earthworms, insects, fungi, bacteria, etc.) inhabiting the soil.

soil expectation value (SEV). The *present net worth* of an infinite series of *rotations*.

soil macropores. Relatively large soil spaces capable of transporting soil water and nutrients by gravitational forces.

soil organic matter. See *organic matter*.

soil porosity. The ratio of the volume of pores to the total volume of soil; this is a major factor affecting structural characteristics, *infiltration capacity*, water storage, and *subsurface flow* in soils.

soil strength. The ability of a soil to resist *shearing* and compacting stresses.

soil structure. The combination or arrangement of primary soil particles into secondary particles or units.

sorption surface. The surface area of particles available for binding substances such as moisture, nutrients, pollutants, etc.

spike camp. A camp with minimum facilities established along a fireline for the subsistence and equipping of firefighters assigned to that portion of the fire perimeter.

splash erosion. Erosion caused by drops of water striking a soil surface and transporting soil particles in the splash droplets; it may degrade or destroy the *soil structure*.

spore. A reproductive body, characteristic particularly of the lower plants (e.g., ferns) and fungi, consisting of one or a few cells and never containing an embryo.

sporophore. A *spore*-producing or spore-supporting structure (e.g., mushroom or conk) in the larger fungi.

spotting. The behavior of a fire producing sparks or embers (*firebrands*) that are carried by the wind and which start new fires beyond the main fire perimeter.

stand. A recognizable area of the forest that is relatively homogeneous and can be managed as a single unit.

steady state (quasi). The stage in development of a fire in which the buildup of *fireline intensity*, heat output, and rate of spread become relatively constant.

stem canker. Diseases of the main *bole* or branches of trees caused by fungi and resulting in deformity and/or girdling of the stem at the point of infection.

stem disease. Abnormal physiological condition in or on the stem of plants; usually caused by fungi.

steppe. An extensive plain or grassland, usually without trees.

stoichiometric process. A chemical reaction process in which the individual elements or compounds are present in the exact proportions necessary for a given reaction to occur.

stratification. In plant propagation, the storing of seeds in (and, strictly, in layers with) a moistened medium, e.g., peat or sand, so as to maintain viability and overcome dormancy.

subsurface flow. That part of the *runoff* that percolates through the soil under the influence of gravity as groundwater (i.e., in contrast to surface runoff) before emerging as seepage or springs.

succession. See *secondary succession*.

surface erosion. The loss of upper layers of the soil profile due to the action of wind, water, or gravity.

surface fire. A fire that burns in the surface *fuel* layer, excluding the crowns of the trees, as either a head fire, flank fire, or backfire.

suspended sediment. Soil particles held in suspension by turbulence of flowing water.

symbiosis. A relationship between two or more kinds of living organisms wherein all (the symbionts) benefit and which is sometimes obligatory for all.

synecology. The study of the ecology of groups or communities of organisms as a unit.

talus slope. Slope consisting of rock fragments derived from cliffs and rock outcrops lying upslope.

10-hr timelag fuels. Dead fuels consisting of roundwood 1/4- to 1-inch in diameter and, very roughly, the layer of *litter* extending from just below the surface of the *forest floor* to 3/4-in below the surface. See *timelag.*

thermal conductivity. The property of a body, e.g., a piece of wood or mass of soil, whereby heat may pass through it; measured as the amount of heat passing in unit time between faces of unit area, unit distance apart, and differing in temperature by 1°C.

thermal cover. Vegetation which is dense enough to have a moderating effect on air temperature and wind velocity to protect wildlife from weather extremes.

thinning. Tree removal in a forest *stand* that reduces tree *density* and tree-to-tree competition. Also, a *felling* made in an immature crop or stand in order primarily to accelerate diameter increment but also, by suitable selection, to improve the average form of the trees that remain, without—at least according to classical concepts—permanently breaking the *canopy.* Trees of merchantable value are cut and removed during "commercial" thinnings whereas trees of nonmerchantable value are thinned and left on site during "precommercial" thinnings.

1000-hr fuel moisture. The moisture content of 1000-hr *timelag* roundwood *fuels.*

1000-hr timelag fuels. Dead *fuels* consisting of roundwood 3 to 8 inches in diameter, or the layer of the *forest floor* more than about 4 inches below the surface, or both. Such fuels take about 1,000 hours to lose approximately two-thirds of the difference between their initial moisture content and their *equilibrium moisture content.*

timber. A general term for forest crops and *stands* or their wood products.

timelag. The drying time, under stated conditions, for dead *fuels* to lose about two-thirds of the difference between their initial moisture content and their *equilibrium moisture content.* The timelag therefore represents the rate of moisture change in a fuel. Dead forest fuels can have timelag values from minutes to months.

tolerance. The ability of an organism or biological process to subsist under a given set of environmental conditions such as shade or fire.

toxicology. The study of the physiological response of organisms to toxic chemicals.

transpiration. The process by which water vapor passes from the foliage or other parts of a living plant to the atmosphere.

trophic level. The level in the food chain hierarchy at which an organism obtains its food. Green plants occupy the first trophic level, *herbivores* a second, carnivores a third, scavengers a fourth, and *decomposers* a fifth.

turbidity. An optical property of a suspension; used to index amount of *suspended* particles in water, such as silt, clay, plankton, microscopic organisms, and *organic matter.*

underburning (or *understory burning*). *Prescribed burning* with a low *fireline intensity* fire under a timber *canopy.*

understory fire (or *burn*). A low *fireline intensity* fire that burns beneath the *canopy* of a *timber stand.* It can occur during the course of a wildfire as well as under *prescribed fire* conditions.

vaporization. The process whereby a substance is converted from a liquid to a gas, usually through the application of heat.

variable source area. Geographic area from which sources of streamflow, sediment, and other pollution emissions vary with time.

volatilization. The rapid evaporation of a liquid.

water repellency. See *hydrophobicity.*

waterbar. A small berm constructed across a potential water channel (e.g., a *skidroad* or fireline) to divert *runoff* and thereby minimize erosion.

weathering. The basic process of soil formation caused by the biological, physical, and chemical decomposition of rock and rock mantle by atmospheric processes involving temperature extremes, precipitation, and wind.

weevils. A group of insects characterized by adults which have a prominent snout.

whole-tree harvesting. *Felling* and transporting the whole tree, i.e., with its crown and sometimes even its roots, for trimming and cross-cutting at a landing or mill.

windrow. *Slash,* brushwood, etc. concentrated along a line, so as to clear the intervening ground between.

windthrow. Uprootal of trees by the wind; also, a tree or trees so uprooted.

witches' broom. An abnormally bushy, local growth of parts of the branch system on woody plants, often characterized by shortening of the internodes and excessive proliferation ("brooming"); generally *pathogenic* in origin, from fungi or *parasitic* seed plants.

wood borer. Insect that attacks trees, logs, and lumber by boring into the wood.

yarding. The operation of the initial haul of cut timber or logs to a collecting point; i.e., of transporting timber from stump to a yard or landing, usually using cable equipment.

yield (stand). The amount of forest produce (e.g., *timber*) that may be harvested periodically from a specified area over a specified period.

YUM. An acronym for "*yarding* unmerchantable material."

Key Sources of Definitions

Deeming, J.E., R.E. Burgan, and J.D. Cohen. 1977. The National Fire-Danger Rating System—1978. USDA For. Serv., Intermt. For. Rge. Exp. Sta., Ogden, UT. Gen. Tech. Rep. INT-39. 63 p.

Esau, K. 1966. Anatomy of Seed Plants. John Wiley & Sons, Inc., New York, NY. 376 p.

Ford-Robertson, F.C. (ed.) 1983. Terminology of Forest Science Technology Practice and Products. Soc. Amer. For., Washington, D.C. 370 p.

Franklin, J.F., K. Cromack, Jr., W. Denison, A. McKee, C. Maser, J. Sedell, F. Swanson, and G. Juday. 1981. Ecological characteristics of old-growth Douglas-fir forests. USDA For. Serv., Pac. Northwest Res. Sta., Portland, OR. Gen. Tech. Rep. PNW-118. 48 p.

GEOMET, Inc. 1978. Impact of Forestry Burning Upon Air Quality. A State-of-the-Knowledge Characterization in Washington and Oregon. Reg. X, U.S. Environ. Prot. Agency, Seattle, WA. EPA 910/9-78-052. 253 p.

Hanley, D.P., D.R. White, D.L. Adams, and D.M. Baumgartner. 1987. Terminology for forest landowners. Coop. Ext., Coll. Agr. Home Econ., Washington State Univ., Pullman, WA. EB 1353. 19 p.

Lyon, C.B. (ed.) 1984. Wildland fire management terminology. FAO-UNESCO Project, Washington, D.C. 250 p.

Merrill, D.F., and M.E. Alexander (eds.) 1987. Glossary of forest fire management terms. Can. Comm. For. Fire Mgt., Nat. Res. Counc., Ottawa, Canada. 91 p.

Morgan, P., and L.F. Neuenschwander. 1988. Shrub response to high and low severity burns following clearcutting in northern Idaho. West. J. Appl. For. 3: 5-9.

Soil Science Society of America. 1975. Glossary of Soil Science Terms. Soil Sci. Soc. Amer., Madison, WI. 34 p.

Stein, J., and L. Urdang. 1973. The Random House Dictionary of the English Language. Random House, Inc., New York, NY. 2059 p.

Stone, C., and D. Carleson. 1983. Wildlife habitat considerations in forest operations. Oregon Dept. Forestry and Oregon Dept. Fish & Wildlife, Salem, OR. 26 p.

Wenger, K.F. (ed.) 1984. Forestry Handbook. 2nd ed. John Wiley & Sons, Inc., New York, NY. 1335 p.

Index

Acreage burned: historical average (Oregon), 35; prescribed burning (Oregon and Washington), 191, 195; slash burning (Oregon), 75

Acrolein, 204, 210

Activity fuels. *See* Slash

Adaptations to fire, 33, 34, 40-49

Air pollution: assessment of, 198-199, 205-206; mitigation strategies, 14, 212, 213-215, 289; technical definition of, 196; urban, 203. *See also* Emission; Particulate emissions; specific pollutants

Air quality: air quality related values (AQRV), general, 264; criteria, 197; in conflict with site productivity, 138; and human health, 13, 14, 16, 191-216, 289; legal requirements for, 263-265; management strategies for, 13, 14, 196-198, 212, 285; protection of rural areas, 215; and smoldering forest floor, 285, 287-289; standards for, 197-198

Aldehydes: combustion product, 204-205; risk assessment for, 209-211

Ash (particulate matter), 130, 202-203

Backing fires, 60, 61, 201

Beetles, 33, 112-113, 115

Benzo-a-pyrene (BaP), 204, 208-210

Biomass consumption, 200-201, 287

Broadcast burning, 4, 60

Brown-and-burn, 63

Brush control (rangelands), 85

Buffer strip (streamside), 224, 225, 226, 241

Burning plans, 58, 63, 65, 264-265

California State Air Resource Board, 264

Carbon dioxide, 201-202

Carbon monoxide, 203

Carbon/nitrogen ratio, 129, 130, 133

Cancer (risk from smoke), 204, 206-210

Cascade Mountains: eastside forests; biomass consumption by fire in, 200; burning and water yield in, 14-15; climate of, 81-82; ecological adaptation in, 7; effects of fire exclusion in, 9, 10; prescribed burning in, 72-73; regeneration in, 8; underburning in, 183-186

Cascade Mountains: westside forests; biomass consumption by fire in, 200; burned vs. unburned sites in, 178-183; burning and water yield in, 14-15; climate of, 81; ecological adaptation in, 7; effects of fire exclusion in, 9, 10; prescribed burning in, 70-74 passim; regeneration in, 8

Cation losses (effects of fire), 134, 228

Ceanothus, 44-45, 71

Center firing, 62-63

Chelators, 145, 153

Chevron burn, 61

"Cigarette burn," 33

Clean Air Act of 1963, as amended, 13, 14, 16-17, 195, 196, 263-265 passim

Climate: eastside of Cascade Mountains, 81-82; westside of Cascade Mountains, 81

Combustion products (chemistry), 14, 201-211

Communities, plant: impacts of prescribed fire on, 7, 9, 10, 82, 84, 89, 186, 244; role of natural fire in, 28-35. *See also* Plant community composition

Contaminant, 196

Convection, 11, 130-131

Costs of prescribed burning, 273-275

Crater Lake National Park, 32, 34

Criteria pollutant, 196-197, 203

Crown fire vs. surface fire, 42, 289-290

Decision making: role of research, 22

Decision analysis, 17-18, 57, 278-280, 284-285

DFSIM, 182, 277

Disease: and fire, 10-11, 46, 117-120

Diversity. *See* Ecological diversity

Dose-response relationship, 205-206

Drip torch, 56, 64

Ecological adaptation to fire, 7, 33, 34, 40-48

Ecological diversity: maintenance on rangelands, 85-86

Economic analysis: current limitations and future prospects, 275; decision analysis example, 278-280; risk assessment, 17-18, 22, 277; stand level example, 277-278; use in prescribed burning, 271-281; value of air quality maintenance, 257, 276-277

Ecosystems: forests, 28-36; rangelands, 81-86; soils, 144-146

Emission: factor, 201, 202, 204; inventory, 198-199; reduction, 14, 212, 213-215; standards, 196, 198-199. *See also* Air pollution; Particulate emissions

Emissions: future predictions (Pacific Northwest forests), 215

Entiat Fire, 11, 134

Erosion: channel erosion, 170; and disturbance frequency, 169-171; earthflows, 168; frost heaving and surface erosion, 163, 166-167; gully erosion, 166; mass wasting, 167-168, 170; overland flow, 161, 162, 164, 165, 166; and prescribed fire, 88, 159-173 passim, 224-225, 239; raindrop splash, 162-166 passim, 221, 225; ravel, 167, 170, 171, 224; rill erosion, 166; sheet erosion, 166, 170; splash erosion, 162-163, 165-166, 170; surface erosion, 165-167

Escape risk (prescribed fire), 9-10, 101, 266, 276-277

Evapotranspiration, 134-135, 220

Exclusion. *See* Fire exclusion